In Pursuit of Marx's Theory of Crisis

Historical Materialism Book Series

The Historical Materialism Book Series is a major publishing initiative of the radical left. The capitalist crisis of the twenty-first century has been met by a resurgence of interest in critical Marxist theory. At the same time, the publishing institutions committed to Marxism have contracted markedly since the high point of the 1970s. The Historical Materialism Book Series is dedicated to addressing this situation by making available important works of Marxist theory. The aim of the series is to publish important theoretical contributions as the basis for vigorous intellectual debate and exchange on the left.

The peer-reviewed series publishes original monographs, translated texts, and reprints of classics across the bounds of academic disciplinary agendas and across the divisions of the left. The series is particularly concerned to encourage the internationalization of Marxist debate and aims to translate significant studies from beyond the English-speaking world.

For a full list of titles in the Historical Materialism Book Series available in paperback from Haymarket Books, visit: www.haymarketbooks.org/series_collections/1-historical-materialism.

In Pursuit of Marx's Theory of Crisis

Samezō Kuruma

Translated and Edited by
Michael Schauerte

Haymarket Books
Chicago, IL

First published in 2024 by Brill Academic Publishers, The Netherlands
© 2024 Koninklijke Brill NV, Leiden, The Netherlands

Published in paperback in 2025 by
Haymarket Books
P.O. Box 180165
Chicago, IL 60618
773-583-7884
www.haymarketbooks.org

ISBN: 979-8-88890-540-1

Distributed to the trade in the US through Consortium Book Sales and Distribution (www.cbsd.com) and internationally through Ingram Publisher Services International (www.ingramcontent.com).

This book was published with the generous support of Lannan Foundation, Wallace Action Fund, and the Marguerite Casey Foundation.

Special discounts are available for bulk purchases by organizations and institutions. Please call 773-583-7884 or email info@haymarketbooks.org for more information.

Cover art and design by David Mabb. Cover art is a development of *Construct 32, Morris, Acorn / Rodchenko, Untitled Textile Design*, wallpaper mounted on linen (2006).

Printed in the United States.

Library of Congress Cataloging-in-Publication data is available.

Dedicated to the memory of Ken Kuruma and Teinosuke Ōtani

∴

Contents

Acknowledgements XI

Introduction 1
    Michael Schauerte
1. Bookish Son of a Merchant 2
2. Aborted Banking Career 4
3. Creation of the Ōhara Institute for Social Research 5
4. Book-Buying Trip to Europe 7
5. Researching 'Crisis' at the OISR 10
6. Move to Tokyo and the War Years 14
7. Postwar Revival 17
8. *Marx-Lexikon zur politischen Ökonomie* 20
9. 'A Mere Interpreter of Marx' 22
10. The Legacy of Kuruma 25
11. Reading *Capital* as Crisis Theory 28
12. A Note on the English Edition 39

PART 1
History and Overview of Crisis Theory

1. An Introduction to the Study of Crisis 43

2. An Inquiry into Marx's Theory of Crisis 72

3. Addendum to 'An Inquiry into Marx's Theory of Crisis': A Response to the Criticism of Kōzō Uno 100

4. An Overview of Marx's Theory of Crisis 117
    1. Marx's General Grasp of Crisis 117
    2. Marx's Theory of Crisis and *Capital* 118
    3. Key Perspective When Contemplating *Capital* as a Theory of Crisis Is to Consider the Developmental Process of Contradictions as a Process Whereby Moments Become Independent 118
    4. Development of the Independence of Moments and the Necessity of Their Real Unity in a Forced and Sudden Form: The Significance of the Explosion, Real Concentration, and Forcible Adjustment of Contradictions 119

5   Moments Becoming Independent and the Elasticity of the Production Process 119
   6   Some Examples from *Capital* (and *Theories of Surplus Value*) of the Emphasis on Moments Becoming Independent 121

PART 2
Marx-Lexikon zur politischen Ökonomie

5 *Marx-Lexikon Crisis I*: Contents and Discussion 135
   1   Part 1: Contents 135
   2   Part 2: Discussion 143

6 *Marx-Lexikon Crisis II*: Contents and Discussion 182
   1   Part 1: Contents 182
   2   Part 2: Discussion 192

7 *Marx-Lexikon Crisis III*: Contents and Discussion 221
   1   Part 1: Contents 221
   2   Part 2: Discussion 232

8 *Marx-Lexikon Crisis IV*: Contents and Discussion 255
   1   Part 1: Contents 255
   2   Part 2: Discussion 264

PART 3
Reviews, Discussions, and Polemics

9   An Evaluation of Condliffe's Analysis of Crisis 293

10 The Contradictions of Modern Wealth 306

11 Capital Accumulation and the Depreciation Fund for Fixed Capital 316

12 Are Prices and Wages in a Vicious Circle? 337

13 Prices, Currency, and Demand 348

14 A Few Problems Concerning Postwar Theories of Crisis 362
    1   'Cycle' and 'Period' 362
    2   On the Theory of 'Intermediate Crisis' – Engels's 'Mistake' etc. 372

15 Yasuma Takada's Theory of Accumulation (Part 1 and 2) 378
    1   Part 1 378
    2   Part 2 391
        2.1 *Gist of Takada's Earlier Theory* 391
        2.2 *Criticism of Arguments Summarised above, Takada's Refutation, and My Counter-Criticism* 396

16 Method for Unfolding a Systematic Theory of Crisis: A Response to Ryōzō Tomizuka (Part 1 and 2) 404
    1   Part 1 404
        1.1 *Relation between the Theory of Reproduction and the Theory of Crisis* 404
    2   Part 2 435

Bibliography 463
Index 472

Acknowledgements

I am grateful to the copyright holders for kindly granting permission to publish this English edition. The table of contents, passage citations, and discussions from *Marx-Lexikon zur politischen Ökonomie* included in Chapter 5 to 8 appear courtesy of the Ōhara Institute for Social Research, Hosei University. Naomi Ishihara, the niece of the author's son, Ken Kuruma, has generously granted permission to translate the 1965 book *Kyōkō ron kenkyū* (An Investigation of Crisis Theory) and content from the 2019 book *Marukusu no kyōkō ron* (Marx's Theory of Crisis). I would also like to express my sincerest appreciation to Hideto Akashi, Kei Ehara, Korefumi Miyata, Kōhei Saitō, Ryūji Sasaki, Soichirō Sumida, and Tsuyoshi Yūki for responding to various translation-related questions. Finally, let me acknowledge my sole responsibility for whatever mistranslations and other mistakes might be lurking in these pages.

Introduction

Michael Schauerte

This book brings together writings on the topic of crisis by Samezō Kuruma (1893–1982) that span nearly half a century, from 1929 to 1975. The earliest works were intended as the initial instalments in a vast project to investigate and extend Marx's incomplete theory of crisis. Kuruma had to scale back his ambitions for the project in the late 1930s, amidst an increasingly repressive political situation, and eventually abandoned the hope of completing the book on crisis he had begun. Nevertheless, crisis remained a central theoretical concern for Kuruma throughout the rest of his life. In the 1970s, he edited four volumes of his *Marx-Lexikon zur politischen Ökonomie*[1] on the topic of crisis. His choice of passages to include in the volumes, and his arrangement of them under various headings and subheadings, reflect his systematic understanding of crisis based on the writings of Marx. This interpretation of Marx's theory of crisis comes into even clearer focus by reading the discussions between Kuruma and his assistant editors that were published as inserts to each of the four volumes. The discussions are included in this English edition, along with the table of contents and list of passages cited for each *Marx-Lexikon* volume. In addition, this book includes the entirety of the 1965 collection of Kuruma's writings on crisis (*An Investigation of Crisis Theory*) and other works not included therein or published subsequently. The wide-ranging content reflects Kuruma's view of the centrality of crisis to Marx's entire 'critique of political economy' centred on *Capital*. This introduction presents some key characteristics of Kuruma's project to construct a systematic Marxian theory of crisis, against the backdrop of important events in his life.[2]

---

1 *Marx-Lexikon zur politischen Ökonomie* is a 15-volume work edited by Kuruma from 1968 until his death in 1982 (with the final two volumes appearing posthumously). The *Marx-Lexikon* volumes contain passages from Marx in the original German with Japanese translations. The volumes are organised around five key topics: competition, method, materialist conception of history, crisis, and money.

2 General biographical information provided here is based on interviews conducted with Kuruma in 1973 (Kuruma 1973c) and 1977 (Kuruma 2015) and his two-part memoir for the journal *Shisō* (Kuruma 1953c and Kuruma 1953d). Other information in English on Kuruma's life is available in Schauerte 2007 and Schauerte 2018.

1 Bookish Son of a Merchant

Samezō Kuruma was born in the city of Okayama in 1893 to a prosperous merchant family that owned a paper and stationary wholesaling business. As the eldest son, Kuruma was expected to take over the business one day, but knew from a young age how ill-suited he was to the world of commerce. Although he described his family as not particularly cultured, Kuruma was an avid reader as a child, influenced in part by his great uncle, who had attended Keio University. At the age of 17, Kuruma insisted on attending Sixth Higher School[3] against the strong opposition of his father, who considered a 'higher vocational school' the more practical option for his future successor.

Under the educational system before the end of World War II, the 'higher school' (*kōtō gakkō*) was a three-year institution that provided college-level instruction to prepare students to attend one of the elite imperial universities. At the time of Kuruma's enrolment in 1911, there were just eight higher schools – and four imperial universities – in the entire country. The broad, liberal-arts curriculum of the higher schools centred on foreign language instruction.[4] Some idea of the calibre of instruction at Sixth Higher School is reflected in the fact that Kuruma was taught English and Latin by Arthur Linsday Sadler, an Oxford graduate who went on to become a distinguished translator and scholar at the University of Sydney.[5] Outside of the classroom, Kuruma and his classmates read original and translated works in English by a wide range of authors, including William James, Thomas Hardy, Herni Bergson, Ivan Turgenev, and Victor Hugo. As a typical 'literary youth' of his day, Kuruma also devoured fictional works by Rohan Kōda, Sōhei Morita, and Doppo Kunikida, not to mention the latest novels by Sōseki Natsume.

In January 1911, a few months before Kuruma entered Sixth Higher School, Shūsui Kōtoku and eleven other anarchists and socialists were executed for their alleged participation in a plot to assassinate Emperor Meiji. What Kuruma knew of this 'High Treason Case' came from the pages of commercial newspapers, as he was unfamiliar with any of the 'dangerous' ideas of the time. Following this sensational event, Kuruma was even less likely to encounter revolutionary ideas, as the government launched a severe crackdown on polit-

---

3   Present-day Okayama University.
4   Henry Dewitt Smith notes that 'one third of the total hours of instruction' at higher schools was directed to the acquisition of foreign languages (Smith 1972, p. 9).
5   Kuruma spent a week at Sadler's traditional Japanese home in Okayama during a summer vacation and recalls being asked for his opinion on the English translation of *The Tale of the Heike* that Sadler was working on at the time (Kuruma 2015, p. 327).

ical dissent and working-class organisations. This 'winter age' (*fuyu no jidai*), when radical activists laid low or fled the movement, continued through to Kuruma's graduation in 1914.

After higher school, Kuruma took the next step along the elite educational path by entering Tokyo Imperial University, where he enrolled in the department of economics, which was still within the Faculty of Law at the time. His interest in economics had been piqued in Okayama by reading *The Wealth of Nations*, a work that convinced him that economic theory was the key to understanding the contemporary world. But the economics courses at university struck Kuruma as terribly boring. One lecture in particular, he recalled, centred on whether the delicious smell of grilled eel, wafting out of a restaurant window to entice passersby, could be considered an 'economic good' or not. Such tiresome classes led Kuruma to transfer to the department of politics, but he continued to read works of political economy on his own. He was influenced in particular by the theory of marginal utility and the ideas of the Austrian economist Eugen von Phillippovich, which conditioned a sceptical attitude toward Marx's labour theory of value.

Kuruma was not a student activist during his university days, as the student movement itself only emerged with the founding of Shinjinkai (New Man Society) in 1918, around the time of his graduation. Kuruma and his classmates thus belonged to what has been described as a 'middle generation', sandwiched between the 'new generation of Meiji Japan' and the generation of student radicals that came on the scene in the early 1920s.[6] His four years at university, which ran parallel to World War I, marked a transitional period in the country as well, as the repressive 'winter age' slowly gave way to a reenergised labour movement. The changing social mood was reflected in the tremendous popularity of *Bimbō monogatari* (A Tale of Poverty), in which the author, Hajime Kawakami, sought to demonstrate that industrialisation is more likely to exacerbate than eliminate poverty. Kuruma was one of the book's many enthusiastic readers around the time of its publication in 1916, after having been serialised in a newspaper the previous year. Kawakami, a professor at Kyoto Imperial University, was beginning to move toward Marxism under the sharp criticism of his former student Tamizō Kushida, who had poked holes in the argument that poverty stems from the production of luxury goods. Kawakami gracefully accepted that criticism and even suspended publication of his bestselling book in 1919. Just a few years later, Kuruma would become personally acquainted with both Kawakami and Kushida.

---

6 Smith 1972, p. x.

2   Aborted Banking Career

In early 1918, with graduation approaching, Kuruma finally began to consider what he might do with his life. An economic boom in Japan during World War I had created an extremely favourable job market. Without even seeking a position, Kuruma received a job offer from the great corporate conglomerate Mitsui but turned it down to look for a teaching position or some job related to China. His intense interest in China was the direct outcome of his connection to Tsuyoshi Inukai, an influential Japanese politician who went on to became prime minister in 1931 and was assassinated the following year in a failed coup d'état. Inukai, a native of Okayama, had been a classmate of Kuruma's great uncle at Keio University, and thus agreed to serve as Kuruma's 'guarantor' during his studies at Tokyo Imperial University.[7] Through this arrangement, Kuruma was able to meet Inukai a number of times at his Tokyo residence, fully absorbing the statesman's views on foreign policy. An ardent supporter of Sun Yat-sen's republican movement in China, Inukai had long urged the Japanese government to pursue closer relations with China and India to counterbalance British imperialism. The conversations with Inukai sparked Kuruma's ambition to pursue a career through which he could contribute to the achievement of such foreign-policy aims.

With no idea how to find such a job, Kuruma consulted one of his professors, Eizō Yahagi, who told him that working for Sumitomo Bank might provide an opportunity to study economics and do work related to China. Yahagi knew the bank's general director, Masaya Suzuki, who happened to be in Tokyo on business, and arranged for Kuruma to meet him. Thrilled by the unexpected opportunity, Kuruma rushed to meet the director, and after swallowing his spiel about how the bank was 'about more than just making money', leapt at an offer to start working at the head office in Osaka. One reason for Kuruma's enthusiasm, besides his interest in China, was the belief that the job would provide an opportunity to study the phenomenon of crisis,[8] which already fascinated him. Kuruma started working in July, but almost as soon as setting foot in the office he began to regret his impetuous decision. The high-minded mission of the bank, as described by the director, bore little resemblance to its everyday operations. This stark contrast raised the first doubts in Kuruma's mind about capitalism. Feeling completely out of place, Kuruma sensed that his life would head toward disaster if he stuck to banking.

---

7   University students at the time required a guarantor.
8   Kuruma 1953d, p. 982.

ical dissent and working-class organisations. This 'winter age' (*fuyu no jidai*), when radical activists laid low or fled the movement, continued through to Kuruma's graduation in 1914.

After higher school, Kuruma took the next step along the elite educational path by entering Tokyo Imperial University, where he enrolled in the department of economics, which was still within the Faculty of Law at the time. His interest in economics had been piqued in Okayama by reading *The Wealth of Nations*, a work that convinced him that economic theory was the key to understanding the contemporary world. But the economics courses at university struck Kuruma as terribly boring. One lecture in particular, he recalled, centred on whether the delicious smell of grilled eel, wafting out of a restaurant window to entice passersby, could be considered an 'economic good' or not. Such tiresome classes led Kuruma to transfer to the department of politics, but he continued to read works of political economy on his own. He was influenced in particular by the theory of marginal utility and the ideas of the Austrian economist Eugen von Phillippovich, which conditioned a sceptical attitude toward Marx's labour theory of value.

Kuruma was not a student activist during his university days, as the student movement itself only emerged with the founding of Shinjinkai (New Man Society) in 1918, around the time of his graduation. Kuruma and his classmates thus belonged to what has been described as a 'middle generation', sandwiched between the 'new generation of Meiji Japan' and the generation of student radicals that came on the scene in the early 1920s.[6] His four years at university, which ran parallel to World War I, marked a transitional period in the country as well, as the repressive 'winter age' slowly gave way to a reenergised labour movement. The changing social mood was reflected in the tremendous popularity of *Bimbō monogatari* (A Tale of Poverty), in which the author, Hajime Kawakami, sought to demonstrate that industrialisation is more likely to exacerbate than eliminate poverty. Kuruma was one of the book's many enthusiastic readers around the time of its publication in 1916, after having been serialised in a newspaper the previous year. Kawakami, a professor at Kyoto Imperial University, was beginning to move toward Marxism under the sharp criticism of his former student Tamizō Kushida, who had poked holes in the argument that poverty stems from the production of luxury goods. Kawakami gracefully accepted that criticism and even suspended publication of his bestselling book in 1919. Just a few years later, Kuruma would become personally acquainted with both Kawakami and Kushida.

---

6 Smith 1972, p. x.

2   Aborted Banking Career

In early 1918, with graduation approaching, Kuruma finally began to consider what he might do with his life. An economic boom in Japan during World War I had created an extremely favourable job market. Without even seeking a position, Kuruma received a job offer from the great corporate conglomerate Mitsui but turned it down to look for a teaching position or some job related to China. His intense interest in China was the direct outcome of his connection to Tsuyoshi Inukai, an influential Japanese politician who went on to became prime minister in 1931 and was assassinated the following year in a failed coup d'état. Inukai, a native of Okayama, had been a classmate of Kuruma's great uncle at Keio University, and thus agreed to serve as Kuruma's 'guarantor' during his studies at Tokyo Imperial University.[7] Through this arrangement, Kuruma was able to meet Inukai a number of times at his Tokyo residence, fully absorbing the statesman's views on foreign policy. An ardent supporter of Sun Yat-sen's republican movement in China, Inukai had long urged the Japanese government to pursue closer relations with China and India to counterbalance British imperialism. The conversations with Inukai sparked Kuruma's ambition to pursue a career through which he could contribute to the achievement of such foreign-policy aims.

With no idea how to find such a job, Kuruma consulted one of his professors, Eizō Yahagi, who told him that working for Sumitomo Bank might provide an opportunity to study economics and do work related to China. Yahagi knew the bank's general director, Masaya Suzuki, who happened to be in Tokyo on business, and arranged for Kuruma to meet him. Thrilled by the unexpected opportunity, Kuruma rushed to meet the director, and after swallowing his spiel about how the bank was 'about more than just making money', leapt at an offer to start working at the head office in Osaka. One reason for Kuruma's enthusiasm, besides his interest in China, was the belief that the job would provide an opportunity to study the phenomenon of crisis,[8] which already fascinated him. Kuruma started working in July, but almost as soon as setting foot in the office he began to regret his impetuous decision. The high-minded mission of the bank, as described by the director, bore little resemblance to its everyday operations. This stark contrast raised the first doubts in Kuruma's mind about capitalism. Feeling completely out of place, Kuruma sensed that his life would head toward disaster if he stuck to banking.

---

7   University students at the time required a guarantor.
8   Kuruma 1953d, p. 982.

That summer, as he was lamenting his poor career choice, a great social event was unfolding that would make it easier for Kuruma to leave banking behind. On 23 July, a protest over soaring rice prices erupted in a small fishing village in Toyama Prefecture. News of the event inspired other uprisings, which soon coalesced into a powerful protest wave that swept the country. The protests and riots reached Osaka on 11 August. As a young unmarried employee, Kuruma was tasked with spending the night at the bank to protect important documents and ward off rioters. As cavalry units patrolled the city streets, Kuruma waited by the phone for updates from the police on the whereabouts of rioters, knowing that if they did show up at the bank his only choice would be to flee. Kuruma made it through the night without incident and spent the next day wandering around the ravaged city, taking in the aftermath of the riot. He was amazed at the impotence of the vast police force in the face of the popular fury. Kuruma took the event as his cue to exit his fledgling banking career, handing in his resignation in October to return to Okayama.

3 Creation of the Ōhara Institute for Social Research

Back in his hometown, Kuruma heard through a wealthy friend and former classmate, Keijirō Hayashi, that the great Okayama textile magnate and philanthropist Magosaburō Ōhara intended to establish a research institute to investigate 'social problems'. A meeting with Ōhara was arranged through Hayashi's father so that Kuruma could learn more about the planned institute. Ōhara explained to Kuruma that the philanthropic activities he had supported to date were like putting a bandage on a tumour. What was necessary, rather, was to locate the causes of social problems, which is a task that cannot be entrusted to governmental bodies. The irony of a powerful capitalist like Ōhara puzzling over the problems of capitalist society goes without saying, but he seems to have been sincere in his motivation, connected to his Christian faith.[9] At the same time, his concern regarding the worsening social problems in Japan reflected a broader anxiety among his capitalist brethren, who were taken aback by the sudden explosion of popular rage during the rice riots. The realisation that social discontent could not be held down by force alone spawned various reformist measures and institutions, such as the establishment in 1919 of the Kyōchōkai (Harmonisation Society), a semi-governmental body to pro-

---

9 Ōhara's was converted to Christianity under the influence of Jūji Ishii, founder of the Okayama Orphanage.

mote 'cooperation and harmony' between labour and capital. Ōhara's eagerness to create an institute to investigate social problems was motivated, one suspects, by a similar desire to smooth over the rough edges of class conflict.

Kuruma was enthused by Ōhara's plan for a research institute and requested an opportunity to take part in it. Ōhara told him to discuss the matter with Iwazaburō Takano, a Tokyo Imperial University economics professor, whom he intended to place at the organisation's helm, along with Jirō Kawata, a scholar of social policy.[10] At a meeting with Takano in Tokyo, Kuruma was told that if the institute were created, he would be hired as a researcher, and that he could make use of Takano's university office for his own studies in the meantime. When the Ōhara Institute for Social Research (OISR) was established in Osaka in February 1919, Kuruma was hired as a full-time researcher, as promised.

Ōhara pledged to 'put up the money and keep my mouth shut'[11] and made good on this promise: lavishly funding the institute without interfering in its operations. The three main aims of the institute were to impartially and fundamentally investigate social issues, archive materials necessary for this research, and educate the public through the publication of research results and other activities. Toward that end, Ōhara provided an enormous initial donation of one million yen as well as an annual operational fund of around 80,000 yen. He also donated 250,000 yen to cover the cost of purchasing land and constructing the OISR facilities, including the main building, modelled after the Solvay Institute in Belgium.[12] From these ample funds, Kuruma drew a fairly regal monthly salary of 120 yen,[13] supplemented by money to purchase books for his research. He was free to pursue his intellectual interests as an OISR researcher, having only to take part in the institute's publishing projects and contribute an article or translation every year to its scholarly journal.

Along with Ōhara's money, the OISR benefited from a sudden influx of talented young scholars from the new Faculty of Economics at Tokyo Imperial University in the wake of the so-called 'Morito Incident'. In December 1919, the inaugural issue of the faculty's journal *Keizaigaku kenkyū* (Economic

---

10 Ōhara first approached Hajime Kawakami to lead the new organisation, but Kawakami was not interested in an administrative position and recommended Takano as better suited to it (Kuruma 1953c, p. 876).
11 Nimura 1989, p. 5. The quotation relies on the English translation by Terry Boardman of Kazuo Nimura's article on the history of the OISR (http://nimura-laborhistory.jp/English/en-70years_oisr.html).
12 Ōhara Institute 2020, p. 34.
13 By way of comparison, an entry-level monthly salary for a career-track civil servant who had graduated from university was around 70 yen at the time.

Research) included an article titled 'A Study of the Social Thought of Kropotkin' by a young economics professor named Tatsuo Morito. The government deemed the article a violation of Article 42 of Japan's 'Press Law' and indicted Morito and the journal's editor Hyōe Ōuchi, leading to their suspension from the university. After serving a three-month jail sentence, Morito was hired by the OISR as a researcher, as was Ōuchi, who had received a year's probation in the case. Other young faculty members resigned in protest and were hired by the OISR, including Tamizō Kushida, Yasunosuke Gonda, and Karoku Hosokawa. The institute thus became what could be described as Tokyo Imperial University's 'Faculty of Economics in exile'.

The young scholars were joined by the man who had been instrumental in creating the faculty, Iwazaburō Takano, who resigned from his university post as a result of a controversy surrounding his selection as a Japanese delegate to the first general assembly of the International Labour Organisation. His elder brother Futasarō had become a labour union leader in Japan, based on experience gained while working in the United States, and he funded the undergraduate and graduate studies at Tokyo Imperial University of Iwazaburō, who also became involved in the labour movement, as a council member of Yūaikai (Friendly Society), the country's largest labour union. As a university professor, Iwazaburō pioneered the field of economic statistics in Japan and pushed for the creation of an independent Faculty of Economics. Following his resignation from the university in October 1919, Takano became the OISR's full-time general director, taking over the functions of the previous administrative committee on which he had served. His academic interests and democratic outlook would play a key role in shaping the direction of the institute.

4 Book-Buying Trip to Europe

In late October 1920, the OISR dispatched Kuruma to Europe with Tamizō Kushida and a budget of 40,000 yen to purchase books for the institute's new library. In his mid-thirties at the time, Kushida already had made a name for himself as one of Japan's first Marxian economists. Around the time of Kushida's departure for Europe, his former professor Hajime Kawakami was plunging into the study of Marx under the influence of his student, and with his customary zeal, Kawakami went on to become an active supporter and then member of the outlawed Japanese Communist Party (JCP). In contrast, Kushida kept radical politics at arm's length, believing that he could contribute more to social change through his scholarly research, to which he remained dedicated until his untimely death in 1934.

During the long sea journey to Europe, Kuruma and Kushida talked from morning to night in their cabin – or rather the garrulous Kushida talked while Kuruma mainly listened. The conversation often veered toward Marx, but Kuruma remained doubtful of the labour theory of value. Despite this scepticism, Kuruma already was heading in a socialistic direction, under the influence of Hitoshi Yamakawa's book *Demokurashī no hanmon* (The Anguish of Democracy), published in 1919. Following their arrival in London in early January 1921, Kushida went on to Germany to purchase books, leaving Kuruma the task of doing the same in England. This division of labour, decided by Kushida during the voyage, came as an unwelcome surprise to Kuruma, who had thought he would only have to serve as his older colleague's assistant. After finding lodgings at a boarding house in Highgate, not far from Marx's grave, Kuruma set about compiling a list of books to purchase, centring on the areas of political economy, socialism, and the history of social movements. Kuruma relied heavily on *Theories of Surplus Value* to find titles related to political economy, thereby taking his first steps toward an engagement with the ideas of Marx.

The task of purchasing books also helped familiarise Kuruma with the labour and socialist movements in England. He was a frequent visitor to Henderson's bookshop on Charing Cross Road, known as the 'Bomb Shop', which stocked radical literature. Kuruma went there to purchase Communist Party pamphlets and other titles banned in Japan. Like many other customers, he had a vivid recollection of the owner, Francis Riddell Henderson, and his trademark red tie. On one visit to the shop, Kuruma was told by Henderson that 'Mister Nosaka would soon be deported'. Henderson, who assumed his customer would know a fellow Japanese, was referring to Sanzō Nosaka, a Yuaikai labour union official who had come to England in 1919 to study economics at the University of London. The following year Nosaka became a founding member of the Communist Party of Great Britain, which was the reason for the deportation order. Kuruma had received a letter of introduction to Nosaka prior to departing for Europe but had not bothered to make use of it, viewing him as a conservative trade unionist. But upon hearing of Nosaka's imminent expulsion, Kuruma visited his flat to help him hastily pack his belongings.[14] During his time in London, Kuruma also met Tom Mann, the chairman of the British Bureau of the Red International of Labour Unions. He had seen Mann often at demonstrations in front of the statue of Nelson in Trafalgar Square, and on one occasion visited his office to obtain some trade-union materials.

---

14   Upon returning to Japan, Nosaka helped found the Japanese Communist Party in 1922.

Apart from these encounters, Kuruma mainly was engrossed in the difficult task of purchasing books. By April, he and Kushida had bought thousands of titles, including a number of rare books, such as first-edition copies of Smith's *The Wealth of Nations* and Malthus's *On Population*, and a signed copy of *Capital* that Marx had presented to his friend Ludwig Kugelmann. Exhausted by the months spent tracking down books, Kuruma travelled to Berlin to meet Kushida, who was staying at a boarding-house in the Charlottenburg district. Acting as tour guide, Kushida showed Kuruma the traces of the recent 1919 Spartacist uprising, including the bullet holes in the wall of the old imperial palace. Realising that Kuruma's nerves were on edge, Kushida suggested that he recuperate in Germany before heading back to Japan. Kuruma took this advice and travelled around Germany with Hyōe Ōuchi, an OISR researcher dispatched to Europe in 1921. The two left Berlin on a trip that took them through Dresden, Leipzig, Wartburg, Weimar, and Frankfurt, before finally arriving in Heidelberg.

Kuruma stayed with Ōuchi in Heidelberg for around eight months, relying on the monthly salary he was still drawing, which was more than enough to live comfortably in inflation-ridden Germany. During the sojourn, Kuruma studied German and pursued his intellectual interests at a leisurely pace, while Ōuchi enrolled in a seminar at Heidelberg University taught by the sociologist and economist Emil Lederer. It was in Heidelberg that Kuruma began to study Marx more seriously and finally accept his labour theory of value, mainly through reading *Theories of Surplus Value*. Kuruma also studied and translated parts of Rosa Luxemburg's *Theory of Accumulation*. Ōuchi observed the Zen-like patience with which his friend approached the task of translation, revising each line multiple times and spending two or three days pondering the meaning of a single passage.[15] After hours spent each day in such study, interspersed with strolls around the countryside, Kuruma would join Ōuchi for an evening meal at the Perkeo Restaurant, where a fresh keg of beer was tapped at the appointed hour. Not surprisingly, Kuruma would look back on his months in Heidelberg as an idyllic time of his life.[16]

In April 1922, Kuruma departed Germany for Paris, where he spent a couple of weeks before returning to London to purchase a few more books for the institute and meet up with Kushida again. Near the end of June, the two embarked

---

15 Ōuchi 1957, p. 394.
16 Kuruma visited Europe a second time after World War II but deliberately avoided Heidelberg, which had become a tourist spot in the meantime, in order to preserve his ideal image of the city (Kuruma 2015, p. 328).

from Southampton on the luxury ocean liner RMS *Aquitania* bound for New York, and then made their way to the west coast, stopping off in Chicago and other cities along the way to buy more books. In San Francisco, Kuruma boarded a ship for Japan, while Kushida travelled to the Soviet Union at the invitation of David Riazanov, director of the Marx-Engels Institute, whom he had encountered in Germany through their friendly book-buying rivalry.

5   Researching 'Crisis' at the OISR

Arriving back in Japan in August, Kuruma settled into his routine as an OISR researcher in Osaka. In 1923, he began teaching the history of political economy as a part-time instructor at Doshisha University, in nearby Kyoto. The position was arranged for him through Kushida's connection to Kawakami, who was also teaching part-time at the university. During those early years at the OISR, Kuruma married Kikuyo Miyake, a fellow native of Okayama. The couple would have four children together, but only their son Ken, born in 1932, would survive to adulthood. A one-year-old son and two-year-old daughter died of illness in 1927, followed by the death of another son in 1936.

Under the broadminded leadership of Takano, the OISR soon became a hub for research related to the labour movement and Marx, which was taboo at most universities. In 1920, the institute began publishing its *Japan Labour Yearbook*, an annual publication detailing working conditions, management policies, and labour relations. OISR researchers with a serious interest in Marxian ideas, apart from Kuruma and Kushida, included Karoku Hosokawa, Tatsuo Morito, and Hyōe Ōuchi, and the OISR journal, established in 1923, regularly published articles on Marx. Kuruma's contribution to the journal in the 1920s included his translations of works by Marx and Marxian writers such as Rosa Luxemburg, Rudolf Hilferding, and Karl Kautsky. Kuruma wrote a few articles of his own for the journal, including a commemoration of the bicentennial of Adam Smith's birth and a comparison of Hegel's history of philosophy to Marx's history of political economy. He also wrote a short history of political economy based on his university lectures that was published in 1927 as a chapter in the first volume of *Shakai mondai kōza* (Lectures on Social Problems).

Kuruma's driving ambition during the 1920s was to investigate crisis. He envisaged writing a book that would present a systematic theory of crisis founded on Marx's writings. Toward that end, he began to gather and organise passages related to crisis from Marx's articles, books, and unpublished manuscripts, centring on the three volumes of *Capital*. In order to keep track of the passages, Kuruma typed them out on notecards that he organised under various headings. Hyōe Ōuchi describes this organisational approach that Kuruma would adhere to throughout his life:

> For an important term in *Capital*, Kuruma would search all of the pages for the definitions of the same term, comparing them to each other, until he had been able to basically confirm its meaning. In order to do this, he would create dozens of notecards for each term. Over the years, as the seasons came and went, he accumulated thousands of these notecards, creating an index for *Capital* in a filing cabinet. In brief, his room in the back of the [OISR] office was a sort of factory, and on his desk, there was always a copy of *Capital* and *Theories of Surplus Value* and a German dictionary, alongside his typewriter. Whenever he was in the room the sound of typing, whether soft or loud, could be heard.[17]

Kuruma's son Ken, who recalled being awoken on many mornings by the typing noise, describes the meticulous approach his father took when setting out to write an article.

> First, he would write detailed notes in the margins of the book he was reading, while also copying almost entire sentences into a notebook, to which he added critical notes and occasionally quotes from *Capital* and other words. And then, finally, he would create notecards organised under particular topics. As a result of this approach, he accumulated a vast quantity of notes for each of his articles, far exceeding the length of whatever work he was critiquing.[18]

In quite literally taking a page out of Marx's book when it came to research, by excerpting and annotating passages from the works he was reading, Kuruma walked a fine line between diligently preparing for his project on crisis and simply procrastinating. The self-critical and conscientious Kuruma was as reluctant as Marx had been to present any idea that had not been fully worked out in his mind. But unlike Marx, who was capable of astounding bursts of creativity when a deadline could be put off no further, Kuruma always found writing to be a painfully slow process. He described this personal affliction in the following way:

---

17   Ōuchi 1957, p. 398.
18   Kuruma 1985, p. 5.

> I'm like a person with a terrible stutter who finds it very hard to speak. Some friends may struggle like me in writing an article, but I feel terribly jealous and sigh in admiration when I see those who actually enjoy writing and can complete five or ten pages in a day. I have complained sometimes that I would have been able to work with more enjoyment had I chosen carpentry or some other profession, but Kōzō Uno commented in a newspaper article somewhere that if I were a carpenter, I probably could only create a few objects that I would find satisfying.[19]

Despite his perfectionist tendencies, Kuruma was able to make steady progress in his investigation of crisis based on the huge collection of notes he gathered from the writings of Marx and from the works of bourgeois economists. He presented the first result of this research in the article 'An Introduction to the Study of Crisis', published in the OISR journal just a month before the October 1929 crash of Wall Street. Kuruma examines how bourgeois political economy as a science came to an end with the emergence of the periodic crises that exposed the fundamental contradictions of capitalism, and then clarifies some of the limitations of crisis theory within the Marxist camp. One gets a sense of the urgency with which the investigation of crisis was undertaken by Kuruma, who foresaw that a 'new crisis ... will soon arrive' that is likely to culminate in another world war. The study of crisis was not an idle, academic pursuit for Kuruma, but a vital task that 'to lay the scientific foundation for [Marxists'] tactics during this momentous period'.[20]

The following year Kuruma presented another part of his crisis-theory project in an article titled 'An Inquiry into Marx's Theory of Crisis'. In it, Kuruma compares Marx's initial plan for a six-book critique of political economy to the actual theoretical scope of *Capital*, considering whether that work is limited to the investigation of 'capital in general' within the first book on 'capital', as originally planned, or rather incorporates content from the entire critique as Henryk Grossman had claimed. Kuruma concludes that *Capital* is fundamentally limited to the elucidation of 'capital in general'. The significance of Kuruma's conclusion, with regard to the investigation of crisis, is that 'Marx's theory of crisis, along with the system of his critique of political economy, was left in an incomplete state', thus leaving us the task of considering 'how to develop a Marxian theory of crisis proper from the various investigations of crisis scattered throughout *Capital*'. Kuruma believed that in order to 'elu-

---

19 Kuruma 1954, p. 106.
20 Kuruma 1929, p. 32. (In Chapter 1 of this book.)

cidate the intrinsic relation between those investigations found in the pages of *Capital* and a proper theory of crisis', we would have to clarify 'Marx's overall approach toward clarifying crisis and its relation to his critique of political economy'.[21]

Kuruma was well aware of the great difficulty surrounding this project, which could not '[i]n all likelihood ... be achieved by a single person',[22] and thus hoped to attract the interest and collaboration of other scholars. However, despite the global depression in the 1930s, the issue of crisis was not a central concern for Marxists in Japan, and Kuruma's articles on crisis had little impact during that decade. The most influential theory of crisis in Japan at the time was that of Moritarō Yamada, presented in the 1931 book *Saiseisan katei hyōshiki bunseki joron* (An Introduction to the Analysis of Reproduction Schema). Yamada concerned himself with the relation of the realm of reproduction to crisis, centring on the examination of the reproduction schema presented in Part 3 of Book II of *Capital*. His linking of crisis theory to the theory of reproduction would continue to be at the core of the understanding of crisis in Japan well into the postwar era.

What captured the attention of Marxian scholars in the late 1920s and early 1930s was not crisis but the debate over the development of capitalism in Japan. The issue centred on the extent to which the Meiji Restoration of 1868 could be seen as a bourgeois revolution that ushered in capitalist production relations in Japan. The debate had a strong political dimension, as it arose out of the 1927 Comintern's 'Theses on Japan', which called for a 'bourgeois-democratic' revolution in Japan led by the proletariat to sweep aside 'feudal remnants' prior to a socialist revolution. The JCP embraced this two-stage theory of revolution, while a dissident faction organised around the journal *Rōnō* (Labour-Farmer), which included former JCP leaders, argued that Japan had already undergone a bourgeois revolution and did not require that first-stage revolution. The Comintern position was bolstered by extensive research on capitalist development by JCP members and sympathisers (including Moritarō Yamada), published in a seven-volume collection titled *Nihon shihonshugi hattatsu shi kōza* (Symposium on the History of the Development of Japanese Capitalism). This JCP-aligned group was thus dubbed the 'Kōza faction', while the other side came to be known as the 'Rōnō faction'.[23] This split among Marxist intellectuals persisted into the postwar period, with the Rōnō faction forming the

---

21 Kuruma 1930, p. 29. (In Chapter 2 of this book.)
22 Kuruma 1930, p. 31.
23 For a detailed account of the debate between the Kōza and Rōnō factions, see the work of Germaine A. Hoston (Hoston 1986 and Hoston 1994).

nucleus of the Japanese Socialist Party (JSP), while the theorists of the Kōza faction supported the reestablished JCP. Probably because Kushida and other OISR researchers were leading Rōnō-faction theorists, Kuruma is often grouped with the Rōnō faction, at least with regard to the prewar period, but he did not take part or express any interest in the debate over Japanese capitalism.[24] Kuruma viewed the dispute as more political than theoretical in nature and did not want to spread himself too thin by taking part in a debate that was outside of his primary interest in crisis.

Despite the political dimensions of the Rōnō-Kōza controversy, which pitted the JCP orthodoxy against a dissident faction, intellectuals on both sides of the debate shared many of the same basic political assumptions, as did Kuruma. It was considered an elementary truth among Japanese Marxists that the Soviet Union was either socialist or headed in that direction, and Lenin was treated as almost infallible. Criticism of the Soviet Union came mainly from the anarchist movement, which relied primarily on the first-hand accounts of Alexander Berkman and Emma Goldmann, rather than any theoretical understanding of the Soviet economy. The absence of any libertarian-socialist or left-communist tendency in Japan ensured that Kuruma never encountered a coherent theory of state capitalism or critique of Leninism. Kuruma's own idolisation of Lenin is clear from his 1929 article on crisis, where he praises the 'ground-breaking significance'[25] of *Imperialism, the Highest Stage of Capitalism*. This deep admiration for Lenin remained throughout Kuruma's life, as is clear from interviews with him in the 1970s and the recollections of his colleagues. One acquaintance, Shizuko Nakabayashi, even recalls Kuruma saying over drinks that, 'If I had had the ability of Lenin, I would have liked to have been an activist myself'.[26] The fact that Kuruma, by his own admission, lacked political acumen no doubt heightened his attraction to Lenin.

6   Move to Tokyo and the War Years

Kuruma, Kushida, and other OISR researchers kept revolutionary politics at arm's length, but the institute came under the scrutiny of the authorities nev-

---

24   For the postwar period, by contrast, Kuruma is often grouped with the Kōza faction, perhaps because he critiqued the ideas of Kōzō Uno, who opposed the JCP and was criticised in turn by JCP-oriented intellectuals like Seikisuke Mita. This view of Kuruma is expressed in Makoto Itoh's *Value and Crisis* (Itoh 1980, p. 33).
25   Kuruma 1929, p. 74.
26   Nimura et. al 1989, p. 41.

ertheless. In March 1928, following a nationwide roundup of JCP activists, the OISR office was searched by police looking for illegal correspondence with Soviet organisations. Takano had in fact been in contact with David Riazanov regarding the translation rights for a possible Japanese edition of the collected works of Marx and Engels,[27] but the investigation was abandoned when the search failed to turn up any evidence. News of this incident, combined with his growing financial concerns, led Magosaburō Ōhara to consider closing the institute. Complaints were also being voiced by his shareholders – and would grow louder as the economic situation worsened in the 1930s. The institute's focus on academic research, rather than the formulation of practical policies, was another source of displeasure to Ōhara, not to mention the fact that an institute bearing his name had become a centre of Marxist thought. If he flipped through the September 1929 issue of the OISR journal, for instance, Ōhara would have come across not only Kuruma's article on crisis (in which he praises Lenin) but also articles on Marx and Engels' theory of ideology, Marx's understanding of currency, and a bibliography of works by Marx and Engels translated into Japanese. And that was a fairly typical issue of the journal at the time.

In the early 1930s, through his negotiations with Ōhara, Takano was able to secure continued subsidies, but it was becoming clear that eventually the institute would have to find a way to support itself. The inevitable parting of the ways came in 1936, after an agreement was reached for the OISR to sell its buildings and land in Osaka to finance operations on a smaller scale in Tokyo. The move to the capital was made in February of the following year, with the institute setting up its offices in the former residence of the painter Tamon Yamauchi. The new location was half the size of the former office in Osaka, and the number of full-time staff (including Kuruma) was reduced to seven.

A few months after the move, the 'Marco Polo Bridge Incident' occurred in China, considered the prelude to Japan's Pacific War, followed by increasing repression of political dissent at home. In December 1937 and February of the following year, hundreds of activists, politicians, university professors, and students were rounded up for their alleged connection to a plan to organise an anti-fascist 'popular front' in Japan. Unlike previous mass arrests that had targeted JCP members, a wider net was cast in this 'Popular Front Incident', as it came to be known, entangling groups and individuals outside of the Party, including supporters of the Rōnō faction. One of those arrested and

---

27   An (incomplete) Japanese edition of the collected works was published by Kaizōsha, not the OISR, in the 1930s.

imprisoned was OISR researcher Hyōe Ōuchi. Kuruma had been tipped off that his colleague might be arrested, but Ōuchi shrugged off the warning, convinced that he had done nothing illegal. The same person who issued the warning claimed that the authorities were going to crush the OISR. Some of the younger researchers panicked upon hearing this rumour and called for the dissolution of the institute to avert the arrests. Kuruma was tasked with quelling the unrest. In the end, the OSIR was not dissolved or crushed. Kuruma later speculated that Takano had used his personal connection to Takio Isawa, a politician known as the 'Cabinet maker', to work out some sort of deal to preserve the institute.

Although the OISR remained in existence through Takano's efforts, the scope of its activities was limited due to inadequate funding and the repressive political environment. The institute had to suspend the publication of its journal and abandoned a project that Ōuchi was to have led to research the history of Japanese labour unions. By 1941, the OISR was no longer able to publish its *Japan Labour Year Book*, after the government deemed labour statistics 'military secrets' and disbanded the labour unions. That same year, the institute launched a new project under the direction of Takano to translate classic works by statisticians, including Ernst Engel, Georg von Mayr, William Petty, and Wilhelm Lexis. The books in the series, which Kuruma helped translate, sold surprisingly well, helping to fund the OISR during the difficult war years.

Even as the situation in Japan went from bad to worse, the OISR remained a sort of oasis for free thought. Ōuchi recalls how after his release from prison, when he was treated as a pariah elsewhere, his OISR colleagues welcomed him back. He found the institute to be a 'quiet and warm place, like a sun-lit rock in a wintry field'.[28] On a typical day, Ōuchi recalled, the researchers would work from morning until around noon, and then share a common meal, over which Takano, who procured the necessary ingredients every day, enjoyed quizzing his colleagues on their knowledge of German and English. Lunch was followed by leisurely games of table tennis in the courtyard, sometimes stretching until two or three in the afternoon. After a few more hours of work, the day was capped off with drinks, again procured somehow by Takano. This routine continued into the final year of the war. No matter how dire the news became, the OISR members kept at their table tennis each afternoon, described by Ōuchi as 'our little act of resistance to the war'.[29]

The outbreak of war itself had come as no surprise to Kuruma, who predicted in his 1929 article on crisis that the upcoming crisis would likely 'once

---

28 Ōuchi 1957, p. 396.
29 Ōuchi 1957, p. 397.

again take the form of a world war'.³⁰ He and his colleagues fully expected the war to end in Japan's defeat and did not think that would necessarily be a negative outcome. Kuruma recalled sitting in on a meeting between Takano and an executive from the Mitsui conglomerate at which he heard the OISR director bluntly declare that Japan was certain to lose the war and that this was the only way for the Japanese people to rid themselves of the militarist fools leading the nation.³¹

In many respects, the war years were fruitful ones for Kuruma in his study of capitalism. Relieved of the pressure to publish articles, he could simply immerse himself in the works of Marx. Kazuo Nimura viewed Kuruma as one of the fortunate ones during the war, as he was 'probably the only scholar in the whole country who was drawing a salary to spend his days reading Marx and creating notecards with excerpts from his works'.³² However, in the final year of the conflict, Kuruma was dealt two terrible blows. In December 1944, his wife died at the age of 42, leaving him to raise his 12-year-old son Ken alone. Then, on 24 May of the following year, a US bombing raid on Tokyo destroyed the OISR offices in the former Yodobashi Ward. Rare books and other materials kept in a stone storehouse survived the attack, but the thousands of notecards on crisis that Kuruma had painstakingly compiled went up in smoke – as did his hope of completing his project on crisis.

7   Postwar Revival

At the war's end, in August 1945, the OISR was running its operations out of the home of Iwazaburō Takano, with few financial resources available. The institute was soon to lose the services of many of its leading members who rose to positions of power on the wave of postwar 'democratisation'. Takano became the director of Japan's public broadcaster NHK; Hyōe Ōuchi was hired by the University of Tokyo to rebuild its faculty of economics; Karoku Hosokawa was elected to the Diet in 1946 as a candidate for the JCP, becoming the head of its parliamentary group; and Tatsuo Morito was elected to the Diet for the JSP and appointed Minister of Education in 1947. This left Kuruma as the institute's administrative director, tasked with keeping the organisation afloat during the turbulent period that followed Japan's surrender.

---

30   Kuruma 1929, p. 80.
31   Kuruma 1973c (Sep. 18 issue of *Ekonomisuto*, p. 89).
32   Nimura et. al 1989, p. 40.

In May 1946, the OISR obtained office space within the facilities of the former East Asia Studies Institute, which was being reorganised as the Institute for the Study of Political Economy. Some funding was secured through contributions and government grants, but the money coming in did not keep pace with inflation. Eventually the OISR found a way out of its financial crisis when Hosei University, where Kuruma was teaching, proposed taking over the organisation. This resulted in the establishment of the Ōhara Institute for Social Research, Hosei University, in 1949, with Kuruma staying on as its director.[33]

Despite his administrative tasks at the time, Kuruma continued his research and before long had built up an extensive new collection of notecards with passages from the writings of Marx. Crisis remained an area of interest for Kuruma, although it was not his primary concern. A collection of his articles on crisis was published in 1949, allowing his views to finally reach a wider audience. Kuruma also organised a study circle in the 1950s that aimed to arrive at a more systematic understanding of crisis. Several participants went on to publish their ideas on crisis, including Kiyoshi Ōshima's long entry on crisis for the dictionary on *Capital* published in 1961 and Yoshio Miyake's 1974 two-volume work on the writings of Marx and Engels related to crises in England.

Kuruma's interest in crisis was rekindled through reading the *Grundrisse der Kritik der Politischen Ökonomie* when the second German edition was published in 1953.[34] The edition sold out immediately in Japan, amidst the intense interest in Marx at the time, forcing Kuruma to literally snatch the book out of the hands of his colleague Sutehiko Uesugi, who had been one of the lucky few to secure a copy.[35] Kuruma spent several months engrossed in the study of this 'treasure trove'.[36] Uesugi recalled that 'Kuruma seemed to have had the feeling that he would discover theoretical ideas in the pages of the *Grundrisse* that he had long pondered'.[37] Reading the work confirmed Kuruma's view that an understanding of crisis requires grasping how capital continually seeks to drive beyond its own immanent barriers. The *Grundrisse* also revealed to Kuruma that Marx's conception of 'capital in general' had changed during the interval between completing that work and writing the manuscripts for *Capital* – as he explains in the introduction to the 1965 edition of *An Investigation of Crisis Theory*.[38]

---

33   He held this position until 1966.
34   The first German edition was published during the war years and was unobtainable in Japan.
35   Nimura et. al 1989, p. 40.
36   Kuruma 1968 (ed.), p. xxxvi.
37   Nimura et. al, p. 41.
38   This part of the introduction is included as an addition to Chapter 2 of this book.

More than crisis, however, it was the theory of money that absorbed most of Kuruma's attention in the 1940s and 1950s. The runaway inflation that was harassing Kuruma as OISR director fascinated him as a scholar. Long before the end of the war, he had turned his attention to the phenomenon of inflation in the expectation that it would run rampant following Japan's defeat. When that prediction came true, an increasingly militant working class responded to the rapidly rising prices with strikes and workplace occupations to secure higher wages and improve working conditions. Many economists and politicians argued that the wage increases won through such struggles were causing inflation to spiral out of control. This was a popular view that Kuruma sought to refute in his 1946 article, 'Are Prices and Wages in a Vicious Circle?', published in the left-wing magazine *Kaizō*.[39]

Kuruma's interest in inflation was connected more broadly to his study of Marx's theory of money. For many years he had been grappling with the 'riddle of money' presented in Marx's analysis of the commodity in Chapter 1 of *Capital*. Kuruma found it particularly difficult to grasp the theoretical task of the theory of the value form in Section 3 of Chapter 1 and its relation to Chapter 2 on the exchange process. None of the interpretations of Part 1 of *Capital* available at the time[40] seemed convincing to him. Kuruma pondered these issues during the war years and by war's end had 'arrived at a view that seemed fundamentally correct'.[41] He was given an opportunity to present his views on Marx's analysis of the commodity and money in the autumn of 1946, when he took part in a series of study meetings on *Capital* organised by the journal *Hyōron*. The monthly meetings, which were held until the following summer, brought together a dozen leading Marxian scholars, including Kōichirō Suzuki, Itsurō Sakisaka, and Hyōe Ōuchi. Kuruma faithfully attended each meeting, attracted as much by the publisher's generous provision of food and drinks as by the discussion itself. During the meetings, Kuruma encountered the radically different perspective of Kōzō Uno, who argued that the value form cannot be understood without taking into consideration the desire of a commodity owner for a specific use value. Kuruma argued against this view, insisting that in order to clarify the mechanism of value expression Marx had to abstract from that want.

---

39   Kuruma 1946 (Chapter 12 of this book).
40   When Kuruma first began studying *Capital* in the 1920s, the two main commentaries available in Japan were *Commentary on Das Kapital* by the Russian economist David Rozenberg and *An Introduction to Das Kapital* by Hajime Kawakami.
41   Kuruma 2018, p. 28.

A transcript[42] of the discussions was published in *Hyōron* and later issued as a book. By examining the book and taking careful notes, Kuruma was able to refine his understanding of the theoretical tasks raised at the beginning of *Capital*. His notes served as the basis for a series of articles for *The Hosei Economic Review* titled 'Theory of the Value Form and Theory of the Exchange Process' – later published by Iwanami Shoten in 1957 as a book under the same title.[43] Kuruma viewed the content as a sort of introduction to a larger work on Marx's theory of money that he hoped to write. Kuruma had in fact received an advance from the publishing firm Kawade Shobō for such a book, but the writing came slowly, as usual, and in the end he fulfilled his contractual obligation by instead submitting a short history of political economy.[44] Even though the book on money, like the book on crisis, was never completed, Marx's theory of money remained a central concern for Kuruma until the end of his life. In 1979, a collection of his discussions with colleagues of money and the commodity was published under the title *Theory of Money*,[45] and five volumes on the topic of money were published in *Marx-Lexikon zur politischen Ökonomie*.

8   Marx-Lexikon zur politischen Ökonomie

Kuruma was already past the age of 70 when he began work on a publishing project to which he would dedicate the remaining years of his life. The project grew out of the enormous collection of notecards on the writings of Marx that Kuruma had amassed after the war. By the early 1960s, the collection numbered around 10,000 notecards, which Kuruma made available to students and colleagues for use in their own research. Hoping to make the notecards more accessible, Kuruma asked his son to help him catalogue the collection. Ken kept putting off the request until his friend Teinosuke Ōtani stepped in to undertake the burdensome task. Ōtani had met Samezō Kuruma at a study meeting on crisis held in 1957, and a few years later enrolled in the same doctoral programme at Rikkyo University as Ken Kuruma.

By late 1965, the diligent Ōtani had finished the task of cataloguing the notecard collection. Soon thereafter, the collection came to the attention of Naoe Kobayashi, an editor at Ōtsuki Shoten, the publisher of the Japanese edition

---

42   Kuruma was dissatisfied with his own remarks at the meeting and received permission from the publisher to extensively rewrite them (Uno 1973, p. 634).
43   Kuruma 1957 (English translation included in Kuruma 2018).
44   Kuruma 1948b (English translation of Chapter 3 published as Kuruma 2007).
45   Kuruma 1979 (English translation of Part 1 included in Kuruma 2018).

of the collected works of Marx and Engels. Kobayashi became interested in publishing the content of the notecards in some form or other. In the end, Ōtsuki Shoten partnered with the Ōhara Institute for Social Research, Hosei University, to publish a multivolume collection of passages from the works the works of Marx (in German with Japanese translations), organised under several key topics.[46] In 1967, an editorial committee headed by Kuruma was formed to publish this *Marx-Lexikon zur politischen Ökonomie*. The choice of the name was influenced by the *Hegel-Lexikon* (Hermann Glöckner, ed.), while the format of arranging passages under headings and subheadings drew on the approach of the *Marx Brevier* (Franz Diedrich, ed.) and the *Friedrich Engels Brevier* (Ernst Drahn, ed.).[47]

The editorial aim of *Marx-Lexikon* was 'to provide readers with a supplemental means to accurately assimilate the theory of Marxian economics … so they can avoid a fragmentary and one-dimensional understanding of Marx's theories and become aware of facts and theoretical points that are easy to overlook but fully merit attention'.[48] The first *Marx-Lexikon* volume, on the topic of competition, appeared in 1968, followed by two volumes on Marx's method (1968–69), two volumes on the materialist conception of history (1971), four volumes on crisis (1972–76), and five volumes on money (1979–85), as well as an index for first nine volumes (1978). Ōtani, who served on the editorial committee, notes that none of the five *Marx-Lexikon* topics are dealt with in a single place within *Capital* or any other work by Marx, so that they can only be understood within the context of his entire oeuvre. This emphasis on bringing together and systematically organising the writings of Marx on a number of key topics sets *Marx-Lexikon* apart from a dictionary of Marxist thought, and accounts for why Kuruma did not seek to include a comprehensive list of topics. The passages chosen from Marx's published works, manuscripts, and correspondence were intended to serve as a resource for exploring topics of fundamental importance to an understanding of capitalism.

The editorial process for *Marx-Lexikon* began with the grouping together of notecards according to the main topic for each volume. The editors examined the typed passages and headings of the cards and then grouped related cards together, creating a heading for each bundle. Various bundles were then grouped together under broader headings. Through this process, the overall

---

46   Kobayashi had suggested a partnership with the Institute of Marxism-Leninism in Moscow, given the international significance of the project, but Kuruma rejected the idea.
47   The format is also similar to Kuruma's 1936 article 'An Overview of Marx's Theory of Crisis' (Chapter 4 of this book), which has been described as a 'prototype' of *Marx-Lexikon*.
48   Ōtani 2003, p. 97.

structure of each volume gradually took shape and was discussed among the editors. Once an agreement had been reached on the basic structure of a volume, a rough manuscript was typed out and the source and page number for each passage were tracked down. With the typed manuscript of the passages in hand, the editors could then again discuss the overall content and the names of headings and subheadings and decide what sentences or words to underline for emphasis. Existing translations of the passages were also copied to create the corresponding Japanese manuscript that was revised under the supervision of Seijirō Usami.

Each *Marx-Lexikon* volume came with an insert that included a discussion of the main topic between Kuruma and the assistant editors.[49] These discussions were based on the recorded meetings of the editorial committee, but since recordings ran to dozens of hours, Kuruma often had to create a semifictional dialogue rather than simply transcribing what had been said. The views expressed in the discussions, and the *Marx-Lexikon* volumes themselves, drew considerable attention from other Marxian scholars in Japan, generating debate, including Ryōzō Tomizuka's criticism of Kuruma's understanding of crisis theory.[50] Kuruma continued to work on the *Marx-Lexikon* project right up to the end of his life, managing to complete the volumes on money around the time he was diagnosed with lung cancer and hospitalised in late August 1982. Kuruma died a little over a month later, on 10 October, at the age of 89. Had he lived a few years longer, Kuruma could have mined his notecard collection for further volumes on the state, credit, or the system of Marx's critique of political economy.[51]

9   'A Mere Interpreter of Marx'

The close association of Kuruma with the *Marx-Lexikon* project led some to label him a 'mere interpreter of Marx' who had few ideas of his own. Such 'doctrinal rather than original work'[52] was contrasted with the creativity of those who were seeking to go *beyond* Marx. Kuruma would hardly have denied that his aim was to interpret the ideas of Marx. But even the 'creative' thinkers who aim to transcend Marx, after finding fault with some of his ideas, must begin

---

49   The discussions for the four *Marx-Lexikon* volumes on crisis are included in this English edition.
50   See Chapter 16 for Kuruma's two-part response to Tomizuka.
51   Ōtani 2003, p. 110.
52   Itoh 1980, p. 33.

from an interpretation of those ideas. If the interpretation itself turns out to be mistaken, the whole creative endeavour can be called into question. The existence of so many conflicting explanations of the first chapter of *Capital* alone attests to the difficulty of interpreting Marx. For his part, Kuruma spent years trying to sort out his understanding of Part 1 of *Capital*, particularly the theory of the value form in Chapter 1, Section 3. Had Kuruma rushed to the conclusion that Marx is needlessly splitting hairs in that analysis, he would never have been able to appreciate the way in which the riddle of money is unravelled through explaining the mechanism of value expression. Kuruma believed that one-sided or incorrect interpretations often stem from a failure to firmly grasp the theoretical question that Marx is posing. Kuruma emphasised that 'a problem can only be solved once it has been posed in a pure, independent form'[53] by setting aside or 'abstracting from' whatever is irrelevant to it. Thus, the crucial task for readers and interpreters of Marx, is to understand how and why he poses a theoretical question in a particular way. Once that has been achieved, the solution to the problem should be nearly self-evident; whereas 'it would be a waste of time, like casting pearls before swine, to present the solution to someone who had yet to grasp the problem'.[54]

Grasping Marx's theoretical questions is easier said than done, however. *Capital* does not provide cut-and-dried definitions of the sort found in a typical economics textbook. What we encounter instead are complexly intertwined concepts and multiple levels of abstraction. Rather than taking economic forms for granted, Marx subjects them to a multifaceted analysis that not only identifies their essential determinations but lays bare the social and class relations that underlie but at the same time are concealed by those forms. It is already a challenge for a reader to follow Marx's presentation in the highly polished Book I of *Capital*, but the difficulty increases by orders of magnitude when reading the manuscripts in which he is working out his ideas on the page. Another challenge for the 'mere interpreter' is how the three books of *Capital* fit into the larger project Marx had envisaged for his critique of political economy. This includes the question of whether the theoretical scope of *Capital* is narrowly limited to the elucidation of 'capital in general', as in Marx's original six-book plan for a 'critique of political economy', or was expanded under a broader conceptual framework.[55] Thus, the interpreter has to grapple with problems that those more eager to 'transcend' Marx may not have even noticed.

---

53 Kuruma 2018, p. 30.
54 Kuruma 2018, p. 55.
55 Kuruma presents his views on the relation of *Capital* to Marx's overall critique of political economy in Chapter 2 and 3.

The label of 'mere interpreter' attached to Kuruma also implies that he was engaged in a scholastic endeavour of no real practical significance, as if his primary aim was 'to study Marx for Marx's sake' rather than to analyse contemporary capitalism. Kuruma responded to such criticism by pointing out that even though it is true, in many cases, that the ideas of Marx cannot be directly applied to the analysis of present-day capitalism, his theories provide vital concepts necessary to arrive at a deeper understanding of the capitalist world:

> Marx of course did not write his works in the form of being immediately applicable to current problems, but I hold the view that within his theory we can find the fundamental thinking needed for such an explanation. In many cases people are saying such things about Marx without understanding the true meaning of what he wrote. What is the point of saying Marx is of little use if one has not understood him? I think that once we have reached an adequate understanding of his ideas, many things become clear. Since I am incapable of doing everything at once, the most meaningful and useful approach for me has been to clarify what has been overlooked or misunderstood within Marx's writings up to now.[56]

For Kuruma, an examination of the ideas of Marx provides us with fundamental concepts necessary for a concrete analysis of capitalism. Kiyoshi Ōshima points out that, far from engaging in a 'superficial explanation of this or that concept of Marx', Kuruma 'sought to clarify how concepts are reflected and unfold in the development of reality and are related to other concepts, as the means of grasping the laws that penetrate the world of capital'.[57] Given his intense interest in the real movement within the capitalist world, Ōshima adds, Kuruma was troubled by what he saw as a trend toward 'nitpicking articles regarding small details in *Capital*' that made him wonder 'what exactly was the aim of scholars in studying economics'.[58]

An example of the relation between theoretical insights gained from reading Marx and the analysis of contemporary reality can be seen in Kuruma's 1946 article on the relation between rising wages and inflation.[59] This was a question of the utmost practical and political significance at the time. Kuruma drew on knowledge gained from reading *Capital* to refute a persuasive argument used by capitalists to reject the demands of workers. Without a theoretical grounding

---

56   Kuruma 1973 (Oct. 2 issue of *Ekonomisuto*, p. 86).
57   Kuruma 1985, p. 14.
58   Kuruma 1985, p. 14.
59   Kuruma 1946.

in the ideas of Marx, Kuruma would not have been able to counter an argument that seemed to be empirically confirmed. A decade earlier Kuruma had drawn on his knowledge of Marx to engage with another pressing economic problem: the unprecedented global depression. Here again theoretical ideas presented in *Capital* provided clues for making sense of contemporary economic reality. The manner in which Kuruma was able to apply fundamental theoretical knowledge to the analysis of contemporary economic reality is demonstrated in his critique of John B. Condliffe's *World Economic Survey*, published by the League of Nations.[60] Kuruma was interested in how the heap of empirical facts presented by Condliffe could be 'illuminated by Marx's theory' so as to 'take on new meaning in their relation to the totality'.

These are two examples of how the study of Marx was not an end in itself for Kuruma, but an indispensable means of understanding concrete reality more precisely. His engagement with the economic problems of his time was also reflected in the decision to focus on money and crisis. He chose those two theoretical topics wisely, knowing their centrality to capitalism and relation to a wide range of economic phenomena. The study of crisis and money was a means for Kuruma to systematically explore capitalism and approach concrete problems in a step-by-step manner. But simply understanding the world was not the limit of Kuruma's ambition. Like Marx, Kuruma wanted to change the world, and saw the understanding of capitalism as essential to that end. Ōtani writes that 'the continued importance to Kuruma of changing the world was why he sought to read and interpret Marx' and that 'this fundamental stance was maintained right up to his final breath'.[61]

10   The Legacy of Kuruma

During his own lifetime, Kuruma's influence was not particularly widespread for a number of reasons. As someone who spent the bulk of his career as a member of a research institute, rather than a university professor, he did not build up a network of former graduate students who shared a similar outlook to his own. The self-effacing nature of Kuruma's work, which aimed to dive deeper into Marx's ideas rather than soar beyond them, also made him less appealing than those who claimed to offer something radically new. And then there was Kuruma's lack of interest in worldly success or leading a tight-knit group of

---

60   Kuruma 1935a (Chapter 9 of this book).
61   Ōtani 2003, p. 41.

followers. Kōzō Uno jokingly said that Kuruma was 'the only person in Japan, apart from the emperor, who was without ambition', which made him 'a fearsome person to debate'.[62] Teinosuke Ōtani describes Kuruma as 'indifferent to personal prestige and self-promotion', and observes that no 'Kuruma school' ever emerged because 'he had no thought of fostering outstanding protégés to be dispatched to universities around the country to form a personal network, nor did he seek to exclude anyone for having a different way of thinking to his own'.[63] Kuruma liked to point to the Buddhist monk Shinran, who claimed to 'have not even one disciple', and he consciously refused the authoritarian role of determining followers and outcasts.[64] Nevertheless, a group of sorts did begin to coalesce around Kuruma in the late 1960s through the *Marx-Lexikon* project. One of the project participants, Hirono Okuda, explains how he and others became 'disciples' of this 'teacher who claimed to have not even one disciple':

> Those who had a genuine interest in examining Marx's critique of political economy, whether they were famous or unknown, gathered around Professor Kuruma. The editors of *Marx-Lexikon* were likewise a group of free individuals who wanted to learn from Marx and sought direction in their reading. The collaborators all had their own views and took their own actions, but we were able to get along in an atmosphere of harmony and mutual understanding because Professor Kuruma was the central figure.[65]

Through the *Marx-Lexikon* project, Kuruma came into contact with many graduate students and young professors. For the students who encountered him in the 1960s and 1970s, the tall, lean, white-haired professor must have seemed a character from another age. Yukihiko Maehata, a seminar student who often visited Kuruma at his home in Kichijoji to assist his work on *Marx-Lexikon*, recalled the sight of Professor Kuruma on strolls to nearby Inokashira Park, dressed in a blue kimono and brown beret, back perfectly straight, and brandishing a walking stick.[66] His indifference to the latest fashions extended to the intellectual world, whose trends and controversies were only a faint blip on his radar. 'Follow your path, and let the people talk', Marx's adaptation of a line from Dante, could have served equally well as Kuruma's maxim. All of this

---

62 Kuruma 1985, p. 6.
63 Ōtani 2003, p. 37.
64 Kuruma 1985, p. 8.
65 Kuruma 1985, p. 14.
66 Kuruma 1985, p. 8.

made Kuruma seem forbidding at first, but on closer acquaintance he proved to be warm-hearted and generous. Recollections of Kuruma after his death touch on many of the same points. Colleagues remember the strong emphasis he placed on being aware of why one is engaged in the study of something and clearly grasping the central theoretical question. The importance of limiting one's research to certain fundamental problems, so as not to spread oneself too thin, is another point he emphasised and considered indispensable in his own particular case. In later life, Kuruma's conversations often drifted toward memories of his trip to Europe in the 1920s and recollections of Kushida's unique personality. His stories were told over the evening drink, a sacred ritual for Kuruma throughout his life. Reading Marx during the day, drinking at night, and smoking all the way through – these were Kuruma's simple requirements for the good life.

What the younger scholars gained through their interaction with Kuruma, above all, was an appreciation of the importance of engaging directly with Marx's writings, without preconceptions. This approach is reflected in the subsequent work of *Marx-Lexikon* editors, most notably Teinosuke Ōtani, who went on to play a central role in editing volumes of the new *Marx-Engels Gesamtausgabe* until his death in 2019.[67] Other scholars involved in the *Marx-Lexikon* project who did important work included his son Ken, whose research centred on the monetary system, inflation, and the environmental limits to capitalism, as well as Tadatoshi Kawanabe, Kazuo Konishi, and Keiko Maehata, who all made important contributions to the understanding of crisis. Through the work of such scholars, and their direct interaction with their own graduate students, a new generation of Marxian economists influenced by the work and approach of Kuruma has emerged over the past decade, including Hideto Akashi, Korefumi Miyata, Kōhei Saitō, and Ryūji Sasaki. The legacy of Kuruma, as reflected in the work of those directly or indirectly influenced by him, centres on freeing the ideas of Marx from the ideology of 'Marxism'.

That is not to say that Kuruma himself was free from that ideology in the realm of his political sympathies, as already touched on. In a 1977 interview, for instance, he responded to a comment about the social stagnation in Eastern Europe at the time by describing the Communist-led countries as transitional societies that should be judged by how much progress they had made to date, rather than how far they were lagging behind other countries, and he even placed some of the blame on the difficulty of changing people's way of think-

---

67 My English translation of Ōtani's textbook introducing the three volumes of *Capital* was published in 2018 under the title: *A Guide to Marxian Political Economy* (Ōtani 2018).

ing.[68] Yet Kuruma did not allow the existence of money, wage labour, profit, etc. in the Eastern Bloc and China to alter his fundamental understanding of socialism as a society in which there would be no room for those economic forms to exist. In his book *Theory of Money*, a section clearly titled 'Commodities and Money Do Not Exist in a Socialist Society' includes his explanation that money would have no reason to circulate under socialism because 'individual labour would be social labour from the outset',[69] rather than only becoming a part of the total social labour through the sale of commodities. Other references to a future socialist society that bears little resemblance to the 'really existing socialism' of his time are sprinkled throughout this book on crisis. For instance, in the discussion regarding the third *Marx-Lexikon* volume on crisis,[70] Kuruma describes a socialist society as one in which 'production is not carried out for the sake of profit but to improve the lives of all members of society', so that after a certain stage it is 'pointless' to produce more of certain goods and instead 'labour time would likely be reduced' to expand the free time needed 'for people to engage in truly creative activities'.

Thus, Kuruma's writings provide some essential ideas needed to demonstrate that socialism (in Marx's understanding of the term) has yet to really exist anywhere, and his younger colleague Teinosuke Ōtani did eventually recognise that the societies that he and so many others had mistaken for socialism were in fact examples of 'state capitalism'. This conclusion, once labelled 'counter-revolutionary', has been accepted by more and more Marxian scholars in Japan over the past decade, providing an example of how we can look to the ideas of Marx to overcome the terrible confusion generated in the twentieth century by the ideology of Marxism. From this perspective, the leather-bound volumes of *Marx-Lexikon*, which seemed destined for the trash bin of history after the collapse of the Soviet Union, are a treasure trove for understanding capitalism and envisaging a real alternative to it.

11 Reading *Capital* as Crisis Theory

Kuruma's fascination with crisis guided his lifelong engagement with the ideas of Karl Marx. This interest fundamentally shaped his approach to reading *Capital* from the time he first encountered that work in the early 1920s. The more Kuruma explored *Capital*, the more convinced he became that 'the system of

---

68   Kuruma 2015, p. 335.
69   Kuruma 1979, p. 191.
70   Kuruma 1975b (ed.) (Chapter 7 of this book).

Marx's critique of political economy is an astoundingly magnificent system of crisis theory, in which *Capital* constitutes the most fundamental part'.[71] Kuruma thus viewed *Capital* as the foundation for a systematic understanding of crisis.

At the same time, Kuruma knew that *Capital* does not contain a theory of crisis *per se*. According to some of the plans Marx sketched for his 'critique of political economy', the sixth and final book was to deal with the world market and crisis, but that book was never completed or even begun. Thus, an important first step in Kuruma's project was to consider the relation of the investigations related to crisis in the published volumes of *Capital* to a 'proper' theory of crisis of the sort Marx may have intended to create. This is linked to the broader question of how *Capital* relates to Marx's overall critique of political economy. The conclusion that Kuruma reached is that the theoretical scope of *Capital* is basically limited to the elucidation of 'capital in general', as per Marx's original plan for the first book in his six-book critique. This is a rejection of the assertion by Henryk Grossman and others that *Capital* incorporates the content originally planned for the other books in the critique.[72] Thus, Kuruma viewed the explanations of crisis in *Capital* as 'no more than points of reference' for clarifying 'problems pertaining to the logical unfolding of Marx's descriptions of "capital in general"' rather than a 'proper theory of crisis', making it necessary to clarify the intrinsic relation between the two. Kuruma believed that positioning the writings on crisis in *Capital* within a systematic theory of crisis requires us 'to trace our way back further to elucidate Marx's overall approach toward clarifying crisis and its relation to his critique of political economy, based on an understanding of the essence of crisis'.[73]

Kuruma's understanding of the essence of crisis, as the starting point for a theory of crisis, is founded on Marx's descriptions of 'crises of the world market' as the 'momentary, violent solutions for the existing contradictions'[74] or the 'real concentration and forcible adjustment of all the contradictions of bourgeois production'.[75] This view of crisis as a violent eruption and temporary resolution of all the contradictions of capitalist production determines

---

71 Kuruma 1953d, p. 984.
72 At the time of his critique of Grossman, Kuruma had not yet read the *Grundrisse* and was thus unaware of the degree to which Marx's concept of 'capital in general' expanded from the late 1850s to the early 1860s. In part of the preface to his 1965 book *An Investigation of Crisis Theory*, (included near the end of Chapter 2), Kuruma discusses what he learned from reading *Grundrisse* with regard to 'capital in general'.
73 Kuruma 1930, p. 30.
74 Marx 1981a, p. 357.
75 Marx 1987a, p. 140.

Kuruma's entire plan for a systematic theory of crisis, as he explains in 'An Overview of Marx's Theory of Crisis':

> Because crisis is the concentrated explosion of all of the contradictions of capitalist production, in order to concretely grasp crisis as such, one must first unfold all of the contradictions of capitalist production according to their internal relations, thereby clarifying the significance of each contradiction as a moment within a totality, and then elucidate what processes the contradictions pass through and in what sense they must explode in a concentrated manner.[76]

Kuruma makes a similar point in 'An Introduction to the Study of Crisis', emphasising the need to grasp 'all the contradictions' of capitalism in their organic interrelation as moments in the dialectical development of capitalist production, so as to clarify the process of their inevitable development to the point of explosion'.[77] This is an approach that Kuruma found lacking among other Marxists, who tended to sever the 'various causes of crisis … from their intrinsic relations' so as to grasp them 'abstractly, in isolation, and therefore as mutually unrelated (or only superficially united) or even in conflict with each other'.[78] In short, a systematic understanding of crisis requires nothing less than the comprehensive understanding of capitalism itself. This also implies that the 'entire system of the critique of political economy (of which *Capital* is the most fundamental part) must at the same time be an enormous theory of crisis – or an enormous system concentrated in the theory of crisis as its summarising or conclusive part'.[79] The vast scale of the task that Kuruma set himself is clear. Where does one even begin to develop such a theory of crisis?

As his methodological guiding thread, Kuruma looked to a passage from *Theories of Surplus Value* in which Marx clarifies that the starting point of a theory of crisis is a recognition of the abstract form of crisis. This is the 'general, abstract possibility of crisis' arising from the contradiction between sale and purchase, which 'may fall apart'.[80] In *Capital*, Marx explains that the possibility for sale and purchase to diverge stems from the obvious fact that 'no one directly needs to purchase because he has just sold'.[81] Marx thus refutes the

---

76   Kuruma 1936, p. 44.
77   Kuruma 1929, p. 80.
78   Kuruma 1929, p. 81.
79   Kuruma 1929, p. 81.
80   Marx 1989b, p. 140.
81   Marx 1976, pp. 208–9.

'foolish dogma' of Jean-Baptiste Say, who insisted that sales and purchases (and hence supply and demand) are in equilibrium 'because every sale is a purchase, and every purchase a sale'. This was the popular argument used to deny the possibility of overproduction and crisis. Granted, as Marx notes, there is a 'direct identity present ... between the exchange of one's own product and the acquisition of someone else's' in the case of a barter exchange; but the mediation of money in that direct exchange splits the unity 'into the two antithetical segments of sale and purchase', so that 'circulation bursts through all the temporal, spatial and personal barriers imposed by the direct exchange of products'.[82] This is an example of how a contradiction is given 'room to move'.[83] Yet sale and purchase still 'form an internal unity', which means that if the 'assertion of their external independence proceeds to a certain critical point, their unity violently makes itself felt by producing – a crisis'.[84] This does not mean that the divergence of sale and purchase within commodity circulation is a direct cause of crisis, however. Marx is careful to note that this divergence merely concerns the 'formal possibility of crisis', which is 'no more than the *most abstract form* of crisis, without content, without a compelling motivating factor'.

A 'second form' of crisis related to the divergence of sale and purchase is presented in the same key methodological passage from *Theories of Surplus Value*. This is the possibility of crisis arising from money's function as a means of payment. In transactions mediated by money in this function, a seller hands over a commodity to a buyer in return for a 'promise to pay money' at a later date, so that the seller becomes a creditor and the buyer a debtor. Thus, there is a temporal gap between the handing over of the commodity and the payment of money, and money 'has two different aspects' ('measure of value' when the commodity is handed over and 'realisation of value' when payment is made). Marx notes that if 'in the interval between them the value has changed' so that the commodity is not worth as much at the time of its sale as it was worth at the moment when money was acting as a measure of value, then 'the obligation cannot be met from the proceeds of the sale of the commodity, and therefore the whole series of transactions which retrogressively depend on this one transaction, cannot be settled'.[85] Given these characteristics, this second form of crisis 'is more concrete than the first', but Marx is careful to note that it is still 'quite abstract'.[86]

---

82   Marx 1976, p. 209.
83   Marx 1976, p. 198.
84   Marx 1976, p. 209.
85   Marx 1989b, p. 144.
86   Marx 1989b, p. 140.

The first and second form of crisis are not a direct, concrete cause of crisis, but simply its 'most generalised expression'[87] or its abstract possibility. A more concrete understanding of crisis requires us to consider 'why *its abstract form*, the form of its possibility, turns from possibility into *actuality*'.[88] Marx explains that the 'factors which turn this possibility of crisis into [an actual] crisis are not contained' in the abstract form of crisis itself, which 'only implies that *the framework* for a crisis exists';[89] for 'the development of this possibility into reality a whole series of conditions is required, which do not yet even exist from the standpoint of the simple circulation of commodities'.[90] Thus, the challenge in pursuing a theory of crisis is to move beyond the general, abstract forms of crisis to locate and examine within 'each sphere of the bourgeois economy', the individual moments that are 'condensed' in a world trade crisis. The 'further one proceeds' in this endeavour, Marx explains, 'the more aspects of this conflict must be traced', revealing that 'more abstract forms are recurring and are contained in the more concrete forms'.[91]

Here we face another difficulty in determining what step to take next in advancing toward a more complete understanding of crisis. Kuruma sought clues for how to proceed in the same key a passage from *Theories of Surplus Value*, where Marx points out that the abstract forms 'receive a content, a basis on which to manifest themselves' in the 'reproduction process of capital (which coincides with its circulation)'.[92] In other words, we need to turn to Book II of *Capital*, where the main aim is to analyse the circulation process of capital. Marx had to set aside the circulation process in Book I in order to purely examine the immediate production process. For the sake of that analysis, he assumes that the circulation process proceeds smoothly so as to allow capitalists unhindered access to the needed means of production and labour power. This is why the analysis of the production process of capital 'does not contribute any new element of crisis', which 'can only emerge in the circulation process which is in itself also a process of reproduction'.[93]

In Book II of *Capital*, Marx returns to the metamorphoses of commodities considered in Book I, but now the process is examined as a circulation process of capital, premised on his analysis of the production process. The

---

87   Marx 1989b, p. 145.
88   Marx 1989b, p. 145.
89   Marx 1989b, p. 140.
90   Marx 1976, p. 209.
91   Marx 1989b, p. 140.
92   Marx 1989, p. 140.
93   Marx 1989b, p. 143.

abstract forms of crisis that Marx identified within the circulation of commodities are 'repeated' but with content that is more developed, reflecting the greater complexity of the circulation of capital compared to simple commodity circulation. Kuruma borrows Marx's term *Inhaltsbestimmung* (content determination)[94] in describing how the abstract forms of crisis become more determined within the circulation of capital. Under Heading VII in the first *Marx-Lexikon* volume on crisis, Kuruma includes nine subheadings dealing with specific cases of the abstract possibility of crisis acquiring such 'content determination'.[95]

The first two subheadings look, respectively, at the metamorphoses M–C and C–M that capital must pass through on its circuit. The same metamorphoses exist in the circulation of commodities (albeit in reverse order), but within the circulation of capital the content is far more concrete. In the first phase, M–C, money capital must be transformed into the elements of productive capital (labour power and the means of production), rather than just a particular commodity that the money holder desires. The second phase is also more concrete, since C–M is at the same time C'–M', which means that a commodity containing surplus value must be sold to realise that surplus value. These are two examples of the abstract possibility of crisis becoming more determined in its content under the circulation of capital.

The fourth subheading in *Marx-Lexikon* considers how, unlike the case of simple commodity circulation, 'the circuits of individual capitals are interlinked, they presuppose one another and condition one another, and it is precisely by being interlinked in this way that they constitute the movement of the total social capital'.[96] This is a complex social relationship in which not only different capitals but also capital and revenue are intertwined (e.g. the variable capital advanced by the capitalist is for the workers simply 'revenue'). The process is thus far more complex than simple commodity circulation, making the possibility of crisis arising from the separation of sale and purchase that much more concrete.

The ninth and final subheading looks at the difficulties that can arise from the shift from simple to expanded reproduction (discussed in Chapter 20 of Book II of *Capital*). In the case of simple reproduction, the rate of accumulation is zero. In other words, the capitalist consumes all of the surplus value appro-

---

94 The passage in which the term appears ('und so erweitert sich schon die Inhaltsbestimmung der Krise') is translated more loosely in the *Collected Works* as 'and thus the definition of the content is already fuller' (Marx 1989b, p. 141).
95 See Chapter 5 of this book.
96 Marx 1978, p. 429.

priated so that the production process is repeated on the same scale. In shifting to a positive rate of accumulation, thereby expanding reproduction, the department producing the means of production (Dept. I) expands in proportion to the department producing means of consumption (Dept. II). Similarly, any change of the rate of accumulation, whether up or down, will bring about a change in the proportion between the two departments. In other words, the change in the accumulation rate is the independent variable, while the proportion is the dependent variable. The friction or difficulties that can arise from the change in proportion is an example of how the possibility of crisis develops further within the circulation (=reproduction) process of capital.

Even though Marx's analysis of the circulation of capital in Book II reveals how the possibility of crisis becomes more developed, this does not yet clarify the 'factors which turn this possibility of crisis into [an actual] crisis'. Kuruma draws an important distinction between the abstract forms of crisis acquiring 'content determination' and the transformation of the possibility of crisis into actuality, describing them as 'two separate dimensions'.[97] He emphasises that, through becoming more determined, the forms of crisis are given a 'basis on which to manifest themselves' and for the possibility of crisis to be realised, but that this does not yet clarify the 'moments' through which the actualisation occurs. Kuruma's distinction may come into clearer focus by considering once more the shift from simple to expanded reproduction. The possible friction between production departments arising from the increased rate of accumulation in Dept. I is an example of how the abstract form of crisis becomes more determined and concrete, providing a basis for its manifestation. But at this stage in the analysis, the specific factors determining the rise in the rate of accumulation have yet to be elucidated. This means that even though the understanding of crisis has developed further, the analysis remains at the level of the *possibility* of crisis, not its actualisation.

The next step in the pursuit of crisis, according to Kuruma, involves clarifying the 'moments that transform the possibility of crisis into reality' – the topic of the second *Marx-Lexikon* volume on crisis. This requires an awareness of 'living contradiction' (*lebendiger Widerspruch*) at the core of capitalism, which is, according to Kuruma, a 'contradiction that is actively moving, with its opposing elements in actual conflicting motion'[98] – in contrast to a latent or static contradiction. The term is used by Marx in the following passage from the *Grundrisse*:

---

97   Kuruma 1973b (ed.), p. 2 (Chapter 6 of this book).
98   Kuruma 1973b (ed.), p. 4.

By its nature, therefore, it [capital] posits a barrier to labour and value-creation in contradiction to its tendency to expand them boundlessly. And in as much as it both posits a barrier specific to itself, and on the other side equally drives over and beyond every barrier, it is the *living contradiction*.[99]

In Book III of *Capital*, Marx describes this fundamental contradiction more clearly in the following passages:

[T]he fact that the capitalist mode of production tends towards an absolute development of the productive forces irrespective of value and the surplus value this contains, and even irrespective of the social relations within which capitalist production takes place; while on the other hand its purpose is to maintain the existing capital value and to valorise it to the utmost extent (i.e. an ever accelerated increase in this value).[100]

The barriers within which the maintenance and valorisation of the capital-value has necessarily to move ... therefore come constantly into contradiction with the methods of production that capital must apply to its purpose and which set its course towards an unlimited expansion of production, to production as an end in itself, to an unrestricted development of the social productive powers of labour. The means – the unrestricted development of the forces of production – comes into persistent conflict with restricted end, the valorisation of the existing capital.[101]

In other words, here we have the fundamental contradiction between capital's tendency to develop the forces of production without limit, and the need for that development to be kept within the realm of profitability. Marx thus identifies the 'true barrier to capitalist production' as 'capital itself'. Once this living contradiction 'has progressed to a certain point', Kuruma argues, 'an extreme tension arises that causes the contradiction to explode' as crisis.[102]

This conception of the living contradiction differs from the typical ways in which the fundamental contradiction of capitalism has been portrayed by Marxists. Many theories of crisis are centred on the notion of a fundamental contradiction between production and consumption, often expressed more

---

99 Marx 1973b, p. 421. [Kuruma's emphasis.]
100 Marx 1981a, pp. 357–8.
101 Marx 1981a, pp. 358–9.
102 Kuruma 1973b (ed.), p. 4.

specifically as the contradiction between the production and realisation of surplus value or the contradiction between the tendency to raise productive power and the limited consumption power of workers (or limited capacity of markets to absorb products). Kuruma considered that manner of framing the contradictions as static rather living and dynamic. He pointed out, for example, that the limit of consumption is not an active factor within a living contradiction, as is clear from the fact that crises are periodic, whereas the restricted consumption of workers under capitalism is continual. Restricted consumption could thus be better described as a 'condition' for crisis, not its cause. For Kuruma, the mistaken theory of underconsumption arises from 'detaching the problem of the restricted consumption of the working class (which is an important problem in itself) from the "living contradiction"'.[103]

Another way of defining the fundamental contradiction of capitalism that struck Kuruma as one-sided and static was Engels's idea that the '[capitalist] mode of production is in rebellion against the mode of exchange' due to a core contradiction between 'socialised production' and 'capitalist appropriation'.[104] Kuruma thought one might make the argument that the notion of 'socialised production' is related to the tendency to develop productive power and that and 'capitalist appropriation' is related to the barrier imposed by capital's self-valorisation, but that even then the theory does not express a living contradiction and thus is 'not directly linked to periodic crises'. Engels's conception of capitalism, according to Kuruma, has 'two conflicting characteristics, and along with [its] development ... each of the two becomes more conspicuous, so that the contradiction is increasingly heightened'.[105] This is an example of a 'fundamental contradiction' in which the two key elements are *not* in an active, organic relation with each other.

In Kuruma's conception of a living contradiction, drawn from the writings of Marx, capital's tendency toward a limitless development of productive power runs up against the need for that development to benefit profitability. This limit imposed by capital itself becomes a barrier to be overcome, and in breaking through that boundary (at least temporarily), the living contradiction is stretched to the point where eventually it must violently contract in a crisis. The analysis of the production of relative surplus value in Book I of *Capital* already clarifies the ceaseless drive of individual capitals to develop productive power as a means of expanding their own market share (at the expense

---

103 Kuruma 1973b (ed.), p. 14.
104 Engels 1994, p. 64.
105 Kuruma 1973b (ed.), p. 11.

of their competitors). Marx explains how a capitalist raising the productivity of labour drives the individual value of the commodity produced below its social value, making it possible to pocket 'extra surplus value' by selling the item above its individual value but below the social value. The 'coercive law of competition' forces competitors to likewise introduce new methods to increase productivity. Through his analysis, Marx concludes in Book I that capital 'has an immanent drive, and a constant tendency, towards increasing the productivity of labour'.[106] He also clarifies important limits imposed by a system of production for profit, such as the need to restrict workers' consumption in order to generate surplus value, and he introduces the concept of the 'organic composition of capital' in relation to the 'general law of capitalist accumulation'. However, in Book I, where 'all secondary influences external to [the immediate production] process' are 'left out of account',[107] Marx is not in a position to concretely present the decisive factors in motion when capital's 'immanent drive' to raise productive power runs up against the immanent barriers of capitalism.

In order to grasp the active 'moments' within the living contradiction, we must look instead to Book III of *Capital*, where Marx examines the concrete forms of capital and surplus value within the total process of capital. Kuruma thought that Part 3 on the law of the tendential fall in the general rate of profit as capital production advances is of primary importance for grasping the active 'moments' within the living contradiction of capitalism and understanding the moving and conflicting forces that transform the possibility of crisis into actuality. Kuruma never fully elaborated those moments and their interrelation in his articles on crisis, but his understanding of the dynamic at play is reflected in the second *Marx-Lexikon* volume on crisis, where passages from Book III and other writings of Marx are grouped under the heading titled 'Moments that transform the possibility of crisis into reality', which includes 14 subheadings presenting those moments in a developmental order.

The first three subheadings deal, respectively, with (1) the 'immanent drive' of capital to raise the productive power of labour, (2) the rise in the organic composition and lowering of the profit rate that result from that increased productive power, and (3) the need for the total quantity of profit to expand as the profit rate falls and the resulting accumulation and concentration of capital. The next two subheadings deal with how (4) accumulation includes 'contradictory tendencies and phenomena' and (5) the absolute overproduc-

---

106 Marx 1976, pp. 436–7.
107 Marx 1981a, p. 117.

tion of capital that can accompany accumulation if the fall in the rate of profit is not outweighed by an increase in the mass of profit. The focus then shifts to overproduction in relation to the limits of consumption, and more specifically: (6) the difficulties facing the 'second act' of the capitalist production process, when the 'total mass of commodities' must be sold; (7) the contradiction between workers' importance as consumers and the need to limit their labour power price to a minimum; (8) the critique of the theory of underconsumption. In the next subheading, (9), Kuruma introduces passages mainly taken from the *Grundrisse* that present the 'living contradiction' in which capital seeks to drive beyond its own barriers to develop productive power. This is followed by subheadings dealing with how that contradiction can be stretched through (10) the elasticity of the production process itself, (11) the functioning of commercial capital, and (12) the role of the credit system. The last two subheadings, which are topics that stand alone, deal with (13) the contradiction of distribution relations arising as the result of production conversely entering production as its prerequisites and (14) the moments within capitalist development that prevent the contradictions of capitalism from exploding in a crisis.

The emphasis within Kuruma's conception of crisis on the conflicting elements within the accumulative drive of capital, outlined above, owes much to his reading of the *Grundrisse* in the 1950s. Prior to that, his investigation of crisis had placed more emphasis on how 'moments' with an essential unity develop in an independent direction to the point where they must be forcibly contracted in a crisis. Through reading the *Grundrisse*, Kuruma came to better appreciate how the limits inherent to capitalism become a barrier that capital seeks to break through in its pursuit of its self-valorisation. As noted above, passages clarifying the 'living contradiction' at the core of capitalism are mainly presented under Subheading 9. At one point in the editorial process, Kuruma had considered positioning those passages as the first subheading, so as to 'indicate the general way of thinking' before considering 'the concrete issue of the unfolding of the contradictions',[108] but ultimately decided to position it as a 'conclusion' for the subheadings that preceded it.

The active unfolding of the moments within the living contradiction between the drive to increase productive power and the limits of capitalism as a system of production for profit is related to the distinctive trajectory of the industrial cycle. The question of the 'distinction and relation' between the theory of crisis and the industrial cycle was described as the 'biggest prob-

---

108 Kuruma 1973b (ed.), p. 5.

lem' confronting Kuruma in editing the *Marx-Lexikon* volumes on crisis.[109] Passages discussing the industrial cycle are presented in the fourth and final volume on crisis, preceded by the three volumes dealing the theory of crisis 'proper'. This reflects Kuruma's view that the theory of the industrial cycle is premised on an understanding of the essence of crisis and the moments within the living contradiction of capitalism. Since crisis itself is the culminating phase of the industrial cycle, it might seem that the analysis of crisis should instead be positioned within the discussion of the industrial cycle, but before the phases of the industrial cycle can be analysed it is necessary to clarify what drives production to collide with the barriers of capitalism in the first place. In other words, an understanding of the industrial cycle and the distinctive pattern of its phases is premised on a theoretical understanding of the living contradiction and its active factors. The task for the theory of the industrial cycle is to clarify more concretely the crisis-culminating process through which capitalism seeks to drive through its immanent barriers, including such issues as the characteristics of each phase and the starting and ending point of the cycle. In short, the analysis of the phases of the industrial cycle is the basis for a more concrete understanding of the phenomenon of crisis.

12   A Note on the English Edition

The translations for Part 1 and Part 3 are based on the 1965 edition of *Kyōkō ron kenkyū* (An Investigation of Crisis Theory) published by Ōtsuki Shoten, except for Chapter 15 and 16, which are based on *Marukusu no kyōkō ron* (Marx's Theory of Crisis), published by Sakurai Shoten in 2019. The translations for Part 3 are based on Volume 6, 7, 8, and 9 of *Marx-Lexikon zur politischen Ökonomie* (1972–76), published by Ōtsuki Shoten, with footnotes added from *Marukusu no kyōkō ron*. Some changes have been made to translations of passages quoted from Marx, particularly when an English translation diverges considerably from the Japanese translation discussed by Kuruma. Such cases are indicated with either an explanation of the change or the simple inclusion of 'Modified translation' in the footnote. Other changes involving spelling, hyphenation, etc. have been made without comment. References made by Kuruma to *Capital* throughout this edition utilise the term 'Book' rather than 'Volume', although the latter term appears in quotations from other writers and in the listings of

---

109   Kuruma 1972b (ed.), p. 3. (In Chapter 5 of this book.)

citations for Part 2, which reflects the terminology of *Marx-Lexikon zur politischen Ökonomie* (including use of the title *Theories of Surplus Value* instead of *Economic Manuscript of 1861–1863*). Footnotes enclosed in brackets are either my own additions as editor or translations of editorial comments added by Teinosuke Ōtani in *Marukusu no kyōkō ron* (with the later indicated by the addition of '– T. Ōtani' at the end). Japanese names are listed with the family name *second*, rather than first (as is the custom in Japan).

Finally a word on the title of the book, which does not appear as the title of any published work by Kuruma. In part, the title was chosen to emphasise the incomplete nature of Marx's theory of crisis, which required Kuruma to track down the 'moments' of crisis within *Capital* and attempt to organise them into a theoretical structure. Although he made considerable progress toward that goal, Kuruma did not ultimately manage to complete the sort of comprehensive work he had envisaged. Thus, the task of pursuing Marx's theory of crisis remains – and this book is intended for anyone undertaking this pursuit. However, the further one progresses along the path leading to a systematic understanding of crisis, the more it becomes clear that the *pursuit* is as important as its ultimately aim. Pursuing the elusive phenomenon of crisis can bring us (as it brought Marx and Kuruma) to a deeper understanding of the essential elements and fundamental contradictions of capitalism as an historical mode of production.

PART 1

History and Overview of Crisis Theory

CHAPTER 1

An Introduction to the Study of Crisis

The problem of crisis is gaining worldwide attention as a crisis of unprecedented scale and unparalleled seriousness and tenacity sweeps the world.[1] Representatives of the two main classes in society have been earnestly engaged in studying this problem with a rare degree of seriousness: economists in order to somehow forge a path toward stable capitalist production, and Marxists to lay the scientific foundation for their tactics during this momentous period.

However, as long as political economy retains a bourgeois outlook it will be incapable of pushing forward in the direction of a thorough understanding of crisis. Indeed, we can see that it was the outbreak of crisis in the proper sense of the term that marked a turning point for political economy, which ceased thereafter to be a science. A crisis in the proper sense of the term is the collective explosion of all of the contradictions of capitalist production, and as such, its outbreak necessarily brought bourgeois political economy as a science to an end in two ways. First, the reality of crisis thrust upon political economy a new problem that was unanswerable from the bourgeois perspective (i.e. a problem that can only be answered by clarifying the contradictions of capitalist production), thus exposing the fundamental flaws of bourgeois political economy and the class-imposed limitations of its understanding. Second, by suddenly throwing out on the street a vast number of wageworkers who had been mobilised from all directions during the preceding boom, crisis vividly revealed the antisocial nature of capitalist production and stimulated the class consciousness of the proletariat. Thus, the clarification of the internal relations of capitalist production was transformed from a weapon of the bourgeoisie to one wielded by the proletariat. Here I would like to consider this historical process at length.

The first major crisis to strike capitalist production occurred in 1815. With the approaching downfall of Napoleon, capitalists in England prepared a massive quantity of goods for export, thinking that the continental market, which had

---

[1] [Originally published as Kuruma 1929 and republished as Chapter 1 of *An Investigation of Marx's Theory of Crisis* (Kuruma 1949). The original article (subtitled 'Preparatory Considerations to Provide a More Developed Basis for the Scientific Investigation of Crisis') included a five-chapter table of contents that lists this article as the introductory first chapter, to be followed by chapters dealing with the essence of crisis, the method of crisis theory, and the system of crisis theory, as well as a concluding chapter to consider problems related to crisis that remain, other issues related to crisis, and recent debates on crisis theory (Kuruma 1929, p. 31).]

long suffered from a shortage of goods due to the blockade, would be reopened. The Battle of Waterloo in July of that year was followed by several months of robust trading and optimistic speculation. However, before the year's end, it became clear that expectations were entirely fictitious. One reason was that industrial development on the continent had been stimulated to an unexpected degree by the blockade, which prevented the import of English goods. On top of this, continental purchasing power had deteriorated as a result of war. Unquestionably people perceived a lack of goods, and products to relieve that scarcity were piled up in warehouses, but the collision between demand without purchasing power and a mountain of unsold goods was fated to result in unmet needs and many bankrupt capitalists. This situation persisted until the spring of 1817, as one bankruptcy followed the next, so that the ranks of the unemployed overflowed in the industrial cities, resulting in the outbreak of riots in many places. The suspension of the Habeas Corpus Act in 1817 reflected the seriousness of the social unrest at the time. In spring of that year, signs of recovery finally began to appear, but business slumped again in 1819, leading to more social unrest that culminated in the horrible Peterloo Massacre. The economic depression and social disturbances continued into the following year, and only in 1821 did a path toward recovery come into view. The business climate then gradually improved, leading production to develop an unprecedented strength. But, near the end of 1825, this culminated in yet another crisis, on an enormous scale.

Needless to say, the upheavals that swept capitalist production in its youthful period like a violent storm inevitably affected the realm of political economy. One economist who experienced his first doubts about existing economic doctrines upon seeing the harsh 'convulsions of wealth', and the shocking social misery that accompanied it, was Simonde de Sismondi (1773–1842), who, like Jean-Jacques Rousseau, hailed from Geneva. At a young age, Sismondi read *The Wealth of Nations* and became strongly attached to Adam Smith's theories. Sismondi is said to have written *De la richesse commerciale ou principes de l'economie politique appliqué à la legislation du commerce* to explain and popularise Smith's doctrine, but after its publication in 1803, he immersed himself for some time in the study of history. Around 1818, he once again turned his attention to political economy, upon being commissioned to write an entry on 'political economy' for the *Edinburgh Encyclopedia*.

This was immediately after the serious economic downturn that followed the first major crisis in 1815. This crisis, as mentioned, cannot necessarily be viewed as a crisis in the proper sense of the term since it was an outcome of the Napoleonic Wars, and thus arose from what might be described as *external* factors. But the breadth and scale of the crisis, and the seriousness of its impact, were sufficient to generate grave doubts in Sismondi's mind about the capitalist mode of production. It became clear to him that, regardless of its underlying factors, the crisis itself and its dreadful aftermath could not have occurred apart from the capitalist mode of production. Sismondi later recalled that his doubts were already growing at the time of writing his encyclopaedia entry, but given the aim of the submission he did not use that opportunity to develop his own ideas. His new doctrine was first presented in 1819, in *Nouveaux principes d'économie politique*. In the foreword to the book, Sismondi writes:

> I was deeply moved by the business crisis Europe had experienced in the last few years; the cruel suffering of the factory workers I witnessed in Italy, Switzerland, and France, and which all public accounts showed to be equally severe in England, Germany, and Belgium. I became convinced that governments and nations were on the wrong track, that they aggravated the distress they were seeking so much to remedy. I had noted with equal sadness the combined efforts of landowners, legislators, and writers, to change cultivation systems which spread so much happiness in the countryside, and to destroy the comfort of the peasants in the hope of increasing the net product. The politicians as well as the writers seemed to me to stray in their quest, sometimes for what could most increase wealth, sometimes for what could most increase population; whereas one or the other, considered by themselves, are only abstractions, and the real problem for statesmen is to find that combination and proportion of population and wealth that would safeguard the greatest happiness to humanity in a given space.[2]

Here already we can clearly sense the motivation for his intellectual conversion, as well as the direction in which it led. But if we look at the foreword to the second edition, published in 1827, his views are presented in an even more acute form:

> Seven years have passed [since the first edition], and it seems to me that the facts have victoriously fought on my side. They have proven, much better than I could have ever done, that the wise men with whom I parted ways have pursued a false prosperity; their theories, where they were put into operation, could well increase material wealth, but they diminished the sum of enjoyments destined for each individual; if these theories ten-

---

2 Sismondi 1991, p. 2.

ded to make the rich even richer, they also made the poor poorer, more dependent and deprived. Entirely unforeseen crises have followed each other in the business world; industrial progress and opulence have not saved those producers who created this wealth from unheard-of suffering. The facts have neither conformed to common expectations, nor to the predictions of the pundits, and despite the implicit trust the disciples of political economy have in the teachings of their masters, they are now forced to seek elsewhere new explanations for events which diverge so much from laws they have believed settled.

Among these explanations, those which I had given in advance have totally agreed with the events. Perhaps one should ascribe to such coincidence the quick sale of my book, and the demand which has brought me to prepare a new edition. I have done so in England. England has brought forth the most celebrated economists; their science is practiced there even today with redoubled ardour. Government ministers, already well versed in the doctrines of public welfare, have been seen to pursue studies with one of the most qualified professors of political economy; they have been heard to invoke his reasonings in Parliament. Universal competition, or the effort to always produce more, and always at a lower price, has been for a long time the English system, a system I have attacked as dangerous. That system has enabled English industry to make giant strides, but it also has, twice, thrown producers into frightful distress. It is in the face of such economic upheavals that I have seen it as my duty to review my arguments and compare them with the facts.

The study I have made of England has proven to me the validity of my *New Principles*. I have seen in that amazing country, which seems to go through a great trial for the instruction of the rest of the world, production increased while happiness decreased. The greater part of the nation, as well as the philosophers, seems to forget that increased wealth is not the goal of political economy, but the means it has to procure happiness for everyone. I have looked for such happiness among all classes, and I do not know where to find it. The upper English aristocracy has actually achieved a measure of wealth and luxury which surpasses everything one could see in all other nations. Nevertheless, it does not at all enjoy the opulence which it seems to have acquired at the expense of other classes; it lacks security, and in every family privation is felt more keenly than abundance. When I visit houses whose splendour is altogether regal, I hear their owners assert that if the corn monopoly they practice against their fellow citizens is abolished, their fortunes will be destroyed, because their estates, which extend over whole provinces, will not pay anymore the cost of production. Around these men I see numerous children, unequalled in any other aristocratic class; often one counts ten, twelve, sometimes more, but all the younger sons, and the daughters, are sacrificed to the glory of the eldest son; their share of the inheritance is not even equal to a year's income their brother receives. They must grow old as bachelors, and their dependence, at the end of their lives, is the high price they must pay for the luxury of their early years.

Below this titled and untitled aristocracy I see business occupy a distinguished position; its enterprises embrace the whole world, its agents brave the icy regions of the poles, and the heat of the equator, whilst every one of its leaders, meeting at the Exchange, can dispose of millions. At the same time, in all the streets of London and of other large English cities, the shops display goods sufficient for the consumption of the entire universe. But has this wealth secured to the English merchant that kind of happiness one would expect? Not at all – in no other country are bankruptcies as frequent. Nowhere are such colossal fortunes, sufficient in themselves to finance a public loan, to support an empire or a republic, destroyed more quickly. Everyone complains that business is scarce, difficult, hardly profitable. Within a span of a few years two terrible crises have ruined part of the bankers and spread desolation among all English manufacturers; at the same time another crisis has ruined the farmers, and its repercussions have been felt in the retail trade. On the other hand, business, despite its immense extent, has ceased to call for the young men who seek a career; all positions are taken, and in the upper, as well as the lower ranks of society most offer their labour in vain, without being able to obtain remuneration.

Finally, has this national opulence, whose material progress strikes every eye, benefited the poor? Not at all! The working classes in England are without comfort now, and without security for the future. There are no more freeholders on the land; they had to yield to day labourers; there are hardly any craftsmen left in the villages, or independent owners of small businesses, but only manufacturers. The factory hand, to use a word the system itself has coined, does not know what it is to have a station in life; he only gains wages, and since these wages cannot suffice equally for all seasons, he is almost every year reduced to ask alms from the poorhouse.

This opulent nation has found it more economical to sell all the gold and silver she possesses, to give up good coinage, and to accomplish its circulation with paper. She has thus voluntarily deprived herself of the most valuable of all the advantages of specie, price stability. The holders of provincial bank notes risk ruin every day from frequent, sometimes epidemic bank failures, and the entire state is exposed to a convulsion in all fortunes if an invasion, or revolution, should shake the credit of the national bank. The English nation has found it more economical to give up crops which demand much manual labour, and she has discharged half the cultivators who lived on the land; she has found it more economical to replace workers with steam engines, and she has dismissed, then rehired, then dismissed again, the workers in the villages; weavers have yielded to power looms, and now succumb to famine; she has found it more economical to reduce all workers to the lowest possible wages on which they can still subsist, and the workers, being no more than *proletarians*, have no fear of plunging themselves into even greater misery by raising ever larger families. She has found it more economical to feed the Irish with nothing but potatoes, and clothe them in rags, and now every packet boat brings legions of Irish who, working for less than the English, drive them from all employments. What are then the fruits of the immense accumulation of wealth? Has it had any other effect than to make all classes share sorrow, privation, and the spectre of total ruin? Has England, by forgetting men over things, sacrificed the end for the means?[3]

Here we get a vivid sense of how the reality of capitalist production in England, the rapidly developing motherland of capitalism, made a deep impression on the humanistic liberal Sismondi, who was raised in the feudalistic atmosphere of Switzerland, and how this experience changed the direction of his thought. Sismondi saw that the accumulation of capitalistic wealth is accompanied by the accumulation of poverty; that farmers and craftsmen are ruined, becoming propertyless wageworkers; and that the use of machinery generates unemployment. He witnessed how frequent crises disturbed the entire range of production, bringing unease, ruin, and famine to members of every class. He also discovered that all of these evils are the outcome of a social system based upon *universal competition*. This completely shattered his belief in Adam Smith's lovely dream, which saw *laissez faire* and the Divine Providence of capitalist production methods as a panacea for every social ill. Sismondi was dismayed that this mistaken doctrine of political economy had led people and governments into such a labyrinth. He was saddened not only for the working class, but for the aristocrats and capitalists as well. Thus, Sismondi offered his 'new principles of political economy' in place of the existing ones, and called for controls to be placed on universal competition.

---

3   Sismondi 1991, pp. 7–10.

From the description above, we can get an idea of the fundamental stance Sismondi took toward the various problems of capitalist production. There seems little need here to explain in detail that his position was well-intentioned and humanistic but at the same time petty-bourgeois, conservative, querulous, and completely ineffective, historically speaking, appearing pitiful when contrasted with the materialist conception of history developed later by Marx; nor is there much need to discuss how the ideas of Marx were a profound development beyond those of Sismondi. It seems sufficient to simply point out that the materialist conception of history is characterised by uncovering, within the problems of the day, the elements necessary for a development toward a new era, rather than simply bemoaning the existence of problems.

In this article, there also seems no particular need to examine in detail Sismondi's analysis of the causes of crisis or the countermeasures he proposed. Instead, we can simply note the following. According to his doctrine, a competitive system of production necessarily brings forth crisis in two senses. First, crisis occurs because the correspondence between supply and demand, or lack thereof, can only be gauged after the fact, through increasing or decreasing prices. Not only is the correspondence between supply and demand necessarily premised on constant disequilibrium, but the reestablishment of equilibrium among industrial sectors prompted by fluctuating prices is severely hindered by the difficulty of transferring capital and labour, making it impossible to reach equilibrium without ruining some capitalists and immiserating their workers. But the system of competition does not merely make such partial crises inevitable. Sismondi notes, secondly, that the only weapon capitalists can wield in their competition under this system, as an indispensable condition for survival, is the lowering of prices, as he explains:

> He will sell more if he sells cheaper, because the other sell less; the attention of the manufacturer is therefore endlessly directed to the discovery of some savings of labour, in the use of materials, that will enable him to sell at a lower price than his competitors. As the materials in their turn, are the product of previous labour, his savings come down at all times, in the last analysis, to the use of less labour for the same product.[4]

---

4   Sismondi 1991, p. 263. [The Japanese translation in Kuruma's article differs somewhat in content from the English translation of Sismondi's work. This seems to be the result of Kuruma translating a citation from Sismondi's book that appeared in Eugen von Bergmann's *Geschichte der nationalökonomischen Krisentheorien* (pp. 318–19 and p. 320), rather than translating it directly from *Nouveaux principes d'économie politique*.]

In other words, as a result:

> Old trades will be lost, and with them that part of the revenue of fixed capital which sprang from their value ... only consumers will have gained; they will make a small profit on the purchase of their needs. But that benefit is in no way proportional to the diminution of labour which causes it.[5]

Thus, Sismondi argues, an inconsistency arises generally between production and the social revenue that determines demand (and therefore consumption), making a general crisis not merely possible but inevitable under unlimited free competition. What, then, were the countermeasures that Sismondi proposed? It is on this point that his stance becomes exceedingly inconsistent and uncertain. Basically, he adheres to the belief that state intervention of some sort is necessary to place controls on unrestricted competition.

It does not seem necessary to explore Sismondi's theory in too much detail in this short article, since the aim is not to present various explanations of crisis; I think that later there will be a suitable moment to examine the defects in his analysis of the cause of crisis. More essential to the purpose of this article is to clarify how Sismondi, despite his impotent stance and incomplete analysis, has great significance to the history of political economy and to the self-awareness of the capitalist class.

As a political economist, Sismondi retained a bourgeois outlook despite his 'new principles'. But even while remaining within that framework, he could already perceive the fundamental contradictions of the capitalist mode of production and posit them as an important problem to consider. His outlook prevented him from posing the problem in a correct form, which in turn made the problem unsolvable, but we can recognise the groundbreaking significance that his way of posing the problem had for the development of political economy. A fundamental characteristic of classical political economy is that, even while adopting a bourgeois perspective, it clarified the internal relations of capitalist production. What made the scientific approach of the pioneers of political economy possible was an unshakable belief in the capitalist mode of production. One example of this was their conviction that this mode of production is ideal for the development of productive power. The view of Adam Smith, needless to say, is strikingly optimistic, but even Ricardo, whom economic historians consider a pessimist, shared the same conviction, which underlies all of his arguments. Marx offers the following description of Ricardo:

---

5 Sismondi 1991, p. 263.

Ricardo, rightly for his time, regards the capitalist mode of production as the most advantageous for production in general, as the most advantageous for the creation of wealth. He wants production for the sake of production and this with good reason. To assert, as sentimental opponents of Ricardo's did, that production as such is not the object, is to forget that production for its own sake means nothing but the development of human productive forces, in other words the development of the richness of human nature as an end in itself. To oppose the welfare of the individual to this end, as Sismondi does, is to assert that the development of the species must he arrested in order to safeguard the welfare of the individual. Sismondi is only right as against the economists who conceal or deny this contradiction. Apart from the barrenness of such edifying reflections, they reveal a failure to understand the fact that, although at first the development of the capacities of the human species takes place at the cost of the majority of human individuals and even classes, in the end it breaks through this contradiction and coincides with the development of the individual; the higher development of individuality is thus only achieved by a historical process during which individuals are sacrificed for the interests of the species in the human kingdom.

Thus Ricardo's ruthlessness was not only scientifically honest but also a scientific *necessity* from his point of view. But because of this it is also quite immaterial to him whether the advance of the productive forces slays landed property or workers. If this progress devalues the capital of the industrial bourgeoisie it is equally welcome to him. If the development of the productive power of labour halves the value of the existing fixed capital, what does it matter, says Ricardo. The productivity of human labour has doubled, Thus here is scientific honesty. Ricardo's conception is, on the whole, in the interests of the industrial bourgeoisie, only because, and in so far as their interests coincide with that of production or the productive development of human labour. Where the bourgeoisie comes into conflict with this, he is just as ruthless towards it as he is at other times towards the proletariat and the aristocracy.[6]

Marx strongly emphasises that one characteristic of Ricardo is his scientific outlook. But at the same time, his overall standpoint is that of the capitalist class. The basis for Ricardo's ability to balance those two perspectives was that the actual development of capitalist production still coincided with the devel-

---

6 Marx 1989a, pp. 347–8.

opment of productive power. As long as this foundation remained in place, the 'sentimental' attack launched by Sismondi was destined to remain impotent, as Marx points out. But we should remember that, as Marx also correctly indicates, this criticism was only powerless as long as a social basis remained in place that allowed orthodox political economy to preserve its original scientific standpoint. Once that basis had deteriorated, not only could the scientific standpoint no longer be maintained, but its ability to resist Sismondi – even his sentimental condemnation – completely vanished. That basis was overturned, fundamentally, by the outbreak of crisis as the explosion of the contradiction between the capitalist relations of production and the development of productive power. Crisis, in other words, is general overproduction, which is first and foremost a manifestation of the products of capitalist production reaching the point where, as a whole, they can no longer be completely consumed within the capitalist relations of production under which they are produced. Thus, a crisis is clear proof that such production relations are not the ideal form for the development of productive power, but rather a fetter to it. David Ricardo, who died in 1823, was fortunate to not have witnessed a crisis in this sense. The first edition of his book *On the Principles of Political Economy and Taxation* was published in 1817, the second edition in 1819, and the third and final edition in 1821, just prior to his death. The crisis that he saw in 1815, as noted already, was determined by external factors, as the outcome of the culmination of the Napoleonic Wars, and was not on the scale of a general crisis in terms of the regions and industries affected. The subsequent crisis of 1819 was even narrower in scope and could be seen as a reverberation of the crisis of four years prior. This is why Ricardo was able, without betraying his scientific conscience, to reject the possibility of general overproduction in *On the Principles of Political Economy and Taxation*, limiting the discussion to 'sudden changes in the channels of trade'. But the possibility of maintaining such a stance was forever swept away with the outbreak of crisis in 1825. Only a dogmatist could deny that this was clearly a case of general overproduction, arising naturally from capitalist production. At that point, there were only two paths left to political economists. If they chose to preserve their sincerity by accepting the truth, they would have to make their way forward while facing doubts about the relations of capitalist production and the principles of political economy. As long as they retained a bourgeois outlook, the path taken could not stray beyond that realm of doubt. This was the path that Sismondi already took in 1819, and he was proud of his foresight, saying: 'seven years have passed, and it seems that the facts have victoriously fought on my side'.[7] We can echo Marx's judgement that, 'whereas Ricardo's political

---

7 Sismondi 1991, p. 7.

economy ruthlessly draws its final conclusion and therewith ends, Sismondi supplements this ending by expressing doubt in political economy itself'.[8] In other words, the only path left to classical political economy after the outbreak of crisis was the blind alley of self-doubt.

Even though the dead end taken by Sismondi may have been the only path left to classical political economy, it was not the main path taken by bourgeois economists. They chose the different path of employing sophistry to deny the stark reality of general overproduction, while misrepresenting, with a guilty conscious, the fundamental relations of capitalist production that they could no longer examine or defend with confidence. We can see this process at play in the shift toward a theory denying the possibility of general overproduction and the complete vulgarisation of the system of political economy.

The basic tenet of the orthodoxy for demonstrating the impossibility of general overproduction is referred to generally as 'Say's Law' (*théorie des débouches*), since it was first advocated in Jean-Baptiste Say's *Traité d'économie politique*, published in 1803.[9] Although Say partially revised the second edition and subsequent editions, it did not alter his main point, which, when applied to the matter at hand, comes down to the following argument: A product is ultimately exchanged for another product, and money is merely the mediator of exchange. Thus, the purchasing power vis-à-vis a product is created by the production of another product, or conversely, the production of a product creates the purchasing power vis-à-vis another product. Therefore, overproduction, or the lack of a sales channel for a product, can only signify that another product is being underproduced, making it inherently impossible to have an excess of pro-

---

8   Marx 1987a, p. 301.
9   Here I make a point of saying 'referred to generally' because in earlier works the same idea can be found. For example, according to the research of Eugen von Bergmann (*Geschichte der nationalökonomischen Krisentheorien*), this was already clarified by Sir Dudley North in *Discourses upon Trade* (London 1691), by Josiah Tucker in *Reflections on the Expediency of a Law for the Naturalisation of Foreign Protestants* (1751–52), and by the physiocrats. Say's achievement (?) was merely to attach the name 'théorie des débouches' to this idea and fashion it into a textbook dogma. Incidentally, in his book *Commerce Defended*, James Mill, independent of Say, concluded that general overproduction was impossible based on his explanation of the 'metaphysical equilibrium of buyers and sellers'. Mill's book was published in 1808, so his explanation clearly appeared after the 'théorie des débouches' presented by Say. However, the theory of the impossibility of general overproduction was derived first from Mill's theory, whereas Say's 'théorie des débouches' was only applied to this question later in his debates with Sismondi and Malthus. In any case, it was the theory of Say that exerted a great influence within political economy, becoming one of the tenets of the orthodoxy, so my discussion here centres on Say's Law.

duction common to all products. Say's argument was later adopted by Ricardo, who writes the following in *On the Principles of Political Economy and Taxation*:

> M. Say has, however, most satisfactorily shown, that there is no amount of capital which may not be employed in a country, because demand is only limited by production. Productions are always bought by productions, or by services; money is only the medium by which the exchange is affected. Too much of a particular commodity may be produced, of which there may be such a glut in the market, as not to repay the capital expended on it; but this cannot be the case with respect to all commodities.[10]

The explanation of Say, which Ricardo adopted in the manner above, later became a long-standing tenet of orthodox political economy. While at first glance the explanation may seem plausible, it is in fact nothing but a heap of misconceptions. At its core is a complete misunderstanding of the essence of money, based on the bourgeois delusion of grasping capitalist production as an absolute, natural, and superhistorical form of production. According to Say and Ricardo, a product is exchanged for a product. However, a product is merely a thing that is produced and nothing more than a use value. Thus, completely overlooked within the concept of a 'product' are the socio-historical relations under which the product is produced, and therefore the specific determinations of the product that reflect these relations. Starting from this superhistorical concept, Say and Ricardo seek to reject the possibility of a general crisis. But what sort of phenomenon is a general crisis? Needless to say, it is a specific historical phenomenon that first occurs once capitalist production has reached a certain level. Clearly, therefore, its basis must be sought within the capitalistic character of production, not the general nature of production; and within the product's character as a capitalistic product, not its character merely as a product. Capitalist production is first and foremost commodity production, and capitalistic products are above all commodities. Say and Ricardo not only ignore the capitalistic character of production, but even overlook its character as commodity production. They treat the commodity – a unity of the mutually contradictory elements of value and use value – as a mere 'product' (use value). The inevitable outcome of failing to understand the dual character of the commodity, in turn, is that the essence of money and the significance of commodity circulation are obscured. Say and Ricardo understand the circulation of commodities as a mere 'exchange of products' and grasp money as a mere 'mediator

---

10   Ricardo 1996, pp. 201–2.

of the exchange of products'. How could a general crisis arise if commodities, the necessity of money, and commodity circulation, not to mention capitalist production, do not exist? The denial of general crisis is the natural conclusion reached from their standpoint. But the naturalness of their conclusion does not mean it has objective validity. Rather, it only signifies that when the fundamental conditions of a general crisis are not recognised, the possibility (not to mention necessity) of a general crisis cannot be recognised either. This merely demonstrates the defect in their understanding of the basic relations of capitalist production.

The denial of general crisis by Say and Ricardo should demonstrate the fundamental defect in their understanding of such basic relations of capitalist production, but that defect could not be demonstrated by reality until the actual occurrence of a general crisis. Until then, it was at least possible for them to insist on their argument without betraying their scientific conscience. The situation changed completely in 1825, when a general crisis did occur. How did the change alter the theory of crisis held by orthodox political economy? With regard to Ricardo there is nothing to be said, since as already mentioned he had died two years earlier, but we can consider the case of Jean-Baptiste Say, the father of the *théorie des débouches*. In countering an attack by Sismondi, who had pointed out the actuality of crisis in England, Say wrote:

> There is an excess of production in England, says M. de Sismondi; but has he formed a sufficiently clear idea of what is understood by the term production? If it means the making of more hats than there are heads, his argument would have some force: but a man who writes upon political economy cannot be ignorant that production is only that which reimburses advances made. The manufacturer who expends to the value of twenty-five shillings in order to create a value of twenty shillings, does not produce – he destroys. True production yields value; an article cannot possess value unless it be in demand by a consumer; and the latter would not bear the expense of it unless he wished to consume it. True production, therefore, is followed by consumption.[11]

Clearly, the whole secret of Say's argument, in seeking to defend his *théorie des débouches* in the face of actual overproduction, lies in an arbitrary determination posited within his concept of production. He states that 'production is only that which reimburses advances made'. Thus, according to Say, production does

---

11   Say 1827, p. 35.

not include cases where prices drop from overproduction so that the expenditure of capital cannot be recouped. Production in the proper sense of the term is limited to production with no overproduction. In a similar vein, Say argues that 'true production yields value' and that 'an article cannot possess value unless it be in demand by a consumer'. From his perspective, a product that does not find a consumer is without value, and the production of a valueless product cannot be considered 'true production'. Therefore, the production of valueless products unable to find consumers cannot be considered 'true production'. In other words, only the production of products that are able to find consumers is 'true production'. Obviously, if only the production of products that find consumers merits the term 'true production', overproduction could not occur, and such 'true production' would always be 'accompanied by consumption'. This new determination of the concept of production may rescue Say's argument, formally speaking, but it comes at the cost of negating the original meaning of production. In the end, his view amounts to nothing more than the tautology that production not in excess cannot be overproduction, and that the production of products that obtain consumers always finds consumers. This tells us nothing about the laws of capitalist production, amounting to a mere papering over of the actual contradictions. We can see that the outbreak of a real crisis not only exposed the errors of orthodox political economy, but also turned errors that had once been made innocently into apologetic arguments made in bad faith.

But the fatal relationship between bourgeois political economy and crisis extends even further. Periodic crises unceremoniously discarded large numbers of wageworkers who had been gathered from all directions during the preceding boom period, throwing them into the ranks of the unemployed and effectively stimulating their rebellious feelings and class consciousness by instilling a keen awareness of their own suffering and of the contradictions of capitalist production. The clearest manifestation of this are the numerous riots that broke out in the wake of every crisis and the emergence of socialistic doctrines. The early socialistic ideas, labelled 'Ricardian socialism', inherited Ricardo's theory of value and used it as a weapon to attack capitalist production. According to Ricardo, labour is the source of value, of which profit and rent are merely its parts. From this perspective, profit and rent can be said to be stolen from labour, meaning that the current organisation of society is an organisation of theft. Ricardian socialists argued that such an amoral way of organising society should be swept aside and replaced by an appropriate society in which distribution is carried out in line with each person's labour. There is no real need here to explain the utter impotence of this moralistic, utopian standpoint. Nevertheless, this attack was at least a menace to the capitalist class at the time and appealed to the proletariat. In the face of this attack, the capitalist class was unable to present an effective counterargument. The outbreak of crises had already robbed economists of the only basis from which to refute such criticism: namely the belief that capitalist production is the ideal form for the development of productive power. The clarification of the internal relations of capitalist production, which had once been a weapon in the hands of the capitalist class, became a weapon to be wielded against them. This situation ultimately determined the transformation of bourgeois political economy from its classical form into a vulgar system. The labour theory of value was discarded, replaced by the emergent 'trinity formula', according to which rent arises from land, profit (and interest, even more so) from capital, and wages from labour.

However, the gradual awakening of the working class that accompanied the periodic outbreaks of crisis could not be stemmed by this dogma that conceals the class nature of capitalist production, or by the sophistry used to deny the possibility of a general crisis. Indeed, a crisis is an example of a stubborn fact that cannot be denied by sophistry. The need to whitewash the internal relations of capitalist production grew with the passage of time, while the awareness of the necessity for policies to prevent or at least alleviate crisis became increasingly acute. This change altered the attitude within the capitalist camp toward crisis. It was no longer feasible to deny the possibility of crisis. Spurred by this new necessity, even bourgeois scholars engaged actively in examining the processes that generate a crisis. However, it was never possible for them to investigate the necessity of crisis as the developmental outcome of capitalist production's fundamental contradictions, since this path leads to a rejection of capitalist production itself. Thus, instead of considering the ultimate cause of crisis (as in the debate between Sismondi and Say), or its internal process of development (as examined in the later system of Marx), a new tendency arose that set itself the task of seeking the superficial relations between the phenomena within the business cycle, which is one aspect of crisis. This tendency represented a shift from a 'metaphysical = deductive' to a 'scientific = inductive' theory of crisis. The historicist school within political economy in general (which at the same time was an orientation toward social policy) was rooted in the same socio-historical necessity. That is to say, reality had developed to the point where both tendencies could no longer conceal the reality of the contradictions of capitalist production (particularly in the case of the former tendency, which was dealing with the extremely contradictory phenomenon of crisis). This development made it impossible to maintain to a hands-off approach. Meanwhile, so as to reject the exposure of the internal significance of the contradictory phenomena as they pursued the self-contradictory goal of preserving capitalist production while avoiding its undesirable outcomes, economists denied comprehensive theoretical research itself, but still attached the label 'scientific method' to their pursuit of historical facts and examination of the superficial relations between them (without touching on the fundamental relations of capitalist production).

The above, of course, is merely an overview of the new stance taken by bourgeois political economy toward crisis. When observed more closely, this certainly does not present a single, uniform appearance. The new tendency passed through various developmental stages, and actually split into different branches. It is not possible here to provide a detailed description, but in very general terms it could be said that the tendency was manifested in three developmental stages, and that the final two stages form the two main contemporary currents. The first, or pioneering stage, is represented by the achievements of Clement Juglar, who forged a new approach that shifted the object of study from 'crisis' to the entire process of the 'business cycle' that encompasses crisis as one of its aspects, replacing the 'abstract = deductive' method of investigation with a 'demonstrative = inductive' method based on historical materials. But Juglar's field of vision was limited primarily to the area of finance and did not encompass the entirety of the national economy. The second stage is represented by continental scholars, most notably Arthur Spiethoff, who, taking his hint from the work of the Russian 'revisionist Marxist' Tugan-Baranowsky at the end of the nineteenth century, and also motivated by the crisis that broke out at the beginning of the twentieth century, developed ideas based mainly on new materials emerging from the research of the German Economic Association (*Verein für Socialpolitik*). The intention of such scholars was to move from the historical study of the process of changes in the business cycle to the elucidation of the cause-and-effect relations within the wave-like movement of the economy. This led to various 'discoveries', although those of any value had already been clarified earlier by Marx. The only difference is that Marx grasped various moments within the total process of capitalist production and revealed their particular relation to that totality, based on a full understanding of the internal relations of capitalist society; whereas these later scholars severed the moments from such relations so as to emphasise them in an isolated, abstract, and therefore one-dimensional manner. Later I will have the opportunity to touch further on this point. Finally, in the third stage, which developed with particular rapidity after World War I, the most urgent matter became the gathering of a large quantity of materials to clarify the process of changes in the business cycle, in place of the meagre and imprecise materials formerly relied on to find the causes of fluctuations within the business cycle. Efforts were made to quantitatively express the process of the business cycle, primarily through the use of complex mathematical methods, in the hope of being able to devise policies related to the business cycle on the basis of knowledge gained from scrutinising the order in which various indicators appeared within the cycle. By its nature, this approach could not rely on the achievements of individual scholars and instead required a collective effort involving enormous expenditures and personnel. In line with the given aim, research centres on the business cycle were established, first in the United States and then in other countries. Some representative American institutions are the Harvard University Committee of Economic Research, established in 1917, and the National Bureau of Economic Research and the Institute of Economics in Washington DC, both founded in 1920. With these institutes as the model, similar research centres were founded elsewhere, including those in Stockholm (1922), London (1923), Paris (1925), and Rome (1926).[12] Considering how recently these research centres have been established, no definite statement can be made about the results of their research, but from the outset it has at least been clear that there is no way to correctly investigate the business cycle without a correct theory of political economy. It is only in accordance with an established theoretical standpoint that one can decide what facts should be observed, in what manner, and from which direction – out of an infinite number of existing economic facts, within an infinite number of relations, open to an infinite range of interpretations.[13] If such a theoretical basis is lacking or

---

12   In opposition to these capitalist business-cycle research centres, a special research cycle on the business cycle was established in Russia in 1920 in order to contribute to the financial and economic policies of the Soviet government. I have great interest and expectations in this organisation but unfortunately do not possess the materials needed to comment on it in detail.

13   This fact is even recognised by the researchers themselves. A recent book by Wesley C. Mitchell, a prominent scholar at the National Bureau of Economic Research in the United States, which is one of the world's foremost research institutes on the business cycle, provides us with a clear glimpse of how perplexed researchers are by the contradiction between their lack of theoretical confidence and the need for theory as the precondition for investigations. In his introduction to his 1927 book *Business Cycles: The Problem and its Setting*, Mitchell writes:

   'It is not advisable to attack the statistical data until we have made this survey of theories. For while the statistics will come to seem scanty as our demands develop, they are sufficiently abundant and diverse, susceptible of enough transformations and combinations, to make hopeless a purely empirical investigation. At every turn, we shall need working hypotheses to guide our selection of data, and to suggest ways of analysing and combining them. Our survey of theories will provide us with the most promising hypotheses which have been invented. Not until we are thus equipped can we begin constructive work upon the problems of business cycles, confident that we are not overlooking the elements already proved to be important' (Mitchell 1927, p. 3).

mistaken, most investigations, no matter how precise or large in scale, will end up being a waste of energy. Granted, some results of value may be arbitrarily generated (just as a dog that walks around, to quote the Japanese saying, may eventually find a bone); although it is more precise to say that such results will be endowed with real value once reorganised according to a correct theory. For this reason, we do not hold out much expectation for the findings of these bourgeois research centres. At the same time, though, it is worth paying attention to see what research results can be utilised, rather than rejecting their work out of hand.

Thus far I have looked at the development of crisis theory within the capitalist camp and the historical significance of that development, but now I would like to turn to the development of the theory of crisis within the camp of Marxism and the current state of this theory.

The great interest that Marx and Engels had in crisis is clear from the pages of *The Communist Manifesto* and *Capital*, as has been pointed out by many commentators. But if we read the direct record of their lives and trace all of the connections within the system of their critique of political economy, we can no doubt renew our sense of wonder on this point. From their correspondence, we get a keen sense of how excited Marx and Engels were by any indication of a crisis and the degree of their practical interest in the topic. The enormity of their theoretical interest in the problem of crisis is demonstrated, I think, by the fact that the entire system of the critique of political economy can be viewed, ultimately, as an investigation of the developmental process of crisis. (This is a point I will address in subsequent chapters.)

However, around the end of the 1870s, for specific reasons (that must be elucidated in the theory of crisis proper), a remarkable change took place in the situation of the world market, and therefore in the conditions for the progression of capitalist production. In line with this change, a shift occurred in the immediate aim of the proletarian movement, and following the death of Marx the original spirit of Marxism was neglected. At least for some time,

---

In other words, the author, lacking theoretical confidence regarding the processes of capitalist production, wanders around in search of anything to fill the gap, like a hungry dog. Thus, the bulk of the first chapter is taken up with a general survey of existing doctrines. But this sort of makeshift compilation has no chance of success. Mitchell even fails to understand the doctrines of others (see his description of Marx's theory of crisis). Needless to say, he also fails to comprehensively synthesise research results (see how in Chapter 2, on economic organisation and the business cycle, he scrounges around among the ideas of various scholars for elements that might bear an important relation to the business cycle, without any regard for their interrelations).

the issue of crisis as a catastrophe for capitalist production was no longer the object of practical or theoretical attention. It was the effort of Eduard Bernstein to 'revise' Marxism that hardened this tendency, turning what had been passive neglect into active rejection.[14] But Bernstein's proposals, unexpectedly provided a great stimulus within the Marxist camp, as many opposed his 'revisionism'. The necessity of debate provided an opportunity to restore the revolutionary theory of Marx centred on the problem of crisis. This situation was reinforced by the presentation in Russia of the work of the 'revisionist Marxist' Mikhail Tugan-Baranowsky,[15] and by the outbreak of crisis at the beginning of the new century. Thus, the problem of crisis frequently came to the fore. Two or three meaningful theories were proposed,[16] but ultimately were limited

14   Bernstein first publicly presented his proposal for a 'revision' in a series of articles titled 'Probleme des Sozialismus' (Problems of Socialism) that appeared from 1896 to 1897 in the SDP journal *Die Neue Zeit*. His famous book published in 1899, Die *Voraussetzungen des Sozialismus und die Aufgaben der Sozialdemokratie* [published in English under the title *Evolutionary Socialism*], was a more systematic presentation of his views in response to the incredible controversy that his articles had sparked within the party.

15   See Tugan-Baranowsky's *Studien zur Theorie und Geschichte der Handelskrisen in England* (Studies on the Theory and the History of Business Crises in England). The original Russian edition was published in 1894, but it was first introduced in Europe through the 1901 German edition. In one aspect, the book displays the same revisionist tendency as that of Bernstein and must be seen as a product of the global situation at the end of the nineteenth century, but it also has the characteristic of being a product of the particular social conditions in Russia at the time. For more on this, see 'Third Round' in Section II of Rosa Luxemburg's *Die Akkumulation des Kapitals* (The Accumulation of Capital.) Having said that, Tugan-Baranowsky's work at least provided a stimulus for discussion within the Marxist camp by considering the previous crises in England in terms of the process of their occurrence and providing important suggestions for the later development of the theory of crisis, while discussing the problem of the reproduction of the total social capital in relation to the problem of crisis (particularly in relation to the reproduction schema in Part 3 of Book II of *Capital*). Critiques of Tugan-Baranowsky's book include Kautsky's essay 'Krisentheorie' (Theories of Crisis; *Die Neue Zeit* 1901-2) and Louis Boudin's 'Mathematische Formeln gegen Karl Marx' (Mathematical Formulas against Karl Marx; *Die neue Zeit* 1906-7). Rosa Luxemburg, in her book *The Accumulation of Capital* (examined later), which seeks to unfold the problem of crisis in relation to the problem of the reproduction of the total social capital, seems to draw many hints from Tugan-Baranowsky, and her discussion revolves around a critique of his ideas.

16   Examples include Rosa Luxemburg's 1898 work *Sozialreform oder Revolution?* (Social Reform or Revolution), Alexander Parvus's *Die Handelskrise und die Gewerkschaften* (Economic Crisis and the Trade Unions), and Karl Kautsky's 'Krisentheorie' (see previous footnote). Luxemburg's work is particularly important in displaying a dialectical grasp of the problem, while the other two works recognise within the developmental process of capitalist production in the nineteenth century a more comprehensive cycle that contains several cycles recognised previously. Kautsky's work in particular implies a certain sig-

by the motivation that called them forth. The time was not yet ripe for the new development of a Marxian theory of crisis.

The opportunity for development ripened with the maturation of a new stage of capitalist production, which Lenin referred to as the 'stage of imperialism'. This stage is characterised by capitalist production undergoing a fundamental formal change during its process of development; namely, the transformation from its 'liberal' to its 'monopoly' form. However, this transformation does not signify the abolishment of capitalist production itself, nor does it signify the overcoming of the contradictions of capitalist production. Rather, it posits a developmental change in the form of contradictions, which in turn necessarily brings about a developmental transformation in the form of crisis as the explosion and self-resolution of the contradictions. This is the transformation from a purely economic crisis to a world war. In other words, within the new form, the contradictions of capitalist production that periodically accumulate explode not merely as an economic crisis but necessarily as a world war. The contradictions take on the quality of only being resolvable through global war. Thus, along with the necessity of economic crisis, the necessity arises of world war as a developed form of crisis.

This shift to a new situation – and the inevitable arrival of world war – was naturally keenly felt even before it was theoretically elucidated. The awareness of this steadily ripening situation gradually drew considerable attention from every direction, including, of course, that of Marxists, as reflected in the heated debates that broke out at the congresses of the Second International over the policy toward war. Among the opinions expressed during those debates, three different tendencies could be seen. The first was a clear jingoistic tendency, the second a utopian pacifist tendency, and the third was a tendency that recognised the inevitability of war as the explosion of the contradictions of capitalist production while also detecting within such a war the final catastrophe of capitalist production. Needless to say, it was the third tendency that took the most active interest in the problem of war. This tendency mainly was composed of those who had experienced the 1905 revolution in Russia that arose from the Russo-Japanese War, represented in particular by Lenin as well as Rosa Luxemburg. It is no accident that these two carried out the most innovative work for developing a scientific analysis of imperialism.

---

nificance of a more comprehensive cycle and attempts to elucidate it with regard to the historical developmental stage of capitalist production; however, this attempt did not bear fruit at the time, nor was it ever achieved by him.

The work by Luxemburg to which I am referring is of course her famous book *The Accumulation of Capital: A Contribution to the Economic Theory of Imperialism* (1913). In it, she begins by critically examining Marx's schema for the process of expanded reproduction for the total social capital, attempting to demonstrate that in a society where capitalist production is universally dominant and monopolistic, it is quite impossible for capital to be accumulated. An indispensable condition for the accumulation of capital, she asserts, is the existence of non-capitalist societies or social layers. Thus, the necessity of capital accumulation at the same time requires the forced advance of capitalist societies into non-capitalist areas and competition among groups of capitalists (states) seeking to make such advances. In a word, it necessitates imperialism. Imperialism is precisely the historical expression of the process of capital accumulation. But the accumulative process manifested under imperialism is sort of double-edged sword. Non-capitalistic areas ultimately disappear as they undergo a transformation to capitalism, so that capitalism robs itself of the possibility to advance further. This is the ultimate limit insofar as the historical process of capital accumulation, and thus the fate of capitalism itself, is concerned. The explanation above covers the gist of what Luxemburg sought to demonstrate in *The Accumulation of Capital*.

Various opinions have been expressed as to whether Luxemburg's way of grasping the problem and of reasoning was on target. I have several doubts myself, and will probably have an appropriate time to discuss each of them later. At any rate, no one can ignore the historical significance of Section I of *The Accumulation of Capital*. Luxemburg's book was the first theoretical work that aimed to sweep aside the petty-bourgeois attitude of the 'Marxist centre' faction so as to put in place a truly proletarian foundation for the Social Democratic Party at a moment when its attitude toward war was becoming increasingly crucial, against the backdrop of the increasingly keen awareness of the approaching crisis of world war in relation to the steady unfolding of contradictions particular to the imperialist stage of capitalism. The historical significance of *The Accumulation of Capital* is demonstrated by the incredible controversy it generated within the Social Democratic Party. In many of the party organs, her work was subject to intense attacks. In response, Luxemburg wrote *The Accumulation of Capital, Or, What the Epigones Have Made Out of Marx's Theory – An Anti-Critique*, which begins as follows:

> *Habent sua fata libelli* – books have destinies of their own. When I was writing my *Accumulation* I was disheartened from time to time by a particular thought: all supporters of Marx's doctrine who take an interest in theory would make the pronouncement that points I was trying so

exhaustively to demonstrate and substantiate were actually self-evident already. Nobody would voice a different opinion: my solution of the problem would be the only one possible or conceivable.

Things turned out quite differently: a whole series of critics in the Social Democratic press declared that my book was totally misguided in its very conception and that such a problem calling for a solution did not exist at all. I had become the pitiful victim of a pure misunderstanding.

There were events connected with the publication of my book that must be called rather unusual. The 'review' of the *Accumulation* [by Gustav Eckstein], which appeared in *Vorwärt* on 16 February 1913, was striking in tone and content even to the less involved reader; and this was all the more astonishing because the criticised book is purely theoretical and strictly objective, nor was it aimed against any living Marxist. But that was not good enough.

Against those who had published a favourable review of my book a highhanded official campaign was initiated, and the central newspaper pursued this campaign with particularly notable warmth.

This was an unparalleled, and in its way rather comical, sequel: With regard to my purely theoretical work about a complicated issue involving abstract scientific analysis, the entire Editorial Board of a political daily paper came forward – although two members, at the most, might have read the book – and as an official body handed down a collective judgment ...

Such a fate has befallen no other party publication as far as I know, and over the decades Social Democratic publishers have certainly not produced all gold and pearls. All these events clearly indicate that, in one way or another, there have been passions at work other than those of 'pure science'.[17]

Near the end of this anti-critique in which she further developed her views on capital accumulation and the necessity of imperialism, Luxemburg explains the practical interests that were the actual cause of the leadership's vehement attack:

The guidelines run in quite a different direction from the standpoint of the 'experts' of official Marxism. Their belief in the possibility of accumulation in an 'isolated capitalist society', their belief that 'capitalism

---

17   Luxemburg 2016b, pp. 347–8.

without expansion is also conceivable' – these theoretical formulas are applied in a particular way in manners of tactics. This conception of the 'experts' is aimed at promoting the view that this phase of imperialism is not a historical necessity, not the occasion for a decisive settling of accounts in favor of socialism, but as a regrettable invention made by a handful of 'special interests'. This conception leads toward the practice of giving advice to the bourgeoisie, assuring them that from the standpoint of their own best capitalist interests, militarism and imperialism are harmful to the bourgeoisie itself. The aim here is to isolate the alleged handful of beneficiaries of imperialism and thus to form a bloc between the working class and the broad strata of the bourgeoisie in order to 'put a wet blanket' on imperialism, to starve out militarism by promoting 'partial disarmament' and thus to remove the stinger from its abdomen!

Just as liberalism in its era of decline appealed from the poorly informed monarchy to those who would better inform it, so, too, the 'Marxist center' wants to appeal from the poorly advised bourgeoisie to those who would give it better advice, from the policy course of imperialist catastrophes to international disarmament treaties.

They want to appeal from the wrenching struggle of the Great Powers to establish a worldwide dictatorship of the sword to a peaceful federation of democratic nation-states. The need for a general settling of accounts to resolve the world-historical contradiction between labour and capital is transformed into the utopia of arranging a 'historic compromise' between the proletariat and the bourgeoisie for the 'mitigation' of imperialist conflicts among the capitalist states.[18]

Luxemburg is hardly expressing an unjust suspicion or emotional vilification of the critics of her book. Rather, she is stating a clear truth that was confirmed by the actual stance toward imperialism taken by those (in the 'Marxist centre' faction) who attacked *The Accumulation of Capital*. The attitude of the central leadership to imperialism echoed the attitude toward crisis of Sismondi, considered earlier. The same fundamental error that Sismondi made nearly a century prior in his attitude toward capitalist contradictions in the form of 'universal competition' was repeated by 'Marxists' in their attitude toward capitalist contradictions in the form of imperialism. What was said earlier regarding Sismondi can be applied directly to the attitude of the 'Marxists' as well, just as Luxemburg's criticism of them in the passage above could be

---

18   Luxemburg 2016b, p. 447.

directly applied to the ideas of Sismondi. The difference is that whereas Sismondi was naive and humanistic to the core, these other gentlemen oddly claim to be 'expert Marxists'. Sismondi's error can be understood from the historical circumstances of his time, characterised by an insufficient development of capitalism, and therefore of its opposing element, the proletariat, which had yet to adequately develop its own distinct way of thinking as a revolutionary class and its own sociopolitical power. But today, long after Marx established the dialectical materialist conception of history, with the power of the proletarian class even reflected strongly in the parliaments of advanced nations, self-described disciples of Marx who are the representatives of this proletarian power have ended up repeating the same errors made a century earlier. How can we account for this? Clearly, this is not some well-intentioned, naive error, but rather must signify a conscious turning away from Marxism, a conscious betrayal of the class interests of the proletariat. In this sense, it is the same as the opportunistic, imperialistic outlook of the right wing. The apostasy and betrayal can no longer be explained by a lack of capitalist development. The basis for this must be sought instead in the modern relations of capitalist production. Herein lies an important problem. In his preface to the French and German editions of his famous book *Imperialism*, Lenin draws the reader's attention to this problem and explains the basis in the following way

> It is precisely the parasitism and decay of capitalism, characteristic of its highest historical stage of development, i.e. imperialism. As this pamphlet shows, capitalism has now singled out a *handful* of exceptionally rich and powerful states which plunder the whole world simply by 'clipping coupons'. Capital exports yield an income of eight to ten thousand million francs per annum, at pre-war prices and according to pre-war bourgeois statistics. Now, of course, they yield much more.
>
> Obviously, out of such enormous superprofits (since they are obtained over and above the profits which capitalists squeeze out of the workers of their 'own' country) it is *possible to bribe* the labour leaders and the upper stratum of the labour aristocracy. And that is just what the capitalists of the 'advanced' countries are doing: they are bribing them in a thousand different ways, direct and indirect, overt and covert.
>
> This stratum of workers-turned-bourgeois, or the labour aristocracy, who are quite philistine in their mode of life, in the size of their earnings and in their entire outlook, is the principal prop of the Second International, and in our days, the principal social (not military) prop of the bourgeoisie. For they are the real agents of the bourgeoisie in the

working-class movement, the labour lieutenants of the capitalist class, real vehicles of reformism and chauvinism. In the civil war between the proletariat and the bourgeoisie they inevitably, and in no small numbers, take the side of the bourgeoisie, the 'Versaillese' against the 'Communards'.

Unless the economic roots of this phenomenon are understood and its political and social significance is appreciated, not a step can be taken toward the solution of the practical problem of the communist movement and of the impending social revolution.[19]

This problem is dealt with in further detail in Lenin's book. But to elaborate on this point would be to stray too far from the aim of this article. Returning to the main point, then, we need to consider the groundbreaking significance of Lenin's *Imperialism* within the history of the development of the theory of crisis.[20] I should point out, incidentally, that we have already clarified the significance of Luxemburg's *The Accumulation of Capital* to that development. Thus, the problem can now be posed in terms of how Lenin's *Imperialism* is a step forward compared to Luxemburg's work.

Essentially, the advance made by Lenin concerns how he grasped the problem. A hint as to the development in grasping the problem can be seen, externally, in the difference between the titles of the two books. Whereas Luxemburg chose the title *The Accumulation of Capital: A Contribution to an Analysis of Imperialism*, Lenin clearly titled his work *Imperialism: The Highest Stage of Capitalism*. I have already noted that both works, in a sense, clarify that imperialism is the product of the modern development of capitalism. The historical backdrop to the appearance of both books was the emergence of imperialism as the outcome of the modern development of capitalism – or the appearance of the modern aspect of imperialism. The particular historical significance of both works is that they seek to provide a foundation for a true proletarian stance toward this new situation. But Luxemburg seems to have lacked an adequate awareness of the historical mission she had undertaken. Indeed, as can be seen in the passage from *An Anti-Critique* quoted earlier, the particular historical significance of *The Accumulation of Capital* only first reached her

---

19   Lenin 1964, pp. 193–94.
20   It should be clear from the discussion thus far that my use of the term 'theory of crisis' is not limited to the theory of economic crisis, since it naturally encompasses the study of the necessity of imperialist world war as the explosion of the contradictions peculiar to modern capitalism. Imperialist world war itself is precisely crisis in its highest form. Thus, the theory of imperialism must be an extension of the theory of crisis.

consciousness through the unexpected impact its publication had within the Social Democratic Party, although she may have been expressing surprise as a rhetorical technique within the context of the controversy. In any case, the problem extends further than that. If we look at the structure of her book, as already noted, its fundamental part is composed of a general analysis of the reproduction process of social capital. She concludes that expanded reproduction (capital accumulation) is absolutely impossible in a purely capitalist society. From this impossibility, she demonstrates that non-capitalist environments are indispensable to capital accumulation in general. This is where she seeks to locate the economic basis of imperialism. It may be possible on such a general basis to explain imperialism as a characteristic of capitalism in general, but this approach is quite unable to explain imperialism as a characteristic of the contemporary stage of capitalism or the particular contemporary aspects of imperialism. What actually motivated Luxemburg and spurred her to write *The Accumulation of Capital* in 1913, on the eve of a world war, must have been the latter, yet what she explained was the former. Herein lies a defect in her work. And this defect highlights the groundbreaking significance of Lenin's *Imperialism*. In this book, the object of study is clearly defined from the outset in terms of 'imperialism as the highest stage of capitalism'. Adopting this perspective, Lenin clearly views his task as examining the 'fundamental economic question, that of the economic essence of imperialism', without which 'it will be impossible to understand and appraise modern war and modern politics'.[21] Thus, instead of posing the question in terms of the general process of capital accumulation, he considers the 'concentration of production and monopolies', 'banks and their new role', and 'finance capital and the financial oligarchy', which were important new developments at the end of the nineteenth and beginning of the twentieth century. Lenin, unlike Luxemburg, does not raise the problem of the general relation between capitalist societies and non-capitalist societies. Instead, he considers the 'export of capital', 'division of the world among capitalist associations', and the 'division of the world among the great powers', which characterise the modern stage of this relation. The consideration of these problems provides Lenin with an essential grasp of imperialist war in its most modern form; i.e. not war in general or a general view of capitalist aggression, as explained by Luxemburg, but rather a world war among great powers to divide up the world, which is indeed the explosion that occurred in 1914 and will again occur so long as capitalism continues to exist. Lenin also reveals the foundation for the tendency of

---

21 Lenin 1964, p. 188.

'social patriotism' that arose along with the necessity of world war. Further, unlike Luxemburg, Lenin from the outset considers where the most dangerous enemies lie, pointing out that 'special attention has been devoted in this pamphlet to a criticism of Kautskyism, the international ideological trend represented in all countries of the world by the most "prominent theoreticians", the leaders of the Second International and a multitude of socialists, reformists, pacifists, bourgeois democrats and parsons'.[22] Finally, unlike Luxemburg, who abstractly speaks of the general self-contradictions of capitalism and explains the ultimate deadlock of capitalism from these self-contradictions, Lenin locates within imperialism, as the modern form of capitalism, a clear sign of the decline of capitalism and a clear transitional aspect leading toward socialism.

Thus, Lenin's theory of imperialism is a study of the historical features of imperialism as a particular aspect of capitalism in its current stage or of the current stage of capitalism that is manifested in imperialistic characteristics. Essential to these historical features, according to Lenin, is the formal transformation that occurs as the outcome of the development of the contradictions of capitalist production. By investigating the new forms of these contradictions, Lenin clarifies the inevitability of world war as the explosion of the contradictions and the decisive significance such wars must have for the fate of capitalism, while clearly discerning the boundaries of the enemy camp within the struggle waged against imperialist war. Thus, his book has great practical significance in establishing general standards for the struggle of the proletarian class against modern capitalism, centred on imperialist war. As is well known, the work provided a guiding principle for the Russian Revolution and then for the Third International, and continues to be useful today.

We need to clarify the value of Lenin's work, while at the same time not overlooking its inherent limitations. This is a work originally written to clarify certain phenomena, so we should not expect it to resolve matters that it did not set out to address.

As noted above, *Imperialism* is a study of the features of the current stage of capitalism, and does not extend beyond the features that characterise this stage. But closer consideration of the current stage of capitalism reveals that it does not have a uniform appearance: encompassed within it are various developmental aspects. In other words, the contradictions of capitalist production in its imperialist stage develop through a wave-like process. From the outset, Lenin's book does not seek to elucidate this process of development. This is

---

22   Lenin 1964, p. 192.

natural, since it was written in the midst of a world war as an urgent response to the situation. The development of contradictions had already gone beyond a certain point. The contradictions, regardless of the nature of their process of development, were exploding in reality. The pressing task was to reveal that the crisis that had actually arrived was in essence a crisis of capitalism in general and had to be realised as such. Clearly, the question of the twists and turns leading up to the arrival of the crisis was a secondary issue at the time. But today the situation has changed. For the moment, the page of the Great War has been turned, with a direct outcome being the receding wave of the worldwide revolutionary movement. Today's task is to prepare for the new crisis that will soon arrive. This new period of crisis will probably once again take the form of a world war. But even prior to that, it is likely to assume the form of an economic crisis. In either case, the crucial task in the current period is to prepare for the major crisis that approaches. How can we accomplish this task in the most efficient and effective manner? First, we must verify the necessity underlying the arrival of the new crisis and the position of the present moment as one step along that path. The theoretical basis for this verification can only be obtained by grasping all the contradictions of capitalism in their organic interrelation as moments in the dialectical development of capitalist production, so as to clarify the process of their inevitable development to the point of explosion. Investigating this theoretical basis is the precise task of a truly Marxian theory of crisis (as will be explained in more detail later). This is exactly what Marx set out to achieve throughout the entire system of his critique of political economy. In this sense, the entire system of the critique of political economy (of which *Capital* is the most fundamental part) must at the same time be an enormous theory of crisis – or an enormous system concentrated in the theory of crisis as its summarising or conclusive part. Yet, many Marxist researchers have not seemed to adequately understand this relationship. In fact, the problem of crisis has mainly been considered from a narrow, one-dimensional perspective. The relationship between crisis and its related problems has not been clarified and at times distorted. In most cases, the various causes of crisis (both the intrinsic and ultimate causes of crisis as well as the forms, conditions, etc. of its realisation) have been severed from their intrinsic relations so as to be grasped abstractly, in isolation, and therefore as mutually unrelated (or only superficially united) or even in conflict with each other. Given this situation, every debate ends up being waged for the sake of debate alone, naturally failing to generate any results that would take us a step forward. This seems to be a reason why no systematic theory of crisis has been completed and that there is not even any sign of progress toward that end. Of course, the completion of a theory of crisis is no easy task. In all likelihood it could not be achieved by a single person, requiring instead the cooperation of many. But effective cooperation among many people requires a common basis or uniform standpoint. We can only look to Marx to provide this. This is the reason why I have taken a look back on Marx here and titled this 'An Introduction to the Study of Crisis.'

CHAPTER 2

An Inquiry into Marx's Theory of Crisis

Sharp differences of opinion exist among Marxists today regarding the question of crisis and related issues.[1] This situation suggests the need for a new inquiry into Marx's theory of crisis, and at the same time indicates that a major obstacle is blocking such an endeavour. Where does the obstacle lie? Various answers can of course be given, from different perspectives, but the most direct obstacle, at least as far as an examination of Marx's theory of crisis is concerned, is that his systematic critique of political economy – and hence his theory of crisis – remains incomplete, and that this fact has not been adequately acknowledged. Hence, our new effort to understand crisis must start from a recognition of this fact as a fact.

We can look to several passages from the works of Marx for important clues regarding his original conception of the overall structure of his critique of political economy. The first is taken from a manuscript that Marx titled an 'Introduction to the Critique of Political Economy':

> The order [of the critique of political economy] obviously has to be (1) the general, abstract determinants which obtain in more or less all forms of society, but in the above-explained sense. (2) The categories which make up the inner structure of bourgeois society and on which the fundamental classes rest. Capital, wage labour, landed property. Their interrelation. Town and country. The three great social classes. Exchange between them. Circulation. Credit system (private). (3) Concentration of bourgeois society in the form of the state. Viewed in relation to itself. The 'unproductive' classes. Taxes. State debt. Public credit. The population. The colonies. Emigration. (4) The international relation of production. International division of labour. International exchange. Export and import. Rate of exchange. (5) The world market and crises.[2]

This manuscript is the 'general introduction' referred to in Marx's preface to *A Contribution to the Critique of Political Economy*, where he notes that 'a general

---

1 [Originally published as Kuruma 1930 and republished as Chapter 2 of *An Investigation of Marx's Theory of Crisis* (Kuruma 1949).]
2 Marx 1973b, p. 108.

introduction, which I had drafted, is omitted'.[3] According to Karl Kautsky, this introduction is dated 23 August 1857.

The second text we can look to, chronologically, is a letter to Ferdinand Lasalle that Marx wrote on 22 February 1858:

> The whole is divided into 6 books: 1. On Capital (contains a few introductory Chapters). 2. On Landed Property. 3. On Wage Labour. 4. On the State. 5. International Trade. 6. World Market ... generally speaking the critique and history of political economy and socialism would form the subject of another work, and, finally, the short historical outline of the development of economic categories and relations yet a third.[4]

About forty days later, Marx discussed the plan in more detail in a letter to Engels, dated 2 April 1858:

> The following is a short outline of the first part. The whole thing is to be divided into 6 books: 1. On Capital. 2. Landed Property. 3. Wage Labour. 4. State. 5. International, Trade. 6. World Market.
>
> 1. *Capital* falls into 4 sections. a) Capital *en general* (This is the substance of the first installment) b) *Competition* or the interaction of many capitals. c) *Credit* where capital, as against individual capitals, is shown to be a universal element. d) *Share capital* as the most perfected form (turning into communism) together with all its contradictions. The transition from capital to landed property is also historical, since landed property in its modern form is a product of the action of capital on feudal, etc., landed property. In the same way, the transition of landed property to wage labour is not only dialectical but historical, since the last product of modern landed property is the general introduction of wage labour, which then appears as the basis of the whole business.
>
> Well (It is difficult for me today to write), let us now come to the *corpus delicti*
>
> I. Capital. First section: Capital in general (Throughout this section. wages are invariably assumed to be at their minimum. Movements in wages themselves and the rise and fall of that minimum will be considered under wage labour. Further, landed property is assumed to be zero, i.e. landed property, as a special economic relation is of no relev-

---

3 Marx, 1987a, p. 261.
4 Marx, 1983, p. 270.

ance as yet. Only by this procedure is it possible to discuss one relation without discussing all the rest.)[5]

Finally, we can refer to the following statement by Marx in his preface to *A Contribution to the Critique of Political Economy*:

> I examine the system of bourgeois economy in the following order: capital, landed property, wage-labour; the State, foreign trade, world market. The economic conditions of existence of the three great classes into which modern bourgeois society is divided are analysed under the first three headings; the interconnection of the other three headings is self-evident. The first part of the first book, dealing with Capital, comprises the following chapters: 1. The commodity, 2. Money or simple circulation; 3. Capital in general. The present part consists of the first two chapters.[6]

A comparison of the four passages above reveals some slight differences. For example, in the 'Introduction' cited initially, the first book was to have dealt with the 'general, abstract determinants', whereas that is omitted as an independent heading in the subsequent plans. Moreover, in that same text, 'capital' is followed by 'wage labour' and 'landed property', whereas in the other passages cited, 'landed property' appears before 'wage labour'. But, setting these points aside, we can see that apart from such details, the basic structure is the same. Furthermore, even though Marx only mentions 'world market' in some places, instead of 'world market and crisis' as he does in the 'Introduction', this could be seen as a mere simplification that does not signify the elimination of the theory of crisis.

Marx's ambitious plan for a critique of political economy was not realised, however. Only one volume was published under the title *Zur Kritik der politischen Ökonomie*.[7] In preparing to write what was to have followed that first volume, Marx felt the need to fundamentally revise his ideas. The result of completely rewriting his manuscripts from the beginning was *Capital*. Marx

---

5 Marx, 1983, p. 298.
6 Marx 1987a, p. 261.
7 [Published in 1859. The first English translation by Nahum Stone was published by Charles H. Kerr & Co. in 1904 under the title *A Contribution to the Critique of Political Economy*. In 1970, Progress Publishers issued a new edition, under the same title, translated by Salo Ryazanskaya and edited by Maurice Dobb.]

only oversaw the publication of the first volume of *Capital*, although based on his manuscripts Engels was able to edit a second and third volume, thus giving a more or less completed form to the work. But what is the relation between the three volumes of *Capital* and Marx's original conception of a critique of political economy? This is of vital importance to us here, and in addressing this question I would like to begin by examining four different viewpoints.

The first is the opinion that the three volumes of *Capital* constitute the most fundamental part of the investigation of 'capital', which itself constitutes the fundamental part of Marx's overall conception of a critique of political economy. In other words, the three volumes are thought to correspond to 'capital in general' within Marx's plan (see the earlier citation from the 2 April 1858 letter). The second view is that the three volumes correspond to 'capital as a whole', rather than 'capital in general', because they include the investigation of specific issues, such as competition and credit. The third position takes the second view a step further by claiming that *Capital* encompasses not only 'capital' but also the content of Marx's originally planned books on landed property and wage labour, because the three volumes include a detailed examination of wages and ground rent. Finally, as the fourth argument, some claim that Marx completely altered his original plan in abandoning the subsequent volumes of *Zur Kritik der politischen Ökonomie*, so that the three volumes of *Capital* can be seen as replacing the original plan for a critique of political economy, encompassing all of the planned content.

Solving this problem, clearly, is pivotal to the study of Marx's economic theory, particularly his theory of crisis. Yet, strangely, this question has hardly been addressed until recently, and the few times it has, only in a superficial manner that yielded no acceptable solution. Here I will examine a few of the discussions of Marx's plan that I have come across, beginning with Karl Kautsky, who writes the following in the preface to his new edition of *Zur Kritik der politischen Ökonomie*:

> The sharp critic Marx was not as critical toward others as he was toward himself. Even when the path of his own thinking displayed no defects, he would turn over the object of investigation to consider it from a different perspective, seeking to make his presentation even more self-evident. Thus, the structure for *Capital* differs from that of *Zur Kritik der politischen Ökonomie*, whose first part [*erestes Heft*] was published in 1859. This fact is immediately clear from the first few lines of his preface to that work [where Marx notes the plan for his critique of political economy, comprising six books from *capital* to the *world market*], and

from a comparison of the plan developed there to the plan he actually followed for *Capital*.[8]

Despite Kautsky's assertion, the difference between the two works is certainly not clear through a simple comparison. For it to seem clear, one must have already assumed that *Capital* as a comprehensive work takes the place of the entire plan for a critique of political economy. On the basis of such a premise, it would be possible to directly compare the entire conception of the critique of political economy to the structure of *Capital* in order to clearly indicate the fundamental differences between them. However, the idea that *Capital* is a comprehensive work that replaced the entire content Marx had planned for his critique of political economy is precisely the problem under consideration here. Moreover, in declaring in his preface to *Zur Kritik der politischen Ökonomie* that he would consider the organisation of the capitalist economy in the order of 'capital', 'landed property', etc., Marx was issuing a sort of public pledge. If he had completely altered his original plan when writing *Capital*, surely Marx would have drawn attention to the change. Yet nowhere in *Capital* can we find any such indication. Instead, he clearly states in the preface to *Capital*: 'The work, the first volume of which I now submit to the public, forms the continuation of my book *Zur Kritik der politischen Ökonomie* published in 1859'.[9] Therefore, absent some other particular reason, the natural assumption is that, in the case of *Capital*, Marx retained the original plan. Anyone claiming that there *is* a particular reason for arguing otherwise should clarify it. Yet Kautsky, in the passage cited above, offers no such explanation, apparently assuming that it is self-evident, somehow, that the basic original plan was abandoned with regard to *Capital*. His attitude is truly baffling. On top of this, Kautsky later presented a substantially different view in his preface to *Theories of Surplus Value*:

> From the outset, putting together this work [the manuscript of *Theories of Surplus Value*] was exceedingly difficult in terms of organisation. It had the same arrangement as in *Zur Kritik der politischen Ökonomie*, with a discussion of theoretical ideas followed by a presentation of their historical development. Moreover, the presentation is not merely descriptive but critical, containing further consideration of the ideas themselves. The more that the work moves from simple phenom-

---

8 Kautsky 1903, p. vi.
9 Marx 1976, p. 89.

ena to progress toward more complex things, the more that the historical descriptions of new thought, theoretical criticism, and positive developments become entangled in a broad, multifold investigation. As a result, even though I tried to bring the historical descriptions of surplus value and its phenomenal forms ... into more exact order, it was unavoidable that the manuscript, whose materials showed no trace of external organisation, would remain chaotic in character for everyone except its author.

My own belief is that because of the increasingly difficulty of shaping the materials into a clear form while preserving the structure of the previous manuscripts, Marx in 1863 abandoned all of the previous manuscripts and followed a new, clear structure that can be seen in the 1867 work *Capital*, so that he decided to start his work over from the beginning. And in the new structure, the history of theory is completely set aside as a special matter to be presented as a final volume.[10]

Kautsky, in other words, basically thinks that Marx discontinued *Zur Kritik der politischen Ökonomie* to write *Capital* from the beginning because of difficulties arising from his initial descriptive method, which sought to interweave logical descriptions and the history of economic doctrines. According to Kautsky's view, there was no reason at all to alter the fundamental plan, at least as it was developed in the 'Introduction to the Critique of Political Economy', so that the difference between the initial plan and *Capital* just comes down to a partial, technical matter regarding how to incorporate the historical content. But that is not the extent of Kautsky's view, since he also writes the following in his introduction to *Capital*:

> Strictly speaking, even the three volumes of *Capital* are not sufficient for grasping the entire process, and thus each of its parts from every direction, because these three volumes are not yet the completed work, which may have been finished in Marx's head but not on paper.[11]

This statement clearly contradicts Kautsky's earlier view. But each of these mutually contradictory views are presented as if self-evident, with no explanation whatsoever. Thus, we cannot look to Kautsky for a solution to the problem at hand, which he does not even pose in a clear way to begin with.

---

10   Kautsky 1905, pp. xi–xii.
11   Kautsky 1914, p. xxxiv.

In contrast, the conclusion reached by Robert Wilbrandt is quite clear. In his book *Karl Marx*, Wilbrandt accounts for the many misunderstandings of *Capital* as stemming from its unfinished nature:

> The noteworthy fate of this extraordinary work [*Capital*] had many ups and downs. Originally it was planned as the first of six books [as indicated in the preface to *Zur Kritik der politischen Ökonomie*] ...
>
> Thus, the only volume of *Capital* that was published by Marx himself, Volume I, is a torso in two senses. First, it was just one of many volumes, that would be hard to understand without the subsequent volumes, which is why it has been misunderstood throughout an entire era. Volume II was published after his death, and then the thick two-set Volume III was issued, which was seen as contradicting Volume I. It was only much later that the mistaken view of Volume I was corrected so that its place within the totality could be understood. The second point is that Volume I itself is only the first volume of one book among six books. The author had in mind the six books together as providing the solution to many other problems, and so in *Capital*, as one book within the entire work, such problems were set aside – or only hinted at or indicated – and left for subsequent volumes.[12]

Wilbrandt is clearly advancing the second of the four views introduced earlier. But he does not provide any explanation of why he has adopted this view. It seems that he never had any doubt that *Capital* corresponds to 'capital' in the original plan.

Unlike Wilbrandt, Hajime Kawakami, in *An Introduction to Das Kapital*, expresses uncertainty regarding the plan, noting his 'inability to say anything definitive about the final form of Marx's plan for the entire structure of his political economy'.[13] Kawakami, after quoting Marx's 2 April 1858 letter to Engels (cited earlier), writes the following:

> Marx's *Zur Kritik der politischen Ökonomie*, published in 1859, corresponds to the first half of Book 1 mentioned in his letter, which he titled 'capital in general'; according to his plan at the time, Book 1 was to contain Chapter 1 on the commodity, Chapter 2 on money, and Chapter 3 on capital in general. The work *Capital* that we have today is a developed version of the

---

12   Wilbrandt 1919, pp. 96–7.
13   Kawakami 1946, p. 52.

book on 'capital in general', but there is the question of whether Marx's plan remained unchanged even after that development. In other words, after bringing the first book on capital to an end by going on from capital to deal with competition, credit, and joint-stock capital, would he have continued his work in the order of going on to Book 2 on landed property and Book 3 on wage labour? Currently I am unable to offer with confidence a definitive answer to that question.[14]

Kawakami's doubts later vanished, however. In an article published in Issue 87 of his journal *Shakai mondai kenkyū* (Research in Social Problems),[15] he clearly argues for the second view introduced earlier:

> *Capital* only corresponds to the first book – 'capital' – among the six main books. Along with capital, there are the problems of landed property and wage labour, and even after the consideration of those problems, there are the additional problems of the state, relations between states, and the global market.[16]

Unfortunately, Kawakami provides no explanation of how he overcame his own doubts to adopt the second view.

Next, we can turn to the book *Toward a Critique of Political Economy*, in which Kazuo Fukumoto considers the 'system of the critique of political economy and the system of *Capital*' (pp. 195–209), and the 'scope of Marx's *Capital* within the critique of political economy' (pp. 290–309). However, the opinions he presents are vague and difficult to grasp. For instance, he presents the following conclusion:

> Thus, this demonstrates that the ultimate 'ascending' stage in *Capital* does not go beyond the boundaries of the second heading Marx lists in the 'Introduction to Critique of Political Economy' [i.e. capital, wage labour, and landed property].[17]

---

14   Kawakami 1946, pp. 55–6.
15   [A monthly journal that Kawakami began issuing in January 1919 (published by Kōbundō Shobō). A total of 106 issues of the journal appeared until its discontinuation in October 1930; up to issue 89, Kawakami was the sole author.]
16   Kawakami 1928, p. 3.
17   Fukumoto 1928, p. 203.

At first glance, this might seem to fall under the category of the third view, but Fukumoto also cites the following passages from Marx to support his conclusion:

> It is assumed throughout, that the commodity is sold at its value. We do not examine the competition of capitals, nor the credit system ...[18]

> [A] critique of [Sismondi's views] belongs to a part of my work dealing with the real movement of capital (competition and credit) which I can only tackle after I have finished this book.[19]

Even setting aside the inappropriateness of using a passage that predates the change in Marx's plan as a basis for considering whether or not the initial plan changed in the case of *Capital*, it must be pointed out that the content of the passages cited certainly does not back up Fukumoto's conclusion. Marx in these passages clearly states that 'competition' and 'credit' belong to a subsequent stage – and notes further on, after the first passage cited, that such problems as the transformation of value into production price (i.e. problems dealt with in Book III of *Capital*) are also set aside. It is difficult to understand how one can adopt the third view based on such clear statements. Here, too, we must regret that the problem not only remains unsolved but is posed in a way that leaves us in confusion.

Henryk Grossman presented an argument in favour of the fourth view in an article titled, 'The Change in the Original Plan for Marx's *Capital* and Its Causes', published in Carl Grünberg's journal *Archiv*.[20] As its title indicates, the article consists of two parts: first Grossman aims to verify the facts regarding the change of the original plan within *Capital*, and then he attempts to set out the reasons for the change. But it is the first part of the article that is of fundamental importance to his argument and directly concerns the problem addressed here.

The first part of Grossman's argument is developed in the form of an attack on the view of Wilbrandt introduced earlier. Although full of confidence, and sometimes even scornful in tone, Grossman diverges from the topic at hand

---

18   Marx 1989b, p. 124.
19   Marx 1989b, p. 245.
20   [Grossman's 1929 article 'Die Änderung des ursprunglichen Aufbauplans des Marxschen *Kapital* und ihre Ursachen' was published in issue 14 of *Archiv für die Geschichte des Sozialismus und der Arbeiterbewegung*, the journal established by Carl Grünberg in 1911 that later became the organ of the Institute for Social Research (*Institut für Sozialforschung*).]

occasionally, so that the point of his argument is not always clear. Nevertheless, since Grossman was the first to address the problem in a substantial way and consider various historical documents in an attempt to find a solution, I want to examine his view in as much detail as possible to obtain some hints on how to develop my own view.

Grossman's main grounds (?) for arguing that Marx completely altered his original plan in writing *Capital* seem to be the following. First, he points to the passage from Kautsky's introduction to the new edition of *Zur Kritik der politischen Ökonomie*, which I examined earlier. Although Grossman is doubtful about Kautsky's 'whole attitude towards Marx's principal work', he uncritically accepts the claim made by Kautsky in his introduction and on that basis mocks Wilbrandt for not perceiving what was clear 'at first glance'.[21] This is truly a baffling attitude for someone who has at least recognised the problem at hand and is seeking the truth.

The second piece of evidence Grossman points to is the following from Marx's 15 August 1863 letter to Engels:

> In one respect, my work (preparing the manuscript for the press) is going well. In the final elaboration the stuff is, I think, assuming a tolerably popular form, aside from a few unavoidable M – C's and C – M's. On the other hand, despite the fact that I write all day long, it's not getting on as fast as my own impatience, long subjected to a trial of patience, might demand. At all events, it will be 100 percent more comprehensible than No. 1. When, by the by, I consider my handiwork and realise how I've had to demolish everything and even build up the *historical* section out of what was in part quite unknown material, I can't help finding Izzy [Ferdinand Lasalle] a bit of a joke; for he has already got 'his' political economy in hand and yet everything he has peddled around hitherto has shown him to be a callow schoolboy who trumpets abroad as his very latest discovery ...[22]

With regard to this, Grossman writes:

> Already in the letter of 15 August we hear further that Marx 'had to demolish everything'. The change in plan appears here as *an already accomplished fact*.[23]

---

21 Grossman 2018, p. 185.
22 Marx 1985, p. 488.
23 Grossman 2018, p. 189.

In other words, Grossman interprets the line *habe alles umschmeissen müssen*[24] as meaning Marx had completely changed his plan; and that the change did not merely involve an improvement in description but a fundamental change of the entire system. However, I cannot fathom how, from that one line, Grossman can infer a change in the fundamental plan.

The third document cited by Grossman in support of his view is a letter from Marx to Ludwig Kugelmann dated 13 October 1866. Grossman has the following to say about this letter:

> Not only because this modification [of the original plan for *Capital*] can be seen 'at first glance' and had already been observed [?] by Kautsky, but because Marx himself – as we are instructed in his correspondence with Kugelmann – emphatically confirmed it.
>
> From the new draft plan, which he tells Kugelmann about and which we cite further below, it is clear that *Capital*, as it is presently available to us in four volumes, *is essentially complete*. In the available volumes, even though the exposition of individual sections has gaps in places, a chapter may be missing here and there, and the logical sequence is often interrupted, on the whole not only is all of the material to be dealt with included, but at the same time, as Engels said, 'what Marx intended to say is said there, in one way or another'.[25]

If we look up exactly what Marx wrote to Kugelmann concerning the change of plan, we find the following passage from the 13 October letter:

> My circumstances (endless interruptions, both physical and social) oblige me to publish *Volume One* first, not both volumes together, as I had originally intended. And there will now probably be 3 volumes. The whole work is thus divided into the following parts:
>
> *Book I. The Process of Production of Capital.*
> *Book II. The Process of Circulation of Capital.*
> *Book III. Structure of the Process as a Whole.*
> *Book IV. On the History of the Theory.*

---

24   Rather than this one line on having to 'demolish everything' signifying a complete change in the original plan, it seems more obvious to interpret it as a reference to overturning conventional doctrines in all realms of political economy. I think there is almost no doubt in this regard when the sentence is read together with the reference to the 'historical section' and Marx's contrasting of his own work to that of Lasalle.
25   Grossman 2018, p. 185.

The first volume will include the first 2 books. The 3rd book will, I believe, fill the second volume, the 4th the 3rd. It was, in my opinion, necessary to begin again *ab ovo* in the first book, i.e. to summarise the book of mine published by Duncker [*Zur Kritik der politischen Ökonomie*] in one chapter on commodities and money. I judged this to be necessary, not merely for the sake of completeness, but because even intelligent people did not properly understand the question, in other words, there must have been defects in the first presentation, especially in the analysis of commodities.[26]

The above seems to be what Grossman is referring to in mentioning the letter to Kugelmann. Apart from this, there is no other information in the letter that seems at all relevant to the point Grossman is making. Where exactly, in the passage above, can it be confirmed that Marx had fundamentally changed his original plan? Marx does indicate that the initially planned two-volume *Capital* was expanded to three volumes. He also notes that he will publish the first volume by itself to begin with, rather than publishing the first two volumes simultaneously as originally planned. Furthermore, instead of continuing from the previous work, as originally intended, Marx decides to start again from the beginning with the analysis of the commodity. Yet no matter how one looks at this information, it cannot be interpreted as confirming a fundamental change of the original plan. The only thing that Marx indicates is the plan to divide *Capital* into four parts ('the process of the production of capital' etc.). Grossman views this as confirming that Marx announced a 'new draft plan' and that 'Marx himself ... emphatically confirmed' the 'modification of the original plan for *Capital*'.[27] But is this in fact true?

First of all, there is no question that Marx writes that 'the whole work [*Das ganze Werk*] is thus divided into the following parts', but there is no reason to necessarily conclude that 'the whole work' is referring to the entire system of Marx's writing on political economy. This should be seen, instead, as a reference to the entire upcoming work that Marx was often discussing in his letters to Kugelmann – i.e. *Capital* as the fundamental part of his critique of political economy. It should be clear from what Marx writes thereafter in the letter that this is the necessary interpretation.

Second, it is completely counter to the truth for Grossman to argue that the plan to divide the parts of *Capital* into 'the process of the production of capital'

---

26   Marx 1987b, pp. 328–9.
27   Grossman 2018, p. 185.

etc. was a 'new draft plan'. Although I cannot say exactly when Marx arrived at this proposal, we can at least come across the following reference made in his 11 March 1858 letter to Lasalle:

> It [the first instalment of *Zur Kritik der politischen Ökonomie*] contains 1. Value, [note] 2. Money, 3 capital in General (the process of the production of capital; process of its circulation; the unity of the two, or capital and profit; interest)[28]

From this we can see that Marx's plan to deal with the production process of capital, etc. was already in place at least as early as March 1858, and that this concerned the content of 'capital in general' as the fundamental part of his critique of political economy.

This is not the extent of the matter, however. As Kautsky notes in his preface to the third volume of *Theories of Surplus Value*,[29] Marx, in a manuscript apparently written in December 1862,[30] called the first section of his work planned at the time 'the process of the production of capital' and the third section 'capital and profit', and he listed the content for both in some detail.[31] If we compare this plan to the actual first and third volumes of *Capital*, we can see that, except for a few differences, the content is essentially the same. Thus, we can know that, at least as of December 1862, Marx had worked out a plan for a work with more or less the same content as *Capital*. Moreover, on 28 December, around the time he was writing the manuscript for *Theories of Surplus Value*, Marx sent a letter to Kugelmann in which he conveyed the following:

> I was delighted to see from your letter how warm an interest is taken by you and your friends in my critique of political economy. The second part [*Teil*] has now at last been finished, i.e. save for the fair copy and the final polishing before it goes to press. There will be about 30 sheets of print. It is a sequel to Part I [*A Contribution to the Critique of Political Economy*], but will appear on its own under the title *Capital*, with *The Critique of Political Economy* as merely the subtitle. In fact, all it comprises is what was to make the third chapter of the first part [*Abteilung*], namely 'Capital in

---

28 Marx 1983, p. 287. Marx later replaces 'value' with 'commodity' but this change is not related to the question we are dealing with here.
29 Kautsky 1910.
30 [This is the date estimated by Kautsky, but it was later revised by the Moscow-based Institute of Marxism-Leninism to January 1863.]
31 [See Marx 1991a, pp. 346–7.]

General'. Hence it includes neither the competition between capitals nor the credit system. What Englishmen call 'The Principles of Political Economy' is contained in this volume. It is the quintessence (together with the first part), and the development of the sequel (with the exception, perhaps, of the relationship between the various forms of state and the various economic structures of society) could easily be pursued by others on the basis thus provided ...

As soon as I have a fair copy of the manuscript (upon which I shall make a start in January 1863), I shall bring it to Germany myself, it being easier to deal with publishers on a personal basis.

There is every prospect that, as soon as the German edition appears, arrangements will be made in Paris for a French version. I have absolutely no time to put it into French myself, particularly since I am going either to write the sequel in German, i.e. to conclude the presentation of capital, competition and credit, or condense the first two books for English consumption into one work.[32]

Based on the content of this letter and Marx's description in the aforementioned manuscript, it becomes clear that, around December 1862, Marx was planning a work whose content is nearly identical to what was eventually published as *Capital*, while at the same time referring to the work he was planning as a 'sequel to Part 1' of *A Contribution to the Critique of Political Economy* that 'comprises ... what was to make the third chapter of the first part, namely "Capital in General"' and therefore 'includes neither the competition between capitals nor the credit system'. These undeniable facts provide what I think is a nearly decisive solution to the problem at hand. But this solution certainly does not coincide with the view of Grossman, and indeed is the very opposite. The published volumes of *Capital* are not, as Grossman imagines, a comprehensive work that takes the place of the entire critique of political economy that Marx originally planned. Rather, it merely encompasses 'capital in general'. The content does not include 'competition and credit' that 'conclude the presentation of capital'. Therefore, it must be assumed that the specific presentations of landed property, wage labour, the state, foreign trade, and the world market are not included either.

The errors of Grossman's view should be evident from the explanation above, but I would like to look at one other argument he offers in support of his view. In expressing his opposition to the position of Wilbrandt, Grossman writes:

---

32   Marx 1985, pp. 435–6.

We must counterpose a question to this account: is it correct that Marx 'consciously refrains' from considering these problems in *Capital*; that he only intended to deal with the questions of ground rent, wages and foreign trade later? Apparently Wilbrandt has not noticed the analysis of all these questions in *Capital*.[33]

For Grossman it seems an unquestionable fact that the analysis of problems such as ground rent, wage labour, and foreign trade was completed in *Capital*. But is that in fact the case? Granted, the third volume of *Capital* includes a part titled the 'Transformation of Surplus Profit into Ground Rent', which provides a detailed analysis of ground rent; and in the first volume there is certainly a rather involved investigation of wage labour. But is it really the case that this analysis of ground rent and wage labour in *Capital* corresponds to the content planned for 'landed property' and 'wage labour' as parts within the initial plan for the critique of political economy? In other words, can it be said that this analysis constitutes the proper analysis of 'landed property' and 'wage labour'? Or could it rather be said that landed property and wage labour are considered only to the extent necessary to clarify the general character of capital? Grossman has completely overlooked the existence of this crucially important question. When Wilbrandt says that the discussion of 'landed property', 'ground rent', and other problems lies outside of the framework of *Capital*, it certainly does not mean that these problems were not pursued at all within *Capital*, but only that the proper consideration of these problems lies outside of the framework of *Capital*. Anyone who has glanced at the table of contents for Book III of *Capital* can see that Marx deals with the 'transformation of surplus profit into ground rent', just as it is clear that a chapter in Book I deals with 'wage labour'. Even the most careless person could perceive this. So the careless person in this case turns out to be Henryk Grossman, who failed to perceive a decisively important question that requires clarification.

Simply indicating the carelessness of Grossman is not enough to dispose of this problem, however. We need to advance toward a solution to the problem itself by considering whether the discussions of wage labour and ground rent in *Capital* constitute the proper theories of 'wage labour' and 'landed property.' The key to solving this problem, of course, should be sought within *Capital* itself. If we examine the relevant sections in the Book I and III[34] of

---

33   Grossman 2018, p. 185.
34   [As noted in the introduction, the term 'Book' will be used throughout for references by Kuruma to *Capital* (although in his early writings he tended to use the term 'Volume'). The former pertains to the division of *Capital* on the basis of content, while the latter indic-

Capital, we can come across indications added by Marx. For instance, in Part 6 ('Wages') of Book I, Marx writes:

> Wages themselves again take many forms. This fact is not apparent from the ordinary economic treatises which, in their crude obsession with the material [*Stoff*], ignore all differences of form. An exposition of all these forms however, *belongs to the special study of wage labour*, and not, therefore, to this work. Nevertheless, we shall have to give a brief description of the two fundamental forms.[35]

According to Marx, the explanation of the various forms of wages clearly lies outside the framework of *Capital*, belonging instead to 'a special study of wage labour' (*in die spezielle Lehre von der Lohnarbeit*).

Turning to Book III, the following passages can be found within Marx's presentation of ground rent:

> The analysis of landed property in its various historical forms *lies outside the scope of the present work*. We are concerned with it only in so far as a portion of the surplus value that capital produces falls to the share of the landowner ...
>
> Our own reason for considering the modern form of landed property is simply that we need to consider all the specific relationships of production and exchange that arise from the investment of capital on the land. Without this, our analysis of capital would not be complete ...
>
> It is one of Adam Smith's great services that he showed how the ground rent for capital applied to the production of other agricultural products, e.g. of flax, of dye-stuffs, in independent stock-raising, etc., is determined by the ground rent yielded by capital invested in the production of the staple crop. In fact, no further progress has been made in this connection since his time. What we should have to keep in mind as a restriction or addition *belongs to the independent treatment of landed property*, and not here.[36]

---

ates the actual published form. In the case of *Cápital* the two terms coincide, as Marx was not able to publish Book I and Book II together as Volume I, as originally intended, and his manuscripts for Book II and Book III were published posthumously as Volume II and Volume III, respectively.]

35   Marx 1976, p. 683. [Kuruma's emphasis.]
36   Marx 1981a, pp. 751–2. [Kuruma's emphasis.]

Interest on capital incorporated into the earth and the improvements that are thereby made to the soil as an instrument of production may form a portion of the rent that is paid by the farmer to the landowner, but it does not constitute ground rent proper, which is paid for the use of the soil as such, whether this is in a state of nature or is cultivated. *In a systematic treatment of landed property, which lies beyond our present scope*, this portion of the landowner's income would be presented in detail.[37]

Similar passages can be found elsewhere, but just from those cited above we can see that various problems concerning 'landed property' are outside the 'scope' of *Capital*; that there was to be an 'independent treatment of landed property', separate from the study of ground rent in *Capital*; and that the 'systematic treatment of landed property' which 'lies beyond our present scope' in *Capital* is included within the future plan.

However, a point remains that can generate doubts related to the problem under consideration. Namely, in his 2 April 1858 letter to Engels cited earlier, Marx clearly states:

> 1. *Capital*. First section: Capital in general (Throughout this section. wages are invariably assumed to be at their minimum. Movements in wages themselves and the rise and fall of that minimum will be considered under wage labour. Further, landed property is assumed to be zero, i.e. landed property, as a special economic relation is of no relevance as yet. Only by this procedure is it possible to discuss one relation without discussing all the rest.)[38]

In this case of 'capital in general', of course, the issue of wages is not raised. And in *Capital* as well, wages are 'invariably assumed to be at their minimum'. But that is not the case for landed property, since in Part 6 of the published edition of Book III, as is well known, Marx discusses the 'transformation of surplus profit into ground rent' and clearly poses the question of 'landed property as a special economic relation', without assuming that landed property is zero. This letter to Engels must be seen as evidence of a change in Marx's initial plan. We need to consider roughly when this change occurred, what factors determined it, and the degree of influence it had on the overall plan. Fortunately, among Marx's letters to Engels we can find some clues for the solution of this problem, starting with an 18 June 1862 letter in which Marx writes:

---

37 Marx 1981a, p. 756. [Kuruma's emphasis.]
38 Marx 1983, p. 298.

> Incidentally, another thing I have at last been able to sort out is the shitty rent business (which, however, I shall not so much as allude to in this part). I had long harbored misgivings as to the absolute correctness of Ricardo's theory, and have at length got to the bottom of the swindle.[39]

Just over a month later, on 2 August, Marx informs Engels:

> I now propose after all to include in this volume an extra chapter on the theory of rent, i.e. by way of 'illustration' to an earlier thesis of mine.[40]

Marx also tells his friend that he intends to then explain the consequent transformation of value into production price, and the related establishment of absolute ground rent, as well as elucidate how the defects in Ricardo's theory of value necessarily led to a violent rejection of absolute ground rent, in contrast to his own theory of value that could consistently clarify ground rent.

Taking these letters into consideration, it is clear that in 1862, between 18 June and 2 August, Marx first altered his original plan by deciding to 'include in this volume [capital in general] ... the theory of rent'. However, this certainly did not mean that Marx directly transferred to the book on 'capital in general' the entire content of 'landed property', which was one of the planned six main books. Rather, the theory of rent would be 'included' to the degree necessary in order to serve as an 'illustration' to Marx's 'earlier thesis'. It is not too hard to imagine why Marx would have perceived the need to alter his plan to that extent. Indeed, without explaining ground rent (and absolute ground rent in particular), at least to some extent, it is quite impossible to adequately discuss the transformation of value into production price, which Marx had decided to include within 'capital in general'. Marx naturally would have had a keen awareness of this necessity in the course of establishing his new theory of absolute ground rent. It was precisely around this time, according to Marx, that he first managed to establish that theory. In his 16 June letter to Engels, he informs his sworn friend of the happy event, and in a 2 August letter provides more detail of the theory's content. Marx's reason for saying in the former letter that he will 'not so much as allude' to the theory of rent in the volume on 'capital in general' seems to be that he had not resolved to alter his original approach, and that the decision to do so only crystallised as the result of careful consideration. In Book III of *Capital*, we can indeed find a part

---

39 Marx 1985, pp. 380–1.
40 Marx 1985, p. 394.

titled 'The Transformation of Surplus Profit into Ground Rent', in which Marx clearly indicates that this part of his work does not signify a special investigation of landed property, since he is concerned with landed property 'only in so far as a portion of the surplus value that capital produces falls to the share of the landowner'.[41] Thus, as before, the 'independent treatment of landed property' or the 'systematic treatment of landed property' lie 'outside the scope of the present work'.

But the problems of 'wage labour' and 'landed property' only constitute one portion of the entire plan. The original plan also called for three main books that would deal, respectively, with 'the state', 'international trade', and the 'world market'. Can it truly be said that the special study of any of these problems is found in *Capital*? We need to subject the ideas of the cross-examiner Grossman to a cross-examination.

Already we have considered all the grounds for Grossman's argument, shown the feebleness of each, and clarified that there is nothing to justify his view that Marx's original plan (or at least its framework) was subsequently changed. We also clarified that *Capital* corresponds to 'capital in general' in the original plan, which was to have been followed by 'competition' and 'credit' (and then 'joint-stock capital' – although there is some room for doubt on this point), thus concluding the book on 'capital', which was in turn to have been followed by books on 'landed property', 'wage labour', 'the state', 'foreign trade', and the 'world market', for an overall critique of political economy consisting of six books.

Given this, the problem naturally reaches a second stage. That is, if Marx's plan for a critique of political economy was only realised to the extent explained above, in what state does this leave his theory of crisis? In considering this problem, the first thing to bear in mind is a main heading in the second volume of *Theories of Surplus Value* titled 'Akkumulation von Kapital und Krisen'. Even though this heading itself was inserted by the editor Karl Kautsky, rather than by Marx himself, the question of crisis is dealt with there in a relatively coherent fashion, providing us with many suggestive arguments. But that does not necessarily mean that this content constitutes Marx's conclusive theory of crisis *per se*. Indeed, the content is actually from a much earlier stage and represents a preliminary consideration. This is clear from the nature of the entire manuscript and from the content of the arguments developed in that particular part, especially the frequent clear indications made by Marx that the concrete study of crisis belongs to a subsequent part. In *Capital* as well, it is true that we can find various explanations of crisis, but they are no

---

41   Marx 1981a, p. 751.

more than points of reference for problems pertaining to the logical unfolding of Marx's descriptions of 'capital in general' (i.e. 'the internal organisation of the capitalist mode of production, its ideal average'[42]), and none of this can be seen as constituting a proper theory of crisis. We can also come across clear indications by Marx regarding how the concrete investigation of crisis belongs to a subsequent work.

Clearly, then, Marx's theory of crisis, along with the system of his critique of political economy, was left in an incomplete state. The problem thus becomes how to develop a Marxian theory of crisis proper from the various investigations of crisis scattered throughout *Capital*. In order to succeed in this endeavour, we must clarify the intrinsic relation between those investigations found in the pages of *Capital* and a proper theory of crisis. Accomplishing that requires us to trace our way back further to elucidate Marx's overall approach toward clarifying crisis and its relation to his critique of political economy. What conception did Marx have to begin with concerning the elucidation of crisis? The fundamental determinant of his conception, needless to say, was his general grasp of the essence of crisis. We can often come across descriptions of the essence of crisis in Marx's works, such as the following:

> The commercial crises of the nineteenth century, and in particular the great crises of 1825 and 1836, did not lead to any further development of Ricardo's currency theory, but rather to new practical applications of it. It was no longer a matter of single economic phenomena – such as the depreciation of precious metals in the sixteenth and seventeenth centuries confronting Hume, or the depreciation of paper currency during the eighteenth century and the beginning of the nineteenth confronting Ricardo – but of big storms on the world market, in which the antagonism [contradiction] of all elements in the bourgeois process of production explodes.[43]

> The world trade crises must be regarded as the real concentration and forcible adjustment of all the contradictions of bourgeois economy.[44]

> In world market crises, all the contradictions of bourgeois production erupt collectively.[45]

---

42   Marx 1981a, p. 970.
43   Marx 1987a, p. 412.
44   Marx 1989b, p. 140.
45   Marx 1989b, p. 163.

These are some of the most direct expressions of the way Marx grasped the 'world market crises' particular to modern production, which are the general crises that rock every sector of production on a global scale. In order to clarify crisis in the proper sense of the term, as a crisis of the world market, what sort of conception is necessary? Since crisis is the collective explosion of all the contradictions of capitalist production, and their real concentration, it should be clear that the problem naturally comes down to how to trace the necessary unfolding of these contradictions that collectively explode and are concentrated in reality, and to then reconstitute this process theoretically. How did Marx actually pursue this problem? And how (and to what extent) was he able to develop his theory? These are the initial questions that we will need to investigate.

∙ ∙ ∙

I wavered about whether to include the article 'An Inquiry into Marx's Theory of Crisis' as a chapter in this book because its textual analysis of the relation between *Capital* and Marx's original systematic plan for a critique of political economy was written in 1930, when most of the content of the *Grundrisse der Kritik der politischen Ökonomie*, published five years later, was still unavailable.[46] Thus, I wrote the article without being able to consult that text of decisive importance to the problem under consideration. In this sense, the article is flawed and requires revision. In fact, it requires a complete rewriting, since a partial rewriting cannot resolve its problems. But that is not something that I have adequate time to do at present. Moreover, since the earlier article is a sort of 'historical document', as the first attempt in Japan to address this issue, it has been quoted from and referred to by many scholars, regardless of their view of its content. Thus, I decided in the end to republish the article as is. But just doing that seemed irresponsible, so I feel obliged to add some remarks here about my impressions from reading the *Grundrisse*.

What I noticed from the *Grundrisse*, first of all, insofar as it relates to the present issue, is that Marx's thinking with regard to 'capital in general' at the time of writing this manuscript (1857–59) was quite different from what I had imagined it to be. In the *Grundrisse*, Marx says that 'to regard the total capital of e.g. a nation as distinct from total wage labour (or, as distinct from landed property)', or to 'regard capital as the general economic basis of a class as dis-

---

46 [What follows are comments related to the foregoing chapter made by Kuruma in his introduction to the 1965 edition *Investigation of Crisis Theory* (Kuruma 1965, pp. i–x).]

tinct from another class' is to 'regard it in general';[47] and that when dealing with capital in general the 'differentiation etc. of capitals does not concern us'.[48]

However, if that is the case, the problem of the equalisation of the profit rate (and the formation of a general profit rate premised on differences in the rate of profit between capitals in different industries), and therefore the problem of the transformation of value into production price, would not belong to the realm of inquiry for 'capital in general' and would instead lie outside of its scope (in the theory of competition). And this is indeed what is clearly stated in the *Grundrisse*.

This differs completely from what I had surmised with regard to 'capital in general'. My conjecture at the time of writing my article was based mainly on two sources from Marx written at the end of 1862 and in January 1863: his letter to Kugelman dated 28 December 1862 and the plan for Book III of *Capital* in the manuscript for *Theories of Surplus Value*.[49] In the letter to Kugelman, Marx notes the following about his plan at the time for *Capital*:

> It is a sequel to Part I,[50] but will appear on its own under the title *Capital*, with *The Critique of Political Economy* as merely the subtitle. In fact, all it comprises is what was to make the third chapter[51] of the first part [*Abteilung*], namely 'Capital in General'. Hence it includes neither the competition between capitals nor the credit system. What Englishmen call 'The Principles of Political Economy' is contained in this volume.[52]

If we look at Marx's plan for Book III of *Capital* written around the same time, it was to have be divided as follows:

---

47   Marx 1973a, p. 852.
48   Marx 1973a, p. 346.
49   This plan is from page 1139 of notebook XVIII. Kautsky estimates the manuscript to have been written in December 1862 but according to the Marx-Engels-Lenin Institute editors the date was January 1863.
50   'Part' clearly refers to the volume of *A Contribution to the Critique of Political Economy* [published in 1859].
51   The published volume of *A Contribution to the Critique of Political Economy* consists of two chapters ('The Commodity' and 'Money or Simple Circulation') under 'Section One: Capital in General' in 'Book One: On Capital'. These are the *Vorchapters* ('pre-chapters') on capital in general that were to have been followed by the proper discussion of capital in general.
52   Marx 1985, p. 435.

> The third section[53] 'Capital and Profit' to be divided in the following way: 1) Conversion of surplus value into profit. Rate of profit as distinguished from rate of surplus value. 2) Conversion of profit into average profit. Formation of the general rate of profit. Transformation of value into prices of production ... [Parts from '3)' omitted.][54]

Considering that both of these sources were written around the same time, it becomes clear that Marx had a plan, on the one hand, to deal with the 'conversion of profit into average profit', the 'formation of the general rate of profit', and the 'transformation of value into prices of production' in Book III of *Capital*; while, on the other hand, the entirety of *Capital* was to encompass only 'capital in general' so that 'it includes neither the competition between capitals nor the credit system'. Based on this, it seems that including the 'transformation of profit into average profit' in Part 2 of the published edition of Book III of *Capital* certainly does not signify that Marx altered his original plan to introduce within it the theory of competition. Therefore, at least to this extent, it does not seem to signify a change in the original plan, thus supporting the view of those who argued that Marx's plan had remained unchanged.[55] And it seems to me that Marx's fundamental ideas regarding the realm of consideration for 'capital in general' is the same as was expressed in the pages of *Capital*, such as in the following:

> In a general analysis of the present kind, it is assumed throughout that actual conditions correspond to their concept, or, and this amounts to the same thing, actual conditions are depicted only in so far as they express their own general type.[56]

> This is because the actual movement of competition lies outside our plan, and we are only out to present the internal organisation of the capitalist mode of production, its ideal average, as it were.[57]

---

53   'Section' (*Abschnitt*) corresponds in this case to 'book' (*Buch*) in *Capital*.
54   Marx 1991a, p. 346.
55   Although I adhered to this idea that the plan did not change, I did not insist that it was unchanged in every aspect. For example, I already recognised that there was a change in Marx's opinion with regard to whether rent should be incorporated within 'capital in general' and if so to what extent. This is dealt with in more detail in Chapter 3 of this book, but here I will limit the problem to competition.
56   Marx 1981a, p. 242.
57   Marx 1981a, p. 970.

My conjecture at the time of writing my article in 1930 was not incorrect, at least with regard to the conception Marx had around 1862 to 1863 (particularly with regard to 'capital in general' and the 'theory of competition'), but I was clearly mistaken in thinking that the plan Marx made around this time was his 'initial plan'. In reading the *Grundrisse*, I could see that the conceptual definition of 'capital in general' – and therefore the realm of consideration particular to it – was far different from what I had imagined, as already explained. This necessarily implies that Marx's conception of a systematic critique of political economy changed greatly between the time of writing the *Grundrisse* and the period around 1862 to 1863. This raises questions that need to be addressed.

First there is the question of Marx's motive for changing the plan. With regard to this, we can point, first, to the seeming difficulty he faced in writing *Theories of Surplus Value*. Previous doctrines of political economy had lacked a clear distinction between surplus value and profit, and between original profit and average profit, so that a distinction between value and production price was also lacking – resulting in the mixing up of all those concepts. Thus, Marx would not have been able to critique the view of value and surplus value within those doctrines unless he also discussed the transformation of profit into average profit (formation of a general profit rate) and the transformation of value into production price, not to mention the transformation of surplus value into profit. This seems to be his direct impetus for going beyond the initially planned framework of 'capital in general'.

Incidentally, the expansion beyond the framework of 'capital in general' under that impetus seems to have led Marx in early 1863 to introduce into his plan for the 'third section' (Book III) of *Capital* the following parts, as introduced earlier:

> 1) Conversion of surplus value into profit. Rate of profit as distinguished from rate of surplus value. 2) Conversion of profit into average profit. Formation of the general rate of profit. Transformation of value into prices of production

This expansion of the scope of consideration also was necessarily accompanied by a change in the conceptual definition of 'capital in general'. Whereas initially the concept of 'capital in general' abstracted from the relations between capitals to consider capital as a single entity (and capital in opposition to wage labour as well as to landed property), Marx came to understand that what the 'English call the principles of political economy were included therein'. It seems likely that Marx realised at the same time that the inclusion within 'capital in general' of the formation of a general profit rate and the transformation of value into price was necessary not only to criticise the 'doctrines regarding surplus value' but also was indispensable to an adequate clarification of the fundamental laws of capitalist production because, with the development of the capitalist mode of production, it is production price, not value, that becomes the point around which market prices continually fluctuate and the thing that determines those fluctuations.

However, as of late 1862, Marx had said, with regard to his new plan for *Capital*, that 'all it comprises is ... "Capital in General"' and what 'Englishmen call "The Principles of Political Economy"'.[58] But in the actual pages of *Capital* expressions with regard 'capital in general' in that sense no longer appear and the conceptual limits are expressed in terms such as those quoted earlier with regard to the assumption that 'actual conditions correspond to their concept or ... are depicted only in so far as they express their own general type'[59] and that 'the actual movement of competition lies outside our plan' that only seeks to present the 'ideal average' of the 'internal organisation of the capitalist mode of production'.[60]

But next we must consider whether the examination of the 'transformation of profit into average profit' in Part 2 of Book III of *Capital* (pertaining to the 'theory of competition' in the original plan) can be said to concern the theory of competition proper. Marx, in Chapter 10 of Part 2, does consider the 'equalisation of the general rate of profit through competition', and this has led some to imagine that he had finished his theoretical consideration of competition. This view seems incorrect to me, however. I do not mean to imply, of course, that competition is *not* considered there. However, what is at issue is not competition *per se*, but its mediation of the 'equalisation of the general profit rate', so that competition is only considered to the extent necessary to clarify this issue. In his 6 March 1868 letter to Kugelmann, Marx notes:

> In volume II ... property in land will be one of the subjects analysed, competition only in so far as called for in the treatment of other themes.[61]

I think this comment can be applied directly to our discussion above (in which the main subject analysed is the 'equalisation of a general rate of profit'). If Marx had been dealing with a theory of competition (where competition is

---

58   Marx 1985, p. 435.
59   Marx 1981a, p. 242.
60   Marx 1981a, p. 970.
61   Marx 1987b, p. 544.

the *central issue*), the problems would have had to be posed in a completely different manner than they are in *Capital*. In Chapter 10, for instance, Marx considers competition between capitals in the same department, but he is merely considering how competition equalises the different individual values into a single market price. However, this competition between capitals in the same department is, on the other hand, a cause of differences that arise between individual capitals. Raising productive power to lower individual values is a means of obtaining a special profit and also a condition for winning out in competition. At the same time, competition combines with credit to be a lever of capital accumulation, etc. If Marx had made competition his main topic and considered the competition between capitals of the same department, such actions would have had to be examined together as the same actions of competition. Another point that may be worth mentioning is the following. As Marx notes in *Theories of Surplus Value*, the fact that 'the value of each individual commodity in a particular sphere of production is determined by the total mass of social labour time required by the total mass of the commodities of this particular sphere of social production and not by the individual values of the separate commodities' is due to the 'competition, partly among the capitalists themselves [in the same sphere], partly between them and the buyers of the commodity, and partly among the latter themselves',[62] not merely from the competition between capitalists in the same sphere. Thus, when Marx solely emphasises competition between capitalists in the same sphere in examining the reduction of individual values to market price in Chapter 10, he does so because this is the competition that is more characteristic in this case than the equalisation of the profit rate through competition between capitals in different departments.

Another issue we can consider is the relation of supply and demand that is an essential moment within the operation of competition. Marx considers this relation in detail from a variety of angles throughout most of Chapter 10, but he did not forget to indicate the limits of this consideration. For instance, he writes:

> Let us note here, but merely in passing, that the 'social need' which governs the principle of demand is basically conditioned by the relationship of the different classes and their respective economic positions; in the first place, therefore, particularly by the proportion between the total surplus value and wages, and secondly, by the proportion between the vari-

---

62   Marx 1989a, p. 430.

ous parts into which surplus value itself is divided (profit, interest, ground rent, taxes, etc.). Here again we can see how absolutely nothing can be explained by the relationship of demand and supply, before explaining the basis on which this relationship functions.[63]

Demand and supply, on further analysis, imply the existence of various different classes and segments of classes which distribute the total social revenue among themselves and consume it as such, thus making up a demand created out of revenue; while it is also necessary to understand the overall configuration of the capitalist production process if one is to comprehend the demand and supply generated among the producers as such.[64]

Furthermore, the relation between this demand for personal consumption and demand for production depends on the proportion at which revenue is transformed into capital, so it cannot be determined without an awareness of the law that governs that transformation, etc. But since all of this understanding is only first posited over the course of the entirety of *Capital*, the consideration of supply and demand along the way must necessarily be more or less abstract and formalistic. In the passage from Chapter 10 quoted above, Marx expressly notes that what he is saying is 'merely in passing' precisely because it is not yet the appropriate place to consider the problem on its own. The substantial consideration of supply and demand, and analysis of its internal determinations, is premised on the various investigations in *Capital* and can only be unfolded thereafter. Needless to say, the 'deeper analysis of these two social driving forces [supply and demand] which we do not intend to give here'[65] was to have been dealt with after *Capital* as one aspect of the 'theory of competition'.

The above are just a few examples, but I think they make clear that the theory of competition remains outside the scope of *Capital*. Moreover, we could see that this does not mean that the general theoretical consideration of competition was already completed in *Capital*, leaving nothing more than the 'detailed research' for Marx to carry out. Rather, the analysis of competition in *Capital* is only dealt with 'in so far as called for in the treatment of other themes', so that the consideration of competition as the main topic had not been carried out generally and theoretically. These are points that can be insisted on irrespective of the fact that, under Marx's initial plan, the problems of the formation

---

63   Marx 1981a, p. 282.
64   Marx 1981a, p. 296.
65   Marx 1981a, p. 291.

of a general rate of profit and transformation of value into production price were to have been dealt with in the theory of competition rather than 'capital in general' – contrary to my understanding at the time I wrote my article in 1930. Thus, with regard to this point, my view has not changed since reading the *Grundrisse*. Moreover, my reason for examining texts related to Marx's plan was not the result of some sort of historical curiosity but rather was intended to clarify that the content of *Capital* is limited to the fundamental part of the overall critique of political economy and to inquire into the development beyond that for the sake of elaborating a Marxian theory of crisis. With regard to these points, as well, I do not think there is a reason to revise my earlier explanation.

CHAPTER 3

Addendum to 'An Inquiry into Marx's Theory of Crisis': A Response to the Criticism of Kōzō Uno

In a 1952 article titled 'Problematic Points in the Theory of Crisis in *Capital*' published in Vol. 3, No. 3 of the journal *Shakai kagaku kenkyū* (Research in Social Science),[1,2] Kōzō Uno argues that a fundamental theory of crisis was not developed in *Capital* due to a certain defect in the way Marx's logic was unfolded in Book III of *Capital*. Uno refers in his article to passages from my own article 'An Inquiry into Marx's Theory of Crisis'.[3] Here I will respond to Uno's criticism, but before getting to the core of my response, I want to introduce his basic argument for the sake of readers who may not be familiar with the article in question. Uno begins by posing the problem as follows:

> In Marx's 'Introduction to the Critique of Political Economy',[4] published as an appendix to the current [Japanese] edition of *A Contribution to the Critique of Political Economy*, 'crisis' is listed at the end of his plan for a critique of political economy, alongside 'world market'. Needless to say, this is a broad outline of Marx's planned work, of which *A Contribution to the Critique of Political Economy* and *Capital* are only the beginning part. The general assumption, in accordance with this plan, has been that the theory of crisis lies outside the boundaries of *Capital*. As I will discuss later, I concur that the theory of crisis was not developed completely in *Capital*, but I do not think that this was a natural outcome due to the theory being outside the scope of *Capital*. Indeed, existing within *Capital* are what could be considered the fundamental determinations of the theory of crisis. What we need to consider is why Marx could not develop these determinations into a full-fledged theory of crisis. Here I would like to offer my frank opinions on this point.[5]

---

1 [Originally published as Kuruma 1953a under the title 'A Reply to Professor Uno Concerning the Relation Between *Capital* and Crisis Theory'] and republished as Chapter 9 in Kuruma 1953b.]
2 [Uno's article was republished as an appendix in his 1953 book *Kyōkō ron* (Theory of Crisis).]
3 [Chapter 2 of this book.]
4 [Marx 1973, pp. 83–111.]
5 Uno 1953 p. 189.

As can be surmised from the passage above, the content of Uno's argument can be divided into two parts. The first part concerns the plan for Marx's critique of political economy, while the second part discusses the defects of Book III. The passages that Uno quotes from my article concern the former, of course, and he develops a critique of my view. Uno's reason for critiquing my article seems to be that my views run directly counter to his idea that Marx erred in not developing the fundamental determinations of crisis into a finished theory in *Capital*. Uno's critique, incidentally, is quite convoluted, including some trains of thought that I was unable to unravel even after pondering them at some length. But setting that aside for the moment, I think that the gist of his argument can be summarised as follows:

1. Kuruma argues that in *Capital* 'it is true that we can find various explanations of crisis, but they are no more than points of reference for problems pertaining to the logical unfolding of Marx's descriptions of capital in general (i.e. 'the internal organisation of the capitalist mode of production, its ideal average'),[6] and none of this can be seen as constituting a proper theory of crisis'; however, the question here centres on the meaning of a 'proper theory of crisis'.

2. Kuruma uses the same term 'proper' [*koyū*] with regard to the theory of 'wage labour' and of 'landed property', but in those cases he writes: 'Granted, the third volume of *Capital* includes a part titled the "Transformation of Surplus Profit into Ground Rent", which provides a detailed analysis of ground rent; and in the first volume there is certainly a rather involved investigation of wage labour. But is it really the case that this analysis of ground rent and wage labour in *Capital* corresponds to the content planned for 'landed property' and 'wage labour' as parts within the initial plan for the critique of political economy? In other words, can it be said that the analysis itself signifies the proper analysis of 'landed property' and 'wage labour'? Or could it rather be said that it is merely the consideration of landed property and wage labour to the extent necessary to clarify the general character of capital?' From this, we can see that Kuruma thinks that a 'proper analysis' pertains to the content envisaged for 'landed property' and 'wage labour' within Marx's original plan for a critique of political economy, whereas the content of the published volumes of *Capital* falls outside that realm.

I have no objection to saying that there is a disparity between the content of 'landed property' and 'wage labour' conceived of as one part of the

---

6 Marx 1981a, p. 970.

original plan for the critique of political economy, and the way *Capital* was later developed. And I also agree that the latter work only considers 'landed property and wage labour to the extent necessary to clarify the general character of capital', but this certainly does not mean that the theory of rent and of wages found in *Capital* are not an unfolding of the general theory of landed property and wage labour, or that the development of those general theories lies outside the scope of *Capital*. The fundamental determinations of capitalistic landed property and wage labour are in fact superbly unfolded in *Capital*. And that is appropriate. Indeed, a relationship exists where the general characteristic of capital certainly cannot be clarified unless those fundamental determinations are clarified. Thus, the theories of landed property and wage labour thought to lie outside the realm of *Capital* certainly do not have a character that could be described as a 'proper' analysis, but rather must be 'particular' research premised on those general theories posited within the theory of capital and developed on that basis. Even if we set aside the appropriateness of Kuruma's use 'proper' so as to assume he is using it to refer to 'particular' research, saying that the 'particular' analysis of landed property and wage labour in this case lies outside the realm of the theory of capital certainly does not negate, and is in fact premised on, the fact that the general theory related to landed property and wage labour is, and naturally must be, developed within the theory of capital.

3. If landed property and wage labour are thought of in that manner, it is natural to think of crisis in the same way. It is not sufficient to simply write, as Kuruma has done, that in *Capital* 'it is true that we can find various explanations of crisis, but they are no more than points of reference for problems pertaining to the logical unfolding of Marx's descriptions of capital in general … and none of this can be seen as a proper theory of crisis'. Kuruma of course is not incorrect insofar as stating this fact regarding *Capital*, but that is not sufficient for dealing with this problem. The structure of *Capital* as such must be posed as a problem. But Kuruma merely quotes from the original plan of the critique of political economy to justify what exists. Doing so does not provide the foundation for saying it is objectively correct. And as long as that basis is lacking, one must imagine the facts he describes signify a defect in *Capital*.

The above is the gist of Uno's critique, insofar as I was able to follow his reasoning. My summary left out the parts I was incapable of understanding, as alluded to earlier, so before replying to the content of his critique I need to touch on those omitted parts.

As indicated in the summary above, Uno begins by considering the significance of what I mean by a 'proper theory of crisis', but in so doing he argues, unexpectedly, that my 'reasoning seems to stem from what Marx writes in three letters to Engels regarding ... landed property'.[7] After introducing those letters and quoting my comments, Uno writes:

> The first doubt I immediately had upon reading Professor Kuruma's explanation is whether it is indeed appropriate to assume that the part on rent in the published edition of *Capital* is, as Marx thought, something that he 'include[d] in this volume [as] an extra chapter on the theory of rent, i.e. by way of "illustration" to an earlier thesis'.[8]

Uno then expresses his own opposing view. If that were the extent of his opposition, it would not be strange to interpret Uno's view as being based on a misunderstanding due to my insufficient explanation (as I will explain later in more detail). What is odd, though, is that on the basis of my explanation of the passages from Marx that he also quotes, Uno seems to think that I hold the same view with regard to wage labour; as if the theory of wage labour in *Capital* had, likewise, merely been 'included to illustrate an earlier thesis'. For instance, Uno writes:

> I have no objection to saying that there is a disparity between the latter [the content of the theories of 'landed property' and 'wage labour' conceived of as one part of the original plan for the critique of political economy] and the way they were later developed in *Capital*. I also agree with Professor Kuruma that 'landed property and wage labour' are only considered there 'to the extent necessary to clarify the general character of capital', but I think they are too important to be included just as 'an "illustration" to an earlier thesis'. Rather, in *Capital* the theory of wages concerns the determination of the fundamental relation between capitalists and workers, while the theory of rent concerns the fundamental determination of the relation between capitalists and landowners. Furthermore, the part within the 'initial plan for the critique of political economy' on wage labour belongs to the 'special study of wage labour' [Marx 1976, p. 683].[9]

---

7 Uno 1953, p. 191.
8 Uno 1953, pp. 192–3.
9 Uno 1953, pp. 193–4.

I should have thought it would be clear from the nature of the problem under discussion, without any room for doubt, that my reference to the inclusion 'by way of 'illustration' to an earlier thesis' solely pertained to rent and was not applicable to wages or anything else. The discussion there was particular to rent because I was considering the changes in Marx's way of thinking as to whether or not to include the theory of rent within *Capital*. The question of whether the fundamental theory of wages should be included within *Capital* was not at issue at all, nor was it something that Marx had pondered. Capitalist production without the premise of wage labour is unthinkable, and without elucidating the law of wages there is no way to elucidate the law of surplus value. In other words, there is no need to wait for Professor Uno's explanation to be aware of the self-evident fact that the fundamental theory concerning wages is an elemental part of *Capital*. But that is not true of the theory of rent. Whereas the basics of capitalist production cannot be understood without having a certain understanding of wage labour and wages, the fundamental relations of capitalist production can be understood without an understanding of rent. This can be seen by the fact that within *Capital*, rent only first appears in Book III, and near the very end, just before the concluding section. This is a clear indication that the relations and laws of capitalist production discussed prior to that can be developed without a theory of rent. This is precisely why, as Marx explains in a letter to Engels dated 2 April 1858, 'landed property is assumed to be zero, i.e. landed property as a special economic relation is of no relevance as yet' at the beginning of his critique of political economy ('First section: Capital in general').[10] In his letter of 18 June 1862, Marx writes that 'another thing I have been able to sort out is this shitty rent business (which, however, I shall *not so much as allude to* in this part)'.[11] And, in yet another letter from that year, dated 2 August, Marx makes clear for the first time a change in that original idea:

> I now propose after all to include in this volume [i.e. 'capital in general'] an extra chapter on the theory of rent, i.e. by way of "illustration" to an earlier thesis of mine.[12]

When I mentioned the '"illustration" to an earlier thesis', I was directly quoting Marx and imagined it would be obvious that this solely pertains to the rela-

---

10   Marx 1983, p. 298.
11   Marx 1985, p. 380.
12   Marx 1985, p. 394.

tion to rent, having no relation whatsoever to wage labour. It is hard to fathom how Professor Uno could have misconstrued me in the manner described above.

But there is more to the mystery than that. Uno's starting point itself is already unclear to me. He begins with the idea that what I meant by the 'proper theory of crisis' is ambiguous, and that the key to clarifying the meaning is to be found in the letters Marx wrote to Engels explaining a change in his conception of how to deal with rent. I have no intention of insisting that my use of the term 'proper' is appropriate, but the basic meaning should have been clear by looking at the two or three examples I offered. For instance, I wrote the following (in a passage quoted by Uno himself):

> But is it really the case that this analysis of ground rent and wage labour in *Capital* corresponds to the content planned for 'landed property' and 'wage labour' as parts within the initial plan for the critique of political economy? In other words, can it be said that those analyses signify the proper analysis of 'landed property' and 'wage labour'? Or could it rather be said that it merely involves the consideration of landed property and wage labour to the extent necessary to clarify the general character of capital?[13]

From this passage alone, it should be clear that the 'proper analysis' of landed property and wage labour refers to the content planned on 'landed property' and 'wage labour' as part of the originally planned critique of political economy. I should have thought it understandable, without the exercise of much imagination, that this proper analysis takes landed property and wage labour as the primary subjects, and would therefore analyse them in detail from every angle, unlike the case in *Capital*, where the 'consideration of landed property and wage labour [is merely] to the extent necessary to clarify the general character of capital'. In any case, the fact that rather than judging from such actual examples, Uno sought the key to the explanation in totally unrelated letters written by Marx, as mentioned earlier, is something that makes no sense to me, no matter how hard I try to fathom the meaning.

Leaving aside such perplexing points within Uno's critique, let me move on as promised to explain in more detail the misunderstanding that may stem from the insufficiency of my explanation. Uno's criticism has shown that some parts of my explanation of the problem were probably too simplistic, thus invit-

---

13 [See p. 86 of this book.]

ing misunderstanding, so I would like to take this opportunity in responding to his criticism to make up for those defects, even if it relates to issues secondary to the primary issue of considering whether it is natural or rather inappropriate for the theory of crisis to not be fully developed in *Capital*. The criticism offered by Uno is as follows:

> On the basis of these letters [from Marx to Engels], Professor Kuruma concludes that, 'it is clear that in 1862, between 18 June and 2 August, Marx first altered his original plan by deciding to "include in this volume [capital in general] ... the theory of rent". However, this certainly did not mean that Marx directly transferred to the book on "capital in general" the entire content of "landed property", which was one of the planned six main books. Rather, the theory of rent would be 'included' to the degree necessary in order to serve as an "illustration" to Marx's "earlier thesis"'.
>
> The first doubt that immediately springs to mind upon reading Professor Kuruma's explanation is whether it is indeed appropriate to assume that the part of *Capital* on ground rent is, as Marx thought, something that he 'include[d] in this volume [as] an extra chapter on the theory of rent, i.e. by way of "illustration" to an earlier thesis'.
>
> Even if it can be said that the discussion in *Capital* of rent, as in the case of wage labour, was a development of the 'earlier thesis', it could hardly be thought that it was a mere 'illustration'. ... [it is] too important to be just brought into *Capital* as 'an "illustration" to Marx's earlier thesis'. Rather ... the theory of rent concerns the fundamental determination of the relation between capitalists and landowners.[14]

My 'interpretation' examined by Professor Uno, as is immediately clear from the passage he quotes, concerns Marx's new conception on how to deal with rent that arose in 1862, between 18 June and 2 August. Moreover, because this is not so much an 'explanation' on my part as an exact conveying of what Marx himself wrote, and the issue itself concerns a clarification of the change in his conception of how to deal with rent, there does not seem much room for 'doubt'. Marx's thoughts on how to deal with rent changed thereafter to a certain extent, but without touching on that, I moved directly to the theory of rent as it is actually dealt with in *Capital*, noting the following:

---

14   Uno 1953, pp. 192–3.

In Book III of *Capital*, we can indeed find a part titled 'The Transformation of Surplus Profit into Ground Rent', in which Marx clearly indicates that this part of his work does not signify a special investigation of landed property, since he is concerned with landed property 'only in so far as a portion of the surplus value that capital produces falls to the share of the landowner'.[15] Thus, as before, the 'independent treatment of landed property' or the 'systematic treatment of landed property' lie 'outside the scope of the present work'.

In this passage as well, I am merely presenting what Marx wrote in the section on ground rent in *Capital*, since my aim was to consider his intentions around the time of writing *Capital*. Here, too, I certainly do not think I am mistaken. However, since I did not comment on how Marx's thinking changed between August 1862 and the time he wrote the section on ground rent for *Capital*, I may have given the impression that I thought Marx at the time of writing *Capital* still fully maintained the idea expressed in August 1862 that the theory of rent would serve as a an 'illustration' to his earlier thesis. In order to make up for that defect, I want to discuss the change in Marx's thinking around that time, relying on direct historical evidence, but since the matter is not of great significance in itself, I will be brief.

Unlike the case of the initial change, no trace can be found of Marx himself clearly indicating the subsequent change, but we can verify what happened based on various documents. It is not clear up to what precise point Marx continued to adhere to the idea of only inserting the theory of rent as an 'illustration' to an 'earlier thesis', as he had expressed in the 2 August 1862 letter announcing the new approach of including that theory within 'capital in general'; but we can see that same way of thinking is expressed in the manuscript for *Theories of Surplus Value*, thought to have been written in the spring of the same year. The manuscript contains the plan for the parts corresponding to the Book III of *Capital*. On page 1139 of the manuscript [Notebook XVIII] (according to Kautsky), Marx writes that the 'third section "Capital and Profit" [is] to be divided as follows':

1. Transformation of surplus-value into profit. The rate of profit as distinct from the rate of surplus value.
2. Transformation of profit into average profit. Establishment of the general rate of profit. Transformation of values into prices of production.
3. A. Smith's and Ricardo's theories on profit and prices of production.

---

15   Marx 1981a, p. 751.

4. Ground rent (illustration of the difference between value and price of production).
5. History of Ricardo's so-called Law of Rent.
6. Law of the fall in the rate of profit. A. Smith, Ricardo, Carey.
7. Theories of profit (question whether or not to include Sismondi and Malthus in *Theories of Surplus Value*).
8. Division of profit into industrial profit and interest. Mercantile capital. Money-capital.
9. Revenue and its sources. Include here the question of the relation of the processes of distribution and production.
10. Reflux movement of money in the process of capitalist production as a whole.
11. Vulgar Economics.
12. Conclusion. Capital and wage-labour.[16]

Heading 4, 'Ground rent (illustration of the difference between value and price of production)', clearly shows that Marx had in mind at the time the same idea expressed in his August letter with regard to introducing the theory of rent as an illustration to his previous thesis, and the position of ground rent within the plan above directly reflects that way of thinking. That is to say, ground rent is placed after the transformation of value into prices of production, with Marx planning to then deal with the law of the fall in the rate of profit and the division of profit into industrial profit.

However, the order is inverted for Book III of *Capital*, so that the theory of ground rent is placed just before the final and apparently concluding Part 7 ('The Revenues and Their Sources'). Clearly, this is a change from the earlier idea of inserting the theory of rent as a sort of 'illustration', and the theory of rent must be understood as thus having a more independent position. Although it is not known precisely when Marx decided to make this change, a trace of it can be seen already in his 13 February 1866 letter to Engels:

> As far as this 'damned' book is concerned, the position now is: it was *ready* at the end of December. The treatise on ground rent alone, the penultimate chapter, is in its present form almost long enough to be a book in itself. I have been going to the Museum in the day-time and writing at night. I had to plough through the new agricultural chemistry in Germany, in particular Liebig and Schönbein, which is more important for this matter

---

16   Marx 1991a, pp. 346–7.

than all the economists put together, as well as the enormous amount of material that the French have produced since I last dealt with this point. I concluded my theoretical investigation of ground rent two years ago. And a great deal had been achieved, especially in the period since then, fully confirming my theory incidentally. And the opening up of Japan (by and large I normally never read travel-books if I am not professionally obliged to) was also important here. So here was the 'shifting system', as it was applied by those curs of English manufacturers to one and the same persons in 1848–50, being applied by me to myself.

Although ready, the manuscript, which in its present form is gigantic, is not fit for publishing for anyone but myself, not even for you.[17]

Judging from the fact that the theory of ground rent is the 'penultimate chapter', it is clear that Marx had already by this point more or less arrived at the conception for *Capital* as it exists in the published version, and since he notes that he 'concluded' his 'theoretical investigation of ground rent two years ago', one can imagine that the change in his thinking dates back that far as well. Based on this, if we look back on the traces of changes in Marx's way of thinking with regard to ground rent, we can state the following.

Marx's initial intention had been to not include rent at all within 'capital in general' for the reason stated in the 'Introduction to the Critique of Political Economy':

> Ground rent cannot be understood without capital. But capital can certainly be understood without ground rent. Capital is the all-dominating economic power of bourgeois society. It must form the starting-point as well as the finishing-point, and must be dealt with before landed property. After both have been examined in particular, their interrelation must be examined.[18]

Another reason can be found in the letter dated 2 April 1858:

> First section: Capital in general. (Throughout this section ... landed property is assumed to be zero, i.e. landed property as a special economic relation is of no relevance as yet. Only by this procedure is it possible to discuss one relation without discussing all the rest.)[19]

---

17   Marx 1987b, p. 227.
18   Marx 1973b, p. 107.
19   Marx 1983, p. 298.

The second approach planned by Marx was to 'include' the theory of rent directly in the theory of production price as an illustration of the distinction between production price and value. The reason can be found in the following passages from two letters written by Marx in August 1862:

> All I have to prove theoretically is the possibility of absolute rent, without infringing the law of value. This is the point round which the theoretical controversy has revolved from the time of the physiocrats until the present day. Ricardo denies that possibility; I maintain it. I likewise maintain that his denial rests on a theoretically false dogma deriving from A. Smith – the supposed identity of cost prices[20] and values of commodities.[21]
>
> Ricardo confuses value and cost price. He therefore believes that, if there were such a thing as absolute rent (i.e. rent independent of variations in the fertility of the soil), agricultural produce, etc., would be constantly sold for more than its value, because at more than cost price (the advanced capital + the average profit). That would demolish the fundamental law. Hence he denies absolute rent and assumes only differential rent.
>
> But his identification of values of commodities and cost prices of commodities is totally wrong and has traditionally been taken over from A. Smith ...
>
> Differential rent as such – which does not arise from the circumstance that capital is employed on land instead of any other field of employment – presents no difficulty in theory. It is nothing other than surplus profit which also exists in every sphere of industrial production wherever capital operates under better than average conditions. It is firmly ensconced in agriculture only because founded on a basis as solid and (relatively) stable as the different degrees of natural fertility of various types of soil.[22]

---

20 This term does not correspond to 'cost price' as used in *Capital*, but rather to 'production price', since Marx's terminology changed subsequently. The term 'production price' appears in the published edition of *Theories of Surplus Value*, which is based on the manuscript written by Marx around the same time (1862–63) as this letter, but that is because the editor, Karl Kautsky, changed 'cost price' to 'production price' in line with the terminology used in *Capital*.
21 Marx 1985, p. 403.
22 Marx 1985, pp. 396–8.

The third planned approach, which Marx ultimately adopted, was to introduce the fundamental theory of rent within *Capital* as one elemental part. The basis for the new conception can be found in the following explanation in Book III of *Capital*:

> Our own reason for considering the modern form of landed property is simply that we need to consider all the specific relationships of production and exchange that arise from the investment of capital on the land. Without this, our analysis of capital would not be complete. We therefore confine ourselves exclusively to the investment of capital in agriculture proper, i.e. in the production of the main plant crops on which a population lives.[23]

These changes in Marx's conception are reflected in the ideas he had for the title of the Book III of *Capital*. In a letter to Lasalle, dated 11 March 1858, Marx describes the book as 'the unity of the [process of production of capital and the process of its circulation] or capital and profit; interest';[24] and in the February 1862 plan quoted earlier, the content corresponding to Book III is titled 'Capital and Profit'. In contrast, in his 13 October 1866 letter to Kugelmann, Marx describes the content more generally as 'Structure of the Process as a Whole',[25] and the published edition of Book III is subtitled 'The Process of Capitalist Production as a Whole'. Moreover, in Book I of *Capital*, Marx notes that the third volume will deal with the 'various mutually independent forms, such as profit, interest, gains made through trade, ground rent, etc.'[26] into which surplus value is split up; i.e. the 'conversion of surplus value into its different forms and separate component parts'.[27]

Each of the three conceptions held by Marx, as outlined above, has its justification, so it does not seem possible to insist that one in particular is absolutely correct. Professor Uno writes, 'How could the theoretical system of *Capital* constitute itself without incorporating the determinations of wages and rent therein?'[28] – which is a matter that of course concerns the appropriate scope of *Capital*. He also writes:

---

23   Marx 1981a, p. 752.
24   Marx 1983, p. 287.
25   Marx 1987b, p. 328.
26   Marx 1976, p. 709.
27   Marx 1988a, p. 21.
28   Uno 1953, p. 197.

As wage labour, of course, constitutes a fundamental determination of the capitalist mode of production, the theoretical elucidation of landed property through the development of the 'thesis' on capital must itself constitute the unfolding and clarification of the capitalistic form of landed property ... Landed property in and of itself cannot develop a capitalistic form. Moreover, capitalism in the process of establishing the modern system of private property establishes the capitalistic form of landed property. This is precisely a process of theoretical development whereby the more capitalistically fundamental relation of distributing surplus value as profit develops into the specific relations vis-à-vis land as a means of production and its form of private property itself.[29]

However, if that is the case, and one views the scope of *Capital* extending up to the 'more capitalistically fundamental relation of distributing surplus value as profit', one could not necessarily say it would be improper in a 'theory of landed property', as a continuation of *Capital* thus defined, to deal with the 'process' whereby this 'develops into the specific relations vis-à-vis land as a means of production and its form of private property itself'.

But that, of course, is not Uno's conclusion. Instead, based on the argument in the passage cited above, he attempts to demonstrate that the general theory of landed property is indispensable to *Capital*, just as in the case of the general theory of wage labour. And, by inferring that the same is true of crisis as in the case of those other two theories, Uno seeks to refute my view and also demonstrate a defect in *Capital* for not developing a theory of crisis. Indeed, after his discussion of wage labour and landed property, partially quoted above, he goes on to argue:

How could the theoretical system of *Capital* constitute itself without incorporating the determinations of wages and rent therein, regardless of what Marx may have originally intended with regard to 'wage labour and 'landed property' within his plan presented in the 'Introduction to the Critique of Political Economy' and elsewhere? If this is the case with regard to wages and rent, how can it be argued with regard to crisis, as Professor Kuruma does, that [the explanations in *Capital*] are 'no more than points of reference for problems pertaining to the logical unfolding of Marx's descriptions of "capital in general" (i.e. "the internal organisation of the capitalist mode of production, its ideal average")'? Of course, in that pas-

---

29   Uno 1953, p. 196.

sage Kuruma is saying that this is the actual case with regard to *Capital*, but he only seeks to justify this according to the plan Marx presents in the 'Introduction to the Critique of Political Economy', without positively clarifying why the necessity of crisis is not demonstrated in a principle theory like *Capital*. Kuruma states that 'Marx's theory of crisis, along with the system of his critique of political economy, was left in an incomplete state'. However, just as in the case of wage labour and capitalistic landed property, Kuruma provides no reason why the fundamental determinations of crisis are not dealt with in a principle theory like *Capital*. Without a fundamental theory of crisis, it is not possible for crisis to be deemed a phenomenon particular to capitalism. Thus, the problem should be posed rather in terms of why a clear and unambiguous theory of crisis was not developed in *Capital*.[30]

As already mentioned, the relation of the theory of wage labour and the relation of the theory of ground rent to *Capital* as a theoretical system of 'capital in general' should not be treated as identical. I must also object to treating those two theories and the theory of crisis in the same way. One certainly should not reason in a mechanical fashion when considering whether the general theory for wages, rent, or crisis should be developed in *Capital* by saying that since such and such is the case for one theory, the same must be true for another theory. Rather, each must be determined on its own. Without a certain degree of understanding of wage labour, it is impossible to know the basics of capitalist production, which is why the theory of wages is included within *Capital* and is developed near the beginning of that work. The theory of rent is different since various other fundamental relations of capitalist production can be understood without it serving as a premise. Therefore, the question of whether to include the theory of rent within *Capital* depends on the conception of the scope of *Capital*. But the essence of crisis is completely different from those other two theories. Instead of being a particular element that forms the 'internal organisation of the capitalistic production method in its ideal average', it is a situation in which the 'antagonism of all elements in the bourgeois process of production explodes'[31] – or at least that was the view of Marx. Insofar as that is the case, crisis is not something that can be elucidated at some midway point within a theoretical system that traces the development of the contradictions of capitalist production, but rather would naturally appear at the end of

---

30 Uno 1953, pp. 197–8.
31 Marx 1987a, p. 412.

the development of all those contradictions as a comprehensive elucidation. Of course, in the development of the system of a critique of political economy, 'all the contradictions of bourgeois production [that] erupt collectively' in the 'crises of the world market'[32] would be 'strikingly revealed'[33] sequentially, and the significance of each contradiction as an element of crisis would have to be clarified, which Marx does in fact do *Capital*. However, the elucidation of each does not form a 'theory of crisis'. It was in this sense that I wrote:

> In *Capital* as well, it is true that we can find various explanations of crisis, but they are no more than points of reference for problems pertaining to the logical unfolding of Marx's descriptions of 'capital in general' (i.e. 'the internal organisation of the capitalist mode of production, its ideal average').

Uno finds it outrageous for me to view this as a natural state of affairs by adding that 'none of this can be seen as constituting a proper theory of crisis'. Even if *Capital* does not extend beyond being a 'principle theory', he argues, it still forms a completed system within that scope, so it is natural to develop the 'demonstration of the necessity' of crisis, even if the system does not include the 'realistic determinations' of crisis; and depending on the approach, it could indeed be developed fully therein. Thus, the lack of such development in the published edition of *Capital* is a clear flaw.

If it were indeed possible within the realm of *Capital* to unfold fully the 'demonstration of the necessity of crisis' (or what Uno also calls 'a clear and unambiguous theory of crisis'), then I would certainly not waver in recognising a flaw in *Capital* for not developing such a theory. But my view is that it is not possible to develop such a theory of crisis at the abstract stage of *Capital* as a theory of 'capital in general', so that the lack of development is natural. Fortunately, Professor Uno did not merely insist that such a theory should and could be developed but actually suggests how it might be done, so here I can consider his views on this matter.

First, Uno locates the 'fundamental determination of crisis' within the 'surplus of capital explained'[34] in Chapter 15 of Book III of *Capital*. The explanation he is referring to seems to be the part in which Marx explains a case where 'no further additional capital could be employed for the purpose of capitalist production', which is when 'capital has grown in such proportion to the working

---

32   Marx 1989b, p. 163.
33   Marx 1989b, p. 131.
34   Uno 1953, p. 198.

population' that a rise in wages occurs that results in a situation where 'the expanded capital produces only the same mass of surplus value as before'.[35] But Uno argues that this alone is not enough to clarify the necessity of crisis. Rather, he argues that 'in order for this to explode as a crisis, it is necessary to plunge into a situation where "it is not possible to pay the interest or rent, etc. on the basis of a certain rate of profit"'.[36] Uno claims that Marx in the end was unable to demonstrate the necessity of crisis because he could not 'explain the clash between the fall in the profit rate of industrial capital and the rise in the interest rate as the moment of the outbreak of crisis',[37] and then he goes on to offer various explanations why Marx was unable to provide such an explanation.

I found the last part of Uno's argument exceedingly hard to understand, with many points that I could not decipher, so I cannot deal with each one. Still, I will attempt to respond to the gist of his argument below

What Uno calls the 'fundamental determination of crisis' – setting aside whether it merits description as such – is certainly an important moment of crisis. But, as he himself recognises, Marx already indicated this determination. Uno criticises Marx for not going further to develop a theory of crisis on that basis, which seems to me an impossible request.

First of all, Marx touches on this matter in Part 3 of Book III of *Capital*, where the aim is not to elucidate a theory of crisis but to clarify the 'law of the tendential fall in the rate of profit' (as the title of this part indicates). Uno's expectation for the development of a theory of crisis in that part was unfulfilled because the expectation itself is mistaken. In Part 3, Marx brings up the points mentioned because, in dealing with the law of the tendential fall in the rate of profit, the following series of phenomena unfold:

Accumulation ⇄ Fall in the rate of profit → Competitive battle → Temporary rise in wages → New sudden fall in profit rate → Crisis.

In dealing there with the 'development of the law's internal contradictions', Marx had to discuss these phenomena as important factors, and thus they were discussed to the extent necessary for that aim. I would have thought that would be obvious.

---

35   Marx 1981a, p. 360.
36   Uno 1953, p. 199. [The passage cited from Uno's book includes a citation of his own book, *Investigations of Capital* (Uno 1973, p. 139).]
37   Uno 1953, p. 205.

But there is more to it than that. The second point is that if one were to posit the fall in the rate of profit from the temporary rise in wages as the 'fundamental determination of crisis', and seek to unfold a theory of crisis on this basis, it would clearly go beyond the limits of *Capital*, even if developed in the final part of that work. This is because all of the problems regarding the divergence of market prices from value or production price are outside the scope of this work. And the same is of course true of wages. In Part 3 of Book III, there is a section on the 'reduction of wages below their value' in the chapter discussing the 'counteracting factors'. In that section, Marx clearly writes:

> We simply make an empirical reference to this point [reduction of wages below their value] here, as, like many other things that might be brought in, it has nothing to do with the general analysis of capital, but has its place in an account of competition, which is not dealt with in this work. It is none the less one of the most important factors in stemming the tendency for the rate of profit to fall.[38]

In other words, Marx mentions that reduction because it is one of the most important factors, but since it belongs outside the realm of *Capital* it is not dwelled upon. If this is the case regarding the reduction of wages below the value of labour power, the same would of course be true for a case where wages rise above their value. Although I do not know what the boundaries might be for what Uno calls a 'principle theory of political economy', the sort of crisis theory he has in mind does at least seem to be outside the scope of *Capital*.

---

38 Marx 1981a, p. 342.

CHAPTER 4

An Overview of Marx's Theory of Crisis

Because it was necessary to write this article quickly, I merely selected some passages directly relevant to crisis from my excerpts from Marx's writings, mainly from the perspective of methodology, and then put them into a bit of order and added some simple commentary. If this can be of some use to researchers I would be quite pleased.[1]

1   Marx's General Grasp of Crisis

Marx's general grasp of crisis, as in the case of other problems he examines, is the outcome of certain investigations he carried out and at same time useful as a guiding principle for future research. His general understanding of crisis is directly expressed in the following propositions:

> The commercial crises of the nineteenth century, and in particular the great crises of 1825 and 1836 [were] big storms on the world market, in which the antagonism of all elements in the bourgeois process of production explodes.[2]

> The world trade crises must be regarded as the real concentration and forcible adjustment of all the contradictions of bourgeois economy.[3]

> In world market crises, all the contradictions of bourgeois production erupt collectively; in particular crises (particular in their content and in extent) the eruptions are only sporadically, isolated and one-sided.[4]

---

1   [Originally published as Kuruma 1936 under the title 'From My Excerpt Notebooks' and republished as Chapter 3 of *An Investigation of Marx's Theory of Crisis* (Kuruma 1949).]
2   Marx 1987a, p. 412.
3   Marx 1989b, p. 140.
4   Marx 1989b, p. 163.

2   Marx's Theory of Crisis and *Capital*

Marx's grasp of crisis expressed in the passages above naturally determines his entire plan for the clarification of crisis. Because crisis is the concentrated explosion of all of the contradictions of capitalist production, in order to concretely grasp crisis as such, one must first unfold all of the contradictions of capitalist production according to their internal relations, thereby clarifying the significance of each contradiction as a moment within a totality, and then elucidate what processes the contradictions pass through and in what sense they must explode in a concentrated manner. This is precisely what Marx sought to achieve throughout his critique of political economy, of which *Capital* is the most fundamental part. In other words, *Capital* can be said to include, as its most fundamental part, a theory of crisis.

3   Key Perspective When Contemplating *Capital* as a Theory of Crisis Is to Consider the Developmental Process of Contradictions as a Process Whereby Moments Become Independent

The contemplation of *Capital* as a theory of crisis naturally requires us to adopt a certain key perspective, however. That is to say, all of the contradictions of capitalist production must be considered from the primary perspective of the relation to their ultimate explosion. The main issue thus becomes how moments that are essentially joined together become independent.

> Crisis is the forcible establishment of unity between elements ['moments'] that have become independent and the enforced separation from one another of elements which are essentially one.[5]

In other words:

> These two processes lack internal independence because they complement each other. Hence, if the assertion of their external independence [*äusserliche Verselbständigung*] proceeds to a certain critical point, unity violently makes itself felt by producing – a crisis.[6]

---

5   Marx 1989b, p. 144.
6   Marx 1976, p. 209.

4 Development of the Independence of Moments and the Necessity of Their Real Unity in a Forced and Sudden Form: The Significance of the Explosion, Real Concentration, and Forcible Adjustment of Contradictions

This reestablishment of equilibrium realised in a crisis is premised on the forceful progression, to a certain extent, of the external independence of moments that are essentially not independent. (The fact that essentially non-independent moments are made externally independent itself means that this occurs through force.) Therefore, crisis necessarily manifests itself in a forceful as well as a periodic and sudden form. In other words, once the independent development of moments has reached a certain limit, the inherent unity of the moments that was suppressed and kept in a latent state is abruptly revealed with tremendous force, like the sudden release of pent-up energy. In this explosive form, which is sudden and forcible, the contradictions that had developed to become more concrete and real as the moments of those contradictions became independent, are again united so as to bring about a new equilibrium. This is precisely why Marx viewed crisis as the 'explosion' of all the contradictions of capitalist production and their 'real concentration' and 'forcible adjustment'.

5 Moments Becoming Independent and the Elasticity of the Production Process

The fact that crisis is periodic and sudden is due to the aforementioned fact that moments are, to some extent, forcefully rendered independent. The basis for the possibility of such forcefulness is the elasticity of the reproduction process. But we should not overlook that, at the same time, the elasticity of the reproduction process is expanded through the moments becoming independent.

> The separation of sale and purchase makes possible not only commerce proper, but also numerous *pro forma* transactions, before the final exchange of commodities between producer and consumer takes place. It thus enables large numbers of parasites to invade the process of production and to take advantage of this separation. But this again means only that money, the universal form of labour in bourgeois society, makes the development of the inherent contradictions possible.[7]

---

[7] Marx 1987a, p. 334.

Now, leaving aside completely the turnovers within the world of commerce, where one merchant after the other sells the same commodity, a kind of circulation which may present a very flourishing appearance in periods of speculation, commercial capital first of all abbreviates the phase C–M for productive capital. Secondly, given the modern credit system, it has a large part of the society's total money capital at its disposal, so that it can repeat its purchases before it has definitively sold what it has already bought; and in this connection it is immaterial whether our merchant has sold directly to the final consumer or whether there are twelve other merchants between the two. Given the tremendous elasticity of the reproduction process, which can always be driven beyond any given barrier, he finds no barrier in production itself, or only a very elastic one. Besides the separation of C–M and M–C, which follows from the nature of the commodity, an active demand is now therefore created. Despite the autonomy it has acquired, the movement of commercial capital is never anything more than the movement of industrial capital within the circulation sphere. But by virtue of this autonomy, its movement is within certain limits independent of the reproduction process and its barriers, and hence it also drives this process beyond its own barriers. This inner dependence in combination with external autonomy drives commercial capital to a point where the inner connection is forcibly re-established by way of a crisis.[8]

If the credit system appears as the principal lever of overproduction and excessive speculation in commerce, this is simply because the reproduction process, which is elastic by nature, is now forced to its most extreme limit; and this is because a great part of the social capital is applied by those who are not its owners, and who therefore proceed quite unlike owners who, when they function themselves, anxiously weigh the limits of their private capital. This only goes to show how the valorisation of capital founded on the antithetical character of capitalist production permits actual free development only up to a certain point, which, is constantly broken through by the credit system. The credit system hence accelerates the material development of the productive forces and the creation of the world market, which it is the historical task of the capitalist mode of production to bring to a certain level of development, as material foundations for the new form of production. At the same time, credit accelerates

---

8 Marx 1981a, p. 419.

the violent outbreaks of this contradiction, crises, and with these the elements of dissolution of the old mode of production.[9]

6 Some Examples from *Capital* (and *Theories of Surplus Value*) of the Emphasis on Moments Becoming Independent

– *The social character of the labour of commodity producers (and social relations between commodity producers) becomes independent as the value character of things (and the value relations between things)*

There seems no real need here to enter a detailed discussion of commodity fetishism, which Marx was the first to clarify. This fetishism steadily develops as commodity value itself becomes independent in the forms of money and capital. Concurrent to this is a development whereby the control of products by human beings is replaced by the control of human beings by products.

– *Value becomes independent within money (division of the commodity into commodities and money)*

The contradiction of the commodity, which must be both a use value and a value, actually unfolds in the exchange process, necessarily bringing forth the division of the commodity into ordinary commodities and money. This means that the value of a commodity comes to have an independent form of existence as money. At the same time, the commodity's internal opposition between use value and value comes to be manifested externally in an oppositional relation between two independent things: commodities and money. This first appears in the form of the oppositions within commodity circulation. (Value becoming independent in the case of money itself has several additional stages. This develops along with the development of the determinations of money, gradually advancing from something formal into something substantial. But we will not enter into the details of this here.)

– *Along with value becoming independent in money, the exchange process splits into the two processes of sale and purchase: General possibility of crisis (general form)*

---

9 Marx 1981a, p. 572.

Along with the commodity splitting into commodity and money, and the value of a commodity becoming independent in the form of money, the direct exchange of products divides into the processes of sale and purchase, which are internally mutually dependent and externally mutually independent. This at the same time posits the most general and the most abstract possibility of crisis.

> Circulation bursts through all the temporal, spatial and personal barriers imposed by the direct exchange of products, and it does this by splitting up the direct identity present in this case between the exchange of one's own product and the acquisition of someone else's into the two antithetical segments of sale and purchase. To say that these mutually independent and antithetical processes form an internal unity is to say also that their internal unity moves forward through external antitheses. These two processes lack internal independence because they complement each other. Hence, if the assertion of their external independence [*äusserliche Verselbständigung*] proceeds to a certain critical point, their unity violently makes itself felt by producing – a crisis. There is an antithesis, immanent in the commodity, between use value and value, between private labour which must simultaneously manifest itself as directly social labour, and a particular concrete kind of labour which simultaneously counts as merely abstract universal labour, between the conversion of things into persons and the conversion of persons into things; the antithetical phases of the metamorphosis of the commodity are the developed forms of motion of this immanent contradiction. These forms therefore imply the possibility of crises, though no more than the possibility. For the development of this possibility into a reality a whole series of conditions is required, which do not yet even exist from the standpoint of the simple circulation of commodities.[10]

The general, abstract possibility of crisis denotes no more than the most abstract form of crisis, without content, without a compelling motivating factor. Sale and purchase may fall apart. They thus represent potential crisis and their coincidence always remains a critical factor for the commodity. The transition from one to the other may, however, proceed smoothly. The most abstract form of crisis (and therefore the formal possibility of crisis) is thus the metamorphosis of the commodity itself;

---

10   Marx 1976, p. 209.

the contradiction of exchange-value and use-value, and furthermore of money and commodity, comprised within the unity of the commodity, exists in metamorphosis only as an involved movement. The factors which turn this possibility of crisis into [an actual] crisis are not contained in this form itself; it only implies that the framework for a crisis exists.

And in a consideration of the bourgeois economy, that is the important thing. The world trade crises must be regarded as the real concentration and forcible adjustment of all the contradictions of bourgeois economy. The individual factors, which are condensed in these crises, must therefore emerge and must be described in each sphere of the bourgeois economy and the further we advance in our examination of the latter, the more aspects of this conflict must be traced on the one hand, and on the other hand it must be shown that its more abstract forms are recurring and are contained in the more concrete forms.

It can therefore be said that the crisis in its first form is the metamorphosis of the commodity itself, the falling asunder of purchase and sale.

The crisis in its second form is the function of money as a means of payment, in which money has two different functions and figures in two different phases, divided from each other in time.[11]

We will not enter into the details of this second form of crisis here.

– *Value becomes independent in the case of capital*

We have already noted that commodity value becomes increasingly independent with the development of the determinations of money, but with the transformation of money into capital the process of value becoming independent develops further at a rapid pace:

> The independent form, i.e. the monetary form, which the value of commodities assumes in simple circulation, does nothing but mediate the exchange of commodities, and it vanishes in the final result of the movement. On the other hand, in the circulation M–C–M both the money and the commodity function only as different modes of existence of value itself, the money as the general mode of existence, the commodity as its particular or, so to speak, disguised mode. It is constantly changing from

---

11   Marx 1989b, p. 140.

one form into the other, without becoming lost in the movement; it thus becomes transformed into an automatic subject. If we pin down the specific forms of appearance assumed in turn by self-valorising value in the course of its life, we reach the following elucidation: capital is money, capital is commodities. In truth, however, value is here the subject of a process in which, while constantly assuming the form in turn of money and commodities, it changes its own magnitude, throws off surplus value from itself considered as original value, and thus valorises itself independently. For the movement in the course of which it adds surplus value is its own movement, its valorisation is therefore self-valorisation [*Selbstverwertung*]. By virtue of being value, it has acquired the occult ability to add value to itself. It brings forth living offspring, or at least lays golden eggs ...

In simple circulation, the value of commodities attained at the most a form independent of their use values, i.e. the form of money. But now, in the circulation of M–C–M, value suddenly presents itself as a self-moving substance which passes through a process of its own, and for which commodities and money are both mere forms. But there is more to come: instead of simply representing the relations of commodities, it now enters into a private relationship with itself, as it were. It differentiates itself as original value from itself as surplus value, just as God the Father differentiates himself from himself as God the Son, although both are of the same age and form, in fact one single person; for only by the surplus value of £10 does the £100 originally advanced become capital, and as soon as this has happened, as soon as the son has been created and, through the son, the father, their difference vanishes again, and both become one, £110.

Value therefore now becomes value in process, money in process, and, as such, capital. It comes out of circulation, enters into it again, preserves and multiplies itself within circulation, emerges from it with an increased size, and starts the same cycle again and again. M–M, 'money which begets money', such is the description of capital given by its first interpreters, the mercantilists.[12]

Capital, as self-valorising value, does not just comprise class relations, a definite social character that depends on the existence of labour as wage labour. It is a movement, a circulatory process through different stages,

---

12   Marx 1976, pp. 255–6.

which itself in turn includes three different forms of the circulatory process. Hence it can only be grasped as a movement, and not as a static thing. Those who consider the autonomisation [*Verselbstständigung*] of value as a mere abstraction forget that the movement of industrial capital is this abstraction in action. Here value passes through different forms, different movements in which it is both preserved and increases, is valorised. Since we are firstly dealing here simply with the forms of movement, we have not considered the revolutions that the capital value may suffer in its circulatory process; it is clear however that despite all revolutions in value, capitalist production can exist and continue to exist only so long as the capital value is valorised, i.e. describes its circuit as value that has become independent, and therefore so long as the revolutions in value are somehow or other mastered and balanced out. The movements of capital appear as actions of the individual industrial capitalist in so far as he functions as buyer of commodities and labour, seller of commodities and productive capitalist, and thus mediates the circuit of his own activity. If the social capital value suffers a revolution in value, it can come about that his individual capital succumbs to this and is destroyed, because it cannot meet the conditions of this movement of value. The more acute and frequent these revolutions in value become, the more the movement of the independent value, acting with the force of an elemental natural process, prevails over the foresight and calculation of the individual capitalist, the more the course of normal production is subject to abnormal speculation, and the greater becomes the danger to the existence of the individual capitals. These periodic revolutions in value thus confirm what they ostensibly refute: the independence which value acquires as capital, and which is maintained and intensified through its movement.

This sequence of metamorphoses of capital in process implies the continuous comparison of the change in value brought about in the circuit with the original value of the capital. The independence of value in relation to the value-forming power, labour power, is introduced by the act M–L (purchase of labour power), and is realised during the production process as exploitation of labour power. But this independence does not reappear in the circuit in which money, commodity and elements of production are only alternating forms of the capital value in process, and in which the past magnitude of the value is compared with the present, changed value of the capital.

'Value', says Bailey, opposing the autonomisation of value which characterises the capitalist mode of production, and which he treats as the illusion of certain economists, 'value is a relation between contemporary commodities, because such only admit of being exchanged with each other.'

He says this in opposition to the comparison of commodity values at different points in time, a comparison which, if the value of money at each period is taken as fixed, is simply a comparison between the expenditure of labour required in different epochs for the production of the same kind of commodities. This derives from his general misunderstanding, according to which exchange value equals value, the form of value is value itself; thus commodity values cease to be comparable once they no longer actively function as exchange values, and cannot actually be exchanged for one another. He does not in the least suspect, therefore, that value functions as capital value or capital only in so far as it remains identical with itself and is compared with itself in the different phases of its circuit, which are in no way 'contemporary', but rather occur in succession.[13]

– *The reification and independent development of the relations of production accompanying the development of capital*

We have already shown in connection with the most simple categories of the capitalist mode of production and commodity production in general, in connection with commodities and money, the mystifying character that transforms the social relations for which the material elements of wealth serve as bearers in the course of production into properties of these things themselves (commodities), still more explicitly transforming the relation of production itself into a thing (money). All forms of society are subject to this distortion, in so far as they involve commodity production and monetary circulation. In the capitalist mode of production, however, where capital is the dominant category and forms the specific relation of production, this bewitched and distorted world develops much further. If we view capital first in the immediate process of production, as a pumper-out of surplus labour, this relationship is still very simple; the real connection impresses itself on the bearers of this process, the capitalists, themselves, and is still in their consciousness. The fierce struggle over the limits of the working day shows this in a striking way. But even within this immediate sphere, the sphere of the

---

13   Marx 1978, pp. 185–6.

immediate process between labour and capital, the matter does not rest at this simple stage. With the development of relative surplus value in the specifically capitalist mode of production, involving the growth of the productive forces of social labour, these productive forces and the social context of labour appear in the immediate labour process as shifted from labour to capital. Capital thereby already becomes a very mystical being, since all the productive forces of social labour appear attributable to it, and not to labour as such, as a power springing forth from its own womb. Then the circulation process intervenes, with all sections of capital, even agricultural, participating in it to the same degree. In this sphere, the conditions of the original production of value fall completely into the background. Even in the immediate production process, the capitalist is active also as commodity producer, as manager of commodity production. This production process thus presents itself to him in no way just as the simple production process of surplus value. Whatever the surplus value capital has pumped out in the immediate production process and expressed in commodities, the value and surplus value contained in these commodities must first be realised in the circulation process. Both the restoration of the values advanced in production, and particularly the surplus value contained in the commodities, seem not just to be realised, only in circulation but actually to arise from it. This appearance is reinforced by two circumstances in particular: firstly, profit on alienation, which depends on cheating, cunning, expertise, talent and a thousand and one market conjunctures; then the fact that a second determining element intervenes here besides labour time, i.e. the circulation time. Even though this functions simply as a negative limit on the formation of value and surplus value, it gives the appearance of being just as positive a ground as labour itself and of involving a determination independent of labour that arises from the nature of capital. In Volume 2, of course, we had to present this sphere of circulation only in relation to the determinations of form it produces, to demonstrate the further development of the form of capital that takes place in it. In actual fact, however, this sphere is the sphere of competition, which is subject to accident in each individual case; i.e. where the inner law that prevails through the accidents and governs them is visible only when these accidents are combined in large numbers, so that it remains invisible and incomprehensible to the individual agents of production themselves. Further, however, the actual production process, as the unity of the immediate production process and the process of circulation, produces new configurations in which the threads of the inner connection get more and more lost, the relations of production becoming independent of one another and the components of value ossifying into independent forms.

The transformation of surplus value into profit is, as we saw, just as much determined by the circulation process as by the process of production. Surplus value in the form of profit is no longer related to the portion of capital laid out on labour, which is where it derives from, but rather to the total capital. The profit rate is governed by its own laws, which permit it to vary while the rate of surplus value remains the same, and even require this variation. All this conceals the true nature of surplus value more and more, concealing therefore the real mechanism of capital. This happens still more with the transformation of profit into average profit and of values into prices. of production, the governing averages of market price. A complex social process intervenes here, the equalisation of capitals, which cuts the relative average prices of commodities loose from their values, and the average profits in the various spheres of production from the actual exploitation of labour by the particular capitals involved (quite apart from the individual capital investments in each particular sphere of production). The average prices of commodities not only seem to differ from their value, i.e. from the labour realised in them, but actually do differ, and the average profit of a particular capital differs from the surplus value this capital has extracted from the workers employed by it. The value of commodities appears directly only in the influence of the changing productivity of labour on the rise and fall of prices of production; on their movement, not on their final limits. Profit now appears as determined only secondarily by the direct exploitation of labour, in so far as, given market prices that are seemingly independent of this exploitation, it permits the capitalist to realise a profit departing from the average. Normal average profit as such seems immanent in capital independently of exploitation; abnormal exploitation or even average exploitation under exceptionally favourable conditions seems only to determine divergences from average profit, and not this average profit itself. The division of profit into profit of enterprise and interest (not to speak of the intervention of commercial profit and money-dealing profit, which are founded in the circulation sphere and seem to derive entirely from this, and not from the production process itself at all) completes the autonomisation of the form of surplus value, the ossification of its form as against its substance, its essence. One portion of profit, in contrast to the other, separates itself completely from the capital relation as such and presents itself as deriving not from the function of exploiting wage labour but rather from the wage labour of the capitalist himself. As against this, interest then seems independent both of the wage labour of the worker and of the capitalist's own labour; it seems to derive from capital as its own independent source. If capital originally appeared on the surface of circulation as the capital fetish, value-creating value, so it now presents itself once again in the figure of interest-bearing capital as its most estranged and peculiar form. This is why the form 'capital-interest', as a third in the series to 'earth-rent' and 'labour-wages', is much more consistent than 'capital-profit', since profit still retains a memory of its origin which in interest is not simply obliterated but actually placed in a form diametrically opposed to this origin.

Finally, besides capital as an independent source of surplus value, there appears landed property, as a limit to the average profit which transfers a portion of the surplus value to a class that neither works itself nor directly exploits workers, and cannot even like interest-bearing capital, launch forth in edifying homilies about the risk and sacrifice in lending capital. Since in this case one part of the surplus value seems directly bound up not with social relations but rather with a natural element, the earth, the form, of mutual alienation and ossification of the various portions of surplus value is complete, the inner connection definitively torn asunder and its source completely buried, precisely through the assertion of their autonomy vis-à-vis each other by the various relations of production which are bound up with the different material elements of the production process.

Capital-profit (or better still capital-interest), land-ground-rent, labour-wages, this economic trinity as the connection between the components of value and wealth in general and its sources, completes the mystification of the capitalist mode of production, the reification of social relations, and the immediate coalescence of the material relations of production with their historical and social specificity: the bewitched, distorted and upside-down world haunted by Monsieur le Capital and Madame la Terre, who are at the same time social characters and mere things ...

In presenting the reification of the relations of production and the autonomy they acquire vis-à-vis the agents of production, we shall not go into the form and manner in which these connections appear to them as overwhelming natural laws, governing them irrespective of their will, in the form that the world market and its conjunctures, the movement of market prices, the cycles of industry and trade and the alternation of prosperity and crisis prevails on them as blind necessity. This is because the actual movement of competition lies outside our plan, and we are only out to present the internal organisation of the capitalist mode of production, its ideal average, as it were.[14]

– *Distribution relations and production relations*

Assuming that the production process repeats itself continuously under the same conditions, in other words, that reproduction takes place under the same conditions as production, which presupposes that productivity of labour remains unchanged, or at least that variations in productivity do not alter the relationships of the different factors of production; thus, even if the value of commodities were to rise or fall as a result of changes in productivity, the distribution of the value of commodities amongst the different factors of production would remain the same. In that case, although it would not be theoretically accurate to say that the different parts of value determine the value or price of the whole [output], it would be useful and correct to say that they constitute it insofar as one understands by constituting the formation of the whole by adding up the parts. The value would be divided at a steady and constant rate into [pre-existing] value and surplus value, and the [newly created] value would be resolved at a constant rate into wages and profit, the profit again being broken down at a constant rate into interest, industrial profit and rent. It can therefore be said that P – the price of the commodity – is divided into wages, profit (interest) and rent, and, on the other hand, wages, profit (interest) and rent are the constituents of the value or rather of the price.

This uniformity or similarity of reproduction – the repetition of production under the same conditions – does not exist. Productivity itself changes and changes the conditions [of production]. The conditions, on their part, change productivity. But the divergences are reflected partly in superficial oscillations which even themselves out in a short time, partly in a gradual accumulation of divergences which either lead to a crisis, [to a] violent, seeming restoration of the old relationships, or very gradually assert themselves and are recognised as a change in the conditions.

Interest and rent, which anticipate surplus value, presuppose that the general character of reproduction will remain the same. And this is the case as long as the capitalist mode of production continues. Secondly, it is

---

14   Marx 1981a, pp. 965–70.

presupposed moreover that the specific relations of this mode of production remain the same during a certain period, and this is in fact also *plus ou moins* case. Thus the result of production crystallises into a permanent and therefore prerequisite condition of production, that is, it becomes a permanent attribute of the material conditions of production. It is crises that put an end to this apparent independence of the various elements of which the production process continually consists and which it continually reproduces.[15]

At the same time, this reveals the significance of the distinction between the forms of production and of distribution. Profit, a form of distribution, is here simultaneously a form of production, a condition of production, a necessary ingrediency of the process of production. How absurd it is, therefore, for John Stuart Mill and others to conceive bourgeois forms of production as absolute, but the bourgeois forms of distribution as historically relative, hence transitory. I shall return to this later. The form of production is simply the form of distribution seen *sub alia specie*.[16] The *differentia specifica* – and therefore also the specific limitation – which set bounds to bourgeois distribution, enter into bourgeois production itself, as a determining factor, which overlaps and dominates production. The fact that bourgeois production is compelled by its own immanent laws, on the one hand, to develop the productive forces as if production did not take place on a narrow restricted social foundation, while, on the other hand, it can develop these forces only within these narrow limits, is the deepest and most hidden cause of crises, of the crying contradictions within which bourgeois production is carried on and which, even at a cursory glance, reveal it as only a transitional, historical form.[17]

---

15   Marx 1989b, pp. 517–8.
16   'From a different aspect'.
17   Marx 1989b, p. 274.

PART 2

Marx-Lexikon zur politischen Ökonomie

CHAPTER 5

Marx-Lexikon Crisis I

1   Part 1: Contents[1]

I.   Essential definition of crisis
   {1} *Communist Manifesto*
        'We see then: the means of production ... the fluctuations of the market'.
        (MECW–6, pp. 489–90)
   {2} *A Contribution to the Critique of Political Economy*
        'The commercial crises of the nineteenth ... bank-notes under these laws'.
        (MECW *Vol.* 29, p. 412)
   {3} *Capital Vol. 3*
        'These different influences may ... restore the disturbed equilibrium'
        (MECW–37, p. 248)
   {4} *Theories of Surplus Value*
        'In the crises of the world market ... excludes contradiction'.
        (MECW–32, p. 131)
   {5} *Theories of Surplus Value*
        'And in a consideration ... the contradictions of bourgeois economy'.
        (MECW–32, p. 140)
   {6} *Theories of Surplus Value*
        'Crisis is the forcible ... elements which are essentially one'.
        (MECW–32, p. 144)
   {7} *Theories of Surplus Value*
        'In world market crises ... sporadical, isolated, and one-sided'.
        (MECW–32, p. 163)

II. Method of crisis theory
   {8} *Theories of Surplus Value*
        'The general, abstract possibility ... conditions of capitalist production'.
        (MECW–32, pp. 140–45)

---

1 [The table of contents and passage sources in *Marx Engels Collected Works* (MECW) for the first volume on crisis of *Marx-Lexikon zur politischen Ökonomie*, Kuruma 1972a (ed.).]

III. **Money sublates the contradictions of direct barter exchange, but only by generalising the contradictions**
    {9} *Grundrisse*
        'In direct barter ... brought about *by force*.' /
        'We see, then, how ... dependent on exchange'.
        (MECW-28, p. 87 / pp. 88–9)
    {10} *Grundrisse*
        'We see that it is in the nature ... two mutually indifferent acts'.
        (MECW-28, p. 135)
    {11} *Grundrisse*
        'We have already seen that money ... underproduction as two periods'.
        (MECW-29, p. 12)
    {12} *A Contribution to the Critique of Political Economy*
        'The division of exchange ... inherent in the bourgeois mode of labour'.
        (MECW-29, p. 332)
    {13} *Capital Vol. 1*
        'We saw in a former chapter ... exist side by side'. /
        'Commodities, first of ... moves and takes place'.
        (MECW-35, p. 113 / p. 114)
    {14} *Capital Vol. 1*
        'Circulation bursts through all ... have as yet no existence'.
        (MECW-35, pp. 123–24)
    {15} *Theories of Surplus Value*
        'In the form of direct barter ... essentially complimentary phases'.
        (MECW-32, p. 139)

IV. **Possibility of crisis that appears under commodity circulation**
    {16} *Grundrisse*
        'The next question which confronts ... trade in the strict sense.)'
        (MECW-28, pp. 84–7)
    {17} *Grundrisse*
        'At first sight, circulation ... corresponding to its concept'.
        (MECW-28, pp. 132–33)
    {18} *A Contribution to the Critique of Political Economy*
        'The division of exchange ... of the bourgeois mode of labour'.
        (MECW-29, p. 332)
    {19} *A Contribution to the Critique of Political Economy*
        'When payments cancel ... mystery surrounding their own relations'.
        (MECW-29, p. 378)

{20} *Capital Vol. 1*
'Circulation bursts through all ... have as yet no existence'.
(MECW-35, pp. 123–24)

{21} *Capital Vol. 1*
'The function of money ... credit money such as bank-notes'.
(MECW-35, pp. 148–49)

{22} *Theories of Surplus Value*
'In the form of direct barter ... essentially complimentary phases'.
(MECW-32, p. 139)

{23} *Theories of Surplus Value*
'The possibility of crisis ... more concrete than the first'. /
'In any case ... their itself merely a *matter of chance'*.
(MECW-32, pp. 138–40 / pp. 142–43)

{24} Marx to Engels, 2 April 1858
'At this point I shall not go ... possibility of crises is expressed'.
(MECW-40, p. 302)

v. **Marx's criticism of theories denying the possibility of crisis (general overproduction)**

{25} *Grundrisse*
'The attempts made from the orthodox ... outside that process'.
(MECW-28, pp. 338–40)

{26} *Grundrisse*
'The nonsense about the impossibility ... therefore from exchange itself'.
(MECW-28 pp. 351–52)

{27} *A Contribution to the Critique of Political Economy*
'If, because the process of circulation ... make a purchase either'.
(MECW-29, pp. 332–33)

{28} *Capital Vol. 1*
'Nothing can be more childish ... have as yet no existence'.
(MECW-35, pp. 123–24)

{29} *Capital Vol. 2*
'The transformation of money-capital ... no overproduction is possible'.
(MECW-36, p. 81)

{30} *Capital Vol. 3*
'Furthermore, capital consists ... moves, and alone can move'.
(MECW-37, pp. 255–56)

{31} *Theories of Surplus Value*
'Most of the writers who ... the people are generally poor"'.
(MECW-31, pp. 178–81.)

{32} *Theories of Surplus Value*
'Here we need only consider ... for which there is no demand"'.
(MECW-32, pp. 124–25)

{33} *Theories of Surplus Value*
'A few more passages from Ricardo ... which are on the market'.
(MECW-32, pp. 130–37)

{34} *Theories of Surplus Value*
'Before embarking on an ... of this mode of production'. /
'Now let us return ... own consumption, seems assured'.
(MECW-32 pp. 147–150 / pp. 152–53.)

{35} *Theories of Surplus Value*
'The word *overproduction* itself ... separation of purchase and sale'.
(MECW-32, pp. 156–61)

{36} *Theories of Surplus Value*
'"A demand means the *will* ... individuals, is quite superfluous'.
(MECW-32, pp. 290–93)

{37} *Theories of Surplus Value*
'Say's earth-shaking discovery ... This is indeed the secret basis of *glut*'.
(MECW-32, pp. 307–09)

VI. **Further development under capital of the possibility of crisis, and the development of the possibility of crisis into reality (Overview)**

{38} *Capital Vol. 1*
'Circulation bursts through all ... have as yet no existence'.
(MECW-35, pp. 123–24)

{39} *Capital Vol. 2*
'So far as the balance is ... spontaneous nature of this production'.
(MECW-36, p. 494)

{40} *Theories of Surplus Value*
'Here we need only consider the forms ... reveals this still more clearly'.
(MECW-32, p. 124)

{41} *Theories of Surplus Value*
'Now before we proceed further ... another, the crisis is there'.
(MECW-32, p. 138)

{42} *Theories of Surplus Value*
'It can therefore be said that the crisis ... conditions of capitalist production'.
(MECW–32, pp. 140–45)
{43} *Theories of Surplus Value*
'The circulation of capital contains ... competitions of capitals and credit.)'
(MECW–32, p. 162)

VII. Further development of the possibility of crisis under the circulation process of capital (abstract form of crisis acquires content determination in the circulation process of capital)

1. In the circulation of capital, the 'C' in M – C is not the object of an individual want but is the elements of productive capital L + mp
   {44} *Capital Vol. 2*
   'M – C represents the conversion ... the other to the labour market'.
   (MECW–36, p. 32)

2. In the circulation of capital, C – M is at the same time C' – M', and the mass of commodities as the bearers of valorised capital must in their totality pass through the metamorphosis of C' – M'
   {45} *Capital Vol. 2*
   'The mass of commodities C' ... form of the universal equivalent'.
   (MECW–36, pp. 46–49)
   {46} *Capital Vol. 2*
   'There is a difference between C – M ... not an afterword'.
   (MECW–36, p. 131)

3. Possibility of interruptions in the reproduction of capital provoked by fluctuations in the value of the elements of production
   {47} *Capital Vol. 2*
   'In order that the circuit ... no overproduction is possible'.
   (MECW–36, pp. 79–81)
   {48} *Capital Vol. 2*
   'Capital as self-expanding ... through its movement'. /
   'In order to study the formula ... other two circuit forms'.
   (MECW–36, pp. 110–11 / pp. 112–14)

{49} *Theories of Surplus Value*
'Meanwhile we just ... principle of the circulation process of capital'.
(MECW-32, pp. 125–26)

{50} *Theories of Surplus Value*
'(A crisis can arise ... but with *values*.)' /
'First phase. The *reconversion* ... as occur in the first case'.
(MECW-32, p. 147 / pp. 145–46)

{51} *Theories of Surplus Value*
'The circulation of capital contains ... competition of capitals and credit'.
(MECW-32, pp. 162)

4. **The intertwinement and combination of capital and revenue**

{52} *Grundrisse*
'Actually, we are not at all concerned ... relation to one another'.
(MECW-28, pp. 346–49)

{53} *Capital Vol. 2*
'In the formula C' ... studies mainly on the first two forms'.
(MECW-36, p. 104)

{54} *Capital Vol. 2*
'The process of circulation of industrial ... all commodity circulation'.
(MECW-36, pp. 117–18)

{55} *Capital Vol. 2*
'The direct process of the production ... aggregate social capital'.
(MECW-36, pp. 349–52)

{56} *Capital Vol. 2*
'For our present purpose ... the wages by the labourers?'
(MECW-36, pp. 391–92)

{57} *Capital Vol. 2*
'We have also seen that in the exchange ... for running abnormally'.
(MECW-36, p. 495)

{58} *Theories of Surplus Value*
'Of the part of the revenue ... as simple commodity owners'.
(MECW-31 pp. 133–37)

{59} *Theories of Surplus Value*
'From the interconnection owners ... can develop into actuality'.
(MECW-32 pp. 141–42)

5. The supply for the capitalist as capitalist exceeds his demand; i.e. the maximum limit of his demand is c + v but his supply is c + v + m. Whence comes the money for the monetisation of the surplus value?

{60} *Capital Vol. 2*
'The capitalist throws less ... relation to his supply'. /
'We now come to ... productive organism'.
(MECW-36, pp. 122–23 / pp. 124–25)

{61} *Capital Vol. 2*
'An opponent of Tooke ... is consumed unproductively'.
(MECW-36 pp. 328–34)

{62} *Capital Vol. 2*
'Since accumulation takes place ... precious metals are mined'.
(MECW-36 pp. 342–44)

{63} *Capital Vol. 2*
'If a capitalist (we have only ... continue deriving it ever anew.'
(MECW-36, pp. 418–20)

{64} *Capital Vol. 2*
'It goes without saying that the more ... not cost him anything'.
(MECW-36 pp. 472–74)

6. Money hoard (and therefore sale without purchase and supply without demand) becomes necessary through the turnover of constant capital. Conditions for the formation of equilibrium in the reproduction process of the total social capital

{65} *Capital Vol. 2*
'The value-part of the productive ... been completely consumed'.
(MECW-36, pp. 170–71)

{66} *Capital Vol. 2*
'Portion c of the value ... discuss this point in particular'.
(MECW-36, p. 395)

{67} *Capital Vol. 2*
'In the analysis of the exchanges ... capital of department'. /
'The following is to be noted ... new to them'.
(MECW-36, pp. 448–64 / pp. 466–69)

{68} *Capital Vol. 2*
'Let us note by the way ... for one another be equal'.
(MECW-36, pp. 493–94)

{69} *Theories of Surplus Value*
'A part of the constant capital ... consumption in other spheres'.
(MECW-32, pp. 111–13)

7. **Money hoard (and therefore sale without purchase and supply without demand) becomes necessary for the accumulation of capital**

    {70} *Capital Vol. 2*
    'Since the proportions which ... individual industrial capitals'.
    (MECW-36, pp. 84–5)

    {71} *Capital Vol. 2*
    'Whether or not m, the surplus-value ... not yet been developed here'.
    (MECW-36, pp. 89–90)

    {72} *Capital Vol. 2*
    'Along with the real accumulation ... annual additional social production'.
    (MECW-36, p. 320)

    {73} *Capital Vol. 2*
    'We have now to investigate the case ... which does not return to him'.
    (MECW-36, pp. 345–48)

    {74} *Capital Vol. 2*
    'It has been shown in ... surplus-product, with B, B', etc.'. /
    'The successive transformation ... later, reflected form'.
    (MECW-36 pp. 488–93 / pp. 497–500)

8. **In the case of a long working period (such as the construction of a railway, etc.) there are purchases without sales and demand without supply**

    {75} *Capital Vol. 2*
    'If we conceive society as being not ... process of production itself'.
    (MECW-36, pp. 314–16)

    {76} *Capital Vol. 2*
    'Inasmuch as the period of turnover ... some equivalent to the circulation'.
    (MECW-36, pp. 355–57)

    {77} *Capital Vol. 2*
    'In all lines of industry ... shipbuilding, large-scale drainage of land, etc.'.
    (MECW-36, p. 476)

9. The inevitable change in the proportion between the two production departments arising from the shift from simple to expanded reproduction, and the difficulties that arise from it [and, *mutatis mutandis*, the same can be said for a general change – whether up or down – in the rate of accumulation]

   {78} *Capital Vol. 2*
   'The surplus-product, the bearer ... elements of productive capital'.
   (MECW-36, pp. 495–97)

   {79} *Capital Vol. 2*
   'We have hitherto assumed that A ... i.e., accumulation'.
   (MECW-36, pp. 501–03)

   {80} *Capital Vol. 2*
   'Let us now take a closer look ... scale cannot take place at all'.
   (MECW-36, pp. 503–05)

   {81} *Capital Vol. 2*
   'We shall now study ... reproduction on an extended scale'.
   (MECW-36, p. 506)

   {82} *Capital Vol. 2*
   'In the exchange of $I_{(v+s)}$ ... circumstances by capitalist class II'.
   (MECW-36, pp. 520–21)

2   Part 2: Discussion[2]

A little secret kept from Professor Kuruma ...

A:[3] It's scorching hot today, isn't it? How are you doing?

B:[4] Not too bad. I saw that *Crisis I* is coming out soon.

A: Yes, we should be able to publish it by early autumn. Are you planning to read this latest volume, too?

---

2   [Fictional dialogue written by Teinosuke Ōtani and published as an insert for the first volume on crisis of *Marx-Lexikon zur politischen Ökonomie*, Kuruma 1972b (ed.).]
3   One of the editors of *Marx-Lexikon zur politischen Ökonomie*.
4   A friend of 'A' who is interested in political economy.

B: Of course, especially since the topic is crisis. I'm aware that, apart from his book *Theory of the Value Form and Theory of the Exchange Process*,[5] Professor Kuruma is best known for *An Investigation of Crisis Theory*.[6] My expectations are even higher considering that he hasn't written a major work on crisis since publishing that book.

A: I'm glad to know of your interest.

B: In every *Marx-Lexikon* volume there an insert, isn't there, with a discussion led by Professor Kuruma?

A: Yes, we call that the 'Lexikon Discussion Room'.[7]

B: Well, I really enjoy those discussions. Reading them makes it much easier for a non-specialist like me to grasp the content of the volumes. Anyway, I make a point of paying attention to whatever discussion or seminar Professor Kuruma takes part in, but since the topic this time is crisis, I'm particularly looking forward to it.

A: Ah ... that's too bad.

B: What is that supposed to mean?

A: Oh, excuse me. What I meant to say is that Professor Kuruma won't be able to take part in the discussion this time. He seems to have worn himself out recently working on editing the second volume on crisis. Once the weather cools down, I'm sure he'll be fine, but I don't know if readers will want to wait that long, so we've been struggling to find some other content for the latest Lexikon Discussion Room insert.

B: That's a shame.

A: I'm sorry to disappoint you. We'll try to make amends by asking Professor Kuruma as many questions as possible in the discussion regarding the second volume on crisis.

---

5 [Kuruma 1957. Complete English translation included in Kuruma 2018.]
6 [Kuruma 1965.]
7 [*Rekishikon sōdan shitsu*.]

B: Well, I guess there's nothing that can be done about it. But I might hold off on buying the first volume and just pick it up with the second volume when it comes out.

B: Hey, hold on, that's not very nice.

B: The thing is, for a layman like me, there's a limit to how much I can grasp of the *Marx-Lexikon* volumes through just relying on the headings. It's thanks to the discussions among the editors that I've been able to follow the content of past volumes. There's not much point in buying a volume if I won't be able to read it.

A: I think you're being a bit stubborn. But if you have questions, why not ask me, I might be able to answer them.

B: Are you saying you can take over Professor Kuruma's role?

A: That's not exactly what I mean.

B: Well, it sounds like an interesting idea. I promise to buy the first *Marx-Lexikon* volume on crisis if you take the place of Professor Kuruma and explain the content. Although I'm not sure you're really up to the task.

A: (*What have I gotten myself into? I suppose it's okay, though, seeing how the sale of the book depends on it. But I'd better not to mention it to Kuruma-sensei.*) Alright, why not. I'll have a go at explaining the content.

B: Great. Let's get started right away. We can sit down and have a discussion over tea.

A: (*A cup of tea sounds nice but trying to explain without any materials at hand could be a nightmare. I need to have some books at hand for sure.*) How about stopping by my house in a little while, so we can have a look at the galleys for *Crisis I* during our talk.

B: Sounds like a plan. And if you could have a few well-chilled beverages ready, I wouldn't complain.

A: There's a good idea. (*That didn't work out so badly in the end, thankfully.*)

Within the phenomenon of the 'business cycle' is the 'industrial cycle' as its essence

B: How many volumes on crisis will be published for *Marx-Lexikon*?

A: Our current plan calls for three volumes. The first two will deal with the systematic development of crisis theory, and the final volume will centre on the industrial cycle as well as the history of crises and industrial cycles. But this plan may change.[8]

B: You just mentioned the 'industrial cycle'. Is that the same as the typical 'business fluctuations' or the 'business cycle'.

A: Well, first we need to distinguish between 'fluctuation' and 'cycle'. The common expression 'business *fluctuation*' or 'economic *fluctuation*' differs from the term 'business *cycle*'. In the case of a 'fluctuation', the emphasis is merely on a change – and it could be an arbitrary change or a necessary and systematic one. In contrast, in the case of a 'cycle' we are dealing with a regular expression of a 'fluctuation'. Then there is the separate question of whether 'industrial cycle' is the same as 'business cycle'? Professor Kuruma, in his book *An Investigation of Crisis Theory*, has the following to say:

> An industrial (or economic) 'cycle' for Marx is not merely the regular repetition of a particular phenomenon or a period of time that elapsed in the interim, but rather the movement *whereby modern industry, in its developmental process, necessarily passes through certain phases* ... Thus, in the case of 'cycle', the issue concerns where is the starting point and where is the ending point. This is something that can and should be objectively determined. In so doing, *the key perspective is that the process of the development of capitalist production is at the same time the process of driving beyond its internal barriers*.[9]

This is what Marx seems to mean when he uses the term 'industrial cycle'. There is a *beginning* at one point and an *end* at some other point, and the movement must pass through a sequence of phases along the way. And this cycle is always *beginning* anew. If the term 'business cycle' were exclusively used in the same

---

8 [Four volumes were in fact published.]
9 Kuruma 1965, p. 223. [In Chapter 14 of this book. Speaker's emphasis.]

sense as that 'industrial cycle', I suppose it would be alright, but in fact the two terms are a bit different.

B: The 'business cycle' calls to mind a cycle moving from one business peak to the next, or from a low point to the next low point.

A: One can start at any point and then trace the cycle from that point. And it repeats itself. This is something that anyone can notice by looking at the real process of business fluctuations.

B: Does the 'industrial cycle' also refer to this sort of noticeable pattern?

A: I suppose you could say that. But I think it could also be said that within the phenomenon of the 'business cycle' lies the 'industrial cycle' as its essence.

B: In that case, from what point does an industrial cycle start and at what point does it end?

A: That's an important question. But since it is a cycle, moving circularly, we could choose any arbitrary point. That same chapter in Professor Kuruma's book on crisis deals with this issue of the starting and ending point of the cycle. Marxian economists generally have thought that a cycle begins with crisis and ends with crisis, but Professor Kuruma argued that this is mistaken, as he explains in the following passage from that same chapter of his book:

> It is correct to say that the cycle ends in crisis, so that crisis is the final phase of a cycle ... But this certainly does *not* mean that crisis also constitutes the starting point, or first phase, of the next cycle? This should be clear from the passage from *Capital* quoted earlier and from various other passages from Marx's writing, such as the following, also from Book I of *Capital*: 'The life of industry becomes a series of periods of moderate activity, prosperity, overproduction, crisis and stagnation'.[10] Marx thought it correct to see the cycle (*Zyklus*) as beginning from the period of 'moderate activity'. This is because the process of the period of rising business activity that inevitably leads to crisis must at the same time be understood as a process of capital breaking through its immanent barrier.[11]

---

10   Marx 1976, p. 580.
11   Kuruma 1965, p. 224. [Speaker's emphasis.]

B: I see. So, the 'period of moderate activity' is the initial aspect, and crisis is the final aspect.

A: That's right.

Crisis must be clarified in general before considering the cyclical process

B: From what you said earlier, it seems that the industrial cycle will only be looked at after the second *Marx-Lexikon* volume on crisis.[12] Isn't that a bit odd? If a crisis occurs within the industrial cycle, as one of its aspects, and is also the cycle's final phase, shouldn't we approach crisis as one part of the theory of the industrial cycle?

A: It's true that in considering the overall structure of the *Marx-Lexikon* volumes on crisis, the biggest problem we faced was how to deal with the distinction and relation between the problems concerning the industrial cycle and those concerning crisis. Professor Kuruma gave the matter a lot of thought before finally arriving at the approach of first dealing with crisis and then dealing with the industrial cycle. This is related to the issue of how to grasp the essence of crisis and the industrial cycle, as indicated in the passages quoted from *An Investigation of Crisis Theory*.

Fundamentally, the *problem of crisis* concerns how the development of capitalist production is only feasible through a certain cycle that culminates in crisis, and in that sense, it already encompasses the *problem of the industrial cycle*. Marx explains this fact inherent to capitalist production from the perspective of the contradictory nature of capitalist production, which has an inherent barrier, but at the same time always seeks expansion by driving beyond it. Marx calls this the fundamental contradiction of capitalist production, and this contradictory character explains the fact of crisis and the industrial cycle. When capitalist production reaches a certain point after driving beyond its immanent barrier, the contradiction explodes as a crisis. At the same time, this explosion brings about a temporary resolution of the contradiction. In this way, the development of capitalist production traces out the pattern of a cycle.

Considered from this perspective, the task for the *theory of the industrial cycle*, where the industrial cycle becomes the primary issue, is to clarify the process whereby production drives beyond its immanent barrier in passing

---

12 [The industrial cycle was in fact examined in the fourth *Marx-Lexikon* volume on crisis – Kuruma 1976a (ed.).]

through the cycle's phases and the way in which contradictions build up until they eventually explode as a crisis. This investigation thus encompasses a concrete analysis of the various phases of the cycle. The effort to clarify the essence of crisis and the essence of the industrial cycle is made to grasp the concrete developmental process of capitalist production, and the theory of the industrial cycle has great significance for us in that sense.

However, before we can concretely analyse the industrial cycle that has this significance, we need to consider various problems, such as: What are the inherent barriers of capitalist production? What compels production to collide with those barriers? And what are the 'moments' that determine this collision? These are problems that can be pondered generally and abstractly without raising the question of the phases of the cycle that lead up to a crisis. And this is something we *must* do. What the investigation of crisis involves, ultimately, is the clarification of such issues. Thus, even though crisis is the final phase of the industrial cycle, a *general* clarification of crisis is necessary before the cyclical process can be analysed.

B: Does this mean that the theory of crisis is at the same time a theory of the industrial cycle or its most fundamental part?

A: I think that could be said. But I also think that the theory of crisis must include the theory of the industrial cycle or become concrete to the point of encompassing it. The key point is not so much what we label the theory but how the theory in its entirety can clarify crisis and the industrial cycle.

Crisis *I* and *Crisis II* are organised comprehensively and systematically, whereas *Crisis III* is organised by topic

B: Basically, then, 'crisis' is the main topic for the *Marx-Lexikon* volumes, and the 'industrial cycle' is included therein. Wasn't it possible to take the opposite approach?

A: This ultimately depends on what is the main focus, with regard to whether crisis is seen as one aspect of the industrial cycle or the cycle is viewed as a process leading up to crisis. According to the latter approach, the theory of the industrial cycle is also one part of the theory of crisis, or one concrete aspect of the consideration of crisis. I should note that even though the industrial cycle will be dealt with in *Crisis III*,[13] that does not constitute the fundamental 'theory of the industrial cycle' in the clear meaning I spoke of earlier.

---

13 [*Crisis IV*, not *Crisis III*, deals with the industrial cycle.]

B: Why is it not the fundamental theory?

A: Even if we tried to present Marx's fundamental theory it was not possible. The issue of the industrial cycle is outside the scope of *Capital*.

B: What do you mean by that?

A: Are you familiar with Marx's plan for his overall critique of political economy?

B: Yes, basically.

A: The last part of his planned critique of political economy, as you probably know, was 'world market and crisis'. But Marx was unable to complete his entire critique and only finished *Capital* in the end. This meant that he did not present a fundamental discussion of *crisis as a central issue in itself* because it falls outside the scope of *Capital*, which, according to his plan, concerns 'capital in general'. Naturally, the concrete analysis of the industrial cycle also lies outside the scope of *Capital*.

B: If that is the case, what characterises *Crisis III*[14] on the industrial cycle?

A: In gathering passages for the Marx-Lexikon volumes on crisis, the main texts utilised were *Capital* and *Theories of Surplus Value*. In seeking to systematically develop the theory of crisis, we could not ignore the systematic limitations of *Capital* insofar as it deals with 'capital in general'. Thus, the first two *Marx-Lexikon* volumes on crisis can be thought of as the theory of crisis within the realm of 'capital in general'.

But, as you are probably aware, the fact that *Capital* corresponds to 'capital in general' does not mean that it never ventures beyond that boundary. Indeed, the case of overproduction, which is related to crisis, naturally extends beyond the realm of 'capital in general' since it involves the divergence of market price from value (or more specifically from production price). Despite that, the topic of overproduction is discussed in some depth in *Capital* and *Theories of Surplus Value*. Although *Capital* concerns capital in general, it was not written by adhering to a strict, systematic framework. This can be said of Book III of *Capital* and *Theories of Surplus Value*, in particular, and is even more the case

---

14   [*Crisis IV*.]

in Marx's earlier work the *Grundrisse*. Since none of those manuscripts were readied by Marx for publication, quite a lot of content goes beyond capital in general. At times some of that content even extends beyond the limit Marx sets himself of only considering such topics to the extent necessary to investigate capital in general. Precisely for this reason much can be learned from those passages regarding issues outside the original framework of *Capital*. Marx did not write a systematic explanation of crisis or of the industrial cycle, but he did leave us various hints that can be used to advance our own research. One of the goals of *Marx-Lexikon* is to use as many passages as possible from *Capital* and other works that help to clarify the problem of crisis and the industrial cycle.

B: Does that mean that the treatment of crisis in *Crisis I* and *II*[15] is incomplete?

A: Certainly, from the perspective of Marx's original plan it is incomplete. However, considering that the system of his critique of political economy has significance, at the same time, as a system of crisis theory, and that *Capital* is the most fundamental part of this critique, it could be said that the most fundamental problems of crisis are included and analysed within *Capital*. But those issues are not dealt with as comprehensively as they would have been in a proper theory of crisis. For the *Marx-Lexikon* volumes on crisis, Professor Kuruma strived to organise the content in the most comprehensive and systematic manner possible to clarify the 'moments' through which the possibility of crisis is actualised.

B: What about the case of the volume on the industrial cycle?

A: The task for that volume, as I touched on, is not so much to carefully trace the concrete process through which contradictions accumulate, but to seek out passages in *Capital* and other works that deal with various problems concerning the industrial cycle, such as what characterises the cycle's phases, what is its starting and ending point, what is its duration, etc. It seems to me that we have managed to bring together the fundamental issues that pertain to the industrial cycle.

---

15   [The content he is referring to also is included in *Crisis III*.]

B: Does that mean that *Crisis I* and *Crisis II*[16] on the theory of crisis have a systematic structure from the outset, whereas the volume with on the industrial cycle is more similar in nature to the earlier *Marx-Lexikon* volumes on method[17] and the materialist conception of history?[18]

A: I think that could be said, which is why editing the first two volumes on crisis has been so difficult. The systematic nature of the volumes on the theory of crisis makes them quite similar to the volume on competition.[19]

Essential determinations of crisis and driving beyond the immanent barrier

A: The first main heading of *Crisis I*, 'Essential definition of crisis', includes Marx's most fundamental descriptions of the essence of crisis. One can respond in various ways to the question *What is crisis?* – but I think the most fundamental answer is that it is the comprehensive explosion of all of the contradictions of capitalist production. Many people are familiar with the points Marx makes in the passages grouped under the first main heading, but they are worth re-reading a number of times, as they pertain to the elements that determine the manner in which we can grasp the essence of crisis and approach the theory of crisis.

B: These points are repeatedly emphasised in Professor Kuruma's book, *An Investigation of Crisis Theory*, I believe.

A: Yes. Chapter 3 of that book, 'An Overview of Marx's Theory of Crisis',[20] is worth reading in particular, as it is a sort of a prototype of the *Marx-Lexikon* volumes on crisis.

B: In the passage from that same book, which you quoted earlier, Professor Kuruma notes the decisive importance, when thinking about the starting and ending point of the cycle, to adopt the perspective that the developmental process of capitalist production is at the same time the process of the driving beyond its own immanent barrier.

---

16 [This also pertains to *Crisis III*.]
17 [Kuruma 1969a (ed.) and Kuruma 1969 (ed.).]
18 [Kuruma 1971a (ed.) and 1971b (ed.).]
19 [Kuruma, 1968 (ed.).]
20 [Chapter 4 of this book.]

A: Yes.

B: Isn't this driving beyond the immanent barrier also essential to the case of crisis?

A: Yes, it is essential, certainly. But capitalist production driving beyond its own barrier is not, in itself, a crisis. As mentioned earlier, a business upswing prior to a crisis is a process whereby capitalist production breaks through its immanent barrier. Within this surmounting process, and as its result, the contradictions of capitalist production are accumulated and deepen. When this progresses to a certain stage the contradictions explode. And that is a crisis. Thus, the immanent barrier is unquestionably a decisively important issue with regard to the essence of crisis. But driving beyond that barrier is a *premise* of crisis as the explosion of accumulated contradictions, rather than being itself an essential determination of crisis. Of course, this is a central issue within the analysis of the accumulation of the contradictions leading up to a crisis and the unfolding of the 'moments' of crisis, so it is dealt with in earnest later – in *Crisis II*.

B: I see.

Two problems related to the method of crisis theory

A: Moving on, we can look at the second main heading, 'Method of crisis theory'. This is the method for unfolding the theory of crisis, determined by the essential understanding of crisis just explained. Because crisis is the comprehensive explosion of all of the contradictions of capitalist production, the fundamental method for theoretically unfolding crisis is naturally that of moving progressively from the most abstract and general of the contradictions to the more concrete ones. In other words, we must pursue the developmental process of the contradictions. This approach is discussed more concretely in the passage under this heading, which is taken from the first section of the second volume of *Theories of Surplus Value*.

B: Was the method Marx describes in that passage followed by Professor Kuruma in editing the *Marx-Lexikon* volumes on crisis?

A: Yes, of course.

B: I plan to read this section carefully on my own, but could you lay out its most important points.

A: Various things are important, but I could point to two in particular. First, the possibility of crisis is already manifested in simple circulation. The analysis of the immediate production process of capital follows the analysis of simple circulation, but with regard to crisis, the immediate production process (dealt with from Part 2 of Book I of *Capital*) does not add anything new to the abstract possibility of crisis within the circulation process. That is the first point.

B: I don't quite understand. What do you mean?

A: In order to analyse the immediate production process, any external factor that might impede this process has to be set aside. Thus, with regard to the circulation process, which here is already the circulation process of capital, our premise must be that circulation progresses normally, without encountering any difficulty. On the basis of this premise, the possibility of crisis within simple circulation can be noted, but the problem does not centre on the development of this potential or any related problem.

B: But doesn't some new potential or 'moment' of crisis emerge in the immediate production process?

A: As you know, the immediate production process is the process of producing and obtaining surplus value. Since this is the process under consideration, the analysis naturally clarifies the essence of capital as something that moves in ultimate pursuit of self-valorisation, which is its determining impulse. This is both the essence and the limitation of capital. Capital is able to move insofar as it is such a thing. However, the analysis of this same process clarifies, on the other hand, the tendency of capital to seek the limitless expansion of production and obtainment of surplus value. A moment ago, I said that the contradictions that explode to become a crisis are accumulated in the course of the breaking through of the immanent barrier of capitalist production. The immanent barrier of capitalist production spoken of concerns how the tendency of capital to seek the limitless development of productive power in pursuit of self-valorisation collides with the essence or limitation of capital's aim of self-valorising, so that this limitation is perceived as a barrier. Capital breaks through this limitation and rushes forward, and thus falls into contradictions that explode as a crisis. Thus, the analysis of the immediate production process, which clarifies the limits of capital and that tendency of capital, includes latent elements of crisis.

B: But you just said a moment ago that it adds nothing new to crisis.

A: That's right. Just now I said that *latent* elements of crisis are included. Marx uses the term *an sich*. In dealing with the immediate production process, he considers the intrinsic tendency of capital to seek the absolute development of productive power, and the essence of capital to pursue self-valorisation, but he does not yet pose the question of the form in which the two collide. Moreover, to mention a point connected to what I said earlier, Marx clarifies the law of the production of surplus value in relation to the immediate production process but sets aside the conditions for its realisation. Not just the conditions for the realisation of surplus value, but all problems generally related to circulation are set aside. Or it could be said that all the conditions for the circulation process of capital are *premised* as givens factors. But you are already aware of this, so let's move on to the second point.

Once the analysis of the immediate production process has been completed, we enter the analysis of the circulation process of capital, and there again the possibility of crisis is manifested. This is a point that merits attention. In passage {8} in *Crisis I*, Marx says that the new element of crisis 'can only emerge in the circulation process which is in itself [*an und für sich*] also a process of reproduction',[21] but we should be careful not to view this circulation process as solely the theory of reproduction presented in Part 3 of Book II of *Capital*. Rather, 'circulation process' here refers to the analysis of the circulation process of capital dealt with in the *entirety* of Book II. Commodity circulation, which was analysed in Book I of *Capital* by abstracting from the capital relation, is analysed by Marx again in Book II as a circulation process of *capital*, but now his analysis of the circulation of the products of capital is premised on the immediate production process of capital, so that the earlier abstract forms of crisis take on certain 'content determination' (*Inhaltsbestimmung*). Here, for the first time, the issue of the *realisation of value and surplus value* is raised. Yet even though the possibility of crisis is further developed through this analysis of the circulation process of capital, it remains just a possibility that has not developed to the point of reality. Its *basis* alone is posited. The analysis of the moments that transform the possibility of crisis into reality is presented in Book III of *Capital*, particularly Chapter 15 ('Development of the Law's Internal Contradictions').

Fundamental perspective to correctly grasp the possibility of crisis

B: So, the method laid out in the passage under Heading II is the basis for organising the passages that appear under the subsequent headings?

---

21   Marx 1989b, p. 143.

A: Yes. I think that there are two main stages: First, Headings III to V include passages addressing problems that pertain to the most abstract possibility of crisis. Then, starting from Heading VI, the problem concerns the development of that potential under capital, so that the possibility is transformed into reality. However, within *Crisis I*, the only passages pertaining to that second stage are those grouped under Heading VI, which provide an overview of the development of the possibility of crisis under capital, and those under Heading VII, which consider what could be called the 'further development' of the possibility of crisis within the circulation process of capital. The next heading, VIII, which deals with the development of the possibility of crisis into reality, is included in *Crisis II* instead.

B: Are we going to discuss all the way up to Heading VII?

A: Certainly. But let's start with Heading III, titled 'Money sublates the contradictions of direct barter exchange but only by generalising the contradictions'. The commodity is a contradiction as the direct unity of use value and value. But this is first manifested as a real contradiction that must be mediated in the actual process of commodity exchange. I'm speaking of the realisation of the commodity as use value and as value. Money is what mediates this contradiction, so that the two 'moments' within the exchange process of handing over and receiving a commodity are divided, respectively, into the two metamorphoses, C–M and M–C. But this does not mean that the contradiction ceases to exist. The two inseparably interconnected [*zusammengehörig*] 'moments' become externally independent as two processes in opposition to each other, and it is through these two processes that the contradiction of the commodity as the unity of use value and value unfolds. The contradictions of the exchange process must be generalised and universalised. This process of becoming independent has the potential to progress to the point where the internal unity must forcefully penetrate. This constitutes the abstract possibility of crisis, although it is still only a potentiality.

B: That reminds me of a passage in Professor Kuruma's book *Theory of the Value-form and Theory of the Exchange Process*.[22]

---

22   Kuruma 1957. [A complete English translation of this book is included in Kuruma 2018. Here 'B' seems to be referring to a passage where Kuruma examines how the contradiction between the realisation of the commodity as use value and as value is mediated by the division into the two metamorphoses of C–M and M–C (Kuruma 2018, pp. 88–91).]

A: You're right. The passage you have in mind does not directly concern the possibility of crisis, but I think it provides the basic perspective needed to correctly grasp the passages under Heading III. Even though Professor Kuruma does not deal specifically with the issue of crisis in that book, he presents the essential basis for correctly grasping the theory of crisis. In *Marx-Lexikon*, the importance of money's mediation of the contradiction is reflected in the editorial decision to insert the separate Heading III, prior to dealing with the possibility of crisis in Heading IV.

The abstract possibility of crisis is a contentless, abstract form of crisis

B: Next there is Heading IV: 'Possibility of crisis that appears under commodity circulation'.

A: Yes. This concerns the possibility of crisis that is linked to what is clarified in the analysis of simple commodity production; which is to say, the most abstract possibility of crisis. In *Theories of Surplus Value*, Marx writes that the 'general, abstract possibility of crisis denotes no more than the most abstract form of crisis, without content, without a compelling motivating factor'.[23] This abstract form of crisis has two forms. The first arises from the division between sale and purchase, and the second from the contradiction of the function of money as a means of payment. Both of these forms are dealt with under Heading IV.

B: From your explanation, it would seem more appropriate to title the heading, 'Possibility of crisis that appears under *simple* commodity circulation'. Is there a reason why the word 'simple' was not added?

A: That word could be added, I think, but this possibility of crisis also applies to capitalist commodity circulation. In the circulation process of capital, the potential comes to be posited with content. This point would not be negated even if the word 'simple' had been added, but a misunderstanding might arise if someone were only to read the heading, so we decided not to add it.

Fallacy of recognising partial overproduction but denying general overproduction

B: Heading V has a lot of pages.

---

23   Marx 1989b, p. 140.

A: Yes, as you can see from its title – 'Marx's criticism of theories denying the possibility of crisis (general overproduction)' – the heading groups together passages in which Marx refers to and criticises mistaken theories that recognise the partial overproduction that arises from disequilibrium between production sectors but deny general overproduction. These mistaken theories are based on the view of money solely as a means of circulation, so that commodity circulation is reduced to barter exchange or the exchange of use values, thereby denying the possibility of crisis. This shows how important the issues in Heading III and IV are to a correct understanding of crisis. In a sense, Heading V is a supplement to those headings with regard to the perspective we need to adopt. And that is also why it required so many pages.

If you read the passages under Heading V carefully, you will see that they include not only Marx's criticism of those who reduced commodity production to production in general, but also those who abstracted from the particular capitalistic, historical character of capitalist production to end up with commodity production in general and, from that perspective, overlooked both the development of the possibility of crisis that arises from the circulation process of *capital* and the 'moments' that transform that possibility into reality. For example, Marx criticises those who, despite the fact that the separation of producers and consumers under capitalist production is an important 'moment' connected to crisis, still equate producers with consumers, thereby negating that 'moment' and erasing the unique character of capitalist production. He also criticises those who recognise the possibility for the overproduction of key products to generate general overproduction but view the core problem as the overproduction of the key products itself, rather than a simple disequilibrium between production sectors. We did not set up a separate heading for Marx's criticism of each of those errors, and this should be borne in mind when reading the passages under Heading V.

Heading VI is an overview of Heading VII and VIII

B: The next heading, VI, is titled 'Further development under capital of the possibility of crisis, and the development of the possibility of crisis into reality (Overview)'. Is this an overview of Heading VII?

A: It is an overview not only of Heading VII but also of Heading VIII in *Crisis II*, which is titled: '"Moments" that transform the possibility of crisis into reality'. Heading VII unfolds the specific content determinations that the abstract form of crisis acquires in the circulation process of capital, while Heading VIII is a systematic unfolding of the 'moments' that transform the possibility of crisis into reality. In contrast, the passages under Heading VI describe the distinction and relation between those two stages of the development of the possibility of crisis, while including passages that can be seen as providing an overview of the topic of each of those two other headings.

Abstract form of crisis acquires content determination in the circulation process of capital

A: Let's look at the next heading, VII, titled: 'Further development of the possibility of crisis under the circulation process of capital (abstract form of crisis acquires content determination in the circulation process of capital)'.

B: The expression in parentheses is not a familiar one.

A: That seems to be the case. Most people use expressions like the 'further development of the possibility of crisis', but actually, for this heading, the expression in parentheses seems more appropriate.

B: Why is that?

A: It is quite abstract to speak of the development of potential. And even if we add 'further', so as to distinguish it from the abstract possibility of crisis under simple circulation, it still seems an expression that includes the entirety of what follows, which is to say, the total development of potential. But the 'further development' in Heading VII, as in Heading VI, is referring to the development of the potential within the circulation process of capital, as compared to the 'transformation of potential into reality'.

B: Isn't the one a 'development' whereas the other is a 'transformation'?

A: It is not quite that simple. Marx of course speaks of the 'transformation (*Verwandlung*) of potential into actuality', 'potential becoming (*werden*) actuality', or the 'realisation (*Verwirklichung*) of potential'. At the same time, he speaks of the 'development (*Entwicklung*) of potential into actuality'. And the content is clear in each of these cases. But in the case of 'further development', the manner of development and its content are not at all clear. The expression does not clarify whether it includes 'development into reality' or not. What Marx is saying, in the case we are dealing with, is that within the circulation process of capital, the abstract possibility of crisis acquires concrete content determination and is posited with a basis that can develop into reality. That is why I said that the expression in parentheses seems more appropriate.

B: So why didn't you use it as the main heading?

A: That was the original plan. But as the editorial work progressed, we decided to place it in parentheses because it was referring to what is typically expressed by the term 'further development of potential'. If Heading VIII had been included in *Crisis I*, it might have been fine to position 'acquire content-determination' as the main heading, but it turned out that Heading VIII ('Development into reality') was placed in *Crisis II*. This meant that someone only looking at the headings of the first volume could not grasp the relation between VI and VII, and we were worried misunderstandings might even arise. Thus, we made the change of putting 'further development of potential' front and centre, while adding the information in parentheses to make the content clear.

B: The heading outside of the parentheses is vague, then?

A: No, because we added the clear determination, 'under the circulation process of capital'. All of the problems dealt with under Heading VII must be clarified in the analysis of the circulation process of capital, which of course is dealt with in Book II of *Capital*, from which most of the heading's passages are taken We basically followed the order of development in Book II for including passages concerning the abstract form of crisis acquiring content determination. As I mentioned when we were discussing the method of crisis theory, it is necessary to look at the entirety of Book II of *Capital*, not just Part 3.

B: I think we still need to discuss the nine subheadings under Heading VII?

First content determination: Content of M – C is concretised

A: OK. I'll try to offer a simple explanation of each one. Subheading 1 is titled: 'In the circulation of capital, the "C" in M – C is not the object of an individual want but is the elements of productive capital L + mp'.[24] Already in the analysis of the simple circulation of commodities, the possibility of crisis is made clear in the split of the exchange process of the commodity into C – M and M – C. In the analysis of the circulation process of capital, C – M and M – C, which are two aspects of circulation, are both studied as phases of the *circuit of capital*. For Subheading 1, M – C concerns the first phase of the circuit of money capital, which is the transformation of money capital into productive capital. In order to bring this about, it is not enough for M – C to be in that form *per se*; rather,

---

24   [labour power + means of production]

it must consist of the material content of C into which M is transformed – in other words, labour power (L) and means of production (mp). Here the content of M–C becomes more concrete, so that the contradiction between sale and purchase unfolds, and the abstract form of crisis takes on further content determination.

Second content determination: C–M becomes C'–M'

A: Subheading 2 is titled: 'In the circulation of capital, C–M is at the same time C'–M', and the mass of commodities as the bearers of valorised capital must in their totality pass through the metamorphosis of C'–M'. Just as M–C in the circulation of capital is the transformation of money capital into productive capital, so does C–M in the circulation of capital signify the reflux of commodity capital into money capital (C'–M'). But whereas M–C formed a phase of the capital circuit as the material content of C, here C–M forms a phase of the capital circuit as C+c–M+m; in other words, a commodity that contains surplus value is sold, thus realising this surplus value. Since the movement of capital is a movement as self-valorising value, it would be meaningless to only seek to sell a portion of the commodities – *the surplus value must be realised.* Therefore, as far as capital is concerned, the life-or-death question is whether C' *in its entirety* can be transformed into M'. What is most important to capital is not M–C (the prelude to the *production* of surplus value), but C'–M' as the *realisation* of the produced surplus value. Not only does the content of C–M become more concrete in this way, but the difference between the two circulation phases of capital (C–M and M–C) is clarified by the passages under Subheading 1 and 2, thus positing the abstract possibility of crisis with that much more content.

Third content determination: Interruptions provoked by fluctuations in the value of the elements of production

A: Subheading 3 is titled: 'Possibility of interruptions in the reproduction of capital provoked by fluctuations in the value of the elements of production'. This subheading deals with the extremely important issue of the possibility of crisis within the circuit of productive capital (P... C'–M'–C... P). The following passage from *Theories of Surplus Value* is a point of reference regarding the significance this has for the possibility of crisis:

> The circulation of capital contains within itself the possibilities of interruptions. In the reconversion of money into its conditions of production,

for example, it is not only a question of transforming money into the same use values (in kind), but for the repetition of the reproduction process [it is] essential that these use values can again be obtained at their old value (at a lower value would of course be even better) ... The reconversion of money into commodity can thus come up against difficulties and can create the possibilities of crisis, just as well as can the conversion of commodity into money. When one examines simple circulation – not circulation of capital – these difficulties do not arise.[25]

Fourth content determination: The intertwinement and combination of capital and revenue

A: Subheading 4, 'The intertwinement and combination of capital and revenue', deals with an extremely important topic that serves as an overview for the five subheadings that follow, so perhaps we should go into a bit of detail. In Chapter 3 of Book II of *Capital* ('The Circuit of Commodity Capital'), Marx deals with the particularities of the circuit form by comparing the circuit of money capital and the circuit of productive capital. He notes that, 'All these peculiarities of the circuit lead us beyond its own confines as an isolated circuit of some merely individual capital', and then indicates the following:

> Hence if this figure [C′ ... C′] is conceived in its particularity, it is no longer sufficient to rest content with the fact that the metamorphoses C′ – M′ and M – C are on the one hand *functionally determined sections of the metamorphosis of the capital*, and on the other hand *links in the general circulation of commodities*. It is necessary to make clear how *the metamorphoses of an individual capital are intertwined with those of other individual capitals, and with the part of the total product that is destined for individual consumption*.[26]

In relation to this, Marx writes the following in Chapter 4 of Book II:

> The way in which the various components of the total social capital, of which the individual capitals are only independently functioning components, alternately replace one another in the circulation process – *both with respect to capital and to surplus value* – is thus not the result of *the*

---

25   Marx 1989b, p. 162. [In passage {43} in *Crisis I*.]
26   Marx 1978, p. 178. [In passage {53} in *Crisis I*. Speaker's emphasis.]

> *simple intertwining of the metamorphoses that occurs in commodity circulation*, and which *the acts of capital circulation have in common with all other processes of commodity circulation*, but rather *requires a different mode of investigation*.[27]

Here, the 'different mode of investigation' refers, of course, to the analysis in Part 3 of Book II of *Capital* ('The Reproduction and Circulation of the Total Social Capital'), which examines 'the circulation process of the individual capitals as components of the total social capital, i.e. the circulation process of this total social capital'.[28] In the first section of Chapter 18 ('The Object of the Inquiry'), which is the first chapter of Part 3, Marx writes:

> However, the circuits of individual capitals are *interlinked, they presuppose one another and condition one another, and it is precisely by being interlinked in this way* that they constitute the movement of the total social capital. Just as, in the case of simple commodity circulation, the overall metamorphosis of a single commodity appeared as but one term in the series of metamorphoses of the commodity world as a whole, now the metamorphosis of the individual capital appears as one term in the series of metamorphoses of the social capital. But if *simple commodity circulation in no way necessarily involved the circulation of capital* – since it can proceed quite well on the basis of non-capitalist production – the circuit of the total social capital, as already noted, also involves a commodity circulation that *does not fall within the circuit of any individual capital*, i.e. the *circulation of those commodities that do not form capital*.[29]

I think it should be clear from the passages looked at thus far that the two stages of the circulation of capital ($C'-M'$ and $M-C$) are each necessarily linked to the other metamorphoses of $M-C$ and $C-M$. This intertwinement in itself is nothing more than the 'intertwining of the metamorphoses' that are generally applicable to commodity circulation, but in fact the 'intertwinement of capital metamorphoses' within the 'intertwinement of commodity metamorphoses' is a complex social relationship that includes not only the relationship between capitals but also the relationship between capital and revenue. Whereas for the capitalist a wage is variable capital that is advanced, for workers it is simply

---

27 Marx 1978, p. 194. [In passage {54} in *Crisis I*. Speaker's emphasis.]
28 Marx 1978, p. 430.
29 Marx 1978, pp. 429–30. [In passage {55} in *Crisis I*. Speaker's emphasis.]

revenue. And surplus value in the case of m–c is simply the expenditure of revenue. The task in Part 3 in Book II of *Capital* is to grasp the social relations that underlie the intertwinement and opposition between capital and revenue by analyzing 'the circulation process of the individual capitals as components of the total social capital, i.e. the circulation process of this total social capital',[30] and grasp the social relations that underlie the intertwinement and opposition of the various C–M and M–C metamorphoses. I think that the relation between the possibility of crisis and such issues is clear, but perhaps we could read two other passages to confirm this:

> [T]hese necessary preconditions all mutually require one another, but they are mediated by a very complicated process which involves three processes of circulation that *proceed independently, even if they are intertwined with one another. The very complexity of the process provides many occasions for it to take an abnormal course.*[31]

> This *intertwining and coalescence of the processes of reproduction or circulation of different capitals* is on the one hand necessitated by the division of labour, on the other hand it is accidental; and *thus the content-determination of crisis is already fuller.*[32]

As for the relationship between Subheading 4 and the five subsequent subheadings, I think that it can be positioned as a premise for the content determinations of the form of crisis that are unfolded through the analysis of the circulation process of the total social capital; or it could be said that subheading 4 is an overview of those headings, as I mentioned earlier.

B: It's gotten a bit difficult now. I'm not sure if I can follow what you are saying.

A: We can go over this again later if you have questions.

Fifth content determination: The divergence between supply and demand for the capitalist as a capitalist

A: Next, Subheading 5, considers the following problem expressed in its title: 'The supply for the capitalist as capitalist exceeds his demand; i.e. the max-

---

30   Marx 1978, p. 430. [In passage {55} in *Crisis I*.]
31   Marx 1978, p. 571. [In passage {57} in *Crisis I*. Speaker's emphasis.]
32   Marx 1989a, p. 141. [In passage {59} in *Crisis I*. Speaker's emphasis.]

imum limit of his demand is $c+v$ but his supply is $c+v+m$. Whence comes the money for the monetisation of the surplus value?'

I think it is best to consider this subheading by looking at each of the two sentences separately. The first sentence concerns the separation of supply and demand for the capitalist as capitalist (as opposed to the capitalist as non-capitalist = consumer) in terms of being the concretisation of the separation of sale and purchase. And the second sentence poses a question that arises as a corollary to that first sentence.

The first issue should be clear from the sentence itself. That is to say, what the capitalist *as capitalist* purchases on the market are the elements of productive capital, i.e. labour power (L) and means of production (mp), which is $c+v$[33] in terms of value. Meanwhile, what the capitalist sells on the market is the commodity C′, consisting of $c+v+s$.[34] Thus, with regard to the capitalist *as capitalist*, there is demand for $c+v$, on the one hand, and supply of $c+v+s$, on the other hand, so that the surplus value (s) is in excess. This does not mean, of course, that a general oversupply arises in the market. From the perspective of the circulation process of the total social capital that includes the exchange between capital and revenue, the part of the surplus value (s) that the capitalist accumulates as a capitalist first of all forms a portion of his demand for additional $c+v$; while, secondly, the part of 's' beyond that portion accumulated constitutes the capitalist's demand on the market as a simple expender of revenue. It should be clear, in any event, that here the split between C−M and M−C, and their intertwinement and opposition, is concretised as the intertwinement and opposition between the supply and demand of the capitalist and the capitalist's demand as the expender of revenue, so that the abstract form of crisis acquires further content determination.

The question thus arises: 'Whence comes the money for the monetisation of surplus value?' Even if there is *demand* on the market by the capitalist as capitalist and as the expender of revenue for commodities corresponding to the new surplus value (s) obtained, the surplus value the capitalist has in the form of commodity capital must first be transformed into money. Thus, the question also arises: What is the exact source of the money to realise this surplus value? This can be answered relatively easily if we correctly follow Marx's theoretical development as it is unfolds in *Capital*. In short, the problem comes down to the issue of where the money comes from to realise the total value of commodities. The answer to this general question is that money as a means of

---

33 [constant capital + variable capital]
34 [constant capital + variable capital + surplus value]

social circulation is always being advanced by the capitalist class, and in a case where the total commodity value is augmented, and this is not covered by an economising of the quantity of circulating money, then hoarded money will be transformed into means of circulation, while gold-producing regions will supply additional gold to increase the quantity of money circulating. 'The problem itself therefore', Marx argues, 'does not exist'.[35]

B: So why does *Crisis I* deal with a problem that does not exist?

A: The reason is related to the following circumstances. Although this relation is a relatively simple matter once understood, it may not be grasped or could be overlooked if the phenomena that arise from capitalist production are the focus of attention. First of all, if capitalists are seen only as the personification of capital, we will end up overlooking that they also advance money for the sake of *consuming* surplus value. Second, if we look at the capitalist class throwing money into circulation in the form of revenue, it will seem as if this class is *paying compensation* vis-à-vis the part of the total product, and we will not be able to understand that this is nothing more than an *advance* made to come into possession of surplus value. Moreover, because commercial capitalists, money capitalists, landowners, the state, and others intervene, the source of the advance of money becomes increasingly difficult to discern.

Correctly understanding the circulation process of the total social capital is essential to grasping the real relations underlying the outside appearance, so it is not surprising that no one prior to Marx had been able to properly solve this problem. Even after Marx fundamentally sorted this out in Book II of *Capital*, many mistaken arguments have been presented, such as the ongoing debate that originated from the views expressed by Rosa Luxemburg. This is the basic reason for Professor Kuruma raising this question in addition to the first issue, and we ended up having more passages concerning this second issue.

Sixth content determination: Money hoard from turnover of constant capital

A: Subheading 6 and 7 both deal with the issue of the money hoard; in other words, C–M not complemented by M–C. This is the issue of the split between sale and purchase acquiring content determination through the circulation process. Subheading 6 is titled, 'Money hoard (therefore sale without purchase

---

35   Marx 1978, p. 407. [In passage {61} in *Crisis I*.]

and supply without demand) becomes necessary through the turnover of constant capital. Conditions for the formation of equilibrium in the reproduction process of the total social capital'.

From the perspective of individual capitals, the turnover of constant capital is carried out in the form of accumulating a depreciation fund[36] during the period in which sales are made without purchases and then throwing that accumulated fund into circulation at once when the period of renewal arrives. But, viewed from the perspective of the circulation process of the total social capital, there is at all times, on the one hand, the capital that is being accumulated as a depreciation fund (forming supply without demand), and on the other hand the constant capital that has reached its renewal time (forming demand without supply). The balance between the two is a condition for the smooth progression of social reproduction.

Seventh content determination: Money hoard for the accumulation of capital

A: Subheading 7 is titled: 'Money hoard (therefore sale without purchase and supply without demand) becomes necessary for the accumulation of capital'. When forming an accumulation fund, individual capitals carry out supply without demand, and when the fund is invested, demand without supply is formed. From the perspective of society, there are capitals carrying out C–M without M–C, on the one hand, and capitals carrying out M–C without C–M, on the other hand. The correspondence between the two is the condition for the smooth progression of social reproduction.

B: I seem to recall that Professor Kuruma dealt with the topics addressed in Subheading 6 and 7 in *An Investigation of Crisis Theory*.

A: Yes, I think you are referring to the chapter titled, 'Capital Accumulation and the Depreciation Fund for Fixed Capital',[37] which addresses the mistaken theory of the Marxian economist Tsunao Inomata as well as the arguments of Rosa Luxemburg. The chapter centres on the question of whether the depreciation fund for fixed capital can also be used as an accumulation fund. Inomata

---

36   [The term 'deprecation fund' is used throughout this book as the translation of the Japanese term *shōkyaku kikin*, but such terms as 'amortisation fund', 'sinking fund', and 'replacement fund' can be found in English translations of the writings of Marx and Engels to refer to this fund to replace the worn-out fixed capital.]

37   [Chapter 11 of this book.]

had argued that the money needed to realise accumulated surplus value is advanced from the capitalist's depreciation fund for fixed capital. Rosa Luxemburg also criticised Marx with regard to this issue, although from a different perspective. Both Inomata and Luxemburg committed an error that seems to be fully addressed by the passages grouped under Subheading 5 (so the content of the chapter in Professor Kuruma's book is a good frame of reference for understanding that subheading). But a question remains: Can the depreciation fund for fixed capital at the same time be an accumulation fund? In passage {69} in *Crisis 1*, taken from the second volume of *Theories of Surplus Value*, Marx seems to be saying that the depreciation fund can be used as a such a fund. Professor Kuruma, in that chapter of his book, raises the question of how we should interpret what Marx wrote, and concludes that, although Marx had stated in *Theories of Surplus Value* that the depreciation fund could be used as an accumulation fund, he later changed his mind, so that by the time he wrote the manuscript for Book II he no longer thought it possible. A footnote is added in *Crisis 1* to the key part of passage {69} to briefly indicate this fact, but readers can refer to the chapter in *An Investigation of Crisis Theory* for more on this issue. However, that chapter cannot serve as a direct explanation of Subheading 6 and 7 since its aim is not to clarify the overall significance of the depreciation fund and accumulation fund.

I should also note that my comments regarding Subheading 6 and 7 did not take the credit system into consideration. There are passages under those subheadings that explain the relation to the credit system, so I hope readers will pay attention to those parts.

Eighth content determination: Long working period during which there are purchases without sales

A: Next is Subheading 8, titled: 'In the case of a long working period (such as the construction of a railway, etc.) there are purchases without sales and demand without supply'. This deals with the problem of the split between sale and purchase or the divergence between demand and supply. Long working periods stem from the material aspects of the production process, so they can occur in any form of society. But in a capitalist society a need arises in such a case for advances made by money capitalists, raising the possibility of crisis. In the case of social production, where the elements of production are allotted to production spheres in a planned manner, production elements that do not supply products over a long period of time, and therefore projects that absorb the means of subsistence, do not present any great obstacle. But that is not the case under anarchic capitalist production, wherein disturbances necessarily arise.

With regard to this, we need to consider the tremendous role played by the credit system, as Marx notes in the following passage:

> At the less developed stages of capitalist production, enterprises that require a long working period, and thus a large capital outlay for a longer time, particularly if they can be conducted only on a large scale are often not pursued capitalistically at all ... Large-scale jobs needing particularly long working periods are fully suitable for capitalist production only when the concentration of capital is already well advanced, and when the development of the credit system offers the capitalist the convenient expedient of advancing and thus risking other people's capital instead of his own.[38]

As we can see, the credit system plays the role of breaking through the limitations of individual capital so as to play a major role in the expansion of large-scale production, but of course this means that contradictions are accumulated further, reaching a new stage.

Ninth content determination: Difficulties accompanying the fluctuation in the rate of accumulation

A: The ninth and final subheading under Heading VII is titled: 'The inevitable change in the proportion between the two production departments arising from the shift from simple to expanded reproduction, and the difficulties that arise from it [and, *mutatis mutandis*, the same can be said for a general change – whether up or down – in the rate of accumulation]'.

B: What does that part added in brackets mean? Up to now, as in Heading V and VII, additional information has been placed in parentheses, not brackets.

A: Ah, you noticed that. The text inside the brackets could be viewed as the opinion of Professor Kuruma or a note regarding the entire subheading. But the significance in terms of content concerns the entirety of the subheading, including the part in brackets. In any case, that is why we adopted a bit of an unconventional approach.

B: I see. Could you tell me more about the significance you just mentioned?

---

38   Marx 1978, pp. 310–2.

A: In Chapter 20 of Book II of *Capital* ('Simple Reproduction'), Marx clarifies the fundamental conditions for the reproduction process of the total social capital, and then moves on in Chapter 21 to consider 'accumulation and reproduction on an expanded scale'. The problem posed in Subheading 9 concerns the central issue of the latter chapter. In order to clarify this issue, we need to correctly grasp the significance that the investigation of simple reproduction in Chapter 20 has to the examination of expanded reproduction in Chapter 21. This involves, on the one hand, clarifying the conditions of simple reproduction as the basis for considering expanded reproduction. At the same time, because simple reproduction is reproduction in which the rate of accumulation is zero, if the zero-accumulation rate in the case of simple reproduction becomes a positive accumulation rate, we are dealing already with expanded reproduction. Thus, it is clear that the point to clarify with regard to Chapter 21 is, first of all, the changes in the conditions for social reproduction resulting from *the accumulation rate going from zero to a positive number*. In other words, what changes in the conditions for social reproduction arise *when there is a shift from simple to expanded reproduction*. Although only a few pages in *Crisis I* are dedicated to this topic, this is the perspective that I think we need to bear in mind when reading Chapter 21, particularly Section 3. In considering this problem, Marx demonstrated that the shift from simple to expanded production is necessarily accompanied by a change in the proportion between Department I and Department II, so that Department I becomes larger, relatively speaking. He also points out the difficulties that necessarily arise from this change in the proportion between the departments.

B: Does this mean that the shift from simple to expanded reproduction is a particular case of an increase in the rate of accumulation?

A: Yes, that's exactly right. If we were to speak in more general terms of Marx's analysis here, it is the idea that *when the rate of accumulation changes*, a need arises for a change in the proportion between production departments, which is inevitably accompanied by certain difficulties.

B: Within the brackets of the subheading, Professor Kuruma specifically notes a 'general change – whether up or down – in the rate of accumulation'. Does that mean that there is a need to think about a fall in the rate of accumulation, too?

A: Yes. In fact, the question of what occurs in the case of a sharp drop in the accumulation rate is quite important with regard to the possibility of crisis.

B: Even in the case of a socialist society, wouldn't there be a change in the proportion between production departments if there were a change in the rate of accumulation?

A: Yes, of course. That in itself could be called a superhistorical, natural necessity. Of course, in that case, the 'rate of accumulation' is not the rate of the *accumulation of capital*, but the rate of production expansion. But under capitalism this law penetrates in a completely different way, as compared to socialism. In the case of social production, people would be able – and indeed would have to – anticipate the various changes that might occur among the different conditions of social reproduction from a modification in the magnitude of the accumulation rate, including a change in the proportion between the production departments, and on that basis they could consciously determine the optimal rate of production expansion in a planned manner. In contrast, under capitalist production, the magnitude of social production, and therefore the rate of accumulation, is determined by the total volume of accumulation that happens to be carried out, as determined by the profit impulse of individual capitals, so the changed proportion between the departments and other changes in the conditions for reproduction merely arise as a result. The rate of accumulation will change depending on changes in the profit rate and interest rate or via other exterior circumstances. Moreover, it can change suddenly. But the issue of how and through what the rate of accumulation is decided is a problem that goes beyond Part 3 of Book II of *Capital*, so even without posing that question, we can just note that the rate of accumulation changes. This means various sorts of friction, as well as changes and difficulties, will arise within social reproduction. By elucidating such things, the abstract form of crisis is posited with content determination, providing a basis for the development from possibility to reality. – This is the significance to the theory of crisis of the theory of reproduction in Part 3 of Book II of *Capital*.

B: I see. Our discussion thus far seems quite different from the sorts of explanations found these days in works of Marxian political economy.

A: I suppose you're right. But what particular points are you referring to?

B: Let's see ... well, for instance, there have been recent books and articles about an 'equilibrium rate of accumulation'.

A: Oh, yes. That seems to be a popular topic, but it is a bit of a strange notion. I believe that is the idea that not only the organic composition and the rate of surplus value but also the proportion between production departments are taken as givens, and upon that basis the issue centres on what rate of accumulation is needed to maintain such an equilibrium or balance. I think from a methodological standpoint it is mistaken. The rate of accumulation is the independent variable, while the proportion between departments is the dependent variable – this is the real manner of the capitalist economy. Since this is the reality, we must think theoretically in the same manner; otherwise ideas won't be of any use for understanding reality.

B: Would you say that the first *Marx-Lexikon* volume on crisis has significance as a critique of that sort of new argument?

A: I think you could say that, but in fact the argument is not so new. Professor Kuruma already criticised a similarly mistaken view in the 1930s.

B: What was that?

A: I am referring to his two articles[39] criticising the views of Yasuma Takada that were published in the first edition of Professor Kuruma's book on crisis.[40] Unfortunately, the two chapters were not republished in the latter editions of that book.

B: What are the titles of the articles?

A: The articles, written in 1932 and 1933, are titled 'A Consideration of Professor Takada's Theory of Accumulation' and 'Professor Takada's Revision of His Theory of Accumulation'. In his preface to the 1953 edition of his book on crisis, Professor Kuruma offered the following reason for not including them:

> There is no need for 50 pages on that subject today. At the time the articles were published, I felt the need to criticise such a view, given the situation back then, but *probably no one still adheres to such a view today, so I feel that there is no longer any necessity to criticise it*.[41]

It is true that there is probably no one employing the exact arguments of Takada these days, but similarly mistaken views are being presented, so I think it was a

---

39   Kuruma 1932 and Kuruma 1933. [Both articles are included in Chapter 15 of this book.]
40   Kuruma 1949.
41   Kuruma 1953b, pp. 2–3. [Speaker's emphasis.]

bit of a miscalculation to leave those two articles out of the new edition on the grounds that they were no longer necessary.

Professor Kuruma also touches on the issue addressed in Subheading 9 in a discussion with Sutehiro Uesugi that was published in the January 1960 issue of the journal *Keizai seminā* (Economic Seminar), which I think many people have read.[42] So, the critique of an 'equilibrium rate of accumulation' is not so new. Nevertheless, quite a few people seem to have been influenced by this concept because it has been incorporated within works on crisis theory considered rather sophisticated. In that sense, it seems worthwhile to explore this issue. But let's not go into any more detail today. I think we have finished our overview of *Crisis I*.

---

42   [In that discussion, Kuruma offers the following comment when asked if there was anything that struck him about recent works of political economy in Japan:

'I can't make a definitive statement, since I'm not so familiar with who has written what, but one thing I have noticed with regard to crisis theory, for example, is that relatively few are thinking in a comprehensive way. That is to say, it seems like there may be a tendency to overestimate the importance of specific factors, resulting in somewhat strained arguments. To take one example, various attempts have been made to demonstrate the necessity of crisis through manipulating the reproduction schema, including those who try to find the necessity of crisis in the unfolding of so-called disequilibrium arising from a change in the ratio [of Department I] to Department II resulting from a change in the accumulation rate. However, the change that arises in the ratio between the two departments from a change in the accumulation rate is a superhistorical or natural necessity, and in this case, it is through the uneven development that equilibrium can first be secured. If it is said that uneven development causes crisis, then it would have to be said that crises would occur in any type of society. However, I am not saying that this has no relation to crisis. This means at the same time that if the accumulation rate suddenly changes drastically, equilibrium will suddenly fall into disequilibrium, as in a case, for instance, where an accumulation rate of 20 percent, around which equilibrium between two departments has been established, suddenly drops to 5 percent; a situation that would likely make Department I far in excess [of Department II]. As a result, many businesses in Department I would be likely to fail, which in turn would reduce demand for goods in Department II, along with other effects. Considered in such terms, it might seem that the theory of unfolding disequilibrium is valid. But is that the case? Moreover, thought of in those terms, a natural question becomes: What determines the rate of accumulation? If it is said that it is the possibility of valorisation, then one must consider what determines that possibility. And this is connected to an endless series of other issues, such as the tendential fall in the rate of profit, intensifying competition, and the further fall in the profit rate, as well as the interest rate, credit system, etc. This is just one example ...'
(Kuruma and Uesugi, 1960, p. 41) – T. Ōtani.]

Does the contradiction between production and consumption pertain to the theory of reproduction in Part 3 in Book II of *Capital*?

B: Hold on a second. Do you mean to say that our discussion of Heading VII is over?

A: Yes.

B: So we're done with issues related to the theory of reproduction?

A: Unless there is something you want to look at.

B: There is, actually.

A: Okay, if you insist. What is it?

B: The general image I have of the relation between the theory of reproduction and crisis is of a contradiction between production and consumption. And the importance of the theory of reproduction to the theory of crisis seems to be that it elucidates this 'immanent contradiction'. However, there does not seem to be a heading in *Crisis I* that deals with this particular issue. What does that fact signify?

A: I can understand your doubt, and I suppose we should discuss it.

B: The contradiction between production and consumption is an important issue to crisis, isn't it?

A: Certainly. On this point, Marx writes the following in Book III of *Capital*:

> [W]hile the consumption capacity of the workers is restricted partly by the laws governing wages and partly by the fact that they are employed only as long as they can be employed at a profit for the capitalist class. *The ultimate reason for all real crises always remains the poverty and restricted consumption of the masses, in the face of the drive of capitalist production* to develop the productive forces as if only the absolute consumption capacity of society set a limit to them.[43]

---

43   Marx 1981a, p. 615. [Speaker's emphasis.]

In other words, capitalist production on the one hand has the impulse or tendency of seeking to absolutely develop productive power by breaking through any barrier. But, on the other hand, this tendency collides and is in contradiction with the distribution relations determined by the essence of capital in its pursuit of valorisation and the capitalist production relations, and therefore it is in contradiction with the severely limited consumption capacity of the working class. When Marx speaks of the 'ultimate reason for all real crises' this is what he means. He also refers to the same thing in *Theories of Surplus Value* as the 'fundamental contradiction' (*Grundwiderspruch*),[44] the 'basis (*Grundlage*) of modern overproduction',[45] the 'essential secret of glut',[46] the 'secret basis of glut',[47] or the 'deepest and most hidden cause (*Grund*) of crises'.[48] We can see from this, in relation to crisis, the degree to which Marx emphasised what has been referred to as the 'immanent contradiction' [*naizaiteki mujun*] since the time Moritarō Yamada first used the term.

B: But this is not dealt with in *Marx-Lexikon*.

A: Hold on. It's not dealt with in *Crisis I*, but it is addressed in *Crisis II*.

B: That seems a bit strange. I thought it was common knowledge that the issue of the 'immanent contradiction' is dealt with in Part 3 of Book II of *Capital*.

A: That may be so, but it seems to me that this 'common knowledge' contains an unexpected pitfall.

B: So that is not the case? I seem to recall that Marx himself clearly indicated this.

A: I think you are referring to a footnote in Part 2 of Book II of *Capital* inserted by Engels, who writes that, 'In the manuscript, the following note is here inserted for future amplification':

> Contradiction in the capitalist mode of production: the labourers as buyers of commodities are important for the market. But as sellers of their

---

44   Marx 1989b, p. 248. [In passage {137} in *Crisis II*.]
45   Marx 1989b, p. 158. [In passage {106} in *Crisis II*.]
46   Marx 1989b, p. 252. [In passage {112} in *Crisis II*.]
47   Marx 1989b, p. 309. [In passage {113} in *Crisis II*.]
48   Marx 1989b, p. 274. [In passage {138} in *Crisis II*.]

own commodity – labour power – capitalist society tends to keep them down to the minimum price. – Further contradiction: the periods in which capitalist production exerts all its forces regularly turn out to be periods of overproduction, because production potentials can never [*nie*]⁴⁹ be utilised to such an extent that more value may not only be produced but also realised; but the sale of commodities, the realisation of commodity capital and thus of surplus value, is limited, not by the consumer requirements of society in general, but by the consumer requirements of a society in which the vast majority are always poor and must always remain poor. However, this pertains to the next part.⁵⁰

B: I see. That is quite clear.

A: It would seem so. And naturally, one assumes that the 'next part' (*nächsten Abschnitt*) refers to Part 3 of Book II. Moreover, to someone not aware of the content of Part 3, it would seem that it must deal with the 'immanent contradiction'. But anyone who reads Part 3 in a straightforward way is likely to have doubts about whether it does in fact deal with the issue touched on in Marx's note. Nevertheless, many, if not most, theorists have assumed that *Marx is saying* the contradiction between production and consumption, which is the 'ultimate reason for all real crises', is a problem pertaining to Part 3 of Book II. Some 'magicians' have even made the feat seem effortless, although for most it is difficult.

As I think you know, there have been various debates on the significance to the theory of crisis of Part 3 of Book II. In Japan, there was the debate between Tokuzō Fukuda (who based himself on Tugan-Baranowsky) and Hajime Kawakami (who drew on the ideas of Rosa Luxemburg). But the first argument that originated in Japan was presented by Moritarō Yamada in his 1931 book, *An Introduction to the Analysis of Reproduction Schema*.⁵¹ This work had a

---

49   [When it later became possible to read Marx's second manuscript for Book II of *Capital*, differences became clear between the content of the original manuscript and this 'note' in the published edition edited by Engels. Among the various differences, one decisively important one concerns Engels use of the word *nie* (never) rather than the original *nur* (only) in the manuscript. This is important because *nur* could not be seen as referring to the so-called 'immanent contradiction' within the note, and thus there would be no reason to think that what 'pertains' to the 'next part' (*nächsten Abschnitt*) would also deal with that contradiction. – T. Ōtani.]

50   Marx 1997, p. 315. [Penguin edition (Marx 1978) p. 391. In passage {109} in *Crisis II*. Speaker's emphasis.]

51   Yamada 1948.

major impact on subsequent debates, which were characterised (regardless of whether participants adhered to Yamada's theory or opposed and sought to revise it) by a special emphasis on the relation to crisis theory of Part 3 of Book II of *Capital*. The debate centred on the relation between the 'immanent contradiction' and the theory of reproduction.

In discussing Subheading 9, we touched on some of the upside-down notions regarding the rate of accumulation, and I think such notions are just the latest variations of the fixed idea that the 'immanent contradiction' pertains the theory of reproduction.

What does the 'next part' (*nächsten Abschnitt*) refer to?

B: But how can we not think along those lines if Marx himself states that he will deal with this in Part 3 of Book II?

A: Yes, but in fact the question revolves around whether he actually said such a thing.

B: Are you implying that the note that you quoted is not genuine?

A: No, that's not what I mean. In the passage in question, the German *nächsten Abschnitt* is translated as the 'next part', and for the *structure* of Book II, Marx did in fact used term *Abschnitt* to indicate its main parts. But the original meaning of the word is 'segment' or 'break', and Marx also used the term in that sense, as in the following passage from Book II:

> What renders this act of the general circulation of commodities simultaneously a functionally definite *section* [*Abschnitt*] in [an] independent circuit of some individual capital is primarily not the form of the act but its material content.[52]

This word, by itself, could also mean some particular section of a text. For example, in Engels's preface to Book II of *Capital*, he writes:

> They are dealt with in passing in the *section* [*Abschnitt*] that forms the main body of the manuscript, pp. 220–972 (notebooks VI–XV): *Theorien*

---

52 Marx 1997, p. 32. [Speaker's emphasis. In the Penguin edition, the term *Abschnitt* is translated as 'part' rather than 'section' (Marx 1978, p. 110).]

> *über den Mehrwert.* This *section* [*Abschnitt*] contains a detailed critical history of the crucial question in political economy ...[53]

In the case above, *Theorien über den Mehrwert* (Theories of Surplus Value) could be either a book, part, chapter, section, etc. In fact, in the *Grundrisse* we can find this sort of flexible usage. In *Capital*, the divisions are along the lines of *Buch–Abschnitt–Kapitel* (Book–Part–Chapter), but that is only for the later editions of *Capital*. The first German edition (1867) was composed of *Buch* and *Kapitel*,[54] and was only changed to Book–Part–Chapter for the second edition (1872). The Chapter–Section divisions in the first edition became Part–Chapter. Thus, *Abschnitt* in the case of the first German edition of *Capital* could be referring to *Buch*. The plan for Marx's critique of political economy found in the first volume of *Theories of Surplus Value*, written around the time Marx was writing the manuscript for *Capital*, refers to the 'production process of capital' as the first *Abschnitt* and 'profit and capital' as the third *Abschnitt*. In the second volume of *Theories of Surplus Value*, Marx also speaks of the first *Abschnitt* that is to deal with 'capital–immediate production process'. In both cases, he is referring to what is *Buch* in *Capital*. The manuscript that includes the note we are discussing now, which Engels calls the 'second manuscript', was written around the same time, in *1870*.

Given all this, I think we cannot say for sure that the *nächsten Abschnitt* is referring to Part 3 of Book II of *Capital*.[55] There is a good possibility that it is referring to the entirety of Book III of *Capital*. Thus, it seems to me that the debate needs to centre on whether the note is, in fact, referring to the content of Part 3. It is through this sort of debate that we may be able to determine what *nächsten Abschnitt* is referring to.

Don't leave the reading of signs to the leader

B: I see. Why is it that no one has questioned this?

---

53   Marx 1978, p. 84. [Speaker's emphasis.]
54   [I.e. there was no 'Abschnitt' in between 'Buch' and 'Kapitel'. – T. Ōtani.]
55   [Later it was learned that in his second manuscript for Book II of *Capital*, Marx had first written *Abschnitt* in this passage but changed it to *Kapitel*, and then Engels decided, in line with the structure of the volume he was editing, to use *Abschnitt*. On the basis of this information, it was possible to confirm that in that published edition, the 'next part' (*nächsten Abschnitt*) is referring to Part 3 of that volume. Meanwhile, as indicated in the earlier footnote, the word 'nie' in the Engels edition was 'nur' in Marx's manuscript, which makes it clear that the 'note' did not include a reference to the 'immanent contradiction' – T Ōtani.]

A: I didn't mean to suggest that no one had raised this doubt before. It's just that I was not personally aware of anyone who has pointed out that precise point. I have some vague sense of the circumstances surrounding this fact. In Japan, Yamada raised this issue generally in *An Introduction to the Analysis of Reproduction Schema*, where he makes a near-definitive statement that *nächsten Abschnitt* refers to Part 3 of Book II. The text is a bit old, but let's take a look at the following passage:

> The 'next part' refers to Part 3 of Book II, titled, 'The Reproduction and Circulation of the Total Social Capital'. *Through this part* Marx *clearly* is incorporating the issue of the limits of consumption within the theory of reproduction.[56]

Yamada says that his own explanation is the same as that of Lenin, and he seeks to reinforce this by quoting a section from 'A Characterisation of Economic Romanticism'. This is a rather subtle point, so first let's read what Lenin wrote:

> This quotation was from a *note inserted in the manuscript* of Part II of Volume II of *Capital*. It was inserted 'for future amplification' and the publisher of the manuscript put it in as a footnote. *After the words quoted above, the note goes on to say: 'However, this pertains to the next part',* i.e. to the third part. What is this third part? It is precisely the part which contains a criticism of Adam Smith's theory of two parts of the aggregate social product (together with the above-quoted opinion about Sismondi), and an analysis of 'the reproduction and circulation of the aggregate social capital', i.e. of the realisation of the product. Thus, in confirmation of his views, which are a repetition of Sismondi's, our author quotes a note that pertains 'to the part' which refutes Sismondi: 'to the part' in which it is shown that the capitalists *can* realise surplus value, and that to introduce foreign trade in an analysis of realisation is absurd ...[57]

Well, it is true that Lenin thinks the 'next part' is Part 3 of Book II, but here Lenin is saying that in the theory of reproduction, the Sismondi-style theory of underconsumption is refuted, making it ridiculous for the romanticists to insist on that theory of underconsumption by quoting this note. Lenin is certainly not saying that the contradiction between production and consumption,

---

56   Yamada 1948, p. 77.
57   Lenin 1972, p. 169.

and therefore the 'limits of consumption', are discussed in the theory of reproduction. In other words, this does not support the entirety of what Yamada was saying. Nevertheless, the 'Lenin-Yamada' explanation was born and widely accepted in Japan as a self-evident truth.

B: This is the 'pitfall' that you referred to earlier?

A: Yes, but instead of a pitfall, it seems more apt to describe it as a case where one leaves the reading of road signs to the leader, and if that leader makes an error, everyone who is following, even the most experienced, can get lost and waste a lot of time trying to find the way out.

B: Once you end up lost in a strange place, even after realising a misinterpretation was made, it seems hard to get back to the original place.

A: Setting aside how hard that might be, it seems to me that there is something worthwhile for you to consider. That is to say, I think you should completely dispense with the preconceived idea that the 'immanent contradiction' pertains to the theory of reproduction. That would involve, on the one hand, carefully considering the content of the theory of reproduction and its significance to the theory of crisis, while also clarifying what it means to say that the 'immanent contradiction' is the 'ultimate basis of crisis'.

B: When was it that Professor Kuruma begin to have doubts about the orthodox interpretation?

A: As far as I am aware, it was rather recently – after the completion of the manuscript for *Crisis I*. As you can see from that volume, Professor Kuruma did not view the 'immanent contradiction' as pertaining to the theory of reproduction, but he seemed to have forgotten about the 'Lenin-Yamada' explanation of the note. I mentioned to him that there are many theorists who have connected the two, and he gave me a quizzical look. He became aware of this issue in re-reading the works of various theorists in relation to the content for *Crisis II*. Although, to be honest, I suspect this may have been a case where Professor Kuruma was thinking anew about something he had looked into before but subsequently forgot about.

B: If the issue of the 'immanent contradiction' does not pertain to the theory of reproduction, it must be an issue concerning Book III of *Capital*, so could we talk a little more about how the issue is dealt with there?

A: That is an issue that concerns *Crisis II*, so Professor Kuruma will probably examine it in detail during the next discussion. I had not even planned to discuss all that we covered today, but you got me a bit carried away.

Really putting away the beer ...

A: That just about ends our discussion of the first volume on crisis. As I told you, the next volume will begin from Heading VIII, 'Moments that transform the possibility of crisis into reality'. This corresponds *directly* to Book III of *Capital*, particularly from Part 3 onward. The manuscript we have put together is too long for a single volume, so we will have to somehow arrange and compress the contents. The editing of this second volume has involved various difficulties related to the subject matter, but Professor Kuruma put his heart and soul into the work, so it is worth looking forward to.

By the way, you really put away the beer while we were talking, but you don't seem tired at all. Was it because you found what I was saying so interesting?

B: It was not so much what you were saying but the times when you got a bit irritated that I found interesting.

A: I suppose I wasn't able to fill Professor Kuruma's shoes so well.

B: Don't get so down about it. In honour of your efforts, and the refreshing beer you provided, I'll purchase a copy of *Crisis I* as soon as it comes out.

A: Really? I am happy to hear that. But next time let's find something else to talk about.

CHAPTER 6

Marx-Lexikon Crisis II

1   Part 1: Contents[1]

VIII. Moments that transform the possibility of crisis into reality

1. Capital's immanent drive is to raise the productive power of labour
   {83}   *Capital Vol. 1*
   'The surplus-value produced by prolongation ... cheapen the labourer himself'.
   (MECW–35, pp. 320–25)

2. With the advance of the productive power of labour, the organic composition of capital inevitably rises, resulting in a lowering of the profit rate
   {84}   *Grundrisse*
   'The general laws we have so far ... (E.g. in the United States.)'
   (MECW–29 pp. 130–32)
   {85}   *Capital Vol. 1*
   'Machinery produces relative ... but of the absolute surplus-labour'.
   (MECW–35, pp. 409–10)
   {86}   *Capital Vol. 1*
   'According to the economists themselves ... the advance of accumulation'.
   (MECW–35, pp. 616–18)
   {87}   *Capital Vol. 3*
   'If it is further assumed that this gradual ... rate must constantly fall'.
   (MECW–37, pp. 210–11)
   {88}   *Capital Vol. 3*
   'The law of the falling rate of profit ... for greater productivity of labour'.
   (MECW–37, p. 214)

---

1   [The table of contents and passage sources in *Marx Engels Collected Works* (MECW) for the second volume on crisis of *Marx-Lexikon zur politischen Ökonomie*, Kuruma 1973a (ed.).]

3. Even if the fall in the profit rate proceeds, the total quantity of profit can expand; not only can it expand, it must expand. But this expansion must surpass the rise in the organic composition of capital. This at the same time inevitably brings about the accumulation and concentration of capital

   {89} *Grundrisse*
   'The GROSS PROFIT i.e. the surplus value ... been consciously formulated'.
   (MECW-29, pp. 132–33)

   {90} *Capital Vol. 1*
   'But, if the progress of accumulation lessens ... formerly employed by it'.
   (MECW-35, pp. 618–23)

   {91} *Capital Vol. 3*
   'The law of the progressive falling ... decrease in the rate of profit'.
   (MECW-37, pp. 214–23)

   {92} *Capital Vol. 3*
   'A fall in the rate of profit and accelerated ... with the rate of profit'.
   (MECW-37, p. 240)

   {93} *Capital Vol. 3*
   'If a certain rate of profit is given ... alongside the centripetal one'.
   (MECW-37, pp. 243–45)

   {94} *Theories of Surplus Value*
   'First, however, a few observations ... cent) yields a total profit of 12'.
   (MECW-32, pp. 170–72)

   {95} *Theories of Surplus Value*
   'What Jones says first of all ... a silver spoon in his mouth'.
   (MECW-33, pp. 366–69)

4. The moments within the accumulation process of capital that are in opposition cannot be considered (as Ricardo did) as existing quietly side by side. They contain a contradiction, and this manifests itself as contradictory tendencies and phenomena. Periodically the collision of the conflicting factors seeks to clear itself in crisis

   {96} *Capital Vol. 3*
   'The development of the social ... and on a more formidable scale'.
   (MECW-37, pp. 245–48)

5. If in the progression of accumulation, the fall in the profit rate is not compensated for by the quantity of profit, an absolute overproduction of capital will arise. The fall in the profit rate is not due to competition arising as a result of the overproduction of capital. Rather, conversely, the fall in the profit rate and the overproduction of capital occur simultaneously, so that the competitive struggle begins from that point. The competitive struggle of course leads to a temporary rise in wages, which makes the profit rate temporarily fall further. How is this conflict to be resolved? How are the relations corresponding to a 'healthy' movement of capitalist production to be restored?

   {97} *Capital Vol. 3*
   'A drop in the rate of profit is ... temporary fall of the rate of profit'.
   (MECW–37, pp. 249–55)

   {98} (note for {97}) *Capital Vol. 1*
   'Adam Smith has already ... governed by the products of his own hand'.
   (MECW–35, pp. 614–16)

   {99} *Capital Vol. 3*
   'If the rate of profit falls, there ... material conditions of production'.
   (MECW–37, pp. 257–58)

6. The overproduction of capital includes the overproduction of commodities. Periodically, too much means of labour and means of subsistence are produced to allow them to function as the means of exploitation of workers at a certain rate of profit. Too many commodities are produced to realise the surplus value contained in them, as well as the surplus value that constitutes a portion of that value, under the conditions of distribution and consumption posited by capitalist production, and to convert this into new capital, or to be able to carry out this process without constantly recurring explosions.

   {100} *Capital Vol. 3*
   'Given the necessary means ... those under which it is realised'.
   (MECW–37, pp. 242–43)

   {101} *Capital Vol. 3*
   'The same occurs when here ... its capitalistic, self-contradictory forms.
   (MECW–37, pp. 255–57)

   {102} *Capital Vol. 3*
   'Let us suppose that the whole ... society constituted their limit'.
   (MECW–37, pp. 482–83)

{103}   *Theories of Surplus Value*
        'Ricardo is of course theoretically right ... on Profits and Interest".)'
        (MECW-32, pp. 101–02)
{104}   *Theories of Surplus Value*
        'But the whole process of accumulation ... often violently, to even out'.
        (MECW-32, pp. 123–24)
{105}   *Theories of Surplus Value*
        'To the best of his knowledge, Ricardo ... commodities, but as capitalists'.
        (MECW-32, pp. 128–30)
{106}   *Theories of Surplus Value*
        'The word OVERPRODUCTION in itself ... basis of modern overproduction'.
        (MECW-32, pp. 156–58)
{107}   *Theories of Surplus Value*
        'The *overproduction of commodities* is denied ... nature of capitalist production'.
        (MECW-32, pp. 162–64)

7. The contradiction of the capitalist mode of production: The worker as the purchaser of commodities is important to the market, but as the seller of his commodity (labour power) there is a tendency to limit the price of his commodity to the minimum, etc.
   {108}   *Grundrisse*
           'In production based on slavery ... as worker is extinguished'.
           (MECW-28, pp. 345–49)
   {109}   *Capital Vol. 2*
           'In the manuscript the following note ... pertains to the next part'.
           (MECW-36, p. 315)

8. Critique of the so-called theory of underconsumption; i.e. the theory that explains crisis directly from the underconsumption of the working class
   {110}   *Grundrisse*
           'To what extent GLUT ... SYNONYMOUS WITH HIGH PROFITS'.
           (MECW-28, p. 344)
   {111}   *Capital Vol. 2*
           'It is sheer tautology ... harbinger of a coming crisis'.
           (MECW-36, pp. 409–10)

{112} *Theories of Surplus Value*
'The anonymous author ... essential secret of "GLUT"'.
(MECW–32, p. 252)

{113} *Theories of Surplus Value*
'"The very meaning of an increased ... secret basis of GLUT'.
(MECW–32, p. 309)

{114} *Anti-Dühring*
'But unfortunately the under-consumption ... did not exist before'.
(MECW–25, p. 272)

9. **The contradiction between the barriers of production that are peculiar to capital and the impulse of capital to drive production beyond every barrier of capital, when it develops to a certain point, reaches an extreme point of tension where it explodes in a periodic crisis**

{115} *Grundrisse*
'We have already seen, in the case ... limits: an endless process'.
(MECW–28, pp. 200–01)

{116} *Grundrisse*
'But since capital represents ... *simple composition* [of capital] *itself*'.
(MECW–28, pp. 259–60)

{117} *Grundrisse*
'Within the production process the ... society and production'.
(MECW–28, pp. 331–38)

{118} *Grundrisse*
'So far, we have in the ... barrier on production and commerce'.
(MECW–28, pp. 341–43)

{119} *Grundrisse*
'Capital as a *barrier to production* ... PRODUCTION AND POPULATION"'.
(MECW–28, pp. 341–42)

{120} *Grundrisse*
'To begin with: capital compels ... objectifies itself in values on the other'.
(MECW–28, pp. 349–51)

{121} *Grundrisse*
'Beyond a certain point, the development ... STATE OF SOCIAL PRODUCTION'.
(MECW–29, pp. 133–34)

{122} 'Results of the Direct Production Process'
'Admittedly, *'production for production's* ... an advantage for himself'.
(MECW-34, pp. 441–42)

{123} *Capital Vol. 2*
'Inasmuch as the period of ... disturbances in the money market'.
(MECW-36, pp. 355–56)

{124} *Capital Vol. 3*
'On the other hand, the rate ... its further development'. /
'Given the necessary means ... which it is realised'.
(MECW-37, p. 240 / pp. 242–43)

{125} *Capital Vol. 3*
'The contradiction, to put it ... corresponding social relations of production'.
(MECW-37, pp. 248–49)

{126} *Capital Vol. 3*
'On the other hand, the fall ... to exceed this immanent barrier'.
(MECW-37, p. 255)

{127} *Capital Vol. 3*
'The limitations of the capitalist ... material conditions of production'.
(MECW-37, pp. 257–58)

{128} *Capital Vol. 3*
'At any rate, it is but a requirement ... moves thus in a contradiction'.
(MECW-37, pp. 262–63)

{129} *Capital Vol. 3*
'A repeated turnover of commercial ... at the disposal of the former'.
(MECW-37, pp. 302–03)

{130} *Capital Vol. 3*
'The credit system appears as the main ... old mode of production'.
(MECW-37, pp. 438–39)

{131} *Capital Vol. 3*
'The industrial cycle is of ... capitalistic limits of the production process'.
(MECW-37, pp. 488–89)

{132}   *Capital Vol. 3*
        'As for the other portion of profit ... in forms that call forth a reaction'.
        (MECW-37, pp. 504–05)
{133}   *Capital Vol. 3*
        'This social character of capital is first ... of crises and swindle'.
        (MECW-37, pp. 601–02)
{134}   *Theories of Surplus Value*
        'When Ricardo says that ... characteristic of this mode of production'.
        (MECW vol. 32, pp. 149–50)
{135}   *Theories of Surplus Value*
        'The word *overproduction* in itself ... basic phenomenon in crises'.
        (MECW-32, pp. 156–57)
{136}   *Theories of Surplus Value*
        'It is the unconditional development ... basis of modern overproduction'.
        (MECW-32, pp. 157–58)
{137}   *Theories of Surplus Value*
        '*Sismondi* is profoundly conscious ... by developing poverty as well'.
        (MECW-32, pp. 247–48)
{138}   *Theories of Surplus Value*
        'At the same time, this reveals ... development of productivity impossible'.
        (MECW-32, p. 274)
{139}   *Theories of Surplus Value*
        'The author also admits ... slowly within its own *bornes*'.
        (MECW-32, pp. 309–10)

10. **Elasticity of the capitalist production process**
{140}   *Grundrisse*
        'It is very important to conceive ... expansion of the productive forces'.
        (MECW-29, pp. 11–12)
{141}   *Capital Vol. 1*
        'In the few remarks I have still ... not here further inquire into'.
        (MECW-35, pp. 453–54)
{142}   *Capital Vol. 1*
        'Although in all branches of ... growing productivity of labour'.
        (MECW-35, pp. 598–601)

{143}   *Capital Vol. 1*
'It has been shown in the course ... "revenue" of the wealthy'.
(MECW-35, pp. 604–06)

{144}   *Capital Vol. 1*
'But if a surplus labouring population ... condition of modern industry'.
(MECW-35, pp. 626–28)

{145}   *Capital Vol. 2*
'The entire advanced capital ... products is elastic and variable'.
(MECW-36, pp. 353–55)

{146}   *Capital Vol. 3*
'However (aside from the turnovers ... at the disposal of the former'.
(MECW-37, pp. 302–03)

{147}   *Capital Vol. 3*
'The credit system appears as the main ... old mode of production'.
(MECW-37, pp. 438–39)

11. **Role of commercial capital in driving production and overcoming consumption barriers**

{148}   *Grundrisse*
'*Thirdly*: With the separation ... from trade in the strict sense.)'
(MECW-28, pp. 86–7)

{149}   *Grundrisse*
'The separation of exchange into ... General fall or rise in prices'.
(MECW-28, pp. 134–35)

{150}   *A Contribution to the Critique of Political Economy*
'The separation of sale and purchase ... inherent contradictions *possible*'.
(MECW-29, p. 334)

{151}   *Capital Vol. 2*
'The only condition which the act ... reproductive process of capital'.
(MECW-36, pp. 81–3)

{152}   *Capital Vol. 3*
'However (aside from the turnovers ... prosperity to an abrupt end'.
(MECW-37, pp. 302–04)

12. The role of the credit system in driving the reproduction process and overcoming its capitalistic limitations. The inner limitations of capital are finally asserted in the form of crisis. The collapse of the credit system in a crisis appears as both the result of overproduction and at the same time as an exacerbating factor of the crisis.

{153} *Grundrisse*
'But, quite apart from the ... (*relativement*) outside that process'.
(MECW–28, p. 340)

{154} *Grundrisse*
'The whole *credit system*, and ... form he has placed his money'.
(MECW–28, p. 343)

{155} *Grundrisse*
'These limits to production ... underproduction as two periods'.
(MECW–29, p. 12)

{156} *Capital Vol. 3*
'The main damage, and that ... a real falling off in reproduction'.
(MECW–37, p. 253)

{157} *Capital Vol. 3*
'We have seen that Gilbart knew ... what credit can accomplish'.
(MECW–37, p. 404)

{158} *Capital Vol. 3*
'The credit system appears as the main ... of swindler and prophet'.
(MECW–37, pp. 438–39).

{159} *Capital Vol. 3*
'In the discussion of money ... interruption of production, etc. part'.
(MECW–37, p. 457)

{160} *Capital Vol. 3*
'However, in addition to this commercial ... the debacle takes place'.
(MECW–37, pp. 483–84)

{161} *Capital Vol. 3*
'It is self-evident that there ... it is less so in centres of production'.
(MECW–37, p. 489)

{162} *Capital Vol. 3*
'But if this new accumulation meets ... forms that call forth a reaction'.
(MECW–37, p. 505)

{163} *Capital Vol. 3*
'It is a basic principle of capitalist ... extreme cases as the sole relief.'
(MECW-37, pp. 513-14)

{164} *Capital Vol. 3*
'As long as the state of business ... have reached £4 to £5 million'.
(MECW-37, pp. 524-25)

{165} *Capital Vol. 3*
'Everybody acquainted with our ... drain of gold increases the crisis'.
(MECW-37, pp. 533-35)

{166} *Capital Vol. 3*
'We have also omitted from ... this bank money, in turn, into gold'.
(MECW-37, pp. 567-69)

{167} *Capital Vol. 3*
'The banking system, so far ... effective vehicles of crises and swindle'.
(MECW-37, pp. 601-02)

{168} *Theories of Surplus Value*
'These are the *formal possibilities* of ... yet the place to do it.)'
(MECW-32, pp. 144-45)

{169} *Theories of Surplus Value*
'The author also admits ... slowly within its own *bornes*'.
(MECW-32, pp. 309-10)

{170} Marx to Engels, 3 February 1851
'I shall now submit to ... aggravate an existing crisis, as in 1847'.
(MECW-38, pp. 274-75)

13. **The contradiction of capitalist production wherein the distribution relations that originally arise as the result of production become fixed to conversely enter production as a prerequisite that conditions production**

{171} *Theories of Surplus Value*
'The *rate of profit* falls because ... Crisis of labour and crisis of capital'.
(MECW-32, p. 146)

{172} *Theories of Surplus Value*
'Profit enters into the *production costs* ... of productivity impossible'.
(MECW-32, pp. 273-74)

{173} *Theories of Surplus Value*
'Thus two forms of surplus-value ... much forms of production'.
(MECW–32, pp. 477–78)

{174} *Theories of Surplus Value*
'Assuming that the production ... which it continually reproduces'.
(MECW–32, pp. 517–18)

14. **Moments within the development of capitalism that in some way prevent the contradictions of capitalist production from exploding in the form of crisis**

{175} *Grundrisse*
'In the *current price lists* ... actual community and universality'.
(MECW–28, pp. 97–8)

{176} *Grundrisse*
'HENCE THE HIGHEST ... developed.) (Similarly, monopolies.)'
(MECW vol. 28, pp. 134–35)

{177} *Capital Vol. 3*
'The chief means of reducing ... without effect on the rate of profit'.
(MECW–37, p. 75)

{178} *Capital Vol. 3*
'This fraudulent procedure remained ... become totally impracticable'.
(MECW–37, p. 407)

{179} *Theories of Surplus Value*
'A large part of constant capital ... these types of fixed capital'.
(MECW–32, p. 123)

2 Part 2: Discussion[2]

Aiming to correctly convey the essence of Marx's theory of crisis

A: *Crisis II* will be published soon. I think this volume could be said to contain the core content of the four volumes on crisis. The result seems a fitting *tour*

---

2 [Discussion published as an insert for the second volume on crisis of *Marx-Lexikon zur politischen Ökonomie*, Kuruma 1973b (ed.).]

de force achieved through your struggle to bring together the fruits of research conducted over many years. I would like to begin by asking what you struggled with most in editing this volume.

KURUMA: It certainly was a struggle, but I am not sure if this volume can be described as the culmination of my research. In any event, looking back, there are many points that I am dissatisfied with, and even now things that I would have liked to have changed had more time been available. As a result of all of your pleading, I got dragged into that interview for the magazine *Shūkan ekonomisuto* (Weekly Economist)[3] and ended up slacking off a bit near the end. That was partly my own fault, of course, but you all bear some responsibility too. [*Laughs.*]

A: Our sincerest apologies. [*Laughs.*] Leaving that aside, what points were particularly difficult in editing this volume?

KURUMA: The main problem stems from the attempt to create something systematic from published works and manuscripts that Marx did not write as part of a systematic theory of crisis, so the task may have been impossible from the outset. In creating the headings to organise the passages, problems always arose at some point. The challenge, at any rate, was to create a volume that would allow the reader to grasp the core of Marx's theory of crisis without falling into any gross errors.

B: In that sense, it must have been more difficult than editing *Crisis I*.

KURUMA: Yes, indeed. *Crisis I* was comparatively easy, with not so many things to worry about; whereas for *Crisis II*, just figuring out the overall structure was quite hard. We had to consider many options before arriving at the structure we ended up adopting. As you know, I sent all of the editors a number of different versions.

A: Yes, there were five in total.

C: Is the relatively long length of the headings related to this issue?

---

3 [In 1973, the magazine published a seven-part interview with Kuruma that ran from the 21 August issue to the 2 October issue, as part of an ongoing series titled *Shakai kagaku gōjū nen no shōgen* (Testimonies on Fifty Years of Social Science).]

KURUMA: Yes. A number of headings were quite long from the beginning, and they grew even longer in our struggle to make sure they would allow readers to grasp the basic content. Do you find that the headings are too long?

B: Personally, I think the length is appropriate. In fact, in some cases, they could have been a bit longer.

A: A German colleague who has been proofreading the German headings that appear in the *Marx-Lexikon* volumes said that the content was fine, but perhaps the headings were too long. However, the headings have special significance, as compared to those in an ordinary book. Moreover, the German headings are particularly important for non-Japanese readers who do not have access to the transcriptions of these discussions we are including as inserts.

E: The West German publishing firm Oberbaum Verlag will issue a German edition of *Marx-Lexikon* for Western Europe, but it will not include a translation of these editorial discussions. Is your German colleague connected to that company?

A: No, he is an East German, Hannes Skambraks, whose short article on *Marx-Lexikon* will be included in the insert for *Crisis II*. He was one of the MEGA editors for *Das Kapital* and *Theorien über den Mehrwert*.

B: How did he come to check the German headings for *Marx-Lexikon*?

A: He read the very first *Marx-Lexikon* volume on the topic of competition, back in 1969, I think. It was around the time the first of the two *Marx-Lexikon* volumes on method was about to be published. That led him to become interested in our project. He contacted Yoichi Murada, who is involved in the Japanese translation of the collected works of Marx and Engels, in order to request from him the latest *Marx-Lexikon* volumes. Hannes sent us some corrections he had made to the German translations of the headings in the volume on competition and offered to check the headings of subsequent volumes. So, starting from the third volume of *Marx-Lexikon*, we sent him the table of contents and asked him to revise anything that seemed unnatural. Since we only sent him the headings, without the passages quoted, there have been some revisions that we could not use because the changes did not correspond to the actual content, but he has been a tremendous help. And now he has also sent us that short article with his impressions of *Marx-Lexikon*.

***Crisis* I clarified the 'basis' for the realisation of the possibility of crisis**

A: Shall we begin our discussion? I would like to have 'B' first lay out for us the differences between *Crisis I* and *Crisis II*.

B: I think that an overview of the theory of crisis is provided in *Crisis* I through the passages under the headings 'Essential determination of crisis' and 'Method of crisis theory', while issues pertaining to the general abstract form of crisis that is common to all crises can be found under the heading titled 'Possibility of crisis that appears under commodity circulation'. Setting those three headings aside, then, it seems that the subsequent content of *Crisis I* is characterised by the heading titled 'Further development of the possibility of crisis under the circulation process of capital (abstract form of crisis acquires content determination in the circulation process of capital)'. In contrast to that, there is a heading in *Crisis II* titled: 'Moments that transform the possibility of crisis into reality.' My first question concerns the difference between the expression 'abstract form of crisis acquires content determination' and 'transform the possibility of crisis into reality'.

KURUMA: That point already is dealt with in *Crisis I* under Heading VI: 'Further development of the possibility of crisis under capital, and the development of the possibility of crisis into reality (Overview)'. If you read the passages under that heading, I think you will find that the issue of the abstract form of crisis acquiring content determination, and the issue of the potential being transformed into reality, are two separate dimensions. What is called the 'abstract form' or 'formal potential' of crisis lies within the commodity metamorphosis; or it could be described as the metamorphosis itself. The two moments of sale and purchase, which are the two complementary moments within the metamorphosis, diverge from each other and thus have the potential to be forcibly united. One example of this potential or form of crisis acquiring content determination is the split between the accumulation of the depreciation fund for fixed capital and the actual renewal of the fixed capital, or the accumulation of an investment fund and the act of investment, since both are cases where the formal split between C–M and M–C takes on new, additional content determination under the circulation process of capital.

C: Hold on a moment. In a passage from the second volume of *Theories of Surplus Value* that appears under the heading 'Method of crisis theory', and also under the heading 'Further development of the possibility of crisis under capital, and the development of the possibility of crisis into reality (Overview)', Marx writes:

To begin with therefore, in considering the reproduction process of capital (which coincides with its circulation) it is necessary to prove that the above forms are simply repeated, or rather, that only here they receive a content, a basis [*Grundlage*] on which to manifest themselves'.[4]

Moreover, with regard to the possibility of crisis that arises from the form of money as a means of payment, Marx writes that, 'capital may provide a much more concrete basis [*reale Grundlage*] for turning this possibility into reality'.[5] Can this 'basis [*Grundlage*]' be considered the same as 'content determination'?

KURUMA: I don't think that the two examples of 'basis' you refer to are exactly the same, but in any case, it can be said that forms acquire 'content determination' and through this are posited 'a basis on which to manifest themselves [*sich manifestieren*]' and a basis for 'potential to be actualised'.

C: Is this the same as the line where Marx says that, 'The process of reproduction and the basis [*Anlange*] for crisis which is further developed in it'?[6]

KURUMA: I think they are similar, although it seems to me that *Anlage* would be better translated as *soji* (groundwork) in Japanese than *kiso* (basis).[7] What is important, at any rate, in speaking of a 'basis' is that it is *nothing more than* a basis. Granted, in the case of individual capital, for both the depreciation fund for fixed capital and the accumulation fund, C–M and M–C are in fact split. However, if we think in terms of the total social capital, there can be agreement between the overall supply and demand. Not only can they be in agreement, but as long as we are considering the normal progression of the total social capital, that agreement is posited as a precondition. When clarifying how social reproduction is carried out (as in Part 3 of Book II of *Capital*), the question of how the two sides might fall out of agreement is not posed – and should not be posed. The actual overall reproduction process progresses in the midst of continual upheaval, of course, so if we look at investment in a particular facility, it will be more or less concentrated during a particular period, depending on a variety of circumstances, such as the discovery of new markets, invention

---

4 Marx 1989b, p. 140. [In passages {8} and {42} in *Crisis I*.]
5 Marx 1989b, p. 141. [In passages {8}, {42}, and {59} in *Crisis I*.]
6 Marx 1989b, p. 143. [In passages {8}, {42}, and {59} in *Crisis I*. Modified translation.]
7 [*Anlage* is translated as 'predisposition' in Marx 1989b.]

of new production methods, or the impact of war, etc. Thus, it is not the case that investment is regularly renewed every year, uniformly. This has important significance for the circular movement of capitalist reproduction but is not at issue in Part 3 of Book II of *Capital*.

C: Can the same be said of expanded reproduction?

KURUMA: Yes. For example, in considering expanded reproduction, the main question is how simple reproduction shifts to expanded reproduction, but in terms of the possibility of crisis acquiring content determination, as dealt with in *Crisis I*, what is important is that in this shift the previous proportion between Department I and Department II changes, and that Department I must expand first, so that this shift involves certain difficulties. In more general terms, if the rate of accumulation changes, then the proportion between the two departments must also change, and certain difficulties arise from this. If the accumulation rate is fixed, then the proportion between the departments is also constant. However, the rate of accumulation is determined by various factors and changes as a result. In a case where the accumulation rate falls precipitously, major problems can arise. Even if this possibility is explained in Part 3 of Book II of *Capital*, which might be described as the abstract form of crisis being posited with content determination, the issue of exactly what causes the rate of accumulation to change is not raised. That is basically the case for the abstract form of crisis acquiring content determination, whereas the transformation of potential into reality might be described as the main characteristic throughout *Crisis II*.

The crux of *Crisis II* is the 'living contradiction' that turns the possibility of crisis into a reality

KURUMA: What basically characterises *Crisis II* is that its core problem is the 'living contradiction [*lebendiger Widerspruch*]', which could be thought of as a 'lively' or 'active' contradiction. In other words, instead of a latent contradiction, we are dealing with a contradiction that is actively moving, with the opposing elements in actual conflicting motion. And once this has progressed to a certain point, an extreme tension arises that causes the contradiction to explode. This is the process at issue in *Crisis II*. The term 'living contradiction' appears in the following part of passage {120}:

> By its nature, therefore, it [capital] posits a barrier to labour and value-creation in contradiction to its tendency to expand them boundlessly.

And in as much as it both posits a barrier specific to itself, and on the other side equally drives over and beyond every barrier, it is the *living contradiction*.[8]

The tendency of capital to develop productive power absolutely is in contradiction with the capitalistic limits of production that stem from capital's nature. This is a sort of 'living contradiction' where, on the one hand, the limit is posited, while at the same time there is the impulse to go beyond it. What transforms the possibility of crisis into reality is precisely the contradiction of the capitalist mode of production as this sort of living contradiction. The central task for *Crisis II* is to pursue this process so as to elucidate the development of the contradiction that transforms the possibility of crisis into reality. – For *Crisis I*, in contrast, this 'living contradiction' is not yet posed as a problem.

What is the overall structure of *Crisis II*?

B: Does this mean that the core of *Crisis II* is Subheading 9 ('The contradiction between the barriers of production that are peculiar to capital and the impulse of capital to drive production beyond every limit of capital, when it develops to a certain point, reaches an extreme point of tension where it explodes in a periodic crisis')?

KURUMA: It is true that the passages under Subheading 9 bring things together, and in that sense could be considered the 'core', but it is not the case that the entire issue of the 'living contradiction' is dealt with there. In passages grouped under earlier subheadings, moments that constitute a living contradiction are frequently unfolded. The role of Subheading 9 was to provide a conclusion.

C: There are quite a lot of pages grouped under that subheading.

KURUMA: Yes, because Marx always had that perspective in mind when he was considering crisis. I tried to limit the page length as much as possible, but he wrote a great deal on that topic.

A: I have heard that at one point you intended to put that subheading at the beginning of the *Crisis II*.

---

8   Marx 1973b, p. 421. [Kuruma's emphasis.]

KURUMA: Yes. And I don't think that such a structure is without merit. But in that case, we would have had to first indicate the general way of thinking and then consider the concrete issue of the unfolding of the contradictions. The question comes down to what the soundest approach is. After taking various factors into consideration, we decided on the current structure.

E: When you say that Subheading 9 provides a conclusion, does that mean *Crisis II* is fundamentally brought to an end by the passages under that heading?

KURUMA: No, that's not the case. Certainly, Subheading 9 concludes the discussion up to that point, but Subheading 10, 11, and 12 – dealing, respectively, with the elasticity of the reproduction process, the role of commercial capital, and the credit system – are a sort of supplement to it. Such issues play a major role in propelling capital as it drives beyond its immanent barrier or seeks to expand its limits. It would have been difficult to indicate the relation of Subheading 9 to those other aspects if it had been moved to the beginning of the volume, which was one factor determining the current structure.

A: Since we are on the topic of structure, I have a question regarding the way *Crisis II* fits together as a whole. Is there any way to separate the subheadings in *Crisis II* into various groups according to their content?

KURUMA: Yes, I think the 14 subheadings under Heading VIII could be divided into around five main groups. Subheading 1 to 3 deal with the accumulation and concentration of capital that progresses as capital seeks to expand the quantity of profit to overcome the limit to itself from the tendential fall in the rate of profit that arises from capital's impulse to raise productive power. Next, the problems at issue in Subheading 4 and 5 concern how the process elucidated in the first three subheadings is not a peaceful advance, but rather encompasses a 'living contradiction' and therefore progresses through the conflicting operation of opposing factors. This group of subheadings also considers the necessity for the process to periodically explode as a crisis. Subheadings 6 to 8 deal basically with overproduction and the limits of consumption. Subheading 9 to 12 centre on what we just discussed regarding the contradiction between the impulse or tendency of capital and its limits (as a 'living contradiction'), and the breaking through, expansion, and advance of the internal contradictions that periodically explode as a crisis. Finally, Subheading 13 and 14 include passages that did not fit into the first 12 subheadings, with the content of each being clear, I think, from the title.

What did Marx mean by 'next part' (*nächsten Abschnitt*)?

C: You briefly explained Subheading 6 to 8. Among those three, it seems clear that Subheading 6 deals with the problem of overproduction and the consumption limits, and that Subheading 8 contains a criticism of underconsumption theories, but I cannot see why Subheading 7 merits a separate section. Given its content,[9] it seems that the passages grouped under this subheading could have been included as one aspect of the consumption limitation dealt with in Subheading 6.

KURUMA: Under Subheading 7 there is a passage from the *Grundrisse* and a famous passage from a note included in Book II of *Capital*. The latter is the source of the subheading's title. This could have been included in Subheading 6, as you just noted, but I thought it was worth drawing attention to the problem as another aspect of the issue of overproduction and consumption limits. Let me also mention here the relation between those two passages. The footnote is a sort of memo Marx jotted down, in which he writes: 'This however belongs rather to the next part [*nächsten Abschnitt*]'.[10] As for Marx's intention in writing 'the next part', it seems to me that the content he had in mind can be seen in passage {108}. In writing Part 2 of Book II of *Capital*, Marx may have recalled what he had written earlier, which is to say, the content of passage {108}, and then added the note as a reminder to himself. In any case, reading passage {108} gives us get a good idea of what Marx has in mind in passage {109}.

Bearing in mind the relation between the two passages also provides us with an important hint regarding the meaning of 'next part' in the note, which was addressed in the discussion on *Crisis I*. There is a view that Marx is referring to Part 3 of Book II of *Capital*, but in passage {108} Marx says that this problem is unfolded in more detail in relation to 'competition'. It could not be said that such a problem is dealt with by Marx in Part 3 of Book II of *Capital*. With

---

9   ['The contradiction of the capitalist mode of production: The worker as the purchaser of commodities is important to the market, but as the seller of his commodity (labour power) there is a tendency to limit the price of his commodity to the minimum, etc.']

10 Marx 1978, p. 391. [In the second manuscript for Book II of *Capital*, which we were able to read later, the corresponding passage reads: 'This whole matter, however, belongs to the next chapter' [*diese ganze Geschichte jedoch gehört erst in das nächste Kapitel*] (MEGA II/11, p. 208.20–21). What Marx is referring to by 'diese ganze Geschichte' may be not merely the content of the note Engels inserted in the published version of *Capital* but rather to the entire preceding passage. In his critique of Tomizuka (Chapter 16 of this book), Kuruma began to examine this issue. – T. Ōtani.]

regard to whether the 'next part' is referring to Part 3 of Book II of *Capital* or to Book III, my view is that it is probably the latter because even if that book's content does not correspond exactly to the 'competition between capitals' in the planned six-book 'critique of political economy', it does deal with many of the problems belonging to the realm of 'competition' as conceived by Marx around the time of the *Grundrisse*. But there is still the question of whether the entirety of what is written in passage {108} pertains to Book III, and it seems to me that there are parts of that passage that do not.

For capital, every 'limit' (*Grenze*) must be a 'barrier' (*Schranke*)

B: Moving forward a bit, I wanted to ask about the term 'barrier' used in the expression 'barriers of production that are peculiar to capital' in Subheading 9. Professor Kuruma, you often talk about 'limit' (*Grenze*) and 'barrier' (*Schranke*).[11] And in Subheading 9 there seems to be a distinction between the two. Does Marx always make a clear distinction between the two?

KURUMA: I think that in the *Grundrisse* there is a clear distinction between the two terms that is easy to understand, as can be seen if you carefully read the passages from the *Grundrisse* under Subheading 9 with this in mind. In *Capital* and *Theories of Surplus Value* the distinction is not so clearly drawn, and in many cases only the term *Schranke* (barrier) is used. However, if we read those works while bearing in mind the distinction made in the *Grundrisse*, I think the matter will become clear in many cases. The term 'barrier' naturally presupposes the term 'limit', so I think that when 'barrier' alone appears in a passage, we can understand that 'limit' is contained within it as the premise.

B: Hegel seems to have drawn a clear distinction between 'limit' and 'barrier.'

---

11 [In his 'Translator's Remarks on Terminology' for the English edition of Rosa Luxemberg's *The Accumulation of Capital*, Nicholas Gray provides the following explanation of the distinction between the two terms: '*Grenze* and *Schranke*: German has two words that can ordinarily be translated into English as "limit" – *Grenze* and *Schranke*. In his speculative philosophy, Hegel makes a distinction between these two terms: a *Grenze* is a limit (or boundary, border, endpoint) that defines a finite entity qualitatively or quantitatively, whereas a *Schranke* implies a barrier, restriction or limitation that is, or ought, to be overcome (a cognate of *Schranke* is *beschränken*, "to restrict"). In Hegel's speculative idealism, the movement of spirit is ultimately infinite, insofar as it overgrasps (*übergreift*) other entities and finds itself at home in them: in this movement, the restrictions or confines of finitude are overcome' (Luxemburg 2016a, p. 3).]

KURUMA: I remember that 'D' pointed this out, but I don't recall the details about how Hegel drew that distinction. Perhaps he could clarify this for us?

D: I'm not such great a student of Hegel and it's a bit hard for me to explain, but I could at least mention what I said to Professor Kuruma before.

A: Sure, go ahead.

D: According to Hegel, 'the finite' (*das Endliche*) always has a 'limit' (*Grenze*) as well as an 'end' (*Ende*). Hegel says that 'Something only is what it is *within* its limit and *by virtue* of its limit',[12] and the 'limit' of a thing is its essential nature, its internal determination. Of course, whether the term is 'limit' or 'determination' it is only a limit or determination in relation to some other thing. In other words, the term 'limit' or 'barrier' means that contained within the given thing is the moment of its negation. Incidentally, when that moment of negation within the thing itself is something that develops, the moment comes to overcome the limit of the thing. Hegel uses the term *sollen* (ought) to refer to this thing within the thing itself that is its negation and seeks to overcome the limit. He says that from the standpoint of *sollen*, or in relation to it, the limit of the thing becomes a 'barrier' or a 'restriction'. This relation is the self-contradiction of the thing, and because of this self-contradiction, the finite thing overcomes the restriction to become another finite thing with a new limit. In other words, the finite (*das Endlich*) meets its end (*Ende*) and is extinguished. Hegel points to living, sentient, organic beings as an example of things that contain within themselves moments seeking to overcome their own internal limits, but I think that what I am talking about here is in fact an explanation of the dialectical contradiction that is the motive force of a thing's movement.

B: Do you think that Marx could be said to have inherited this way of thinking?

D: Marx did not make use of the concept of *sollen* in relation to a barrier, so it cannot be said that he simply takes over Hegel's idea, but it does seem fairly certain that he took over the idea of limit, barrier, contradiction, the finite, etc.

B: Is that point made clear in any passages in the second *Crisis II*?

---

12   Hegel 1991, p. 148.

D: As Professor Kuruma noted, Marx clearly distinguishes between 'limit' and 'barrier' in the *Grundrisse*. Examples of the clear distinction made include passage {70}[13] in the second *Marx-Lexikon* volume on the materialist conception of history,[14] as well as the following two passages from *Crisis II*:

> However, as representative of the general form of wealth – money – capital is the *endless and limitless drive to go beyond its limiting barrier. Every boundary [Grenze] is and has to be a barrier [Schranke] for it.*[15]

> But from the fact that capital posits every such *limit* as a *barrier* and hence gets ideally beyond it, it does not by any means follow that it has really overcome it, and, since every such *barrier contradicts its character*, its production moves in contradictions which are constantly overcome but just as constantly posited. Furthermore. The *universality towards which it irresistibly strives encounters barriers in its own nature*, which will, at a certain stage of its development, allow it to be recognised as being itself the greatest barrier to this tendency, and hence will drive towards its own suspension.[16]

In *Capital*, the distinction between 'limit' and 'barrier' is not as clearly made, but even there the concept of 'barrier' is fundamentally used in the same way as in the *Grundrisse*, as can be seen in passages from Book III under Subheading 9:

> Thus economists like Ricardo, who take the capitalist mode of production as an absolute, feel here that this mode of production *creates a barrier for itself* and seek the source of this barrier not in production but rather in nature (in the theory of rent). The important thing in their horror at the falling rate of profit is the feeling that *the capitalist mode of production comes up against a barrier to the development of the productive forces which has nothing to do with the production of wealth as such*; but this characteristic barrier in fact testifies to the restrictiveness and the solely historical and transitory character of the capitalist mode of production; it bears witness that this is not an absolute mode of production for the

---

13   Marx 1973, pp. 649–52.
14   Kuruma 1971b (ed.).
15   Marx 1973, p. 334. [In passage {116} in *Crisis II*. Speaker's emphasis.]
16   Marx 1973, p. 410. [In passage {117} in *Crisis II* Speaker's emphasis.]

production of wealth but actually comes into conflict at a certain stage with the latter's further development.[17]

The *true barrier to capitalist production is capital itself*. It is that capital and its self-valorisation appear as the starting and finishing point, as the motive and purpose of production; production is production only for capital, and not the reverse, i.e. the means of production are not simply means for a steadily expanding pattern of life for the society of the producers. The barriers within which the maintenance and valorisation of the capital-value has necessarily to move – and this in turn depends on the dispossession and impoverishment of the great mass of the producers – therefore *come constantly into contradiction with* the methods of production that capital must apply to its purpose and which set its course towards an *unlimited expansion of production*, to production as an end in itself, to an *unrestricted development of the social productive powers of labour*. The *means* – the unrestricted development of the forces of social production – comes into persistent conflict with the *restricted end*, the valorisation of the existing capital. If the capitalist mode of production is therefore a *historical means* for developing the material powers of production and for creating a corresponding world market, it is at the same time the *constant contradiction* between this *historical task* and the *social relations of production* corresponding to it.[18]

B: With regard to the 'historical task' in the passage just quoted, can the creation of a world market in response to the development of material productive power be seen as corresponding to Hegel's *sollen*?

D: Marx thought that it was the 'historical task [*Aufgabe*]' of the capitalist mode of production to create a high level of material productive power that becomes the basis for a new mode of production. In addition to passage {125} cited above, there is passage {127} in *Crisis II*, where Marx notes that, 'The development of the productive forces of social labour is capital's historic mission [*Aufgabe*] and justification [*Berechtigung*]',[19] as well as passage {130}, where he says that the 'credit system hence accelerates the material development of the productive forces and the establishment of the world market, which it is the

---

17   Marx 1981a, p. 350. [In passage {124} in *Crisis II*. Speaker's emphasis.]
18   Marx 1981a, pp. 358–9. [In passage {125} in *Crisis II*. Speaker's emphasis.]
19   Marx 1981a, p. 368.

historical task [*Aufgabe*] of the capitalist mode of production to bring to a certain level of development, as material foundations for the new form of production'.[20] Also in Book III of *Capital*, although it is not included in *Crisis II*, there is a passage where Marx says that the 'historical mission' of the capitalist mode of production 'is ruthlessly to expand the productivity of human labour'.[21] Marx said that for this 'historical task' of the capitalist mode of production, the mode of production itself becomes a barrier, and from this perspective, he saw the historical contingency of this mode of production, its temporary and transitional character, and therefore the necessity of its sublation. The perspective for grasping this sort of 'historical task' is of course a higher perspective than that of capitalist production; in other words, a perspective that is within capitalism and at the same time negates it, so in terms of this point it correlates to the perspective of Hegel's *sollen*.

But if I may add my own opinion: When Marx spoke of 'barriers' in relation to crisis, he was not saying that we would arrive at socialism the moment the barriers were overcome. As he notes in {125}, the contradiction between the 'historical task' of capital and the capitalistic contradiction is a constant (*beständig*) contradiction. The impulse of capital in seeking to develop productive power expands the various barriers or drives beyond them to advance production, but ultimately the barrier penetrates so that a crisis arises to bring things back to within that framework – and this is repeated periodically. This is the relation denoted by Marx's use of the term *barrier*. I think that he is dealing with the contradiction from the perspective that Professor Kuruma calls a 'living contradiction', but that is not Hegel's view, at least as far as *sollen* and *Schranke* are concerned. In any case, that is the decisively important point with regard to crisis, so I don't think we have to be overly concerned about what Hegel thought.

Marx's 'fundamental contradiction' and Engels's 'fundamental contradiction'

C: What can be said about the relation between the 'living contradiction' that you discussed and the so-called 'fundamental contradiction (*Grundwiderspruch*) of capitalism'.

---

20   Marx 1981a, p. 572.
21   Marx 1981a, p. 371. [The description in the passage quoted comes at the end of a part that Engels placed in parentheses because, he explains, 'it is re-edited from a note in the original manuscript', but no such note can be found in the relevant part of the first manuscript for Book III of *Capital* that the MEGA editors suppose Engels relied on. – T. Ōtani.]

KURUMA: Are you referring to Engels's use of the expression the 'fundamental contradiction' of capitalism'?

C: That's right. I was thinking of his notion of the contradiction between the social character of production and the private capitalistic character of appropriation. Many books on the theory of crisis have sought the necessity of crisis in this contradiction or in its development. In what way does this coincide or differ from what you spoke of earlier?

KURUMA: I think that Engels in *Anti-Dühring* and in *Socialism: Utopian and Scientific* spoke of the 'fundamental contradiction' (*Grundwiderspruch*).

C: Yes. Prior to the final paragraph of *Socialism: Utopian and Scientific*, Engels inserts a summary of his argument up to that point, in which he notes the 'fundamental contradiction, whence arise all the contradiction in which our present-day society moves, and which modern industry brings to light'.[22] The concept of the contradiction referred to here as the 'fundamental contradiction' was already developed in *Anti-Dühring* but it was in *Socialism: Utopian and Scientific* that Engels first used that specific term.

KURUMA: Marx also used the term 'fundamental contradiction'. For instance, we can point to the following two passages in *Crisis II* from the *Grundrisse* and *Theories of Surplus Value*:

> It is enough here to demonstrate that capital contains a *particular restriction of production* – which contradicts *its general tendency* to drive beyond every barrier to production – in order to have uncovered the foundation of *overproduction*, the fundamental contradiction [*Grundwiderspruch*] of developed capital [*entwickeltes Kapital*]; in order to have uncovered, more generally, the fact that capital is not, as the economists believe, the *absolute* form for the development of the forces of production.[23]

> He [Sismondi] is particularly aware of the fundamental contradiction [*Grundwiderspruch*]: on the one hand, *unrestricted development of the productive power* and *increase of wealth* which, at the same time, consists of commodities and must be turned into cash; on the other hand,

---

22 Engels 1994, p. 73.
23 Marx 1973a, p. 415. [In passage {118} in *Crisis II*. Kuruma's emphasis.]

the system is based [*Grundlage*] on the fact that *the mass of producers is restricted to the necessaries.*[24]

In both passages, Marx's use of the term of 'fundamental contradiction' differs from that of Engels. In the case of Engels, the 'social character of production' refers to production carried out on a social scale or large-scale production, in contrast to the small-scale individual production prior to capitalist production.

E: Isn't there also a view of the 'social character of production' not in terms of large-scale production but rather as the combination of producers via the social division of labour?

KURUMA: I'm not sure about that point. At least in the case of *Socialism: Utopian and Scientific* such an idea does not appear. Marx at times expressed a similar idea to Engels, by the way, such as in the following passage from *Theories of Surplus Value*:

> And if we strip this fact of the contradictory character which, on the basis of capitalist production, is typical of it, what does this fact, this trend towards centralisation, indicate? Only that production loses its private character and becomes a social process, *not formally – in the sense that all production subject to exchange is social because of the absolute dependence of the producers on one another and the necessity for presenting their labour as abstract social labour* ([*by means of*] *money*) – but in actual fact. For the means of production are employed as communal, social means of production and therefore not [determined] by [the fact that they are] the property of an individual, but by their relation to production, and the labour likewise is performed on a social scale.[25]

I think we can see from this that the view presented by 'E' is not correct. That is, the social character of production means that the production process has become social, and this then constitutes an indispensable condition for the development of the productive power of social labour. In this sense, the 'social character of production' is a corollary of the tendency of capital to pursue the absolute development of productive power, so that both can be seen as an expression of the aspect of productive power.

---

24 Marx 1989b, p. 248. [In passage {137} in *Crisis II*. Kuruma's emphasis.]
25 Marx 1991a, p. 368. [In passage {95} in *Crisis II*. Kuruma's emphasis.]

Meanwhile, if the 'private, capitalistic character of appropriation' is thought of in terms of appropriation as the concentrated expression of the capitalist production relations that aim for valorisation, then this can also be seen as representing the particular restriction of capitalist production. To that extent, it does not differ completely from Marx's understanding of the 'fundamental contradiction' and could be described as a different expression of the same contradiction. But in Engels's manner of speaking, a 'fundamental contradiction' does not express a 'living contradiction' and therefore is not directly linked to periodic crises.

The same content that corresponds to what Engels called the 'contradiction between socialised production and capitalistic appropriation'[26] was described by Marx as the 'cardinal facts about capitalist production' (although unlike Engels he did not label this the 'fundamental contradiction of capitalism'). Marx uses that expression in passages {67}[27] and {68} in the second *Marx-Lexikon* volume on the 'materialist conception of history',[28] and I would like to quote from the latter, which is taken from *Theories of Surplus Value*:

> Two cardinal facts about capitalist production: [First,] concentration of the means of production in a few hands so that they no longer appear as the immediate property of the individual labourer, but as factors of social production, even though in the first instance they appear as the property of the non-working capitalists, who are their trustees in bourgeois society and enjoy all the fruits of this trusteeship. Second: Organisation of labour itself as social labour brought about by cooperation, division of labour and the linking of labour with the results of social domination over natural forces. In both these ways, capitalist production eliminates private property and private labour, even though as yet in antagonistic forms.[29]

As we can see from the passage quoted, Marx is emphasising the 'cardinal facts' not in relation to periodic crises but rather to the historical mission of the capitalist mode of production, in terms of paving the way, in a contradictory manner, to a more advanced form of socialist production. I think that it can be said, at least in relation to periodic crises, that Marx's usage of 'fundamental contradiction' is more direct and appropriate than Engels's usage. It seems to me that, according to Engels's way of grasping the problem, capitalism has two con-

---

26   Engels 1994, p. 59.
27   Marx 1981a, p. 375.
28   Kuruma 1971b (ed.).
29   Marx 1991a, pp. 342–43.

flicting characteristics, and along with the development of capitalism each of the two becomes more conspicuous, so that the contradiction is increasingly heightened. But, even if he clarifies this contradiction, the two characteristics do not appear as a living contradiction. That is my opinion, in any case.

The *barrier* of capitalist production and the *barrier* of the consumption of the producing masses

C: Was Marx using the term 'fundamental contradiction' in the same way in both of the passages you quoted earlier?

KURUMA: What do you mean?

C: Well, in the second passage he contraposes the 'unrestricted development of the productive power' to the fact that the 'mass of producers is restricted to the necessaries'. This seems to concern the so-called 'consumption limit of the working masses'. Marx also speaks of the 'restricted consumption of the masses' in a famous passage from Book II of *Capital* where he proposes the 'ultimate foundation (*Grund*) of crisis' in the following way:

> The ultimate reason for all real crises always remains the poverty and restricted consumption of the masses, in the face of the drive of capitalist production to develop the productive forces as if only the absolute consumption capacity of society set a limit to them.[30]

Quite a few passages in *Crisis II* seem to make this same basic point. Is this idea the same as the 'particular restriction of production' mentioned in the first passage you quoted, or the same as what you spoke of generally as the immanent barriers of capitalist production?

KURUMA: Marx drew a distinction between the (singular) 'barrier' or 'restriction' of capitalist production, generally speaking, and the (plural) 'barriers' or 'restrictions'; and I think that when he is speaking of the barrier in general it could be thought that the restricted consumption of the producing masses constitutes one of its moments; whereas in the case of barriers, in the plural, it can be said that the restricted consumption of the producing masses is one of the barriers.

---

30 Marx 1981a, p. 615. [Passage {102} in *Crisis II*.]

This probably goes without saying, but in the first of the two passages quoted from Marx, he speaks of the 'particular restriction on production', while in the later he speaks of how the 'mass of producers is restricted to necessaries', and terrible confusion will arise if one were to carelessly think that meaning of 'restrict' is the same in both; and I have in fact encountered such views. So, to avoid such confusion, it should be noted that in the former case 'restriction' is being used in the sense that capital is a particular factor that limits the free development of production. In contrast, 'restriction' in the latter case signifies that the consumption of the producing masses is limited to the goods necessary to sustain their lives. Thus, in that latter case, the restriction – the restriction of the consumption of the producing masses – is thought of as one of the factors within the restriction by capital of the free development of production. Conversely, if the aim of production were to raise the standard of living for the producing masses, crises appearing in the form of overproduction would not be possible. But in reality, production is carried out for capitalists to obtain profit and is not intended to raise the standard of living. Thus, even though the consumption needs of the producing masses are not fully met, crises arise, manifested as a surplus of products in the form of commodities. And so, the consumption restriction of the producing masses can be said to be one condition of crisis because, if it did not exist, a crisis of overproduction certainly could not arise. However, that is not a positive and active factor in motion when a crisis occurs; i.e. it is not a cause of crisis. This should be clear from the fact that even though there is always a restriction on consumption as long as capitalism continues to exist, crisis only occurs periodically. As Marx points out, it is not the case that crises are always in existence, but rather that they are periodic. If one thought of the restriction on consumption as the active factor of crisis, believing that crises occur because wages are low, one would fall into the mistaken underconsumption theory of crisis. The error of this theory is clear just from the fact that immediately prior to a crisis, at the peak of prosperity, wages rise to a higher-than-normal level, so that the consumption of the workers is higher than usual. Thus, the restriction on the consumption of the working masses is a condition for crisis manifested as overproduction, but it is not a factor that is actively in movement. What is the active factor, then? Marx always points to another moment that is in relation to the production barrier peculiar to capital as the active factor that transforms the possibility of crisis into reality. This is the general tendency of capital to advance despite that restriction, seeking to overcome it, as referred to in the passage quoted earlier. The tendency is manifested directly as the impulse of capital to seek as much profit as possible, but ultimately, via the competition between capitals, it is manifested as the tendency of capital to develop productive power to the greatest extent possible. When this tendency breaks through the original barriers under the impetus of various moments so as to progress to a certain point, it brings the tension of the contradiction to such an extreme that it explodes as a crisis. This is the fundamental thinking underlying Marx's theory of crisis, and I think we can view Chapter 15 of Book III of *Capital* ('Development of the Law's Internal Contradictions'), as the place where we can see how Marx sought to clarify the moments through which capital seeks to overcome its internal barriers, given its tendency to pursue the unrestricted development of productive power.

C: As you pointed out, in dealing with the production restrictions specific to capital, Marx speaks of the 'barrier' or 'restriction' in the singular as well as 'barriers' or 'restrictions' in the plural, but in any case, I don't think we can come across passages where he exhaustively lists up all of the particular barriers of capitalist production. What does often appear in his writings are references to the 'consumption restriction of the producing masses' that we have discussing (which more precisely can be described as the barrier on capitalist production due to the restriction of the consumption of the producing masses) and sometimes, along with this, references to the 'barrier set up by ... profit'.[31] I think a question that naturally arises is the nature of the relation between these two problems. What are your thoughts on this?

KURUMA: As for the 'barrier set up by ... profit', I think that the meaning can be understood if we carefully consider the context in which the expression is used, whereas it can be misunderstood if treated on its own. So, for the sake of those unfamiliar with the subject, let me introduce the passage in which Marx clearly explains the meaning:

> The barrier [*die Schranke*] to the capitalist mode of production shows itself as follows:
> (1) in the way that the development of labour productivity involves a law, in the form of the falling rate of profit, that at a certain point confronts this development itself in a most hostile way and has constantly to be overcome by way of crises;
> (2) in the way that it is the appropriation of unpaid labour, and the proportion between this unpaid labour and objectified labour in general – to put it in capitalist terms, profit and the proportion between this profit and the capital applied, i.e. a certain rate of profit – it

---

31 Marx 1989b, pp. 157–8. [In passages {106} and {136} in *Crisis II*.]

is this that determines the expansion or contraction of production, instead of the proportion between production and social needs, the needs of socially developed human beings. Barriers to production, therefore, arise already at a level of expansion which appears completely inadequate from the other standpoint. Production comes to a standstill not at the point where needs are satisfied, but rather where the production and realisation of profit impose this.[32]

If we read this passage carefully, not only does the meaning of the 'barrier set up by ... profit' become clear, but at the same time the relation between it and the 'consumption restriction of the mass of producers' is also elucidated.

E: It seems to me that there are relatively few theories of crisis that emphasise the 'living contradiction' that you have spoken of between the impulse of the development of productive power and the limitations of capitalist production. Of course, there are various ways that this idea might be expressed. If we look at your book *An Investigation of Crisis Theory*, this perspective was not yet clearly indicated in the 1949 and 1953 editions, but in your 1962 article 'A Few Problems Concerning Postwar Theories of Crisis'[33] that was included in the 1965 edition, you first indicated that the contradiction is the fundamental perspective from which to grasp crisis and the industrial cycle. And here again, in *Crisis II*, you adopt that unique way of framing the problem. At what point did you begin to adopt this viewpoint?

KURUMA: I realised how important this is to a theory of crisis when I read the *Grundrisse* after the war. Then, when I reread *Capital* and *Theories of Surplus Value*, I could understand well that this perspective of 'barrier' and 'limit' is playing an extremely important role, along with the 'accumulation and explosion of contradictions' and the 'restoration of the unity of moments that had become independent', which I had emphasised up to that point, so I began to copy passages related to this viewpoint on notecards. That was in the early 1950s. Kiyoshi Ōshima used those notecards to write his article 'The Barrier of Capitalist Production and Crisis',[34] published in *Problems of Political Economy*,[35] and I also relied on the notecards when editing *Crisis II*.

---

32 Marx 1981a, p. 367. [In passage {127} in *Crisis II*.]
33 Kuruma 1965, pp. 221–41. [In Chapter 14 of this book.]
34 Ōshima 1957.
35 Ōuchi and Morito, eds., 1957.

C: It was just mentioned by 'E' that not many works on crisis theory emphasise that contradiction, but aren't there quite a few works that emphasise the 'consumption restrictions of the masses' or the 'contradiction between production and consumption'?

E: That's true enough, but viewing what opposes the impulse for developing productive power as 'barriers' and then grasping this as a 'living contradiction', in the manner spoken of by Professor Kuruma, is quite different from reducing the oppositional factor to the 'restriction on consumption'.

KURUMA: I'm not familiar with what people are writing these days, and I have forgotten about things that I read some time ago, but I would not deny the importance of the contradiction between the tendency toward the unrestricted development of productive power and the restricted consumption of the working class. However, as I said earlier, I think there is a need to clearly position this contradiction within the unfolding of the 'living contradiction' between the tendency of the development of productive power and the barriers arising from the aim of valorisation. Subheading VIII in *Crisis II* contains passages criticising the theory of underconsumption, but I think that theory (very generally speaking) arises from detaching the problem of the restricted consumption of the working class (which is an important problem in itself) from the 'living contradiction'.

Why does the term 'moments' appear in Heading VIII?

B: From the discussion so far, I can understand well the reason for Professor Kuruma placing particular emphasis on the 'living contradiction'. I have another question that seems related to what was just asked now. My question concerns Heading VIII, under which are gathered all the subheadings in *Crisis II*. The heading's title is 'Moments that transform the possibility of crisis into reality' (although the German heading might be directly translated as 'Moments through which the possibility of crisis becomes reality'[36]). I can basically understand what the passages under this heading deal with from the comments made by Professor Kuruma thus far, but I would like to know why the term 'moments' appears in its title. Couldn't the term 'conditions' or 'causes' have been used instead?

---

36 ['Momente, wodurch die Möglichkeit der Krise zur Wirklichkeit wird'.]

KURUMA: I think the term 'conditions' could be used instead of 'moments'; but I preferred to use 'moments' instead because it expresses the interrelation between them and the specific role of each in actualising a form – whereas 'conditions' implies a separateness.

D: Does that mean that each of the 14 subheadings grouped under Heading VIII can be seen as an individual moment, or are there various moments within each subheading?

KURUMA: There are cases where a subheading expresses a particular moment. For example, the first subheading deals with the inherent impulse of capital to raise the productive power of labour. Other examples include Subheading 10 on the elasticity of reproduction, Subheading 11 on the role of commercial capital, and Subheading 12 on the role of the credit system. Each of those three subheadings is a moment for breaking through a capitalistic barrier or expanding the barrier itself. However, not every subheading represents a specific moment. The expression 'moments that transform' in the heading title was used in a very comprehensive sense, as I mentioned.

B: Why does the page header in Japanese have the full title of VIII, whereas the page header on the opposite German page is simply *Ursache der Krise* (factors of crisis)?

KURUMA: By positioning each of the moments in an organic relation to the whole and clarifying them as such, it becomes clear why the form of the possibility of crisis moves from being a possibility to a reality, so when we think of these moments as things that are moving as a totality toward actualisation it becomes possible to speak of the 'cause of crisis'. We tried to come up with a page header for VIII that was as compact as possible and considered various options, but it turned out to be quite difficult. But the German *Ursache der Krise* seemed to work rather well with regard to content, so it ended up that the page headers differed between the two languages.

Why wasn't the problem of the 'necessity of crisis' posed?

B: Now I have a better understanding of the meaning of Heading VIII, 'Moments that transform the possibility of crisis into reality', but I have another question related to the choice of that title. In conventional works on crisis theory, rather than that sort of heading title one often finds headings about the 'necessity of crisis'. I'm curious why, instead of that more common expression, you chose the more unusual expression 'moments that transform the possibility of crisis into reality'?

KURUMA: The basic reason we did not use 'necessity of crisis' as the heading is that Marx himself, to the best of my knowledge, never used that expression. It was natural, from the perspective of the basic aim of *Marx-Lexikon*, to avoid using expressions that Marx himself had not used, particularly for a major heading.

B: I see. That makes sense as for why the 'necessity of crisis' was not chosen, but I wonder why it is that this expression is used so often in works on crisis theory. What are your thoughts regarding this?

KURUMA: Actually, I would like to ask those who *have* used the expression the 'necessity of crisis' to explain why, if their aim was to elucidate Marx's theory of crisis, they have chosen an expression that he did not use, particularly in the case of a title for an important heading. I'm also curious about the exact meaning of 'necessity' in that expression. Without clarifying those points, it is a bit difficult for me to provide a simple answer to your question.

B: As far as I am aware, no reasons have been given to explain why the expression 'necessity of crisis' has been used as a heading despite Marx never using the expression himself. It seems that there is an accepted idea that it is natural within a theory of crisis to speak of the 'necessity of crisis'. I also think that there has not been any clear account of the exact meaning of 'necessity'.

C: Although it isn't a book on crisis theory, there was a review of *Marx-Lexikon* in the March 1973 issue of the journal *Keizai hyōron* (Economic Critique), in which by Tetsu Yoshikawa argues that 'this new structure [in *Marx-Lexikon*] is directly related to the Marxian definition of the *philosophical categories of potential, actuality, and necessity*.' He then adds:

> It is interesting that Professor Kuruma uses the expression 'development of potential' but does not use the term 'necessity', either as a concept corresponding to potential or as a concept that excludes potential and its development. However, establishing the heading 'Moments that trans form the possibility of crisis into reality', in distinction from the heading titled 'Further development of the potential' gives rise to the problem of the nature of the relation between the form of this possibility and the

> *demonstration of its necessity* (=transformation into actuality) through grasping the form's foundation or basis.[37]

Yoshikawa also writes:

> Doesn't it invite a careless misunderstanding and confusion into the explanation of *necessity as a strict categorical system* to use the expression of 'not being able yet to develop to the point of actuality' to explain the distinction and relation between the formal determination of the externalisation of the contradiction and the logic of the movement of development that should recur?[38]

Judging from these passages, Yoshikawa's *Voruteil* (preconceived notion) seems to be that within the system of Marx's theory of crisis, 'necessity' is naturally one of the indispensable philosophical terms along with 'possibility' and 'actuality', so it probably never even occurred to him to consider why Marx did not use the expression 'necessity of crisis'. If forced to speculate, I imagine that Yoshikawa would say that had Marx developed his theory of crisis systematically he would have established the heading of 'necessity of crisis'.

As for books seeking to systematically develop a theory of crisis that actually explain the significance of establishing a heading on the 'necessity of crisis', we can point to the rare example of *An Investigation into Crisis Theory* by Ryōzō Tomizuka.[39] In Chapter 2 ('Fundamental Structure of Crisis Theory within the System of *Capital*') within the book's Introductory Part ('Method and Structure of Crisis Theory'), there is Section 3, titled 'Necessity of crisis (transformation of the "possibility" of crisis into its "reality")', in which Tomizuka writes the following:

> I think it is necessary to proceed from the fundamental principles of capitalist accumulation when *showing the internal necessity through which the 'possibility' of crisis is transformed into 'reality', and* to demonstrate the *necessity of crisis rooted* in the essence of capitalist production in the sense of how 'capital itself becomes the barrier to capitalist production'.[40]

---

37 Yoshikawa 1973, pp. 216–7.
38 Yoshikawa 1973, p. 218.
39 Tomizuka 1965.
40 Tomizuka 1965, p. 31. [Speaker's emphasis.]

Incidentally, the meaning of 'necessity of crisis' in that section heading can be understood as equivalent to the 'transformation of the possibility of crisis into reality', but judging from what Tomizuka writes in the passage just quoted about 'showing the internal necessity through which the "possibility" of crisis is transformed into "reality"', what he calls the 'transformation of the possibility of crisis into reality' should more precisely be considered the *'necessity of the transformation'*, and I cannot really understand why he did not use that sort of description.

In Tomizuka's case, he uses the title 'Necessity of crisis (transformation of the "possibility" of crisis into "reality")' for the third and final section, following the first section 'General, abstract possibility of crisis (fundamental form of crisis)' and the second section 'Possibility of developed crisis (expansion of the content determination of latent crisis)'; all of which make up what he refers to as the 'fundamental structure of crisis theory within the logic of "capital in general" that is the standard for the organisational = logical structure of *Capital*'. It could be imagined he chose 'Necessity of crisis' as the main heading – even though the parenthetical 'Transformation of the "possibility" of crisis into "reality"' would have made the relation to the other two sections clearer – in order to elucidate his critical attitude toward the opinion that negated the necessity of crisis as the manifestation of the 'immanent contradiction' in the original sense that is rooted in the formal determinacy of capitalist production, instead of grasping the 'immanent contradiction' of crisis in its internal necessity as the 'explosion of the internal contradictions of capitalistic production'.[41]

KURUMA: Of the two views just introduced, I'm particularly interested that Yoshizuka deals with 'necessity' as a philosophical category, but since this is outside the range of Marx's theory of crisis dealt with in *Marx-Lexikon* I won't comment on his view here. As for Tomizuka, while I understand his desire to adopt a critical standpoint toward the theories of crisis presented within modern economics [*kindai keizaigaku*],[42] I don't understand why he has to introduce the heading 'necessity of crisis'. While the expression 'necessity of crisis' may be self-evident to some, it is not always the case and hence problematic. For instance, it has been interpreted to mean that as long as capitalism continues crisis will always occur. And along with this the belief has been added that

---

41   Tomizuka 1965, p. 17.
42   [The term *kindai keizaigaku* (modern economics) is used by Marxian economists in Japan to refer to 'bourgeois' (= non-Marxian) economic theory from around the time of the emergence of the theory of marginal utility in the late nineteenth century.]

the demonstration of the necessity of crisis is at the core of Marx's theory of crisis. This meant that when, from the 1870s, periodic crises of the sort that had been seen before no longer occurred, Marx's theory of crisis was considered mistaken or irrelevant, leading to strained efforts to demonstrate that periodic crises were in fact still occurring.

The term 'necessity' used by Tomizuka differs from that case; it seems to express the idea that the periodic crises that have broken out since 1825 have arisen from a necessity related to the internal contradictions of capital, rather than being random. But if that is the case, what would become of his 'necessity of crisis' in the era starting from around 1870, when severe periodic crises were not seen for some time? Would the idea of necessity no longer apply, or would it still be applicable in some sense? This sort of doubt naturally arises. And Tomizuka seems to have anticipated it in writing the following:

> However, the periodic crises that had regularly engulfed capitalist economies every 10 years or so since 1825, underwent a particular change in form from the 1870s, when the monopoly stage was reached. Along with the transformation in the structure of capitalism and its laws of motion upon entering the monopoly stage, the way in which the internal contradictions of capitalism are manifested in a crisis underwent a particular change. But the systematising of the determinations of crisis must first be done on the basis of the original phenomenon of nineteenth century crisis – of the sort that occurred up to the 1860s in the classical form of the industrial cycle. In this way, we can have the theoretical premise and the standard for analysing the monopoly stage.[43]

Even reading this, it is not clear to me whether he thinks that the 'necessity of crisis' still applies even after that 'transformation', and therefore I am not sure why he uses 'necessity of crisis' in the heading that concludes the part on 'the fundamental structure of the theory of crisis in the system of *Capital*'.

B: Does this mean you can avoid that sort of troublesome problem in *Crisis II* through using the heading: 'Moments that transform the possibility of crisis into reality' instead?

KURUMA: That does seem to be one outcome. However, that's not all. If we clarify the factors involved in the actualisation of crisis – and the manner in which

---

43 Tomizuka 1965, p. 13.

each is involved – I think that we will be able to posit the fundamental viewpoint needed to understand the problem of the 'change in the form' of crisis posted by Tomizuka (who also raises various other points to account for why a long period of time elapsed without a chronic crisis after 1870).

Learning from Marx in an ambitious yet humble way

A: Today I had hoped we could get Professor Kuruma's views on the specific content of *Crisis II*, but I'm afraid that we will have to bring our discussion to a close, as we have already surpassed our allotted space for the discussion transcript by speaking at such length on broad issues. Does anyone have anything they would like to add?

E: I have gotten a lot of helpful hints for reading and studying *Crisis II* from this discussion, but I must say that I don't have the impression of gaining a totally clear idea of Marx's systematic theory of crisis from reading the first two *Marx-Lexikon* volumes on crisis. [*Laughs.*] And a specialist on crisis theory, reading *Crisis II*, might even raise the criticism that the system is not adequately constructed.

KURUMA: I can understand that feeling well. [*Laughs.*] As I mentioned at the outset, we have tried to put the various fragments that Marx left us into some kind of a system.

E: What is your understanding, then, in simple terms, of the fundamental framework of Marx's system of crisis theory? [*Laughs.*]

KURUMA: Please don't ask the impossible of me! [*Laughs.*] To answer that question would require an entire book, titled *The System of Crisis Theory*. Neither here in the *Marx-Lexikon* volumes on crisis, nor in my book *An Investigation of Crisis Theory*, did I attempt to provide a definitive statement along the lines of: *This* is Marx's theory of crisis.

For *Crisis II*, a great many passages come from Chapter 15 of Book III of *Capital*, since that content seems extremely important and convincing. But it is not necessarily the case that what is written there can be easily understood. There are several places where one can offer some conjecture as to the meaning but not a definitive judgment. And that is even more the case for the *Grundrisse*. There are also passages related to crisis from *Capital* and other works that were not included; a lot of things were left out of *Crisis II*. It would be dangerous, I think, to take one passage from *Grundrisse* and feel like one had a grip on crisis theory. Not only is there the danger of misinterpreting Marx, but he himself had not put things in order, so there is the possibility at times that his presentation is inadequate.

A great effort was made for *Crisis II* to bring the content together in a systematic way, and I think that if Marx himself had organised his presentation it would be roughly similar. Still, there are many points that require further clarification. Also, some passages important to the issue of crisis that Marx left us cannot be easily incorporated in a systematic way, so they were not included under the headings up to and including VIII. I gave a good deal of thought to how such passages could be dealt with, and decided that the most important of them will be included in *Crisis III*. So, instead of giving you a hasty explanation of the system of crisis theory, perhaps it would be best for all of you to examine the *Marx-Lexikon* volumes on crisis and then provide me with the answer. [*Laughs.*]

A: It seems that we have a responsibility to tackle the study of Marx in a way that is ambitious but at the same time humble. And I think we have reached some conclusions today, so I would like to end our discussion here.

CHAPTER 7

Marx-Lexikon Crisis III

1 Part 1: Contents[1]

IX. World market and crisis

1. Limits of use value: A specific use value is only needed in a certain quantity
   - {180} *Grundrisse*
     'As a specific use value, its ... (in so far as it is not money)'.
     (MECW-28, p. 332)
   - {181} *Grundrisse*
     'All the contradictions of [simple ... objectified labour in general'.
     (MECW-28, pp. 333–34)
   - {182} *Capital Vol. 2*
     'So long as we looked upon ... value, their material shape'.
     (MECW-36, pp. 392–93)
   - {183} *Capital Vol. 3*
     '*Second*, to say that a commodity ... the amount of this social want'.
     (MECW-37, pp. 183–84)
   - {184} *Capital Vol. 3*
     'Although the labour of the direct ... do not explain ground-rent.
     (MECW-37, pp. 629–30)
   - {185} *Theories of Surplus Value*
     'Of the part of the revenue ... the whole of commodity exchange'.
     (MECW-31, pp. 133–134)
   - {186} *Theories of Surplus Value*
     'Say's earth-shaking discovery ... that I previously paid for one'.
     (MECW-32, p. 307)

---

1 [The table of contents and passage sources in *Marx Engels Collected Works* (MECW) for the third volume on crisis of *Marx-Lexikon zur politischen Ökonomie*, Kuruma 1975a (ed.).]

2. The capitalist through competition is always raising the productive power of labour and expanding the scale of production, and therefore steadily increasing the quantity of products. From this arises the need to expand the market. The continual expansion of the market and the formation of the world market is a condition for the existence of industrial production and at the same time the historical mission of the capitalist mode of production. The contradiction herein

{187} *Manifesto of the Communist Party*
'The need of a constantly expanding … world after its own image'.
(MECW–6, pp. 487–88)

{188} *Wage Labour and Capital*
'Finally, as the capitalists … exploited the disturbed equilibrium'.
(MECW–9, p. 228)

{189} *Wages*
'While the growth of the productive … more and more violent'.
(MECW–6, pp. 429–30)

{190} *Grundrisse*
'Capital's creation of *absolute* … transcendence through itself'.
(MECW–28, pp. 334–37)

{191} *Grundrisse*
'The simple concept of capital … as already latent within it'.
(MECW–28, p. 341)

{192} *Grundrisse*
'The same is true of the *productive* … made on consumption rise'.
(MECW–28, p. 351)

{193} *Grundrisse*
'Let us now return to the *circulation* … earlier conditions of production'.
(MECW–28, p. 466)

{194} *Grundrisse*
'Within a society itself … capital establishes its mode of production'.
(MECW–29, p. 115)

{195} 'Preface to the English Edition of *Capital*' (Engels)
'The working of the industrial system … peaceful and legal revolution'.
(MECW–35, pp. 35–6)

{196} *Capital Vol. 2*
'With the development of capitalist … commodity supply also grows'.
(MECW–36, p. 148)

{197} *Capital Vol. 3*
'The conditions of direct exploitation ... under which it is realised'.
(MECW-37, p. 243)

{198} *Capital Vol. 3*
'The *real barrier* of capitalist ... social relations of production'.
(MECW-37, pp. 248–49)

{199} *Capital Vol. 3*
'Since the aim of capital ... reconverts itself into capital for him'.
(MECW-37, pp. 255–56)

{200} *Capital Vol. 3*
'There is no doubt ... groundwork of Asiatic production untouched'.
(MECW-37, pp. 331–32)

{201} *Capital Vol. 3*
'Originally, commerce was the precondition ... over industrial capital'.
(MECW-37, pp. 334–35)

{202} *Capital Vol. 3*
'Since Marx wrote the above ... whole of society, the nation'.
(MECW-37, pp. 435–36)

{203} *Capital Vol. 3*
'Hence, the credit system accelerates ... old mode of production'.
(MECW-37, p. 439)

{204} *Capital Vol. 3*
'The statistics of exports ... world market is still expanding'.
(MECW-37, pp. 499–500)

{205} *Theories of Surplus Value*
'Furthermore, the influence ... and therefore FOREIGN TRADE'.
(MECW-32, p. 58)

{206} *Theories of Surplus Value*
'Secondly [he overlooks] ... expansion of the world market'.
(MECW-32, p. 101)

{207} *Theories of Surplus Value*
'This ARGUMENT, HOWEVER ... itself) in the internal market'.
(MECW-32, pp. 153–54)

{208} *Theories of Surplus Value*
'One sees that he accepts ... result of capitalist production'.
(MECW-32, pp. 387–88)

{209}   *Theories of Surplus Value*
        'Originally, trade is the precondition ... over productive capital'.
        (MECW–32, pp. 466–67)
{210}   Marx to Engels, 8 October 1858
        'There is no denying that bourgeois ... over a far greater area?'
        (MECW–40, pp. 346–47)
{211}   Engels to Danielson, 22 September 1892
        'Your calculation that the ... consequences of their own doings'.
        (MECW–49, pp. 537–38)

3. **Export of capital. Its motive and operation. Its two forms**

{212}   'British Commerce'
        'The simple fact of the excess ... and industrial supremacy'.
        (MECW–15, pp. 429–30)
{213}   *Grundrisse*
        'The whole credit system ... form he has placed his money'.
        (MECW–28, p. 343)
{214}   'Manufacturers and Commerce'
        'By comparing tables A and B ... manufacturer and merchant'.
        (MECW–16, p. 492)
{215}   *Capital Vol. 3*
        'If capital is sent abroad ... mutually influence one another'.
        (MECW–37, p. 255)
{216}   *Capital Vol. 3*
        'The following points are important ... colonies or the United States'.
        (MECW–37, pp. 571–77)
{217}   *Capital Vol. 3*
        'India alone has to pay 5 million ... insignificant in comparison'.
        (MECW–37, pp. 585–86)
{218}   *Theories of Surplus Value*
        'We disregard here the case ... short, speculative investments'.
        (MECW–32, p. 116)
{219}   *Theories of Surplus Value*
        'The author also admits ... slowly within its own *bornes*'.
        (MECW–32, pp. 309–10)

4. **International repercussions of crisis**
    {220} Review: May to October [1850] (Marx and Engels)
    'The first repercussions ... revolution to the commercial crisis'.
    (MECW-10, pp. 496–97)
    {221} *Capital Vol. 2*
    'Finally, inasmuch as the length ... production and reproduction'.
    (MECW-36, pp. 316–17)
    {222} *Capital Vol. 3*
    'It should be noted in regard ... for the good of England'.
    (MECW-37, pp. 490–92)
    {223} *Capital Vol. 3*
    'In the case of two individuals ... same phenomena are repeated'.
    (MECW-37, pp. 514–15)
    {224} *Capital Vol. 3*
    'In 5144 the esteemed Wilson ... supplies of bullion from America."'
    (MECW-36, pp. 530–31)
    {225} *Capital Vol. 3*
    'The question, so far as ... supplies of bullion from America"'.
    (MECW-37, pp. 530–31)

5. **World market and crisis within the drafted plan**
    {226} 'Introduction' to *Grundrisse*
    'The arrangement has evidently ... (5) World market and crises'.
    (MECW-28, p. 45)
    {227} *Grundrisse*
    '(In this first section ... adopt a new historical form.)'
    (MECW-28, p. 160)
    {228} *Grundrisse*
    'I. (1) General concept of capital ... as social and vice versa.)'
    (MECW-28, pp. 194–95)

x. **Various types of crises**
    {229} Review: March to April [1850] (Marx and Engels)
    'What threatens "order" in England ... and an agricultural crisis'.
    (MECW-10, pp. 338–40)
    {230} Review: May to October [1850] (Marx and Engels)
    'In the years of prosperity ... gold reserves of six million'.
    (MECW-10, pp. 491–96)

{231} '18th Brumaire of Louis Napoleon'
       'In the year 1851, France ... by French local influences'.
       (MECW-11, pp. 173–75)
{232} 'Pauperism and Free Trade'
       'What, then, follows this enormous ... into workable condition'.
       (MECW-11, pp. 360–61)
{233} 'Monetary Crisis in Europe'
       'The general commercial crisis ... symptom and the forerunner'.
       (MECW-15, p. 113)
{234} 'The British Revulsion'
       'What English writers consider ... roots of the national prosperity'.
       (MECW-15, p. 390)
{235} 'The Trade Crisis in England'
       'The European crisis has so far ... heart of English production'.
       (MECW-15, pp. 401–02)
{236} 'The Financial Crisis in Europe'
       'The arrival yesterday morning ... fluctuations in the rate of interest'.
       (MECW-15, pp. 404–06)
{237} 'The English Banking Act of 1844'
       'The Hamburg crisis has scarcely ... Christian Matthias crashed'.
       (MECW-15, pp. 411–12)
{238} 'The English Banking Act of 1844'
       'What other proof was wanted ... Act, the Committee say:'
       (MECW-16, p. 5)
{239} *Grundrisse*
       'Before 1845, when the English ... other country in the world'.
       (MECW-28, p. 71)
{240} *Grundrisse*
       'As exchange itself splits ... trade in the strict sense.)'
       (MECW-28, pp. 86–7)
{241} Original text of Ch. 2 and beginning of Ch. 3 of *A Contribution*
       'Without any further anticipation ... practised in effecting them.
       (MECW-29, pp. 432–34.)
{242} *A Contribution to the Critique of Political Economy*
       'When payments cancel ... surrounding their own relations'.
       (MECW-29, pp. 378–79)
{243} *A Contribution to the Critique of Political Economy*
       'The commercial crises of the ... notes under these laws'.
       (MECW-29, p. 412)

{244} 'Afterword' to Second edition of *Capital*
       'The contradictions inherent ... holy Prusso-German empire'.
       (MECW–35, p. 20)
{245} 'Preface' to English edition of Capital (Engels)
       'The working of the industrial ... again vanish into air'.
       (MECW–35, p. 35)
{246} *Capital Vol. 1*
       'The function of money as ... money such as banknotes'.
       (MECW–35, pp. 148–49)
{247} *Capital Vol. 1*
       'Before I turn to the regular ... other London industries'.
       (MECW–35, pp. 660–61)
{248} *Capital Vol. 2*
       'The following is to be noted ... something new to them'.
       (MECW–36, pp. 466–69)
{249} *Capital Vol. 3*
       'The main damage, and ... falling off in reproduction'.
       (MECW–37, p. 254)
{250} *Capital Vol. 3* (Engels)
       'Since Marx wrote the above ... regulation of production'.
       (MECW–37, p. 435)
{251} *Capital Vol. 3*
       'Should circulation as a ... interruption of production, etc.'
       (MECW–37, pp. 456–57)
{252} *Capital Vol. 3*
       'It is self-evident that there ... so in centres of production'.
       (MECW–37, p. 489)
{253} *Capital Vol. 3*
       'What appears in one country ... come to the fore there'.
       (MECW–37, p. 491)
{254} *Capital Vol. 3*
       'It is a basic principle of ... extreme cases as the sole relief'.
       (MECW–37, pp. 513–14)
{255} *Capital Vol. 3* (Engels)
       'As long as the state of business ... reached £4 to £5 million'.
       (MECW–37, pp. 524–25)
{256} *Capital Vol. 3*
       'Everybody acquainted ... drain of gold increases the crisis'.
       (MECW–37, pp. 533–35)

{257} *Capital Vol. 3* (Engels)
       'The crisis of 1837 with ... of 1844 and 1845 was passed'.
       (MECW–37, p. 550)
{258} *Capital Vol. 3*
       'Sixthly, with the exception ... did not come until October'.
       (MECW–37, p. 563)
{259} *Capital Vol. 3*
       'Palmer, ex-Governor and a Director ... crisis or money panic'.
       (MECW–37, p. 564)
{260} *Theories of Surplus Value*
       'Ricardo himself ... PLETHORA of CAPITAL and OVERPRODUCTION'.
       (MECW–32, pp. 128–29)
{261} *Theories of Surplus Value*
       'But now the further ... existence as commodity and money'.
       (MECW–32, pp. 128–29)
{262} *Theories of Surplus Value*
       '1) The general *possibility* ... yet the place to do it.)'
       (MECW–32, pp. 144–45)
{263} *Theories of Surplus Value*
       'It goes without saying ... etc., admit this form of crisis'.
       (MECW–32, pp. 150–51)
{264} *Theories of Surplus Value*
       'Adam Smith did not yet ... itself) in the internal market'.
       (MECW–32, p. 154)
{265} *Theories of Surplus Value*
       'In world market crises ... isolated and one-sided'.
       (MECW–32, p. 163)
{266} 'Preface' to second German edition of *The Condition of the English Working Class*
       'The recurring period of the great ... of which more anon'.
       (MECW–27, p. 314)
{267} 'Preface' to second German edition of *The Condition of the English Working Class*
       '"This, then was the position ... Trade, thou universal panacea'.
       (MECW–27, pp. 318–19)
{268} Engels to Marx, 24 August 1852
       'At all events, whether ... deal of stuff to get through'.
       (MECW–39, p. 165)

{269} Engels to Marx, 10 March 1853
'The Austro-Prussian tariff ... face of the general débâcle'.
(MECW-39, p. 286)

{270} Marx to Engels, 23 April 1857
'He was assured by ... TURN to all his disquisitions'.
(MECW-40, p. 165)

{271} Engels to Marx, 15 November 1857
'This time the crisis ... most will be recovered'. /
'We can only hope ... these gentlemen will see'.
(MECW-40, pp. 200–01 / p. 203)

{272} Marx to Engels, 24 November 1857
'The MONETARY PANIC in London ... English are concerned'.
(MECW-40, pp. 208–09)

{273} Marx to Engels, 8 December 1857
'I've had a gratifying ... out of the COMMERCIAL WORLD'.
(MECW-40, p. 215)

{274} Engels to Marx, 27 September 1873
'I hope that the American PANIC ... sting out of it'.
(MECW-44, p. 536)

{275} Marx to Danielson, 15 November 1878
'The most interesting field ... official Yankee reports'.
(MECW-45, p. 344)

{276} Marx to Danielson, 10 April 1879
'And now, primo ... lead me too far at present'.
(MECW-45, pp. 354–55)

{277} Marx to Danielson, 12 September 1880
'The present crisis was ... longer or shorter interval'.
(MECW-46, pp. 31–2)

{278} Marx to Danielson, 19 February 1881
'I wrote you some time ago ... a very narrow escape."(!)'
(MECW-46, pp. 62–3)

{279} Engels to Bernstein, 31 January 1882
'That crises are one of ... shown as a five-year one'.
(MECW-46, pp. 189–90)

{280} Engels to Marx, 30 November 1882
'Encl. a letter from Bebel ... suffer worse than any other'.
(MECW-46, pp. 390–91)

{281} Engels to Marx, 22 December 1882
'The crisis in America would ... much before it is due'.
(MECW-46, p. 415)

{282} Engels to Bebel, 10–11 May 1883
'Your view of the business ... crash will quite surely come'.
(MECW–47, p. 23)

{283} Engels to Danielson, 13 November 1885
'That crisis of which ... prairies remains unexhausted'.
(MECW–47, pp. 349–50)

{284} Engels to Bebel, 20–23 January 1886
'Six weeks ago there ... earnest – and not before'.
(MECW–47, p. 390)

{285} Engels to Kelly-Wischnewetzky 3 February 1886
'But it strikes me ... necessary as it is desirable'.
(MECW–47, pp. 396–97)

{286} Engels to Danielson, 8 February 1886
'Here the industrial crisis ... *Uns kann recht sein*'.
(MECW–47, p. 402)

{287} Engels to Schmidt, 27 October 1890
'Your money market man ... history of the last 20 years'.
(MECW–49, p. 58)

{288} Engels to Oppenheim, 24 March 1891
'It's the old story ... crisis of 5 or 6 year's duration'.
(MECW–47, p. 402)

{289} Engels to Bebel, 8 March 1892
'However, unemployment might ... another acute one'.
(MECW–49, p. 373)

XI. **False theories of crisis**

{290} 'The Vienna Note'
'It is now the fourth time ... severity of the approaching crisis'.
(MECW–12, pp. 295–300)

{291} 'The Bank Act of 1844 and the Monetary Crisis in England'
'As to the reserve of notes ... beyond Government control'.
(MECW–15, pp. 379–83)

{292} 'The Trade Crisis in England'
'Still the very recurrence ... true cause of all maladies'.
(MECW–15, p. 401)

{293} 'English Bank Act of 1844'
'It will be recollected ... by a Government ukase'.
(MECW–16, pp. 3–7)

{294} 'Commercial Crises and Currency in Britain'
'There is, perhaps, no point ... discarded as altogether imaginary'.
(MECW–16, pp. 8–12)

{295} 'British Commerce and Finance'
       'In reviewing the Report on ... put it in its adequate terms'.
       (MECW-16, pp. 33-4)
{296} *A Contribution to the Critique of Political Economy*
       'The commercial crises of ... Cabinet on its own responsibility'.
       (MECW-29, pp. 412-15)
{297} *Capital Vol. 1*
       'Just as the currency of money ... give rise to such stagnation'.
       (MECW-35, p. 131)
{298} *Capital Vol. 2*
       'The successive transformation ... bourgeois economists understand'.
       (MECW-36, p. 497)
{299} *Capital Vol. 3*
       'Furthermore, capital consists ... moves, and alone can move'.
       (MECW-37, pp. 255-56)
{300} *Capital Vol. 3*
       'We revert now to the accumulation ... "on their own account"'.
       (MECW-37, pp. 484-87)
{301} *Capital Vol. 3*
       'It is characteristic of ... Germany and France the day after'.
       (MECW-37, pp. 491-92)
{302} *Capital Vol. 3*
       'In times of stringency ... continue with their swindles'.
       (MECW-37, p. 513)
{303} *Capital Vol. 3* (Engels)
       'In a former work, Ricardo's ... above-mentioned Bank Acts'. /
       'The critique of this school ... Peel's Bank Acts (B.C. 1857)'.
       (MECW-37, pp. 542-43 / pp. 545-55)
{304} *Capital Vol. 3* (Engels)
       'The crisis of 1837 ... symbols of value with its credit'.
       (MECW-37, pp. 550-51)
{305} *Theories of Surplus Value*
       'To the best of his knowledge ... commodities, but as capitalists'.
       (MECW-32, pp. 128-30)
{306} Marx to Engels, 3 February 1851
       'I shall now submit to you ... Hamburg in the eighteenth century'.
       (MECW-38, pp. 274-78)
{307} Marx to Engels, 25 February 1851
       'In any case, I have ... itself is quite unexceptionable'.
       (MECW-38, pp. 299-300)

2 Part 2: Discussion[2]

How does *Crisis III* Differ from *Crisis I* and *II*?

A: What shall we begin by discussing today?

B: In the previous discussion on *Crisis II*, we started off with how it differs from *Crisis I*, so perhaps a good place to start here would be to consider the difference and relation of *Crisis III* to the first two volumes. After that, it seems we should look at the structure of this latest volume on crisis, which consists of three main headings (IX. World market and crisis; X. Various types of crises; XI. False theories of crisis) and consider why only the first heading is divided into subheadings. In relation to that, we might also consider the significance of each subheading and the relations between them. I think those are points worth discussing.

A: As our discussion develops, we are likely to touch on all sorts of issues, so perhaps we can begin by asking Professor Kuruma for his thoughts on the relation between *Crisis III* and the first two volumes

KURUMA: For *Crisis I* and *Crisis II*, we generally assumed a closed society in which the capitalist mode of production fully dominates, so our editorial focus was on tracking down the development of the contradictions of capitalist production and clarifying how those contradictions are in movement up to the point of exploding as a crisis. However, the societies that have actually existed up to now have not been that sort of pure capitalist society. The realm of capitalist production relations that have been established, although they are expanding as history progresses, still only encompasses a portion of the globe. Non-capitalistic realms remain, to a greater or lesser extent. What significance do such realms have to the development of capitalistic production, and in what form have economic relations connected to those realms been established? These are the sort of factors that have to be taken into consideration when dealing with the actual processes of capitalist development. More concretely, not only is the population of the world divided between those who have been absorbed within the realm of capitalist production relations and those who have not, but it is also divided into nationalities under different

---

[2] [Discussion published as an insert for the third volume on crisis of *Marx-Lexikon zur politischen Ökonomie*, Kuruma 1975b (ed.).]

states. Capitalist society does not exist as a unity but rather as different capitalist states, interwoven in various oppositional relations; the same is true of the non-capitalist societies as well as societies where capitalism has yet to develop. Naturally, therefore, we must consider the role played by the state within global economic exchange. The economy cannot be understood without examining that reality.

Those problems are abstracted from in *Crisis I* and in *Crisis II*. At that stage, as I mentioned, a purely capitalistic, closed society is premised in order to clarify whether crisis would necessarily occur under such conditions; whereas in *Crisis III*, we chose several headings thought to be important for taking the next step toward a concrete understanding of crisis, in the sense just spoken of, and under those headings we gathered passages from Marx and Engels that could be of use to researchers. This is basically the reason why we chose to position 'World market and crisis' as the central heading of this volume. Of course, there is not necessarily such a clear line dividing the passages included in *Crisis II* and in *Crisis III*. A clear distinction could not be made because passages are included as they exist, so that mixed in with the passages in *Crisis II* are elements that belong to the realm of *Crisis III*, and vice versa. That was simply unavoidable.

Difference between demonstrating the necessity of crisis and clarifying the conditions under which crisis inevitably arises

A: I think that Professor Kuruma clarified the character of *Crisis III* clearly, so perhaps we can move on to the next topic.

C: Hold on a moment. One thing caught my attention in those remarks that I would like to ask about, although it doesn't concern the main issue here.

A: Go ahead.

C: Just now, Professor Kuruma, you said that a purely capitalistic, closed society is assumed in *Crisis II*, with the aim being to clarify the inevitable occurrence of crisis under such conditions. But I believe that for some time you have expressed doubts about posing the question in terms of the 'necessity of crisis'. It strikes me that there could be some contradiction between what you just said now and your view in the past. Could you say a word about that?

KURUMA: Clarifying the conditions under which crisis necessarily occurs, and emphasising that crisis will always arise as long as capitalism continues, are not the same thing. In speaking of 'crisis' here, I mean, of course, periodic crises, not crisis in the sense of more or less bringing about the end of capitalism and characterising its demise. If someone were to say that crisis in that latter sense is inevitable, I would not raise any objection. When I say that I cannot concur with those who insist on demonstrating the necessity of crisis, I am not referring to a crisis that signifies the downfall of capitalism, but to the periodic crises that occur with a certain regularity. Instead of seeking to demonstrate that such crises will always occur as long as capitalism continues to exist, it seems to me more scientific to clarify the conditions under which they occur and why and how they occur. One can also seek to explain why an expected crisis did not in fact occur. *Crisis II* includes passages on how, despite its immanent barrier, capitalism has an impulse to drive beyond that barrier, with crisis occurring as a result of it actually being driven beyond. So, it could be said that if those impulses weaken, the barrier will not be broken through, so that crisis also will not occur. Marx actually wrote the following in Book III of *Capital*:

> The rate of profit, i.e. the relative growth in capital, is particularly important for all new off-shoots of capital that organise themselves independently. And if capital formation were to fall exclusively into the hands of a few existing big capitals, for whom the mass of profit outweighs the rate, the animating fire of production would be totally extinguished. It would die out.[3]

Here, of course, Marx is saying that capitalism has an inherent tendency in that direction, not that such a period will definitely arrive, so it would be mistaken to think that production could become completely lethargic and that capitalism would continue in such a state. However, it is possible for production to remain stagnant over a long period of time (during a depression), and that does in fact occur. That is a period of 'chronic crisis' (*chronische Krise*), which has been translated as *mansei kyōkō* in Japanese. Using the Japanese term *kyōkō*, which corresponds more closely to the 'panic', in order to translate 'crisis' in this particular case, creates the strange impression that for years on end people are running around in a stunned and alarmed state. 'Crisis' does not originally have that meaning of 'panic' expressed in the Japanese term *kyōkō*, but I think that later someone may talk more about this translation issue.

---

3 Marx 1981a, p. 368. [In passage {128} in *Crisis II*.]

At any rate, to return to the subject at hand, it is not the case that crises always have periodically occurred up to now. The last quarter of the nineteenth century, in particular, was a period of chronic crisis, so even if there were small fluctuations, no great business upturn occurred as in the earlier periods, and therefore the turbulent crises also did not occur as they had before. This situation continued until the outbreak of World War I, a conflict that resulted from intensifying competition over the world market. So, there have been such cases. Recently, as well, a situation has arisen where we have gone through quite a long period without a genuine sort of crisis. Why is this the case? Marxian economists have a responsibility to answer this question. But the issue centres on how we go about doing that. No matter how much one may speak of the 'necessity' of crisis, it will not bring us closer to answering that question. In my view, the question of why crisis has not occurred recently can be answered, abstractly and generally, by saying that some of the conditions that would make a crisis necessary are lacking. Of course, we have to clarify the actual situation, but it seems to me that in order to accomplish this we must start from the sort of conception I just mentioned. We can progress in our analysis of the problem by considering the conditions that are lacking. Of course, it is not the aim of this discussion to answer such a question, nor could it be accomplished here, but one factor that comes to mind is the extraordinary influence of the state on the capitalist economy. As for the direction in which that influence is manifested, the first thing to mention is the massive investment in undertakings that would not be profitable for private capitalists, such as the construction of roads and ports or large-scale projects for river management and irrigation. One classic example is the Tennessee Valley Authority project carried out in the United States during the period of the New Deal. Such projects remove, to some extent, the barrier posed by the profit rate under capitalist production.

A second factor is the prodigious waste on the part of the state that is unimaginable for individual capitalists, tasked as they are with accumulating capital. Expenditures on armaments have reached extraordinary levels (even outside of the great wars that have occurred between large capitalist states). It is a far cry from the age when there were just munitions and tanks. Not only are there continual improvements in military aircraft, but weapons are being developed with no end in sight, extending to nuclear bombs and satellites. Such military expenditures are astounding, and such colossal expenditures by the state can be thought to lessen the restriction on consumption by capitalists, which is one underlying factor of crises of overproduction.

However, such expenditures certainly cannot be covered by tax revenue alone, which means that inflation necessarily occurs. Under the system of convertibility, the development of the credit system allows for fictitious purchasing power to be created, whereas there is a limit to such creation as long as the obligation of convertibility remains. When the limit was exceeded, the issuing bank faced bankruptcy if it failed to meet the demand for convertibility. The only way to create as much fictitious purchasing power as desired was to end the obligation of convertibility. This means the abolition of the convertibility system. This allowed the creation of fictitious purchasing power without limit, laying the foundation for inflationary policies. This meant that those in charge of governmental policy were the ones to decide how far inflationary policies would be pursued and the extent to which fictional purchasing power would be created so as to drive beyond the inherent barriers of capitalism, but such decisions certainly are not something that can be freely chosen. Inflationary policies of the sort that have become the norm today (setting aside the temporary policies implemented during and after a war to deal with a state's budgetary crisis) originally arose from the need to break out of recession, and it has become increasingly necessary to pursue inflation to prevent the resulting prosperity from sinking back into crisis. If these policies were to be halted, it would lead to a ferocious crisis or a severe recession. The only way to prevent that is to prolong the inflationary policies. But that does not mean, by any means, that all will be well as long as inflation is pursued. There is no need for me to explain the problems that can arise, because everyone can perceive this today, although of course how it affects them will vary depending on their particular circumstances. In other words, there are problems if inflation is pursued, and problems if it is not pursued. Herein lies the dilemma that could be described as the disease of the late-capitalist economy.

Relation between the 'limits of use value' and the 'necessity of market expansion'

C: My question seems to have led the discussion off on something of a tangent. I am sorry about that. Shall we return to the main subject and move on to discuss something new?

A: Perhaps we can consider the structure of *Crisis III*. First, there is Heading ('World market and crisis'), which is divided into the following five subheadings:
1. Limits of use value: A specific use value is only needed in a certain quantity
2. The capitalist through competition is always raising the productive power of labour and expanding the scale of production, and therefore steadily

increasing the quantity of products. From this arises the need to expand the market. The continual expansion of the market and the formation of the world market is a condition for the existence of industrial production and at the same time the historical mission of the capitalist mode of production. The contradiction therein.
3. Export of capital. Its motive and operation. Its two forms
4. International repercussions of crisis
5. 'World market and crisis' within the drafted plan.

Regarding these subheadings, I would like to know Professor Kuruma's basic thoughts on the relation between the first subheading 'Limits of use value' and the seemingly closely related second subheading regarding the 'need to expand the market'.

KURUMA: If we assume a closed society in which the capitalist mode of production is in complete operation (and that assumption is indispensable to purely elucidate the fundamental laws of capitalist production), the expansion of production in one department must be thought to be restricted to some extent by the 'limit of use value'. This is the limit where even if it is possible to increase production there is no way to use those products. Of course, this is not a rigid restriction, but rather more or less flexible, and the degree of flexibility will depend on the particular product. What can generally be said is that there is more flexibility for luxury goods and less for daily necessities. And the department that corresponds to large-scale production, and thus occupies the main position within the historical development of capitalism, is clearly the production department for daily necessities, not luxury goods.

Of course, here we have excluded the production department for the means of production. Ultimately, however, the expansion of that department cannot be considered to be independent of the expansion of the production department for daily necessities. But, under certain conditions, it is not only possible but inevitable for the former to expand more rapidly than the latter over a certain period of time, although that is not an issue that can easily be discussed here so I will have to leave it for a separate discussion. Thus, under the assumed conditions I mentioned, even if there is scope for the accumulation of capital and an expansion of production in the sector for daily necessities, the range is limited.

However, if we look at historical reality, we can see that even a primary industry that has existed since ancient times, such as the cotton industry, is able to expand remarkably at a later date. This is possible, it seems, because a purely capitalist society of the sort assumed theoretically has not existed in reality from the outset, given the existence of non-capitalistic areas outside the realm dominated by the capitalist mode of production. Also, if we take into consideration the existence of nation states, abstracted from before, there are advanced capitalist states, developing states, and non-capitalist states – and even within the advanced states there are sectors of production at an early stage of capitalist development or in a non-capitalistic condition (although these tend to develop in a capitalistic direction). Looking at the world as a whole, we encounter a vast expanse of non-capitalistic area. And capitalism has developed by incorporating those areas within capitalist production relations. Meanwhile, markets are expanded through countries importing products they do not produce or that are not suited to domestic production, while exporting their own products to other countries. To get an idea of the acute necessity of market expansion, we need only consider what the advanced capitalist countries have done to open up markets, such as the waging of the Opium Wars to secure the treaties to open up the ports of China. The following account by Engels, included in Book III of *Capital*, gives us a sense of the lofty expectations for market expansion among Manchester factory owners at the time:

> At the end of 1842 the depression which English industry had been suffering almost uninterruptedly since 1837 began to ease. In the two following years the export· demand for English industrial products rose even more; 1845–6 marked the period of greatest prosperity. In 1843 the Opium War had opened up China to English trade. The new market offered a new pretext for an expansion that was already in full swing, particularly in the cotton industry. 'How can we ever produce too much? We have 300 million people to clothe', I was told at the time by a Manchester manufacturer.[4]

This extravagant expectation ended as a mere dream, but it is quite interesting in revealing the ferocious desire of capitalists for market expansion. Such a 'continual expansion of the market and the formation of the world market is a condition for the existence of industrial production', but this at the same time is the 'historical mission [*historische Aufgabe*] of the capitalist mode of production'[5] Marx called this the 'propagandistic [*propagandistisch*]' or 'civilising [*zivilisierend*]' tendency'[6] of capital.

---

4 Marx 1981a, pp. 533–4.
5 Marx 1998, p. 439. [In passage {203} in *Crisis III*.]
6 Marx 1973, p. 542. [In passage {193} in *Crisis III*.]

What does 'contradiction therein' mean?

C: You just spoke of the first two subheadings under Heading IX ('World market and crisis'), and at the end of the second subheading there is the expression the 'contradiction therein'. I do not quite understand that meaning, judging from the subheading alone. What is the content of the contradiction to which you are referring?

KURUMA: The subheading is based on the following passage in Book III of *Capital*:

> If the capitalist mode of production is therefore a historical means for developing the material powers of production and for creating a corresponding world market, it is at the same time the constant contradiction between this historical task and the social relations of production corresponding to it.[7]

Since Marx does not explain the concrete manner of the contradictions in that passage it is not possible to say anything definitive, but I think it is something along the following lines. As mentioned earlier, the market is able to expand by incorporating into itself non-capitalistic areas, thereby making expanded production possible. However, at the same time as expanded production becomes possible, it necessarily comes to pass that large-scale production is carried out, which raises productive power. This heightens the contradiction between productive power and production relations, which is the peculiar barrier of capitalist production, enhancing the need for accelerated market expansion, which in turn rapidly reduces the space for further market expansion. This is one aspect of what Marx might have meant. For instance, in 'Wage Labour and Capital', he writes:

> Finally, as the capitalists are compelled, by the movement described above, to exploit the already existing gigantic means of production on a larger scale and to set in motion all the mainsprings of credit to this end, there is a corresponding increase in earthquakes, in which the trading world can only maintain itself by sacrificing a part of wealth, of products and even of productive forces to the gods of the nether world – in a word, crises increase. They become more frequent and more violent, if

---

7 Marx 1981a, p. 359. [In passage {198} in *Crisis III*.]

only because, as the mass of production, and consequently the need for extended markets, grows, the world market becomes more and more contracted, fewer and fewer markets remain available for exploitation, since every preceding crisis has subjected to world trade a market hitherto unconquered or only superficially exploited.[8]

Meanwhile, as market expansion progresses, elements that promote disequilibrium based on the anarchic character peculiar to capitalism begin to function more and more strongly, as seen in the expansion of speculative production and speculation at the circulation stage. In Book III of *Capital* Marx explains that, 'The market, therefore, must be continually extended, so that its relationships and the conditions governing them assume ever more the form of a natural law independent of the producers and become ever more uncontrollable'.[9] I think that this passage can serve as a point of reference for the issue we are considering.

Relation between the preceding issues and the realisation problem due to the consumption restriction in capitalist society

A: Before we move on to the next issue, would anyone like to raise a point related to what has been discussed so far?

C: I understand fairly well what has been explained up to now, but another important issue that seems closely related is the realisation problem stemming from the consumption restriction particular to capitalist production. This is an issue that was treated in Subheading 6 of *Crisis II*, but I do not have a clear understanding of its relation to what we have been discussing here. What are your thoughts on this, Professor Kuruma?

KURUMA: Overall, *Crisis II* deals with the 'moments that transform the possibility of crisis into reality', as indicated by the title of Heading VIII, and one of the items positioned under that heading is Subheading 6, which is as follows:

> The overproduction of capital involves the overproduction of commodities. Periodically an excess of means of labour and subsistence are produced to allow them to function as the means of exploitation of workers

---

8 Marx 1977, p. 228. [In passage {188} in *Crisis III*.]
9 Marx 1981a, p. 353. [In passage {197} in *Crisis III*.]

at a certain rate of profit. Too many commodities are produced in order to be able to realise the surplus value contained in the commodities and the surplus value that constitutes a portion of that value under the conditions of distribution and consumption posited by capitalist production, and to convert this into new capital, or to be able to carry out this process without constantly recurring explosions.

As we can see from this title, the particular restriction on consumption of capitalist production is considered as the most fundamental condition of the periodic crises of overproduction, without which a crisis of overproduction would not be possible. In contrast, in our discussion here, this same restriction on consumption is premised as a fundamental condition creating the need for market expansion. Of course, this is just the basic yardstick we followed when editing the volumes, and no perfectly clear distinction can be drawn between the passages grouped under the former and latter subheading since we are including passages in their given state, as was noted earlier. However, if I had to compare the respective role of each, with regard to the particular consumption restriction of capitalist production, I could offer the following explanation.

First, the restriction on the consumption of the working class under capitalist society is that their consumption is limited, fundamentally, to the range of life's necessities. And there is an upper limit in the demand for such necessities. There are of course differences in population size, and the larger the population, the greater the demand for necessities, and therefore the greater scale of production necessary to meet that demand, but in any case, the restriction will be posited by the given magnitude. This is true of any social system, rather than being particular to capitalist society. What is unique to capitalism is not the mass of daily necessities, but the question, after that demand has been met, of what production will be invested in, using the surplus value that is to be newly capitalised. If we call all the other means of subsistence besides those daily necessities 'luxury goods', there would be no alternative but to increase production of those luxury goods. Those are the materials of life for the capitalist class. As for what would determine the demand for those materials, the limit is the total quantity of surplus value. However, the capitalist is unable to use all of the surplus value obtained for personal consumption, since it is also necessary to accumulate. The accumulation of capital is a necessity that stems from the essential nature of capital, manifested as the condition for survival imposed by the law of competition. The expansion of production through accumulation is, of course, first directed at the production department producing the means of production. This is because expanding the means of subsistence requires, to begin with, increasing the means of production needed to produce them; or at least in principle that is the case. The greater the scale of the means of production, particularly the fixed capital, and therefore the longer the period needed for their creation, the more likely that accumulation proceeds without being accompanied by an increase in the production of the means of consumption, and that business conditions improve during that time. But ultimately the production of the means of production cannot be independent of the production of the means of subsistence. The increase in the production of the means of production will sooner or later lead to an increase in the production of the means of subsistence. In that case, who will buy the means of subsistence whose production has been increased? As long as more workers are employed because of this increase in production, so that more wages are paid, demand from this direction will increase, but that alone is of course insufficient. Moreover, if demand for labour power increases too precipitously, so that wages become abnormally high, profit will contract, coming into contradiction with the motive for expanding production, which is to obtain greater profit. Since profit is constituted upon the restriction of workers' consumption, it would be fatal to capital for that consumption to increase beyond an ordinary level. This is because the accumulation of capital is not aimed at enriching workers but obtaining greater profit. The consumption of the additional means of subsistence from the increase in their production can only be done by the capitalist class, but it is not possible for the bulk of their income to be directed toward personal consumption. Capitalists who consumed their revenue individually would no longer be capitalists. In order to remain a capitalist, one's mission must be accumulation for accumulation's sake, and production for production's sake. Thus, as long as we are considering a closed, capitalistic society, there is a limit to increasing production, and if production is increased beyond that point overproduction will inevitably occur. At the same time, because of this, the desire to expand the market into the remaining realms outside of the capitalist realm is also inevitable. In this way, a world market gradually is created. And productive power develops to an astounding extent as a result, so that ultimately a new mode of production naturally takes the place of the old. I think that this roughly summarises the relation to the particular consumption barrier of capital in the headings that 'C' brought to our attention. This becomes even clearer in the case of a socialist society. In such a society, production is not carried out for the sake of profit but to improve the lives of all members of society, so once the demand for the necessities of life is adequately met, production of useful things would likely be carried out to further improve the standard of life. In the case of those things as well, there would be an upper limit for each as a use value, but once production of a given thing was sufficient, other useful things would be produced in turn. And if it then became clear that it was pointless to produce other things beyond a certain point, labour time would likely be reduced. Through this, 'free time' would be increased, creating the space for people to engage in truly creative activities. The sort of contradiction that arises under capitalism between production and consumption would basically cease to exist. In any case, that seems to me to be the gist of Marx's thinking.

'Export of capital'

A: It seems we have basically explained the content up to and including Subheading 2, so I'd like for us to move on to Subheading 3, 'Export of capital'. Shall we begin by considering the positioning of this subheading under the main heading 'World market and crisis' and its relation to the other subheadings?

KURUMA: The passages under the heading 'World market and crisis' in *Crisis III* deal with a problem that remains outside the original scope of *Capital*. Thus, we could not arrange passages according to the same approach as *Crisis I* and *Crisis II*. In those first two volumes, we created headings and subheadings to arrange the moments of crisis more or less in the order in which they appear in *Capital*, in line with the fundamental thinking of Marx regarding the method of crisis theory. That was not possible for 'World market and crisis' because, as I just mentioned, the problem is not originally within the scope of *Capital*. Although various discussions of world market and crisis do appear in the pages of *Capital*, they are only addenda to the primary problems under examination, rather than constituting the primary subject matter. Even if we had dealt with the descriptions related to this topic in the order in which they appear in *Capital*, it would not have amounted to presenting the various problems related to the world market and crisis in the order of importance as the main topic. This left us no choice, as already touched on, but to select a few headings that seemed worthy of consideration when examining the world market and crisis, and to gather passages from Marx and Engels under those headings for readers to refer to. That, at any rate, is the basic approach we took for *Crisis III*. Thus, there is no particular developmental relation between the subheadings, but it would seem problematic to alter the given order, which is: 'Necessity of market expansion', 'Export of capital', and the 'International repercussions of crisis'. For instance, it would be odd to have the export of capital come before the necessity of market expansion, just as it would be strange to start from the international repercussions of crisis. Also, needless to say, not all of the matters that need to be considered with regard to the problem of the world market and crisis are grouped under this heading. In particular, the role of the state within the scene of competition between capital on the world market, which is a matter indispensable to understanding the actual economic situation today, could not be dealt with as a heading in *Marx-Lexikon* because the necessary materials were lacking. Marx made various drafts of his plan for the system of a critique of political economy, and all of them included a section on the state, with some of the plans drawing a distinction between the internal and external role of the state. Although there is a possibility that he wrote some sort of memo regarding this problem, no such manuscript has been discovered thus far. For this reason, even if I were able to write something on the subject myself, it would not be possible to include a related heading within *Marx-Lexikon*. This is one point I wanted to mention.

A: From your explanation just now, the circumstances related to the structure of the heading 'World market and crisis' are clear, so I think we can move on to look at the content of the subheading 'Export of capital'. The full title of the subheading is: 'Export of capital. Its motives and effects. Its two forms'. Could we begin by discussing why those three words – *motives*, *effects*, and *forms* – are mentioned in relation to the export of capital?

KURUMA: In the case of *Capital*, the problem of the export of capital discussed by Marx in the passages gathered under this subheading basically can be divided between those three terms, but it was not worth dividing the passages into further subheadings. One reason is that there are not so many passages related to each of the three terms, and in any case the issue discussed for each is clear at a glance. Given this, we decided to just include them all together, while also listing the three terms just to be clear.

A: Let's begin, then, by looking at the motives for the export of capital.

D: I think that two motives can be pointed to regarding the export of capital. One is the creation of markets and the other is that 'more capital is accumulated than can be invested in production'[10] domestically; in other words, an overaccumulation of capital. But I'm not sure if it can be thought of in such simple terms, since there are various related problems. For instance, with regard to exporting capital 'in order to create markets', the need to create markets outside the country is premised on there not being adequate room for an

---

10   Marx 1989b, p. 116. [In passage {218} in *Crisis III*.]

expansion of production based solely on domestic demand, so the issue cannot be considered completely apart from the issue of more capital being accumulated than can be invested in domestic production. Furthermore, in speaking of the export of capital 'in order to create markets', it would be an exceptional case for the industrialists who perceive the need to expand markets to make loans themselves to foreign countries in order for their products to be purchased; in principle, the capital would be raised on the London financial market (in the form of government and corporate bonds and stocks), and that money then used to purchase English products, so it seems a bit peculiar in such a case to speak of the export of capital 'in order to create markets'. Marx, in addressing the problem of the export of capital to create markets, also deals with the related problem of the role of the credit system, which is the role in breaking through the immanent barrier of capital, so instead of the perspective of the individual capitalists, I think it can be said that the perspective is that of capitalist production as a whole. In any case, if we take into consideration those intermediary relations, all sorts of difficult problems come to light.

KURUMA: What 'D' just said is quite reasonable, and certainly by reading the passages gathered in *Crisis III* regarding the motives for the export of capital, one would not be able to understand every problem related to those motives, nor could everything in those passages be understood without some doubts arising. One reason – and this is true not merely of the *motives* for the export of capital and its *effects* and *forms* but also of issues raised in the subsequent subheading on the 'international repercussions of crisis' – is that Marx is merely referring to these issues in connection to the main topics he is considering, rather than treating them systematically as the main topics in themselves, so such doubts are unavoidable. The second reason is that Marx of course wrote about all of those issues in connection with the conditions of the world market at the time, so they cannot be understood without an awareness of those conditions. It is not possible to go into all those problems in a discussion of this length, nor is it appropriate considering the fundamental *Marx-Lexikon* policy of gathering the writings of Marx in relation to specific issues as a resource for scholars, rather than offering our own explanations.

A: If we move on from this issue of 'motives' just discussed, there are the terms 'effects' and 'two forms' under the same subheading on the export of capital. I think that we should try to at least clarify what each is referring to. But before doing so, perhaps someone could indicate the problem at hand. How about you, 'D'?

D: In reading the passages on the export of capital in *Crisis III*, it seems to me that issues related to the effects of the export of capital come down to three basic aspects, the most important of which is that when England supplied massive amounts of credit to other industrialised countries on the European continent, it ended up cultivating its own competitors, and in this way, England's function as credit provider developed more rapidly than its function as factory owner and merchant. Since what was true of England can more or less be said of the leading capitalist nations today, those passages are quite enlightening. Another effect is that, as a result of the export of capital, the export of commodities becomes possible. This corresponds to the export of capital to create markets, related to the *motives* for exporting capital, but as I noted earlier, it seems unnatural when seen from the standpoint of the individual capitalist to export capital in order to create a market, so it is more natural to say, from this perspective, that the creation of the market is the 'effect' or 'result' of the export of capital. Furthermore, one circumstance when considering the 'operation' of the export of capital is the influence exerted by the money market of the country exporting the capital, and therefore the influence of the interest rate and exchange rate. Marx discussed this in the passages where he distinguishes between the 'two forms' of the export of capital, so that seems the best place to consider this circumstance.

The two forms of exported capital that Marx speaks of are capital exported in the form of precious metals and capital exported in the form of railways etc., and his discussion of the two forms is developed in relation to the debate between the English parliamentary committee members Wellstone and Newmarch. Wellstone did not distinguish between the two forms, but Marx explained that the distinction was important. Central to this issue was that in the case of exporting capital in the form of railways etc., as compared to the form of precious metals, there is an influence exerted by certain conditions in the money market of England as the country that is exporting capital, and therefore an influence resulting from the interest and exchange rates; but in entering into the actual content of this discussion there are points that cannot be fully understood with regard to the influence of exchange rates, setting aside the issue of interest rates. However, since, as Professor Kuruma pointed out, a conclusion cannot be clearly reached without adequately understanding the concrete circumstances of that time, I will simply note that Marx emphasised the importance of distinguishing the two forms and move on to the next point.

Ah ... one other thing just came to mind that seems worth mentioning. In an article for the *New York Daily Tribune*, included as passage {212} in *Crisis III*, Marx writes that, 'The enormous and increasing amount of British capital invested in all parts of the world must be paid for in interest, dividends and profits';[11] but interest, dividends, and profit are each premised on a different from of investment. In other words, interest is usually interest-bearing capital, dividends are stock capital, and profit stems from the direct operation of a business, but in this case, Marx only premises those distinct forms of investment without going into further detail. In any case, I wanted to bring some attention to this point.

About the 'international repercussions of crisis'

A: Next, why don't we look at the topic of the 'international repercussions of crisis'.

C: This heading deals with the 'balance of trade' and 'balance of payments'. Here Marx emphasises the problem that occurs during a period of general crisis when, as a result of the excessive exporting and importing between all countries,[12] the balance of payments for every country becomes unfavourable, and in relation to this gold steadily flows out of each country like a 'volley firing'.[13] In this discussion he distinguishes between the 'balance of trade' and the 'balance of payments'. In drawing that distinction, Marx notes that the 'balance of payments' is a 'balance of trade that must be settled at a particular date'.[14] England, for instance, commonly provides long-term credit for its exports, but pays cash for imports, and therefore even if its balance of trade is in order, its balance of payments is the opposite.

B: The passages under this heading, as in the passages under the heading 'Export of capital', can be difficult to understand in many cases unless the concrete circumstances of the time when Marx was writing are adequately understood, but going into such issues here will get us too bogged down, so perhaps we can move on.

---

11   Marx 1986b, p. 429.
12   [Marx explains in Book III of *Capital* that it becomes evident that all the countries have 'simultaneously over-exported (i.e. over-produced) and over-imported (i.e. over-traded)' (Marx 1981, p. 624).]
13   Marx 1981a, p. 623.
14   Marx 1981a, p. 649.

'World market and crisis' within Marx's plan

A: What was the reason for placing 'World market and crisis within the drafted plan' as the last subheading under Heading IX ('World market and crisis')?

KURUMA: As I mentioned before, the problems dealt with under Heading IX are outside the original scope of *Capital*, but Marx does deal with them in *Capital* in relation to the main problems under examination, and they are also dealt with in his articles on current events for the *New York Daily Tribune*, where he analyses the actual world market of the time. Those passages are the basis for the content of Heading IX, but of course they were not written as part of a system Marx was arranging, nor do they cover all of the relevant problems, so the composition of this heading necessarily is extremely limited. Thus, at the end, as a point of reference, we wanted to provide readers with some idea of the conception Marx had regarding 'world market and crisis' by including several of the plans he drafted.

B: Although Marx includes 'World market and crisis' as a planned book within his critique of political economy, he did not in fact complete it, nor are there many details about what he had intended to write. Another question is whether he intended to systematically bring together a proper theory of crisis at the end of his critique of political economy.

KURUMA: With regard to that question, it is hard to imagine that Marx had intended to again bring together at the end everything he had written on crisis to date. Rather, it seems to me that, on the basis of what he had developed up to that point, he would have discussed the explosion of crisis under the main theme of 'world market and crisis'. In other words, Marx would have shown that all of the contradictions of bourgeois political economy are in motion as a totality and collide, so that they collectively explode. Through the periodic repetition of global crises, the historical mission of capitalist production would come to an end, replaced by a society that is compatible with the material foundation that was developed within capitalist society. I imagine that this was the sort of thing that Marx had intended to write. But my comments here are so abstract that I doubt they answer your question. [*Laughs.*]

'Various types of crises'

A: Let's turn now to the Heading x, 'Various types of crises'. I think that you struggled with the editing of the passages under this heading and that it underwent various changes along the way. Could you explain more about that?

KURUMA: At first, I alphabetically listed the various types of crises that Marx mentions in his writings, but in so doing there was a great deal of repetition of the same passages. After trying various approaches, I ended up simply listing the passages from works of Marx in chronological order, while including his correspondence separately at the end. But since this approach creates considerable inconvenience for the reader, Teinosuke Ōtani created an index for the passages under the heading.[15] None of the volumes up to this point had included an index within the text itself, but given the circumstances just explained we decided to add this at the beginning of the heading. Actually, I wavered quite a bit about whether to include this heading in *Crisis III* and only finally decided to do so in response to the urging of the editorial committee members. In any case, we discussed many issues in our editorial meetings, including of course the question of how to translate the terms in the index indicating the types of crises.

A: That's right. As Professor Kuruma just said, we thought the subheading should be retained because we realised that the passages included a lot of interesting points that are normally overlooked, some of which are surprisingly important. Marx use of terms to refer to various types of crises is one point that is already quite interesting in itself, but we also realised that some of the expressions we use so casually were hardly used at all by Marx or used in a somewhat different sense, and that Marx and Engels each had his own preferred terms. These are some of the many points that we discussed at our editorial meetings. Since we are not able here to cover everything that we discussed, perhaps we can limit ourselves to a few representative examples?

B: One major issue concerned the meaning of *Handelkrise* and how to translate it. As you can notice right away if you look at the beginning of the index, the term *Handelkrise* was translated as either *keizai kyōkō* (economic crisis) or *shōgyō kyōkō* (commercial crisis). The term 'commercial crisis' was used only

---

15   [The index for Heading x is not included within the *Crisis III* contents in this English edition.]

in the case of the expression *Produktions und Handelskrise*, whereas in the other cases it was translated as 'economic crisis'. Normally *Handelkrise* has been translated in Japanese as *shōgyō kyōkō* (commercial crisis), but in most cases Marx seems to use the term to refer to what is very generally a crisis of the economy. Marx uses the separate term *kommerzielle Krise* to clearly refer to a 'commercial crisis' as opposed to a crisis of industry or agriculture, whereas *Handelskrise* is not a 'commercial crisis' in that sense.

A: Another issue that arose in our discussions concerned the term *Krise* itself.

B: That's right. In England, terms like 'commercial distress' or 'commercial difficulties' were at first to express the phenomenon of crisis, but starting from around the 1840s the term 'commercial crisis' came into frequent use. The term 'crisis' originally referred to the peak of an illness that is its turning point. A person might reach that peak in the evening and would be likely to recover if able to make it through the night. The term was later used to refer to various sorts of critical situations within society. In applying the term to society, adjectives were added to indicate the sort of social phenomenon in question, such as a 'political crisis' or 'commercial crisis'.

C: The use of the term 'commercial' in that case is not in opposition to industry or agriculture, but rather refers to a crisis of the economy manifested generally in the realm of circulation, isn't that correct?

B: Yes, I think so. Under Heading X in *Crisis III*, there are many passages written originally in English by Marx, and he mainly uses the term 'commercial' in the sense just explained. In other words, it would be translated as *Handels-* in German. But there are also cases where the English term 'commercial crisis' corresponds to *kommerzielle Krise* in German or to *shōgyō kyōkō* in Japanese.

A: The Japanese term *kyōkō* (crisis) stems from the kanji characters in the verb *osoreawateru*, which corresponds in meaning to the English verb 'to panic', and in this sense, as Professor Kuruma explained earlier, the term is not always appropriate as a translation of 'crisis'. Incidentally, the *Marx-Lexikon* editors were curious about when the term *kyōkō* was first used in a translation. As far as we could determine, its first appearance was in Sadamasu Ōshima's 1883 translation of *Money and the Mechanism of Exchange* by William Stanley Jevons. In that case, *kyōkō* was used to translate 'panic'. The term was also used in Kōhei Makiyama's 1894 translation of *Éléments d'économie politique* by Émile Louis

Victor de Laveleye. The translation was based on the English edition of the book, with *kyōkō* used to translate 'crisis'.

C: Another issue that we discussed was who was the first to use the term 'crisis' to refer to the economic phenomenon of crisis. The scholar Minokichi Hirase has claimed that Sismondi first used the terms *crise* and *crise commerciale* in his 1819 book *Nouveaux principes d'économie politique*.

D: In addition, there was the issue regarding the decision to translate Marx' use of the English term 'industrial crisis' as *kōgyō kyōkō* rather than *sangyō kyōkō* (although I won't go into the reason here).[16] Also, the Japanese term *kajōseisan kyōkō* (overproduction crisis) does not have a direct equivalent as *Überproduktionskrise* in the writings of Marx, who instead used the expression *Krise aus Überproduktion* (crisis from overproduction) or *Krise der Überproduktion* (crisis of overproduction). One other thing is that only Engels used the term *Zwischenkrise* (intermediate crisis).

B: Many of the passages from Marx and Engels included in *Crisis III* deal with current events and were written at different moments over a long period of time, so naturally the content and expressions used changed in line with actual developments and the progress in their own research. In order to study systematically what Marx and Engels thought of the crises they actually encountered or the crises they anticipated, readers can consult the two-volume collection by Yoshio Miyake titled, *Marx and Engels's History of Crisis in England*.[17] In addition, readers can consult the section 'On the theory of 'intermediate crisis' in Professor Kuruma's article 'A Few Problems Concerning Postwar Theories of Crisis',[18] which deals with the concept of 'intermediate crisis' that arose in the debate following World War II over the changes in the form of crisis and the industrial cycle. In that article, Professor Kuruma points out that Jürgen Kuczynski's criticism of Engels was based on a misinterpretation. We can also find a discussion of the concept of 'intermediate crisis' in Miyake's article 'On J. Kuczynski's Mistaken Theory of Intermediate Crisis', which is included as an appendix in the second volume of *Marx and Engels's History of Crisis in England*.[19]

---

16 [Whereas *sangyō* corresponds to 'industry' in such general usage as the 'advertising industry' or 'automotive industry', *kyōkō* refers more specifically to industry in the sense of processing raw materials and manufacturing goods.]
17 Miyake 1974a and Miyake 1974b.
18 [See Section 2 of Chapter 14 of this book.]
19 Miyake 1974b, pp. 283–397.

'False theories of crisis'

A: The final heading in *Crisis III* is 'False theories of crisis'. Some of the mistaken theories were already dealt with in passages included in *Crisis I* and *II*, such as the passages under Heading V ('Marx's criticism of theories denying the possibility of crisis') in *Crisis I* and under subheading 8 ('Critique of the so-called theory of underconsumption') in *Crisis II*.

KURUMA: Those passages in *Crisis I* are Marx's critique of theories that denied the possibility of a general crisis. Ricardo, in particular, never actually experienced a periodic crisis, so he did not perceive the contradictions. But once periodic crises had occurred, it was no longer possible to deny the possibility of crisis. It thus became necessary to explain the cause of crisis somehow. This heading on false theories concerns the incorrect theories that sought to explain the real crises that were encountered.

B: In that sense, the underconsumption theory dealt with in *Crisis II* is one such theory.

KURUMA: That's right. It would be best to read that part along with the passages under this final heading of *Crisis III* as constituting the critique of false theories. From the time of Marx's death up to the present, all sorts of other false theories have appeared in a new guise, such as the ideas of Keynes, but in dealing with such recent theories the passages under those headings offer us a good basic frame of reference, even if, naturally, we cannot directly apply Marx's criticism. One thing I should point out is that, unlike the passages under other headings in *Crisis III*, there is no underlining of important sentences in the passages under Heading XI. This is because we would have had to underline both the description of the false theory and the critique of it, meaning that nearly everything would have been underlined. Also, I should note that we included a letter from Marx to Engels dated 3 February 1851, even though there are some problems with the view expressed in it, as Engels points out in his response. Our reason was that the letter, as the first example of Marx's critique of the Currency school, seemed too important to ignore. I hope, in any case, that readers will take these points into consideration.

A: Could someone briefly introduce a few of the views criticised by Marx in this part of *Crisis III*?

C: There are many passages here from Marx criticising the mistaken theories that were raised against the backdrop of the Bank Charter Act of 1844, but there is more than just that. Since we don't have time to go into detail, let me just give a brief overview. Marx's critique centres on the ironic role played by that law in worsening the panic during the crisis of 1847 and 1857. The idea that crisis could be averted by government artificially determining the quantity of currency and its circulation was criticised by concrete reality itself. The fallacy of Ricardo's theory of currency underlying the Bank Charter Act also came to light, fundamentally refuting the idea that the source of crisis could be found in the realm of money circulation. In addition, with regard to the 'Report on the Crisis of 1857–58' of the House of Commons, which concluded that 'the recent commercial crisis ... was mainly owing to excessive speculation and abuse of credit', Marx responds by saying:

> What are the social circumstances reproducing, almost regularly, these seasons of general self-delusion, of over-speculation and fictitious credit? If they were once traced out, we should arrive at a very plain alternative. Either they may be controlled by society, or they are inherent in the present system of production. In the first case, society may avert crises; in the second, so long as the system lasts, they must be borne with, like the natural changes of the seasons.[20]

Marx points out that this report, as well as the 'Report on the Commercial Distress of 1847' and 'all the other similar reports which preceded them', share the same 'essential defect' in that:

> They treat every new crisis as an insulated phenomenon, appearing for the first time on the social horizon, and, therefore, to be accounted for by incidents, movements and agencies altogether peculiar, or presumed to be peculiar, to the one period just elapsed between the penultimate and the ultimate revulsion.[21]

Such passages express well, I think, one aspect of Marx's fundamental attitude when investigating crisis.

---

20   Marx 1981b, p. 34. In passage {295} in *Crisis III*.
21   Marx 1981b, p. 34. In passage {295} in *Crisis III*.

B: Yes, and there's also the following scathing criticism by Marx of those who sought the cause of crisis in speculation.

> Still the very recurrence of crises despite all the warnings of the past, in regular intervals, forbids the idea of seeking their final causes in the recklessness of single individuals ... The political economists who pretend to explain the regular spasms of industry and commerce by speculation, resemble the now extinct school of natural philosophers who considered fever as the true cause of all maladies.[22]

D: Another mistaken theory that Marx criticises is the view that denied or overlooked the overproduction of commodities, focusing instead on the increase in the 'additional virtual money capital'[23] that accompanies capitalist development, and seeking to centre the problem on the excess production of money capital, such as the view of Fullarton. There are also passages in which Marx criticises the view of crisis solely as the fault of insufficient capital or means of payment, or the related view that sought the cause of crisis in the export of gold; as well as the view (held by Hodgson) that crisis is caused by the 'absorption of floating [circulating capital] into fixed capital'.[24]

A: I think Professor Kuruma must be a little tired by this point, so we should probably end today's discussion here. Thank you everyone.

---

22 Marx 1986a, p. 401. In passage {292} in *Crisis III*.
23 Marx 1978, p. 574.
24 Marx 1981a, p. 617.

CHAPTER 8

Marx-Lexikon Crisis IV

1   Part 1: Contents[1]

I.   Fundamental problems of the cyclical movement of industry

1.   What gives production the impetus for its rapid expansion?
> {316}   *Capital Vol. 1*
> 'The enormous power, inherent ... cheapening commodities'.
> (MECW-35, pp. 455–56)
>
> {317}   *Capital Vol. 1*
> 'Since the capital produces yearly ... wages may rise'.
> (MECW-35, pp. 608–09)
>
> {318}   *Capital Vol. 1*
> 'The mass of social wealth ... development of the old ones'.
> (MECW-35, pp. 626–27)

2.   Under what conditions is the sudden expansion of production possible?
> {319}   First manuscript for *Book II of Capital*
> 'In dem fixen Kapital ist ein ... increase of actual capital'.
> (MEGA II/4.1, pp. 352–53)
>
> {320}   *Capital Vol. 1*
> See {316}
>
> {321}   *Capital Vol. 1*
> 'But if a surplus labouring ... or half-employed hands'.
> (MECW-35, pp. 626–27)
>
> {322}   *Capital Vol. 3*
> 'Jones emphasises correctly ... in fixed capital grows, etc.'
> (MECW-37, p. 265)

---

1   The table of contents and passage sources in *Marx Engels Collected Works* (MECW) for the fourth volume on crisis of *Marx-Lexikon zur politischen Ökonomie*, Kuruma 1976b (ed.).]

3. The expansion by fits and starts of the scale of production is the precondition for its equally sudden contraction; the latter again evokes the former. Effects become causes in their turn, and the various vicissitudes of the whole process, which always reproduces its own conditions, take on the form of periodicity

{323}   See {316}

{324}   *Capital Vol. 1*
'The course characteristic ... condition of modern industry'.
(MECW-35, pp. 627–28)

{325}   *Capital Vol. 3*
'The industrial cycle is of ... impulse has been given'.
(MECW-37, p. 488)

II. Order of the phases of the industrial cycle – From what phase does the industrial cycle begin, what phases does it pass through, and where does it end?

{326}   'Review May to October [1850]'
'However, this much at least ... to £713 million (1848)'.
(MECW-10, p. 497)

{327}   'Pauperism and Free Trade'
'Modern industry and commerce ... again in quiescence'.
(MECW-11, p. 357)

{328}   'Russian Policy Against Turkey'
'Without the great alternative ... now ruling bourgeoise'.
(MECW-12, p. 169)

{329}   'Manufacturers and Commerce'
'Having considered, in ... likely again to recede'.
(MECW-16, p. 492)

{330}   'Value, Price and Profit'
'All of you know that ... regulated by their values'.
(MECW-20, p. 143)

{331}   'Preface to English Edition of *Capital*' (Engels)
'The decennial cycle ... recurrent from 1825 to 1867'.
(MECW-35, p. 35)

{332}   *Capital Vol. 1*
'The life of modern industry ... of the industrial cycle'.
(MECW-35, p. 455)

{333}   *Capital Vol. 1*
'The course characteristic ... agents of its reproduction'.
(MECW-35, p. 627)

{334} *Capital Vol. 1*
       'Before I turn to ... cycle periodically ends'.
       (MECW–35, p. 660)
{335} *Capital Vol. 1* (French edition)
       'Mais c'est seulement ... se raccourcira graduellement'.
       (Marx 1993, p. 710)
{336} *Capital Vol. 1*
       'This much is evident ... for the next turnover cycle'.
       (MECW–35, p. 455)
{337} *Capital Vol. 2*
       'This shows the way in which ... after the end of a crisis'.
       (MECW–36, p. 282)
{338} *Capital Vol. 3*
       'The ensuing stagnation ... increased productive forces'.
       (MECW–37, p. 254)
{339} *Capital Vol. 3*
       'If we observe the cycles ... corresponds to the period of crisis'.
       (MECW–37, p. 358)
{340} *Capital Vol. 3*
       'On the whole, then, the ... is still self-supporting'.
       (MECW–37, p. 488)
{341} *Capital Vol. 3*
       'We have already seen ... terms to the money capitalist'.
       (MECW–37, p. 493)

III. **Descriptions of the various phases of the industrial cycle**
{342} 'Review [January–February 1850]'
       'While the Continent has ... ÉGALITÉ, FRATERNITÉ'.
       (MECW–10, pp. 263–67)
{343} 'Review [May– October 1850]'
       'The political turmoil ... as certain as this crisis'.
       (MECW–10, pp. 490–510)
{344} 'The Eighteenth Brumaire of Louis Napoleon'
       'In the year 1851, France ... *terror without end!*'
       (MECW–11, pp. 173–76)
{345} 'Pauperism and Free Trade'
       'Modern industry and commerce ... statistics of *The Economist*'.
       (MECW–11, p. 357)
{346} 'Pauperism and Free Trade'
       'But the most superficial ... subject of my next letter'.
       (MECW–11, pp. 360–63)

{347} 'Russian Policy Against Turkey'
'Without the great alternative ... Ancient Greece and Rome'.
(MECW–12, p. 169)

{348} 'The Monetary Crisis in Europe'
'The general commercial crisis ... the revolutions of 1848'.
(MECW–15, p. 113)

{349} 'The Causes of the Monetary Crisis in Europe'
'The monetary crisis in Germany ... the people was wrong'.
(MECW–15, pp. 117–19)

{350} 'The British Revulsion'
'The British commercial revulsion ... of 1837 to 1847'.
(MECW–15, pp. 385–87)

{351} 'The Trade Crisis in England'
'Still the very recurrence ... heart of English production'.
(MECW–15, pp. 410–02)

{352} 'The English Bank Act of 1844'
'What other proof was ... Act, the Committee say'.
(MECW–16, p. 4)

{353} *Grundrisse*
'Similarly, capital may lie ... after the water brooks'.
(MECW–29, p. 10)

{354} *A Contribution to the Critique of Political Economy*
'Under conditions of advanced ... their own relations'.
(MECW–29, pp. 378–79)

{355} 'Manufactures and Commerce'
'From the first table ... likely again to recede'.
(MECW–16, p. 493)

{356} 'Value, Price and Profit'
'All of you know that ... regulated by their values'.
(MECW–20, p. 143)

{357} 'Afterword to the Second German Edition of *Capital* Vol. 1'
'The contradictions inherent ... Prusso-German empire'.
(MECW–35, p. 20)

{358} 'Preface to the Second German Edition of *Capital* Vol. 1' (Engels)
'The working of the industrial ... again vanish into air'.
(MECW–35, p. 35)

{359} *Capital Vol. 1*
'The enormous power ... 1863 complete collapse'. /
'We find then ... note subjoined'
(MECW–35, pp. 455–58 / pp. 461–62)

{360} *Capital Vol. 1*
'The course characteristic ... condition of modern industry'.
(MECW-35, pp. 627–28)

{361} *Capital Vol. 1*
'Before I turn to the regular ... other London industries'.
(MECW-35, pp. 660–61)

{362} *Capital Vol. 2*
'This much is evident ... next turnover cycle'.
(MECW-36, pp. 187–88)

{363} *Capital Vol. 2*
'This shows the way ... the end of a crisis'.
(MECW-36, pp. 282)

{364} *Capital Vol. 2*
'Every crisis at once lessens ... harbinger of a coming crisis'.
(MECW-36, pp. 409–10)

{365} *Capital Vol. 3*
'The main damage ... and increased productive forces'.
(MECW-37, pp. 254–55)

{366} *Capital Vol. 3*
'In spite of its independent ... to an abrupt end'.
(MECW-37, pp. 303–04)

{367} *Capital Vol. 3*
'If we observe the cycles ... during the crisis of 1847'.
(MECW-37, p. 358)

{368} *Capital Vol. 3* (Engels)
'We have seen that Gilbart ... crash of 1857'.
(MECW-37, pp. 404–06.)

{369} *Capital Vol. 3*
'In times of prosperity ... and the latter increases'.
(MECW-37, pp. 444–48)

{370} *Capital Vol. 3*
'Fullarton quotes the discovery ... follows after a storm'.
(MECW-37, pp. 450–51)

{371} *Capital Vol. 3*
'Should circulation as ... return to this question later'.
(MECW-37, pp. 456–58)

{372} *Capital Vol. 3*
'Therefore, when the money ... of centralising fortunes'.
(MECW-37, pp. 467–68)

{373} *Capital Vol. 3*

'As long as the reproduction ... debacle takes place'.
(MECW-37, pp. 481–84)

{374} *Capital Vol. 3*
'We revert now ... on their own account"'.
(MECW-37, pp. 484–87)

{375} *Capital Vol. 3*
'After the reproduction ... solvency of their owners'.
(MECW-37, pp. 487–92)

{376} *Capital Vol. 3*
'We have already seen ... not relative to profit'.
(MECW-37, pp. 493–94)

{377} *Capital Vol. 3*
'In countries with a developed ... coin or paper money'.
(MECW-37, p. 498)

{378} *Capital Vol. 3* (Engels)
'The statistics of exports ... is still expanding'.
(MECW-37, pp. 493–94)

{379} *Capital Vol. 3*
'The accumulation of all ... of the reproduction process'.
(MECW-37, pp. 500–01)

{380} *Capital Vol. 3*
'Thus, the accumulation ... capacity as middleman'.
(MECW-37, p. 503)

{381} *Capital Vol. 3*
'In the discussion on ... phenomena are repeated'.
(MECW-37, pp. 509–15)

{382} *Capital Vol. 3* (Engels)
'As long as the state ... £4 to £5 million'.
(MECW-37, pp. 524–25)

{383} *Capital Vol. 3*
'Everybody acquainted with ... gold increases the crisis'.
(MECW-37, pp. 533–35)

{384} *Capital Vol. 3*
'It should be noted ... vaults of the Bank'.
(MECW-37, pp. 559–60)

{385} *Capital Vol. 3*
'Before the gold mines ... of the increased wealth'.
(MECW-37, pp. 560–61)

{386} *Capital Vol. 3*
'Sixthly, with the exception ... against Europe and America'.
(MECW-37, pp. 563–65)

{387} *Capital Vol. 3*
       'An import of precious ... production is in full swing'.
       (MECW-37, pp. 565–67)

{388} *Capital Vol. 3*
       'He then says in ... bank credit relatively low'.
       (MECW-37, pp. 580–84)

{389} *Theories of Surplus Value*
       'Meanwhile we just note ... to their further fall'.
       (MECW-32, pp. 125–26)

{390} Engels to Marx, 15 November 1857
       'This time the crisis is ... most will be recovered'.
       (MECW-40, pp. 200–01)

{391} Marx to Engels, 8 December 1857
       'I've had a gratifying ... than a PRIVATE CAPITALIST'.
       (MECW-40, pp. 215–16)

{392} Marx to Sorge, 27 September 1873
       'I hope that the American ... the sting out of it'.
       (MECW-44, p. 536)

{393} Marx to Danielson, 15 November 1878
       '[The] English crisis which ... the white producers'.
       (MECW-45, p. 344)

{394} Marx to Danielson, 12 September 1880
       'The present crisis was ... me too far at present'.
       (MECW-46, p. 31)

{395} Marx to Danielson, 19 February 1881
       'I wrote you some time ... a very narrow escape'.
       (MECW-46, pp. 62–63)

{396} Engels to Bebel, 22 December 1882
       'The crisis in America would ... before it is due'.
       (MECW-46, p. 415)

{397} Engels to Danielson, 13 November 1885
       'The crisis of which ... prairies remains unexhausted'.
       (MECW-47, pp. 349–50)

IV. Fixed capital and the industrial cycle

1. The average time of renewing fixed capital and the duration of the industrial cycle

{398} *Grundrisse*
       'The total time in terms ... unique to large-scale industry'.
       (MECW-29, pp. 104–05)

{399} *Capital Vol. 2*
'In the illustration under ... next turnover cycle'.
(MECW-36, pp. 187–88)

{400} Marx to Engels, 2 March 1858
'Apropos. Can you ... consolidation of big industry'.
(MECW-40, p. 278)

{401} Engels to Marx, 4 March 1858
'As to the question of machinery ... less than 10 years'.
(MECW-40, pp. 279–81)

{402} Marx to Engels, 5 March 1858
'My BEST THANKS ... replace itself completely'.
(MECW-40, p. 282)

2. Which phase of the industrial cycle is the starting point for large new investment and in what phase is it carried out?

{403} *Capital Vol. 2*
'But a crisis always forms ... next turnover cycle'.
(MECW-36, pp. 188)

{404} *Capital Vol. 3*
'We revert now to ... Royal Bank of Liverpool)'.
(MECW-37, pp. 484–85)

{405} *Capital Vol. 3*
'After the reproduction ... absence of loan capital'.
(MECW-37, p. 487)

3. It is mainly crisis that forces the premature renewal of constant capital on a large social scale

{406} *Capital Vol. 2*
'The instruments of ... catastrophes or crises'.
(MECW-36, p. 173)

4. The direct consequences for the reproduction of the means of subsistence will be very different according to whether a greater or smaller part of the surplus products is converted into one of the types of fixed capital.

{407} *Theories of Surplus Value*
'A large part of constant ... types of fixed capital'.
(MECW-32, p. 123)

v. **Changes in the course of the industrial cycle arising from the development of capitalist production**

{408} *Capital Vol. 1* (French edition)
'Mais c'est seulement ... cycles se raccourcira graduellement'.
(Marx 1993, p. 710)

{409} *Capital Vol. 3*
'But much is already ... in the process of reproduction'.
(MECW–37, p. 120)

{410} *Capital Vol. 3*
'Herewith follow ... and the subsequent commercial crisis"'.
(MECW–37, pp. 123–24)

{411} *Capital Vol. 3* (Engels)
'As I have already said ... powerful future crisis"'.
(MECW–37, p. 488)

{412} 'Preface' to second German edition of *The Condition of the English Working Class*
'"For England, the ... right in the end'. /
'"This, then was ... Which is it to be?'
(MECW–27, p. 317 / pp. 318–20)

{413} 'On Certain Peculiarities in England's Economic and Political Development'
'The absence of crises since ... giant crisis in the making'.
(MECW–27, pp. 324–25)

{414} Marx to Lavrov, 18 June 1875
'The trade crisis goes ... of the bourgeois world'.
(MECW–45, p. 78)

{415} Engels to Danielson, 13 November 1885
'The crisis of which ... prairies remains unexhausted'.
(MECW–47, pp. 349–50)

{416} Engels to Danielson, 8 February 1886
'Here the industrial crisis ... *Uns kann's recht sein*'.
(MECW–47, p. 402)

2   Part 2: Discussion[2]

The next volume will include the full index for the crisis volumes

A: This volume, *Crisis IV*, subtitled *The Industrial Cycle*, is the last of the main volumes on crisis. I say 'main volumes', because the next installment of *Marx-Lexikon* will include a full index for the four volumes on crisis.

B: I believe that the next volume with the index will bring to an end the first round of the *Marx-Lexikon* volumes.

A: Yes, that's right. Actually, our original plan was to include the index within *Crisis IV* because it is not just a supplement but something that compliments the main content. For example, despite the importance of the relation between the phases of the industrial cycle and changes in the rate of interest rate, there is no independent heading on that topic in the four volumes on crisis. We thought that including an index would be a way for readers to locate that issue. And there are a lot of other similar issues. Starting last summer, Sukeyoshi Kimura, Yoshio Komatsu, and Noriko Maehata handled the fundamental task of compiling this index.

The content of *Crisis IV* expanded beyond what we had initially expected, and the index was clearly going to be quite large too. Simply incorporating the content from the previous volumes on crisis alone would have resulted in a huge index. If we had created the same sort of index as we had made for the two *Marx-Lexikon* volumes on the materialist conception of history[3] it would probably have ended up being twice as long, since there are three volumes on crisis. There was not much point in creating a limited index, so it was going to end up being quite large no matter how much we tried to condense and organise it. In the end, after consulting the publisher, we decided to create an entirely separate volume for the index.

C: The index will be published as the tenth volume of *Marx-Lexikon*, but does it include entries for volumes other than crisis?

---

2 [Discussion published as an insert for the fourth volume on crisis of *Marx-Lexikon zur politischen Ökonomie*, Kuruma 1976b (ed.).]
3 [Kuruma 1971a (ed.) and Kuruma 1971b (ed.).]

A: Yes. Our current plan is to include the headings for all nine volumes and a topic index, but if more space is available, we may include other things, so readers can look forward to that content.[4]

Theory of crisis proper and theory of the industrial cycle: Characteristics and structure of *Crisis IV*

A: Shall we begin by discussing the position of *Crisis IV* within the four volumes on crisis?

D: We can see that the main title of the volume includes, in parentheses, 'industrial cycle', and that the roman numerals for the headings start from the beginning, at I, II, etc., even though the number of the passages cited continue on directly from *Crisis III*. So perhaps we could begin by explaining this.

KURUMA: I think the situation for the passage numbers is clear since we decided to have the numbering continue throughout all four volumes. As for the roman numerals used in the headings, we felt that since the fourth volume presents key writings from Marx and Engels on the industrial cycle, premised on the theory of crisis proper presented in the first three *Marx-Lexikon* volumes, we wanted to make a clear distinction from the earlier volumes by starting the roman numerals over from the beginning.

B: It seems rather difficult to pin down the difference between this volume and the three previous ones. In a sense, the theory of crisis could be said to be a theory of the industrial cycle, and conversely, the theory of the industrial cycle naturally encompasses an elucidation of crisis.

KURUMA: That's exactly right. Distinguishing the two is quite difficult. I'm not exactly sure if a clear line can be drawn between them. One thing we have had to take into consideration when organising the writings Marx has left us is that his descriptions of the industrial cycle are often a commentary on current events, rather than being a well-developed, proper theory of crisis. If it were just a matter of jotting down quotes from Marx's writings for myself, it

---

4 [This tenth volume, published in January 1977, included the headings and indexes for Competition (vol. 1), Method (vols. 2–3), Materialist Conception of History (vols. 4–5), Crisis (vols. 6–9), as well as an index of books and periodicals cited within the passages quoted, a name index, and a list of the sources used from the works of Marx and Engels corresponding to the passage numbers in each volume. – T. Ōtani.]

would be a different matter, but for *Marx-Lexikon* it seemed more appropriate to draw the distinction between the two. I think this point was touched on in the discussion for *Crisis 1*, so perhaps readers can refer to that discussion.

B: This might be a bit of an extreme statement, but it seems that even though we speak of the *theory* of the industrial cycle, it actually come down to the *history* of crisis or of the industrial cycle. Already, in the theory of crisis proper, it is explained that the fundamental law of the cyclical fluctuations of industry is the collision with barriers, the accumulation of contradictions, and the temporary resolution of those contradictions. So, when discussing the industrial cycle, the task becomes the investigation of how each of those laws penetrates the historical cyclical process, only leaving us the task of historically investigating crisis and the industrial cycle. Does that seem fair to say?

KURUMA: I'm not so sure about that. Granted, each industrial cycle has its own particular characteristics. And there are many differences between them with regard to what factor drove prosperity and how it began. And it is crucial to analyse each cycle to clarify its characteristics and particularities. But, at the same time, there are elements common to every cycle. It seems to me that a theoretical task is to bring out these generalities of the circular movement of industry.

B: But aren't the common elements and generalities already made clear in the theory of crisis proper? In the case of capitalist production, even though there are intrinsic barriers, there is a tendency to overcome those barriers to develop productive power absolutely, resulting inevitably in the accumulation of contradictions. Once the barriers have been broken through to a certain extent, the contradictions collectively explode as a crisis, thereby temporarily dissolving the contradictions. Since this process is repeated, the movement of capitalist production always takes the form of cyclical fluctuations accompanied by crisis. This is already clarified in the theory of crisis proper.

KURUMA: That is correct, to the extent of what you just described. This is precisely why, in a sense, the theory of crisis is also a theory of the industrial cycle, and why the theory of crisis, in the proper sense of the term, could also be said to constitute the most fundamental aspect of the theory of the industrial cycle. However, that it is not sufficient in itself to cover the aspects that all industrial cycles have in common. The issues that you just mentioned are covered in the first three volumes, but there remain problems common to each industrial cycle, which are not addressed in those volumes. For *Crisis IV (Industrial Cycle)*, I sought gather passages regarding such problems.

The sudden contraction of production in a crisis is the precursor to a sudden expansion of production, but what sets the stage for this sudden expansion? – Of course, if we look in detail at each industrial cycle to date, there would be various differences between them, but from a general perspective we should be able to locate a number of factors common to most cases. In the passages included in *Crisis IV*, Marx presents those main factors. These passages can be seen as conveying the important results from his own detailed investigation of the industrial cycle, and the problems involved are not addressed in the first three *Marx-Lexikon* volumes on crisis. Those earlier volumes also do not examine cases where, even though there is an impulse posited for the sudden expansion of production, a corresponding rapid expansion of production does not occur. The production conditions are posited as a given at a particular time, so the question becomes: What makes possible a sudden expansion of production under the given conditions? There is also the question of what phase the industrial cycle begins from, what phases it passes through, and where it ends. Such problems differ from the question of the characteristics of individual industrial cycles. Furthermore, it goes without saying that new and renewed investment in fixed capital has great significance for the cyclical movement of capitalist production, and this is an issue that must be treated generally, apart from any historical analysis. Also, the time span of the industrial cycle changes as capitalist production develops, and although in one respect it is an historical change, it differs from the question of the particularity of individual cycles deriving from various random circumstances. Instead, the change in the time span must be grasped in relation to the development of capitalist production itself, and in this sense concerns the general circumstance. Those are the sorts of problems dealt with in *Crisis IV*.

A: I think that Professor Kuruma has nicely summarised the content of this volume. That gives us a basic idea of the structure of the volume, including the significance of each of the five headings. So why don't we move on and look at the content of each heading?

What gives production an impetus for sudden expansion?

C: The first heading in this volume, titled 'Fundamental problems concerning the cyclical movement of industry', is divided into the following three subheadings.

1. What gives production the impetus [*Anstoß*][5] for its rapid expansion?
2. Under what conditions is the sudden expansion of production possible?
3. The expansion by fits and starts of the scale of production is the precondition for its equally sudden contraction [...]

What topic does this first main heading deal with?

KURUMA: We begin here – in turning our attention to the industrial cycle after having dealt with the theory of crisis – by bringing together the main matters at hand. In the theory of crisis, the industrial cycle was considered from the perspective of capitalist production driving beyond its own barrier and then being brought back within its limitations. Since crisis is the *temporary dissolution* of contradictions, it might be said, abstractly, that the same process should repeat itself, but it is only when we clarify how the business climate revives from a phase of stagnation following a crisis, and more particularly, the motive or opportunity that leads to the beginning of a sudden expansion of production, that we will be able to understand theoretically the phenomena that concern the cyclical movement of industry. In other words, as expressed in Subheading 3, we become able to grasp that the sudden expansion of production is the premise of its sudden contraction, and that the latter calls forth the former, so that 'effects become causes in their turn' and 'the various vicissitudes of the whole process, which always reproduces its own conditions, take on the form of periodicity'. I don't want to say that this problem is the starting point when considering the systematic unfolding of the theory of the industrial cycle, but in treating the industrial cycle itself as a problem, the first thing to consider is what impetus (*Anstoß*) stimulates the sudden expansion of production or what makes possible the sudden expansion of production.

E: In considering this, don't we need, on a more fundamental level, to consider not only the impetus to expanded production but also such conditions as the low level of wages, prices of raw materials, and interest rates?

KURUMA: Of course, those are the premises. However, even if wages or the price of raw materials are low, capitalists will not be willing to make new investments unless there is a prospect of selling products through expanded repro-

---

[5] [The title for Subheading 1 is taken from a passage in the edition of Book III of *Capital* edited by Engels. It was later learned that Marx in his original manuscript had used the term impetus *Stoß* (impact), not *Anstoß* (impulse) (see MEGA II/4.2, p. 542.39). However, this does not change the meaning here significantly. – T. Ōtani.]

duction. Thus, the prospect of being able to sell products must be premised. There has to be some sort of impetus, such as a discovery of a new production method, the 'moral [*moralisch*] deterioration'[6] of the old means of production, or the discovery of a new use value. Of course, the pioneering of new markets or the discovery of new use values do not occur at random (although in the process of an actual industrial cycle, random circumstances do exert a major influence), but rather should be viewed as arising through capital's efforts for valorisation. That does not occur at any given phase of the industrial cycle, however. It takes place during a slump, not during the boom times when products are selling well, and the outcome is an upturn in the business climate. Clearly, the issue of the impulse (*Anstoß*) is important to the consideration of the industrial cycle, at least if premised on the theory of crisis.

What makes a sudden expansion of production possible?

D: The title of the second subheading is 'What conditions make possible a sudden expansion of production?' In other words, this concerns the flexibility of production. There are just four passages under this subheading (including one from the first manuscript for Book II of *Capital*), followed by a footnote referring to eight passages that appear in *Crisis II* under Subheading 10 ('Elasticity of the capitalistic production process') within Heading VIII. What was the reason for that footnote?

KURUMA: Whereas the first subheading looks at what sort of impulses trigger a sudden expansion of production, the second subheading centres on what makes that sudden expansion possible. The relation between the two should be clear. As you pointed out, the issue concerns the elasticity or flexibility of the production process. As to why there is a passage from the first manuscript for Book II of *Capital* and just a few other passages, the reason is very simple. At the time we were editing *Crisis II*, we had not yet been able to see that manuscript and were thus unaware of the descriptions therein. The manuscript was published a year ago as Volume 49 of the Russian language edition of the selected works. We were able to see the original German manuscript in connection to the project to translate it for the Japanese language edition of the collected works of Marx and Engels. Had we known of the manuscript at the time we were editing *Crisis II*, we naturally would have included the passage from it. Indeed, it can be considered the best overall description of the issue of 'flexibility'. Given its importance, we added the passage to *Crisis IV*, while also including

---

6 Marx 1978, p. 250.

c: Is there a difference between the treatment of the issue in *Crisis IV* as compared to *Crisis II*?

a footnote to refer to all of the related passages in *Crisis II*. We did not want to include all of those citations again to avoid taking up too much space.

c: Is there a difference between the treatment of the issue in *Crisis IV* as compared to *Crisis II*?

KURUMA: In *Crisis II*, the issue centres on the flexibility of the production process that makes it possible for production to expand by *surmounting the barrier* of capital, assisted by commercial capital and the credit system. In contrast, for *Crisis IV*, the issue becomes the *sudden expansion* of the scale of production and what makes that expansion possible. However, the two are not separate. Rather, they can be viewed as the consideration of the same thing from a different perspective. Thus, the question of where the issue of flexibility should be treated among the four volumes on crisis, had it been placed in a single volume, is rather difficult. We positioned it in *Crisis II* because it was related to the main theme of that volume and because at that point we did not know the exact content of *Crisis IV*, which had yet to be assembled.

A: That passage from the first manuscript for Book II of *Capital* is quite interesting. It examines many issues that are not dealt with in the current edition of Book II.

KURUMA: It is quite interesting. The manuscript includes some suggestive ideas related to the relation between fixed capital investment and the industrial cycle, as well as extremely interesting passages regarding the significance of Part 1 and Part 3 of Book II in relation to the theory of crisis. But if we enter into those issues there will be too much to say.

A: I'm sorry, shall we get back to the main topic?

How should the cyclical movement of expansion and contraction be understood?

c: The third subheading has the following title: 'The expansion by fits and starts of the scale of production is the precondition for its equally sudden contraction; the latter again evokes the former. Effects become causes in their turn, and the various vicissitudes of the whole process, which always reproduces its own conditions, take on the form of periodicity'. It deals with something that seems very much on the phenomenal level, in line with Professor Kuruma earlier comment about the *phenomena* that concern the cyclical movement of industry'. Does this mean that the various movements – such as the rapid contraction that arises as an outcome of rapid expansion, and then becomes the cause of the next expansion – can be superficially observed from the actual circular movement? Is this an issue that pertains to the 'fundamental problems' of the industrial cycle?

KURUMA: We chose that title for third subheading because it is based on a line from Marx,[7] but certainly if we just take it on its own, detached from the relation to the problems that precede and follow it, it seems to be describing the sudden *contraction* to trigger a *sudden* expansion. In fact, an actual contraction causes a sudden expansion under certain conditions, and those conditions are themselves created out of the process of the industrial cycle, but since the heading is detached from that relation, only looking at it by itself could create the impression that 'C' just mentioned. Moreover, that citation from Marx is excerpted from a longer discussion, so the meaning is unlikely to be fully understood without the preceding parts. Our reason for including a citation in such an incomplete form is that the entire passage is included as passage {144} in *Crisis II* under Subheading 10 ('Elasticity of the capitalist production process') of Heading VIII, and because we also included a footnote under Subheading 2 in *Crisis IV* to refer to that passage. The content presented under Subheading 3 is premised on everything elucidated earlier, and it presents phenomena that were clarified as a result, namely that capitalist production always repeats a circular motion of expansion and contraction, just as a celestial body, once thrown into motion, continually retraces the same orbit. Moreover, in discussing the industrial cycle, the sudden contraction of production also becomes an issue, whereas before the issue had centred on the sudden expansion. The problem pertains to the theory of crisis proper, which was the focus in the previous volumes, particularly *Crisis II*. What is being discussed with regard to Subheading 3 is only first given a theoretical basis by taking all of those other points into consideration. If detached from those points, it will seem to be a mere phenomenal description.

F: In relation to what 'C' mentioned, modern theories of the business cycle also include investigations of fluctuations that seek the cause of sudden expansions of production in the stimulus of the automotive industry or railway construction. Is that different from what you had in mind regarding the impulse for expansion?

---

7   Marx 1976, pp. 785–86.

KURUMA: Insofar as dealing with that sort of particular issue, there is not much difference. It seems to me that the difference to Marx concerns whether the contradictions of capitalist production are posited as the basis for explaining a case where the expansion of production due to some impulse sends out ripples that ultimately lead to overproduction and crisis. I cannot offer much more than that sort of vague comment because I am not so familiar with modern economics. But as one gets closer and closer to the surface phenomena, our own way of treating a problem becomes similar to the way it is dealt with by modern economics [*kindai keizaigaku*], so just because a problem is dealt with in the manner of modern economics is not in itself problematic.

A: I don't think there's a need for further discussion of Heading I ('Fundamental problems of the cyclical movement of industry'), but I would like to ask one more question before we move on. With regard to the 'fundamental problems' of the industrial cycle, it seems to me that one such problem concerns fixed capital. Could you explain the reason for only treating certain problems as the fundamental ones in *Crisis IV*?

KURUMA: We did not mean to imply that only the included content is fundamental, whereas everything else is not. However, the reason that fixed capital is important to the industrial cycle is that its actual investment is not equal year after year, but rather is concentrated during a particular period of time. In considering why this concentrated investment occurs, one must of course first take as one's premise a sudden expansion of production. The issues gathered under Heading I are *more* fundamental in this sense. The problems related to fixed capital, as can be seen in the passages grouped under Heading IV ('Fixed capital and the industrial cycle'), are multifaceted, so we set up that separate heading. I hope it is clear that the passages grouped under Heading I are fundamental to the problems dealt with in *Crisis IV*.

B: From the discussion so far, I can understand well that the content of *Crisis IV* differs from a history of crisis or a history of the business cycle.

KURUMA: I think it should also be noted, though, that the theory of the industrial cycle must be backed by research on the history of crisis. Without that backing it would be an abstract theory. But in researching individual industrial cycles, one has to consider the perspective from which to examine a cycle's phases, as this will greatly influence how crisis or the industrial cycle is grasped and the manner in which a theory of crisis or the industrial cycle is unfolded.

B: It seems significant, in that respect, that Marx and Engels wrote many articles on current events in which they analyse the course of the industrial cycles of their own time. Yoshio Miyake's two-volume *Marx and Engels's History of Crisis in England*[8] and other works take up those writings as the subject of analysis.

KURUMA: Actually, as you know, for *Marx-Lexikon* we had planned to deal with the history of crisis and gathered passages to create a quite lengthy manuscript. But the content for the other volumes of crisis expanded so much that, in the end, there was not sufficient space to include everything. Moreover, the content on the history of crisis would have overlapped with Miyake's work, so we abandoned our plan. But if he had not published that two-volume book, we might have included passages on the history of crisis.

Descriptions of the various aspects of the industrial cycle

A: Let's move on to look at the next two main headings:

> Heading II 'Order of the phases of the industrial cycle – From what phase does the industrial cycle begin, what phases does it pass through, and where does it end?'
> Heading III 'Descriptions of the various phases of the business cycle'

A good place to start might be to consider the relation and distinction between these two headings.

KURUMA: Yes, well, both of them deal with the phases of the industrial cycle. Heading II includes passages from Marx and Engels that list the phases of the industrial cycle and show the order of those phases as a point of reference for where a cycle starts and ends. But here we are not yet dealing with the particular nature of each phase. In contrast, the passages under Heading III include descriptions of the characteristics of each phase and their mutual relation. The title of Heading III is '*Descriptions* of the various aspects of the business cycle', but in German the term used *Bemerkungen* because the passages are meant to serve as a sort of *indicator*. It would have been too difficult to include comprehensive descriptions of each phase, so our approach was to gather descriptions of what characterises each phase. However, such content began to pile up during the editing process, as suggestions were made to include this or that pas-

---

8 Miyake 1974a and 1974b.

sage, resulting in a huge number of passages. We also ended up with quite a variety of different expressions used by Marx to describe the phases.

E: It really surprised me how many different expressions Marx used. In addition to using different terms to describe what seemed to be the same phase, he wrote an article titled 'Pauperism and Free Trade' for the *New York Daily Tribune* in which he lists 11 different 'states' that are passed through:

> Modern industry and commerce, it is well known, pass through periodical cycles of from 5 to 7 years, in which they, in regular succession, go through the different states of quiescence – next improvement – growing confidence – activity – prosperity – excitement – over-trading – convulsion – pressure – stagnation – distress – ending again in quiescence.[9]

C: That article was written in English originally, wasn't it?

E: Yes. As in the case of Heading X ('Various types of crises') in *Crisis III*, quite a few passages were written in English, most notably the articles Marx wrote for *The New York Daily Herald*. For this reason, after the German (translated from English) we included the original English in brackets.[10] These can also be a point of reference for those who are not so familiar with German. Another reason was that the German terms do not always perfectly correspond to the English. We decided that adding English in that way would be helpful.

A: Unless someone has another question regarding Heading II, shall we concentrate on Heading III, since we seem to be discussing it already.

KURUMA: Editing the passages under Heading III in *Crisis IV* – 'Descriptions of the various phases of the industrial cycle' – presented us with a similar situation as for Heading X in *Crisis III*. That is to say, given the overlapping of passages

---

9   Marx 1979, p. 357. Passage {327} in *Crisis IV*. [The list of the 'states' (phases) of the industrial cycle in the passage quoted are in fact taken from an 1837 pamphlet by Samuel Jones-Loyd Overstone, with Marx only adding 'activity'. This fact was not noted in the collection of Marx's articles published in MEGA I/11. This is explained in more detail in Ōtani 2016 (pp. 254–55), where it is also noted that Marx's article was written in 1863 – not 1852 as it was incorrectly listed in the collected works of Marx and Engels. – T. Ōtani.]

10 [This is referring to the index (in German and Japanese) created for Heading X in *Crisis III*, which is not included in this English edition.]

regarding the phases of the industrial cycle, we had no choice but to list the passages chronologically and add an index at the beginning. Do you have anything to add regarding the index 'G'?

G: One thing is that we also included subjects in the index that are not phases of the industrial cycle in themselves but are closely connected to the phases in the sense of occurring in a concentrated manner within a certain phase. Conversely, there were items related to crisis that were not included, even if they were phases of the industrial cycle, because they were included under Heading X ('Various types of crises') in *Crisis III*, unless they characterised crisis itself or were related to other phases. In addition, we drew attention to descriptions of 'speculation' and 'swindles' within the main text through bold underlining of those parts. But those terms were only included in the index when they directly concerned a specific phase because, even though those issues are deeply related to the process of an industrial cycle, they aren't phases themselves and appear within every phase. In the case of those two terms, as well as 'crisis' and 'prosperity', the passages containing them are not comprehensively listed in the index. For the descriptions of prosperity, we only included those passages that seemed to characterise the term. The index in German also includes entries for the original terms used by Marx or Engels in English or other languages, along with the German translations that appear in MEGA. However, in cases of terms that are nearly identical in both languages – such as 'Depression' and 'depression' or 'Panik' and 'panic' – we did not bother to list them side by side each time.

A: Consistency among translated terms was a problem, it seems.

G: Yes, very much. If you look at the Japanese index this becomes even clearer. In the process of creating the index, the issue of consistency was one that we struggled with. For instance, consider the expression *Produktion unter Hochdruck*. Previous Japanese editions had rendered this term as *seisan no hanbō* (the busyness of production), as *kōatsu no motode no seisan* (production under high pressure), or as *kōatsu-ryoku no motode no seisan* (production under the power of high pressure). None is wrong in itself, but none is exactly right, either, so we ended up going with *zenryoku o tsukushite no seisan* (production that uses all its force). We had to make all sorts of adjustments of this sort.

D: Speaking of translation issues, it was mentioned in our previous discussion for *Crisis III*, that the Japanese term *kyōkō* is not so appropriate as an equivalent for *Krise*, and that issue has been much debated these days.

C: In Chinese, instead of using the characters for *kyōkō*, the term *wēijī* is used, which is equivalent to the Japanese *kiki* [meaning 'crisis' or 'emergency']. The German term *allgemeine Krise* (general crisis) can be translated in Japanese as *ippanteki*[11] *kyōkō* or *ippanteki kiki*, whereas in Chinese it is always translated as *wēijī*. Perhaps the alternative term *kiki* could be used to indicate 'dangerous period'[12]?

B: But in that case the two uses of *kiki* would be indistinguishable, since they are pronounced the same.

F: In that case, perhaps the term *kikyoku*[13]–in the sense of 'dangerous phase' – would be appropriate?

KURUMA: That sounds like be a good option.

A: Another issue was whether to use 'period' or 'phase' to refer to the aspects of the industrial cycle. This was discussed when trying to figure out what headings to use for this volume. In the end, we decided to exclusively use 'phase', but at one point we thought of using 'period' instead, since Marx had used that term as well (although there seemed a slight difference in nuance between the two).

Where does the cycle begin from?

A: Various issues related to Heading III have arisen, but shall we return to Heading II?

B: Heading II centres on the question of the starting and ending point of a cycle. This is something that Professor Kuruma discusses in detail in the first section of his article 'A Few Problems Concerning Postwar Theories of Crisis,'[14] titled 'Cycle and period', so I would encourage readers to refer to that discussion. The view that has generally been held regarding the cycle is that it *begins from crisis* and ends with crisis, but as the article points out, such a way of looking at things

---

11   [*Ippanteki* means 'general'.]
12   [The proposed term *kiki* (危期) and its homonym *kiki* (危機), which corresponds to the Chinese *wēijī*, have the same first character meaning 'danger' (危), but the second characters differ, meaning 'period' (期) and 'opportunity' (機), respectively.]
13   [The first character of *kikyoku* (危局) means 'danger', while the second character means 'phase' or 'aspect'.]
14   [Chapter 14 of this book.]

confuses the terms 'period' and 'cycle', thus impeding the understanding of the cyclical process through which capital drives beyond its own immanent barrier. Professor Kuruma notes that the cycle should be seen as starting from 'middling activity' instead.

E: In relation to this issue, passage {335} in *Crisis IV* contains an addition that Marx made to the French edition of *Capital* that includes the line:

... une crise générale, fin d'un cycle et point de départ d'un autre.[15]

If this is read on its own it could lead to misunderstandings. Professor Kuruma argues that the 'point de départ' is not the point where the crisis begins or where it continues, but rather the point *from which it has ended*, with the next cycle then beginning from that point. But the expression in the French edition implies that *crisis itself is the starting point*.

C: I suppose that misunderstanding is unavoidable, because 'point de départ' could only be translated as 'starting point'. The only way around this is to understand the content Marx is trying to convey.

D: If the starting point of the circuit is the point at which the *crisis* ends, this would not seem to correspond exactly to the 'moderate activity' that Professor Kuruma considers the starting point. Since crisis also includes stagnation, would a certain process of revival be needed to reach the point of *moderate activity*?

KURUMA: You spoke of my 'opinion', but it is based on what Marx wrote rather than being my own view. When Marx spoke of 'moderate activity' he was referring to an upward phase of an ongoing 'slack' (*Abspannung*)[16] period. Thus, it includes the phase of 'revival' that you just mentioned. The term 'moderate activity' or 'moderate prosperity' is a translation of *mittlere Lebendigkeit*, and in translating *Lebendigkeit* as 'activity' or 'prosperity', it could be said to encompass the entirety of that part of the upward phase in which some slackness remains. In this sense, 'moderate activity' or 'moderate prosperity' is some-

---

15   Karl Marx 1993, p. 710. ['... a general crisis, end of the cycle and departure point of another cycle'.]
16   [The term *Abspannung* is translated into English in a number of different ways in *Marx Engels Collected Works*, including: 'slack' in passages {375} and {388}; 'dullness' in passages {328} and {347}; and 'depression' in passages {336} and {362}.]

where around the middle of the upward phase, rather than including its initial period. But there is the question of whether it is correct to understand *Lebendigkeit* in that sense. The word *lebendig* has the original meaning of 'living', and later came to be used in the sense of 'lively' or 'full of vitality'. Thus, in the former sense, a person could be considered *lebendig* even if ill, and the period that covers recovering from the illness and regaining vitality could be described as *mittlere Lebendigkeit*. That sort of understanding seems natural, but I do not think that it is the sense in which Marx is using the expression. If this point is not understood, there will seem to be a contradiction with what he is saying elsewhere.

C: In other words, during the period of stagnation, the *Lebendigkeit* is at a low level, whereas it is high during the period of prosperity. And then during the phase where the business conditions begin to recover and head in the direction of prosperity, it is at a middling level. If that is the case, the term 'activity' can lead to misunderstanding, it seems. Perhaps 'vitality' would be a better translation in this case.

A: Good point. We still have time to revise the galleys, so let's change it to 'moderate *vitality*' (*chūi no kakki*).[17]

Index clarifies the relation of various factors to the phases of the industrial cycle

D: In *Marx-Lexikon*, only Heading II and III of *Crisis IV* concern the phases of the industrial cycle, but it seems to me that in dealing with the phases, it is important to clarify the process whereby the various economic factors undergo changes as they are intertwined with and influence each other during the changing phases of the cycle. If we look at the passages under Heading III, we can see that Marx wrote various things about what occurs at each phase to such factors as prices and wages, the relative surplus population, the profit and interest rates, the quantity of the means of circulation, the magnitude of stock, imports and exports, currency exchange, gold reserve, etc. Wasn't it possible to create headings for each of these factors or to create a heading for each phase?

KURUMA: We did consider doing that, but if we had, there would have been considerable repetition and the length of the volume would have swelled.

---

17 [This is indeed the Japanese term used to translate *Lebendigkeit* in *Crisis IV*.]

Moreover, even if it is useful for a limited aim to look at the industrial cycle by separating out each factor, there was the risk that it would make it impossible to comprehensively grasp the characteristics of the cycle's phases. In many cases, Marx describes how the factors concerning each concrete process of the cycle are intertwined, so it seemed questionable to treat them separately. The approach would have been different for writing a book on the theory of the industrial cycle, but in the case of *Marx-Lexikon* we had to take such issues under consideration in seeking to bring together the various things that Marx wrote. As for the approach of separating the passages according to phase, even if we could broadly divide the phases into 'recovery, prosperity, crisis, and stagnation', there is the question of whether we would have been able divvy up the various descriptions made by Marx into each category. We would have had to muster a lot of courage for that task and been willing to accept a great deal of repetition. I think it would have been quite difficult.

G: Another problem we faced concerned the index created for the entries in Heading III.[18] What we came up with was a German index in alphabetical order and a Japanese index in *gojūon* order,[19] but at one point we had tried to divide the index into the phases of the industrial cycle, from beginning to end, and gather the concepts thought to pertain to each. It turned out to be very hard to decide where to place each concept. It did not seem like a good idea to forcefully arrange fragmentary descriptions, so in the end we abandoned that approach.

KURUMA: We would rather allow readers to make use of the passages for their own research. That suits the basic aim of *Marx-Lexikon*, and it seems to me that *Crisis III* is quite useful for researching the phases of the cycle.

B: Nevertheless, the relation between real capital and money capital, and therefore the relation of changes in the interest rate to the industrial cycle, are important, and Marx seems to have written quite a lot about this.

KURUMA: That's true. As you know, some time ago we had created a manuscript with passages concerning that issue. However, when we created Heading III, all of those passages were placed within it. It will be possible to look up that

---

18 [This index is not included under Heading III of *Crisis IV* in this chapter.]
19 [The *gojūon* order ('fifty-sound ordering') refers to the 5×10 grid in which the order of the *hiragana* characters are displayed, similar to alphabetical order.]

issue using the index – not the index for Heading III, but the separate index volume.[20] I would also hope that the various factors mentioned by 'D', such as excess population, wages, etc., could also be searched for in that index.

G: We'll have to keep that point fully in mind when we edit the index volume.

Relation between durability period of fixed capital and the period of the industrial cycle

A: Let's move on to Heading IV ('Fixed capital and the industrial cycle').

F: The first subheading under Heading IV is titled 'Average renewal period of fixed capital and the duration of the industrial cycle'. This subheading groups together Marx's descriptions of the period of reproduction of fixed capital, which is to say, the relation between the period of durability and the period of the industrial cycle or the period of crisis. Judging from these passages, Marx seems to be merely confirming the relation with regard to empirical facts, without offering a logical explanation.

KURUMA: I'm not so sure about that. What was confirmed by Marx as an empirical fact was the period of crisis, which is to say how many years an industrial cycle would last. In passage {398}, he writes that 'the cycle which industry has passed through' has been 'at more or less 10-yearly intervals',[21] so he seems to be saying that *logically* this period must correspond to the average reproduction period for types of machinery. This subheading consists of five passages – one from the *Grundrisse* and from Book II of *Capital*, as well as a letter from Marx to Engels, the response of Engels, and Marx's letter of thanks. Among those passages, the passage from the *Grundrisse* and the three letters were written at nearly the same time. The part quoted from the *Grundrisse* appears on the seventh page of notebook VII, whose fifth page is dated 'March 1858'. Meanwhile, the letters are dated from 2 to 5 March of the same year. It is not clear which was written first, but in terms of content they are exactly the same.

Bearing this in mind, if we look at the exchange between Marx and Engels, we can notice the following. Marx observed that an industrial cycle was around

---

20   [The index for the first nine volumes of *Marx-Lexikon* that was published as a separate tenth volume, Kuruma 1978 (ed.).]
21   Marx 1973, p. 720.

10 years long and thought that it must be related to the number of years for the durability of fixed capital. However, Babbage claimed that this period was five years. Marx was doubtful about this claim and asked Engels about it. The response from Engels was that, in terms of the common sense of calculations for individual capital, Babbage's assumption was not tenable, and that in fact it would be from 10 to 13 years. Marx wrote to thank Engels and said that his explanation regarding the years of durability *corresponded theoretically* to his idea that this period was the important moment determining the cycle.

C: However, in the passage from the *Grundrissse*, Marx writes:

> According to Babbage, the average reproduction of machinery in England takes 5 years; hence, the real, probably 10 years'.[22]

This seems to run counter to what Professor Kuruma just said.

A: But I think this same passage that 'C' just cited was translated in *Crisis IV* as:

> '*Hence*, although according to Babbage the average reproduction of machinery in England is 5 years, the real one is *perhaps* 10 years.

In other words, the construction is not, 'Babbage said this, and hence ...', but rather:

> There is a necessary relation between the reproduction time for fixed capital and the *repetition* of turnovers, and hence, although Babbage said this ...

C: It's the difference, I think, between the Japanese word *moshikashite* (perhaps) and *tabun* (probably).

A: That is a translation of the German *vielleicht*. This is usually – or nearly always – translated into Japanese as *tabun* (probably), but that leads to many

---

22   Marx 1987c., p. 105. [The passage from *Marx Engels Collected Works* is quoted from because it corresponds more closely to the Japanese translation discussed here than the Penguin edition translation, which reads: 'According to Babbage, the average reproduction of machinery in England 5 years; the real one hence perhaps 10 years' (Marx 1973, p. 720).]

misunderstandings. This word is *hardly ever* used in German for a supposition that is quite possible, as in the construction 'probably', which corresponds instead to the German *wahrscheinlich*. In the case of *vielleicht*, the possibility is not so high, and thus more like 'perhaps'. Although Professor Kuruma said that it 'was not clear' whether the *Grundrisse* or the letters were written first, it seems probable (or *wahrscheinlich*) to me that Marx first wrote 'perhaps 10 years' in the *Grundrisse* and then wrote the letter to Engels. On the same page of notebook VII, just prior to that sentence in the *Grundrisse*, there is an equation on the turnovers of fixed capital that uses five years as the period of time, whereas it would have been natural to use ten years after the exchange of letters with Engels, which is another reason for thinking that he wrote the passage in the *Grundrisse* first.

F: Can the passage from Book II of *Capital* also be viewed as dealing with the same basic issue.

KURUMA: I think so, fundamentally speaking. However, in *Capital* Marx already displays great *theoretical* confidence regarding this issue as well as confidence that it *corresponds to empirical facts*. This is the part of Book II that Engels added to the current edition from Marx's second manuscript, but what is interesting is that in the first manuscript, which we referred to earlier, this issue is also dealt with and the content is similar to that of the passage in the *Grundrisse*.

D: What did he write in that manuscript for Book II?

KURUMA: I think that 'G' has a more precise recollection of the content than I do, so perhaps he could answer.

G: Basically, the content is the following: Say that a given capital is invested in an industrial sector with a high proportion of fixed capital, with a turnover time of 12 years or more. In that case, circulating capital must also be repeatedly invested in this part, so it will also be restricted like that sector. Thus, it would be more subject to 'fateful events' (*Schicksalsfälle*) than a capital that was withdrawn after, say, three months (and transferred to another sector); this term recalls the word *fata* (fate) that appears in passage {398} from the *Grundrisse*. 'Fateful events' in this case concerns changes in the price of materials, changes in market conditions and the money market, rising or falling product prices as a result of competition, changes in the productive power of labour, etc. etc., but such factors alternate or cancel each other out or amplify each other, thus bringing about fateful changes to this capital. It is from this perspective that Marx, in the first manuscript for Book II of *Capital*, describes a further development in how 'the industrial turnover cycle conditioned through fixed capital creates a material basis for the cyclical nature of crisis'.[23]

D: I see. One does get an idea of how that serves to connect the *Grundrisse* and the published edition of *Capital*.

E: In the passage you just read, there isn't an indefinite article *ein* before 'material foundation'

G: That's right.

E: In the current edition of Book II the phrase reads, '*a* material basis for the periodic crises [*eine materielle Grundlage der periodischen Krisen*]'.[24] How much emphasis is being placed on the significance of that indefinite article?

G: I think it is clear that it means 'one out of many'. For instance, in passage {402}, Marx writes:

> Needless to say their [crises] course is also determined by factors of a quite different kind, depending on their period of reproduction. For me the important thing is to discover, in the immediate material postulates of big industry, *one* factor that determines cycles.[25]

And Marx himself emphasises that word 'one'. In passage {398}, taken from the *Grundrisse*, Marx similarly notes:

> 'We shall find *other determinate causes as well*. But this is *one of them*'.[26]

And in passage {400}, he writes:

---

23 Marx 1988b, pp. 268–9.
24 Marx 1997, p. 187. [In passage {399} in *Crisis IV*. Speaker's emphasis. In the Penguin edition of Book II, the translation reads: 'one of the material foundations for the periodic cycle' (Marx 1978, p. 264).]
25 Marx 1983, p. 282.
26 Marx 1973a, p. 720 [Speaker's emphasis].

The average period for the replacement of machinery is *one* important factor in explaining the multi-year cycle which has been a feature of industrial development ever since the consolidation of big industry.[27]

In this letter to Engels, Marx himself again underlines 'one' for emphasis.

B: The passage in the published edition of *Capital* has the sentence in question regarding how 'a crisis is always the starting-point of a large volume of new investment'.

A: That problem concerns our next two topics, so shall we move on?

At what phase is major new investment carried out?

B: The second subheading is titled 'What phase of the industrial cycle is the starting point for large new investment and in what phase is it carried out?' Three passages are grouped under this subheading. In the first, taken from Book II of *Capital*, Marx comes right out and says that, 'a crisis always forms the starting point of large new investments ...';[28] this gives the impression that large new investment begins at the time of a crisis, which seems unlikely to occur.

C: This was a topic raised at several of our editorial meetings, and the translation in *Crisis IV* was changed to '*creates* the starting point for a large volume of new investment'.[29]

KURUMA: Yes, we did discuss that. If the verb *bilden* is translated as 'to form', one cannot help getting the impression that Marx is saying that large new investment begins from the time of crisis. The translation problem centres on the word *Ausgangspunkt*, which is translated as 'starting point', but in this context should be understood as meaning the point of exiting from some place. Thus, the starting point of large new investment can be understood here as

---

27 Marx 1983, p. 278.
28 Marx 1997, p. 188. [Passage from *Marx Engels Collected Works* is quoted because it corresponds more closely to the Japanese translation discussed here. The translation in the Penguin edition reads: '... a crisis is always the starting point of a large volume of new investment' (Marx 1978, p. 264).]
29 [Original German is: *Indessen bildet die Krise immer den Ausgangspunkt einer großen Neuanlager.*]

the point *where crisis ends*. Since there seemed no alternative to using the term 'starting point' to translate *Ausgangspunkt*, 'D' suggested that we translate *bilden* as *tsukuri-dasu* (to create) rather than *nasu* (to form) in order to avoid misunderstanding.

C: In the 1965 edition of *An Investigation of Crisis Theory*, Professor Kuruma takes up issues related to the term *Ausgangspunkt* with regard to the place from which the industrial cycle begins.[30]

B: Even saying that it 'creates' the starting point, however, does not make it clear where the large new investment is carried out. I know this occurs after the end of a crisis, but that is about all.

KURUMA: I can understand how that might be unclear. For that reason, we included two related quotes. In the first, which is passage {404}, taken from Book III of *Capital*, Marx notes that 'in the phase of the industrial cycle immediately after the crisis, when loan capital lies idle on a massive scale', which is 'when the production process has undergone a contraction ... when commodity prices stand at their lowest point, and when the entrepreneurial spirit is crippled', 'there is no question yet of new capital investment'.[31] In other words, this is the phase of 'stagnation'. I think that after reading this passage, one will not end up misconstruing the meaning of 'starting point' in passage {403}. The third passage under this subheading, {405}, is also from Book III of *Capital*. It is where Marx points out that the 'flourishing stage that precedes that of overexertion' is 'the *only* point in time at which it may be said that a low rate of interest, and hence a relative abundance of loanable capital, coincides with an actual expansion of industrial capital', and that there is also 'a great *expansion of fixed capital in all forms and the opening of large numbers of new and far-reaching undertakings*'.[32]

Thus, according to Marx, the movement of the investment of fixed capital becomes more active at the point where the phase of stagnation has given way to an upturn, so that business vitality is on the rise, and then reaches its greatest scale in the phase of prosperity. My comments here concern what Marx himself wrote, but it would be necessary to back them up with concrete studies of the history of industrial cycles. If the reality turns out to be different, it would mean that Marx had been wrong.

---

30   Kuruma 1965, p. 225. [In Chapter 14 of this book.]
31   Marx 1981a, p. 616.
32   Marx 1981a, pp. 619–20. [Kuruma's emphasis.]

A: We are almost out of time and will have to bring today's discussion to a close soon, but before we do, I would like to ask Professor Kuruma if he has anything to add on this topic of 'fixed capital and the industrial cycle' under Heading IV?

KURUMA: As is mentioned in the passages under Subheading 2, at some point large-scale investment of fixed capital is carried out, but it is important to be aware that this is connected to the issue of the impulse (*Anstoß*) that brings about a sudden expansion of production, as discussed under Subheading 1. The other point concerns the central issue for Subheading 3, which is titled, 'It is mainly crisis that forces the premature renewal of constant capital on a large social scale'. This is the problem of how, as the outcome of crisis, competition is intensified, the search for new production methods is promoted, and 'moral [*moralisch*] deterioration'[33] is brought about, making necessary renewal on a social scale prior to the expiration date. This gives us some hints, I think, as to what Marx had in mind when he wrote that crisis creates 'the starting-point of a large volume of new investment' which furnishes 'a new material basis for the next turnover cycle'.[34] If we bear those two points in mind, I think it will be clear that the correspondence between the lifespan of fixed capital and the period of the cycle is something that is being discussed *theoretically*.

What can be learned from Heading V?

A: Finally, we can discuss Heading V, titled 'Changes in the course of the industrial cycle arising from the development of capitalist production'.

E: Earlier, when Professor Kuruma was summarising the overall content of this volume, he noted that this heading deals with historical change regarding issues that must be grasped generally in relation to the development of capitalism, not with the particularity of individual cycles. But it seems to include descriptions of historical processes that concern the history of crisis in the previous century.

A: In relation to what 'E' just said, I would like Professor Kuruma to say a few words about what he had in mind in creating this heading.

---

33 Marx 1978, p. 250.
34 Marx 1978, p. 264. [In passage {399} in *Crisis* IV.]

KURUMA: Marx and Engels spared no effort to precisely grasp the industrial cycles that were actually progressing in front of their eyes. This has been left to us in the form of articles on current events and other writings. From our perspective today, these are descriptions of the *history of industrial cycles* in the past century, but for them it was the *analysis of the current situation*. Our interest in these writings today is certainly not a mere historical interest. Like them, we must clarify the *current* movement of the capitalist economy, and a key for doing so is the research Marx and Engels have left us. However, there is no doubt that capitalism today is different in many respects from the capitalism of their time. Although it is a type of development in a sense, capitalism has entered a stage in which it displays an unprecedented pathology. This may raise some doubts about how useful the analysis of *their* current situation is to our effort to analyse the different situation we confront today. But my response to such doubts is to note that Marx and Engels certainly never sought to impose their own *theory* on the current situation by only gathering facts that suited that theory. Rather, they always respected the facts and sought to objectively grasp them. And when they discovered a new situation that differed from the developments they had observed up to that point, they connected it to the *development* of capitalist production and sought to understand it within that development. This applies precisely to their observation of the duration of the industrial cycle. By becoming familiar with how they sought to explain the changes that arose in the duration of the industrial cycle as a development of capitalist production, we can use this knowledge for *our own* analysis of the current situation; or at least we can employ it to consider how to grasp and explain the changes in the current forms of the cycle. This was one point we had in mind in deciding to conclude the *Marx-Lexikon* volumes on crisis with Heading V.

C: Listening to what you just said reminds me of the chapter titled 'An Introduction to the Study of Crisis'[35] in your book *An Investigation of Crisis Theory*. I think you were the first to say at the time, after the end of World War I, that the contradictions of capitalism would again explode in the form of world war, rather than a global crisis.

KURUMA: I was not saying that world war would take the place of crisis, but that in some cases crisis would take the form of war.

---

35   Kuruma 1965, pp. 3–42. [In Chapter 1 of this book.]

C: What was it that led you to write that?

KURUMA: The direct motive was the existence of a widespread view at the time that war would not reoccur, given the bitter experience of World War I and the formation of the League of Nations. I thought that a war was quite likely to occur, and that the labour movement should prepare for that eventuality, which led me to make that comment. My belief was also based on reading Lenin's *Imperialism*. And, indeed, World War II did break out later as expected.

B: That passage from *An Investigation of Crisis Theory* is the following:

> For the moment, the page of the Great War has been turned, with a direct outcome being the receding wave of the worldwide revolutionary movement. Today's task is to prepare for the new crisis that will soon arrive. This new period of crisis will probably once again take the form of a world war. But even prior to that, it is likely to assume the form of an economic crisis. In either case, the crucial task in the current period is to prepare for the major crisis that approaches. How can we accomplish this task in the most efficient and effective manner? First, we must verify the necessity underlying the arrival of the new crisis and the position of the present moment as one step along that path. The theoretical basis for this verification can only be obtained by grasping all the contradictions of capitalism in their organic interrelation as moments in the dialectical development of capitalist production, so as to clarify the process of their inevitable development to the point of explosion. Investigating this theoretical basis is the precise task of a truly Marxian theory of crisis.[36]

Incidentally, what point do you think is most important when you look at capitalist production today.

KURUMA: One thing, which I mentioned earlier, is the problem of inflation. There is a contradiction in which the effort to get inflation under control leads to a rise in unemployment, while the effort to reduce unemployment triggers inflation. This issue and the issue of war that was just brought up both are related to the state.

---

36 Kuruma 1965, p. 41. [In Chapter 1 of this book.]

F: To return to the earlier point: In Heading v, what do the 'changes in the course of the industrial cycle' refer to?

KURUMA: What are your own thoughts on this, 'B'?

B: This is just off the top of my head, since we don't have much time left, but various phenomena appear, such as the contraction or extension of the period of the cycle, the disappearance of financial panic as the peak of the cycle, chronic recession, and so on. Marx and Engels pointed to various circumstances to account for this, including changes in the period for constructing fixed capital and its lifespan, the destruction of England's industrial monopoly, the appearance of rival industrial nations, and the formation of a world market. In addition, Engels, while continuing to say that these factors were preparing the way for an unprecedented crisis, also wrote about the theory of 'chronic crisis', 'intermediate crisis', and a 'deadlock'.

E: All of those points are traced in detail in Part 4 of the second volume of Yoshio Miyake's *Marx and Engels: History of Crisis in England*,[37] so readers can consult that work along with *Crisis IV*.

A: There are still a lot of things to discuss, but we are out of time. In our last moments, I wonder if Professor Kuruma might share his impressions now that the first round of the *Marx-Lexikon* volumes is nearing completion,[38] as well as his thoughts on the plan for the subsequent volumes?

KURUMA: At times I wonder why it has been my fate to suffer like this at my advanced age, but it is a relief that we somehow managed to complete the first round of the *Marx-Lexikon* volumes. For a while I want to take a break and attend to other work that I had been unable to accomplish during the editing process. Once I have regained my strength, I will probably get started on the next round. Although I am not exactly sure when that will be.

---

37   Miyake 1974b, pp. 159–282.
38   [The 'first round' refers to the first 10 volumes (including a one-volume index). This was followed by the publication of five volumes on the topic of money.]

PART 3

Reviews, Discussions, and Polemics

∴

CHAPTER 9

An Evaluation of Condliffe's Analysis of Crisis

Here I want to convey some of my impressions from reading the League of Nations' *World Economic Survey*.[1]

---

1   [Originally published as Kuruma 1935a under the title 'A Review of the League of Nation's *World Economic Survey*' and republished as Chapter 4 of *An Investigation of Marx's Theory of Crisis* (Kuruma 1949). In the preface to that book, Kuruma notes the following regarding the chapter's content:
    'Reading Condliffe's *World Economic Survey* considerably piqued my interest, so I attempted to introduce that work along with some of my own criticisms of it. The article was written before "An Overview of Marx's Theory of Crisis" [Kuruma 1936; Chapter 4 of this book], but it was an attempt to apply to reality some of the same fundamental concepts of crisis from Marx as my guide. Bourgeois political economy since the collapse of the Classical school has been a steady process of vulgarisation, but in individual areas there is empirical work of value. One well-known example is Tooke's *History of Prices*, which Marx esteemed. Condliffe's *World Economic Survey* is not on par with that book, but it is an outstanding work related to the history of crisis, and at the very least was of interest to me at the time. Marx, in criticizing the theories of Tooke, Wilson, and Fullarton, wrote: "None of these writers take a one-sided view of money but deal with its various aspects, though only from a mechanical angle without paying any attention to the organic relation of these aspects either with one another or with the system of economic categories as a whole" (Marx 1987a, p. 416). The same sort of criticism applies, in a sense, to Condliffe's opinions. His approach also is certainly not one-sided, since he examines various moments in his analysis of the process of crisis, and even if in many cases his viewpoint is off the mark, it is not by much. However, he does not grasp the internal relations of the various moments and processes he examines, and thus also fails to grasp their interrelation. But when the results of his analysis are illuminated by Marx's theory, the various facts take on new meaning in their relation to the totality. That was my main interest in presenting an overview of Marx's theory of crisis and adding my own critique of Condliffe. I think that this applies not only to his particular views but to many other theories of crisis. The error of most theories is not that they claim that things totally unrelated to crisis are in fact relevant, but that they insist that one moment among the various moments of crisis is the sole or main cause of crisis. If we are able to be aware of this when reading such works, they can be useful references for a theory of crisis, at least in terms of backing up the theory with factual observations. I was keenly aware of this when reading works on the theory or history of crisis at the time, and I took notes on such works with the intention of using them for a future systematic consideration of the moments of crisis. I accumulated a large quantity of these notes, but they were all destroyed, along with my excerpts from Marx, when the office of the Ōhara Institute for Social Science was destroyed in an air raid [in May 1945]. One reason for speaking here at such length of these personal matters is not only to explain why, after having announced an ambitious plan for a study of crisis, I was only able to complete the prefatory works gathered in this published collection, but also because I think it could be useful in some way to those who intend to pursue the study of crisis on their own'. (Kuruma 1949, pp. 2–4).]

This report on the preceding year has been published every autumn since 1931, in line with resolutions passed by the Assembly of the League in 1930 and 1931. The author of the report for the past three years has been Professor John B. Condliffe.[2] The report's aim, of course, is to conduct an annual survey of the world economy, but its clearly stated general approach for observing the economy is not so much to record 'dramatic' events that occurred as to examine a huge quantity of underlying phenomena, concentrating on describing the facts themselves rather than offering opinions or policy proposals regarding them. However, as Condliffe himself recognises, the selection of the facts to describe, as well as arrangement and explanation of them, cannot be done without having some sort of viewpoint (at least when it comes to facts with some degree of significance); this makes it necessary to suggest how one is posing the questions and what methods are being used to answer them Indeed, although the discussion of facts in the surveys is quite limited, a certain opinion is expressed with regard to the world economy and the global economic crisis, and based on that opinion an analysis from a certain angle is carried out, yielding results that form the basis for a certain understanding of the moments that constitute the deepening of today's unprecedented crisis or depression.

The first thing that many readers may have noticed in looking through the surveys is that, in the analyses of trends in the world economy for such areas as production, prices, wages, profits, finance, credit, trade, and balance of payments, the author is always guided by a series of fundamental concepts: one is the concept of equilibrium and disequilibrium, another is the concept of flexibility and inflexibility, and a third is the concept of interaction. The author's general view of the processes that generate a crisis or depression seems to be as follows.

Since the world economy is an organic system made up of mutually dependent elements, the disturbance of this system comes from the destruction of the equilibrium between those elements. In a normal state, this system functions through automatic regulation, and as long as those operations are smooth and effective, disequilibrium can be rectified on its own, thereby avoiding major disturbances. But when a disequilibrating force is abrupt or powerful enough to overwhelm that functioning, or when one of the internal elements stiffens for some reason so as to lose its original flexibility, it becomes difficult to restore equilibrium, so that not only does disequilibrium continue and build up but a

---

2 J.B. Condliffe, of the Economic Intelligence Service of the League of Nations, formerly professor of economics at Canterbury College, New Zealand; later research secretary of the Institute of Pacific Relations and professor of economics at the University of Michigan, U.S.A. [Kuruma's original English footnote.]

given case of disequilibrium progressively induces other cases and intensifies the initial disequilibrium, eventually throwing the world economy into hopeless confusion.

Thus, the overall aim of the surveys is to clarify such developmental processes for the given period examined. In other words: What sort of disequilibrium can be found within the system of the world economy during the current period? What tendencies did each case of disequilibrium display and how did the cases affect each other? What were the main elements of inflexibility within the system that impeded the readjustment of that chain of disequilibrium, and therefore what can be looked to for breaking out of the depression? – These are the questions that the author explicitly or implicitly seeks to clarify.

According to the results of Condliffe's analysis, the most important type of disequilibrium within the current crisis or depression is the disequilibrium between production sectors, particularly between agriculture and manufacturing, between industries extracting raw materials and those producing finished products, and between industries producing consumer goods and those producing production goods. Such disequilibrium is perceived in the characteristic gap between the fall in prices and the decline of production in those different production sectors. That is to say, generally speaking, it is assumed that there is a conspicuous fall in prices and a relatively small decline in production (or even a production increase) for each of the production sectors listed first in the opposing pairs above, whereas the sector listed second is assumed to have a remarkable fall in production but a relatively small price decline.[3] Condliffe indicates that the primary and most general cause of this is that agricultural producers are in a weak negotiation position and that it is relatively easy to reduce production in manufacturing, particularly given the cartels in the sector of manufactured goods.[4] The opposition between agriculture and manufactur-

---

3 This is of course just a summation. Considered more closely, the abovementioned movement of price and production in the case of raw materials, for example, would mainly reflect that of agricultural raw materials, and many exceptions would exist among non-agricultural products. Moreover, the price drops in Japan after the outbreak of the crisis were more conspicuous for production goods than for consumer goods.

4 The abovementioned collapse of prices for raw materials amidst disequilibrium is not particular to the current crisis, but rather is a phenomenon widely seen in previous crises, as Condliffe explains: 'The reasons for this discrepancy (which occurs in every period of depression) between price-movements of raw materials and finished goods, are fairly clear. Moreover, this lag is increased by the fact that merchants and manufacturers carry reserve stocks of raw materials' (Condliffe 1932, p. 130). But this price disequilibrium that occurs is usually adjusted for by a decline in the production of raw materials. Nevertheless, in the current crisis, this adjustment has not easily taken place.

ing above, as well as the distinction between industries extracting raw materials and those producing finished products, corresponds at the same time to the distinction between colonial debtor nations and advanced capitalist lender nations, and therefore the price disequilibrium between the production sectors coincides with the irregular global movement of capital and necessarily destroys the equilibrium between national economies, and is said to be a primary cause of the collapse of the world economy.[5] The author also recognises the particular importance of how the disequilibrium between the sectors producing consumer and production goods impedes the establishment of new competitive companies, thereby becoming a major obstacle to a business recovery.[6] We thus learn that in fact the unequal development of monopolies promotes inflexibility among some industries that exerts a major role in the unpreced-

---

5 Of course, the disequilibrium between these production departments and the international disequilibrium is not as unilateral as spoken of here. The latter is the result of the former, and at the same time its cause. For the debtor nations, which are in a disadvantageous position for the balance of foreign trade and face difficulties from restrictions on main exported goods, the only method available to secure a balance of international payments is to aim for an export surplus, which further drives down the prices of their products.

6 Condliffe notes the following:
'In previous depressions, producers' goods destined for capital equipment fell more heavily in price than consumers' goods ...
These facts point to one of the main obstacles that stands in the way of recovery from the present depression. Previous depressions were gradually overcome when capital goods became cheap enough in relation to the prices of consumers' goods, to tempt business enterprise once more to expand its operations. The preceding boom period in such cases was most marked in the industries devoted to producers' goods. When depression developed, therefore, there was an expanded production of these capital goods and a strong tendency for prices to fall. Moreover, general purchasing power was never before so badly affected as it has been in the present depression, and consumers' demand kept up relatively well, so that the prices of consumer goods were less affected.
The present depression, on the other hand, was preceded by a marked boom in consumption and particularly by an inflated demand for articles of durable consumption, accompanied by widespread growth of debt encouraged by instalment selling. The collapse of purchasing power in the depression, aggravated by the unusual debt commitments, has been unprecedented, so that the prices of consumer good have fallen heavily. On the other hand, there has been strong resistance from the powerfully organised capital-equipment industries, many of which are cartellised and, in the process of organisation have been loaded with excessive capital obligations. Capital costs, labour costs, and prices have remained much more rigid in these industries. Demand has fallen off and production decreased to what in former depressions would have been regarded as catastrophic levels; but prices have been slow to fall. The steel industry, particularly in the United States, is a good example of this development.
Until this deadlock is broken in some way, either by the prices of consumers' goods rising, or by a reduction in the prices of producers' goods, there is little possibility that industrial profits will re-emerge, tempting business to expand. There is a fundamental maladjustment

ented severity of the current crisis; but turning this argument over we can see that the author fails to consider the essential significance that this development of monopoly has for capitalist production. Thus, instead of perceiving the historical significance of some of the facts he presents, he merely laments the current situation while glorifying the natural regulation of free competition and preaching the need to restore equilibrium as a precondition for a business recovery.[7]

The next example of disequilibrium to which the author directs his attention basically concerns the disequilibrium between production and distribution based on the inability to adjust distribution demands with regard to the sudden fall in the national income produced, particularly with regard to capital (ownership), labour, and tax collection:

> The maintenance of wage-rates, dividend payments, debt service and governmental expenditures in face of shrunken national incomes, however, was rendered possible only by drawing upon or failing to replenish capital reserves. As the depression persisted it became clear that there was proceeding a distributive struggle of profound significance, and that upon the issue of this struggle depended the possibility of replenishing capital resources.[8]

The battle within the realm of distribution over the value produced annually in each country by labour, in terms of wages as well as profit and all of its subdivided forms, is of course not something that first emerged in the present crisis. This is a phenomenon that arises from the capitalist mode of production

---

at this point which blocks the efforts of governmental or monetary or business leaders to start the process of recovery'. (Condliffe, 1932, pp. 132–33.)

7 The statements here mainly concern the views expressed by Condliffe in the first and second published surveys, whereas the most recent survey covers a period (1933–34) during which the business conditions have been thought to be generally good, with the author pointing out some statistics for the period that do indeed seem to indicate trends toward a business recovery. It also cannot be denied that some of the types of disequilibrium mentioned above have been rectified in certain countries. In particular, the robust situation for raw materials is conspicuous. But the author is not so rash as to conclude from these facts that a sustained business recovery will occur. Indeed, not only has there not been a general restoration of equilibrium, but the restoration of equilibrium in some sectors has even increased disequilibrium elsewhere; and some cases of restored equilibrium have not necessarily been the normal outcome of an adequate resolution through the process of crisis but seem instead to have resulted from unnatural governmental policies and unproductive government expenditures. But the author makes no attempt to adequately pursue this issue. Generally, the first two surveys contain analysis of greater theoretical interest and of richer content.

8 Condliffe 1933, pp. 123–24.

and takes on more intensity during a crisis. However, in the current crisis the 'normal' progression of this struggle has encountered unprecedented obstacles, which in turn has presented unprecedented difficulties. This is because the various elements have come to have an unprecedented inflexibility, as the author describes:

> Not only the actual levels of wages, but their flexibility, prove to be important in periods of fluctuating prices ... levels of wages are not only relatively higher than they were [after the war], but they are more resistant to reductions in a time of falling prices. So large a part is played now in the determination of wage-levels by collective agreements, and in some cases by legislation, that not even severe and prolonged unemployment brings about the reduction that used to be relied upon as one measure of adjustment in crises.
>
> This rigidity at a higher level is, of course, paralleled by other developments of the economic structure, particularly by the greatly increased volume of debt and high rates of interest. The distributive struggle which is a necessary part of any economic order based upon free enterprise has taken a new turn with the development of the contractual idea in wage payments as well as in debt commitments. It has been argued earlier that the greater proportions of the national income claimed, on the one side, for debt service and, on the other, for wage payments, both of which categories are regarded as fixed and invariable, have concentrated the pressure of deflation, after the breakdown of the credit expansion in 1929, upon the more variable shares in national income, and particularly upon the profits of business enterprise, with the result that the mainspring of economic effort under the present system has been weakened. Restoration of the profits of enterprise, in default of a rise in prices, necessitates a reduction either of the debt claims or of the standard of living of the workers, perhaps of both. In the crisis as it stands in the spring of 1932, schemes and projects of a more permanent character, such as the various proposals, on the one hand, for a reversion to a freer, or, on the other, progress towards a more completely planned economic organisation, must necessarily wait upon a measure of recovery from depression. Economic activity must be revived before it can be reorganised, and any restorative measures involve some sacrifice of claims at present rigidly maintained in face of shrunken national incomes.[9]

---

9 Condliffe 1932, pp. 226–27.

The view of the author expressed above, in comparing national income and wages etc., is that a sharp contraction of the former will naturally lead to a corresponding fall in the latter,[10] but there is significant room for doubt on this point.

It is not clear whether the position expressed by Condliffe in the passage above is based on a particular opinion regarding such fundamental matters as the definition of national income, its source, the laws of its production and distribution, as well as the relation between those laws. What is certain, in any case, is that he thinks it possible for the diminution of what he calls national income to not signify a reduction in productive power. Indeed, he says that it is precisely because productive power increases to result in 'surplus' production that a crisis occurs and national income declines. But this idea that he finds so self-evident leads to a conclusion that is peculiar at first sight; namely that because the productive power of labour has risen to allow more useful goods to be produced within the same period of time, workers should be satisfied with a lower standard of living. How can this be explained? In my opinion, such a strange conclusion is certainly not the product of a peculiar way of thinking on the part of the author himself as an individual. It stems rather from a fundamental, inherent contradiction that is active within the capitalist mode of production itself, and as long as this mode of production is taken as the natural premise, every theory must end up in the same contradictory conclusion. The basis of the contradiction is that under the capitalist mode of production, the motive of production and its aim is not to satisfy the needs of the producers but

---

10   The opinion of Condliffe regarding wages is expressed from a variety of other perspectives besides the one above. This springs from the fact that wages pertain, intrinsically, to various relations within the aspects of the developmental process of capitalist production, and are manifested in various forms, but Condliffe does not clarify that process, and therefore is unable to grasp the different aspects in their appearance as different aspects of the same process. Thus, he is also unable to clearly convey the distinctions and unity of the various relations of wages within those aspects (i.e. the various perspectives when considering wages). As a result, his view necessarily falls into confusion and contradiction. According to Condliffe, wages should be in proportion to national income, but also must be in proportion to the minimum level to ensure the life of the working class, the value of products, the cost of living, the labour performed (in terms of labour time and labour intensity), and productive power (on this point he stands outside the bounds of capitalist production but is not aware of this himself), and when it comes to production cost it is better for wages to be low, while as a source of demand it is better if they are high. And in line with each of these different viewpoints, wages might either be seen as having already fallen dramatically or not to have done so. However, despite confusing all of this, the absolutely decisive idea for Condliffe, in the end, seems to be that the lowering of wages is an indispensable condition for overcoming the depression.

to obtain profit (and not just any arbitrary profit but one that it above a certain rate posited at the time), and that the competition to obtain this profit inevitably leads to the development of productive power, while the development of productive power necessarily brings down the general rate of profit. The 'surplus' is certainly not a surplus in terms of the aim of consumption, but a surplus vis-à-vis the conditions for the valorisation of capital. Despite the capitalist mode of production being a mode of production that is driven by and aims for profit, it must develop productive power as if its aim were to produce for consumption. This fundamental contradiction, along with its development, brings increasing tension to all of the contradictions of capitalist production, which makes the periodic eruption of crisis inevitable. In this way, crisis is the collective explosion of contradictions that are brought to this state of extreme tension, and at the same time their forcible adjustment. The essence of this adjustment, needless to say, establishes the conditions whereby it is possible to again secure a certain rate of profit. And the reduction of wages and devaluing of debt that the author emphasises (along with the lowering of the price of productive assets just referred to) are merely the classic methods to achieve this aim.

But these means face unprecedented obstacles in the current crisis. The author laments that, although unemployment has risen to an unprecedented level, '[s]o large a part is played now in the determination of wage-levels by collective agreements, and in some cases by legislation, that not even severe and prolonged employment brings about the reductions that used to be relied upon as one measure of adjustment in crises'.[11] Not only is the capitalist mode of production incompatible with the improvement of workers' standard of living beyond a certain point, it demands the occasional reduction in wages to 'accommodate' fluctuations in the business conditions. However, the common sense of workers is that they should share in the profits resulting from the increase in productive power, and they do not see why their lives should be shaken by capital's moneymaking drive. Through their solidarity the power of workers advances, making it hard from the standpoint of capital to demand wage cuts. Moreover, once unemployment has reached a certain level, it immediately threatens the capitalist social order, raising the need for various measures to be taken to address the situation. Thus, spending on social policies actually increases during a depression, along with military spending, so that, at the very moment when a contraction is most necessary, the *faux frais* of capitalist production swell instead, making it hard to implement reductions. But an even bigger obstacle to the adjustment of the current crisis is the inflexibility of capital ownership, as Condliffe explains:

---

11   Condliffe 1932, pp. 226–27.

Opportunities for profitable new investment as interest rates and prices fall have, in past depressions, been an important factor in forcing capital reconstruction of existing industries ...

The failure of such new enterprises to emerge up till the present appears to be due to a variety of factors partly connected with the price of investment goods relative to the price of finished consumption goods, but partly due also to general insecurity. For the reasons set out in previous chapters, the discrepancy between the prices of production and consumption goods has constantly tended to widen, so that costs of production have remained high and investment has not been profitable. Moreover, though credit has been abundant and short-term interest rates have fallen to exceptionally low levels, the rates of interest charged upon industrial loans have not fallen greatly. In many countries, the banks have been afraid to endanger their liquidity by extending industrial loans which are not self-liquidating within a short period. In addition, there has persisted a heavy risk premium in consequence of the continued extension of Government interference with industry and trade in an effort to protect existing industries from new or aggravated competition. There has been little incentive to new investment in a world which has multiplied tariffs, quotas, exchange controls and other forms of interference with private initiative.

The failure of new competing enterprises to emerge and force a readjustment of existing businesses is therefore partly due to the pressure upon public authorities from those who are reluctant to face such a readjustment and are able to secure public support to a degree never known in any previous depression. The reluctance to face drastic revaluations of invested capital has been in part due to the combination of factors to which attention was drawn in the preceding sections of this chapter. The greater volume of indebtedness, especially that part of it which was borrowed in foreign countries and came to industry through bank advances, the increased use of debentures and preference shares and the general demand of small investors and financial institutions for continuity of dividends are very important factors in the situation. The plight of the financial institutions and banking systems in many countries, to which attention is drawn in a later chapter, is a further powerful influence in the direction of conserving the existing capital structure.

In addition, however, there must be reckoned the widespread disposition to shrink from the catastrophic solution of the crisis by means of bankruptcy and to invoke the aid of the banking systems and, in certain cases, of the public credit in staving off the hardships which would be involved therein. There has been a disposition to seek a solution along other lines, by monetary action designed to raise the price-level, by protective governmental intervention, or by organisation to restrict and regulate production and trade.

Such solutions had not been found in effective measure by the end of 1932 and, in many countries, the continued aggravation of the crisis had led to a situation in which financial and currency difficulties were beginning to force both a diminution of dividends and capital revaluation. The banking crisis in the United States in February 1933 was the most important example … Capital reconstruction, both of the banks and of industry in general, proved necessary in many cases.

This example, however important in itself and significant also because of its far-reaching effects, by no means exhausts the consequences that followed from the extreme difficulty of maintaining intact the capital structure that had been built up in the course of the boom. The burden of ownership claims upon the product of industry contributed its large share to the combination of forces that has driven many countries to abandon or restrict the working of the gold standard. A particularly difficult situation has been created where industrial expansion was largely based upon foreign capital and where the inability of industry to carry the charges thus imposed upon it has resulted in a paralysis, not only of domestic production, but of international financial transactions. The manner in which the effort to discharge foreign debt obligations and, at the same time, maintain currency stability has led to the increased trade restrictions which are throttling international commerce is treated elsewhere, but its obvious connection with the over-capitalisation of industry is relevant here. A further important consequence of the maintenance of existing capitalisation has been the difficulty of reducing the unit-price of goods produced in manufacturing industry and of thereby reducing the discrepancy between the prices of finished goods and raw materials, which is an outstanding obstacle to recovery from the depression. From many points of view, therefore, the disproportion of the claims of ownership to the earning capacity of industry proved a serious obstacle to recovery.[12]

The view introduced above by Condliffe is indeed correct. The disproportion between the claims of ownership and the earning capacity of industry are a

---

12   Condliffe 1933, pp. 148–50.

fundamental obstacle to a true recovery. Not only is this a fundamental obstacle to recovery, but also, in a sense, a fundamental cause that leads to crisis. Up to a point Condliffe recognises this as well. That is to say, he recognises that there was excessive credit expansion and excessive investment during the period of prosperity prior to the crisis, and that therein lies a primary source of the disproportion manifested after the crisis and the accompanying inflexibility in the economic system. But we need to take a further step forward in our thinking by questioning why exactly excessive credit and excessive investment occur. This is clearly the result of the excessive loanable capital. And the phenomenon of excessive loanable capital is nothing more than the manifestation of the disproportion between the demand of capital ownership as self-valorising value and the actual possibility for valorisation posited by the process of production and distribution. The excessive loanable capital based on this disproportion necessarily leads to the enormous expansion of credit and expansion of production at a certain stage in its development, and at the same time the internal limits of capitalist production that form the basis of the disproportion are what posit the swelling of credit and expansion of production with an 'excessive' character. This is not an 'excess' with regard to the life needs of humanity, but an excess in proportion to the possibility of value augmentation at a certain rate. One of the great contradictions of this mode of production is that the credit system always periodically brings about an enormous collision with the immanent barrier of capitalist production; this is one of the main moments to accelerate and aggravate a crisis, and also an important lever to hasten the accomplishment of the historical mission of capitalist production. Instead of excessive credit and excessive investment bringing about a disproportion between capital ownership and the function of capital, it is rather the disproportion between the capital ownership and the function of capital that leads to the swelling of credit and the excessive expansion of production. Rather than economic inflexibility arising from the swelling of credit, the internal limits of capitalist production are broken through by the swelling of credit, and the reproduction process of capital is able through this to expand its inherent elasticity to an extreme point, as Marx explains in Book III of *Capital*:

> If the credit system appears as the principal lever of overproduction and excessive speculation in commerce, this is simply because the reproduction process, which is elastic by nature, is now forced to its most extreme limit; and this is because a great part of the social capital is applied by those who are not its owners, and who therefore proceed quite unlike owners who, when they function themselves, anxiously weigh the limits of their private capital. This only goes to show how the valorisation of cap-

ital founded on the antithetical character of capitalist production permits actual free development only up to a certain point, which, is constantly broken through by the credit system. The credit system hence accelerates the material development of the productive forces and the creation of the world market, which it is the historical task of the capitalist mode of production to bring to a certain level of development, as material foundations for the new form of production. At the same time, credit accelerates the violent outbreaks of this contradiction, crises, and with these the elements of dissolution of the old mode of production.[13]

The crisis that is the forced explosion of this contradiction at the same time constitutes the moment of its forced resolution. The solution, of course, signifies bringing equilibrium into the fundamental disequilibrium noted above. This can be arrived at from two directions. First, the function of capital can be reduced. And second, the demands of capital ownership can be lowered. What Condliffe is discussing with regard to the devaluing and destruction of capital, in the passage quoted above, belongs to the latter category, and represents the classic method that is the most thorough and at the same time the most forceful. This is not a mere demand to raise prices, but the reduction of the subject of this demand itself. At the same time, this can only be brought about by the forcible negation of that sacred thing, private property. This negation does not challenge the sanctity of the principle of private ownership itself, however. Rather, it is carried out according to the responsibility of individuals, in line with the principles of private ownership. And yet this classic method (like the other main classic methods discussed earlier) is facing unprecedented obstacles in the current crisis. Overall and partial destruction has taken place on an abnormal scale, but this is completely insufficient compared to the liquidation needed. What is the fundamental cause that is impeding the adequate progression? This is the central concern of Condliffe in the passage quoted above, where he argues that this is the precise outcome of the development of finance capital. The profits of finance capital require the blocking of the forced settlement exercised by crisis, and the power of finance capital makes this obstruction possible. However, the impediment of a forced settlement does not abolish its necessity: it merely builds up the contradiction further by postponing the solution, ultimately creating the need for a settlement on an even larger scale. The author, as his proof of this, points to the 1933 banking crisis in the United States, but this is a mere opening act. The succession of

---

13   Marx 1981a, p. 572.

inflationary policies that followed were the negation of capital ownership on an even more general scale. Not only was this on a more general scale, but it took a more forceful shape. This can be seen, for instance, in the revoking of the gold clause, which is in fact the legal removal of the sacred contract – that highest legal principle of private ownership – with regard to gold, the fetish of modern production relations. Such circumstances indicate the enormity of the disproportionality underlying the current crisis, and at the same time the fundamental contradictions of finance capital and its policies.

This concludes my discussion and observations regarding several main types of disequilibrium and the causes of inflexibility that prolong that disequilibrium, which are indicated in the *World Economic Survey* as the characteristics of today's unprecedentedly severe crisis or depression. Unfortunately, there is not adequate space here to also consider the disequilibrium within the international economy, to which Condliffe attaches extreme importance. However, it can briefly be said that in this realm as well he basically adopts the impotent, orthodox position of not setting foot outside of the fortress of doubt, nostalgia, and didacticism; while at the same time indicating to some extent many important contradictions particular to recent developments. This evaluation applies to the survey as a whole. Its content includes many facts that will even interest those whose standpoint is different than that of the author – and the more advanced a person's standpoint, the deeper the interest will be. In this sense, I do not hesitate to widely recommend Condliffe's survey.

CHAPTER 10

The Contradictions of Modern Wealth

This spring a study group was organised for those with an interest in Ricardo. The following is a summary of the discussion at one of the meetings. An enthusiastic member of the group was unable to attend that day, so in the relevant places I have inserted some of his views regarding the discussion and ask for the indulgence of the other participants in this respect. The discussion started from a critique of Ricardo's distinction between use value and value, then examined his concept of 'riches' in Chapter 20 of On the Principles of Political Economy and Taxation, *before gradually veering off into problems related to crisis, dumping, economic national power, national wealth accounting, etc. Here I will just present the first half of the discussion, as that is the only part that has been edited thus far.*[1]

s:[2] Simply put, Ricardo did not grasp the essential relation between use value and value. He only knew that they were completely different from each other, and that the former was the indispensable condition for the latter's existence. As a result, he was unable also to grasp the contradiction of the commodity. It is not merely that use value and value are different from each other, and that the former is the condition for the latter's existence. They are the opposite aspects or oppositional moments within a given commodity. As such, they are in a relation of mutual presupposition, in which they supplement and at the same time exclude each other. Here we have the contradiction of the commodity as a unity of use value and value. This is what makes money, as well as the division of commodities into ordinary commodities and money, necessary. Yet Ricardo failed

---

1 [Originally published as Kuruma 1935b under the title 'Questions and Answers about Wealth' and republished as Chapter 5 of *An Investigation of Marx's Theory of Crisis* (Kuruma 1949). In the preface of that book, Kuruma notes the following regarding the chapter's content:

'This article was the fruit of a study group set up at the Ōhara Institute for Social Research for those interested in Ricardo. Although the content stems from that group, it is not a transcript of an actual discussion but rather mainly my own creation, and the initials of participants are not a reference to actual names. The group was organised just after the Manchurian Incident [of 1931]. At the time, a foolish argument was being made that if the state confiscated the wealth of the conglomerates Mitsui and Mitsubishi it could easily wage war for many years, and one of my aims for the article was to unfold an aspect of crisis theory while bearing that argument in mind. However, my limited skills as a writer did not allow me to accomplish that aim in time for the submission deadline' (Kuruma 1949, pp. 4–5).]

2 Presenter at the study meeting. This is the summation of his presentation.

to grasp the essential relation between use value and value, which is also why he failed to grasp the contradiction of the commodity and the true significance of money and of all its developed forms.

K:[3] Shall we move on to the questions and discussion now? I hope that we can have a lively debate.

Z: My question does not concern the presentation itself, but if we look at the content of Ricardo's *On the Principles of Political Economy and Taxation*, we can see that Chapter 20 is titled 'Value and Riches, Their Distinctive Properties'. I am embarrassed to admit that I have not yet read this chapter, but what is Ricardo referring to in using the term 'riches'? And what does he mean by the 'distinctive properties' of value and riches? Perhaps I am on the wrong track, but I thought that discussing this topic could help clarify the problem just posed by 'S' regarding Ricardo's understanding of the relation between use value and value.

S: I can't offer a definite answer since I haven't given the matter much thought, but my basic view is that Ricardo speaks of 'riches' in the objective sense to indicate use value or the abundance of use values, and in the subjective sense to indicate a certain power of a subject to command riches. What Ricardo is saying in Chapter 20 is connected to various problems that are in fact distinct from each other and can be introduced from a variety of perspectives, but in terms of the problem we are dealing with here, we can consider how he is primarily indicating the reciprocal influence that changes in productive power have on wealth and value, while emphasising the essential difference between wealth and value. In so doing, Ricardo on the one hand attacks the view of Say, who mistakes riches for value, and thus places utility or use value, which is merely an element of riches, alongside labour as a determining factor of value; while on the other hand, criticising the view that mistakes value for riches, so as to erroneously view an increase in value as immediately signifying an increase in riches. Ricardo emphasises that the increase of wealth that is the goal of economic development is the augmentation of use values, not value, and suggests in a sense that value would decrease as a result. But Ricardo's recognition that changes in productive power have opposite effects on use value and value does not necessarily mean that he had a clear understanding of the fundamental contradiction of the commodity that I mentioned earlier, regarding the essential opposition between use value and value.

---

3 The moderator.

z: Thank you. Your explanation has cleared up that point regarding Chapter 20. But according to your explanation, it would seem that Ricardo thought that riches consist of use value. Is that view correct? I would like to hear more of your opinion on this.

s: It's a bit ambiguous and difficult to answer a question posed in terms of whether his view is correct or not, but the key issues seem to be: Was Ricardo's view of the determinations of riches different from the general or traditional view of wealth? Did he grasp the essence of the problem? And is his view applicable to every situation?

z: That's exactly what I'd like to know.

s: In that regard, at least, I think there can be no room for doubt regarding the correctness of Ricardo's definition of riches. This definition was not originally created by Ricardo nor is it unique to him. Rather, he inherited it from that great common-sense thinker, Adam Smith. Chapter 20 begins by quoting the following line from *The Wealth of Nations*: 'A man is rich or poor in the degree to which he can afford the necessaries, conveniences, and amusement of human life'.[4] Ricardo treats this proposition from Smith, which had stood the test of time, as a correct proposition to be assimilated as is. Smith himself was not consistent in adhering to this definition of wealth, contradicting himself at times by raising the proposition that a man 'must be rich or poor according to the quantity of that labour which he can command, or which he can afford to purchase'.[5] Ricardo already pointed out that this 'description differs essentially from the other, and is certainly incorrect',[6] but there are two errors contained in Smith's view. First, he confused value with wealth, and second, he confused the merely extrinsic measure of value according to commanded labour with the intrinsic measure according to necessary labour. By confusing the extrinsic measure of commanded labour with the intrinsic measure of necessary labour when he argued that value is determined by labour, Smith slipped into the fallacy that commanded labour is somehow a constant measure of value. This is well known and requires little additional explanation, and that confusion is clearly manifested in the second proposition within his theory, quoted above. If we set aside the characteristic confusion within Smith description, the second pro-

---

4   Smith 1937, p. 30.
5   Smith 1937, p. 30.
6   Ricardo 1996, p. 193.

position can ultimately be reduced to the general idea that wealth is composed of value, so that the magnitude of wealth is determined by the magnitude of value. The error within this view is clear when we consider what occurs when there are fluctuations in productive power, as was mentioned in the overview of Ricardo's discussion of the difference between value and wealth. For instance, we can consider a case where, as a result of a fall in productive power, there are fewer products but value augments (not only value per product but aggregate value as well). In this case, could it really be said that wealth has increased? Or should it rather be said that wealth has contracted? If value is said to be the measure of wealth, then the natural conclusion would be that wealth had increased, but this clearly goes against our conventional notion of wealth. I think this demonstrates the truth of the generally held concept of wealth as being composed of use value.

z: What you said makes sense to me, but if that is the case, our normal view of national wealth in terms of so many billion yen or our definition of a wealthy person as someone with a great deal money would be a mere appearance, rather than a plain truth.

s: It is quite strange to call it an appearance, but what I'm trying to say is that if we pursue this question further, we will see that deep down everyone thinks of wealth in terms of use value, including the examples you just raised. However, we are not always aware of this in our daily lives; or I should say that in many cases we fall into the illusion that wealth is composed of value. And I think this derives from two circumstances. First, as long as we assume that productive power is unchanged, the magnitude of value will correspond to the magnitude of wealth. Therefore, if we set aside changes in money, the most realistic expression of the magnitude of wealth can be found in price. This is in fact convenient, but it leads us, unknowingly, into the fallacy just mentioned. To that extent, this illusion can be rectified by reflecting on the example I mentioned of a change in productive power. In so doing, we can see for ourselves that wealth is composed in fact of use value. The second circumstance is that, when seen from the restricted viewpoint of an individual, the magnitude of one's own wealth is determined by the magnitude of the relative value of the money and property that is possessed. In other words, the larger that magnitude, the greater the portion of the social products that a person will be able to command. This is of course a justified view when seen from the standpoint of a specific individual, but if we do not recognise the limitation of its significance, we can slip into the illusion that value is somehow the general measure or substance of wealth. This illusion will dissolve if we shift from the individual viewpoint to a more comprehensive, social perspective. From that perspective, as long as the total product of society is a given, the plus in wealth on one side from a simple augmentation of value would be a minus in wealth on the other side, so that value only determines the distribution of social wealth and bears no relation to the determination of its magnitude. In other words, when viewed from the perspective of society as a whole, it becomes clear that wealth is solely determined by the quantity of use value.

z: Does that mean, according to Ricardo and according to you, that wealth is different when viewed socially as opposed to individually? In other words, when seen individually, value is wealth, but when seen from a social perspective, use value is wealth. Is that right?

s: Not exactly. Essentially, wealth is composed of use value. But seen from the standpoint of the individual, the quantity of use values that can be commanded and enjoyed by that person depends on the relative magnitude of the value possessed, so value becomes the measure of wealth.

z: Is that really the psychology of a wealthy person? Not being rich myself, or likely to ever become rich, I wouldn't know exactly, but if the aim is merely to 'enjoy the necessaries, conveniences, and amusements of human life', what need would there be to save up an enormous amount of money? For people accumulating money, the aim itself is not to enjoy more use values but to accumulate more value itself. In other words, for them, money is the true shape of wealth. Aren't there extremely rich people in Japan, such as moneylenders, who, apart from the 'necessaries' of human life, do not consume that much in the way of the 'conveniences and amusements' that money can bring?

s: Certainly, that is true. But I don't think it is sufficient to deny that wealth is essentially composed of use value. Even in the extreme case of such a moneylender, it is very unlikely that he would be saving money were it not capable of buying things. His reason for accumulating money lies in its ability to make purchases. The moment that money would no longer be able to do that, it would cease to be money and could not be the object of his accumulative desire. Even if he does not purchase anything, that just means that he has opted for money's latent rather than its actual purchasing power.

z: You say it is simply a matter of choice, but I think an important problem lies precisely within the choice between the two. Doesn't this demonstrate the undeniable difference between a thing and the power to purchase a thing.

s: There is of course an important difference between the two, but it cannot be denied that there is something in common between them as well, because purchasing power is the power to buy a thing, and that power ultimately can only be realised through the transformation into that thing.

z: Then, according to your logic, the wealth of the money hoarder is also essentially composed of use value.

s: Yes, ultimately.

z: Doesn't that contradict the presentation you made today. You seemed to criticise Ricardo for not grasping the necessity of money and for viewing money simply as a means of circulation?

s: Well, if you put it that way you might be right ... but wouldn't it be far stranger to say that wealth is composed of value. Consider again the example I gave earlier of a change in productive power.

z: Yes, that is certainly the case ...

s: We seem to have both reached a dead end. Is there someone here who might help us solve this problem?

M: I think the issue will clear up naturally if the crux of the report presented by 'S' is thoroughly considered. He pointed out that Ricardo had only seen the external relation between use value and value, without grasping the inherent oppositional relation between them, and that this made it impossible for him to grasp the fundamental contradiction of the commodity. What is the exact source of this defect of Ricardo and what does it ultimately signify? Principally, he (and Classical political economy in general) mistook the capitalist mode of production for a natural mode of social production, and thus did not perceive the historical character of the commodity and value, which are the most general forms that historically characterise this mode of production. Thus, Ricardo was unable to grasp these historically particular forms in their nature as such or distinguish the forms as such from their natural content. The Classical economists managed to analyse value and discover that its content was labour. But from the outset they did not even attempt to ponder the core form-related problems, such as: What is the characteristic of labour insofar as it forms value? Why does labour take the form of the value of a product rather than directly appearing as labour? In other words: Why do products of labour not appear simply as products but in the particular form of commodities? By not pondering such questions, they were unable to clarify the oppositional relation between the labour that forms value and the labour that forms use value, and in turn failed to grasp the two-fold character of commodity-producing labour. This also made it impossible to grasp the contradiction of the commodity by clarifying the oppositional relation between value and use value. It seems to me that this same defect is manifested in Ricardo's conceptual grasp of wealth. Granted, wealth is merely products if considered separate from all of its specific social forms and is no different than use value if considered separate from all of its relations to production. Similarly, in the case of the commodity, if its particular characteristic form is overlooked, it is reduced to a mere product. And if then stripped of its qualities as a product, it simply becomes a use-value – a mere 'good' (*Güter*) as a desired object. But, of course, these are abstractions. If one aims to speak of the wealth of society, we first need to consider what mode of production dominates in the society and therefore what is the social form of this wealth. In this sense, we should pay attention to the opening lines of *Capital*, where Marx writes:

> The wealth of societies in which the capitalist mode of production prevails appears as an. 'immense collection of commodities'; the individual commodity appears as its elementary form. Our investigation therefore begins with the analysis of the commodity.[7]

This is a clear declaration of the fundamental standpoint of Marx's examination in *Capital*, and at the same time the opening statement in a declaration of war that perfectly suits his critique of the 'political economy' that is based on the fundamental fallacies that have been mentioned. Those opening lines also provide us with the key for solving the problem we face here. The idea that wealth is composed of use value, and the idea that wealth is composed of value, both contain an element of truth, but to take a one-sided truth and claim it is the whole truth is to fall into a fundamental error. Use value is the material content of wealth (i.e. material wealth) in any form of society, while the commodity (and therefore value) is the most abstract and at the same time the most general social form of wealth under the capitalist mode of production. If the understanding of this essential relation is lacking, so that the question is posed in terms of whether wealth is composed of use value or of value, we will end up talking at cross purposes, like the dialogue between a fisherman

---

7 Marx 1976, p. 125.

and a woodcutter.[8] The opposition between different theories of wealth reflects the fundamental contradiction of modern wealth, which is the contradiction between the commodity as use value and value. It is by recognising that modern wealth itself is a contradictory thing that a theory can free itself from its own contradictions.

z: I see what you mean now. That removes the doubts I had.

s: My thought has also cleared up thanks to your explanation. But now it seems that my criticism of Smith might be a bit strange. What do you think about that?

m: I think you might have gotten carried away by Ricardo's criticism of Smith. But if we read the passage before and after the line Ricardo quotes from *The Wealth of Nations*, we can see that Smith did not carelessly juxtapose two definitions of wealth. Smith writes:

> Every man is rich or poor according to the degree in which he can afford to enjoy the necessaries, conveniences, and amusements of human life. But after the division of labour has once thoroughly taken place, it is but a very small part of these with which a man's own labour can supply him. The far greater part of them he must derive from the labour of other people, and he must be rich or poor according to the quantity of that labour which he can command, or which he can afford to purchase. The value of any commodity, therefore, to the person who possesses it, and who means not to use or consume it himself, but to exchange it for other commodities, is equal to the quantity of labour which it enables him to purchase or command. Labour, therefore, is the real measure of the exchangeable value of all commodities ...
>
> What is bought with money or with goods is purchased by labour as much as what we acquire by the toil of our own body. ... They contain the value of a certain quantity of labour which we exchange for what is supposed at the time to contain the value of an equal quantity.[9]

---

8 [Kuruma is referring to the short philosophical prose treatise *Yuqiao wendui* ('Fisherman and Woodcutter Dialogue') – commonly but perhaps erroneously attributed to the Chinese philosopher Shao Yong (1011–1077) – in which two allegorical figures converse along a riverbank.]

9 Smith 1937, p. 30.

In this passage, Smith clearly is discussing the fundamental change wealth undergoes through the establishment of commodity production relations. In other words, Smith is saying that the wealth of commodity producers is no longer composed of the products of their own labour but rather of the quantity of the labour of others that the products command, and the quantity of this labour is determined by the amount of labour contained within one's own products. Upon even closer inspection, the wealth of commodity producers no longer consists of the fruit of their labour in its natural character (as use value), but rather consists of the fruit of their labour insofar as it is equal to the labour of others, as social labour; in other words, it consists of value. Smith does not perceive this, however. He does not clarify the relation of value and exchange value, and therefore the relation between invested labour and commanded labour, and thus he also overlooks that in the case of commanding the labour of another person, there is a distinction between the objectivised labour of the other person and that person's living labour. The result is that he falls into a serious misunderstanding, as we are well aware of from what 'S' explained. But here as well we cannot overlook that there is great significance underlying this fallacy. Smith was certainly mistaken, as Ricardo pointed out, for thinking that with the accumulation of capital, the original theory of value is no longer applicable. But there was a much deeper reason for this than Ricardo could surmise. First, the exchange between capital and wage labour is basically an exchange of unequal quantities of labour, since objectified labour is exchanged for a greater quantity of living labour. This seems to contradict the original theory of value, making it is hard to see how one might explain this exchange on the basis of that theory. As long as the value of labour power is grasped in a distorted form as the value of labour, this problem can never be solved. And, of course, Ricardo was also incapable of solving it. But Ricardo did not even notice the existence of the problem, whereas Smith was aware of a contradiction, which is why he thought that the original law of value was no longer operative. There is a second unspoken motive that seems to underlie Smith's decision to limit the determination of value by invested labour to the period of simple commodity production, while thinking that, with the accumulation of capital, value is solely determined by commanded labour. That is, with the development of capitalist production, commodities (or money as their transformed form) generally become capital, or at least can be transformed into capital (and are thus latent capital). However, the value of a commodity as capital is not determined merely by its value as a commodity, but by its augmented value when it can develop into capital; in other words, it is not determined by the quantity of labour that it contains itself but by the larger amount of living labour that it can command. This seems to be the hidden impetus that confused Smith. I should note that although I said earlier that the social form of modern wealth is the commodity, it is certainly not limited to the commodity. The commodity is merely the most fundamental, the most universal, and at the same time the most abstract form of modern wealth. But more concretely the commodity appears in many forms with more determinations, whether in the mere commodity form, in the form of money, or the form of capital – or further as capital itself. And the modern social form of wealth also takes those many forms. This also applies to what I said earlier about the contradiction of modern wealth. The contradiction between use value and value within the commodity is the most fundamental and the most general but also the most abstract form. The contradiction of the commodity develops into the modern contradiction of wealth by developing into money, capital, and other forms.

CHAPTER 11

Capital Accumulation and the Depreciation Fund for Fixed Capital

The most fundamental and theoretically interesting part of Tsunao Inomata's book, *Research on Imperialism*,[1,2] is Part 1 ('The Theoretical Basis for the Collapse of Capitalism'), the main content of which is a brilliant polemic aimed at Rosa Luxemburg's *Accumulation of Capital*, containing many characteristic ideas. But the most striking idea, it seems to me, is his response to the question: 'Where does the money to realise the surplus value to be accumulated come from?'. Inomata writes:

> According to Rosa Luxemburg, the capitalised surplus products cannot be bought back by the capitalists or the workers ... If we look at the case of the capitalists, in order for some of them (A, A', A", etc.) to purchase the new means of production required for expanded production from other capitalists (B, B', B", etc.), the A-group capitalists have no choice but to first sell their surplus products and use the money received to pay the B-group capitalists. However, even if the A-group capitalists want to sell what they have, since the ones to purchase those surplus products are the B-group capitalists, who will not be able to purchase the products

---

1 [Originally published as Kuruma 1931 and republished as Chapter 6 of *An Investigation of Marx's Theory of Crisis* (Kuruma 1949). In the preface of that book, Kuruma notes the following regarding the chapter's content:

'This article is a critique of Tsunao Inomata's book *Research on Imperialism*. At the time in Japan, as elsewhere, there was a lively debate over accumulation that centered on what could be called the tendential way Rosa Luxemburg posed the problem based on her mistaken interpretation of the core of the theory of reproduction in Part 3 of the Book II of *Capital*, in terms of how she understood the particular problem Marx sought to clarify and therefore of the particular significance of Part 3 within the overall system of *Capital*. Inomata took part in this debate and presented a novel opinion on the question of where the money to realise surplus value comes from. His opinion was respected among quite a few observers at the time and was seen as one of his most brilliant theoretical contributions. When I first read his book, I had doubts about his view and took some notes at the time in preparation for writing my planned work on the theory of crisis, but since I was not able to bring that plan to fruition and there was pressure to publish, I ended up presenting this as a separate article (Kuruma 1949, pp. 5–6).]

2 Inomata 1928.

until they have sold their own surplus products to the A-group capitalists seeking to sell their own products, the problem has no solution. Therefore, the capitalists are unable to transform their surplus value into money through mutual transactions so as to purchase the means of production they require to expand production, thus making it absolutely impossible to carry out capital accumulation. Here we have the position of Luxemburg.

Next, we can consider the case where workers purchase surplus products from capitalists ... In this case, the workers to whom the capitalists want to sell are all newly added workers. They are wageworkers precisely because they have no money, so their purchasing power is zero apart from the wages received from a capitalist. Thus, only one method is available. It is necessary for the capitalist to advance wages to the workers prior to the surplus products being transformed into money in order for the workers to be able to purchase them. But where can the capitalist obtain the money needed for those wages? There is no source from which it can arise. Seen from either perspective, then, as long as we are dealing with a purely capitalist society, it is impossible for either the capitalists themselves or the workers they hire to obtain the money needed to purchase the surplus products, and therefore expanded production as well as the accumulation of capital are inherently impossible.[3]

After that introduction on how Luxemburg poses the problem, Inamoto goes on to argue the following:

The problem here, in short, concerns the source of the money needed to purchase the surplus product. Is this a problem Marx failed to pose? Not at all. He theoretically supposed the difficulty that could arise in the process of circulation with regard to the problem of the realisation of surplus products, and after rejecting all makeshift answers was able to provide the following solution. Marx recognised that, generally speaking, in order for capitalists to reciprocally to turn their surplus products into money, a portion of them must first hand over money to other capitalists or workers prior to realising their own surplus products. But they would have stored up the money needed to pay that advance as long as they have an adequately large amount of fixed capital. This is because fixed capital is in fact renewed after a long period of time, and the portion of value that

---

3 Inomata 1928, pp. 37–8.

is allocated annually for the renewal of fixed capital is not transformed every year into means of production, but rather accumulated as a depreciation fund. This is the money that can be used by capitalists to make an advance payment.[4]

As is clear from the passage above, Inomata argues that the problem posed by Luxemburg was not worth raising since Marx had solved it quite some time earlier by identifying the money accumulated to cover the depreciation of fixed capital as the source of the money capitalists use to make the advances necessary to realise surplus value. Inomata claims that Marx presents this idea in the following passage from Book II of *Capital*:

> There [in the case of simple reproduction] the money whose only use was to be spent as revenue on means of consumption returns to the capitalist to the extent that they advanced it for the exchange of their respective commodities; here the same money similarly reappears, but with the function changed. The *A*'s and *B*'s (Dept. I) supply one another with the money for transforming their surplus products into additional virtual money capital, and alternatively cast the newly formed money capital into the circulation sphere as a means of purchase.[5]

Inomata uses this passage to back up his idea, but does it really have the significance he ascribes to it? The gist of his argument is that the 'the same money' Marx mentions in this passage refers to the depreciation fund for fixed capital. But such an assertion, it seems to me, is completely unfounded. Just prior to the passage quoted by Inomata, Marx writes:

> We already know, however, from considering simple reproduction, that a certain quantity of money must exist in the hands of the capitalists in department I and II so that they may exchange their surplus product. There the money whose only use was to be spent as revenue on means of consumption returns to the capitalists to the extent that they advanced it for the exchange of their respective commodities.[6]

This immediately precedes the part that begins with 'here the same money ...', and no matter how one might scrutinise Marx's argument, no trace can be

---

4   Inomata 1928, p. 39.
5   Marx 1978, p. 575.
6   Marx 1978, p. 575.

found of him posing the issue of the depreciation fund for fixed capital. How Inamoto could have picked up such an idea from that passage is not clear. In any case, it seems to me that Marx is simply noting in that section of his book that in observing simple reproduction, which constitutes the premise of expanded reproduction, it is evident that there must already be money in the hands of the capitalists of a quantity sufficient to realise surplus value.[7] Thus, as long as simple reproduction is premised, that amount of money must naturally be premised as well. Therefore, in the initial progression from simple to expanded reproduction, the question of the money needed to realise surplus value does not present any new difficulty at all. Indeed, in this case, there is not yet an increase in the quantity of the surplus value to be realised. What is different from before is merely the purpose of expending money and the function of the expended money (setting aside whatever change there might be in the type of product, which concerns the direct production process). The money that was formerly expended for the personal consumption of the capitalist as revenue is now invested as capital to purchase new elements of production. That is the fact Marx is referring to when he writes, 'the same money similarly reappears, but with its function changed'. Interpreted from this perspective, the situation is quite clear. Not only can we find no reference to the depreciation fund of fixed capital, but there is absolutely no need to raise such an issue here. Inomata's explanation strikes me as a complete misinterpretation.

But this misinterpretation did not originate with Inamoto: it can already be found in Rosa Luxemburg's *The Accumulation of Capital*. Her remarks on the subheading in Book II of *Capital* titled 'Hoard Formation' (Chapter 21, Section 1), reflect a misunderstanding that is similar to that of Inomata:

> This marks a regression to simple reproduction. It is quite true that capitalists *A* and capitalists *B* are always gradually accumulating a reserve of money for the periodic renewal of their constant (fixed) capital, and thus mutually help each other to realise their product. Yet this reserve that is amassed does not fall from the sky. It is merely the gradual precipitation of the value of the fixed capital that is transferred incrementally to the products and realised piecemeal through their sale. In this way, the reserve that has been built up can only ever be sufficient for the renewal of the former capital, and cannot serve for the purchase of an additional constant capital over and above this. This scenario remains within the confines of simple reproduction. Alternatively, a part of the means of

---

[7] This already was clarified in more detail in Book II of *Capital* (Ch. 17, Sec. 1; Ch. 20, Sec. 5).

circulation that had previously served the personal consumption of the capitalists now appears as a new, additional source of money to be capitalised. However, this merely marks a reversion to the brief, exceptional moment that is only conceivable in theory the transition from simple to expanded reproduction. No headway has been made beyond this original leap; in fact all that has been achieved is to go round in a circle.[8]

It should be clear from what I explained earlier that most of Luxemburg's criticism of Marx in the passage above is based on a pure misunderstanding of what is written in the part of *Capital* under consideration.[9]

In defending Marx from the criticism of Luxemburg, Inamoto makes no attempt whatsoever to clarify that her criticism is based on a pure misinterpretation of the ideas of Marx, so that what she is attacking is not Marx's doctrine

---

[8] Luxemburg 2016, p. 99.

[9] However, near the end of the passage quoted, Luxemburg adds a sort of ancillary comment that seems to anticipate that someone could offer an explanation similar to mine, by noting that even if that were so, Marx's explanation would still be incorrect. But the following response can be made to Luxemburg. Granted, the answer that Marx posits here only applies to 'the transition from simple to expanded production' and would no longer be the case later under expanded production. But we need to remember, at the same time, that Marx is certainly not saying that the answer he provides is applicable to every case or that it is basically the only answer that can be posited. Rather, he is focusing in particular on the 'transition' case under consideration. In Chapter 17, Section 2, Marx had already provided a general explanation of the circulation of surplus value under expanded reproduction. The passage criticised by Luxemburg is merely a supplement to that. Whereas that earlier chapter presented a detailed investigation of continual expanded reproduction, it only dealt with the transition from simple to expanded production in very simple terms. This seems to be the circumstance for Marx only dealing later with that issue in detail. (Incidentally, we should also take into consideration that Book II of *Capital* was not completed by Marx himself.) In Chapter 17 Section 2, Marx examines in detail the question of money in relation to continual expanded reproduction, and posits the following answer:

'The general reply is again the same. The total price of the mass of commodities in circulation has increased, not because the price of a given mass of commodities has risen, but rather because the mass of commodities now in circulation is greater than that of the commodities circulating earlier, without this having been balanced by any fall in prices. The additional money required for the circulation of this increased commodity mass of a greater value must be created either by a more economic use of the quantity of money in circulation – whether by directly balancing payments, etc., or by means that accelerate the circulation of the same pieces of money – or alternatively by the transformation if money from the hoard form into the circulating form … To the extent that all these means together are not enough, there must be additional production of gold, or, what comes to the same thing, a part of the additional product must be exchanged either directly or indirectly for gold' (Marx 1978, pp. 419–20).

This explanation is exceedingly clear, so it is hard to imagine there could be any room for doubt.

but an illusion she herself concocted. Inamoto is captivated, in fact, by her illusion and seems to find in it a clue for constructing his own unique theory of accumulation, thus requiring him to safeguard that aspect from the rest of his attack on Luxemburg.

> If we have already recognised the existence of fixed capital within the problem of expanded reproduction, then we must likewise recognise the existence of the accumulation fund for fixed capital therein. When considering whether this fund is used in the process of accumulation to realise surplus products or not, it is of no concern whether the fund might 'fall from the sky' or instead be a 'gradual precipitation'. The question centers not on the history of its generation but rather the function it can currently play. In order to play the role necessary, it must of course take the shape of money and be of a certain magnitude of value. Incidentally, if we express this using the figures in Marx's reproduction schema, even if half of the 4000 units of total constant capital in Dept. I is assumed to constitute fixed capital, of which half must be replenished every year, there would still be a value of 1000 units in the shape of accumulated money. Meanwhile, the total added constant capital is only 400 units of value. It is clear, without using an abacus, that advancing the former would be more than enough to realise all of the surplus value embodied in the latter.
>
> What does Luxemburg mean when she says that the reserve accumulated can only be 'sufficient for the renewal of the former capital'? This signifies that she has committed the error of viewing all 2000 units of value as expressing the value of the fixed capital that should be actually replenished. Even if one were to accept this standpoint, her argument is still impossible unless we accept a second error of viewing the 2000 units as being replenished all at once at some point in the year. Just as the 'value of the fixed capital', as Luxemburg recognises, is realised piecemeal through the sale of products, rather all at once, so is the replenishment of fixed capital carried out bit by bit, by individual capitalists successively.
>
> This is not limited to fixed capital. All the replenishments and conversions to money are only carried out gradually, in a piecemeal fashion. For the sake of investigating the conditions for expanded reproduction to be carried out without any hindrance, in perfect equilibrium – which is the investigation in the two senses often referred to – the circulation process is rightfully set aside as long as we are in the abstract stage where the various magnitudes are merely considered numerically, so that everything is just seen as a mass. At that stage, the *Warenbrei*

['undifferentiated mishmash of commodities'[10]] offered by Luxemburg is allowable. However, once one proceeds beyond that stage to pose the problem more concretely, so as to touch on the process of the conversion of value into money, one cannot avoid scrutinising the circulation process in its primary shape, which is to view it in its successive, partial segments. This is the stance that Marx justifiably took. And so, when dealing with the problem of fixed capital as well, even if it is replenished in its entirety annually, the capital that would carry out that replenishment at the end of the fiscal year would have to accumulate its value over 12 months by being 'realised piecemeal through [the products'] sale'. Even if the period were relatively short, say 10 months or 8 months, it would still be rather clumsy, even as sophistry, to argue that these funds would be insufficient to advance the relatively small sum, vis-à-vis the whole, needed for the additional constant capital (approximately 400 units). Moreover, just as the replenishment of the existing constant capital is done gradually, bit by bit, so is the purchase of the new constant capital also gradually and partially carried out. In the entire process of the commodity circulation to complete the mutual exchange whereby the means of production of various types and methods that embody the value of 400 units pass from the hands of the suppliers to the demanders, which is thus carried out simultaneously as a two-sided process whereby each capitalist realises surplus value and replenishes the necessary material conditions, the quantity of money needed as means of circulation and means of purchase is certainly, as the common sense of political economy holds, not equivalent to the 400 units that are the total commodity value. Would not a third, a fifth, or even a tenth suffice? If it were one-fourth, the money needed would be 100 units. Yet the author *The Accumulation of Capital* holds the position that a capitalist society that recovers 4000 in constant capital every year would be unable to advance a mere 100 in money![11]

This is Inomata's rejoinder to Luxemburg's attack on Marx. I have quoted from it at length because, even though in one aspect the attack and the rejoinder have been dealt with already by clarifying his fundamental misunderstanding of the passage in *Capital* that forms his starting point, the basis for his new theory of accumulation is not limited to that passage. Inomata also quotes from a passage in *Theories of Surplus Value*, which we will examine more closely later.

---

10   [Luxemburg 2016, p. 65.]
11   Inomata 1928, pp. 44–7.

Since the crux of the matter, obviously, is not to clarify a particular doctrine of Marx, but to elucidate the relations of what is being examined, for the time being I would like to detach the problem from its original relations to view Luxemburg's commentary in the passage cited earlier as a critique of Inomata's own doctrine, so that his reply quoted above is a counter-critique to defend his view. Based on this assumption, I would like to consider, in sequential order, whether the grounds he offers for his refutation of Luxemburg are justified or not.

First of all, Inomata states that '[w]hen considering whether this fund is used in the process of accumulation to realise surplus products [?] or not, it is of no concern whether the fund "falls from the sky" or is instead a "gradual precipitation"', since the 'question centers not on the history of its generation but rather the function it can currently play'. That is true enough in itself. However, when Luxemburg grasps the depreciation fund for fixed capital and says that it is not something that 'falls from the sky' and is instead a 'gradual precipitation', she should not be understood as merely posing the irrelevant question of the history of the fund's generation. Rather, she is trying to say that the fund is not some new element suddenly added from somewhere else in the expansion of production, but rather the product of the gradual transformation of the value of the old constant capital and the indispensable element for the replenishment of the former fixed capital; in other words, the fund existed as an irreplaceable moment for the reproduction process at its former scale, and is premised to the extent necessary as such, so that it cannot be sufficient for the 'purchase of an additional constant capital'. – That is merely what Luxemburg is saying.

Second, as the next stage in his argument, Inomata calculates the overall depreciation fund for fixed capital and the overall amount of money newly required to purchase additional constant capital for expanded reproduction, numerically showing that the former is a small percentage of the latter in order to demonstrate that the small amount needed could be taken from the large fund available. However, the figures he advances to support his argument are not, by their nature, useful to his aim for several reasons.

First, Inomata looks for the basis of his calculation in the reproduction schema of *Capital*, even though it is perfectly clear that the numeral relations within the schema are arbitrary and hypothetical (such as the ratio of variable to constant capital, the ratio of surplus value to variable capital, the proportion accumulated within the total surplus value, and therefore the proportion of additional to existing constant capital). The figures, in other words, are by no means an expression of real relations, nor do they express necessary relations, so they should not form the basis of such a rough calculation.

Furthermore, one struggles to even make sense of what Inamoto is trying to argue when he says that, 'even if half of the 4000 units of total constant capital in Dept. I is assumed to constitute fixed capital, of which half must be replenished every year, there would still be a value of 1000 units in the shape of accumulated money'. Indeed, in the case of the reproduction schema, as Marx himself clearly indicates, the part of constant capital that is not used up within the year is completely set aside. Thus, there is no way to suppose, as Inomata does, that half – or any other amount – of the 4000 units of total constant capital in Dept. I constitutes the fixed capital. If 'fixed capital' were understood as the part of the fixed capital that is worn out, the problem would at least become clear. In that case, though, what follows in his argument ('of which half must be replenished every year') would be completely incomprehensible. But that is not the only part of his argument that eludes understanding. Inamoto also says that 'if half of the 4000 units of total constant capital in Dept. I is assumed to constitute fixed capital', there would be 'a value of 1000 units in the shape of accumulated money', but it is not clear at all to me why that should be the case. If the total amount of the depreciation fund for fixed capital were naturally equal to the total amount of fixed capital replenished every year, such a thing would occur. But it is impossible to imagine that these two sums would naturally be equal. In short, his calculation seems to be thoroughly mistaken.

Another flaw in Inomata's argument, more fundamental than the issue of his calculations, concerns his belief that such calculations can be used as the basis of his argument. That is to say, the nature of the problem itself is not such that the problem can be decided by the greater or lesser proportion between the sum of the depreciation fund for fixed capital and the sum of additional money needed. If Inomata were able to offer some reason why this fund would suddenly bear an additional function at the time of accumulation the situation might be different, but otherwise just comparing the overall amount of the fund to the quantity of new money needed does not change the fact that the fund will not able to fulfill a new need, no matter how much larger it might be than the additional money required. One can only state that if a larger amount new money were required, the shortfall would also be larger; just as if it were not so large, the shortfall would not be so large either. But the problem is not the size of the shortfall, but whether it arises in the first place.

The third main basis for Inomata's argument concerns his interpretation of Luxemburg's statement that the reserve amassed 'can only ever be sufficient for the renewal of the former capital'. He believes that this 'signifies that she has committed the error of viewing all 2000 units of value as expressing the value of the fixed capital that should be actually replenished'. I think that this argument is clearly an expression of his own error, for the reasons already presented.

As the fourth basis for his argument, Inomata asserts that, 'Even if one were to accept this standpoint, her argument is still impossible unless we accept a second error of viewing the 2000 units as being replenished all at once at some point in the year'. But why is this impossible? This does not make any sense to me. Luxemburg's position is merely, as already explained, that the depreciation fund for fixed capital exists to begin with as an essential element within the current scale of production and is premised as such to the extent it is necessary, so that the fund cannot serve as a fund for new expanded production. How can it be said that this position is only tenable on the premise that the fixed capital is 'replenished all at once'? Needless to say, depending on whether the fixed capital is replenished all at once or successively, differences in the quantity of money necessary for reproduction to progress at a certain scale will likely arise. In a case where it is replenished all at once, the amount of the money hoard for the depreciation of fixed capital would rise or fall around the period of replenishment, and just prior to this period would have to be equal to the total value of the fixed capital. In contrast, for the case of successive replenishment, during the time that some capitalists are hoarding, others would have already reached the time to replenish, so that their hoarded money would be conversely thrown back in circulation. Therefore, in this case, seen from the perspective of society as a whole, the need for the money hoard to replace the fixed capital – and therefore the overall need for money – does not have to reach an enormous sum as in the former case. But this problem is certainly not particular to expanded reproduction. If the various replenishments of fixed capital are carried out successively, so that the money hoard needed for this is a small amount of the total, that relatively small depreciation fund is premised at the time of expansion. This does not in the least reduce the difficulty of realising surplus value. In other words, Inamoto's framing of the discussion in terms of 'all at once' or 'successively' has no essential significance to the problem at hand.

The fifth and final point concerns his argument that begins, 'This is not limited to fixed capital ...', which is basically a reiteration of all the errors criticised thus far, requiring no further criticism. In other words, at issue is whether the depreciation fund for fixed capital can at the same time serve as a fund for capital accumulation; not the question of whether the fund exists in a greater or lesser magnitude or what it is that determines the size of the fund.

The above is my detailed examination of each of the theoretical grounds offered by Inomata in his attempt to refute Luxemburg, so as to clarify that none of his arguments can be considered sufficient. That does not bring the matter to a close, however. Inomata goes on to present a passage from the second volume of *Theories of Surplus Value* as an important basis for his argument, saying that

Marx 'offers the clearest articulation of the role played in the accumulation process by the reserve fund for replenishing fixed capital'. Inomata then writes:

> Since the problem first was raised by Marx himself, Luxemburg as well as Professor Kawakami and Professor Takada would not have been likely to fall into error had they relied on the key he had provided. Just considering the fact that Marx in *Theories of Surplus Value* calls the fund for fixed capital an *Accumulationsfonds* (accumulation fund) should make clear that he did not dismiss it as those three did.[12]

Let's take a look at that passage that Inomata is referring to:

> A part of the constant capital which is calculated to be used up annually and enters as wear and tear into the value of the product, is in fact not used up. Take, for example, a machine which lasts 12 years and costs £12,000; its average wear and tear, which has to be charged each year, = £1,000. Thus, since £1,000 is incorporated into the product each year, the value of £12,000 will have been reproduced at the end of the 12 years and a new machine of the same kind can be bought for this price. The repairs and patching up which are required during the 12 years are reckoned as part of the production costs of the machine and have nothing to do with the question under discussion. In fact, however, reality differs from this calculation of averages. The machine may perhaps run more smoothly in the 2nd year than in the first. And yet after 12 years it is no longer usable. It is the same as with an animal whose average life is 10 years, but this does not mean that it dies by 1/10 each year, although at the end of 10 years it must be replaced by a new individual. Naturally, during the course of a particular year, a certain quantity of machinery, etc. always reaches the stage when it must actually be replaced by new machines. Each year, therefore, a certain quantity of old machinery, etc. has in fact to be replaced *in natura* by new machines, etc. And the average annual production of machinery, etc., corresponds with this. The value with which they are to be paid for, lies ready; it is derived from the [proceeds of the] commodities, according to the reproduction period (of the machines). But the fact remains, that although a large part of the value of the annual product, of the value which is paid for it each year, is needed to replace, for example, the old machines after 12 years, it is by no means actually

---

12   Inomata 1928, p. 44.

required to replace 1/12 *in natura* each year, and in fact this would not be feasible. This fund may be used partly for wages or for the purchase of raw material, before the commodity, which is constantly thrown into circulation but does not immediately return from circulation, is sold and paid for. This cannot, however, be the case throughout the whole year, since the commodities which complete their turnover during the year realise their whole value, and must therefore replace the wages, raw material and used up machinery contained in them, as well as pay surplus value. Hence where much constant capital, and therefore also much fixed capital, is employed, that part of the value of the product which replaces the wear and tear of the fixed capital, provides an accumulation fund, which can be invested by the person controlling it, as new fixed capital (or also circulating capital), without any deduction whatsoever having to be made from the surplus value for this part of the accumulation. (See MacCulloch [sic][13]) This accumulation fund does not exist at levels of production and in nations where there is not much fixed capital. This is an important point. It is a fund for the continuous introduction of improvements, expansions etc.[14]

This is the passage from *Theories of Surplus Value* that Inomata is referring to, but does the opinion Marx expressed really back his position? Here, as well, I cannot help but express a contrary opinion. The problem Marx poses here in his discussion is simply whether it is possible to use the depreciation fund for fixed capital – i.e. one part of the old capital itself – to expand the original scale of production later to a certain extent. In other words, the issue in this case clearly concerns the possibility of expanded reproduction. However, the possibility of this expanded production does not depend on the capitalisation of surplus value but rather is carried out within the range of the existing capital. Thus, Marx is recognising the possibility of such expanded production, and when he calls the depreciation fund for fixed capital that makes this expansion possible the 'accumulation fund', he is certainly not using the term 'accumulation' in the sense of the capitalisation of surplus value. Therefore, the 'accumulation fund' cannot (as Inomata imagines) signify a fund for the capitalisation of surplus value. In other words, Inomata is justified in saying that, in considering the question of the source of the money to capitalise surplus value, 'Luxemburg as well as Professor Kawakami and Professor Takada would not have been

---

13   Scottish economist John Ramsay McCulloch (1789–1864).
14   Marx 1989b, pp. 111–3.

likely to fall into error had they relied on the key he [Marx] had provided', but the grounds for his argument, in saying that Marx's use of the term 'accumulation fund' in *Theories of Surplus Value* shows that he 'did not dismiss it' as those three had done, is clearly based on a misunderstanding of how Marx is using the term. In the passage quoted above, Marx is not dealing with the problem of the capitalisation of surplus value, and therefore there is no reason for him to pose the problem of the source of money. One could say instead: 'Since the problem first was raised by Marx [in *Capital*], Luxemburg as well as Professor Kawakami and Professor Takada [and Inomata] would not have been likely to fall into error had they relied on the key he had provided [in *Capital*]'. The fact that this key is fully provided within *Capital* is a point I have already touched on.

This concludes the presentation of my thoughts on the view of Inomata, but it has raised a new problem to consider. This is the question of whether the idea that Marx presents in *Theories of Surplus Value* is, in fact, correct.

First of all, Marx claims that the depreciation fund for fixed capital can be used generally for the expansion of production. Assuming for the moment that it can be used as such, could the fund in this case truly be referred to as an 'accumulation fund'? This is the first doubt I had. In Book I of *Capital*, Marx defines the 'accumulation of capital' as the 'employment of surplus value as capital, or its reconversion into capital'.[15] According to this definition, the central concept of 'accumulation' is clearly not the expansion of production but the capitalisation of surplus value. It is true that, from the outset, the capitalisation of surplus value in principle takes the form of expanded production, and the expansion of production (in capitalist society) is carried out in principle through the capitalisation of surplus value; but expanded reproduction and accumulation are completely distinct from each other, conceptually, and they do not necessarily coincide in reality either. One example of this is the question we are dealing with here. That is, as already noted, the capitalisation of surplus value does not necessarily exist even if expanded production exists. This should be clear from the passage quoted earlier where Marx notes that that expanded production is carried out 'without any deduction whatsoever having to be made from the surplus value'. In other words, when he calls expanded production 'accumulation' in that case, and refers to the fund that makes it possible as the 'accumulation fund', it is clearly a misuse of terms. Indeed, in Book II of *Capital*, Marx describes the same case using the following terms:

---

15   Marx 1976, p. 725.

This reproduction on an extended scale does not result from accumulation – the transformation of surplus value into capital – but from a retransformation of the value, which branches into two parts, and in its money form has separated itself off from the body of the fixed capital into new fixed capital of the same time, either additional or more effective.[16]

My second doubt regarding the passage from Marx relates to a more fundamental problem. This is the question of whether the depreciation fund for fixed capital can, in principle, be at the same time a fund for expanded production. As already noted, Marx affirms this possibility in *Theories of Surplus Value*, writing that it 'can be invested by the person controlling it, as new fixed capital (or also circulating capital)'. But can this opinion be unconditionally accepted? Granted, as Marx notes, the depreciation fund for fixed capital generally is only first actually needed after a long period of time, prior to which it lies dormant, in a useless state. Therefore, unless some difficulty arises, the fund should be divertible, in the interim, to the purpose of expanded production. But if that is done, what sort of problem would a capitalist confront when it came time to replenish the fixed capital? At that point, the capitalist would be in the position of having replenish the entirety of the former fixed capital. In order to do so, the capitalist would have to be in possession of its full value in the form of money. Normally that would be covered by the depreciation fund accumulated year after year. But in this example, the capitalist has already invested all or part of that fund on expanded production. How would the capitalist then be able to meet the pressing need to replenish the old capital? The only method available would, of course, be to again build up the fund that was thrown into expanded production. But the capitalist would have had to invest in some way for the fund to have been recovered, without any loss, prior to the date of replenishment. The situation, of course, would be different if the initial premise is altered, so that, instead of replenished all at once (e.g. machinery that must be completely replaced after 12 years), we are dealing with fixed capital that can be partially replaced. In other words, in such a case, each time the depreciation fund had reached a certain amount, it could be invested in newly establishing the same kind of fixed capital, so that the entirety of the gradually established new fixed capital would already be in operation as the replacement of the former fixed capital by the time the original replenishment date for the old fixed capital had arrived so that it would no longer be utilisable (refer to the letter from Engels quoted later). Therefore, in this case the need to

---

16   Marx 1978, p. 251.

recover the depreciation fund spent on expanded production would not arise. But this is a special case that does not generally apply. In other words, one cannot assume that the depreciation fund for fixed capital can generally be used for expanded production (setting aside here, of course, the existence of the credit system).

The above are my basic doubts that arose with regard to how the issue is dealt with in *Theories of Surplus Value*, but Marx seems to have had his own doubts about the view he had expressed in that manuscript, as can be surmised from the following letter to Engels:

> Can't you come down for a few days? In my critique I have demolished so much of the old stuff that there are a number of points I should like to consult you about before I proceed. Discussing these matters in writing is tedious both for you and for me.
>
> One point about which you, as a practical man, must have the answer, is this. Let us assume that a firm's machinery at the outset = £12,000. It wears out on an average in 12 years. If then £1,000 is added to the value of the goods every year, the cost of the machinery will have been paid off in 12 years. Thus far, A. Smith and all his successors. But, in fact, this is only an average calculation. Much the same applies to machinery having a life of 12 years as, say, to a horse with a life – or useful life – of 10 years. Although it would have to be replaced with a new horse after 10 years, it would in practice be wrong to say that 1/10 of it died every year. Rather, in a letter to factory inspectors, Mr. Nasmyth observes that machinery (at least some types of machinery) runs better in the second year than in the first. At all events, in the course of those 12 years does not 1/12 of the machinery have to be replaced *in natura* each year? Now, what becomes of this fund, which yearly replaces 1/12 of the machinery? Is it not, in fact, an accumulation fund to extend reproduction aside from any conversion of revenue into capital? Does not the existence of this fund partly account for the very different rate at which capital accumulates in nations with advanced capitalist production and hence a great deal of *capital fixe*, and those where this is not the case?[17]

This letter of Marx is dated 20 August 1862, and there is reason to believe that around the same time he wrote the passage quoted from *Theories of Surplus Value*. It seems, in other words, that when Marx was writing that part of his

---

17   Marx 1985, pp. 411–2.

manuscript, he felt many doubts and sought the opinion of Engels. We can get some idea of the sort of answer Engels provided to Marx in a reply dated 9 September:

> What with the cotton pother, the theory of rent a has really proved too abstract for me. I shall have to consider the thing when I eventually get a little more peace and quiet. Likewise the question of wear and tear where, however, I rather suspect you have gone off the rails. Depreciation time is not, of course, the same for all machines. But more about this when I get back.[18]

Although Engels told Marx that he would write more later, he seems to have been too busy with work at the time to explain in detail so that no such reply can be found among his correspondence. However, in the letter just quoted, we can at least see that Engels was opposed to Marx's explanation of that point. Marx wrote back to Engels on the following day, but simply noted: 'As to the economic stuff, I don't propose to burden you with it on your journey'.[19] The exchanges between Marx and Engels regarding this problem seem to have broken off here, at least as far as can be determined from the extant correspondence. However, around five years later, in a letter to Engels dated 24 August 1867, Marx again brings up the issue. This was right around the time he was correcting the proofs for Book I of *Capital*. Judging from this fact, one could surmise that – having finished his work on that book and taking up right away his preparations for Book II – Marx was seeking to sort out the issue of the depreciation fund that had bothered him for some time. In that August letter, he writes

> For the conclusion to the 2nd book (Process of Circulation), which I am writing now, I am again obliged to seek your advice on one point, as I did many years ago.
> Fixed capital only has to be replaced *in natura* after, say, 10 years. In the meantime, its value returns partially and *gradatim*, as the goods that it has produced are sold. This progressive return of the fixed capital is only required for its replacement (aside from repairs and the like) when it becomes defunct in its material form, e.g., as a machine. Prior to that, however, these successive returns are in the capitalist's possession.

---

18 Marx 1985, p. 414.
19 Marx 1985, p. 416.

> Many years ago I wrote to you that it seemed to me that in this manner an accumulation fund was being built up, since in the intervening period the capitalist was of course using the returned money, before replacing the *capital fixe* with it. You disagreed with this somewhat superficially in a letter. I later found that MacCulloch [*sic*] describes this sinking fund as an accumulation fund.[20] Being convinced that no idea of MacCulloch's [*sic*] could ever be right, I let the matter drop. His apologetic purpose here has already been refuted by the Malthusians,[21] but they, too, admit the fact.
>
> Now, as a manufacturer, you must know what you do with the returns on capital fixe before the time it has to be replaced *in natura*. And you must answer this point for me (without theorising, in purely practical terms.)[22]

Here we can see Marx clearly state that he 'let the matter drop'. His claim that he had abandoned his earlier view because he 'later found that MacCulloch [*sic*] describes this sinking fund as an accumulation fund' is somewhat doubtful since already in *Theories of Surplus Value*, Marx refers to McCulloch holding the same view. In any case, the fact that someone held this or that view is not the essential point. No matter how much Marx might have despised someone, that would not be the real reason for altering his own opinion. Mentioning McCulloch in that way just seems an example of Marx's sense of humor. What is clear from the letter, as an unshakeable fact, is that Marx 'let the matter drop'. The first thing that comes to mind, with regard to the 'matter' in question, is that it concerns the use of the term 'accumulation fund'. It should be clear from the passage in *Capital* quoted earlier, where Marx cautions the reader that 'reproduction on an extended scale does not result from accumulation – transformation of surplus value into capital',[23] that he realised that the use of

---

20 McCulloch 1825, pp. 181–2.
21 It is not clear to me which Malthusians Marx is referring to in the passage quoted above, but I can provide one example of such a refutation. In the book [by John Cazenove] *Outlines of political economy, being a plain and short overview of the laws relating to the production, distribution and consumption of wealth* (London 1832), there is a refutation in Chapter 20 ('On the Effect of Machinery') of (what Marx calls) the 'apologetic purpose' of McCulloch, who is described as such because in advocating his theory of the 'accumulation fund' he was seeking a basis to support his position that the introduction of machinery would not ultimately reduce demand for labour. Marx also discusses this issue in a passage in *Theories of Surplus Value* (Marx 1989b, pp. 257–58).
22 Marx 1987b, p. 408.
23 Marx 1978, p. 251.

the term 'accumulation fund' was incorrect. However, what changed as the result of Marx's long deliberation was more than just this matter of terminology. Indeed, Marx puts to Engels the question of what is done with the 'returns on *capital fixe* before the time it has to be replaced *in natura*'. It seems clear that Marx recognised the need to fundamentally reflect on this issue, and the first step he took was to seek direct knowledge from a practical capitalist, Engels. The answer provided to Marx can be seen in the two letters Engels wrote in late August 1867:

> On the question of the replacement-fund, full details with accompanying calculations tomorrow. You see, I must ask some other manufacturers whether our practice is the customary one or an exception. The question is whether, with an original outlay of £1,000 on machinery, where £100 is written off in the 1st year, the rule is to write off 10% of the £1,000 in the 2nd year, or of £900, etc. We do the latter, and understandably the matter goes on thereby *in infinitum*, at least in theory. This complicates the arithmetic considerably. But, otherwise, there is no doubt that the manufacturer is using the replacement-fund on average for 4½ years before the machinery is worn out, or at least has it at his disposal. However, this is included in the calculations, by way of what one might call a certain guarantee against moral wear and tear, or alternatively the manufacturer says: the assumption that in 10 years the machinery will be completely worn out is only approximately correct, i.e. it presupposes that I receive the money for the replacement-fund in 10 annual instalments from the outset. At all events, you shall have the calculations; regarding the economic significance of the matter, I am none too clear about it, I do not see how the manufacturer is supposed to be able to cheat the other partners in the surplus value, that is, the ultimate consumers, by thus falsely representing the position – in the long run. *Nota bene*, as a rule, machinery is depreciated at 7½% which assumes a useful life of approximately 13 years.[24]

After that letter sent on 26 August, Engels wrote another letter the following day:

> Enclosed two schedules for machinery, which will make the matter fully clear to you. The rule is that part of the original sum is written off each

---

24 Marx 1987b, p. 409.

1860 1 Jan.	Purchases..	£	1,000
1861 1 Jan.	Written off 10%...	"	100
		£	900
	New purchase...	"	200
		£	1,100
1862 1 Jan.	Written off 10% £1,200 (£1,000+£200)...........	"	120
		£	980
	New purchase...	"	200
		£	1,180
1863 1 Jan.	Written off 10% £1,200 (£1,000+£200+£200) etc......	"	140
		£	1,040

year, usually 7½%. but to simplify the calculation I have kept to 10%, which is not excessive for many machines either. Thus, e.g.,

In schedule No. 1 I am now assuming that the manufacturer puts his [money] out at interest for writing-off purposes; on the day when he has to replace the old machinery with new, he has not £1,000 but £1,252–11s. Schedule No. 2 assumes that he puts the money straight into new machinery, each year. As is shown in the last column giving the value of the total purchases as it stands on the last day of the 10 years, it is true that the value of his machinery then does not exceed £1,000 (and he cannot have more, as he has, after all, only invested the value of what has been worn out, and the total value of the machinery cannot thus grow by the process), but he has extended his factory from year to year, and as an average over the 11 years he has employed machinery which cost £1,449 in investment, in other words, he has produced and earned substantially more than with the original £1,000. Let us assume he is a spinner and every £ represents one spindle together with the roving-frame; in that case, he has on average spun with 1,449 spindles instead of 1,000, and, after the original spindles have ended their useful lives, he begins the new period on 1 January 1866 with 1,357 spindles that he has purchased in the meantime, to which is added a further 236 from the writing off as per 1865, which makes 1,593 spindles. The money advanced for writing off has thus enabled him to increase his machinery by 60% and without putting a farthing of his actual profit into the new investment.

Repairs have been disregarded in both schedules. At 10% write-off, the machine should cover its own repair costs, i.e. the latter should be included. Nor do they affect the issue, as they are either included in the

10%, or else they prolong the useful life of the machine in proportion, which amounts to the same thing.

I hope schedule No. 2 will be sufficiently clear to you; if not, just write, I have a copy of it here.[25]

As Engels points out, there are two tables in his letter. The first is not of direct relevance to our discussion, but we can look at the second table:[26]

II. The renewal fund is reinvested in machinery every year

	Reinvestment			Wear and tear %	Value on 1 Jan. 1866
1856 on 1 Jan. machinery purchased			£1,000	100%	£–
1857 1 Jan. 10% written off and reinvested			£100	90%	£10
1858 1 Jan. 10% write-off	£1,000	£100			
	£100	£10	£110	80%	£22
			£210		
1859 1 Jan. 10% write-off	£1,000	£100			
	£210	£21	£121	70%	£36
			£331		
1860 1 Jan. 10% write-off	£1,000	£100			
	£331	£33	£133	60%	£53
			£464		
1861 1 Jan. 10% write-off	£1,000	£100			
	£464	£46	£146	50%	£73
			£610		
1862 1 Jan. 10% write-off	£1,000	£100			
	£610	£61	£161	40%	£97
			£771		
1863 1 Jan. 10% write-off	£1,000	£100			
	£771	£77	£177	30%	£124
			£948		
1864 1 Jan. 10% write-off	£1,000	£100			
	£948	£95	£195	20%	£156
			£1,143		
1865 1 Jan. 10% write-off	£1,000	£100			
	£1,143	£114	£214	10%	£193
			£1,357		
1866 1 Jan: 10% write-off	£1,000	£100			
	£1,357	£136	£236	0%	£236
Nominal value of the new machinery			£1,593		
Real value of the machinery					£1,000

---

25   Marx 1987b, pp. 410–1.
26   Marx 1987b. pp. 412–3.

	@ £1 per spindle he has employed:		
1856 .... 1,000 spindles	Brought forward .... 9,486 spindles		
1857 .... 1,100 "	1863 .... 1,948 "		
1858 .... 1,210 "	1864 .... 2,143 "		
1859 .... 1,331 "	1865 .... 2,357 "		
1860 .... 1,464 "			
1861 .... 1,610 "	In 11 years .... 15,934 spindles		
1862 .... 1,771 "			
	On average 1,449 spindles		
Bring forward 9,486 spindles			
and begins 1866 with			
1,357			
236			
1,593 spindles			

In these examples provided by Engels on spinning, we can see one case where the partial replenishment of fixed capital is allowed. And to the extent of dealing with such a case, Engels's explanation is extremely clear and extremely suggestive as information provided by a practical capitalist. It seems to have been 'sufficiently clear', as Engels had hoped, since Marx did not ask any further questions for clarification and simply informed his friend that he had '[r]eceived both your letters with the calculations'[27] and expressed his thanks. What view, then, did Marx arrive at in the end? We can see the answer in the passage quoted from Book II of *Capital* (Chapter 8, Section 2).[28]

Note: A separate discussion is necessary to deal with the importance of the depreciation fund for fixed capital with regard to crisis and the industrial cycle.

---

27 Marx 1987b, p. 416.
28 Marx 1978, p. 251.

CHAPTER 12

Are Prices and Wages in a Vicious Circle?

Since the sort of professors whom readers might be interested in hearing from have been too busy lately to get together, I have decided to try something new here by creating a hypothetical discussion. Although this is a sort of substitute, it may be a worthwhile endeavour insofar as it allows me to gather together whomever I like and have them express themselves after careful deliberation, with no time limit (except for the article's deadline).[1]

CHAIRMAN: Since the end of the war, demands for higher wages have been spreading like wildfire. According to newspaper articles, those demands have met with considerable success up to now, but it is frequently argued, as you know, that a vicious circle exists between wage and price increases. It is said that a rise in prices stimulates wage increases, while higher wages drive up prices in turn, with each triggering the other, resulting in a spiralling tendency that, if left unchecked, leads to a limitless rise in general prices, including wages. The need arises to put an end, somehow, to this vicious circle, and the central concern for most people is where and how to do so in the most rational way. What are your thoughts on this 'C'?

C: The situation is just as you described. In newspaper articles we can read about the labour disputes waged since last autumn, and the demands of the workers are reasonable, at least with regard to the call for higher wages. It might seem outrageous to demand a three- or five-fold increase in wages, but if one considers the prices on the black market, on which we must depend now to some extent, it is certainly not an excessive demand. However, that does not mean that it is unreasonable for capitalists to also demand a suitable level of profit. Thus, in a case where wages are raised, and the sale of products at the current price would result in a loss or at least the absence of profit, one would have to approve of a price increase. But this would signify the vicious circle you just mentioned, raising an alarming prospect for the future of Japan. I have been giving this matter some thought lately but have not managed to sort it out, so the invitation to take part in this discussion arrives at an opportune time, and I am looking forward to hearing all of your valuable contributions.

---

[1] [Originally published as Kuruma 1946, under the title 'Wage Increases and Inflation' and republished as Chapter 9 of *An Investigation of Marx's Theory of Crisis* (Kuruma 1949).]

CHAIRMAN: That lays things out quite clearly. From what you have said, it seems that our task is taking on increasing importance. My own view is that the most appropriate approach in addressing this issue would be to begin by clarifying whether a wage increase and price increase are indeed, as it would seem at first glance, in a relation that can be described as a vicious circle. How does that sound to everyone?

PARTICIPANTS: *Agreed!*

CHAIRMAN: Could you tell us your views, 'E'?

E: My understanding is that a rise in wages does not become the cause of a general rise in prices, and thus does not lead to a vicious circle. Ricardo already clarified this a long time ago in pointing out that the quantity of labour needed to produce a commodity is what determines its value, so that wages and profit are merely parts of the given value distributed to the two main classes involved in production. Ricardo thus argued that even though a wage increase necessarily leads to a fall in profit, it will not have any impact on the value of the commodity. If wages and profit were in fact the elements that compose value, instead of being its distributed parts, an increase in one of the elements would increase the value of the product, rather than decrease the other element. However, given the essence of value, that is not the case. This is the basic argument presented by Ricardo. And, despite various defects in his theory, I think that his view is not mistaken, at least as it concerns this particular issue. Marx can be said to share the same basic view on this point, although he introduced the separate term 'surplus value' to avoid the confusion that arose in Ricardo's case from using the term 'profit' to describe two distinct relations.

However, it is important to note that the law of value just explained is the most fundamental but at the same time the most general and abstract principle concerning the commodity, so it does not have direct validity with regard to the various phenomena under developed capitalist production relations. That is to say, as the simple commodity develops into the capitalistic commodity, the standard for commodity exchange becomes production price, not value. That is not to suggest, in any way, that the law of value or the law of surplus value based upon it somehow becomes meaningless. Production price, as you all know, is the sum of the capital expended on production plus average profit, but average profit itself is the total profit of society distributed in accordance with the amount of capital advanced. And that total profit is simply the total surplus value viewed from a different perspective. It is only on the basis of the law of value that the existence and quantitative determination of surplus value first can be elucidated, so ultimately production price cannot be clarified without the law of value.

However, the law of value and the law of surplus value only operate indirectly as the fundamental laws that ultimately determine production price. As I mentioned, the average profit that characterises production price is nothing but the total surplus value redistributed in line with the magnitude of the capital advanced, so the total amount of average profit is equal to the total amount of surplus value. Clearly, then, the total amount of production price is equal to the total amount of value. And this means that as long as we are dealing with the total product of society, the law of value and the law of surplus value continue to apply, without any change, even when value is transformed into production price. This also means that the argument of Ricardo, which I mentioned a moment ago as the fundamental answer to the issue of the vicious circle, continues to be applicable even when value develops into production price, as long as we are dealing with the total product of society. Thus, to repeat the argument while now employing the term production price, it could be said that a rise in wages will bring about a decrease in surplus value (and therefore a decrease in the general rate of profit), but it will certainly not be the cause of a rise in the production prices of all commodities.

Y: I have a question.

E: Go ahead.

Y: Your explanation touched on various points, but would it be fair to say that the argument comes down to the idea that a rise in wages cannot be the cause of an overall price rise?

E: Yes, I think it's acceptable to think along those lines.

Y: But that doesn't seem to be the case judging from the current situation in Japan. Isn't this precisely why the problem we have gathered together to discuss has arisen? We've seen large-scale price increases in train fares that were explained as the result of wage increases, carried out not only generally by many capitalists but also by the government that is implementing various measures to stem inflation. This general situation today – if it is indeed the general situation – seems to be in clear contradiction with the explanation you just offered. I think it goes without saying that theory must account for reality. How useful can a theory be that says wage increases cannot be the cause of an overall rise in prices when it comes to explaining the polar opposite reality? Or do you mean to suggest that the theory just described pertains to the fundamental principles whereas there are particular conditions at present that have led to the opposite situation? Since our aim is to clarify the problem we are facing, and explaining the fundamental principle seems somewhat beside the point, shouldn't we begin with the particular conditions? What are your thoughts on this?

E: I think the doubt you have expressed is natural. It is true, of course, that the fundamental laws I mentioned do not explain the particular phenomena generally thought to constitute a 'vicious circle'. Nevertheless, elucidating those laws is, I believe, the primary requirement for thoroughly clarifying the issue at hand, because our task is to determine whether the vicious circle, generally thought to exist, is indeed a vicious circle. My view is that the apparent vicious circle, which most people uncritically accept, stems from a fundamental misperception: namely the mistaken idea that the value of a commodity is composed of wages and profit (along with the value of the means of production). Clearly, this view is based on the error of directly conflating production price with value, instead of analysing production price so as to reduce it to value. That is a natural view to take as a capitalist, but even those who are not capitalists find it quite difficult to shake free of this fetishism. Indeed, the brilliant economist Adam Smith – who arrived at a firm understanding of the fundamental law whereby the value of a commodity is determined by the quantity of the labour needed for its production – could not free himself of the mistaken idea that the value of a commodity is composed of wages and profit, and he advanced a mistaken economic doctrine on that basis. The argument of Ricardo, which I mentioned a moment ago, was mainly introduced to point out this contradiction within Smith's thought and drive out the mistaken view. Ricardo indicated this contradiction and rejected the vulgar notion swayed by phenomenal reality, emphasising the fundamental principle instead. Yet Ricardo proved incapable of explaining (on the basis of the fundamental principle) why such phenomena arise. Therefore, he fell into a contradiction that ultimately led to the collapse of the Classical school of political economy. This attests to the difficulty of shaking free of the fetishism particular to the capitalist mode of production. Marx later clarified the basis of this fetishism, thereby solving the problem of production price. But since relatively few people are familiar with Marx's theory, most still think a rise in wages causes a general rise in prices – or at least there are precious few people with an adequate theoretical grounding to confirm that this is not the case. Without arriving at that understanding, however, it is not possible to truly grasp of the problem at hand.

We need that understanding as the basis for correctly posing the problem and putting our analysis on the right track. And so ...

Y: I don't think you need to go any further. You've convinced me. I didn't understand that reason, and I'm sorry to have taken up so much time.

CHAIRMAN: Alright, why don't we listen to some more of the explanation from 'E', while bearing in mind the points he just made.

E: Okay, I'll continue then. A moment ago, I tried to clarify that a rise in wages not only will exert no influence on value, but that when viewed from the perspective of the total product of society it will exert no influence on the total sum of production price either, so that no vicious cycle, nor any phenomena that would seem to constitute one, should arise. We need to consider, then, why phenomena thought to constitute a vicious circle do in fact appear. One could only think that such phenomena arise due to elements of price other than value or total production price, and I want to consider what each of those elements are so that we can investigate the potential for such phenomena to arise.

The first factor to consider is the influence that a rise in wages will have on the production price of different types of commodities. I think that if we reflect on the point I made earlier about the relation between value and production price it should be self-evident, but to make this even clearer I will offer the following details. The value of a commodity consists of the value of the means of production that are used up for its production and the new value added in production, and the latter can be broken down further into the part of compensated value paid to workers as wages and the part of surplus value created above and beyond that paid labour. Given this, if we assume that the same quantity of labour is paid the same wage, the ratio of the surplus value to the part of the value paid as wages (in other words, the 'rate of surplus value') will always the same; but this does not necessarily mean that the rate of surplus value to the total capital advanced (in other words, the 'profit rate') will be the same. This is because the advanced capital is made up of the value of the means of production and the value paid as wages, and the proportion of each is not the same in every industry. If the rate of surplus value is the same, then the profit rate will be lower in those industries where the proportion of the value of the means of production to the total capital advanced is larger – just as the opposite will hold true in the opposite case. Therefore, if a product is sold in line with its value, the rate of profit will vary among industries as a result. This is a natural outcome in terms of the law of the production of surplus value. Yet in terms of the essential instinct of capital as self-valorising value, this is an unjust and intolerable state of affairs, since the differences in the rate of profit do not arise from differences in the individual capacities of the capitalists themselves. Somehow this must be rectified, and it is in fact through redistributing the surplus value according to the amount of capital advanced, rather than returning it directly to the hands of the capitalist under which it was produced. Of course, having said that, the redistribution is not carried out through some sort of arrangement among all of the participants, based on some sort of impartial observation. Like every other relation between commodity producers, it takes place beyond the realm of a capitalist's consciousness, as the functioning of an economic law, thus arising as the outcome of the law of things. If there is a difference in profit rates among production sectors, capital will leave those sectors with a low rate and gravitate toward those where the rate is high. As a result, supply for the former will fall so as to increase prices, whereas supply in the latter will be excessive, causing prices to fall. This movement of capital will continue, unless hindered by some special circumstance, until rates of profit in the various sectors are averaged out. And 'production price' is the price that makes it possible to secure an average profit, which is the ultimate objective of the entire process.

As for the influence a rise in wages would have on production prices, it would mean that in sectors where a relatively high proportion of the capital advanced goes to wages, the production prices of products would rise higher, whereas products of sectors in the opposite situation would see their production prices fall. I think this should be clear from what I have said thus far, but I will demonstrate this numerically. Here 'c' will stand for constant capital (the value of the means of production used up in production), 'v' for variable capital (the part of value spent on wages), 's' for surplus value, and 'p' for profit. To simplify matters, I will assume that there are only two 'organic compositions of capital' (which refers to the ratio between constant and variable capital), and that all of the industries of society are divided into Dept. A or Dept. B according to their compositions. Such assumptions, of course, do not correspond to direct reality, but that does not matter as far as the present task is concerned.

First, let's look at the production for the total capital of society, from Dept. A and Dept. B, in terms of the following value relations.

$$\text{Dept. A} \quad 9{,}000c + 3{,}000v + 3{,}000s = 15{,}000$$
$$\text{Dept. B} \quad 3{,}000c + 3{,}000v + 3{,}000s = 9{,}000$$
$$\overline{\phantom{\text{Dept. B }}12{,}000c + 6{,}000v + 6{,}000s = 24{,}000}$$

The average profit rate would thus be:

$$6{,}000s \div (12{,}000c + 6{,}000v) \times 100 = 33\tfrac{1}{3}$$

Therefore, production price would be as follows:

Dept. A   9,000c + 3,000v + 4,000p = 16,000
Dept. B   3,000c + 3,000v + 2,000p = 8,000
―――――――――――――――――――――――――――――――――
           12,000c + 6,000v + 6,000p = 24,000

Clearly, the production price is higher than value in Dept. A; whereas the opposite is the case for Dept. B. Now, let's consider what happens to the value relation if there is a 20% increase in wages:

Dept. A   9,000c + 3,600v + 2,400s = 15,000
Dept. B   3,000c + 3,600v + 2,400s = 9,000
―――――――――――――――――――――――――――――――――
           12,000c + 7,200v + 4,800s = 24,000

In this case, the average profit rate would be:

$$4{,}800s \div (12{,}000c + 7{,}200v) \times 100 = 25\%$$

And production prices would be:

Dept. A   9,000c + 3,600v + 3,150p = 15,750
Dept. B   3,000c + 3,600v + 1,650p = 8,250
―――――――――――――――――――――――――――――――――
           12,000c + 7,200v + 4,800p = 24,000

We can see in the equation above that the production price for Dept. A decreases from 16,000 to 15,750, while the production price increases in Dept. B from 8,000 to 8,250. I think that this generally shows that the outcome of a rise of wages is that the production prices will fall in those sectors where the organic composition of capital (c/v) is higher than average, and will increase in those sectors where the organic composition is lower than average.

Let's consider whether this can in fact become the cause of a vicious circle or of phenomena that appear as such. What is at issue in this case, needless to say, is the increase in production price in Dept. B, but if the increase in wages only leads to an increase in the prices of some products, that alone would not immediately constitute a vicious circle. That problem would only occur if it so happened that the bulk of the industries producing goods for workers belonged to Dept. B. In such a case, part of the impact of the rise in wages would be counteracted by the rise in the prices of goods that the wage increase would cause, and so, in order to meet the original goal wages would have to rise again, bringing about a phenomenon that at first glance would resemble a vicious circle. However, this is certainly not a true vicious circle because the total sum of the increase in the production prices of the goods used by workers would certainly not reach the same level as the total sum of the increase in wages. If we look at the figures mentioned a moment ago: the increase in wages was 1,200 (as the difference of 6,000 from 7,200), while the increase in the production prices of all products in Dept. B was only 250 (as the difference of 8,000 from 8,250). (This gap between the wage and production-price increase would be even larger considering that one could assume that the products in Dept. B would also include some goods for use by non-workers, just as there would be some goods for workers in Dept. A.) The figures used here are based on arbitrary, hypothetical numerical relations, so of course various differences could occur depending on the assumptions made. In any case, unquestionably there would be a considerable gap between the wage increase and the price increase. Therefore, we are not dealing with a process that has the propensity to unfold in a spiral, spinning round and round. Rather, at some point it would have to settle down. If the initial wage increase was made in expectation of a price rise, it would have the character of being able to reach its expected goal at once.

However, the influence exerted on prices from a rise in wages is not solely from the change in production prices arising from the relations just described. A rise in wages would also increase the demand for goods used by workers, which would likely bring about a certain increase in the market prices of those goods. Hence, we need to examine whether or not a vicious circle can arise from this relation.

The first thing that one notices is that a price increase in this case is essentially different from the sort of case generally considered to be a vicious circle. The general theory of a vicious circle is based on the idea that a rise in wages will lead to an increase in the cost of production that will in turn cause an increase in prices. But in the case here, the rise in prices arises solely from the disequilibrium between supply and demand. It is not a rise in market prices that stems from the rise in the cost of production (and hence the rise in the production price), but rather the divergence of production price from market price. According to the general theory of a vicious circle, an overall rise in wages triggers an overall rise in the price of goods, whereas in our case it only brings about an increase in the prices of goods for use by workers. And because the rise in wages should necessarily bring about a decrease in surplus value, if all other conditions are the same, it will at the same time reduce demand among capitalists and therefore decrease the prices of the goods for their use. (In the case of goods consumed by both workers and capitalists, the increase in demand on the one side would be offset by the decrease in demand on the other, so the fluctuation of market prices would be diminished to that extent.) Moreover, the rise in prices that occurs from the disequilibrium between supply and demand is essentially a transitory state of affairs, with an intrinsic propensity to be eliminated. That is, when the market price of a certain commodity rises above its production price, the production sector of that commodity will attain higher than average profit, drawing capital into that sector so that the supply of the commodity increases and thus brings the market price back in line with the production price.

However, this does not guarantee that increasing the supply will in every case be easily carried out. Depending on the situation, there may be cases where a temporary phenomenon can pose a major problem. For instance, when a rise in wages occurs along with a rise in the prices of primary foodstuffs due to a poor harvest, an increase in supply through increased production might not be possible until the next harvest. Thus, if importing food is not an option, those in possession of the previous harvest would be likely to secure an advantageous position as monopoly suppliers for an entire year. In this case, the market prices of agricultural produce could continue to rise as long as the purchasing power directed towards that demand would rise, so that the bulk of the rise in wages might end up having little effect. Thus, there would once again be felt the need to increase wages, and if they were raised, the outcome would again be an increase in the market price of food products, so that a sort of vicious circle would arise, albeit different from the proper sense of the term. The same case resulting from a poor harvest would occur in a situation where a country that had tended to import most of its food suddenly did not have that option. Whereas in the case of a poor harvest the market price will return to the level of production price once a decent harvest has been obtained, in the latter case, as long as imports are not available, the only option is to expand domestic agricultural production, which would likely require more time to restore the equilibrium between supply and demand than in the case of even a very poor harvest. Moreover, the production price would likely remain some degree higher than the previous production price even after the state of equilibrium had been reached. Yet whether relatively high or low, once the market price settles around that level, wages would be decided with that price as the standard, thus dissolving the problem of the vicious cycle. The problem, in short, is limited to a temporary period from the time the equilibrium between supply and demand is lost, to the point where it is recovered, and during that time a sort of vicious circle would seem to occur, as I described. However, like all other conceptions regarding a vicious circle, that is an illusion due to the confusion arising from the overwhelming operation of inflation. The situation we have assumed here is a major disequilibrium between productive sectors, and what necessarily emerges from that situation is a sort of economic crisis, not an economic boom. Normally people would not imagine that in the case of a crisis, even a crisis based on a poor harvest, a vicious circle would arise that is due in part to a rise in wages. Nevertheless, that way of thinking does emerge because of the illusion created by inflation. Indeed, inflation leads to a variety of other illusions as well, and we could look at one of the many examples from contemporary economic theory. In order to avoid such illusions, we need to examine various phenomena in clear distinction from the operations of inflation. And we should not forget to critically examine the operation of inflation that gives rise to those various phenomena. In other words ...

CHAIRMAN: I'm sorry to interrupt just as you are raising an interesting point, but we will have to leave the discussion of inflation for another day, as our primary aim here is to sort out the issue of the vicious circle as quickly as possible.

E: As for our topic today, I have already more or less expressed my conclusion, which is that wages and prices certainly do not rise together in a vicious circle, and that the idea of a vicious circle is a mere illusion generated by the operation of inflation. But I would like to conclude by also expressing my view regarding the simple question of why such an illusion arises. My view is that inflation ultimately signifies a lowering in the quantity of gold that forms the unit of price, which brings about a general rise in prices. In the case of wages as well, which is the price of a type of commodity called 'labour power', the price increases for the same reason as in the case of prices of other commodities. However, the overall rise in prices in the case of labour power does not occur all at once – for instance, in the form of the quantity of gold represented by 'yen' being lowered from .750 g to .375 g. Rather the increase is in waves, where the price of one commodity rises and then the prices of related commodities rise in turn, and then other commodities related to those commodities increase, and so on – like a rising tide. Therefore, with the continuation of inflation and the repetition of that process, it seems that a vicious circle has emerged. But to think, in the case of a rise in the price of goods due to inflation, that prices are higher because wages have increased, is like thinking that because the tide is higher during a typhoon it must be high tide at that moment. Moreover, wages certainly do not increase more than the rise in the price of goods. It is in fact the contrary, where wages struggle to keep up with the rising prices of goods.

CHAIRMAN: Thank very much for your observations. I would like to bring our meeting to a close now, as I'm sure everyone is a bit worn out. Normally I would suggest that we all relax and have a cigarette, but that has become a precious item these days, unfortunately, so let's just have a cup of *socha*[2] instead.

---

2 [Low-grade tea.]

CHAPTER 13

Prices, Currency, and Demand

Many works on inflation have appeared since the end of the war, but one that has gained considerable attention is *Studies on Inflation*.[1,2] This book is the fruit of research conducted by the brightest stars of the Japanese Economic Association, often referred to as the 'Professors' Group', centred on Hyōe Ōuchi. Not only has this group set itself apart through the multifaceted and suggestive content of its work, but several of its members were offered important governmental posts by the head of the former conservative cabinet as the only hope of shouldering the grave responsibility of Japan's postwar economic reconstruction. Although they did not accept this offer, it is expected they will receive a similar request from the progressive political camp. Thus, the opinions of this group on inflation and the policies to deal with it must be thought to have significance for the future of the country.

Given the importance of the group, it seems a sort of public duty to criticise their work as long as I have doubts about their views, even if what I have to offer is not of much practical use. Another, and in fact more pressing reason for my criticism, is that I want to make use of this extremely multifaceted and suggestive research as the basis for my contribution to the collection of articles to be published in honour of Professor Takano that I have been struggling to put together as one of the editors.[3]

In Part 2 of *Studies on Inflation*, titled 'The Theory of Inflation', Masao Takahashi poses the central question in the following way:

> Let's take a closer look at the theory of inflation. One thing that I am always thinking about is the position of the theory of inflation within the system of political economy. In other words, in putting together a theory of inflation, what concepts or laws should be brought in from so-called theory of political economy and how should they be organised? Conduct-

---

1 [Originally published as Kuruma 1948a, under the title 'A Review of Studies on Inflation' and republished as Chapter 10 of *An Investigation of Marx's Theory of Crisis* (Kuruma 1949).]
2 Ōuchi 1946.
3 [A collection of articles commemorating the 77th birthday of Iwasaburō Takano, former director of the Ōhara Institute for Social Research (Kuruma and Ōuchi, eds., 1948).]

ing such a study seems useful to me. And I think it is best to begin with the theory of value.[4]

This problem that Takahashi poses is one that I imagine anyone seeking to theoretically grasp inflation would confront. Finding out what answer he and his colleagues would provide to this question in their book was something that I was looking forward to.

After posing the problem in the manner above, Takahashi says that when products become commodities in a society that has private property and a division of labour, money is discovered at some point as a medium of exchange to eliminate the inconvenience of barter exchange, first using things like shells or grain, and eventually arriving at the use of metallic money. Takahashi then writes:

> The next question to consider is what role money plays, and its first role is as the means of purchase. This involves, needless to say, obtaining money in return for handing over a commodity, or, from the perspective of the purchaser, handing over money to obtain a commodity in return. In other words, this is a case where a commodity and money change hands at the same time. Another role of money is as the means of payment ... It might seem pedantic to distinguish money as the means of purchase from money as the means of payment, but that is certainly not the case. For example, there are often cases where an explanation will encounter difficulty as a result of treating all of the currency issued by the Bank of Japan as circulating money. For example, if there were more money that is immediately exchanged for goods, the price of those goods will rise, but that would not occur when the money is only used for the payment of goods that have already been sold. Thus, it seems necessary to distinguish between those two terms when engaging in a discussion on latent or actual inflation.[5]

Various points are raised in the passage above that could be addressed, but since it is too difficult to touch on each one, I will limit myself to points of particular importance to the discussion that ensues in the book.

The first thing that strikes me as strange is that, despite declaring that one should begin with the theory of value, Takahashi has nothing to say about

---

4 Ōuchi 1946, p. 113.
5 Ōuchi 1946, pp. 114–5.

value at all. Not only is there no explanation of the essence of value, he does not provide an explanation of the value form. In addition, when Takahashi deals with money, he explains it as a medium of exchange that is discovered to remove the inconveniences of barter exchange, rather than being the inevitable product of the contradiction of the commodity. And, in line with that explanation, Takahashi states that the primary function of money is not as a measure of value but as the means of purchase. Since *Studies on Inflation* is not intended as a textbook but a record of a discussion between specialists, it cannot be taken to task for failing to lay out the ABCs of political economy. Moreover, one must naturally take into consideration that the book, as the transcript of a discussion, will include unguarded remarks or imprecise expressions. But those circumstances do not seem to account for why the series of relations just mentioned were overlooked. In the discussion below, for example, there seems to be confusion between the function of money as the measure of value and as the means of circulation, and I think that this confusion indicates the absence of a clear understanding of the function of money as the measure of value. (Below, my comments are bracketed within the quoted passage.)

> ŌUCHI: At that time [*period of German inflation after World War I*], prices would double or triple between morning and evening, so that within a week they had risen fifty- or a hundred-fold. Moreover, a phenomenon presented itself where if food was not available on the market people would be left with no goods; this was a phenomenon, in other words, where there was nothing to purchase with money [*this signifies the function of the Papiermark (paper mark) as the means of circulation – or more restrictedly as the means of purchase – had ceased to function*] so that unless one brought some other thing to the market, items would not be sold to a person, meaning there was no use for money as such [*since it is said here that prices doubled or tripled or rose fifty- or a hundred-fold, and that the prices were indicated in marks, one must imagine that the mark continued to function as the unit of price or unit of account, even if paper money was not functioning as the means of circulation*], which placed people in a situation where they could only survive through barter. Meanwhile, since it was preferable to have something more stable than barter exchange, the dollar was increasingly used in contracts as the unit of account. [*To the extent that the functioning of the dollar was limited to the function as the unit of account, it would have replaced the mark as such, but would not have been likely to replace the mark as the means of circulation (including as the means of payment in the broad sense) or to replace barter. His example of a restaurant, brought up later, shows that*

after the dollar in the function as the unit of measure is substituted for the mark, the Papiermark continues to function as the means of circulation as before. Moreover, barter is not likely to be abolished through the appearance of the dollar as mere unit of measure. Barter solely signifies the deficiency of money as the means of circulation, regardless of the existence or non-existence of money as a unit of measure (as explained in my earlier bracketed comment). This being the case, barter cannot be abolished as long as money as the means of circulation does not appear.]

In addition, companies, regional organisations, banks, and unions all issued their own temporary currency. In fact, those currencies had a more stable price [*value?*], and the dollar basically was the unit of measure. In short, by the final stage, people had to bring an enormous amount of money to purchase anything. Even if a person filled up a bag with notes, it would not be enough to buy a single beer. [*This seems to be different from the earlier example, where 'unless one brought some other thing to the market, items would not be sold', because it concerns the inconvenience of using the money as the means of purchase, not the loss of the function as the means of purchase. This inconvenience could likely have been removed by making the face number on the bill larger.*] In response, efforts were made to maintain economic order through barter exchange and the use of the dollar as a central currency. [*All of this concerns money as the means of circulation.*]

MINOBE: In that case, what appeared at first was gold price, I imagine? [*I interpret this question to concern the unit of price.*]

ŌUCHI: Yes, I think so. When merchants sold goods in foreign countries, they quickly became priced in gold. Foreign contracts could not be entered without being set in gold, so all traders followed that method.

MINOBE: That must have been what first appeared to replace the marks previously used. [*Given the context here, this must be referring to the mark as the unit of price.*]

ARISAWA: No, I think that first it would have been barter. Having said that, the exact order is not clear, but there would have been barter and then gold prices because the exporters would have been dealing with people with gold and thus set gold prices [*this would have likely been prices in units of dollars in reality*], but within the country circulation would have been through barter. [*As noted earlier, barter only signifies that there is no money as the means of circulation and does not impede money as the unit of price. Indeed, in a modern society that already has a developed monetary system, barter itself could not be generally carried out without something indicating value as the unit of price. The opposition is between whether price is indicated through a certain definite quantity of gold being made the unit of price (e.g., the dollar) or through some other unit of price; or the opposition is between whether a transaction is mediated by barter or by the means of circulation; whereas if one poses the question in terms of gold price or barter there is no way to arrive at an answer.*]

ŌUCHI: At that time, the exchange rate with the dollar was listed in the newspapers every day. Since there was this information, unlike the case in Japan, it was possible to enter contracts based on the dollar exchange rate. For instance, the cost of a meal at a restaurant was agreed to be set at one dollar, which might be 10,000 marks today and increase to 12,000 marks by evening, depending on the daily exchange rate. [*In this case, as already noted, the dollar functions as the unit of calculation or unit of price, while the Papiermark functions as the means of payment or purchase.*]

TAKAHASHI: This was demonetisation. In other words, the mark progressively lost its role as money. And because of its insufficient quantity, [*this clearly concerns the means of circulation*], barter [*also concerns the means of circulation*] or gold [*concerns money as the unit of price or account*] ...

ARISAWA: That's not quite right. On top of perceiving its insufficient quantity [*concerns the means of circulation*], the mark could not be the unit of account because it was constantly fluctuating [*concerns money as the unit of price or of account*].

TAKAHASHI: That demonetisation occurred when there was not enough currency. [*The 'demonetisation' spoken of here concerns the function as the means of circulation, and this would not signify that the Papiermark no longer functions as the means of circulation, but simply that its monopoly circulation as the general means of circulation had ceased – otherwise the issue of 'insufficiency' would not arise in the first place.*]

ARISAWA: Theoretically speaking, the fluctuation [*concerns the unit of price*] was the primary cause, I think. Added to this, as a contributing factor, was the insufficient quantity [*concerns the means of circulation*].

TAKAHASHI: Really this is barter exchange [*if it really is a case of barter exchange, then one would have to think in terms of there being nothing to function as the means of circulation*], but phenomenally [?], there were things that became money, like coal, potassium, wheat ...

ARISAWA: There was the rye mark, the potassium mark, the potato mark, you could say. [*If that is the case, then it should not be considered barter exchange.*]

TAKAHASHI: What would those things be in the case of Japan? Rice, I suppose.

ŌUCHI: I had considered that too and wanted to ask about it. I don't think rice would come to play that role. That is, unless the commodity is freely exchanged, it is not much use for a contract ... At the same time, since rice is sold on the black market perhaps it could. I'm not really sure.

TAKAHASHI: If it were rice, I wonder if the market price of rice would be similar to gold regardless of whether the rice enters from the system of obligatory deliveries or the system of rationing. Or perhaps it would be the price of rice on the black market? [*Here they seem to think that rice would play a completely different role from the rye or potassium that is the 'rye mark' or 'potassium mark' etc. Since I am not familiar with the exact character of the rye or potassium mark etc., or the method for their issuance, I do not know for sure, but I think it can be imagined they did not have the character of convertible notes, nor did they enter circulation as such, but rather were a sort of credit money issued as collateral. However, since they say that rice would be the same as gold, it can be imagined that they are thinking it becomes the spontaneously generated measure of value or means of circulation. If that is the case, then the question of the route does not enter the question at all. Since rice, unlike coins, would not enter circulation after being stamped by the government, it would freely enter circulation from whatever source. Moreover, regardless of the route, it would not alter the use value of the rice. If this question is posed from the perspective of the difference between the official price and the black-market price, one should recollect that the money commodity itself does not have a price, and that price is nothing more than the value of a commodity expressed in the quantity of the use value of the money commodity.*]

ARISAWA: In any case, if we accept that rice could come into this role, couldn't it be said that rice would *not* have to actually be put into movement? That is, just as gold can be merely ideal gold, couldn't there also be ideal rice? [*Gold is only able to be ideal in its function as the measure of value: i.e. money as the unit of price or of account. However, price must be realised. And when it is realised, real gold (or its token) is needed.*]

ŌUCHI: But there would need to be some sort of connection ...

ARISAWA: It can't be said that there is no connection at all. Since it can be purchased on the black market. [*The ability to purchase it on the black market is premised on something else functioning as the standard of price or means of circulation. I cannot see out how one could say on this premise that rice is money. At most, one could say that it is an equivalent with a certain degree of generality.*]6

Let's return now to the ideas Takahashi presented at the meeting. My second doubt concerning the passage quoted earlier is that money as the means of circulation is grasped from the outset as the means of purchase. At first glance, this might just seem a squabble over terminology, but it is more than that. Within the two opposing metamorphoses that form the circuit of a commodity – i.e. the sale (C–M) and purchase (M–C) – the term 'means of purchase' only directly expresses the determination of money in the latter. Grasping the 'means of circulation' from the outset as solely the 'means of purchase' amounts to treating the determination of money within the second metamorphosis as if it were unrelated to the first metamorphosis, and therefore as if it were unrelated to the commodity metamorphosis in general. Instead of seeing the 'M' in M–C as the result of C–M, which is to say, as the shape of value after casting off the commodity itself, it is instead understood as an independent existence in itself. As a result, instead of understanding the movement of money as a phenomenon within the movement of the commodity metamorphosis, the commodity's movement is seen as the result of the movement of money. One thus loses track of the path leading toward a correct understanding of the circulation of money. This is why Marx, in considering the circulation of money, begins with a critique of money as the means of circulation appearing phenomenally as the means of purchase. For instance, in *A Contribution to the Critique of Political Economy*, he writes

---

6   Ōuchi 1946, pp. 75–80.

In the first instance real circulation consists of a mass of random purchases and sales taking place simultaneously. In both purchase and sale commodities and money confront each other always in the same way; the seller represents the commodity, the buyer the money. As a means of circulation money therefore appears always as a means of purchase, and this obscures the fact that it fulfils different functions in the antithetical phases of the metamorphosis of commodities.[7]

Why does such a phenomenon arise? In other words: Why does the movement of commodity metamorphoses, which passes through two opposing stages, always appear as a monotonous movement whereby money changes places with commodities? Why does money, which comes to have two different determinations in the two stages of the commodity metamorphosis, only appear to be a means of purchase? Why is it that, even though the movement of money is a manifestation of commodity circulation, commodity circulation appears to be the result of the movement of money? These are the upside-down phenomena that Marx sought to explain. Earlier economists had accepted these phenomena uncritically, resulting in the projection of an inverted theory within their minds,[8] whereas Marx grasped them as the necessary appearance of an underlying essence. This brilliantly crystallised in his theory of money circula-

---

[7] Marx 1987a, p. 334.

[8] Marx describes the defect of conventional political economy in being taken in by phenomena related to actual circulation, thus overlooking the movement of the underlying commodity metamorphosis:

'This change of form has been very imperfectly grasped as yet, owing to the circumstance that, quite apart from the lack of clarity in the concept of value itself, every change of form in a commodity results from the exchange of two commodities, namely an ordinary commodity and the money commodity. If we keep in mind only this material aspect, that is, the exchange of the commodity for gold, we overlook the very thing we ought to observe, namely what has happened to the form of the commodity, We do not see that gold, as a mere commodity, is not money, and that the other commodities, through their prices, themselves relate to gold as the medium for expressing their own shape in money' (Marx 1976, p. 199).

'The seller has his commodity replaced by gold, the buyer has his gold replaced by a commodity. The striking phenomenon here is that a commodity and gold, 20 yards of linen and £2, have changed hands and places, in other words that they have been exchanged. But what is the commodity exchanged for? For the universal shape assumed by its own value. And what is the gold exchanged for? For a particular form of its own use value. Why does gold confront the linen as money? Because the linen's price of £2, its money-name, already brings it into relation with the gold as money' (Marx 1976, p. 203).

In other words, the fundamental flaw in this case is an insufficient understanding of the value form and of the most fundamental function of money that arises from the development of that form (i.e. the function of money as the measure of value).

tion that developed out of his theory of commodity metamorphosis, one aspect of which is his law of the quantity of circulating money.[9]

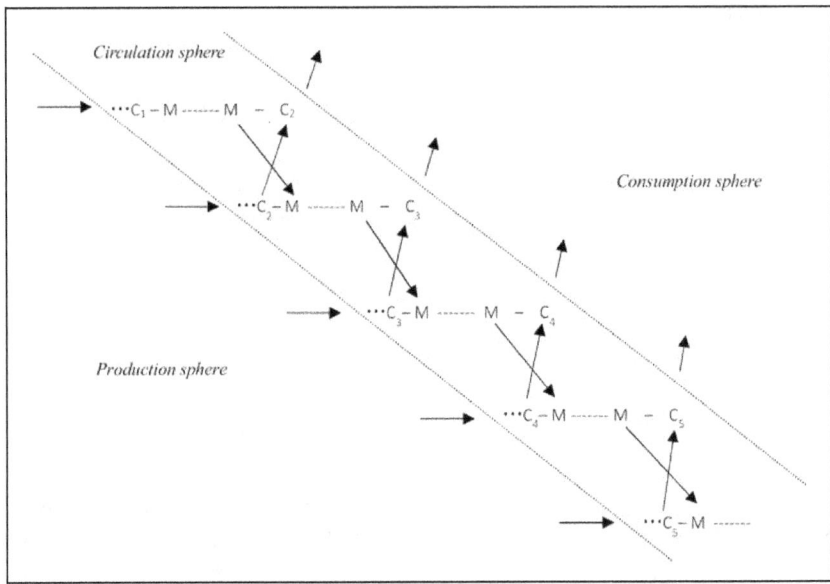

Diagram: Commodity metamorphoses and money circulation

Diagram Legend

⟶ ... C

The initial arrow indicates that a commodity as the unity of use value and value enters the sphere of circulation from the sphere of production (however, in this case, value has already been posited with the form of price, and therefore it is presumed that the commodity is entering circulation as a two-fold form, insofar as it has a natural form and a price form). The three dots followed by a 'C' indicate the period from when the commodity enters circulation up to the point it is sold.

C–M ------- M–C

Expresses the movement of the commodity as value (movement of commodity metamorphosis).

---

[9] The diagram above presents what I think is a relatively easy-to-understand depiction of the movement of commodity metamorphoses and the determinations of the circulation of money intertwined with those metamorphoses. In addition to depicting those relations, the diagram aims to comprehensively illustrate the other fundamental relations of commodity

Indicates the relation in which the opposing metamorphoses of two commodities are mutually realised, which manifests itself in people's eyes as the possessor of money and the possessor of the commodity changing positions.

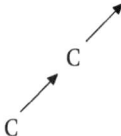

Indicates the movement of the commodity as use value. In other words, this is the commodity moving from the hands of the seller, for whom it is not a use value, into the hands of the buyer for whom it is (the so-called social material metamorphosis), and is therefore the movement whereby the commodity exits the sphere of circulation to enter the sphere of consumption.

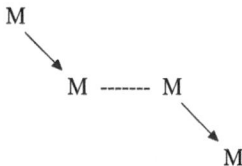

Expresses the circulation of money. The broken line between the two M's (M ------- M) expresses the period of time between obtaining money through a sale and expending it on a purchase. During this period, the money is in a state of *suspendierte Münze* (suspended coin; Marx 1987a, p. 360) or *Münzreserve* (reserve funds of coin; Marx 1987a, p. 370). The length of this time period is determined (in an inverse relation) by the velocity of currency. If one were to write another M – C above the C_1 – M at the top of the diagram, one would also have to insert an M – C to the left of it, so that could go on *ad infinitum*. Contrarily, if we were to consider the M in the first C – M as not being the result of another commodity's metamorphosis (C – M), we would have to set this exchange outside the realm of the circulation process, which would correspond to the case of exchange between a commodity and newly produced gold. This is the direct exchange transaction between gold as a newly produced commodity (not as the means of circulation) and another commodity, and thus does not pertain to circulation. The reason that

---

circulation in a concise way, but since the diagram still has various flaws, I hope that it can be revised by someone more adept at such things.

M – C does not follow the last C – M is that the value of the commodity congeals in the form of *M*, so that the commodity becomes hoarded money. In this diagram, C – M shifts *en masse* to M – C (i.e. the commodity producer uses the entire sum received from the sale of the commodity to purchase one type of other commodity), but in reality the second metamorphosis of a commodity can be divided into numerous M – C transactions, intertwined with the initial metamorphosis of multiple other commodities. But if this fact were incorporated into the diagram, then the entirety of the movement within the area of the 'sphere of circulation' would express nearly the entirety of the 'commodity circulation'.

∙ ∙ ∙

Takahashi explains the gist of the law put forth by Marx in roughly the same way right after the passage quoted earlier. But unlike Marx, who established the law from a critique of the phenomenon of money as the means of circulation manifesting itself as the means of purchase (and of related inverted phenomena within real circulation), Takahashi adopts an uncritical concept of money as the means of purchase and even sets out from the assumption that this is the primary function of money. Did Marx engage in a futile endeavour in drawing a distinction, or is it Takahashi who has overlooked a necessary step? My own view, not surprisingly, is that Marx (not Takahashi) is correct. I think that this is demonstrated in the following way that Takahashi tried to distinguish between the function as the means of purchase and as the means of payment:

> For example, if there were more money that is immediately exchanged for goods, the price of those goods will rise, but that would not occur when the money is only used for the payment of goods that have already been sold.[10]

In other words, Takahashi argues that the quantity of money in its function as the means of payment has no effect on prices, whereas the quantity of money in the function as the means of purchase does affect prices. To most people this must seem a subtle difference, but Takahashi's view is a sort of quantity theory of money[11] that collides head on with the theory of Marx. In examining the

---

10   Ōuchi 1946, p. 115.
11   The quantity theory of money is a conclusion that arises from understanding money directly as the means of purchase, rather than as the means of circulation. In other words, instead of grasping money as determined by the movement of commodity metamorphoses, it is seen as an independent entity in itself. Thus, the standard version of the quantity

'circulation of money' (where he has yet to deal at all with money as the means of payment), Marx clearly states that, 'Prices are thus high or low not because more or less money is in circulation, but there is more or less money in circulation because prices are high or low', and that this 'is one of the principal economic laws'.[12] But there is no need to rely heavily on quotes from Marx. The following statement by Takahashi himself on the quantity of circulating money clearly contradicts his statement quoted above.

> ŌUCHI: Recently the question has arisen of what quantity of money is needed in society, or what determines the overall quantity of money. [*Here the expression 'quantity of money' or 'overall quantity of money' is not the total quantity of money actually in society (since some of it exists as hoarded money), but the amount that is actually in circulation.*]

> TAKAHASHI: As is clear from what I said earlier, the amount needed would be the total of the commodities exchanged at a given time in the society plus the relation between the claims and obligations after payments had been settled. In other words, if 10 billion in commodities were sold and 5 billion in claims and obligations settled, then 15 billion in money would be necessary. Of course, each unit of money can circulate a number of times, which is to say, each has a certain frequency, and depending on that the quantity of money can decrease. In our example, if the number of times was 10, then 1.5 billion in money would be sufficient for the economy to function.[13]

This is obviously (apart from the unfortunate lack of clarity of expression) identical to Marx's law regarding the amount of circulating money, and thus incompatible with the quantity theory of money. Not only is this incompatible with the ordinary quantity theory of money, it is in twofold contradiction with the previous statement of Takahashi. The law stated above is, first of all, founded on the premise of the given commodity prices. In other words, to borrow

---

theory of money is in fact based on limiting the function of money to the means of purchase. Marx critiqued the quantity theory of James Mill in the following way:

'Incidentally, the whole concept of a direct confrontation between commodities and money and their direct exchange is derived from the movement of simple purchases and sales or from the function performed by money as means of purchase. The simultaneous appearance of commodities and money ceases even when money acts as means of payment' (Marx 1987a, p. 412).

12 Marx 1987a, p. 341.
13 Ōuchi 1946, pp. 116–7.

Takahashi's manner of expression, the basis of the theory is that 'if 10 billion in commodities were sold and 5 billion in claims and obligations settled, then 15 billion in money would be necessary'. But this 10 billion must be understood, not as the quantity of commodities or their value, but as of course indicating their price as expressed in yen, dollars, or pounds, etc. In other words, price is clearly the given premise here. In addition, although the 5 billion must be understood as the sum that remains after the claims and obligations cancel each other out when the day of payment arrives, what originally determines the debts must be thought of as the price of commodities at the time they are sold, as long as these debts arise from the sale of commodities. In other words, in this case as well, price is the given premise. Thus, the law of circulating money that Takahashi explains in the passage quoted is generally founded on taking price as the given. This view that commodity prices determine the quantity of circulating money is utterly incompatible with the quantity theory of money, according to which the quantity of circulating money determines commodity price. Moreover, this view seems to contradict what Takahashi had stated with regard to the need to distinguish between the means of purchase and the means of payment. If there is a difference with regard to prices between money as the means of purchase and as the means of payment, as he had stated, that difference should naturally be reflected in the law of the quantity of circulating money. Yet in his explanation of this law, no trace can be found of such a difference. Instead, he argues that circulating money is determined by prices, rather than being what determines prices, with no mention made of the functions of money.

Why is it that Takahashi explains this law on the one hand, while on the other hand advocating the opposite view of a quantity theory of money? It is not at all clear to me why he adopted the law just mentioned, but I imagine that his adherence to the quantity theory stems from the idea that the market prices of commodities are decided by the relation of supply and demand, and that the amount of demand is determined by the quantity of money as the means of purchase. (The quantitative theory of money arises fundamentally from the abstract observation of the function of money as the means of purchase, as noted earlier, but here I want to consider more concretely the form through which this manner of understanding ultimately leads to the quantity theory of money as its conclusion. In short, I want to at least consider what the direct reason for that conclusion might be.)

Assuming that Takahashi's reason for adopting the quantitative theory is as stated above, even if there is no doubt that the market prices of commodities are decided by the relation of supply and demand, it is not correct to assert that the quantity of demand is decided by the quantity of money as the means of purchase. Rather than the quantity of the means of purchase being the given from the outset, which then determines the magnitude of demand, the actual premise is the market prices determined by the relation of supply and demand, with contracts to buy and sell established on the basis of those determined prices, and money exchanged to fulfil those contracts. In other words, with regard to this point, there is no difference between cash- or credit-based transactions, apart from whether the money is handed over at the same time as the commodity is delivered or handed over later. In the former case, the money handed over functions as the means of purchase, while in the latter it functions as the means of payment. There is no way, as far as I can tell, for a difference to arise so that the quantity of money in the function as the means of purchase is determined prior to the transaction, while the quantity of money as the means of payment is only first determined through the transaction. Of course, in the case of a cash payment, the purchase cannot be made without having cash, whereas in a deferred payment one does not need cash at the time of the transaction. However, to begin with, even if it is said that one must have cash to make a purchase, the person who possesses money is not obliged to use it to purchase something (or to purchase regardless of the price). It can be used to purchase something or saved in a bank or just kept on hand. Whether it will be used to buy something depends on the person's desires at the time (or the needs of reproduction in the case of capital) and on the level of price. In other words, in the process whereby money is handed over for commodities, money is first posited with the determination as the means of purchase. On the other hand, in the case of money as the means of payment, even if the money does not have to be in the hands of the buyer at the time the sales contract is entered, that buyer must have the prospect of coming into possession of the money in the future in order for a contract to be made. No one would be likely to sell to a person who did not have that prospect, and it would be a swindle for someone to enter such a transaction without the prospect of acquiring the money needed. In other words, even a credit transaction is premised on the buyer possessing money (not in the present but at a certain point in the future), and the contract can only first be entered on that premise. At the same time, the person representing this future money is no different from the person who enters the market already possessing the cash in hand (of course, in this case too, the possibility for a purchase on credit does not mean that such a purchase necessarily has to be carried out right away). This fact can be ascertained from the influence exerted on prices by a massive government order, regardless of the payment method.

CHAPTER 14

A Few Problems Concerning Postwar Theories of Crisis

During this year's summer holiday, I read a few of the key works on the theory of crisis published since the end of the war, writing comments in the margins (as is my custom) and adding other thoughts in a separate notebook when necessary. I had not intended to publish these notes, either in their original form or with revisions, but given the lack of articles for the latest issue of the journal of the Ōhara Institute for Social Research, I suggested that they might be used if someone could put them into some sort of readable form. Seijirō Usami volunteered to help, and the result is the article published here. (Included are not only my original notes but also references that Usami added.) Since this article stems from notes made to myself, the language used to refer to other authors may be impolite at times, but I hope that this will be excused since there was not adequate time to revise everything.[1]

1   'Cycle' and 'Period'

One of the debates regarding crisis theory has centred on the starting point of the postwar industrial cycle in Japan. This is the question of whether it began from 1947 or 1949, or from some other year. Many of the participants in this debate seem to have taken as their natural premise the idea that crisis marks the starting point of a cycle (or its initial phase), so that an industrial cycle begins and ends with crisis.[2] But is this way of thinking in fact correct? Another

---

1   [Originally published as Kuruma 1962 and republished as Chapter 10 of *An Investigation of Crisis Theory* (Kuruma 1965).]
2   For example, Johann Lorenz Schmidt writes in *New Problems of Crisis Theory*: 'The cycle begins with crisis and ends with the next crisis that forms the starting point of a new cycle. For this reason, we can call the economic cycle within capitalism a crisis cycle' (Schmidt 1956, p. 19). Similar arguments are made by Japanese scholars, such as the following: 'One cycle consist of the period between one crisis as starting point to the next crisis as starting point' (Ikumi 1961, p. 49); 'Crisis forms the starting point of the cyclical movement of capital' (Imai 1958, p. 85). The direct source of these explanations seems to be scholars such as Fred Oelssner or the textbook *Political Economy* published by the Economics Institute of the Academy of Sciences of the USSR, which includes the following: 'The period from the beginning of one

related problem concerns the understanding among the participants of the term 'period' (*shūki*), which is often used within the debate, as well as the distinction and relation between 'period' and 'cycle' (*junkan*). I want to begin by considering these points, which seem to have been unclear.

The second chapter of Takuichi Ikukmi's book *Modern Capitalism and the Business Cycle*, is titled 'Cycle and Period', but unfortunately, he does not provide a clear explanation of the distinction between the two terms. However, we can begin by looking at the arguments he makes in that chapter, whose opening paragraph begins with the following:

> What determines a periodic [*shūkiteki*] crisis as such is that it brings to an end the period [*shūki*] that had lasted until then and thus posits the starting point of the next period.[3]

This is a mere tautology. We could use the same reasoning to say (even though the argument runs counter to Ikumi's meaning): 'What determines a periodic boom as such is that it brings to an end the period that had lasted until then, and thus posits the starting point of the next period. In using the expression 'what determines a periodic crisis as such', his intention seems to be to distinguish a 'periodic crisis' from an 'intermediate crisis' etc. His proposition could be correctly revised as follows: 'What determines a periodic crisis as such is that it is the end of an industrial cycle [*sangyō junkan*] and at the same time creates the conditions needed for the recommencement of the next cyclical movement [*junkan undō*]'.

At the root of the problem is the lack of a clear distinction between 'period' and 'cycle'. An industrial (or economic) 'cycle' for Marx does not merely indicate the regular repetition of a particular phenomenon or the period of time that elapsed in the interim, but rather the movement whereby modern industry, in its developmental process, necessarily passes through certain phases. For instance, in Book I of *Capital*, Marx writes:

---

crisis to the beginning of another crisis is called a cycle. A cycle is made up of four phases: crisis, depression, recovery and boom. The fundamental phase of a cycle is the crisis, which provides the starting point for a new cycle' (Dutt and Rothstein, eds., 1957) [page number unknown]; 'The terms crisis, depression, recovery, and boom are commonly used to express the four fundamental phases of a crisis' (Oessler 1949, pp. 94–5); 'Marx reached the conclusion that crisis is the starting point of the cycle' (Figurnov 1939) [page number unknown]; 'Each crisis brings a cycle to an end, but at the same time it starts a new cycle' (Mendelson 1959) [page number unknown].

3   Ikumi 1961, p. 49.

> The path characteristically described by modern industry, which takes the form of a decennial cycle (interrupted by smaller oscillations) of periods of average activity, production at high pressure, crisis, and stagnation, depends on the constant formation, the greater or less absorption, and the re-formation of the industrial reserve army or surplus population.[4]

Thus, in the case of 'cycle', the issue concerns where is the starting point and where is the ending point. This is something that can and should be objectively determined. In so doing, the key perspective is that the process of the development of capitalist production is at the same time the process of driving beyond its immanent barrier. In the case of 'period', by contrast, it is not an absolute necessity to have the phases in a particular order. Instead, when the repetition of a given phenomenon occurs, one merely focuses on the period that elapsed in the interim. Thus, as already mentioned, this is not limited to crisis but could include the consideration of the period from the beginning of one boom to its end.

The reason that the passage quoted from Ikumi above is a tautology stems from his use of the term 'period' instead of 'cycle' in the following: 'it brings to an end the *period* that had lasted until then and posits the starting point of the next *period*'. In using that term, it is not clear what period he is referring to. It would seem to indicate the period of crisis, but if so, it can only be a tautology. This is why the term should be replaced by 'industrial cycle' (*sangyō junkan*).

However, this raises a new problem. Namely, what phase is the beginning of an industrial cycle, and what phase is its end? Even if it is correct to say that the cycle ends in crisis, so that crisis is the final phase of a cycle (setting aside for the moment the fact that Marx speaks of the last phase of a cycle as 'crisis' in some places and as 'crisis and stagnation' in other places), but this certainly does *not* mean that crisis also constitutes the starting point, or first phase, of the next cycle. This should be clear from the passage in *Capital* quoted earlier and from various other passages from the writings of Marx, such as the following, also from Book I of *Capital*: 'The life of industry becomes a series of periods of moderate activity, prosperity, overproduction, crisis and stagnation'.[5] Marx thought it correct to see the cycle (*Zyklus*) as beginning from the period of 'moderate activity'. This is because the process of the period of rising business activity that inevitably leads to crisis at the same time should be understood as a process of

---

4   Marx 1976, p. 785.
5   Marx 1976, p. 580.

capital breaking through its immanent barrier (whereas during the period of 'stagnation' that breakthrough had yet to occur).⁶

---

6 Those who argue that a cycle begins from crisis (as L.A. Mendelson clearly does) seem to base their view on a footnote Marx added to the French edition of the first volume of *Capital*. In that note, Marx speaks of '... une crise générale, fin d'un cycle et point de départ d'un autre' [a general crisis, end of one cycle and the starting point of another cycle] (Marx 1993, p. 710). This supplemental note was not included in the third or fourth German edition of *Capital*, the Russian edition published in the collected works of Marx and Engels, the English edition, or the Marx-Engels-Lenin Institute edition, nor was it included in the Japanese edition translated by Fumio Hasebe or by Itsurō Sakisaka. But the footnote was included in Kautsky's edition of *Capital* and the edition published by Karl Dietz Verlag. The translation in the former is along the lines of 'a general crisis that brings one cycle to an end and *starts* a new cycle', while in the latter it is something like, 'a general crisis that is the end of one cycle and the starting point [*Ausgangspunkt*] of a new cycle'. In the monograph by Schmidt quoted earlier, he seems to be basing himself on this note when he writes that, 'crisis constitutes the starting point [*Ausgangspunkt*] of a new cycle' (Schmidt 1956, p. 963). However, *Ausgangspunkt* and *Anfangspunkt* are not the same. The former has the meaning of departing from a place, so that it is the 'exit' from the perspective of the one who is departing. This is the idea of passing through the exit to start out on a new journey. According to the Muret-Sanders dictionary, the expression 'den Ausgangspunkt eines Ereignisses bilden' has the meaning of 'to lead up to an event' or 'to introduce an era' [in English in original]. Thus, it does not mean that the next period starts from that point. In other words, the process of the cycle starts in the phase after the 'crisis' that constitutes the *Ausgangspunkt* in that sense. That is also the sense for Marx in Book III of *Capital*, where he uses the expression 'at the beginning of the cycle after the crisis' (Marx 1981a, p. 626). It seems mistaken to speak of crisis as 'initiating the cycle' (Kautsky) or 'constituting the starting point of the cycle' (Schmidt), not to mention saying that the cycle starts from 'crisis as the origin' (Ikumi). Marx is using *Augangspunkt* in the same sense in Book II of *Capital*, where he writes that, 'a crisis is always the starting point [*Ausgangspunkt*] of a large volume of new investment' and 'more or less a new material basis for the next turnover cycle' (Marx 1978, p. 264). It would of course be foolish to think that 'a large volume of new investment' would be made in the phase of crisis. Such new investment would take place after the phase of crisis had ended, whereas crisis is what creates the 'material basis' for the next turnover cycle, generating the conditions for the next cycle. Crisis itself does not constitute the phase that is the starting point of the next cycle, however. In referring to the starting point of a cycle, Marx uses such expressions as 'at the beginning [*Anfang*] of the industrial cycle' (Marx 1981a, p. 620) and 'at the beginning [*Beginn*] of the cycle after the crisis' (Marx 1981a, p. 626), and in all those cases the phrase is not referring to crisis itself.

In addition, Schmidt uses the term *Krisenzyklus* (crisis cycle), saying that the 'economic cycle within capitalism is a crisis cycle' (Schmidt 1956, p. 19). As far as I am aware, Marx never used such a term, but it was used by Engels in an 8 November 1884 letter to Kautsky. ['Even the fluctuations inseparable from the ten-year cycle of crises have become habitual conditions of existence' (Engels 1995, p. 213).] If the term is used to mean 'the cycle that ends in crisis' or 'the cycle in which crisis is the phase of important or decisive significance' then I could understand, but it seems mistaken for Schmidt (and many other theorists) to use the term 'crisis cycle' in the sense that the 'cycle begins and ends with crisis'.

As indicated above, the confusion of the terms 'period' and 'cycle' can lead to the mistaken view that the cycle begins from crisis, but it is also linked to the idea that a cycle not preceded by a crisis cannot be considered a proper cycle. This results in utterly confused arguments. For instance, Johann Lorenz Schmidt, in *Neue Probleme der Krisentheorie* (New Problems of Crisis Theory), writes:

> Cyclical developments since the end of World War II ... have not begun necessarily from crisis, and for this reason we cannot speak of the initiation of a complete cycle ... The cycles since war's end have been *incomplete cycles*, and so we can refer to them as *Rumpfzyklus* [truncated cycles].[7]

Ikumi has the following to say regarding Schmidt:

> Schmidt criticised the view that took the *basically correct formula that 'the cycle begins with crisis and ends with the next crisis that forms the starting point of a new cycle'*, which is based on the fundamental idea that a cycle must begin from crisis, and then sought to directly apply it to understand the postwar situation in particular. Schmidt argued that such a view was schematic and dogmatic because in so doing the conclusion was reached that the period after World War II was a 'transitional period outside the cycle' during which the cycle would not reoccur until a crisis of overproduction occurred, since immediately after the war it was not possible economically for cyclical overproduction to occur.[8]

As already noted, the error is not as described above, but rather stems from the fundamental notion that a cycle begins from crisis. It is self-contradictory for Ikumi to agree with that idea but then criticise its natural application as schematic and dogmatic. He goes on to argue that, according to Schmidt, the postwar cycle was a deformed or truncated cycle because it did not start from crisis. However, he adds that, 'As a cyclical process, as Schmidt himself insists, it was complete'.[9] In saying that the postwar 'cycle' (*junkan*) was incomplete because it did not begin from crisis, but that the 'cyclical process' (*junkan katei*) was complete, what exactly is the distinction between those two terms? I should

---

7   Schmidt 1956, p. 29.
8   Ikumi 1961, pp. 93–4. [Kuruma's emphasis.]
9   Ikumi 1961, p. 94.

have thought it clear that Marx uses the term *Zyklus* (cycle) to refer what is being discussed here as a 'cyclical process', as in the following passages:

> The path characteristically described by modern industry, which takes the form of a decennial cycle ... of periods of average activity, production at high pressure, crisis, and stagnation'.[10]

> But the industrial cycle of a number of years, divided into characteristic periods, epochs, is peculiar to large-scale industry.[11]

Thus, to use the term 'cyclical process' in distinction from 'cycle' (*Zyklus*) goes against Marx's own use of terminology. But, setting that aside, the problem here centres on whether it is complete nonsense to describe the postwar cycle as 'incomplete' because it did not start from crisis, or if that is just an imprecise way of describing a significant fact.

The proposition that the postwar cycle is incomplete for not beginning from crisis is based on a misunderstanding of the term 'cycle', but if we set aside the bias of seeing crisis as the 'starting point' of the cycle, this idea comes down to viewing the postwar cycle as abnormal for not starting from the conditions posited as the outcome of crisis (or of a global market crisis). In other words, a normal relation between the postwar cycle and the cycle that preceded it was lacking. And this is an undeniable fact. Nevertheless, this fact does not justify the argument that the postwar cycle was an incomplete or 'truncated' cycle. A cycle, at least as far as Marx is concerned, must be considered satisfactory as long as it encompasses a movement that passes through 'moderate activity' and the other phases. The question of whether the conditions needed for this movement to occur were posited by the previous crisis or not is merely an external circumstance as far as the subsequent cycle is concerned.

In the second paragraph of Chapter 2 of his book, Ikumi continues his argument as follows:

> From the beginning of one crisis to the beginning of the next crisis constitutes a period [*shūki*]. The initial crisis, through interrupting the cyclical [*junkanteki*] development up to that point, brings its period to an end, and through the crisis creates the conditions – the material foundation – necessary for a new period. From there, the phase of a new industrial

---

10 Marx 1976, p. 785.
11 Marx 1973, pp. 720–1.

cycle [*sangyō junkan*] begins. The new rising development of the cycle [*junkan*] continues until it is interrupted by the next crisis. That length of time constitutes one period.[12]

What I noted earlier also applies to the statement made by Ikumi above that 'the beginning of one crisis to the beginning of the next crisis constitutes a period'. Since the term 'period' [*shūki*] simply refers to the period of time for a given phenomenon to reappear, it is not limited to crisis. What 'the period' is referring to must be clarified. If it is referring to crisis, then it is a tautology in that sentence, as already noted.

Next, we need to consider the meaning of 'cyclical development' in the sentence: 'The initial [?] crisis, through interrupting the cyclical development up to that point, brings its period to an end, and ...' – One can imagine that this probably means the fluctuating development of the economy or industry as it passes through certain phases of activity. But if that is the case, what is the meaning of 'interrupt' here? Crisis is also just one phase of the cyclical development of the economy. What crisis 'interrupts' is not the 'cyclical development' of the economy, but rather the upward movement of the economic or business activity. If one is speaking of a cycle, the crisis does not 'interrupt' the cycle up to that point, but rather 'terminates' it, constituting its 'conclusion'.

Thus, the expression 'brings its period to an end' is also inappropriate. As already explained, a 'period' can be based on any of the phases of the industrial cycle. Thus, the meaning of 'period is not clear unless it is specified that it is the circuit of crisis or of prosperity, etc. And if it means the 'period of crisis', it is completely tautological and nonsensical to speak of the crisis bringing the period of crisis to an end.

But here Ikumi uses the expression 'its period'. The 'its' seems to indicate the 'cyclical development up to that point.' In other words, the meaning would be that crisis 'brings to an end the period of the cyclical development up to that point', which is also strange. What crisis brings to an end is not the period of the cyclical development up to that point, but the movement of rising business activity up to that point, so that crisis could be described as the final phase in the process of the industrial cycle that progressively passes through a series of other phases.

In the sentence, 'The initial crisis ... and through the crisis creates the conditions – the material foundation – necessary for a new period', setting aside the grammatical oddity, the term 'cycle' (*junkan*) should again replace 'period'

---

12   Ikumi 1961, p. 49.

(*shūki*). The reason for this should be clear from the explanation thus far. Indeed, the author himself, right after that sentence, writes: 'From there, the phase of a new industrial cycle [*sangyō shunkan*] begins.' That is correct. But the 'phase of a new industrial cycle' here is not crisis, but rather a separate phase, subsequent to crisis, that uses the relations created through the crisis as its own material foundation. What is the connection of this to the idea that 'the beginning of one crisis to the beginning of the next crisis constitutes a period'? Does Ikumi think that there is a difference between period and cycle If so, where does he draw a distinction between the two? That is not at all clear in his book. After this, Ikumi writes:

> From there, the phase of a new industrial cycle begins. The new rising development of the cycle continues until it is interrupted by the next crisis. That length of time constitutes one period.

Here the harm caused by the confusion between 'cycle' and 'period' manifests itself as Ikumi's self-contradiction. The sentences just quoted clearly contradict his earlier proposition that the 'beginning of one crisis to the beginning of the next crisis constitutes a period'. It seems to me that the term 'period' in the sentences quoted earlier refers to the 'period of a crisis', while the use of the term above with regard to the 'length of time' refers the period of one continuous cycle. With regard to the question of length, Marx writes:

> The figure of 13 years corresponds closely enough to the theory, since it establishes a unit for one epoch of industrial reproduction which *plus ou moins* coincides *with the period in which major crises recur.*[13]

> One truly remarkable phenomenon is the decrease in the *period between general crises*. I have always regarded that number not as a constant, but as a decreasing magnitude.[14]

The term 'period' above is used more in the sense of the Japanese *kikan* ('interval of time'), than in the sense of *shūki*. In speaking of length, expressions like 'duration' of the cycle are often used, as in the following note inserted by Engels in Book III of *Capital*:

---

13   Marx 1983, p. 282. [Kuruma's emphasis.]
14   Marx 1991b, p. 78. [Kuruma's emphasis. Modified translation.]

> The acute form of the periodic process with its former *ten-year cycle* seems to have given way to a more chronic and drawn-out alternation, affecting the various industrial countries at different times, between a relatively short and weak improvement in trade and a relatively long and indecisive depression. Perhaps what is involved is simply an extension of the *cycle's duration*. When world trade was in its infancy, 1815–47, *cycles of approximately five years* could be discerned; between 1847 and 1867 the cycle was *definitely a ten-year one* ...[15]

> And there it is constantly apparent that for the period over which English industry moved in *ten-year cycles* (1815–70) ...[16]

In the third paragraph of Chapter 2, Ikumi writes:

> The question of what sort of relations posit the starting point is a concrete issue, just as each cycle and crisis is a concrete issue. At the same time, the concrete form of each cycle is fundamentally characterised by the relations at its starting point.[17]

In speaking of 'what sort of relations posit the starting point', that 'starting point' must be the starting point for the next 'cycle' after the crisis has ended. The given 'relations' are posited by the crisis that is the culminating phase of one cycle, and what they are posited for is a separate phase that constitutes the starting point of the next cycle. Next, Ikumi writes:

> Therefore, the question of whether or not a period has ended or not can be verified by whether the character of that period has fundamentally changed or not.[18]

The expression 'whether the period has ended or not' is incorrect. Unless he writes something along the lines, 'whether that period is a new period or not', the meaning cannot be grasped. But even when revised in that way, it is not a precise manner of expression. The correct expression would be something like,

---

15   Marx 1981a, p. 620. [Kuruma's emphasis.] Later in this chapter I will consider the issue of the 'typographical error' or 'mistranslation' related to the expression 'cycles of approximately five years' in the passage quoted here.
16   Marx 1981a, p. 633. [Kuruma's emphasis.]
17   Ikumi 1961, p. 49.
18   Ikumi 1961, pp. 49–50.

'Whether a phase is the phase of a new cycle or not'. Or perhaps something like the following would better suit his intentions given the context:

> Whether a crisis is a cyclical crisis or not can be determined by whether the subsequent phase has the characteristic of being the starting point of a cycle with a character fundamentally different from that which came before.

Setting aside the best manner of expression, is the content itself acceptable? When Ikumi speaks of whether the 'character of that period has fundamentally changed', the use of 'character of that period' and 'fundamentally' is so abstract as to be nearly meaningless. For example, over the course of the 10-year cycles from 1825 to 1867 indicated by Engels, what sort of 'change in fundamental character' might have occurred? In relation to this point, Ikumi writes:

> If each period is understood as a stage in the development of the production relations of capitalism, it can be understood that there should be certain production relations pertaining to each period. This could be referred to as the 'principles' with regard to the unity of those relations in forming a totality ... For the 1920s, the unified principles could be thought of as the principles of the 'Versailles system'. The governing principles in the 1950s after World War II could be called the principles of the US-centred 'NATO system'.[19]

But can such 'principles' listed by Ikumi really be described as principles that characterise one 'economic cycle' or what the author calls 'one period' spanning from one crisis to the next? I think not. The interval during which the principles he lists governed do not necessarily correspond to the interval of a continued industrial cycle (or to 'one period', to borrow Ikumi's manner of expression). The two do not have such an intrinsic relation. What can be generally said about the alternation of industrial cycles is that there is a development of productive power, an increase in production, and a concentration of capital, and that once this has progressed to a certain point, through repeated cycles, quantitative change gives way to qualitative change, bringing about the so-called stage of monopoly capital.

Ikumi's descriptions on page 50 and 51 of his book are an effort to provide some theoretical grounding for his precipitous idea presented in the passage

---

19 Ikumi 1961, p. 52.

just quoted, which he probably views with pride as an original conception. But in those descriptions he ends up rephrasing the idea in an even more abstract and empty form that fails to demonstrate its correctness. A justification cannot be provided through such a method in the first place, since the problem, given its nature, can only be verified by looking at past 'periods' to clarify the point at which each was replaced and what sort of fundamental change in character' – or in 'unified principle' – took place.

Marx had the following to say, generally, about the contradiction between productive power and the relations of production (that makes crisis necessary):

> To express this contradiction in the most general terms, it consists in the fact that the capitalist mode of production tends towards an absolute development of the productive forces irrespective of value and the surplus value this contains, and even irrespective of the social relations within which capitalist production takes place ; while on the other hand its purpose is to maintain the existing capital value and to valorise it to the utmost extent possible (i.e. an ever accelerated increase in this value) ...
>
> Capitalist production constantly strives to overcome these immanent barriers, but it overcomes them only by means that set up the barriers afresh and on a more powerful scale.[20]

2   On the Theory of 'Intermediate Crisis' – Engels's 'Mistake' etc.

In the debate over the 'nature' or 'transformation' of the postwar industrial cycle, the issue of the distinction and relation between a 'general crisis' (*Allgemeine Krise*) and an 'intermediate crisis' (*Zwischenkrise*) has been raised. In particular, many academic papers have been presented on whether the crisis that began in the latter half of 1957 in the United States was an 'intermediate crisis' or a 'periodic crisis.' Jürgen Kuczynski holds the position that in order to understand the distinction between a general crisis and an 'intermediate crisis', it is necessary to clearly grasp the character of the latter concept, and in 1956 he presented his ideas on this subject in an article titled 'Zum Problem der Zwischenkrisen' (On the Problem of Intermediate Crisis).[21]

---

20   Marx 1981a, pp. 357–8.
21   Kuczynski's article was first published in the French journal *Économie et politque*. He later revised it, based on a lecture he delivered in Moscow in the autumn of 1956, and the revised version was published in issue No. 3 (Nov./Dec.) of the East German journal *Wirtschaftswissenschaft*. That version was slightly revised in turn and included in his 1957

In his article, Kuczynski begins by introducing passages from various works of Engels, to which he adds his own remarks, in order to summarise the development of Engels's views on the length of the industrial cycle. Kuczynski divides that development into the following four periods:[22]

(1) Up to 1847: View that an industrial cycle lasts 5 years or 5 to 7 years.
(2) 1847 to 1882: View that an industrial cycle lasts around 10 or 11 years.
(3) 1882 to 1884: Indeterminate view on the length of industrial cycle and the nature of an intermediate crisis.
(4) From 1884: View on length of industrial cycle is clarified and definition of intermediate crisis completed. This is formulated in an extremely clear form in Engels's appendix to the 1886 American edition of *The Conditions of the English Working Class*, and this can again be clearly confirmed in the preface to the second German edition of the work (dated 21 July 1892), which is the German translation of that appendix.

Setting aside a number of problems with the summary provided above, we can consider the note that Kuczynski inserts at the end of list cited above:

> But even after that, in the third volume of *Capital*, Engels inserted the following surprising footnote: 'When world trade was in its infancy, 1815–47, crises of approximately five years[23] could be discerned; between 1847 and 1867 the cycle was definitely a ten-year one ...'[24]
>
> Does this mean that Engels, near the end of his life (his preface to Volume III of *Capital* is dated 4 October 1894), again rejected the existence of an intermediate crisis? Or was the formulation inserted in the footnote a careless oversight?
>
> My view is that the problem stems from a thoughtless formulation combined with the added thoughtlessness of including that footnote within *Capital*. One reason for supposing an oversight on the part of Engels is that, generally speaking, the formulation in this footnote is noticeably less precise than in other passages he wrote. As the editors of Volume III indicate, the term 'cycles' should have been used instead of

---

book *Studien zur Geschichte des Kapitalismus* (Studies on the History of Capitalism), from which my citations are taken.
22   Kuczynski 1957, p. 123.
23   [See Kuruma's subsequent remarks on the translation of 'fünfjährige Krisen'.]
24   Marx 1981a, p. 620. [English translation altered to correspond to the Japanese translation Kuruma analyses.]

'crises'. However, this is not a 'clear typographical error', as they state, but an evident mistake on the part of Engels. Moreover, Engels speaks of the period of 'infancy' for world trade as 1815 to 1847, but he must have meant from 1825 to 1847, as he had written elsewhere.

A final fact that bolsters the view that Engels was thoughtless in his formulation is that in the same Part 5 of Volume III of *Capital*, he adds the following explanation: 'The crisis of 1837 with its long aftermath, added to which was a further regular crisis in 1842'.[25] Therefore, although Engels uses the term 'further regular crisis' here instead of 'intermediate crisis', it is perfectly clear that he starts from the idea of a crisis cycle lasting 10 or 11 years.

In any case, Engels's footnote should be deleted from the popular edition of *Capital*.[26]

In his comment, Kuczynski describes Engels's footnote in *Capital* as 'surprising' and says that it should be deleted, but in fact it is his own ideas that are mistaken and his comment that is 'surprising', for reasons that will be subsequently explained. In the popular edition of *Capital* published by the Marx-Engels-Lenin Institute, the editors point out that 'crises' is a clear typographical error that should be replaced by 'cycles' in the sentence: 'When world trade was in its infancy, 1815–47, crises of approximately five years could be discerned'. The original German is *fünfjährige Krisen*, meaning a 'five-year crisis' (or 'crisis that lasts five years'), which is indeed strange; hence the editorial note regarding the typographical error for 'cycles of approximately five years'. In the Japanese translation, this term *fünfjährige Krisen* was mistranslated as *go nen goto no kyōkō* ('crises every five years'). In translating it as a 'crises every five years', it can be understood as having the same meaning as 'cycles of five years'. But in that case there seems no need to add an editorial note in the Japanese edition indicating a 'clear typographical error' and change the translation to 'cycles of five years'. That is, since the mistranslation of *fünfjährige Krisen* as 'crises every five years' was a *de facto* correction of the mistake in the original German, some readers must have been perplexed as to why the editorial note was translated into Japanese.

Although it is certain that Engels's use of the term *fünfjährige Krisen* is odd, were the editors in fact correct in stating that 'crises' was a typographical error for 'cycles'? Kuczynski argues that it was not a *typographical error* but a *clear*

---

25 Marx 1981a, p. 688.
26 Kuczynski 1957, p. 123.

mistake on the part of Engels. And it does seem natural to think so, as it is hard to imagine that the typesetters would have mistaken *Zyklen* for *Krisen*. Thus, the note added by the editors is odd. However, that is not Kuczynski's main reason for advancing the idea that Engels had been careless. He uses this example to suggest a general carelessness on the part of Engels at the time he wrote the footnote for *Capital*. Kuczynski uses this to bolster his claim that Engels had certainly not again rejected the existence of intermediate crisis (or thrown out the theory of a 10-year cycle), but rather was simply careless when he wrote that '[cycles] of approximately five years could be discerned' from 1815 to 1847. However, is Kuczynski correct in claiming of a string of careless acts on the part of Engels? I think not. Indeed, my view is that the carelessness lies with Kuczynski himself, not Engels.

First, there is the question of whether the mistake was a typographical error or a mistake on the part of Engels. Both the Marx-Engels-Lenin Institute editors and Kuczynski start from the assumption that the mistake lies in using the term 'crises' rather than 'cycles'. But that is not the only view possible. Rather, it seems more likely that what should have been *fünfjährliche Krisen* (crises every five years) was published as *fünfjährige Krisen* (crises of five years). Thus, it is not unnatural to suppose the possibility of a typographical error. But even if it had been a mistake on the part of Engels, one could hardly point to it as evidence of a general carelessness regarding his footnote for *Capital*. If it is thought that 'crises' should have been 'cycles', then the difficulty could be overcome, formally speaking, by replacing 'crises every five years' with 'cycles of five years'. But in that case a problem in content would remain for Kuczynski. The theory of intermediate crisis based on the theory of a ten-year period is incompatible with the notion of 'cycles of five years', which would mean that the period only lasts five years. Engels, in his 1886 appendix to the American edition of *The Condition of the Working Class in England*, and in his 1892 introduction to the second German edition of that book, looks back on the theory of a five-year period that he held at the time of writing the book in 1845 in the following way:

> The recurring period of the great industrial crises is stated in the text as five years. This was the period apparently indicated by the course of events from 1825 to 1842. But the industrial history from 1842 to 1868 has shown that the real period is one of ten years; that the intermediate crises were secondary and tended more and more to disappear.[27]

---

27   Engels 1975, p. 404.

A great mystery arises here for Kuczynski, who poses the following question to himself:

> Did Engels near the end of his life (the preface to Volume III of *Capital* is dated 4 October 1894) again abandon his recognition of the existence of intermediate crises, or was his formulation in his note added to that volume an oversight resulting from carelessness?[28]

Determining the exact answer is not easy, but for Kuczynski it is hard to imagine that Engels could have abandoned the idea of intermediate crisis to return to the theory of a five-year period. On that basis, he settles the matter by blaming everything on Engels's carelessness, as if there was something a bit wrong with his mind at the time of writing the footnote for *Capital*. In other words, Engels mistakenly wrote 'crises' for 'cycles', and similarly wrote 'five years' instead of 'ten years'. Kuczynski desperately seizes on this conjecture, which does a great disservice to Engels, based on the assumption that 'crises' was a mistake for 'cycles'. But if we think that 'crises of five years' was a mistake or a typographical error for 'crises every five years', there would have been no room for doubt from the beginning. Since an 'intermediate crisis' is also a crisis, indicating that crises occur every five years or so did not signify that Engels had again rejected the existence of intermediate crises or that he abandoned his theory of a ten-year period. Indeed, from 1815, crises (even if not always 'general crises') occurred in 1819, 1825, 1829–30, 1837, 1841–42, and 1847. In other words, phenomenally speaking, '*crises occurring approximately every five years* could be discerned' between 1815 and 1847. Nothing about that statement goes against reality at all. Granted, if we consider the duration of the cycle, 1825 was the first general crisis, and since then the average cycle was around ten years, so that it seems correct to consider the crises in between, occurring every five years on average, as 'intermediate crises'. But this view is based on certain reasons that would need to be explained. Engels spared himself the trouble of doing so in the footnote in *Capital*, and in his role as editor that was natural. This is why he simply presented a fact that would have been clear to anyone by writing that 'crises occurring approximately every five years could be discerned'. There is no contradiction at all between saying that the duration of a cycle is ten years and that prior to 1847 crises occurred around every five years.

Another complaint that Kuczynski directs at Engels is that he was mistaken to say that the 'infancy' of the world trade was from 1815 to 1847, instead of 1825

---

28   Kuczynski 1957 [page number unknown].

to 1847. However, dating the beginning of the industrial cycle from 1815 in the footnote was not some whim on the part of Engels. Rather, this is an idea stemming from Marx, who wrote, for example:

> One measure for the accumulation of genuine capital, i.e. productive and commodity capital, is provided by the statistics of exports and imports. And there it is constantly apparent that for the period over which English industry moved in ten-year cycles (1815–70), the maximum. for the final period of prosperity before the crisis reappeared as the minimum for the period of prosperity that followed next, only to rise then to a new and much higher maximum.[29]

The fact that the first general crisis of world trade occurred in 1825 certainly does not exclude the possibility that the cycle which culminated in that crisis began in 1815. Not only is it possible, but the 1825 crisis would have had to be premised on passing through the other phases such as 'middling activity' etc. Kuczynski views a cycle as beginning from crisis, so he probably thinks that the cycle began from the 1825 crisis, but the mistake in adopting that view should be clear from the preceding discussion.

---

29 Marx 1981a, p. 633. [Kuruma's emphasis.]

CHAPTER 15

Yasuma Takada's Theory of Accumulation

1 Part 1[1]

The February issue of the journal *Keizai ronsō* (Economic Debate)[2] included an article by Professor Yasuma Takada titled 'A Consideration of the Theory of Accumulation'.[3] According to the author's explanatory note, the 'theory of accumulation' referred to concerns the examination of capital accumulation in Part 3 of Book II of *Capital* ('The Reproduction and Circulation of the Total Social Capital'). As for the 'consideration' involved, it is Takada's typical effort to find fault with Marx's ideas. The article can be broadly divided into two parts: the first presents Takada's argument that the necessity of crisis cannot possibly be explained on the basis of Marx's 'theory of accumulation', while the second puts forth his idea that this theory contains a certain 'defect or oversight'. The discussion of the former can be left to another day because that argument has been presented by others in various forms and from various perspectives, and

---

1   [Originally published as Kuruma 1932 and republished as Chapter 7 of *An Investigation of Marx's Theory of Crisis* (Kuruma 1949) along with a second critique of Takada included as Chapter 8. In the preface to that book, Kuruma writes the following about the two articles: 'These articles were written in a sort of fury that is out of character for me that arose from Yasuma Takada's way of arguing in the typical style of a "debunker of Marx", and looking back I can see that I expressed myself in an unpleasant way that is quite immature. Moreover, the second article comes to an abrupt end due to the circumstance of the worsening health and subsequent death of my brother. Although I had not intended to include the articles in this book, given those reasons, I eventually yielded to the advice of a friend who suggested that the content of the articles made them worthy of inclusion' (Kuruma 1949, p. 6). However, Kuruma decided to not include the articles in the 1953 (or 1965) collection of writings on crisis, noting his impression that "there is no longer a need for such a critique since no one these days is following this line of argument anymore" (Kuruma 1953b, pp. 2–3). Teinosuke Ōtani included both articles in the collection of writings by Kuruma and others in *Marx's Theory of Crisis*, noting that in fact the same sort of arguments presented by Takada reappeared in the postwar period in the shape of the theories centred on the concept of an 'equilibrium rate of accumulation'. Ōtani writes that 'the articles show that Kuruma's subsequent critique of Ryōzō Tomizuka [see Chapter 16 of this book] is clearly based on a serious consideration of Marx's theory of expanded reproduction during the prewar years' (Ōtani and Maehata, eds., 2019, p. 4).

2   [A journal established in 1915 by Kyoto Imperial University (present-day Kyoto University).]

3   Takada 1935a.

Takada does not offer anything particularly new. I will concentrate instead on examining the characteristic content of his article, presented in its second part. But let me begin, for the reader's convenience, by quoting the relevant passage from the article:

> From my perspective, there is one defect or oversight in Marx's theory of capital accumulation [*Capital* Book II, Part 3, 'The Reproduction and Circulation of the Total Social Capital']. This is not, in my opinion, merely an oversight on the part of Marx because the same oversight has been made by the epigones of the Marxian school and by the critics of Marx. Moreover, the overlooked point is the most important issue regarding the theory of accumulation. The content of this point, once singled out, is so commonplace that everyone should have been aware of it, but in fact it has been neglected. And once overlooked, it becomes quite difficult to clarify the progression of accumulation.
>
> The point that has been overlooked is the following. For Marx, as well as for all of his adherents (and therefore all Marxian scholars in Japan), the fundamental condition posited for accumulation to progress smoothly is that the sum of the constant capital used up and the additional constant capital in the consumer-goods production department should be equal to the sum of the variable capital, the part consumed by capitalists, and the additional variable capital in the producer-goods production department. However, this is not sufficient for accumulation to progress smoothly. It is not enough, on its own, to ensure equilibrium or proportionality between the production departments. Although it is correct to consider proportionality between the departments as a premise for the smooth progression of accumulation, this proportionality has greater content than what is assumed under the aforementioned fundamental condition posited by Marx. And this is a point that has been overlooked up to now ...
>
> Here we will make use of the symbols introduced by Bukharin.[4] The constant capital for each department is represented by c, variable capital by v, and surplus value by s, while α is the consumed surplus value and β is the accumulated surplus value (of which the constant capital and variable capital are indicated as β_c and β_v, respectively). Thus, in the two departments, we have $c_1\ v_1\ s_1\ \alpha_1\ \beta_{1c}\ \beta_{1v}$ and $c_2\ v_2$, etc. This means that the products of the two departments, or p_1 and p_2, can be indicated as follows:

---

4 [Bukharin 1972.]

$$c_1 + v_1 + \alpha_1 + \beta_1 c + \beta_1 v = p_1$$
$$c_2 + v_2 + \alpha_2 + \beta_2 c + \beta_2 v = p_2$$

... [Thus,] the condition for the smooth progression of accumulation would be seen as: $c_2 + \beta_{2c} = v_1 + \alpha_1 + \beta_{1v}$.

But here a problem emerges. Marx does not posit any other fundamental conditions necessary for the progression of expanded reproduction. However, is it really possible on that basis alone for accumulation to progress smoothly? ...

I will demonstrate subsequently that the smooth progression of accumulation cannot be ensured on the sole basis of the fundamental condition required under Marx's schema of expanded reproduction, and thereby seek to reveal what conditions he overlooked. Following this, I want to point out, in addition, how overlooking this point accounts for Rosa Luxemburg falling into error, and that being aware of the overlooked point allows us to clarify the contradiction between production and consumption that accompanies overaccumulation.

Let's accept the fundamental condition premised by Marx for the smooth progression of accumulation. In line with this, accumulation should be able to advance smoothly no matter how great its magnitude. However, since Marx says that the magnitude of accumulation in the consumer-goods production department (Dept. II) is determined by the magnitude of the accumulation in the producer-goods production department (Dept. I), the magnitude of accumulation cannot deviate from that limit. In Marx's example, accumulation in Dept. I is 500, which is half the amount of the department's surplus value, while accumulation in Dept. II, in line with that, is 150.

We need to be aware that the same fundamental condition could be met even in a case where, for example, the capitalists in Dept. I consume 30 percent of the surplus value and accumulate the remaining 70 percent. In that case, the 70 percent of the 1000 in surplus value would be divided at a ratio of 4:1 between β_{1c} and β_{1v}, according to Marx's assumption. On this basis, the amount of accumulated surplus value in Dept. II would then be determined.

Marx indicates the product for the first year in the two departments as the following:

I. $4000c_1 + 1000v_1 + 1000s_1 = 6000p_1$
II. $1500c_2 + 750v_2 + 750s_1 = 3000p_2$

But even under this same assumption, one could suppose cases such as (a), (b), or (c) below:

(a) $\begin{cases} \text{I. } 4000c_1 + 1000v_1 + 500\alpha_1 + 400\beta_{1c} + 100\beta_{1v} = 6000 \\ \text{II. } 1500c_2 + 750v_2 + 600\alpha_2 + 100\beta_{2c} + 50\beta_{2v} = 3000 \end{cases}$ $\Big| 1500c_2 + 100\beta_{2c} = 1000v_1 + 500\alpha_1 + 100\beta_{1v}$

(b) $\begin{cases} \text{I. } 4000c_1 + 1000v_1 + 400\alpha_1 + 480\beta_{1c} + 120\beta_{1v} = 6000 \\ \text{II. } 1500c_2 + 750v_2 + 720\alpha_2 + 20\beta_{2c} + 10\beta_{2v} = 3000 \end{cases}$ $\Big| 1500c_2 + 20\beta_{2c} = 1000v_1 + 400\alpha_1 + 120\beta_{1v}$

(c) $\begin{cases} \text{I. } 4000c_1 + 1000v_1 + 900\alpha_1 + 80\beta_{1c} + 20\beta_{1v} = 6000 \\ \text{II. } 1500c_2 + 750v_2 + 120\alpha_2 + 420\beta_{2c} + 210\beta_{2v} = 3000 \end{cases}$ $\Big| 1500c_2 + 420\beta_{2c} = 1000v_1 + 900\alpha_1 + 20\beta_{1v}$

Generally, in such cases, the capital composition as well as productive power are seen as not changing. The person who emphasised this the most was Rosa Luxemburg. But in fact the capital composition changes remarkably throughout the industries of society. For the first year, the capital composition is:

$$\frac{v_1 + v_2}{c_1 + c_2} = \frac{1000 + 750}{4000 + 1500} = \frac{5}{22} [(= 0.227)]$$

New capital composition in the case of (a):

$$\frac{1900}{6000} = \frac{19}{60} = 0.316$$

New capital composition in the case of (b):

$$\frac{1800}{6000} = \frac{47}{150} = 0.313$$

New capital composition in the case of (c):

$$\frac{1980}{6000} = \frac{33}{100} = 0.33$$

The failure to recognise a change in the capital composition is the basis for overlooking an important point. All three of the cases above, (a) (b) (c), meet the fundamental condition for accumulation to proceed smoothly ($c_2 + \beta_{2c} = v_1 + \alpha_1 + \beta_{1v}$). However, let's look at the elements of the newly added capital and the proportions of the expansion of each department.

(a) $\frac{400\beta_{1c}+100\beta_{1v}}{100\beta_{2c}+50\beta_{2v}}$ (b) $\frac{480\beta_{1c}+120\beta_{1v}}{20\beta_{2c}+10\beta_{2v}}$ (c) $\frac{80\beta_{1c}+20\beta_{1v}}{420\beta_{2c}+210\beta_{2v}}$

In the case of (a), 500 is invested in Dept. I and 150 in Dept II; for (b), 600 is invested in Dept. I and 30 in Dept II; and for (c), 100 is invested in Dept. I and 630 in Dept II. Each of the three cases is the outcome of the Marxian theory regarding the smooth progression of accumulation. However, the production of producer goods must necessarily correspond to the production of consumer goods in terms of production technologies (setting aside the magnitude of variable capital). If the production methods are fixed, then in line with those production methods there should be a certain scale of the production of production goods that corresponds to a certain scale of the production of consumer goods. If the production methods change, then of course the proportion between those two scales of production would also change. Such circumstances have been placed out of consideration, however. Apart from the relation of $c_2 + \beta_{2c} = v_1 + \alpha_1 + \beta_{1v}$ between Dept. I and Dept. II, therefore, the proportion between $\beta_{1c}\, \beta_{1v}$ and $\beta_{2c}\, \beta_{2v}$ should also be fixed. Those who would deny this should ponder the following.

Consider the case of (b) above. Let's calculate the shift from the second to the third year based on the Marxian assumption. In the second year, 300 in surplus value is consumed in Dept. I:

2nd year:

$$\begin{cases} \text{I. } 4480c_1 + 1120v_1 + 1120s_1 = 6720 \\ \text{II. } 1520c_2 + 760v_2 + 760s_2 = 3040 \end{cases} \begin{array}{l} 4480c_1 + 1120v_1 + 300\alpha_1 + 656\beta_{1c} + 164\beta_{1v} = 6720 \\ 1520c_2 + 760v_2 + 664\alpha_2 + 64\beta_{2c} + 32\beta_{2v} = 3040 \end{array}$$

3rd year:

$$\begin{cases} \text{I. } 5136c_1 + 1284v_1 + 1284s_1 = 7704 \\ \text{II. } 1584c_2 + 792v_2 + 792s_2 = 3168 \end{cases}$$

If we compare this to the first year, we can see that the products for Dept. I increased from 6000 to 7704, whereas the increase in Dept. II was merely from 3000 to 3168. The increases in capital for Dept. I and Dept. II are as follows:

I. $4000c_1 + 1000v_1 = 5000$ $5136c_1 + 1284v_1 = 6420$ ↑28.4%
II. $1500c_2 + 750v_2 = 2250$ $1584c_2 + 792v_2 = 2376$ ↑5.4%[5.6%][5]

$\dfrac{c_2+v_2}{c_1+v_1} = 45\%$ $\dfrac{c_2+v_2}{c_1+v_1} = 37\%$

If the production methods are assumed to be the same, there is no way that capital should increase by 28% in the producer-goods production department but only 5% in the consumption-goods production department. Production equilibrium could not be maintained in the case of such a lopsided increase. Yet this is permissible according to the fundamental condition required under Marx's reproduction schema. My claim

---

5   [Correction by Kuruma.]

is that this occurs because of an oversight in the position of Marx. As long as the production methods are fixed, the proportion between each of the capital parts after the expansion of production, or the proportion between the additional capital, is also fixed at a certain proportion. Needless to say, this would basically be required by the circumstances of production technology. Let's assume here that the proportion within the department under consideration is 4:1. It would be hard to say that this proportion is only determined by the situation for technology, since there is an influence from the rate of surplus value and the rate of accumulation, but we will not consider those factors here. If the proportion of the capital within the two departments is fixed, then it is not possible to calculate the additional capital on the basis of a certain accumulation rate in Dept. I. The accumulation rate of Dept. I must be treated as an unknown figure. Thus, there are only the following sorts of combinations for accumulation to progress smoothly.

1st year:

$$\begin{cases} \text{I. } 4000c_1 + 1000v_1 + 545\alpha_1 + 364\beta_{1c} + 91\beta_{1v} = 6000 \\ \text{II. } 1500c_2 + 750v_2 + 546\alpha_2 + 136\beta_{2c} + 68\beta_{2v} = 3000 \end{cases}$$

2nd year:

$$\begin{cases} \text{I. } 4364c_1 + 1091v_1 + 1091s_1 = 6816[6546]^6 \\ \text{II. } 1636c_2 + 818v_2 + 818s_2 = 3272 \end{cases}$$

In this case, there are six unknown figures: $\alpha_1 \alpha_2 + \beta_{1c} \beta_{2c} \beta_{1v} \beta_{2v}$. These can be calculated based on the following six formulas:

$$\begin{cases} c_2 + \beta_{2c} = v_1 + \alpha_1 + \beta_{1v} \quad \text{or} \quad 1500 + \beta_{2c} = 1000 + \alpha_1 + \beta_{1v} \\ \\ \alpha_1 + \beta_{1c} + \beta_{1v} = 1000 \\ \\ \alpha_2 + \beta_{2c} + \beta_{2v} = 750 \\ \\ \frac{\beta_{2c}}{\beta_{1c}} = \frac{3}{8} \quad \text{(in the hypothesis of Marx this equation is replaced by } \alpha_1 = 500) \\ \\ \frac{\beta_{1v}}{\beta_{1c}} = \frac{1}{4} \\ \\ \frac{\beta_{2v}}{\beta_{2c}} = \frac{1}{2} \end{cases}$$

---

6 [Correction by Kuruma.]

If accumulation were to be carried out at different proportions than these, a deadlock would necessarily arise. For instance, Marx's assumption is that accumulation is 500[7] in Dept. I and 150 in Dept. II, but even if it seems that things are progressing smoothly, numerically speaking, in order for the expansion of Dept. I to coincide with that of Dept. II, it would be necessary for its additional constant capital to be 266 rather than 400 and its additional variable capital 66 rather than 100. Thus, the producer goods are being overproduced by that corresponding amount. Let's consider a case where the accumulation in both departments exceeds my assumptions, so that accumulation is 700 in Dept. I and 525 in Dept. II. The rate of accumulation in both departments is 70%.

I. $4000c_1 + 1000v_1 + 300\alpha_1 + 560\beta_{1c} + 140\beta_{1v} = 6000$
II. $1500c_2 + 750v_2 + 225\alpha_2 + 350\beta_{2c} + 175\beta_{2v} = 3000$

This would mean a surplus of 410 for consumption goods and a deficit of 410 for production goods.[8] However, even if that deficit were solved through expanding production, there would be no way to find a sales outlet for the consumer goods, since they are already in excess by 410 in a year with no expanded production. Since this is a lack of production goods needed to make products that could not be sold, it is not a true deficit. Ultimately, it means there is a production surplus left over.[9]

The above covers all of the aspects of Takada's argument that will be examined here. In some places, the point of his argument seems somewhat unclear, but that does not impede an understanding of the gist of what he is saying.

First of all, he indicates that Marx merely points to $c_2 + \beta_{2c} = v_1 + \alpha_1 + \beta_{1v}$ as the fundamental condition for the smooth progression of accumulation. In other words, the sum of the already used and newly added constant capital in Dept. II must be equal to the sum of the existing and additional variable capital and the part of surplus value personally consumed by the capitalists in Dept. I. It will probably be necessary to say a word about this later when dealing with the issue of crisis, but for now we can accept this assertion as is.

---

7 In the text of Takada's article, the figure is 600 but this must be an error.
8 [Takada arrives at this figure of '410' as the difference between '$1000v_1 + 300\alpha_1 + 140\beta_{1v} = 1440$' in Dept. I and '$1500c_2 + 350\beta_{2c} = 1850$' in Dept. II.]
9 Takada 1935a, pp. 285–300.

Next, Takada indicates his discovery that if only this condition raised by Marx is posited, the composition of capital across all the industries of society can change in various ways depending on the outcome of accumulation. This point has remarkable value in the eyes of Takada, who looks on it as a completely new discovery. An ordinary person might have felt ashamed at his own ignorance in only having just discovered this fact, and humbly reflected on its significance to learn a new truth from Marx. But instead of reflecting on his own thoughtlessness, Takada blindly assumes that since he had overlooked it, everyone else must have done the same, and instead of seeking to learn from a great thinker, impatiently searches for Marx's flaws. Having only just noticed the overlooked fact, he triumphantly announces:

> Generally, in such cases, the capital composition as well as productive power are seen as not changing ... But in fact the capital composition changes remarkably throughout the industries of society ... The failure to recognise a change in the capital composition is the basis for overlooking an important point.

He speaks here of the 'failure to recognise a change in the capital composition', but who is he referring to, exactly? Granted, Marx in this case assumes that generally there is no change in production technology, so that the capital composition in each production department remains unchanged. However, if someone imagines from this that Marx thought that there was no change in capital composition throughout the industries of society, that person is measuring others by his own foolishness. To the extent that the composition of capital depends on production technologies, it is reliant on the particular material characteristics of the given product and will have to be determined individually according to the given production department. The capital composition throughout all of the industries of society is given from the outset as an average magnitude that is the sum of the compositions that are individually determined in that manner. Thus, changes in the proportion between the production departments whose capital compositions differ can arise even if there is no general change in production technologies or any change in the capital composition of a given department. This should be something natural and self-evident, at least to anyone with an average degree of intelligence. Yet Takada, as if he has discovered something unexpected, writes:

> Generally, in such cases, the capital composition as well as productive power are seen as not changing ... But in fact the capital composition changes remarkably throughout the industries of society.

I am not quite sure what he means by 'generally', but if his point is that the *general person*, starting with Marx, considers that there is no change in capital composition *in individual departments*, and that they would surely have been surprised to discover that in fact 'the capital composition changes remarkably throughout the industries of society', then we are the ones who should rather be taken aback at the incredible delusion from which Takada suffers. I am not sure about his case, but for the general person there is nothing unexpected about this fact at all, as already noted. If the gist of what he is saying is that Marx thought that there was no change *generally in the capital composition* – or in the compositions of capital within individual sectors or across all industries – then this must be described as an astounding delusion. As already mentioned, neither Marx nor anyone else confuses, for even a moment, the capital composition of individual sectors with the capital composition of all production departments so that, 'Generally, in such cases, the capital composition as well as productive power is seen as not changing'.

However, that delusion of Takada is not the 'important' delusion. It is rather just the 'basis' for the unfolding of the important delusion; for he goes on to argue:

> The failure to recognise a change in the capital composition is the basis for overlooking an important point. All three of the cases above, (a) (b) (c), meet the fundamental condition for accumulation to proceed smoothly $(c_2 + \beta_{2c} = v_1 + \alpha_1 + \beta_{1v})$. However, let's look at the elements of the newly added capital and the proportions of the expansion of each department.
>
> (a) $\frac{400\beta_{1c}+100\beta_{1v}}{100\beta_{2c}+50\beta_{2v}}$ (b) $\frac{480\beta_{1c}+120\beta_{1v}}{20\beta_{2c}+10\beta_{2v}}$ (c) $\frac{80\beta_{1c}+20\beta_{1v}}{420\beta_{2c}+210\beta_{2v}}$
>
> In the case of (a), 500 is invested in Dept. I and 150 in Dept II.; for (b), 600 is invested in Dept. I and 30 in Dept II.; and for (c), 100 is invested in Dept. I and 630 in Dept II. Each of the three cases is the outcome of the Marxian theory regarding the smooth progression of accumulation.

Here again Takada seizes on a matter that, objectively speaking, is not strange at all (and otherwise would have been considered strange by others from the outset), and takes a comical pride in labelling it odd. As he points out, the proportion of accumulated value between Dept. I and Dept. II in those three examples differs remarkably. But how is it that this remarkable difference arises in the first place? As the person who set up those three examples, Takada should be fully aware of the following. First, a different accumulation rate is assumed for (a) (b) (c), respectively, in Dept. I; namely: 50% for (a), 60% for (b), and 10% for (c). Second, despite that, the constant capital, variable capital, and surplus capital for the two departments that is the premise for that accumulation – and therefore the proportion of the scale between the two departments as well – are treated as givens, so that the following is assumed in all three cases:

I. $4000c + 1000v + 1000s = 6000$
II. $1500c + 750v + 750s = 3000$

Takada should be aware that this difference in the proportion of the amounts accumulated in the two departments, which he finds so strange, arises from the aforementioned premises that he himself established. *Under these assumptions*, the amounts accumulated must be 500 for (a), 600 for (b), and 100 for (c) in Dept. I, and 150 for (a), 30 for (b), and 630 for (c) in Dept. II; accumulation could not progress smoothly by any means unless those proportions were kept (which he calls the 'outcome of the Marxian logic'). Yet he raises the following objection:

> However, the production of producer goods must necessarily correspond to the production of consumer goods in terms of production technologies (setting aside the magnitude of variable capital). If the production methods are fixed, then in line with those production methods there should be a certain scale of the production of production goods that corresponds to a certain scale of the production of consumer goods. If the production methods change, then of course the proportion between those two scales of production would also change. Such circumstances have been placed out of consideration, however. Apart from the relation of $c_2 + \beta_{2c} = v_1 + \alpha_1 + \beta_{1v}$ between Dept. I and Dept. II, therefore, the proportion between $\beta_{1c} \beta_{1v}$ and $\beta_{2c} \beta_{2v}$ should also be fixed.

The core of the issue here, clearly, concerns that second proposition. Incidentally, when Takada claims that, 'If the production methods are fixed, then in line with those production methods there should be a certain scale of the production of production goods that corresponds to a certain scale of the production of consumer goods', is he in fact correct? In order to answer this, we must clarify first the meaning of 'production methods' in this case. If the gist of what he is saying is that as long as the organic composition of capital and the rate of surplus value in the two departments are fixed, then the proportion of scale between the two departments must always be fixed, this is an astounding delusion. For instance, if we assume a rate of 100% surplus value in both departments, with an organic composition of capital of 4:1 in Dept. I and of 2:1 in Dept. II, and then raise the question of what the corresponding proportion between the scales of the two departments would be, I would have to say that no one would be able to answer. Consider the following examples.

$$A \begin{cases} \text{I. } 4400c + 1100v + 1100s = 6600 \\ \text{II. } 1600c + 800v + 800s = 3200 \end{cases} \frac{\text{I}}{\text{II}} = 2\frac{1}{16}$$

$$B \begin{cases} \text{I. } 4480c + 1120v + 1120s = 6720 \\ \text{II. } 1520c + 760v + 760s = 3040 \end{cases} \frac{\text{I}}{\text{II}} = 2\frac{4}{19}$$

$$C \begin{cases} \text{I. } 4080c + 1020v + 1020s = 6120 \\ \text{II. } 1920c + 960v + 960s = 3840 \end{cases} \frac{\text{I}}{\text{II}} = 1\frac{19}{1632}$$

$$D \begin{cases} \text{I. } 4000c + 1000v + 1000s = 6000 \\ \text{II. } 1500c + 750v + 750s = 3000 \end{cases} \frac{\text{I}}{\text{II}} = 2$$

In all of the equations above, the organic composition of capital and the rate of surplus value perfectly match the earlier stated premise. Yet the proportion of the scale between the departments (if expressed as the proportion of product values) are all different. Moreover, based on the same premise, we could come up with a limitless number of other examples of different proportions of scale between the departments. And one could certainly not come up with a reason why some are possible while others are not. This demonstrates the insufficiency of saying that in order for the proportion of scale between the two departments to be fixed it must be premised that the organic composition of capital and the rate of surplus value in the two departments are also fixed. What else would have to be premised, then? Let's work our way backwards to consider what sort of premised fact would be demanded in a case where the c, v, and s in both departments are givens.

(1) The total amount of constant capital for the current year in both departments has to be equal to the total amount of product value in Dept. I for the previous year.
(2) The total product value of Dept. I in the previous year should, in line with the premise, be divided into c, v, and s at a ratio of 4:1:1.
(3) The total value accumulated in Dept. I for the previous year must be equal to the result from subtracting the same department's capital in the previous year from its capital in the current year.

In line with the principles above, the figures for Dept. I in the previous year in A, B, C, and D would necessarily be of the following sort:

A. $4000c_1 + 1000v_1 + 1000s_1[500\alpha_1 + 400\beta_{1c} + 100\beta_{1v}] = 6000$

Accumulation rate $= \dfrac{400\beta_{1c} + 100\beta_{1v}}{1000s_1} = \dfrac{1}{2} = 50\%$

B. $4000c_1 + 1000v_1 + 1000s_1[400\alpha_1 + 480\beta_{1c} + 120\beta_{1v}] = 6000$

Accumulation rate $= \dfrac{480\beta_{1c} + 120\beta_{1v}}{1000s_1} = \dfrac{3}{5} = 60\%$

C. $4000c_1 + 1000v_1 + 1000s_1[900\alpha_1 + 80\beta_{1c} + 20\beta_{1v}] = 6000$

Accumulation rate $= \dfrac{80\beta_{1c} + 20\beta_{1v}}{1000s_1} = \dfrac{1}{10} = 10\%$

D. $3666\tfrac{2}{3}c_1 + 916\tfrac{2}{3}v_1 + 916\tfrac{2}{3}s_1\left[500\alpha_1 + 333\tfrac{1}{3}\beta_{1c} + 83\tfrac{1}{3}\beta_{1v}\right] = 5500$

Accumulation rate $= \dfrac{333\tfrac{1}{3}\beta_{1c} + 83\tfrac{1}{3}\beta_{1v}}{916\tfrac{2}{3}s_1} = \dfrac{5}{11} = 45\tfrac{5}{11}\%$

From this we can understand that a fixed proportion in the scale between the two departments is premised not only on a certain organic composition of capital and rate of surplus value in both departments but also a certain rate of accumulation in the previous year in Dept. I. Moreover, if we were to contrast the accumulation rate calculated in the schema above for Dept. I with the proportion of scale between the two departments indicated in the previous schema, we would see that $\dfrac{I}{II}$ would increase or decrease in proportion to the size of the accumulation rate in the previous year for Dept. I, but this is the natural result of the fact that the larger the accumulation rate of Dept. I, the larger the proportion of the products in that department which would remain in it for use in the subsequent year as means of production, and consequently the smaller the part that could be provided as means of production to Dept. II in the subsequent year. This is not irrational or incomprehensible, but an exceedingly clear and natural necessity.

For Dept. II, unlike Dept. I, we can simply state with confidence that the capital of the current year should be equal to the capital of the previous year plus the part accumulated from the surplus value; there is no basis for determining within that how much of this is old capital and how much is new. If the scale of production of the previous year happened to be relatively large, then one could suppose that a large amount would likely be consumed, and a smaller amount accumulated, and in the opposite case the opposite would occur. This suggests that the given proportion between Dept. I and Dept. II is not premised on what was fixed in Dept. II in the previous year. We can verify this in the case of equation A. above.

Previous year:

$$\begin{cases} \text{I. } 4000c + 1000v + 1000s[500\alpha + 400\beta c + 100\beta v] = 6000 \\ \text{II. } \begin{cases} 1500c + 750v + 750s[600\alpha + 100\beta c + 50\beta v] = 3000 \\ 1400c + 700v + 700s[400\alpha + 200\beta c + 100\beta v] = 2800 \end{cases} \end{cases}$$

Current year:

$$\begin{cases} \text{I. } 4400c + 1100v + 1100s = 6600 \\ \text{II. } 1600c + 800v + 800s = 3200 \end{cases}$$

Within the equations above, the current-year figures for Dept. I and Dept. II are givens, the previous year figures for Dept. I (as clarified earlier) are based on the given assumptions, and the previous year figures for Dept. II are new suppositions. The two-fold assumption is that the same result can be arrived at for Dept. I and Dept. II in the current year regardless of the scale of Dept. II in the previous year, within a certain range – and therefore regardless of the proportion between the scale of the two departments in the previous year. (Incidentally, this arises from the fact that one portion of the products of Dept. II can be flexibly used for either 'productive' or 'unproductive' purposes.) Through this, we can confirm that there is no necessary relation that exists between the proportion of the scale between the two departments of the current year and that of the previous year. In other words, the proportion of the scale between the two departments in the current year (assuming that the organic composition of capital and the rate of surplus value in both departments do not change), will wholly be determined by the rate of accumulation in Dept. I in the previous year. Likewise, the proportion of scale between the two departments in the previous year was wholly dependent on the rate of accumulation in Dept. I in the year that preceded it. If it so happens that the scale between the two departments in the current year is the same as in the previous year, that would simply mean that in the previous year the rate of accumulation in Dept. I was the same as in the year that preceded it. And in this case – and only in this particular case – the proportion between the accumulated sums in both departments could be equal to the proportion of old capital between the two departments. Indeed, it would have to be equal. In contrast, if the rate of accumulation in Dept. I in the previous year increases or decreases compared to the year prior to that, then $\frac{I}{II}$ for the current year will necessarily increase or decrease compared to the previous year. For it to increase it is necessary that $\frac{\beta_{1c}+\beta_{1v}}{\beta_{2c}+\beta_{2v}} > \frac{C_1+V_1}{C_2+V_2}$, and for it to decrease it is necessary that $\frac{\beta_{1c}+\beta_{1v}}{\beta_{2c}+\beta_{2v}} < \frac{C_1+V_1}{C_2+V_2}$, which should be obvious. The difference in the proportion of the accumulated sums in the case of (a) (b) and (c) that Takada found strange arises precisely from this. And this necessity, as already noted, is based on his own two assumptions. There is nothing strange about this. If there is something that could be considered strange, it must be Takada's own way of thinking, whereby he finds the natural result of his own assumption to be strange when it does not correspond to a result that could only arise from an opposite assumption. I do not think there is any need to delve further into what he says after the part we have examined already. Basically, it is the same sort of delusional ideas that have been exposed, or what might simply be described as the 'expanded reproduction' of those illusions.

2 Part 2[10]

Previously I wrote an article titled 'A Consideration of Professor Takada's Theory of Accumulation'[11] in response to Yasuma Takada's attempt by to denounce Marx in his article 'A Consideration of the Theory of Accumulation',[12] but recently Takada has published another article, titled 'A Revision of the Theory of Accumulation',[13] in order to 'fill out some of the incomplete details and rethink them, while also adding new findings', in addition to 'addressing the criticism made by Samezō Kuruma'. My aim here is to respond to that criticism and critique Takada's revisions to his earlier article.

2.1 Gist of Takada's Earlier Theory

It is necessary to begin by introducing the gist of Takada's theory presented in 'A Consideration of the Theory of Accumulation', which is as follows.

 I. The fundamental condition within Marx's schema of expanded reproduction for equilibrium to exist between the two main departments of social production (i.e. the department of producer goods and the department of consumer goods) or for accumulation to proceed smoothly (which has the same

---

10 [Originally published as Kuruma 1933 and republished as Chapter 8 of *An Investigation of Marx's Theory of Crisis* (Kuruma 1949), but not included in subsequent editions (Kuruma 1953b and Kuruma 1965).]
11 Kuruma 1932.
12 Takada 1935a.
13 Takada 1935b.

meaning as equilibrium as far as Takada is concerned) is discovered to be nothing more than the requirement that the sum of the existing and additional capital in the consumer-goods production department is equal to the sum of the existing and additional variable capital the part of surplus value consumed by the capitalists in the producer-goods production department. In other words, if the constant capital, variable capital, surplus value, personal consumption of capitalists, additional constant capital, and additional variable capital in the department for producer goods (Dept. I) are expressed, respectively, as c_1, v_1, s_1, α_1, β_{1c}, β_{1v}, and those same elements in the department for consumer goods (Dept. II) are expressed as c_2, v_2, s_2, α_2, β_{2c}, β_{2v}, then $c_2 + \beta_{2c}$ must be equal to $v_1 + \alpha_1 + \beta_{1v}$. This is the only fundamental condition recognised by Marx and his epigones for equilibrium between the two departments.

II. That being the case, as long as this condition is met, equilibrium between the two departments can be perfectly maintained, so that crisis could only be explained from the unplanned nature of production. However, an explanation of crisis based on the unplanned nature of production certainly does not make it possible to explain the necessity of crisis. This suggests a great defect in Marx's schema of expanded reproduction.

III. In order to explain the source of that defect, the following reasons are presented:

1. If one assumes that the sole condition for equilibrium between the two departments is $c_2 + \beta_{2c} = v_1 + \alpha_1 + \beta_{1v}$, as recognised by Marx, then there are various ways for accumulation to proceed in the case where the constant capital, variable capital, and surplus value of each department that form the premise of accumulation are givens. Let's assume that the given amounts are as follows:

$$\text{I. } 4000c_1 + 1000v_1 + 1000s_1 = 6000$$
$$\text{II. } 1500c_2 + 750v_2 + 750s_1 = 3000$$

In this case, accumulation could proceed in a number of different ways:

(a) $\begin{cases} \text{I. } 4000c_1 + 1000v_1 + 500\alpha_1 + 400\beta_{1c} + 100\beta_{1v} = 6000 \\ \text{II. } 1500c_2 + 750v_2 + 600\alpha_2 + 100\beta_{2c} + 50\beta_{2v} = 3000 \end{cases}$ $\bigg| 1500c_2 + 100\beta_{2c} = 1000v_1 + 500\alpha_1 + 100\beta_{1v}$

(b) $\begin{cases} \text{I. } 4000c_1 + 1000v_1 + 400\alpha_1 + 480\beta_{1c} + 120\beta_{1v} = 6000 \\ \text{II. } 1500c_2 + 750v_2 + 720\alpha_2 + 20\beta_{2c} + 10\beta_{2v} = 3000 \end{cases}$ $\bigg| 1500c_2 + 20\beta_{2c} = 1000v_1 + 400\alpha_1 + 120\beta_{1v}$

(c) $\begin{cases} \text{I. } 4000c_1 + 1000v_1 + 900\alpha_1 + 80\beta_{1c} + 20\beta_{1v} = 6000 \\ \text{II. } 1500c_2 + 750v_2 + 120\alpha_2 + 420\beta_{2c} + 210\beta_{2v} = 3000 \end{cases}$ $\bigg| 1500c_2 + 420\beta_{2c} = 1000v_1 + 900\alpha_1 + 20\beta_{1v}$

2. 'Generally, in such cases, the capital composition as well as productive power are seen as not changing ... But in fact, the capital composition changes remarkably throughout the industries of society'.

Capital composition in the first year:

$$\frac{v_1 + v_2}{c_1 + c_2} = \frac{1000 + 750}{4000 + 1500} = 0.227$$

New composition in case of (a):

$$\frac{1900}{6000} = 0.316$$

New composition in case of (b):

$$\frac{1800}{6000} = 0.313$$

New composition in case of (c):

$$\frac{1980}{6000} = 0.33$$

'The failure to recognise a change in the capital composition is the basis for overlooking an important point'.

3. If this is the case, what is the 'important point' that is overlooked on this 'basis'? According to Takada, that point is the following:

> The failure to recognise a change in the capital composition is the basis for overlooking an important point. All three of the cases above, (a) (b) (c), meet the fundamental condition for accumulation to proceed smoothly ($c_2 + \beta_{2c} = v_1 + \alpha_1 + \beta_{1v}$). However, let's look at the elements of the newly added capital and the proportions of the expansion of each department.
>
> (a) $\frac{400\beta_{1c}+100\beta_{1v}}{100\beta_{2c}+50\beta_{2v}}$ (b) $\frac{480\beta_{1c}+120\beta_{1v}}{20\beta_{2c}+10\beta_{2v}}$ (c) $\frac{80\beta_{1c}+20\beta_{1v}}{420\beta_{2c}+210\beta_{2v}}$
>
> In the case of (a), 500 is invested in Dept. I and 150 in Dept II; for (b), 600 is invested in Dept. I and 30 in Dept II; and for (c), 100 is invested in Dept. I and 630 in Dept II. Each of the three cases is the outcome of the Marxian theory regarding the smooth progression of accumulation. However, the production of producer goods must necessarily correspond to the production of consumer goods in terms of production technologies

(setting aside the magnitude of variable capital). If the production methods are fixed, then in line with those production methods there should be a certain scale of the production of production goods that corresponds to a certain scale of the production of consumer goods. If the production methods change, then of course the proportion between those two scales of production would also change. Such circumstances have been placed out of consideration, however. Apart from the relation of $c_2 + \beta_{2c} = v_1 + \alpha_1 + \beta_{1v}$ between Dept. I and Dept. II, therefore, the proportion between $\beta_{1c} \beta_{1v}$ and $\beta_{2c} \beta_{2v}$ should also be fixed.

Unfortunately, I have no choice here but to quote Takada at length. (I hope that he will not hold it against me.) This was necessary because the object of criticism must of course be clarified in order for the suitability of the criticism to be evident. Since Takada's way of framing the argument remains difficult to understand, I was not able to summarise his ideas without adding my own inferences. If I had tried to infer his meaning, I suspect many readers – instead of mocking his exceedingly foolish argument – would have questioned whether I had presented his views accurately. For example, as quoted above, Takada claims that the 'failure to recognise a change in the capital composition is the basis for overlooking an important point', but let's carefully examine the meaning of this claim. First of all, the 'basis' here does not signify the grounds of an argument. As far as I can perceive, this merely signifies a moment within a process of association where not perceiving a given fact leads to overlooking another fact. In other words, Marx and his followers, in only considering the need for $c_2 + \beta_{ac} = v_1 + \alpha_1 + \beta_{1v}$ as the condition for equilibrium between the two departments, fail to perceive the fact that the capital composition throughout all the industries of society changes in various ways as a result of accumulation. Therefore, they in turn overlook the changes in the proportions between the accumulated sums in the departments that would arise in this case, or overlook that if the production methods are fixed, the proportion of scale between the departments must also remain unchanged or (what amounts to the same thing) that the proportion of the accumulated amounts in Dept. I and of Dept. II must be equal to the proportion between the former capital of the two departments. Those are the only sorts of significance that the sentence quoted above could have as far as I can tell. But this amounts to nothing more than Takada imagining the psychological processes of Marx and his followers. However, his imaginings exceed the imagination, and no matter how we may ponder what he has said it seems to have no objective validity. If I were to venture further into imagining why he came up with his supposition, it may be that he only realised recently that the capital composition changes, which led him to conceive of his so-called 'important point'. Of course, as stated above, this is only my guess, and I would not hesitate to withdraw it at any time if it is incorrect, but at least at present I have no choice but to rely on my imagination to explain the 'basis' of which Takada speaks.

In any case, the fact that, in adhering to the condition set by Marx, the composition of the total capital of society could change in various ways as a result of accumulation certainly does not provide a basis (by the very nature of the matter) for the claim that the proportion of the scale between the two departments must remain unchanged as long as the productive methods are fixed. (Incidentally, this claim seems to be the core of Takada's so-called 'important point'.) In other words, his claim is just a spur-of-the-moment idea or dogma. But in presenting this claim to the public, Takada must offer some proof. How does he attempt to do so?

4. In order to provide a proof (or something resembling one), Takada, after the passage quoted above, writes that, 'anyone who would deny this must consider the following', and then points to the following 'lesson in arithmetic':

1st year (accumulation in Dept. I assumed to be 600; accumulation rate = 60%):

$$\begin{cases} \text{I. } 4000c_1 + 1000v_1 + 1000s_1[400\alpha_1 + 480\beta_{1c} + 120\beta_{1v}] = 6000 \\ \text{II. } 1500c_2 + 750v_2 + 750s_2[720\alpha_2 + 20\beta_{2c} + 10\beta_{2v}] = 3000 \end{cases}$$

2nd year (accumulation in Dept. I assumed to be 820; accumulation rate = $73\frac{11}{14}\%$):

$$\begin{cases} \text{I. } 4480c_1 + 1120v_1 + 1120s_1[300\alpha_1 + 656\beta_{1c} + 164\beta_{1v}] = 6720 \\ \text{II. } 1520c_2 + 760v_2 + 760s_2[664\alpha_2 + 64\beta_{2c} + 32\beta_{2v}] = 3040 \end{cases}$$

3rd year:

$$\begin{cases} \text{I. } 5136c_1 + 1284v_1 + 1284s_1 = 7704 \\ \text{II. } 1584c_2 + 792v_2 + 792s_2 = 3168 \end{cases}$$

From this example, we can also obtain the following figures:

First fiscal year *Second fiscal year*
I. $4000c_1 + 1000v_1 = 5000$ $5136c_1 + 1284v_1 = 6420$ ↑28.4%
II. $1500c_2 + 750v_2 = 2250$ $1584c_2 + 792v_2 = 2376$ ↑5.4%[5.6%][14]

$\frac{c_2+v_2}{c_1+v_1} = 45\%$ $\frac{c_2+v_2}{c_1+v_1} = 37\%$

---

14 [Correction by Kuruma.]

Based on this, Takada says the following (with my italicised comments in brackets):

> If the production methods are assumed to be the same, there is no way that capital should increase by 28% in the producer-goods production department but only 5% in the consumer-goods production department. [*Isn't the precise issue here to demonstrate whether there is 'no way' for this to happen or not?*] Production equilibrium could not be maintained in the case of such a lopsided increase. [*Isn't the precise issue here to demonstrate whether there 'is no way' or not?*] Yet this is permissible according to the fundamental condition required under Marx's reproduction schema. My claim is that this occurs because of an oversight in the position of Marx. [*This only clarifies that Takada is not satisfied with views that do not conform to his own dogma because they produce results that run counter to that dogma.*] As long as the production methods are fixed, the proportion between each of the capital parts after the expansion of production, or the proportion between the additional capital, is also fixed at a certain proportion. Needless to say, this would basically be required by the circumstances of production technology [*This is merely the repetition of the same dogma as before.*] Let's assume here that the proportion within the department under consideration is 4:1. [*What is the point of making this assumption of the 4:1 ratio?*] It would be hard to say that this proportion is only determined by the situation for technology, since there is an influence from the rate of surplus value and rate of accumulation, but we will not consider those factors here. [*In the example Takada raised earlier, it was assumed that the accumulation rate in Dept. I changes in the following year. (In other words, the first year it was 60% and in the second 73%.) And he found it strange that the proportion of capital between the two departments would change as a result of accumulation carried out under this assumption, whereas here he says that 'this proportion' (between the capital of the two departments) would also be influenced by 'the rate of accumulation, but we will not consider those factors here'. How are we supposed to understand this?*]

2.2 *Criticism of Arguments Summarised above, Takada's Refutation, and My Counter-Criticism*

The summary above presents the gist of Takada's previous article, 'A Consideration of the Theory of Accumulation', and my previous criticism of it can be summarised as below [following the same order].

I. The way that Takada poses the question, in terms of saying that Marx only recognised the necessity of $c_2 + \beta_{ac} = v_1 + \alpha_1 + \beta_{1v}$ as the fundamental condition for accumulation to proceed smoothly is somewhat problematic, but we can accept it for the time being with regard to the issue at hand (i.e. as long as the problem is limited to the fundamental conditions of equilibrium between the two departments).

II. The idea that if one accepts Marx's reproduction schema there is no way to recognise the necessity of crisis has been put forward by others previously, from a variety of angles and in a variety of forms, so it cannot be seen as content unique to Takada's article. For this reason, it is a point that can be discussed separately, at a different time.

III. Listed below are the responses I made to the points within his argument.

1. I had no objection to this first point.

2. With regard to the second point, my criticism was as follows. Takada speaks of the failure to perceive that the 'capital composition throughout all the industries of society changes in various ways as a result of accumulation', but who exactly failed to recognise this? Granted, Marx clearly premised no change in the production techniques, generally speaking, so that the capital composition within the production sectors is unchanged. But if Takada imagines from this that Marx had thought there is also no change in the capital composition of all the industries of society, then he must be described as judging Marx by his own stupidity. As long as the composition of capital depends on production techniques, it naturally has to be dependent on the material characteristic of products and will be individually determined for each production sector. The capital composition for all of the industries of society, as the sum of those individually determined compositions, is given from the outset as the average magnitude. Thus, even if the production techniques do not generally change, so that the capital composition within each department remains unchanged, a change of the capital composition throughout all the industries of society will naturally arise if a change occurs in the proportion between the departments with different capital compositions. This should be natural and self-evident, presenting nothing unexpected as far as an ordinary, rational observer is concerned. Takada's idea that no one had ever perceived this before clearly runs counter to reality, so it must be based on some misconception. And I offered my own imaginings about this as my criticism.

However, in response, Takada writes that, 'The person who measured others by his own stupidity would answer in the following way to the wise Kuruma':

> Basically, as long as the fundamental condition stated by Marx is met, things function regardless of the proportion between the scale of the

departments. But it is certainly not possible for production techniques, and therefore the productive power of labour, to remain constant. Thus, this is naturally a change in the productive power of labour. Nevertheless, that is not generally recognised, and labour is treated as if its productive power does not change. This is a view that is hard to accept. That is the gist of my opinion. As can be seen from this, I am posing the problem in terms of the change in the composition of capital signifying a change in the productive power of labour ... Kuruma responds by asking: Who wouldn't recognise that is the case? It seems to me that the most appropriate example of such a person would be Kuruma himself. [*His basis for saying this is to quote the following from my article: 'Granted, Marx clearly premised no change in the production techniques, generally speaking, so that the capital composition within the production sectors is unchanged'.*] ... Kuruma does not recognise this. What is so strange about me saying that productive power in such cases is generally seen as not changing? Can Kuruma even understand the nature of the question I am posing? The question is: 'Even if the fundamental conditions posited by Marx are met, the composition of the entire capital can change in various ways. How is this possible in the first place if productive power does not change?' In responding to my view, Kuruma says that I suffer from an 'incredible delusion'; that 'instead of reflecting on [my] own thoughtlessness' I had 'blinding assume[d] that since [I] had overlooked it, everyone else must have done the same]'; and that I had gaped in wonder with a 'comical pride', but since Kuruma does not even recognise the problem at hand it is difficult to respond to his view. Frankly, I don't even know where to start. Such abusive remarks make me wonder if he even tried to understand my view.[15]

The frank comments of an uncultivated person seem to have stirred Takada's emotions somewhat, but before rashly speaking of someone else's 'abusive' behaviour, he should calm down and reflect on how he has posed the argument. As should be evident from passages I have already quoted, he clearly set up the three examples of (a) (b) (c) and points to the fact that, in the case where the fundamental condition posited by Marx is met, the capital composition between the departments will change in various ways. He then says that this self-evident fact was not recognised by any number of people before and that not recognising it was the basis for overlooking an important point. So

---

15 Takada 1935b, pp. 339–41.

before considering his so-called 'important point', I found it necessary first to examine what he calls its 'basis' and to question who had not recognised that clear fact. Here, of course, we have to be careful not to conflate two questions. First, there is the question of whether the aforementioned fact was recognised as such or not; and second, the question of whether one recognises the necessity of a change in productive power as the premise of this fact. The comment by Takada about the basis of an important point that was overlooked – and my response questioning who, exactly, had overlooked this point – undoubtably concerns the former question. And my response to that question was quite natural and clear in asking him who had failed to recognise the fact of changes in capital composition throughout all industries, so that in the first year $\frac{v_1+v_2}{c_1+c_2}$ could be 0.227, while in the second year it could be (a) 0.316, (b) 0.313, or (c) 0.33.

In the face of my natural and clear response, Takada claims that I was not able to even understand the question at hand and notes that his original question concerned whether a change in capital composition is possible without a change in productive power. Takada then argues that the best example of a person who did not recognise a change in the productive power of labour in this case was Kuruma himself.

(Incidentally, although Takada says that this is precisely the problem at hand, in fact it does not constitute the problem at all, as I think my earlier explanation sufficiently demonstrates. Simply put, to repeat the point made before, the change in the overall capital composition is not premised on a change in the productive power of the labour involved in the production of a given use-value – or the change in the production techniques or the change in the capital composition – but rather stems solely from a change in the proportion between the scale of the two departments that have different capital compositions. Thus, supposing that the capital composition in each department is the same, no matter how much the proportion between the scale of the two departments might change, the composition of the overall capital would always remain the same. This, incidentally, can be considered a counter-proof to Takada's statement that 'as long as the composition of capital is fixed in the true sense (?!) … accumulation could progress in just one pattern'. The condition for smooth accumulation involves more than just the condition of equilibrium between the two departments.)

Professor Takada's answer mixes chalk and cheese, and clearly substitutes the first question, mentioned above, with the second question, and he is unable to offer any proof apart from saying that the other person has base intentions. It should be quite clear from what I have argued thus far (without any need for further explanation) that the issue first concerns the path leading up to the conclusion, not the conclusion itself. To borrow his own expression, this 'concerns the basis of the important point that was overlooked'. And yet Takada, in response to my posing of this problem, first says that I did not understand the issue at hand. How can he make such an absurd statement? In fact, I sought to trace each step in his reasoning, respecting the question he had posed, and precisely because I did not in the least disrespect the content of the 'basis' he had indicated, I pondered what its meaning could be until finally arriving at what seemed to me the only possible explanation, which I then endeavoured to express in the criticism summarised above. Whatever one might think of my critical remarks, they could hardly be considered 'abusive'. If Takada finds it difficult to respond, he should by all means reflect on the true cause of that. He should adopt the manly stance of owning up to his own mistake of speaking nonsensically of a 'basis', instead of clumsily trying to dodge the problem and doubting the motives of another person whom he unfairly accuses of ignorance in order to wave off a knowledgeable attack.

3. If we set aside the aforementioned 'basis', which seems to have no meaning except to provide his argument with an air of plausibility, as well as the ideas presented after he states that 'Those who would deny this should ponder the following',[16] the remaining problem with regard to Takada's first article concerns what he calls the 'important point'. This centres on his claim that, 'If the production methods are fixed, then in line with those production methods there should be a certain scale of the production of production goods that corresponds to a certain scale of the production of consumer goods'.

In considering this claim, I first noted the need to clarify the meaning of 'production methods' in this case. There is no question in this case that the expression 'if the production methods are fixed' is premised on the capital composition and rate of surplus value being fixed in each department. But the issue is whether, beyond that, a fixed rate of accumulation in the previous year is premised in Dept. I. If the latter is at the same time assumed, then the claim made by Takada could indeed be described as correct. As long as all three of the conditions above are assumed, the proportion between the scales of the two departments would naturally have to be fixed. But the reason that this has to be fixed in this case is solely due to the fulfilment of the Marxian equilibrium conditions and does not signify that there exist separate conditions for equilibrium along with it. Thus, Takada's claim may be justified in the limited sense stated above, but it cannot at the same time be the foundation for attack-

---

16   Regarding this second point, readers can consult my bracketed comments interspersed in the previously quoted passage.

ing Marx. Therefore, he needed to append to his original argument the idea that the fixity of the 'production methods"' excludes the fixity of the accumulation methods. In other words, Takada's claim above can only be understood as meaning that the proportion of scale between the two departments must always be fixed as long as the capital composition and rate of surplus value in each department is fixed. But understood in that way, it is a clear fallacy. For instance, if we suppose that the capital composition is 4:1 in Dept. I and 2:1 in Dept. II, and that the rate of surplus value is 100% in both departments, no one would be able to say what the corresponding scale between the two departments would be. Various proportions in the scale between the departments are possible when the capital composition and rate of surplus value are fixed in each. Moreover, the proportion would have to vary in line with the rate of accumulation in Dept. I in the previous year. As long as this is the case, the Marxian condition has to be considered valid. (Takada himself cannot help harbouring at least a small doubt as to whether the Marxian condition might not in fact be the fundamental condition for the progression of accumulation.) The fixity of the proportion of the scale between the two departments is certainly not posited by the fixity of the capital composition and rate of surplus value in each department. In addition to that a certain rate of accumulation in Dept. I in the previous year is posited. I sought to clarify this using the four equations that appear in his first article. But in response to that, Takada writes:

> Here no consideration is given to the circumstances of the production technology at all. Kuruma mistakenly treats the issue of the composition of the overall capital of the economy as a calculation problem. As long as it is treated as a problem of calculation, it is possible to calculate the scale of each department in line with the accumulation rate, insofar as the Marxian condition is posited ... But the problem of the economy is not a problem of arithmetic. Even if the proportion of capital calculated thusly meets the fundamental Marxian condition, whether this will comply with economic reality or not is a separate issue. The latter is the question of whether the technical conditions will allow for this or not. This is what could be called the economic problem, which is the problem with which I am primarily dealing. Kuruma does not take one step toward considering this problem. Indeed, he does not even understand the need to do so. This is why I said there was nothing to be done.[17]

---

17 Takada 1935b, pp. 343–4.

Here Takada earnestly laments my lack of understanding, but really I am the one who must regret his inability even to understand his own explanation. When he said before that the proportion between the two departments had to be fixed, and based on this insisted on the indispensable condition of $\frac{\beta_{2c}+\beta_{2v}}{\beta_{1c}+\beta_{1v}} = \frac{c_2+v_2}{c_1+v_1}$, what sort of condition was it proposed as? Clearly, it was proposed as something parallel to the Marxian condition or something on par to it, which is to say, something other than $c_2 + \beta_{2c} = v_1 + \alpha_1 + \beta_{1v}$. That is precisely why he also claimed that the Marxian condition was insufficient and that there was a flaw in the Marxian theory of accumulation. But now what does he say? He nonchalantly mentions that, 'Even if the proportion of capital calculated thusly meets the fundamental Marxian condition, whether this will comply with economic reality or not is a separate issue. The latter is the question of whether the technical conditions will allow for this or not.' If that is truly the case, then the condition he raised for the problem that he posed is not a separate condition alongside the Marxian condition, but rather a subordinate condition naturally absorbed within the Marxian condition in order to realise it, making it possible for what is required under the Marxian condition to be manifested within economic reality. Thus, no matter how justified and important the conditions are as such, it certainly does not signify that the Marxian condition is insufficient. Indeed, this should lead Takada to praise the adequacy of the Marxian condition – and the astounding genius of encompassing in one formula all of the requirements for equilibrium between the two departments. But if he had done so, it would run completely counter to what he had argued up to that point. This is why I said that the one who does not understand Takada's explanation is Takada himself. The one who is suffering from the other's misunderstanding is not Takada but Kuruma; while the one who is beyond hope is Takada, not Kuruma.

∙ ∙ ∙

Finally, in the space available here at the end, let me propose a few other points that seem necessary when further considering this problem.

1. Stating that equilibrium between the two departments can be maintained if the Marxian condition is met is not akin to saying that accumulation will proceed smoothly if the condition is met.
2. Stating that meeting the Marxian condition will bring equilibrium between the departments does not mean that this condition will be met in reality, nor does it exclude the existence of moments that can necessarily make the fulfilment of the condition impossible.
3. Takada's claim that the production of producer goods cannot expand without relation to the production of consumer goods, because 'produ-

cer goods should have the power to ripen the consumer goods', is in itself justified. But this certainly does not contradict Marx's theory of accumulation. In the case of this problem, the greater expansion rate of Dept. I compared to Dept. II is premised on a cumulative expansion of social production, and the cumulative expansion of social production necessarily must be preceded by the cumulative expansion of the producer-goods production department. (Moreover, as long as the productive power of society is a given, the progressive expansion of one department necessarily limits the expansion of the other department.) Given this, if the power of that cumulative expansion were halted, you would be able to perceive the ultimate 'ripening' to the consumer goods from the previously accumulated productive power of Dept. I.

4. One point to emphasise regarding the issue just discussed is that pointing out, in the case of the cumulative expansion of social production, that it is natural for the rate of expansion in Dept. I to be greater than that of Dept. II (based as this is on a natural necessity that applies to any social form) does not signify that there is no contradiction within the cumulative expansion of production under capitalism. But we should be aware that the elucidation of this contradiction is not the theoretical task for Marx in his investigation in Part 3 of Book II of *Capital*.

5. Takada's position that the Marxian condition is insufficient for equilibrium between the two departments has the strange appearance of seeming at first sight to be a leftist revision of Marx, when in fact it arises from a single-minded longing to find fault with Marx (that calls to mind the dialectical notion that what is originally a means takes on such force as to become an aim in itself) and from his seeking (consciously or unconsciously) to reduce the particular historical contradictions of capitalist production to superhistorical, natural circumstances. (Consider how frequently Takada treats the issue mentioned parenthetically in my comment '4' above as a 'technical' problem.)

CHAPTER 16

Method for Unfolding a Systematic Theory of Crisis: A Response to Ryōzō Tomizuka

1   Part 1[1]

Tomizuka-san, I had intended to respond as soon as possible to your article, 'Method for Unfolding the System of Crisis Theory: An Open Letter to Professor Kuruma',[2] which you sent me a copy of last year in a letter dated, I believe, 10 September, but my editorial work for *Marx-Lexikon* ended up taking up too much of my time (as I told you it might in my response to that personal letter). But now that the final volume in the first round of *Marx-Lexikon*[3] is nearing completion, I have time to write this reply. Your article had three sections: (1) Relation between the theory of reproduction and the theory of crisis, (2) Concept of the equilibrium rate of accumulation, (3) Necessity of crisis; and my response will follow that same order.[4]

1.1   *Relation between the Theory of Reproduction and the Theory of Crisis*

The first question you aimed at me takes the following form:

> For example, there is a well-known passage from Chapter 17 in Volume II of *Theories of Surplus Value* that is included as passage {42} under Heading VI in the sixth volume of *Marx-Lexikon* (*Crisis* I) ... in which Marx states that the elements of crisis that are included *an sich* within the pro-

---

1   [Originally published as Kuruma 1975c and republished as Chapter 8 in *Marx's Theory of Crisis* (Ōtani and Maehata, eds., 2019).]
2   [Tomizuka 1974.]
3   [The 'first round' refers to the first 10 volumes of *Marx-Lexikon zur politischen Ökonomie* (including a one-volume index), which were followed by a second round of five volumes on the topic of money.]
4   [In his two-part response to Tomizuka, Kuruma only ended up addressing issue (1) on the relation between the theory of reproduction and the theory of crisis. However, in the discussion included in the third *Marx-Lexikon* volume on crisis (in Chapter 7 of this book), Kuruma touches on issue (3) by explaining his reluctance to use of the expression 'the necessity of crisis'. Issue (2) was responded to subsequently by Kuruma's colleagues Teinosuke Ōtani and Noriko Maehata in an academic presentation and an academic paper republished, respectively, as Chapter 9 and Chapter 11 of *Marx's Theory of Crisis* (Ōtani and Maehata, eds., 2019).]

duction process do not appear within that process but rather 'can only emerge in the circulation process which is in itself also a process of reproduction'.[5] And on pages 8 and 11 of the transcript of the discussion inserted in that *Marx-Lexikon* volume it is stated that the circulation process is *not* referring to the theory of reproduction in Part 3 of Volume II of *Capital* but rather to the 'circulation process of capital' in general presented in the entirety of that volume. This explanation seems rather farfetched.[6]

As is clearly stated in this passage, your first question refers to the discussion included as the insert for *Crisis I* of *Marx-Lexikon*.[7] You refer to two separate parts of that discussion, on page 8 and page 11, but fundamentally the argument centres on the latter, which examines the passages grouped under Heading VII, titled: 'Further development of the possibility of crisis under the circulation process of capital (abstract form of crisis acquires content determination in the circulation process of capital). Nine subheadings with relevant passages from Marx are positioned under that heading, mainly taken from Book II of *Capital*. Many of the passages are from Part 3 of Book II, but there are also passages from Part 1 and Part 2, and some subheadings only include passages from Part 1 or Part 2. This circumstance was borne in mind by one of the participants in the discussion, who made the following remark when considering the meaning of the title for Heading VII and its content:

> [W]e added the clear determination, 'under the circulation process of capital'. All of the problems dealt with under Heading VII must be clarified in the analysis of the circulation process of capital, which of course is dealt with in Book II of *Capital*, from which most of the heading's passages are taken We basically followed the order of development in Book II for including passages concerning the abstract form of crisis acquiring content determination. As I mentioned when we were discussing the method of crisis theory, it is necessary to look at the entirety of Book II of *Capital*, not just Part 3.[8]

This part of the discussion to which you drew attention concerns the explanation of the content of Heading II in *Crisis I* ('The method of crisis theory'), and the following comment seems to be at issue.

---

5   Marx 1989b, p. 143.
6   Tomizuka 1974, pp. 240–1.
7   Kuruma 1972b (ed.). [In Chapter 5 of this book.]
8   Kuruma 1972b (ed.), p. 11.

> Once the analysis of the immediate production process has been completed, we enter the analysis of the circulation process of capital, and there again the possibility of crisis is manifested. This is a point that merits attention. In passage {8} in *Crisis I*, Marx says that the new element of crisis 'can only emerge in the circulation process which is in itself [*an und für sich*] also a process of reproduction',[9] but we should be careful not to view this circulation process as solely the theory of reproduction presented in Part 3 of Book II of *Capital*. Rather, 'circulation process' here refers to the analysis of the circulation process of capital dealt with in the *entirety* of Book II.[10]

The statement above is apparently what grabbed your attention in particular, and you view the warning against misinterpreting Marx's remark about the 'circulation process' being 'in itself also a process of reproduction' as an unjustified, dogmatic statement. But I would like you to understand that this was unavoidable. That part of the discussion is looking at the topic of the 'method of crisis theory', dealt with under Heading II, and considering Marx's remark about the circulation process being 'in itself also a process of reproduction' because of its crucial importance to that question of method. We were concerned that the remark could be misunderstood, so it was necessary to first indicate this possibility. But at that point we could not yet provide the basis for explaining why the anticipated misunderstanding was in fact a misunderstanding. That is first clarified in relation to the passages grouped under Heading VII of *Crisis I*. And since that explanation was to be provided later, we merely issued a warning at that earlier point in the discussion regarding a possible misunderstanding. That was our intention, at any rate. (Since some readers may find it strange, I should mention, although there is no point to explain this to you again, that I did not take part in that discussion for *Crisis I* due to an illness, so unlike the other *Marx-Lexikon* discussions, it was the responsibility of Teinosuke Ōtani.) In the part of the discussion presented on page 11, which you have apparently read since you quote from it, there is the following comment on the editorial policy for the passages grouped under Heading VII:

> We basically followed the order of development in Book II for including passages concerning the abstract form of crisis acquiring content determ-

---

9   Marx 1989b, p. 143.
10 Kuruma 1972b (ed.), p. 8.

ination. As I mentioned when we were discussing the method of crisis theory, it is necessary to look at the entirety of Book II of *Capital*, not just Part 3.[11]

Thus, if you had wanted to clarify the actual situation, you could have examined the content under Heading VII. Had you done so, you would likely have seen that there are many passages from prior to Part 3 of Book II of *Capital*, and that some of the nine subheadings include no passages from Part 3 at all. Seeing this, I think three paths would have been left to you.

First, you could have viewed the existence of subheadings entirely made up of passages prior to Part 3 as demonstrating that the 'abstract form of crisis takes on content determination within the process of the circulation of capital'. Second, if you did not accept this as proof, and insisted that Marx, in speaking of 'the circulation process which is in itself [*an und für sich*] also a process of reproduction', had intended the 'circulation process' to refer to the theory of reproduction presented in Part 3, you could have concluded that he had fallen into self-contradiction. This is because, although according to your own explanation Marx had stated that the further development of the possibility of crisis is only first manifested in the circulation process examined in Part 3 of Book II of *Capital*, he ended up discussing this prior to Part 3. Thus, your question should have been aimed at Marx, but since he is dead and buried, all that can be done is to criticise his contradiction. The third option, if you did not have the courage to make that criticism, naturally would have been to reconsider the validity of your original interpretation of the remark made by Marx about 'the circulation process which is in itself [*an und für sich*] also a process of reproduction.'

However, instead of reconsidering your view, you suddenly pick out a comment from a discussion and ask me to respond to your view that the explanation is 'farfetched?' It's quite troublesome that you put the onus on me to explain a point that you should reconsider yourself. After quoting from the discussion of *Crisis I*, you attempt to reinforce your argument in the following way:

> The issue of the 'realisation of value and surplus value' is fundamentally posed within the 'circulation process as a whole or the reproduction process of capital as a whole' (*Der Gesamt-Zirkulationprozeß oder der Gesamt-Reproduktionprozeß des Kapitals*), and what Marx refers to as the

---

11   Kuruma 1972b (ed.), p. 11.

'circulation process which is in itself [*an und für sich*] also a process of reproduction'[12] is the object of analysis in Part 3 of Volume II of *Capital* ('Reproduction and Circulation of the Total Social Capital'), so that the 'circulation and reproduction process as a whole' must be understood in this sense. It does not seem suitable to say that this only concerns the 'circulation process' in general. Otherwise, why would Marx have used expressions like the 'circulation process which is in itself [*an und für sich*] also a process of reproduction' and the 'circulation process as a whole or the reproduction process of capital as a whole', rather than merely speaking of the 'circulation process of capital'?[13]

Here you again quote the passage about 'circulation process as a whole or the reproduction process of capital as a whole' in an attempt to bolster your argument, and a bit later in your article you quote an extensive passage from *Theories of Surplus Value* that culminates in the following:

> The circulation process as a whole or the reproduction process of capital as a whole is the unity of its production phase and its circulation phase, so that it comprises these processes or phases. Therein lies a further developed possibility or abstract form of crisis.[14]

After this, you write:

> What is at issue for the moment here is the 'further development of latent crisis', which is the further development insofar as it stems from the formal determinations of capital (rather than the mere existence of capital as commodity or money), in distinction from the contradictions inherent to the circulation of commodities and money merely reappearing on the basis of capital's possibilities of crisis [– ?]; and Marx says that the 'elements of crisis' that are included *an sich* within the production process of capital as the production of surplus value are not manifested within that production process itself but rather 'can only emerge' for the first time 'in the circulation process which is in itself [*an und für sich*] also a process of reproduction' (where the issue precisely concerns the 'realisation of the reproduced value and surplus value'). Is it appropriate to say, as was argued in the discussion for the *Marx-Lexikon* insert, that this

---

12 Marx 1989b, p. 143.
13 Tomizuka 1974, p. 241.
14 Marx 1989b, p. 143.

circulation process is the 'circulation process of capital' in general rather than the 'circulation process as a whole or the reproduction process of capital as a whole' presented in Part 3 of Volume II of *Capital* ('Reproduction and Circulation of the Total Social Capital')? If one reads in a normal way what Marx wrote in the last paragraph above [quoted from *Theories of Surplus Value*] – regarding the 'further developed possibility or abstract form of crisis' that lies within the 'circulation process as a whole or the reproduction process of capital as a whole' as the 'unity of its production phase and its circulation phase' that 'comprises both these processes or phases' – it should be self-evident that the 'circulation process' is in this sense precisely the 'circulation process or the reproduction process as a whole' of the total capital.[15]

In the first of the two passages I quoted from your paper, you ask me:

> [W]hy would Marx have used expressions like the 'circulation process which is in itself [*an und für sich*] also a process of reproduction' and the 'entire circulation process or the entire reproduction process of capital', rather than merely speaking of the 'circulation process of capital'?[16]

And in the second you add:

> If one reads in a normal way what Marx wrote in the last paragraph above [quoted from *Theories of Surplus Value*] – regarding the 'further developed possibility or abstract form of crisis' that lies within the 'circulation process as a whole or the reproduction process of capital as a whole' as the 'unity of its production phase and its circulation phase' that 'comprises both these processes or phases' – it should be self-evident that the 'circulation process' is in this sense precisely the 'circulation process or the reproduction process as a whole' of the total capital.[17]

You have sought to persuade me with those arguments but the only thing you have convinced me of is that you hold the fixed idea that Marx was referring to Part 3 of Book II of *Capital* ('The Reproduction and Circulation of the Total Social Capital') in speaking of 'the circulation process which is in itself also a

---

15   Tomizuka 1974, pp. 244–45. Some aspects of this passage are irrelevant to the issue at hand but have been included to present the given context.
16   Tomizuka 1974, p. 241.
17   Tomizuka 1974, pp. 244–5.

process of reproduction' or '[t]he circulation process as a whole or the reproduction process of capital as a whole' as 'the unity of its production phase and its circulation phase', and that you think this is a natural view that everyone must accept, requiring no further explanation. Earlier I noted that the last of the three paths open to you was to reconsider whether your interpretation of the passages quoted from Marx is correct or not, but it seems I cannot hold out any hope on that score. If this was just for the sake of debate, I would merely say that I cannot agree with your unfounded view, but since I have heard that there are many who share your opinion, it is possible that this mistaken view (as I frankly consider it) will gain even wider currency if I do not address it. In order to prevent that from happening, I am going to undertake the troublesome task of conveying my understanding of the passages from Marx in question, even though it is not my personal responsibility.[18]

It seems necessary to begin with what might seem a lengthy detour by clarifying Marx's positioning of 'The Metamorphoses of Capital and Their Circuit' as Part 1 of Book II of *Capital*, which is subtitled, 'The Process of the Circulation of Capital'. In other words, why does Marx begin his examination of the circulation of capital with the metamorphoses of capital and their circuit? The beginning of Book II does not offer any explanation of that reason, but in Book I of *Capital*, at the beginning of Part 7 ('The Process of Accumulation of Capital'), Marx writes:

> The transformation of a sum of money into means of production and labour power is the first phase of the movement undergone by the quantum of value which is going to function as capital. It takes place in the market, within the sphere of circulation. The second phase of the movement, the process of production, is complete as soon as the means of production have been converted into commodities whose value exceeds that of their component parts, and therefore contains the capital originally

---

18   I want to say a word about what seems to me a doubtful use of terminology in your argument quoted above. This is your expression regarding 'the "total circulation process or reproduction process" of the total capital'. (My comment here assumes that you neglected to add 'social' before 'total capital'.) In using the expression regarding 'the "total circulation process or reproduction process" of the total capital', you would seem to be recognizing, on the one hand, that even in the case of the 'total capital' there is a partial 'circulation process or reproduction process' that is not the 'whole', while on the other hand recognizing that even in the case of partial rather than 'total capital' there is a 'circulation process or the reproduction process as a whole'. If that is the case, though, it contradicts the argument you have made. Or perhaps there is a deeper meaning in your use of that expression that my superficial thought has failed to grasp?

advanced plus a surplus value. These commodities must then be thrown back into the sphere of circulation. They must be sold, their value must be realised in money, this money must be transformed once again into capital, and so on, again and again. This cycle, in which the same phases are continually gone through in succession, forms the circulation of capital.[19]

From this we can come to know why Book II of *Capital* on the circulation process of capital must begin by grasping the metamorphoses of capital and their circuit, while at the same time, in grasping that circulation process as such, we can understand the fundamental difference between the 'circulation of capital' and 'simple commodity circulation.' That difference is as follows.

(1) The circuit that 'forms the circulation of capital' is a circular movement that passes through three transformations. Two of those transformations take place in the market (i.e. within circulation), but the other takes place in the process of production. That is to say, the circuit of capital includes, in addition to the original circulation process (the process of buying and selling within circulation), the process of production; or to borrow the expression from *Theories of Surplus Value* that you quoted: 'The circulation process as a whole or the reproduction process of capital as a whole is the unity of its production phase and its circulation phase, so that it comprises both these processes or phases'.[20] This is not something that should be discussed first in Part 3 ('The Reproduction and Circulation of the Total Social Capital') of Book II, but rather from Part 1. (Indeed, anyone who reads Part 1 'in a normal way' should be able to easily grasp this.)

(2) In the three metamorphoses that constitute the three phases of the circuit of capital, the two metamorphoses within the sphere of circulation are themselves, if viewed in isolation, the same as the metamorphoses of the simple commodity; but when viewed as the specific phases of the circuit of capital, a fundamental difference between the two becomes clear. The initial phase M–C in the circuit of money capital is no different from the M–C of simple commodity circulation, but when grasped as the first phase of the circuit of money capital, the C is shown, more specifically, to consist of the elements of production (C = L + mp). In other words, the M–C in the case of capital is not, as in the case of simple commodity circulation, the use of the money obtained from selling one's own com-

---

19 Marx 1976, p. 709.
20 Marx 1989b, p. 143.

modity to purchase some good for one's own life, but rather the stage of preparing for the upcoming production process. The final phase of the circuit of money capital, C'–M', is the same as C–M in content when viewed as a mere formal transformation of value in a given magnitude from the commodity form to the money form, but when viewed as the last link in the circuit of capital, C' is shown to be the commodity that includes the surplus value newly created in the production process, so that the sale encompasses a new condition not seen in the sale of the simple commodity. All of these points are related to the abstract form of crisis acquiring 'content determination' (*Inhaltsbestimmung*) in the circulation process of capital, as I will touch on later.

(3) As I indicated, Marx in the passage quoted from Book I of *Capital* brings up the form of the circuit of money capital, but we learn that this circuit is the reproduction process of money capital, where the capital invested in the form of money passes through three metamorphoses to then return to the money form. (However, since there is the possibility in the case of this circuit of money capital that the capital that returns to the money form will not be reinvested, it should, strictly speaking, be referred to as the 'process of potential reproduction'.)

As noted above, in Marx's prefatory remarks in Part 7 of Book I of *Capital* ('Accumulation Process of Capital'), he indicates that the circuit of capital must pass through the production process (analysed prior to Part 7) and two phases pertaining to the circulation sphere, but he does not offer any further explanation regarding the two phases of circulation. It is naturally assumed (*voraussetzen*) here is that Marx will enter into a detailed consideration of this in Book II. In relation to this, Marx writes the following at the beginning of Book II:

> The circuit of capital comprises three stages. As we have depicted them in Volume 1, these form the following series:
> *First stage*: The capitalist appears on the commodity and labour markets as a buyer; his money is transformed into commodities, it goes through the act of circulation $M-C$.
> *Second stage*: Productive consumption by the capitalist of the commodities purchased. He functions as capitalist producer of commodities; his capital passes through the production process. The result: commodities of greater value than their elements of production.
> *Third stage*: The capitalist returns to the market as a seller; his commodities are transformed into money, they pass through the act of circulation $C-M$.

Thus the formula for the circuit of money capital is

$M-C...P...C'-M'$

The dots indicate that the circulation process is interrupted, while C' and M' denote an increase in C and M as the result of surplus value.

In Volume 1, the first and third stages were discussed only in so far as this was necessary for the understanding of the second stage, the capitalist production process. Thus the different forms with which capital clothes itself in its different stages, alternately assuming them and casting them aside, remained uninvestigated. These will now be the immediate object of our inquiry.[21]

After this, needless to say, Marx goes on to fully examine the 'three figures' of the 'circuit of capital', beginning with a detailed consideration of the 'circuit of money capital', followed by his examination of the 'circuit of productive capital' and the 'circuit of commodity capital', but in the passage quoted above he can be seen as reconfirming the three circuits that were implied in the passage from Book I and discussing how in relation to each circuit there is a further development of the possibility of crisis. We can consider this by following the same order of the three points introduced earlier.

(1) The circuit of capital includes not only the original circulation process but also the production process and is the unity of these processes. This is confirmed quite literally in the following:

The circuit of capital is thus a unified process of circulation and production, it includes both.[22]

Taking Tc to stand for the total circulation process, we can depict the three figures as follows:

(I) $M-C...P...C'-M'$
(II) $P...Tc...P$
(III) $Tc...P(C')$.

If we take all three forms together, then all the premises of the process appear as its result, as premises produced by the process itself. Each moment appears as a point of departure, of transit, and of return. The

---

21 Marx 1978, p. 109.
22 Marx 1978, p. 139.

total process presents itself as the unity of the process of production and the process of circulation; the production process is the mediator of the circulation process, and vice versa.[23]

The real circuit of industrial capital in its continuity is therefore not only a unified process of circulation and production, but also a unity of all its three circuits.[24]

(2) I already indicated two points with regard to this second issue. The first is that the circuit of money capital appears in its first phase as M–C, which is no different, formally, from the M–C of simple commodity circulation, but in the case of the circuit of capital, the M–C is different in essence because it is the metamorphosis of money into the production elements (L+mp) and the preparation for the production process. However, it becomes clear in considering the circuit of capital that the process of the retransformation into the production elements includes an important problem. First of all, during the circuit, the value of the elements of the productive capital can appreciate so that production cannot be initiated at the same scale.[25] This problem does not occur in the circuit of money capital because the M that forms the starting point could be capital invested for the first time. The problem appears graphically in the case of the circuit of productive capital. There the given magnitude of capital value starts in the form of the productive capital that exists as a certain quantity of use values, so there is the problem of whether it can return to the same form of productive capital as before. If the value of the productive materials appreciates during the period of the circuit, it will not be possible to buy the same productive elements as had been purchased at the outset; thus, additional money will have to be newly invested to continue production at the same scale.

In the case of the circuit of commodity capital: $C'-M'<{}^{M-C<{}^L_{mp}\cdots P\cdots C'}_{m}$, the same problem can occur. This circuit begins with C′, not P, but (unlike the case of the circuit of money capital) since C′ in the first phase is the outcome of the $C<{}^L_{mp}\cdots P\cdots C'$ in the circuit that precedes it, the C (productive elements) in the circuit's second phase $M-C<{}^L_{mp}$ necessarily signifies the reproduction of $C<{}^L_{mp}$ within the preceding circuit. Thus, in Book II of *Capital*, Marx first discusses this problem that could impede the normal progression of the process

---

23   Marx 1978, p. 180.
24   Marx 1978, p. 183.
25   In a case where the value of the elements of productive capital depreciates, the value magnitude of the capital necessary to continue production at the same scale would be less, so that capital would be 'released', but this is a problem we will set aside here.

in Part 1, Chapter 2 ('Circuit of Productive Capital'), and then discusses it again in Chapter 3 ('The Three Figures of the Circuit'). This is a problem that must naturally be considered when pondering the 'further development of the possibility of crisis within the circulation process of capital' or the 'abstract forms of crisis taking on content determination within the circulation process of capital'. This is why in *Marx-Lexikon*, under Heading VII ('Further development of the possibility of crisis under the circulation process of capital'), there is Subheading 3: 'Possibility of interruptions in the reproduction of capital provoked by fluctuations in the value of the elements of production'. This subheading includes passages from Part 1 of Book II of *Capital* quoted above, but no passages from Part 3 because there are no such passages there corresponding to the topic. This should of course be understood as meaning that the problem itself, by its very nature, could not have been elucidated in that part of Book II.

There are, by the way, three passages under Subheading 3 from the second volume of *Theories of Surplus Value*, one of which (pp. 516–17 of the *Marx-Engels Werke* edition) begins with the following paragraph from page 716 of Marx's manuscript:

> (A crisis can arise: 1. in the course of the reconversion [of money] into productive capital, [2.] through changes in the value of the elements of productive capital, particularly of raw material, for example when there is a decrease in the quantity of cotton harvested. Its value will thus rise. We are not as yet concerned with prices here but with values.)[26]

This is a paragraph that in Marx's manuscript comes immediately after a passage that you cite after introducing it in the following way:

> The description by Marx in Chapter 17 of Volume II of *Theories of Surplus Value* that we are considering here, as the core of problems pertaining to reproduction and crisis, has great significance to the method for developing a systematic theory of crisis, and is a passage that can be referred when considering the validity of establishing the term 'necessity of crisis'; so for the sake of the convenience of the general reader as well, let me quote a rather long passage from it here.[27]

In the paragraph I quoted, it is clearly written that, 'A crisis can arise … in the course of the reconversion [of money] into productive capital. And in the

---

26 Marx 1989b, p. 147.
27 Tomizuka 1974, p. 242.

Marx-Engels Werke edition[28] around a page and a half taken from manuscript 770a is added here, where Marx examines more closely this possibility of crisis. However, although you speak of the importance of this to the theory of crisis and go to the trouble of including a long passage from *Theories of Surplus Value*, you do not include the part that carries on from that cited passage. This is very odd, but upon further thought it seems to me that you ignored the part where Marx deals with this matter because it does not correspond to the particular bias you have regarding how to treat the issue of the further development of the possibility of crisis under the circulation of capital.

The bias of which I am speaking is your preconceived idea (*Voruteil*) that the further development of the possibility of crisis within the circulation process of capital only pertains to the realisation of value and surplus value in $C'-M'$, which is one of the two phases of circulation that capital passes through in its circuit – along with the phase of $M-C$ $(L+mp)$. I do not know if this is your own particular idea or if you picked it up somewhere else, but the important point here is the basis of that idea, and it seems to me that you make the following misreading of the passage from *Theories of Surplus Value* that you quote. Although it is rather long, I will quote that entire passage, since it is related to the basis of your main objection to my view. Here I am citing your revised translation in which you 'made suitable changes in order to more exactly grasp the meaning of the original passage', but I have added some of Marx's German terms for vital parts in brackets so that the original passage can be more correctly understood:

> However, the issue here [*Es handelt sich aber nun darum*] is to trace the further development of the potential crisis – the real crisis can only be deduced from the real movement of capitalist production, competition and credit – in so far as crisis arises out of [*hervorgeht*] the special aspects of capital which are peculiar to it as capital, and not merely comprised in its existence as commodity and money.
>
> [XIII-716] The mere (direct) production process of capital in itself, cannot add anything new in this context. In order to exist at all, its conditions are presupposed. The first section dealing with capital – the direct process of production – does not contribute any new element of crisis. Although it does contain such an element, because the production process implies appropriation and hence production of surplus value.

---

28   Marx 1989b, pp. 144–45.

METHOD FOR UNFOLDING A SYSTEMATIC THEORY OF CRISIS 417

> But this cannot be shown when dealing with the production process itself, for the latter is not concerned with the realisation either of the reproduced value or of the surplus value.
>
> This matter [*die Sache*] [regarding this problem] can only emerge [*hervortreten*] in the circulation process which is in itself [*an und für sich*] also a process of reproduction.[29]

I think that the passage above is crucial to understanding the way Marx develops his theory of crisis, but what is decisively important is to grasp what *die Sache* in the final paragraph is referring to. In your translation, it is rendered as 'This matter [regarding this problem]' and since right before it there appears the line, 'is not concerned with the realisation of either the reproduced value or the surplus value', *die Sache* can only mean the *problem of the realisation of value and surplus value*.[30] Figuring out how to translate this sentence is no simple matter, but the issue comes down to what *die Sache* is referring to. If I may express my view on the matter, starting directly with my conclusion, I would say that it is *not* referring to the problem of the realisation of value and surplus value that is mentioned just prior, although it encompasses that problem. Rather, it is more generally referring to the beginning of the train of argument where Marx establishes the fundamental problem at hand:

> However, the issue here [*Es handelt sich aber nun darum*] is to trace the further development of the potential crisis – the real crisis can only be deduced from the real movement of capitalist production, competition and credit – in so far as crisis arises out of [*hervorgeht*] the special aspects of capital which are peculiar to it as capital, and not merely comprised in its existence as commodity and money.[31]

In terms of the relation between words: *die Sache* corresponds to *Es heldelt sich aber nun darum*, and *hervortreten* corresponds to the *hervorgeht* that appeared earlier. If that is the case, how can *die Sache* be translated in a way that leaves

---

29   Marx 1989b, p. 143. [Modified translation.]
30   In the Japanese edition of *Capital* published by Ōtsuki Shoten, this part is translated as 'That matter [*sono kotogara*] can only emerge in the circulation process which is in itself also a process of reproduction'. Although this is not as explicit as saying 'the problem', the average reader would imagine that it is referring to the matter indicated immediately prior. In *Marx-Lexikon*, the sentence is translated as, 'That [*sore wa*] can only emerge in the circulation process which is in itself also a process of reproduction', which is not that different from the version quoted earlier.
31   Marx 1989, p. 143.

no room for misinterpretation? That is quite difficult. But if I borrow your own approach of adding words to the translation, it could be rendered as: 'The matter [that was posited above as the problem at hand] ...'; or, to be a bit more concise, 'The matter [posited above] ...'

To avoid possible misunderstanding, I should again note that in saying that *die Sache* should be understand in the manner just explained, I do not wish to imply that this is absolutely correct from the literal meaning of the word. Rather, my point is that, with regard to the term itself, there is no reason for saying that it must necessarily be understood as referring to what *directly* precedes it, as you have done. My point is merely that it could also include what was written prior to that. Without confirming this point, it is not possible to proceed with the matter at hand. What I mean by that is that if the problem is thought to concern the realisation of value and surplus value, as you imagine, then the context of the argument unfolded by Marx prior to and after that point could not be understood at all, whereas the relation does become clear on the basis of my explanation.

Below I will explain my reason for saying this, but first I need to draw attention to the fact that Marx inserted a paragraph break between the sentence 'But this cannot be shown when dealing ...' and 'This matter [*die Sache*] can only emerge [*hervortreten*] ...' I think that the reason he does so is that in seeking to 'trace the further development of the potential crisis ... in so far as crisis arises out of [*hervorgeht*] the special aspects of capital which are peculiar to it as capital', Marx seeks to again state his fundamental understanding with regard to where this development unfolds.

Incidentally, after Marx develops his argument to this point, he makes a digression in the paragraph that follows, again pointing out the limitations of the investigation at this stage by noting that the issue at hand, regarding the 'further development of the possibility of crisis' that can 'emerge in the circulation process which is in itself also a process of reproduction', is still far from actuality, requiring 'further elaboration in the chapter on "Capital and Profit"'. This is in turn is followed by the following paragraph:

> The circulation process as a whole or the reproduction process of capital as a whole is the unity of its production phase and its circulation phase, so that it comprises both these processes or phases. Therein lies a further developed possibility or abstract form of crisis. The economists who deny crises consequently assert only the unity of these two phases. If they were only separate, without being a unity, then their unity could not be established by force and there could be no crisis. If they were only a unity without being separate, then no violent separation would be possible

implying a crisis. Crisis is the forcible establishment of unity between elements that have become independent and the enforced separation from one another of elements which are essentially one.[32]

In the *Marx-Engels Werke* edition, this is followed by a passage inserted from manuscript 770a of around one printed page and a half in length. Four items are included in that inserted passage: starting with an item that provides an overview on the main matters discussed up to that point with regard to the 'general possibility of crisis' or the 'formal possibilities of crisis',[33] and ending with the fourth item on how the '*general conditions* of crises ... as distinct from fluctuations in value, must be explicable from the general conditions of capitalist production'.[34] I think this should be seen not as a step forward in unfolding the problem at hand, but as a preparation for taking the next step. After this, in that *Marx-Engels Werke* edition, there is the following paragraph from page 716 of the manuscript, which brings us back to the main point:

> (A crisis can arise: 1. in the course of the reconversion [of money] into productive capital, [2.] through changes in the value of the elements of productive capital, particularly of raw material, for example when there is a decrease in the quantity of cotton harvested. Its value will thus rise. We are not as yet concerned with prices here but with values.)[35]

Following this, on pages 516 to 517 of that edition, there is a passage from manuscript 770a, where, based on the general description above of how crisis 'can arise ... in the course of the reconversion [of money] into productive capital', Marx further considers the possibility of crisis arising in this 'first phase' of the 'reconversion of money into capital' as a result of value fluctuations in the elements of productive capital, particularly raw materials. This, in turn, is followed by a section inserted from yet another manuscript (page 861a from notebook XIV),[36] but since the upper left corner of that page was ripped, it could not be fully included. The *Marx-Engels Werke* editors offer the following conjecture on the content of the missing part:

---

32   Marx 1989b, pp. 143–4.
33   Marx 1989b, p. 144.
34   Marx 1989b, p. 145.
35   Marx 1989b, p. 147.
36   Marx 1989b, p. 147.

However, it is possible to assume that Marx is discussing crisis arising from 'changes in the value of variable capital'. For example, an 'appreciation in the necessary means of subsistence' resulting from a poor harvest, would lead to a rise in costs for workers 'mobilised by variable capital'. At the same time, this appreciation would lead to 'a decline in demand for *all other commodities*', including those not involved 'in the consumption' of workers. Because of this, it becomes impossible to 'sell these commodities at their value' upsetting the 'first *stage* of reproduction for these products', which is the transformation of commodity into money. As a result, the appreciation of the means of subsistence can lead to 'a crisis in other departments' of production.

The last two lines of this missing part of this page present the following idea summarising the entire subject Marx had pondered; in other words, the idea that crisis can result from the appreciation of raw materials whether 'these materials enter into to the constant [capital] as materials' or enter the cost of workers 'as means of subsistence'.[37]

From this we can see that what Marx is discussing with regard to the possibility of crisis arising from value fluctuations of the elements of productive capital at the time money is reconverted into the elements of productive capital ($M-C < {}^{L}_{mp}$) is the possibility of crisis arising from value fluctuations of the means of subsistence and therefore of labour power (L) – as opposed to the possibility of crisis arising from the value fluctuation of the means of production (mp) within the elements of productive capital. And we can also see from the final paragraph quoted above the commonality of both in terms of arising from a fluctuation in the value of the elements of productive capital at the time of the reconversion of money into productive elements.

Right after the missing part, the case of crisis arising from 'overproduction of fixed capital' is discussed:

> Or they [the crises] are due to an *overproduction of fixed capital* and therefore a relative underproduction of circulating capital.

---

37 Marx 1967, p. 517. [In volume 32 of *Marx-Engels Collected Works*, the following editorial note is included: 'The top left-hand corner of the page has been torn off in the manuscript so that only the right-hand side of the first seven lines has been preserved, making it impossible to reproduce the text in full. From what has survived it can be assumed that the passage deals with crises occurring as a result of changes in the value of variable capital. The passage in question has been omitted from the present volume' (Marx 1989b, p. 147).]

> Since *fixed capital*, like *circulating*, consists of commodities, it is quite ridiculous that the same economists who admit the *overproduction of fixed capital*, deny the *overproduction of commodities*.[38]

Then Marx writes:

> 5) *Crises arising from disturbances in the first phase of reproduction*; that is to say, interrupted conversion of commodities into money or *interruption of sale*. In the case of crises of the first sort the crisis arises from interruptions in the *flowing back* of the elements of productive capital.[39]

This paragraph is the last of the passages transferred from 861a of notebook XIV, after which we return to the order of the previous manuscript (page 716 of notebook XIII), where Marx begins to consider the case mentioned above of 'crises arising from disturbances in the first phase of reproduction; that is to say, interrupted conversion of commodities into money'.

Judging from this, we can see that Marx believed that crisis in this case could be classified into three types: (1) crisis arising from fluctuations in the value of the elements of productive capital, particularly raw materials, (2) crisis arising from the overproduction of fixed capital, and (3) crisis arising from disturbances in sales.

Incidentally, anyone reading the text without any preconceived idea should find it natural that Marx in his description of these three types of crisis is clarifying the results arrived at through pursuing the problem posed at the outset of the discussion with regard to tracing the 'further development of the possibility of crisis' insofar 'as crisis arises out of the special aspects of capital which are peculiar to it as capital' within the 'circulation process which is in itself also a process of reproduction'. Once this has been understood, the relation between the different parts of the passage becomes clear. However, based on your interpretation examined earlier, it is not possible to understand why Marx discusses crisis that can arise from fluctuations in the value of the elements of productive capital during the reconversion to productive capital as the 'first type of crisis', or why after that he offers a simple explanation of crisis arising from the overproduction of fixed capital. This is because you distinguish those two types of crisis from crisis arising from the difficulty to realise surplus value and value (i.e. the third type of crisis described by Marx as 'crisis arising from disturb-

---

38 Marx 1989b, p. 147.
39 Marx 1989b, p. 147.

ances in sales'). Therefore, according to your explanation, those first two types do not belong within in the category of crises that 'emerge in the circulation process which is in itself also a process of reproduction'.

The first type of crisis above, which is crisis emerging from value fluctuations in the elements of productive capital, particularly raw materials, is considered quite extensively in Part 1 of Book II of *Capital*, and through Marx's discussion the degree to which he emphasised this moment of crisis should be clear.[40] Thus, under Heading VII in *Marx-Lexikon* we set up Subheading 3 ('Possibility of interruptions in the reproduction of capital provoked by fluctuations in the value of the elements of production'), where we gathered passages from *Capital* and *Theories of Surplus Value* on this issue. But none of the passages were taken from Part 3 of Book II of *Capital*. As I already noted, this is a fact that was mentioned in the *Crisis I* discussion. Thus, your following criticism is completely off target:

> That explanation [in the discussion on *Crisis I*] seems to have been made to in order to negate the view that the 'developed possibility of crisis' is clarified in Part 3 of Volume II of *Capital*, which has held sway since it was first clarified by Moritarō Yamada in his book *An Introduction to the Analysis of the Reproduction Schema*,[41] but that view is not mistaken if Part 3 is understood as providing an *overview* of the circulation process from the perspective of grasping the process of the reproduction of the total capital. The validity of the view is not negated by the fact that a number of passages outside of Part 3 can be found that have descriptions related to crisis and deal with problems that can be seen as moments of crisis. The crux of the matter, it seems to me, centers on clearly understanding that those moments cannot be grasped as moments determining the 'further development possibility of crisis' (i.e. 'potential crisis ... in so far as crisis

---

40   One reason why Marx paid special attention to this problem in *Theories of Surplus Value* and in *Capital* may have been that he had in mind the great influence that agricultural harvests had on fluctuations in business conditions (as Tooke clarified in *History of Prices*) or the so-called 'cotton crisis' – or if not that, the great concerns of textile owners for the annual cotton crop, as he learned through Engels in particular. Unlike system-makers who treat facts carelessly and are only concerned with an orderly system, Marx always respected the truth and struggled to figure out how to incorporate it theoretically – and I think you would recognise that this is one of his great qualities. If he were alive today, he most likely would have taken a very strong interest in such issues as the influence on the global economy of the recent fluctuations in oil prices (although this is a question of the price and not the value of raw materials).

41   Yamada 1948.

arises out of the special aspects of capital which are peculiar to it as capital'[42]) in Part 1 and 2 of Volume II of *Capital*, where the issue revolves around the movement of individual capital in the circulation process, but rather must be grasped at the logical stage of Part 3, where the intertwined movement of those individual capitals, along with the interlinked circulation of capital and revenue, are grasped as a totality, so that the realisation of value and surplus value is fundamentally considered for the first time.[43]

First of all, although it is a trifling matter, I cannot overlook in a published statement the supposition that an explanation was 'made in order to negate' the view that has been held since it first clarified by Moritarō Yamada. In editing the first *Marx-Lexikon* volume on crisis, I read *Capital* without prejudice to extract passages that seemed to pertain to the issue of the 'further development of the possibility of crisis in the circulation process of capital' or to how the 'abstract form of crisis acquires content determination in the circulation process of capital', and then I organised those passages under the most appropriate headings and subheadings possible. That was my only concern. I was not in the least bit motivated by a petty-minded desire to react to a view held since the time of Moritarō Yamada or to any other view. But even had I reacted in such a way, it would have been ineffectual insofar as the nature of *Marx-Lexikon* is concerned, since only materials written by Marx (and in some cases Engels) are included. If the result has turned out to be incompatible with the position held since the time of Yamada, as you stated, then that is simply the result of the editorial approach just described. From my perspective, your supposition reflects a sort of persecution complex.

Moving on from that trivial matter, I would like to consider the crux of the matter.

First of all, you write that, 'if Part 3 is understood as providing an *overview* of the circulation process from the perspective of grasping the process of the reproduction of the total capital', then it is not mistaken to say that the further developed possibility of crisis is elucidated in the analysis of the reproduction process in Part 3. But can it in fact be said that Part 3 provides an 'overview' of crisis that can emerge through the value fluctuations of the elements of productive capital during the retransformation into productive capital (examined in Part 1 of Book II of *Capital*)? My view is that not only is there no such overview, but such an issue is not even raised in Part 3.

---

42   Marx 1989b, p. 143.
43   Tomizuka 1974, pp. 241–42.

Second, I agree of course that 'a number of passages outside of Part 3 can be found that have descriptions related to crisis and deal with problems that can be seen as moments of crisis', but I cannot agree with your claim that the 'crux of the matter ... centers on clearly understanding that those moments' must be 'grasped as moments determining the "further development possibility of crisis" (i.e. "potential crisis ... in so far as crisis arises out of the special aspects of capital which are peculiar to it as capital")' at the 'logical stage of Part 3, where the intertwined movement of those individual capitals, along with the interlinked circulation of capital and revenue, are grasped as a totality, so that the realisation of value and surplus value is fundamentally considered for the first time'. But isn't the possibility of crisis that can emerge through the value fluctuations of the elements of productive capital during the retransformation to productive capital clearly a 'further development of the possibility of crisis' that 'arises out of the special aspects of capital which are peculiar to it as capital'? Of course, that issue is separate from the problem of the realisation of value and surplus value. But doesn't this demonstrate that the 'potential crisis ... in so far as crisis arises out of the special aspects of capital which are peculiar to it as capital' is not found in the process of the 'realisation of value and surplus value' ($C'-M'$) but rather in the process of the 'reconversion to productive capital ($P...P$), which is the process of the circuit of productive capital; and that therefore it is a fallacy to seek to find the further development of latent crisis in the process of $C'-M'$. At any rate, that is my view. What do you think of this idea?

Another part of your paper that prompted reflection on my part is the following:

> If I say such a thing, Professor Kuruma will likely point to a passage a bit before the passage from *Theories of Surplus Value* quoted earlier, where Marx (after saying that 'the transformation of one capital from the form of commodity into the form of money, must correspond to the retransformation of the other capital from the form of money into the form of commodity ... [so that] one capital leaves the production process as the other capital returns into the production process') notes that this 'intertwining and coalescence of the processes of reproduction or circulation of different capitals is on the one hand necessitated by the division of labour, on the other hand it is accidental, and thus the content determination [*Inhaltsbestimmung*] of crisis is already fuller'.[44] But in this passage

---

44 Marx 1989b, p. 141. [Modified translation.]

Marx is merely trying to say that 'the general possibility of crisis, which is contained in this form [the movement of the formal metamorphosis of commodity circulation] – i.e. the falling apart of purchase and sale – is thus contained in the movement of capital, in so far as the latter is also commodity and nothing but commodity'.[45] *In contrast to that* is the issue of the 'further development of the possibility of crisis ... in so far as crisis arises out of the special aspects of capital which are peculiar to it as capital, and not merely comprised in its existence as commodity and money'.[46] I should have thought that the development of the argument would have been clear from a careful reading of the part prior to the passage quoted.[47]

Setting aside some doubts I have about your interpretation of the citations from Marx, let me state that I cannot figure out why you went to the trouble of refuting an imaginary theory of Kuruma of your own construction. Had you simply looked at the table of contents for *Crisis I*, you would have seen that under Heading VII, 'Further development of the possibility of crisis under the circulation process of capital (abstract form of crisis acquires content determination in the circulation process of capital)', one can find the following nine subheadings:

1. In the circulation of capital M – C is not the object of an individual want but is the element of productive capital L + mp
2. In the circulation of capital, C – M is at the same time C' – M' and the mass of commodities as the bearer of valorised capital must in their totality pass through the metamorphosis of C' – M'
3. Possibility of interruptions in the reproduction of capital provoked by fluctuations in the value of the elements of production
4. The intertwinement and combination of capital and revenue
5. The supply for the capitalist as capitalist exceeds his demand; i.e. the maximum limit of his demand is c + v but his supply is c + v + m. Where does the money for the monetisation of the surplus-value come from?
6. Money hoard (therefore sale without purchase and supply without demand) becomes necessary through the turnover of constant capital. Conditions for the formation of equilibrium in the reproduction process of aggregate social capital

---

45 Marx 1989b. p. 141.
46 Marx 1989b, p. 143.
47 Tomizuka 1974, pp. 247–48.

7. Money Accumulation (and therefore purchase without sale and supply without demand) becomes necessary for the accumulation of capital
8. In a case where the labour period is long (such as for building a railway, etc.) there are purchases without sales and demand without supply
9. 'The inevitable change in the proportion between the two production departments arising from the shift from simple to expanded reproduction, and the difficulties that arise from it [and, *mutatis mutandis*, the same can be said for a general change – whether up or down – in the rate of accumulation].

All of the content of these subheadings concerns matters that naturally must be considered when tracing the 'further development of crisis ... in so far as crisis arises out of the special aspects of capital which are peculiar to it as capital, and not merely comprised in its existence as commodity and money'.[48] Why do you seek to refute an imaginary theory you created, in the manner of Don Quixote, instead of dealing with the subheadings I actually created? Your approach does not make any sense to me. I hope you can understand that this is why I will return now to the main point, without addressing that critique.

(3) The third point concerns the fact that the circuit of the metamorphoses of capital that forms the circulation of capital is at the same time a process whereby capital returns to the form it had at the starting point of the circuit, and in this sense is a process of reproduction. This takes on specific meaning in the formula of the 'circuit of productive capital' as the 'periodically repeated function of the productive capital', which is the manifestation of reproduction in the original sense:

> The circuit of productive capital has the general formula:
> $$P \ldots C' - M' - C \ldots P.$$
> It signifies the periodically repeated function of the productive capital, i.e. reproduction. In other words it signifies that its production process is a reproduction process in respect of valorisation; not only does production occur, but also the periodic reproduction of surplus value. It signifies that the function of the industrial capital that exists in its productive form does not take place once and for all, but is periodically repeated, so that the new beginning is given by the point of departure itself.[49]

---

48 Marx 1989b, p. 143.
49 Marx 1978, p. 144.

Although each of the three circuits of capital has its own significance, all are processes whereby capital returns to the form it had at the outset, and as such can be grasped as a process of reproduction. And since the movement of the realisation of capital involves the three circuits carried out simultaneously, it is also the unity of those forms.

> In so far as each of these circuits is considered as a particular form of the movement in which different individual industrial capitals are involved, this difference also exists throughout simply at the individual level. In reality, however, each individual industrial capital is involved in all three at the same time. The three circuits, the forms of reproduction of the three varieties of capital, are continuously executed alongside one another. One part of the capital value, for example, which for the moment functions as commodity capital, is transformed into money capital, while at the same time another part passes out of the production process into circulation as new commodity capital. Thus the circular form of C' ... C' is constantly described, and the same is the case with the two other forms. The reproduction of the capital in each of its forms and at each of its stages is just as continuous as is the metamorphosis of these forms and their successive passage through the three stages. Here, therefore, the entire circuit is the real unity of its three forms.[50]

> The three forms (I) M ... M', (II) P ... P, and (III) C' ... C' are distinguished in the following ways. In form II (P ... P) the repetition of the process, the process of reproduction, is expressed as a reality, whereas in form I it is only a possibility.[51]

From this, I think it is clear that you were over hasty to write:

> The issue of the 'realisation of value and surplus value' is fundamentally posed within the 'circulation process as a whole or the reproduction process of capital as a whole', and what Marx refers to as the 'circulation process which is in also a process of reproduction' is the object of analysis in Part 3 of Volume II of *Capital* ('Reproduction and Circulation of the Total Social Capital'), so that the 'circulation and reproduction process as a whole' must be understood in this sense. It does not seem suitable to me

---

50 Marx 1978, p. 181.
51 Marx 1978, p. 234.

to say that this only concerns the 'circulation process' in general. Otherwise, why would Marx have used expressions like the 'circulation process which is in itself also a process of reproduction' and the 'circulation process as a whole or the reproduction process of capital as a whole', rather than merely speaking of the 'circulation process of capital'?[52]

However, in order to avoid any misunderstanding, I will respond to the question you pose to me at the end of this passage. As for why, first of all, Marx spoke of the 'circulation process which is in also a process of reproduction', rather than merely the 'circulation process of capital', I would argue the following.

If Marx had only mentioned the 'circulation process of capital', there was a danger that he would have been understood as referring solely to the movement of capital within the circulation process, i.e. $M-C$ and $C'-M'$, in distinction to the production process of capital. If understood in that way, the 'further development of the potential crisis ... in so far as crisis arises out of the special aspects of capital which are peculiar to it as capital' would not be manifested. The circulation process of capital only first manifests itself as such as the circuit of the metamorphoses of capital, and therefore only when grasped as a process of the reproduction of the forms of capital. As I noted earlier, the 'C' in $M-C$, in the case of capital, is the specific commodity: $C(L+mp)$. However, when separated from the relation to the circuit of capital to be seen by itself in isolation, it is reduced to the transformation into money of a commodity with a particular use value; in other words, $M-C$. When seen as the circuit of capital, the issue is posed for the first time of capital value of a certain magnitude starting off from the form of productive capital existing as a certain quantity of use values $(L+mp)$ to then return in the same form as before as productive capital. Therefore, the problem arises of what obstacles to that return are encountered when the value of the elements of productive capital changes during the course of the circuit. In the case of $C'-M'$, similarly, when this metamorphosis is viewed as one link in the total circuit of capital, rather than in isolation, the further development of the possibility of crisis can be manifested, as above. Marx's use of the expression 'circulation process which is in itself also a process of reproduction' should be understood in this precise sense. Your way of understanding, as I have noted several times, contradicts that of Marx.

---

52 Tomizuka 1974, p. 241.

The second point concerns how we should interpret the following passage:

> The circulation process as a whole or the reproduction process of capital as a whole is the unity of its production phase and its circulation phase, so that it comprises both these processes or phases. Therein lies a further developed possibility or abstract form of crisis.[53]

One circumstance concerning this issue is that the expression the 'circulation process as a whole or the reproduction process of capital as a whole' cannot be found in the published version of *Capital*. Another related issue is that unlike in the earlier case regarding the interpretation of 'die Sache', it is not possible to reliably ascertain the meaning from the sentences that come before and after. The passage above appears two paragraphs after the sentence examined earlier ('This [*die Sache*] can only emerge in the circulation process which is in itself also a process of reproduction'). In between them is a paragraph in which the following sentence appears:

> The process of reproduction and the predisposition to crisis which is further developed in it, are therefore only partially described under this heading and require further elaboration in the chapter on 'Capital and Profit'.[54]

This is immediately followed by the paragraph that begins with the sentence under consideration ('The circulation process as a whole or the reproduction process of capital as a whole ...'). In the original order of Marx's manuscript, that paragraph was followed by the paragraph that begins:

> (A crisis can arise: 1) in the course of the reconversion [of money] into productive capital ...[55]

As noted earlier, this seems to indicate the first moment with regard to Marx's description that, 'This matter [*die Sache*] can only emerge in the circulation process which is in itself also a process of reproduction', but I do not know for certain why Marx inserted the passage under consideration about the 'circula-

---

53 Marx 1989b, p. 143.
54 Marx 1989b, p. 143. 'Capital and Profit' here corresponds to the content of Book III of *Capital*.
55 Marx 1989b, p. 147.

tion process as a whole or the reproduction process of capital as a whole'. You declare that, just as in the case of the line, 'This can only emerge in the circulation process which is in itself also a process of reproduction', Marx is referring without doubt to the process considered in Part 3 of Book II of *Capital*, and I have already explained why I think that line does not refer specifically to Part 3. If we adopt your view, it becomes impossible to explain the relation to what follows in Marx's argument. However, I lack your courage to make a definitive statement about what is being referred to

Incidentally, this spring I had the opportunity to look at the first manuscript for Book II of *Capital* and came across the expression *Betrachtung des gesamten Zirkulationsprozesses = Reproduktionsprozesses*. It appears in the following sentence near the beginning of 'Chapter 3' (or 'Part 3' in the published edition of *Capital*);

> Bei der bisherigen Betrachtung des gesamten Zirkulationsprozsesses = Reproduktionsprozess[es] des Kapitals, haben wir die Momente oder Phasen, die er durchläuft, nur formell betrachtet. Wir haben jetzt dagegen die realen Bedingungen zu untersuchen, unter denen dieser Proseß vorgehn kann.[56]

> [In the previous consideration of the overall circulation process = reproduction process of capital, we only considered formally the moments or phases that are passed through. On the other hand, now we have to examine the real conditions under which this process can take place.]

From this we learn the following. First, the 'overall circulation process = reproduction process of capital' was already considered prior to what corresponds to Part 3 of Book II of *Capital*, rather than being discussed in Part 3 for the first time. The second point is that the consideration prior to Part 3 is only a formal consideration of the moments or phases that the process passes through. Third, Part 3, in contrast, examines the real conditions for this process to progress. These three points can be understood without any room for doubt based on the passage quoted above. Thus, it should also be clear that you were premature to declare:

> Within the description in Chapter 17 of the second volume of *Theories of Surplus Value*, where Marx notes that within the 'circulation process as a

---

56   Marx 1988b, p. 302.

whole or the reproduction process of capital as a whole' lies the 'further developed possibility or abstract form of crisis', the 'circulation process as a whole or the reproduction process of capital as a whole' is referring precisely to 'the reproduction and circulation of the total social' analysed in Part 3 of Volume II of *Capital*.[57]

However, judging only from the passage you quote above, it is not clear what specific determination is being expressed by the line about the 'circulation process as a whole or the reproduction process of capital as a whole' with regard to the mere circulation or reproduction process of capital – although it is clear that it is not limited to the case of the total social capital. If this is interpreted as meaning that the circulation and reproduction process of capital is understood comprehensively, rather than partially, as a continual process, then it could be referring to each of the three circuit forms of capital. In that case, it would mean seeing them comprehensively as a continuing process, instead of treating each stage of the circuit separately. However, if that were the extent of the matter, the question arises as to why it was necessary to for Marx to have gone to the trouble to express himself as he did in the passage quoted from *Theories of Surplus Value*. I think that the following sort of explanation could be proposed with regard to this question. Prior to the sentence in question, Marx writes that, 'now the further development of the potential crisis has to be traced', which 'can only emerge in the *circulation process* which is in itself also a *process of reproduction*'.[58] Then, after going on a bit of a digression to mention the consideration of the circulation process or reproduction process of capital and the relation to the subsequent part on 'capital and profit', he returns to the main topic at hand and, before concretely considering how crisis 'can only emerge in the circulation process which is in itself also a process of reproduction', he repeats for emphasis what he said before the digression. And in this case, the meaning of 'circulation process which is in itself also a process of reproduction' and 'circulation process of capital as a whole or the reproduction process of capital as a whole' are the same in terms of content.

There is one sentence in the first manuscript for Book II of *Capital* that is similar to those expressions. There may be other such expressions in that manuscript, too, but I have not had time to read it carefully to determine whether this is the case. The sentence I came across is the following:

---

57   Tomizuka, p. 246.
58   Marx 1989b, p. 143.

Mit der Betrachtung des Umschlags des Kapitals ergiebt sich, was schon an sich in der Betrachtung der verschiednen Umlaufszeit, Produktionszeit under überhaupt des gesamten Zirkulations-und Reproduktionsprozesses enthalten war, eine neue Bestimmung des Mehrwerts.[59]

[With the consideration of the turnover of capital, a new determination of surplus value results, which was already contained in the consideration of the various periods of circulation, time of production, and in general the entire process of circulation and reproduction.]

Judging from this, it would seem that the 'entire process of the circulation and reproduction process' (*gesamten Zirkulations-und Reproduktionsprozesses*) is considered in Part 1 ('The Turnover of Capital') of Book II of *Capital*. For the sake of those investigating the theory of the reproduction schema, I also should note that in this first manuscript Marx makes no use of such schema.

That will have to suffice for dealing with the problem above, so I would like to go on to look at a footnote included in your published article, where you present the following argument:

> In *Marx-Lexikon*,[60] a note is included with regard to the reference [in *Theories of Surplus Value*] to 'the chapter on "Capital and Profit"'. Based on the view of the editors of *Marx-Engels Werke*, the note says that, 'Marx is referring to the part of his research that was later expanded to form Volume III of *Capital*'. However, it seems to me that the chapter on 'Capital and Profit' does not correspond to the entirety of Volume III of *Capital*, which also includes the theory of credit, ground rent, etc. Rather, it seems to correspond to the content under the heading 'Chapter 3. Capital and Profit' that appears from notebook XVI to the beginning of notebook XVII, which follow the notebooks that form *Theories of Surplus Value* (VI–XV), among the 23 notebooks dated between August 1861 and April 1863. 'Chapter 3' corresponds to Part 1 to Part 3 of Volume III of *Capital*, particularly Part 3. I think that in *Capital*, Marx presents his theory of reproduction and accumulation (Marxian system of dynamics) in Part 7 of Volume I, Part 3 of Volume II, and Part 3 of Volume III, each from a different vantage point. From this perspective, I think we can understand well why there would 'require further elaboration in the chapter on "Capital and Profit"'. My

---

59   Marx 1988b, p. 244.
60   [Passage {8} in *Crisis I*.]

view is that Marx's theory of reproduction and accumulation (his theoretical system of reproduction/accumulation) is a pivotal part of the entire system of *Capital* and at the same time the fundamental framework that supports its system of crisis theory.[61]

As is well known, a note from the editors of the *Marx-Engels Werke* edition of *Theories of Surplus Value* mentions that a plan for Book I and Book III of *Capital* was found within notebook XVIII, so I cannot understand why you ignored that plan to bring up the content developed in notebook XVI and XVII that form Parts 1 to 3 of Book III of *Capital*. The fact that the content of those notebooks does not extend beyond the scope of Part 1 to Part 3 of the published third volume of *Capital* certainly does not mean that the planned 'chapter on "Capital and Profit"' was only intended to contain that much content. Rather, it seems to suggest that Marx had only finished that much of the chapter at that point. I fail to see the relation between the fact that Marx in that manuscript had only written up to the part corresponding to Part 3 of Book III of *Capital* and the question of the scope of 'the chapter on "Capital and Profit" that Marx refers to in the passage in *Theories of Surplus Value* as providing a 'further elaboration'. In the plan corresponding to Book III of *Capital*, the 'third section "Capital and Profit"' is divided into 12 headings. Following Heading 6 ('Law of the fall in the rate of profit. A. Smith, Ricardo, Carey') and Heading 7 ('Theories of profit ...'), there are the following three headings:

8. Division of profit into industrial profit and interest. Mercantile capital. Money-capital.
9. Revenue and its sources. Include here the question of the relation of the processes of distribution and production.
10. Reflux movement of money in the process of capitalist production as a whole.[62]

Do you mean to imply that Marx did not yet have this structure in mind when he wrote notebooks XVI–XVII? Unless that is your view, it would seem natural to emphasise the content of that plan, rather than the content developed that 'from notebook XVI to the beginning of notebook XVII', so I am completely at a loss as to what to think. I will have to chalk this up to my own senility and turn to consider the significance to the theory of crisis of the three headings

---

61   Tomizuka 1974, pp. 246–47.
62   Marx 1991a, pp. 346–47.

listed above, which correspond to the part of Book III of *Capital* that follows Part 3, and also ponder whether Marx had that content in mind when noting in *Theories of Surplus Value* that 'further elaboration' would be provided in 'the chapter on "Capital and Profit"'.

Having no way to confirm the extent to which Marx at the time had intended to discuss 'mercantile capital' and 'money-capital', I will have to set aside Heading 8 above, but it is possible to surmise to some degree the content corresponding to Heading 9. Also, it seems unmistakable that the latter half of that heading – regarding the 'question of the relation of the processes of distribution and production' – includes problems related to crisis. In *Crisis 1*, Heading VIII ('Moments that transform the possibility of crisis into reality') includes Subheading 13, which is titled: 'The contradiction of capitalist production wherein the distribution relations that originally arise as the result of production become fixed to conversely enter into production as the prerequisites that condition production'. Under that subheading are four passages from *Theories of Surplus Value*, and the content of those passages can be thought to be what Marx had intended to discuss in the part of the plan introduced above.

The next item in Marx's plan for Book III of *Capital* is Heading 10: 'Reflux movement of money in the process of capitalist production as a whole'. One cannot find a similar heading in the published edition of *Capital*. The content seems to have been used in some form or another for Book II of *Capital*, particularly Part 3, and I do not think you would deny its relation to the theory of crisis either.

You are probably already aware of such matters, which makes it seem even odder that you would insist the reference to 'further elaboration' in 'the chapter on "Capital and Profit"' corresponds to 'to Part 1 to Part 3 of Volume III of *Capital*, particularly Part 3'. You then go on to offer what seems like your own 'trinity formula', in talking about 'Part 7 of Volume I, Part 3 of Volume II, and Part 3 of Volume III of *Capital* ...'. My impression is that you imagine this provides some sort of basis for your argument. While being impressed by your confidence, I could not help but recall the Greek myth of the 'bed of Procrustes'. Although I do not recall the exact story, Procrustes would catch his victims and lay them out on a bed. If someone was too long, he would cut off part of a leg, or if too short, stretch the person out, forcibly adjusting each to the size of the bed. This is the image that sprang to my mind, fatigued from trying to work out your true intentions. I would be pleased, though, if the anguish I suffered was just due to my own senility, rather than your coerciveness. I sincerely hope that is the case.

I seem to have already surpassed the space allotted for this article and also feel exhausted, so I will have to leave it here for now. If I recover my energy, I will ask the editors for permission to continue this critique. Please excuse some of my candid remarks here.

2   Part 2[63]

Although my intention was to continue my response to your published 'open letter' by writing a second article as soon as possible, due to various circumstances the editing of the second round of *Marx-Lexikon* began right away without the originally planned break. Personally, I would prefer to make use of the little time left to me in this world to work on editing the *Marx-Lexikon* volumes, but if I did not respond to all of the questions in your open letter, some might think I am unable to respond and thus conclude (as some already have) that your position is correct. In order to avoid that misconception, and because of the goading of my friends, I feel obliged to continue my counter-critique.

Let me begin by responding to some of the questions in your open letter that my initial article did not address. The first concerns your criticism of the following comment I made in the discussion with the other *Marx-Lexikon* editors for *Crisis II*:

> Granted, in the case of individual capital, for both the depreciation fund for fixed capital and the accumulation fund, C–M and M–C are in fact split. However, if we think in terms of the total social capital, there can be agreement between the overall supply and demand. Not only can they be in agreement, but as long as we are considering the normal progression of the total social capital, that agreement is posited as a precondition. When clarifying how social reproduction is carried out (as in Part 3 of Book II of *Capital*), the question of how the two sides might fall out of agreement is not posed – and should not be posed.[64]

With regard to this, you begin with the following:

> At first glance this seems easy to understand, but if the statement is read carefully and pondered it turns out to be quite difficult to grasp exactly because it is such an oversimplification.[65]

---

63 [Originally published as Kuruma 1976c and republished as Chapter 10 in *Marx's Theory of Crisis* (Ōtani and Maehata, eds., 2019).]
64 Kuruma 1973b (ed.), p. 3. [In Chapter 6 of this book.]
65 Tomizuka 1974, p. 80.

You then proceed to dedicate two pages to speculating on what I was trying to say, offering various interpretations. Many readers are likely to be impressed by your cognitive abilities and the thoroughness of this discussion. Normally I would share that assessment, as someone who has long respected your mental powers, but in this particular case I cannot help but find it strange that you engage in such a lengthy discussion of the passage quoted without considering what immediately followed those remarks. Just after where you cut off the passage, I went on to say:

> The actual overall reproduction process progresses in the midst of continual upheaval, of course, so if we look at investment in a particular facility, it will be more or less concentrated during a particular period, depending on a variety of circumstances, such as the discovery of new markets, invention of new production methods, or the impact of war, etc. Thus, it is not the case that investment is regularly renewed every year, uniformly. This has important significance for the circular movement of capitalist reproduction but is not at issue in Part 3 of Book of *Capital*.[66]

I should have thought that this would make clear my intended meaning with regard to the comment you quoted, without any need for speculation. Did you in fact read this part too? I do not see how you could not have read it, so what exactly was your aim in introducing my comments without including it, so as to create the impression that my meaning was unclear? Perhaps you are right to say, with regard to the part you cited, that I was imprecise in saying that 'the question of *how* the two sides might fall out of agreement is not posed'. Maybe I should have said *in what way* or *why* instead of *how*. Nevertheless, what I was trying to say, and therefore my view on the problem that is outside the realm of Part 3 of Book II, should be easily understood from what was said immediately thereafter. I have heard that you have been making much of your 'debate' with me. Certainly, I would welcome any debate that can bring clarity to important issues that had been unclear, but if the aim is simply to find fault by critiquing abridged citations, it becomes a nuisance for the other person – or at least it seems so to me. Not only is this a waste of energy, but it compels me to write the sort of things that I have just written, which I find truly depressing. This is why my previous response to the points that you seem to have put so much effort into writing remained incomplete. But given the circumstances, as explained

---

66 Kuruma 1973b (ed.), p. 3.

earlier, I am in the unfortunate predicament of having no choice but to continue my response.

Incidentally, the problem I referred to in the discussion as having 'important significance for the circular movement of capitalist reproduction', but not being 'at issue in Part 3 of Book II of *Capital*', is dealt with in *Crisis IV*, which examines the industrial cycle. That volume is divided into five main headings, the first of which, 'Fundamental problems of the cyclical movement of industry', includes three subheadings. The first two subheadings are: 1. What gives production the impetus for its rapid expansion? and 2. Under what conditions is the sudden expansion of production possible? (The third subheading, as well as Heading II, III, and V, can be set aside because they are not directly related to the issue at hand.) The other related part is Heading IV ('Fixed capital and the industrial cycle'), which is made up of four subheadings (that I will not list here). Those are all of the parts of *Crisis IV* that directly concern the issue at hand. I will not enter into an explanation of the relation between them, which I think can be judged from the titles alone, but for clarity's sake I will quote the following exchange from the discussion for *Crisis IV*:

> A: I think we can leave our discussion there with regard to Heading 1 ('Fundamental Problems'), but I would like to ask just one more question before we move on. In speaking of the fundamental problems of the industrial cycle, it seems to me that one of them concerns fixed capital. Could you explain the reason for only treating certain problems as the fundamental ones in *Crisis IV*?
>
> KURUMA: We did not mean to imply that only the included content is fundamental, whereas everything else is not. However, the reason that fixed capital is important to the industrial cycle is that its actual investment is not equal year after year, but rather concentrated during a particular period of time. In considering why this concentrated investment occurs, one must of course first take as one's premise a sudden expansion of production. The issues gathered under Heading 1 are *more* fundamental in this sense. The problems related to fixed capital, as can be seen in the passages grouped under Heading IV ('Fixed Capital and the Industrial Cycle'), are multifaceted, so we set up that separate heading. I hope it is clear that the passages grouped under Heading 1 are fundamental to the problems dealt with in *Crisis IV*.[67]

---

67   Kuruma 1976b (ed.), p. 6. [In Chapter 8 of this book.]

You then consider an important issue concerning the understanding of the footnote that Engels added when editing the second volume of *Capital*. That is a well-known footnote that has been considered by many people to date, but I will quote it again for the convenience of readers:

> Contradiction in the capitalist mode of production: the labourers as buyers of commodities are important for the market. But as sellers of their own commodity – labour power – capitalist society tends to keep them down to the minimum price. – Further contradiction: the periods in which capitalist production exerts all its forces regularly turn out to be periods of overproduction, because production potentials can never be utilised to such an extent that more value may not only be produced but also realised; but the sale of commodities, the realisation of commodity capital and thus of surplus value, is limited, not by the consumer requirements of society in general, but by the consumer requirements of a society in which the vast majority are always poor and must always remain poor. However, this pertains to the next part [*nächsten Abschnitt*]'.[68]

How should this be understood? Engels cites the note after mentioning that it was inserted in the manuscript for 'future elaboration'. And in the note itself, Marx says at the end that this 'pertains to the next part'. The common understanding, of course, has been that Marx is referring to Part 3 that follows. But such an 'elaboration' is nowhere to be seen in that part of *Capital*. Not only is there no 'elaboration', there is no passage that even bears any relation to the issues in question. Given this fact, various discussions of the note have been carried out since the time Book III was published, and you present various sides of the issue from pages 251 to 257 of your article. My impression is that what you wrote was the result of careful deliberation, rather than being a forced argument. However, because of that, the conclusion to your discussion does not present a definitive answer as to how the note by Marx should be understood. Although your discussion stretches on for nearly eight pages, in order to know what you are saying I think the last part of the penultimate paragraph is sufficient. There you write the following:

> [In this note,] I think that Marx is merely saying that the 'realisation of commodity capital, and thus of surplus value' is restricted – ultimately (to be more precise) – by the restricted consumption of the working class.

---

68 Marx 1997, p. 315. [Penguin edition (Marx 1978) p. 391.]

But frankly I cannot help but have some doubts about the definitive statement that this could not or should not have been discussed in Part 3 of Volume II. It seems to me, rather, that this is an issue that cannot be discussed without the mediation of the theory of reproduction in Part 3 of Volume II, which clarifies the intertwining and interconnection of the circulation of capital and revenue. This seems to be what the part added at the end of the note is saying. In addition, considering that Part 3 of Volume II is from the incomplete 'eighth manuscript' that was the final manuscript written for *Capital*, even if Marx did not develop the argument he had originally intended there, it does not mean that it was a problem that was not appropriate to deal with and should not have been dealt with there. Thus, no matter how one might look at it, the idea that the next 'Abschnitt' is referring to Volume III *instead of* Part 3 of Book II is not convincing at all. At best, I think it is nothing more than one of the possibilities that we might consider.[69]

Judging from this, it seems to me that you have fundamentally misunderstood my way of thinking. I certainly am not writing on the basis of a preconceived idea that that Part 3 of Book II of *Capital* should or should not have discussed this or that topic. What I noted was that, no matter where one looks in Part 3 of Book II, no discussion can be found that seems to correspond to what is indicated in the note. One cannot help, then, but conclude that the next part (*Abschnitt*) is referring instead to the published edition of Book III. This is certainly not a farfetched explanation, since up to one point Marx used the term *Abschnitt* to refer to what corresponds to *Buch* in the published edition of *Capital*. In addition, the term *Abshnitt* means some 'part' of a whole, and there are examples in various places where Marx uses the term to refer to parts, whether large or small.[70]

However, you take the opposite approach by starting from the preconceived idea that the 'next part' [*nächsten Abschnitt*] in Marx's note definitely refers to Part 3 of Book II, and then search for some corresponding passage. Even after the search proved futile, you hold tight to your idea on the basis of the following reasoning.

> In addition, considering that Part 3 of Volume II is from the incomplete 'eighth manuscript' that was the final manuscript written for *Capital*, even

---

69 Tomizuka 1974, p. 254.
70 [This issue is discussed in Ōtani 1973.]

if Marx did not develop the argument he had originally intended there, it does not mean that it was a problem that should not have been dealt with there. Thus, no matter how one might look at it, the idea that the next 'Abschnitt' is referring to Volume III *instead of* Part 3 of Book II is not convincing at all.

How you could go to such lengths to read into Part 3 of Book II something that is not written anywhere there is beyond my understanding. Instead of taking that approach, you could have actually looked at what is written in Part 3 to see that Marx provides a decisive solution of fundamental problems that no one prior to him had been able to solve, which is why others had been unable to understand the reproduction of the total social capital. Placing an emphasis on Part 3 of Book II is all fine and good, but I fail to see the point in trying to read into it something that is just not there. You have ended up doing Marx a disservice by showing him too much partiality.

Leaving that aside, recently I have begun to wonder if the great effort you seem to have exerted on this problem has not gone to waste. I say this because new materials have become available that allow us to reconsider the issue concerning footnote 32. What I am referring to is the second manuscript for Book II of *Capital*.[71] As you know, the passage that was inserted as footnote 32 is taken from this second manuscript, but if we look at that original manuscript, we can see that Engels in editing the published edition of *Capital* committed a major mistake that concerns an important point. The decisive thing is that Marx had not detached that passage from the rest of the text to make a note. The Marx-Engels-Lenin Institute kindly sent me one page of the deciphered second manuscript (for the part inserted as a note in *Capital*). In places the meaning is unclear, since it begins in the middle of a sentence and the deciphered manuscript has not yet been subject to further analysis, but I will present it here in the form I received it:[72]

---

71   MEGA II/11 (Marx 2008).
72   I realised subsequently that decades ago, when I was director of the Ōhara Institute for Social Research, there was a request from the International Institute of Social History in Amsterdam to send the microfilm of some materials we had. In return, we asked for the microfilm they had of Marx's handwritten manuscript for Book II of *Capital*, which they sent us right away. I had forgotten about that microfilm, and for that reason ended up requesting the passage in the manuscript from the Marx-Engels-Lenin Institute. But after doing so I remembered the earlier microfilm we had received, and taking a look at it realised it was indeed Marx's second manuscript for Book II. However, as you know, Marx's handwriting is not easy to decipher. Teinosuke Ōtani has been making progress in transcribing the manuscript, and in the near future some of the results of that work will be presented.

Durchschnittsstufenleiter – entziehn dem Arbeitsmarkt ein bestimmtes Quantum Kräfte, das nur aus gewissen Zweigen, wie Agrikultur etc herkommen kann, wo **starke** Burschen angewandt. Ein teil der latenten Arbeiter [blank space] offen [Surplus] Reservearmee absorbiert, deren Druck den Lohn niedriger hält. Selbst [Teile der] gut↔bisher beschäftigte Teile des Arbeitsmarkts affiziert. Hence Steigen der Arbeitslöhne.[73] (der später wieder, in andren Zweigen steigt, wegen des bewirkten Steigens im Preis der notwendigen Lebensmittel.) Das Minimum des Steigens = der grössern Masse variable Kapitals dem grössern **Gesamtlohn**, den jetzt die gesamte Arbeiterklasse erhält. Widerspruch in der kapitalistischen Produktionsweise. Arbeiter als Käufer von Ware wichtig für den Markt. Als Verkäufer seiner Ware – der Arbeitskraft – Tendenz ihn auf Minimum zu beschränken. Fernerer Widerspruch: Die Epochen, worin die kapitalistische Produktion alle ihre Potenzen anstrengt, up to the mark produziert, turn out as periods of overproduction: weil die Produktionspotenzen nur[74] soweit anzuwenden, als dadurch nicht nur **Mehrwert** produziert, sondern **realisiert** werden kann; die Realisation (Verkauf der Waren) des Warenkapitals, also auch des Mehrwerts aber **begrenzt, beschränkt** ist nicht durch die **konsumtiven** Bedürfnisse der Gesellschaft, sondern durch die **konsumtiven**[75] Bedürfnisse einer Gesellschaft, wovon die grosse Mehrzahl stets **arm** ist und **arm** bleiben muss etc. Diese ganze Geschichte jedoch gehört erst in das nächste [Abschnitt[ ]][76] Kapitel.

So weit die grössre oder kürzre Länge der **Umschlagsperiode** von der [wirklichen] **Arbeitsperiode im wirklichen**[77] Sin abhängt, id est die Periode, nötig um das Produkt für den Markt fertig zu machen, beruht sie auf die[78] jedesmals gegebnen **materiellen Produktionsbedingungen** der verschiednen Kapitalan-

---

73 [According to MEGA II/11 (Marx 2008, p. 308), 'der Arbeitslöhne is 'd. Arbeitslohns' in Marx's manuscript. – T. Ōtani.]
74 [This 'nur' (only) is 'nie' (never) in the edition of Book II of *Capital* edited by Engels, creating the opposite meaning for the sentence in which it appears. At the time of writing this paper, neither Kuruma nor Ōtani (who translated the text into Japanese) was aware of the importance of this fact. Ōtani later perceived this significance, after Kuruma's paper was published, and wrote his own paper on this topic. – T. Ōtani.]
75 [According to MEGA II/11 (Marx 2008), the word 'konsumtiven' was not underlined in Marx's manuscript. – T. Ōtani.]
76 [According to MEGA II/11 (Marx 2008), this mark in the manuscript was two large closed brackets. – T. Ōtani.]
77 [According to MEGA II/11 (Marx 2008), 'wirklichen' was 'eigentlichen' in Marx's manuscript. – T. Ōtani.]
78 [This 'die' is 'den' in MEGA II/11 (Marx 2008). – T. Ōtani.]

[... **average scale** ..., withdraw a certain amount of [labour] power from the labour market that can only arise from certain departments such as agriculture etc. in which **strong** young workers are employed. One part of the potential labourers or open reserve army whose pressure keeps down wages is absorbed. This affects even the labour market that had formerly had good employment conditions. Hence, rising wages. (then later again, as a result of rising prices of necessary means of subsistence caused by this, wages rise in other departments as well.) The minimum of this increase = the larger mass of variable capital, the greater **total wage** received by the entire working class. A contradiction of the capitalist mode of production. Workers as commodity buyers are important to the market. But as sellers of their commodity – labour power – there is a tendency to limit them to the minimum. Further contradiction: The periods in which capitalist production expends all of its potential force to produce up to the limit turns out as periods of overproduction: because the potential power of production can only[79] be applied to the extent that it not only produces **surplus value** but also can **realise** it. However, the realisation (commodity sale) of commodity capital and of surplus value as well is **limited** and **restricted**, not by the **consumption** demand of society but by the consumption demand of a society in which the great majority is *poor* and must remain *poor*. However, this whole matter will first be dealt with in the next [part chapter.

In as much as the greater or lesser length of the **turnover period** depends on the [real] **working period in the strict sense**, i.e. the period needed to prepare the product for the market, it depends on the **material conditions of production** in the various spheres of capital investment, as these are given at the time.][80]

---

79 [The original text from Marx's manuscript – 'weil die Produktionspotenzen *nie* soweit anzuwenden, als dadurch nicht nur Mehrwert produziert, sondern realisiert warden kann ...' (because the potential power of production can *only* be applied to the extent that it not only produces surplus value but also can realise it ...) – is altered in the Engels edition of Book II of *Capital* by changing *nie* to *nur*, thus creating the following meaning: 'because the potential power of production can *never* be applied to the extent that it not only produces surplus value but also can realise it'. – T. Ōtani.]

80 [An original translation of the German manuscript, with reference to the Japanese translation by Teinosuke Ōtani (Ōtani and Maehata, eds., 2019, p. 366), with the exception of the final paragraph that corresponds to the content of the published edition of Book II of *Capital* (Marx 1978, p. 391).]

First, I want to say a word about a few questions that arise from reading this passage. The passage from the manuscript is presented as we received it, including a blank space that is probably a place where Marx's handwriting could not be deciphered.[81] The words in brackets, [Surplus], [Teile der], [Abschnitt] and [wirklichen] are words that Marx wrote and then deleted. The person transcribing the text made a mistake and typed 'gut bisher' instead of the 'bisher gut' as Marx had written, and the arrows indicate the need to reverse the order. Those are points I wanted to note to avoid misunderstanding, and among them was Marx's deletion of 'Abschnitt' to replace it with 'Kapitel'. But one thing that was strange in this case is that in the transcription of the manuscript the definite article 'das' seems to be included from the outset, which would make it naturally seem that Marx had written 'Kapitel' initially rather than 'Abschnitt'. However, I think this must have been a case where he had just written the abbreviation 'd.' and the person deciphering the text added the 'as' to make 'das'.[82]

What is clear from the passage to begin with is that in footnote 32 from the second volume of *Capital* edited by Engels, 'the next part [*Abschnitt*]' is referring to Part 3 of the same volume, since *Abschnitt* in the published edition corresponds to *Kapitel* (chapter) in the second manuscript for Book II. This has eliminated the problem of what the 'next part' is referring to in the note.

What becomes clear at the same time is that the passage that Engels adds as footnote 32, preceded by his description of it as a 'note for future elaboration' that is 'inserted in the manuscript', does not appear as such in Marx's

---

81   The blank space (in the sentence 'Ein teil der latenten Arbeiter [blank space] offen [Surplus] Reservearmee absorbiert, deren Druck den Lohn niedriger hält.') was later presented in the published text of the second manuscript for MEGA II as: 'Ein Theil der latenten Arbeiterarmee od. offnen Reservearmee absorbirt, deren Druk den Lohn niedriger hält' (MEGA II/11, S. 308.) ['A downward pressure is exerted on wages by the absorption of part of the latent army of labourers or the unemployed reserve army'. – T. Ōtani.]

82   [The editors deciphering texts in Moscow took the approach in the case of the abbreviation 'd.' of deciding whether it should be *der*, *die*, or *das*. Because of this approach, there were cases where mistakes were made. In this particular case pointed out by Kuruma, Marx had in fact used the abbreviation 'd.' so it was not a case of changing the accusative masculine article 'den' to the accusative feminine 'das'. (In addition, Marx had erased the 'n' from the adjective *nächsten* to change it to *nächste* in line with that other change). In short, Kuruma's supposition in this case was correct. For many years, the MEGA editors followed that practice of determining what definite article Marx was referring to, but at the international conference held to decide editorial practices when the responsibility for MEGA passed over to the Internationale Marx-Engels-Stiftung [in 1990], a proposal by Ōtani was adopted to underline part of the article filled in by the editor, and that policy has been followed for all of the manuscripts published for MEGA since then. – T. Ōtani.]

own manuscript, where it in fact carries on from the main text. Therefore, in the final line in the published edition of *Capital*, 'Dies gehört jedoch erst in den nächsten Abschnitt' (However, this pertains to the next part), the 'Dies' seems to refer not only to the content of the fragment that Engels positioned as footnote 32 but to the entire problem that Marx had been discussing in that part of his manuscript.[83] This view seems natural, rather than arbitrary, if we also consider the fact that the 'Dies' in the published version was 'Diese ganze Geschichte' [this whole matter] in the original manuscript. In order to confirm this, I looked at the part of the first manuscript corresponding to this same passage and (although it does not have the same content as that of footnote 32 in the published edition of Book II) it does say at the end, 'Die ganze Bemerkung gehört in ch. III vom Reproduktionsproceß' (Everything mentioned here belongs to chapter 3 on the *reproduction process*). Since the description in the first manuscript is quite different from the second manuscript, here I will quote a somewhat lengthy passage to avoid any possible confusion.

> Ausser dem Einfluß des Verhältnisses **von circulirendem** und **fixem** Capital kommt in Betracht der längre Aufenthalt in dem **Productions-proceß**; der aus doppelten Gründen herrühren kann:
> **Entweder: Verschiedne Länge des Arbeitsprocesses obgleich continuirlich**, dauert länger, um das **Product** fertig zu machen. Mehr Zeit ist erheischt, um ein Haus zu bauen, also x lbs Garn zu spinnen. Manche Productionen von fixem Capital, z. B. Eisenbahnen, (auch Vieh etc) mögen sich über ein Jahr und mehr erstrecken. Kein Theil des Products kann in die Circulation eingehn, oder also Gebrachswerth dienen. Das ganze vorgeschossene Capital realisirt sich in einem Product, dessen Arbeitsproceß über das Maaß der Umschlagszeit, der Jahreszeit sich hier ver-

---

83 [Based on the page of deciphered text he was working with, Kuruma could only know at the time that a line break came after the sentence 'Diese ganze Geschichte jedoch gehört erst in das nächste Kapitel' (However, this whole matter will first be dealt with in the next chapter') and that it was thus the last sentence of a paragraph. If we look at the published edition of the manuscript (MEGA II/11) we can see that this was a long, 83-line paragraph that begins on line 21 on page 304 and continues until line 21 on page 308 (although page 305 is taken up with photo of the manuscript and no text and page 306 is blank). Moreover, the bracket that is missing from the page of text Kuruma was referring to closes a 26-line portion of bracketed text that stretches from line 37 on page 307 to line 211 on page 308. What Kuruma refers to as the 'entire problem that Marx had been discussing in that part of his manuscript' could correspond to the entire paragraph or more limitedly to the bracketed text. – T. Ōtani.]

längert. [Diese so engagirte Arbeit liefert also **kein** Product das während des Jahres circulationsfähig ist, oder in die **Masse der Producte** eingeht, die die jährliche Revenu bilden, oder als Productionselement in einen neuen Productionsproceß eingehn kann. Der so während des Jahres angewandte Theil der nationalen Arbeit, ersetzt also nicht während des Jahres angewandte Theil der nationalen Arbeit, ersetzt also nicht während des Jahres die consummirten Lebensmittel der Arbeiter, oder die used up raw materials, machinery u. s. w. Es stellt sich während des Jahres in keinem nutzbaren Gebrauchswerth dar, auch in der Circulationsfähigen Form des Werths. Dieß spielt eine Hauptrolle bei der sogenannten **Conversion of circulating into fixed capital**. Die so angewandte Arbeit mag noch so productiv sein ihrer Bestimmung nach; diese bildet kein Element des Consumtions- oder Reproductionsprocesses während des Jahres. Sie befähigt die Nation weder während des folgenden Jahres zu leben, noch die aufgenutzten Productionsmittel zu ersetzen. Sie bildet auch kein Product, das im Verlauf des Jahres oder nach Ende des Jahres ins Ausland geschickt und dort für Lebens oder Productionsmittel ausgetauscht werden kann. Nähme sie also einen unproportionellen Theil der jährlichen Gesammtarbeit ein, so existirte am Ende des Jahre sein unverhältnißmässig grosser Theil der labor spent in einer Form momentan nutzlos, so weit dert Gebrauchswerth, und unrealisirbar, so weit der Tauschwerth in Betracht kommt; während der Theil des Gesammtproducts, woraus Capital ersetzt, nur accumulirt, der Consumtionsfonds erneuert werden muß, zu klein wäre. Mit Ausnahme einiger Luxusartikel, ist es immer fixes Capital, dessen Production die Jahresfrist so überschreitet. (mit Vieh auch der Fall) Ein zweiter Umstand kommt bei diesem fixen Capital hinzu. Besteht es in Baulichkeiten, Docks, Brücken, Eisenbahnen, Kanälen, und selbst improvements fixed in the soil (such as drainings oder clearings, Bewässerungsanstalten u. s. w.), so eigne Art, worin sie Revenu abwerfen. (Dieß gehört jedoch nich hierher. Die ganze Bemerkung gehört in ch. III vom **Reproductionsproceß**.)]

Oder: **Underbrechung der Arbeit während des Productionsprocesses**, aber **bedingt** durch denselben.[84]

[In addition to the influence of the proportion between **circulating** and **fixed** capital there is also the problem of the longer stay within the **production process** that can arise for two reasons:

---

84   Marx 2008, pp. 290–91.

Either: Different lengths of the labour process, even if carried out continually, take longer to finish the **product.** It takes more time to build a house than to spin X pounds of yarn. Most production with fixed capital, e.g. railways (also cattle, etc.) may extend to a year or more. No part of the product [in this case] can enter into circulation or be useful as use value. Here the entire capital advanced is realised in a product, whose labour process is extended beyond the one-year turnover time. [Thus, the labour thus engaged does not supply **any** product capable of circulating during that year, or that can enter the **mass of products** that form the annual revenue, or *any* product that can enter some new production process as an element of production. Therefore, this portion of the annual national labour expended does not replenish the means of production consumed by the workers that year or the used-up raw materials, machinery, etc. During the year it does not appear in any useful use value or in any form of circulating value. This plays a major role in the so-called **conversion of circulating into fixed capital.** No matter how productive this expended labour might be with regard to its planned purpose, it does not constitute an element of the reproduction process during that year. It does not provide the nation with the means of subsistence during the next year nor does it replace the used-up means of production. Nor is it a product that can be sent abroad in the course of the year after the end of the year and exchanged for means of subsistence or production. Therefore, if that labour takes up a disproportionately large part of the total labour of that year, at year's end this disproportionately large amount of labour expended would exist in a form that would be useless as far as use value is concerned and not realizable as far as exchange value is concerned; meanwhile, the part of the total product that has to replenish capital simply accumulates, and the part of consumption funds that must be renewed, would be too small. With the exception of a few luxury goods, the production that exceeds one year is always fixed capital. (Livestock also included therein.) A second circumstance comes with this fixed capital. When capital takes the form of buildings, docks, bridges, railways, and canals, and even improvement fixed in the soil (such as drainings, clearings, irrigation facilities, etc.), then there is a special way in which they earn revenue. (But that is not at issue here. Everything mentioned here belongs to chapter 3 on the **reproduction process.**)]

Or: Interruption of work that arises during the production process, but **conditioned** by that production process.]

We can see that the content here differs significantly from the second manuscript (upon which the published edition of *Capital* was based), but both manuscripts address the circumstances that arise from the establishment of fixed capital necessary for production carried out over a long period of time. Whereas in the second manuscript there is the supplemental part that was later inserted as footnote 32 in the published edition of *Capital*, no such passage exists in the first manuscript at all; instead there is the passage that begins with 'Ein zweiter Umstand ...' (A second circumstance ...). What both manuscripts have in common is the final reference to the 'next chapter' (corresponding to Part 3 in the published edition).

If we set aside the comparison of what problems are generally dealt with in the two manuscripts as well as the conclusions reached, it at least seems clear that the common indication of what pertains to a third 'chapter' (or 'part') does not correspond to the content of footnote 32.

Once we have understood that the content included as footnote 32 was added to the second manuscript and did not exist in the first manuscript, the question becomes what relation this addition has to the overall discussion in that part of the manuscript. My view is that what is written there is not completely separate from what was written before but is rather an addition to deal with a problem that naturally arises in relation to that previous content. Severing this segment from what comes before and positioning it as an independent footnote in the published edition not only obscures the relation to the earlier part but also makes it seem that the reference at the end of the footnote to the 'next part' only concerns the content of the footnote. This has spawned many brilliant theories, but as I noted earlier, they seem to end up in pointless discussions by starting from mistaken presumptions.[85] Various other problems remain regarding the line that 'this pertains to the next part', but I will not go further into this here and rather move on to the next problem.

The next problem to consider is the argument that spans from page 257 to 261 in your article. Whereas the discussion of the previous problem was not fruitless, since it had objective significance for solving the problem raised regarding the understanding of footnote 32 and did not get lost in digressions, the same cannot be said of this next problem, so it is with a heavy heart that I pick up my pen, resigned to my fate. You begin with the following:

> Finally, I want to pose to you the following question regarding the relation between the theory of reproduction and the theory of crisis. This concerns the great emphasis you place on the issue of the change in

---

85 [Now that we can read the entire second manuscript for Book II of *Capital*, it is clear that the speculation Kuruma presents in this paragraph was not off target. – T. Ōtani.]

the proportion between the two departments that accompanies the shift from simple to expanded reproduction, which you generalise, so to speak, by raising the proposition that the proportion between the departments changes along with the change in the rate of accumulation, and that this change presents 'certain difficulties', insisting that this is the main topic addressed by Part 3 of Volume II of *Capital*, which also elucidates the significance of the theory of reproduction vis-à-vis the theory of crisis.[86]

Here you argue that I raise 'the proposition that the proportion between the departments changes along with the change in the rate of accumulation and that this change presents "certain difficulties"', and insist that 'this is the central problem addressed by Part 3 of Volume II of *Capital*', but it is not true that I hold or have ever held the outrageous view that that is the 'main topic' of Part 3. As is perfectly clear from the title of Part 3, the 'main topic' is to clarify the process of the reproduction and circulation of the total social capital. The most fundamental problem that must be clarified to begin with is how the reproduction of constant capital is carried out. This is a problem that no one from the time of Adam Smith onward had been able to clarify, making it impossible to understand the reproduction of the total social capital.

Granted, it is true that in drawing on the results of Marx's investigation developed in Part 3 to better understand crisis (and the industrial cycle in particular), I thought it necessary to place more emphasis on what Marx wrote about the case of a change in the accumulation rate, which has been surprisingly overlooked. For that reason, I included Subheading 9 in *Crisis I* ('The inevitable change in the proportion between the two production departments arising from the shift from simple to expanded reproduction, and the difficulties that arise from it [and, *mutatis mutandis*, the same can be said for a general change – whether up or down – in the rate of accumulation]'). Grouped under this subheading are five passages from Part 3 of Book II of *Capital*, but if you think that this means I 'insist' on this as the 'main topic' of Part 3, I stand in amazement at your extraordinary powers of imagination.

After starting off in that manner, you then devote the next three pages to unfolding all sorts of arguments. I should have liked to summarise them, followed by my response to each, but to do so would run the risk of being taken to task for incorrectly conveying your ideas, so I will have to use a good deal of the limited space here to quote that lengthy passage in full. However, in order to

---

86   Tomizuka 1974, p. 257.

avoid citing the same passages again later, I have inserted numbers in brackets, from [1] to [6], to indicate the parts that I will address:

> The proportion between the departments changes along with the change in the accumulation rate. 'Friction' and 'difficulties' accompany the change in the proportion between the departments. And you argue that in this way that 'the abstract form of crisis acquires content determination'. But isn't such a way of arguing ultimately an attempt to see the content of the 'expanded possibility of crisis' as solely involving the difficulty of the movement of capital between the departments? [1] Based on this line of argument, the rate of accumulation is said to be the 'independent variable' and the proportion between the departments the 'dependent variable'.[87] But is it in fact correct to take an arbitrary value for the rate of accumulation – 'arbitrary' in the sense of not being restricted by the 'conditions of reproduction', even though it is determined by such factors as the rate of profit and interest – and then argue that it is fine (even if accompanied by friction and difficulties) as long as the proportion changes between the departments in line with this figure. [2] If that sort of argument is correct, overall, then the concept of overaccumulation (*Überakkumulation*) – which is I think a central concept within Marx's theoretical system of crisis – would be something that could not be determined from the aspect of the problem of 'realisation' related to the 'conditions of reproduction'. If one unconditionally establishes the proposition that the situation is fine no matter how high the rate of accumulation may rise, provided that the proportion between the departments is adjusted, then there would be no way for 'overaccumulation' to exist. [3] Conversely, this logic would suggest that even if a 'major problem' arises from a 'precipitous drop' in the rate of accumulation, it could be dealt with by a change in the proportion between the departments in the opposite direction (with capital shifting from Dept. I to Dept. II)? [4] If one were to generally and unconditionally accept this logic, it would be impossible, first of all, to grasp 'overaccumulation' as something that should result from a 'sudden drop in the rate of accumulation', or to clarify the process in which 'comprehensive overproduction would be manifested through this 'precipitous drop' in the rate of accumulation'. [5] Thus, it seems to me that the proposition itself must be reconsidered. However, it is a fact that in the real process of the capitalist economy, the rate of accumulation

---

87 Kuruma 1972b (ed.), p. 19.

is continually changing, and in line with these changes the proportion between the departments also changes. Therefore, to that extent, the proposition can be said to reflect one aspect of a phenomenal process of the capitalist economy. I am not seeking to deny this. Nonetheless, it seems problematic to treat this proposition as having general and unconditional validity by viewing it as a 'general law of reality' and positioning it as the main topic of Part 3 of Volume II of *Capital*. I say this because the view is almost identical in content to the position held by Tugan-Baranowsky, apart from some differences in the manner of expression. For instance, in his book *Studies on the Theory and the History of Business Crises in England*, Tugan-Baranowsky writes:

> 'By comparing simple and expanded reproduction of social capital, one can draw a very important conclusion: In the capitalist economy, the demand for commodities is, in a sense, independent from the total magnitude of social consumption. The latter can decline and, at the same time, the global social demand for commodities can grow, as absurd as this may appear from the standpoint of "common sense". The accumulation of social capital leads to a reduction in the social demand for means of consumption and, at the same time, to an increase in the total demand for commodities'.[88]

The increase in the total social demand spoken of here is related to his claim after this that the total social commodity production in the second year (expanded production) 'rose considerably' compared to the first year of simple reproduction but that the 'production of means of consumption declined without at all disturbing the equilibrium between supply and demand'.[89] Whereas Tugan-Baranowsky argues from the perspective of the change in the structure of social demand, Professor Kuruma develops his argument from the perspective of the rate of accumulation 'going from zero to a positive', so there are differences in the manner of expression regarding this point, but in terms of content it basically comes down to the same thing. This is because the change in the structure of social demand arises precisely from the change in the rate of accumulation. Both of them totally coincide: whether the generalisation of the logic of the shift from simple to expanded production, or the idea that the

---

88   Tugan-Baranowsky 2000, p. 71.
89   Tugan-Baranowsky 2000, p. 72.

change in the accumulation rate (and the accompanying change in the total social demand) can be accommodated as long as the 'distribution of social production' (*die Einteilung der gesellschaftlichen Produktion*) – i.e. the 'proportion between the departments' – is adjusted (even if 'Clearly, this is not an easy thing'[90]). This is why in my recent letter addressed to Professor Kuruma I asked him the extent to which he had been conscious of Tugan-Baranowsky's explanation in stating that the rate of accumulation is the 'independent variable' and the proportion between departments the 'dependent variable'. (According to the answer I received, he had not had that explanation in mind at all; but given the strong resemblance between the two arguments, an explanation would be welcome (not only for me but for the general reader) regarding the similarities and differences between his explanation and that of Tugan-Baranowsky). [6] Of course, I am not trying to say that Professor Kuruma's explanation is completely mistaken on the sole basis that it is in essence the same as the explanation of Tugan-Baranowsky. I think that the explanation of Tugan-Baranowsky has value in highlighting one aspect of the reality of the capitalist economy. But it seems mistaken to one-dimensionally adhere to that proposition as the 'approach to the capitalist economy'. What is clarified in Part 3 of Volume II of *Capital* is in fact the very opposite of such a proposition: namely, that an arbitrary amount of accumulation or rate of accumulation cannot be taken as the 'condition of reproduction'. This is closely related to whether the concept of an 'equilibrium rate of accumulation' can be established, which is the topic I will address in the next section of this paper.[91]

Regarding point [1]

A simple look at the table of contents of *Crisis I* should have left no room for the doubt you express. Does this mean that you did not even bother to examine the contents of the volume of *Marx-Lexikon* you are critiquing? A glance at the contents would reveal Heading VII, titled 'Further development of the possibility of crisis under the circulation process of capital (abstract form of crisis acquires content determination in the circulation process of capital)'. Under this heading are nine subheadings, the final one of which addresses this issue you raise regarding the change in the rate of accumulation. You

---

90 Tugan-Baranowsky 2000, p. 69.
91 Tomizuka 1974, pp. 258–61.

should have been able to realise, in other words, that besides that particular subheading there are eight others dealing with the 'further development of the possibility of crisis'. When you ask whether 'such a way of arguing ultimately come[s] down to the attempt to see the content of the "expanded possibility of crisis" as solely involving the difficulty of the movement of capital between the departments', is this because you think that 'ultimately' the first eight subheadings 'come down' to the content of the ninth? (Just looking at the titles of the subheadings should demonstrate that such a view is untenable.) I cannot fathom why you would pose such a question and can only stand in silent amazement, once again, before your extraordinary powers of imagination.

Regarding point [2]

My argument is not along the lines that '*it is fine as long as the proportion changes* between the departments' at the very least. What I am saying is that if the rate of accumulation changes, the proportion between the departments *must change*.

Regarding point [3]

This idea that overaccumulation could not occur appears as the immediate result (or benefit?) of your misunderstanding with regard to [1] and [2] (setting aside the possibility that I am the one who has misunderstood an exceptional explanation beyond the grasp of ordinary minds). If one *assumes* that I hold the outrageous view that 'no matter how high the rate of accumulation may rise' everything will be fine 'provided that the proportion between the departments is adjusted', then indeed there would be 'no way for overaccumulation to exist'. But this *assumption* is a fiction you created, unrelated to my own view, as should be clear from what I have already written with regard to [1] and [2].

From those explanations it should be clear how outrageous it is to suppose that there would be 'no way for overaccumulation to exist' under my way of thinking, but of course even if that point is clear, it does not clarify why 'overaccumulation' does occur. It would also be a terrible error, however, to think that this question of 'why' could or should be elucidated in Book II of *Capital*. This issue is rather first discussed in Chapter 15 of Book III, where Marx examines the development of the contradictions of the law of the tendential fall in the rate of profit. At the stage of Book II, in contrast, this question is completely set aside since it is premised on a series of other laws (such as the transformation of surplus value and the rate of surplus value into profit and the rate of profit, the development of the productive power of labour, the rise in the organic composition of capital, the tendential fall in the rate of profit, the movement to compensate for that fall through a greater quantity of profit, and the intensification of competition). The question of *why* overaccumulation arises is only first discussed, and can only first be discussed, once those other issues have been elucidated. However, the question of *why* regarding overaccumulation, is not the same as the question of *what* overaccumulation itself is. Marx addresses this latter question in the following way in his draft for Book III of *Capital*:

> Overproduction of capital (=plethora of capital) and not of individual commodities (although this overproduction of capital always involves the overproduction of commodities) is nothing more than over-accumulation of capital. To understand what this over-accumulation is (a closer investigation of it will form part of our consideration of the apparent movement of capital in which interest capital, etc., and credit, etc., will be examined in more detail) we have only to take it as an absolute. *When would* the overproduction of capital be absolute? And indeed we refer there to an overproduction which does not just extend to this or that or a few major areas of production, but is rather itself absolute in scope, so that it involves all fields of production.
>
> There would be an absolute overproduction of capital as soon as the amount of additional capital that could be employed for the purpose of capitalist production became equal to 0. But the purpose of capitalist production is the valorisation of capital, i.e. the production of surplus value, of profit, the appropriation of surplus labour. Thus as soon as capital has grown in such proportion to the working population that neither the absolute labour time that this working population supplies nor its relative surplus labour time can be extended (the latter would not be possible in any case in a situation where the demand for labour was so strong, and there was thus a tendency for wages to rise); *where*, therefore, the expanded capital *produces* only *the same* mass of surplus value as before, *or even less* – we are speaking here of the absolute mass, not the rate of profit – *than* capital did *before* it grew, there will be an absolute overproduction of capital; i.e. the original C, with the addition of ΔC, would produce only P (this represents the total amount of profit produced by C), or even P – x. In both cases there would even be a sharp and sudden fall in the general rate of profit, but this time on account of a change in the composition of capital which would not be due to a development in productivity, but rather

to a rise in the money value of the variable capital and a corresponding decline in the proportion of surplus labour to the labour objectified in the variable capital.[92]

From this passage we can understand that the problem Marx is addressing is a case where, even if more capital is accumulated, the rise in the demand for labour power that accompanies this accumulation would surpass the increase in the working population, making it impossible to increase the production of surplus value. Not only would an increase in surplus value become impossible, but the rise in wages would in fact bring about a fall in the mass of surplus value obtained. Thus, if this problem, regarding *what* is overaccumulation, is separated from the earlier question of *why* overaccumulation occurs, it could probably be dealt with prior to Book III. From that perspective, it might be possible to go so far as to deal with the overaccumulation of capital in Part 3 of Book II. However, Marx does not deal with that problem there, and only first addresses it in Book III. This is a fact, but we need to consider why Marx took that approach. Such a question naturally arises, and all I can do is imagine that Marx did so because he did not believe that the problem belonged in Part 3 of Book II. But in your case, starting from the assumption that Part 3 is the place for elucidating the sort of cases in which the overaccumulation of capital arise, you propose the establishment of the concept of an 'equilibrium rate of accumulation' to elucidate this. Such a concept, however, is completely alien to Marx's way of thinking. You insist that Marx should have posited the conceptual definition of the overaccumulation of capital in Part 3 of Book II, and to do so you seek to 'establish' that 'concept of an equilibrium rate of accumulation' as the standard for defining overaccumulation, but such a conceptual definition of overaccumulation is completely different from that of Marx.

At the end of point [3] in the passage quoted above, you write that, 'If one unconditionally establishes the proposition that the situation is fine no matter how high the rate of accumulation may rise, provided that the proportion between the departments is adjusted, then there would be no way for "overaccumulation" to exist'. First of all, this attack on me is founded on a complete a complete misinterpretation of my view. Second, you seem to think that Marx should have posited the conceptual definition of the overaccumulation of capital in Book II rather than in Book III of *Capital*. And third, for that reason,

---

92 Marx 2017, pp. 360–1. [Kuruma's emphasis.]

you 'establish' your own 'concept of an equilibrium rate of accumulation' even though the determination of overaccumulation based on it has nothing to do with Marx's own determination. Those are the points I was trying to make above.

Since the next section of your article is where you present the brilliant elucidation of the error in thinking that everything will be fine no matter how high the rate of accumulation rises, thus 'establishing your concept of an equilibrium rate of accumulation' (that purports to show the upper limit beyond which the accumulation rate cannot rise), I will have to leave the consideration of that concept until later, and first deal with the remaining issues concerning the first problem.

Regarding point [4]

The fact that a 'precipitous fall' of the rate of accumulation brings about a 'major problem', unlike the case of a rising accumulation rate, requires little consideration to understand, but you make the facile statement – as your critique of the idea of a major problem occurs in the case of fall (unlike the case of a rise) – that my logic would suggest the fall could 'be dealt with by a change in the proportion between the departments in the opposite direction (with capital shifting from Dept. I to Dept. II)'. Seeing this argument makes me think I was wrong to imagine that the issue would become clear to you upon a bit of reflection, so let me try to explain again in a way that a novice might understand.

In a case where the rate of accumulation increases, reproduction on an expanded scale can be carried out if the proportion between the departments is adjusted to suit the new rate of accumulation. (However, this is not a problem that is handled through the movement of existing capital between the departments – although this point will not be dealt with here.) In other words, in this case, *the issue for the moment* comes down to how the adjustment in the proportion between the departments is carried out. That is not what happens in a case where the accumulation rate drops suddenly, however. The influence in such a case is first manifested in a contraction in demand for products in Dept. I (means of production), and the corresponding decline in 'v' and 's' in Dept. I is manifested in lower demand for products in Dept. II, forcing Dept. II to contract in turn, thereby generating general overproduction. This is certainly not a problem that can be dealt by 'capital shifting from Dept. I to Dept. II'.

Regarding point [5]

Thus, what you write with regard to point [5] is the complete opposite of the natural conclusion reached from my outlook. Far from it being impossible to 'clarify that 'comprehensive overproduction would be manifested through this precipitous drop in the rate of accumulation', it is only through that way of thinking that the actualisation of general overproduction can be clarified.

Regarding point [6]

You make the extremely bothersome request that I explain, for your sake and that of the general reader, 'the similarities and differences' between my explanation and that of Tugan-Baranowsky. Please excuse me for not taking up your request, as I simply lack the energy to go through his book to examine each point and determine what is similar and what is different. Judging from what you have written, however, it seems that the basis for grouping my views together with those of Tugan-Baranowsky is your idea that, like him, I argue that as long as there is a change in the distribution of the social product, which is to say, a change in the proportion between the departments, which corresponds to the change in the rate of accumulation (and to the accompanying change in the structure of social demand), then everything will be fine. If this is indeed your idea, it is based on a terrible misunderstanding of my position. As noted already, I have never claimed that *everything will be fine as long as* the proportion between the departments is adjusted. The problem I posed in the case of a change in the rate of accumulation concerns the change in the proportion between the departments *that must occur* as a result, what sort of change in the proportion between the departments *must occur* in line with the magnitude of the rate, and *how this change is brought about* (through a change in the internal composition of Dept. I).

You seem quite taken aback by me saying that the accumulation rate is the independent variable and the composition between the departments is the dependent variable, but this is not something I came up with based on a personal whim, but rather a recognition of reality. And as long as that is the reality, it is natural – for anyone who thinks the aim of scholarship is to elucidate the state of reality – to clarify what becomes necessary when the rate of accumulation changes and how this necessity is fulfilled. That was my motivation in emphasising this problem. That was also my motivation for creating Subheading 9 in *Crisis I* ('The inevitable change in the proportion between the two production departments arising from the shift from simple to expanded reproduction, and the difficulties that arise from it'). I did so because it seemed to me that Marx's description of the shift from simple to expanded reproduction, surprisingly, had either been neglected, despite its importance, or presented in a distorted manner. The central question in this case is how it is possible to increase the production of the means of production in Dept. I (which is the key precondition since the means of production in Dept. II cannot be increased otherwise) in a case where the scale of Dept. I has yet to expand and thus remains the same as before (i.e. without any premise of an *a priori* increase in the total amount of the means of production). It is clear that if the total amount of the means of production in Dept. I is unchanged from before, any increase in the means of production for Dept. I will come at the expense of the means of production for Dept. II. At the same time, it also becomes clear that as long as this is done (through the reconfiguration of Dept. I – by switching the production of means of production for Dept. II to the production of the means of production for Dept. I), accumulation can be carried out without the premise that the 'surplus means of production' already exist, i.e. without premising the existence of accumulation prior to accumulation. This is the central problem Marx deals with in examining the shift from simple to expanded reproduction. For instance, he writes the following in Book II of *Capital*:

> If we simply consider the level of reproduction on the part of department I in value terms, then we still find ourselves within the limits of simple reproduction, for no additional capital has been set in motion in order to create this virtual excess of constant capital (the surplus product), and no more surplus labour than was performed on the basis of simple reproduction. The distinction here lies only in the form of the surplus labour applied, the concrete character of its particular useful mode. It has been spent on means of production for Ic instead of IIc, on means of production for means of production instead of on means of production for means of consumption. In the case of simple reproduction, it was assumed that the whole of the surplus-value in department I was spent as revenue, i.e. on commodities from department II; it consisted only of those means of production needed to replace the constant capital II_c in its natural form. Thus in order to make the transition from simple reproduction to expanded reproduction, production in department I must be in a position to produce fewer elements of constant capital for department II, but all the more for department I. This transition, which can never be achieved without difficulty, is made easier by the fact that a number of the products of department I can serve as means of production in both departments.

It follows therefore that – simply considering the values involved – *the material substratum for expanded reproduction is produced in the course of simple reproduction.*[93]

Marx makes the same basic point in various other passages, such as the following:

> The reason why a smaller sum has been chosen than in the earlier schema is precisely to draw attention to the fact that reproduction on an expanded scale (which is conceived here simply as production pursued with a greater investment of capital) has nothing to do with the absolute size of the product, that for a given volume of commodities it simply assumes a different arrangement or a different determination of the functions of the various elements of the given product, and is thus in the first instance only simple reproduction, as far as its value goes. *It is not the quantity, but the qualitative character of the given elements of simple reproduction that is changed, and this change is the material precondition for the ensuing reproduction on an expanded scale.*[94]

Marx attaches the following footnote 58 to the passage above in Book II:

> This puts an end once and for all to the conflict over the accumulation of capital between James Mill and S. Bailey, which we discussed from a different angle in Volume 1 (Chapter 24, 5, p. 759, note 52), i.e. the dispute over whether it is possible to extend the operation of an industrial capital without any alteration in its size. We shall come back to this later.[95]

For reference's sake, here is the passage from Book I of *Capital* that Marx is referring to in the note above:

> 'Political economists are too apt to consider a certain quantity of capital and a certain number of labourers as productive instruments of uniform power, or operating with a certain uniform intensity ... Those ... who maintain ... that commodities are the sole agents of production ...

---

93 Marx 1978, pp. 572–3. [Kuruma's emphasis.]
94 Marx 1978, p. 582. [Passage {81} in *Crisis I*. Kuruma's emphasis.]
95 Marx 1978, p. 582.

prove that production could never be enlarged, for it requires as an indispensable condition to such an enlargement that food, raw materials, and tools-should be previously augmented; which is in fact maintaining that no increase of production can take place without a previous increase, or, in other words, that an increase is impossible' (S. Bailey, *Money and Its Vicissitudes*, pp. 58, 70). Bailey criticises the dogma mainly from the point of view of the process of circulation.[96]

The theory expressed above and the theory presented in Part 3 of Book II have a point in common in their critique of premising accumulation on *a priori* accumulation or on the idea that 'no increase of production can take place without a previous increase'. The difference between them is that the criticism above indicates that the ability to use the elements of production is flexible rather than fixed,[97] whereas the point in Part 3 of Book II is to clarify how, in a case where the process of reproduction is not flexible, the material foundation for expanded reproduction can be created within the scale of simple reproduction (i.e. without premising a previous expansion). When Marx writes in footnote 58, quoted above, that 'This puts an end once and for all to ... the dispute over whether it is possible to extend the operation of an industrial capital without any alteration in its size', he is saying that the debate was resolved in the sense of clarifying the possibility to shift from simple to expanded reproduction when there is no flexibility, since the flexibility in the use of the production elements is not boundless but rather has a limit that, once reached, prevents further movement.

Thus, Marx emphasises the question of how the shift is made from simple to expanded reproduction, while at the same time emphasising in Part 3 of Book II the significance of the solution of this problem to the history of political economy; whereas you seem not to have grasped the significance of this achievement. On page 71 of your book *An Investigation into Crisis Theory*, you write:

> In order for expanded production to be developed, where one part of the surplus product 'S' is set aside for accumulation, first there must be surplus means of production beforehand in Dept. I in the sense of being more than what is necessary to replenish the constant capital in Dept. I and Dept II. In other words:

---

96   Marx 1976, p. 759.
97   Marx's view of the flexibility of the reproduction process can be seen in the passages gathered under Subheading 2 of Heading I in *Crisis IV*, titled: 'Under what conditions is a sudden expansion of production possible?'

$$C'_I > IC + IIC$$
Or:
$$I(V+S) > IIC$$

This is the 'material basis' or 'material precondition'[98] that constitutes the condition for the unfolding of expanded production.[99]

You argue that expanded reproduction requires, first of all, the existence beforehand of surplus means of production in Dept. I beyond the amount needed to replenish the constant capital in both departments, and that this is the 'material basis' or 'material precondition' of expanded reproduction, while suggesting that this is what Marx said by pointing to a passage in *Capital*. But in the passage you cite, Marx is certainly not saying, as you suggest, that 'there *must be beforehand* surplus means of production in Dept. I in the sense of being more than the necessity to replenish the constant capital in Dept. I and Dept II', which is '*the "material basis" or "material precondition" that constitutes the condition for the unfolding of expanded production*'. Quite the contrary, Marx is seeking to correct that erroneous view. Instead of saying that the production of the means of production necessary to expand production must be increased *beforehand*, he is rather clarifying *how the material conditions for expanded production can be created within the range of simple production*, and pointing out that the *reconfiguration of Dept. I within the range of simple reproduction is in this case the material basis for the subsequent expanded reproduction*. In short, he is criticising the doctrine that 'no increase of production can take place without a previous increase'.

If you had read that part of *Capital* without any preconceived ideas you should have been able to understand at least that much easily, so I am at a loss to understand how you could have gone from what Marx says to end up in the polar opposite view examined above. Perhaps my inability to grasp your logic is a sign of my own senility. If so, that is all the better for you, I suppose.

In any case, setting that aside, although up to now we have looked at the shift from simple to expanded reproduction, what is clarified there is applicable, with necessary changes, to a general change of the rate of accumulation. What I mean by 'necessary changes' is that what is clarified in the case of the shift from simple to expanded reproduction cannot always be applied generally, as is, to a case where the accumulation rate changes. In the case of the

---

98   Marx 1978, p. 582.
99   Tomizuka 1965, p. 71.

shift from simple to expanded reproduction, there is an *absolute* contraction in Dept. II that temporarily occurs, but that does not necessarily happen when the accumulation rate increases under reproduction already taking place on an expanded scale.[100] However, even in such a case there is a *relative* contraction in Dept. II. Therefore, the proportion between the two departments must change. And in terms of this point, it is the same as the shift from simple to expanded reproduction.

However, this is certainly not a characteristic particular to capitalist production. Rather, it is a superhistorical law that would be common to socialist production, where this law would always have to be taken into consideration when formulating an economic plan (since the necessity for expanded production will vary depending on the given circumstances at the time). But it is an astounding leap of logic to argue that a natural outcome of recognising this law is the proposition that everything will be fine, no matter what the change in the accumulation rate might be, as long as the proportion between the departments is adjusted in line with the change. However, Tugan-Baranowsky made that sort of outrageous argument, based on his analysis (?) of the reproduction schema in Part 3 of Book II. Moreover, he thought that this proposition was applicable elsewhere, and in seeing Marx discussing in Book III of *Capital* why overaccumulation occurs, he seems to have thought this was incompatible with the conclusion Marx reached from his analysis of the reproduction schema (?) in Part 2 of Book II, so that the train of argument in Book III must have been mistaken. I say that he 'seems' to have thought that because, although I've read parts of his book, it has been a while and I am basing this on a vague memory. If my memory is not mistaken, this is a decisive point of difference between my view and his.

Through my consideration above, I have been able to see how my ideas differ from those of Tugan-Baranowsky on all points, while also becoming aware of some points he has in common with you. One example, as already mentioned, is the idea that recognising that the proportion between the departments *must change* if the accumulation rate changes, naturally generates the proposition that no matter how the accumulation rate might change, *all will be fine if there is a change* in the proportion between the departments. An even more fundamental point in common between you and Tugan-Baranowsky is the idea that it is possible to discuss and determine whether there is a *limit* to capital accumulation as an investigative dimension of Part 3 of Book II. Tugan-Baranowsky

---

100 The expression 'not necessarily' is added here because the necessity for an absolute contraction of Dept. II arises under already expanded reproduction when the previous accumulation rate rises suddenly beyond a certain point.

thought one could demonstrate the possibility of a limitless progression of capital accumulation based on an analysis (?) of the reproduction schema, while you, again based on the analysis (?) of the schema, think that this limit can and should be elucidated there. This is what can be surmised from the last part of the long passage from your article quoted earlier, but there you argue that this 'is closely related to whether or not a concept of an "equilibrium rate of accumulation" can be established', so it seems more appropriate to leave this point for when I consider that section.[101]

---

101   [As noted in the footnote at the beginning of this chapter, Kuruma did not complete a critique of Tomizuka's concept of an 'equilibrium rate of accumulation'.]

Bibliography

Bukharin, Nikolai 1972 [1925–26], *Imperialism and the Accumulation of Capital*, with Rosa Luxemburg, *The Accumulation of Capital: An Anti-Critique*, edited by Kenneth Tarbuck, translated by Rudolf Wichmann, New York: Monthly Review Press.

Condliffe, J.B. 1932, *World Economic Survey: 1931–32*, Geneva: League of Nations.

Condliffe, J.B. 1933, *World Economic Survey: 1932–33*, Geneva: League of Nations.

Condliffe, J.B. 1934, *World Economic Survey: 1933–34*, Geneva: League of Nations.

Dutt, C.P. and Andrew Rothstein (eds.) 1957, *Political Economy: A textbook issued by the Institute of Economics of the Academy of Sciences of the USSR*, London: Lawrence and Wishart.

Engels, Friedrich 1975 [1887], 'Appendix to the American Edition of *The Condition of the Working Class in England*', in Karl Marx and Frederick Engels, *Collected Works*, Volume 26, New York: International Publishers, pp. 399–405.

Engels, Friedrich 1994 [1891], *Socialism: Utopian and Scientific*, New York: International Publishers.

Engels, Friedrich 1995, Correspondence 1883–1886, Karl Marx and Frederick Engels, *Collected Works*, Volume 47, New York: International Publishers.

Figurnov, P.K. 1939, *Марксистско-ленинская теория кризисов* (Marxist-Leninist Theory of Crisis), Moscow: Gospolitizidat.

Fukumoto, Kazuo 1928, *Keizaigaku hihan no tame ni* (Toward a Critique of Political Economy), Tokyo: Kaizōsha.

Grossman, Henryk 2018 [1929], 'The Change in the Original Plan for Marx's *Capital* and Its Causes', translated by Geoffrey McCormack, in *Henryk Grossman Works, Volume 1*, edited by Rick Kuhn, Leiden: Konninklijke Brill NV, pp. 183–209.

Hegel, Georg Wilhelm Friedrich 1991 [1817], *The Encylopaedia Logic: Part 1 of the Encyclopaedia of Philosophical Sciences*, translated by T.F. Geraets, W.A. Suchting, and H.S. Harris, Indianapolis: Hackett.

Hoston, Germaine 1986, *Marxism and the Crisis of Development in Prewar Japan*, Princeton, New Jersey: Princeton University Press.

Hoston, Germaine 1994, *The State, Identity, and the National Question in China and Japan*, Princeton, New Jersey: Princeton University Press.

Ikumi Takuichi 1961, *Gendai shihonshugi to keiki junkan* (Modern Capitalism and the Business Cycle), Tokyo: Nihonhyōron-sha.

Imai Noriyoshi 1958, 'Sengo nihon no keiki junkan' (Business Cycle in Postwar Japan) in *Kōza kyōkō ron II: Sengo no keiki junkan* (Lectures on Crisis Theory Vol. II: Postwar Business Cycle), Tokyo: Tōyō Keizai Shinpōsha.

Inomata, Tsunao 1928, *Teikokushugi kenkyū* (Research on Imperialism), Tokyo: Kaizōsha.

Itoh, Makoto 1980, *Value and Crisis*, London: Pluto Books.
Kautsky, Karl 1903, 'Vorwort des Herausgebers', in Karl Marx, *Zur Kritik der politischen Ökonomie*, Stuttgart: Verlag J.H.W. Dietz Nachf., pp. vi–viii.
Kautsky, Karl 1905, 'Vorrede', in Karl Marx, *Theorien über den Mehrwert, Erster Band*, Stuttgart: Verlag J.H.W. Dietz Nachf., pp. vii–xx.
Kautsky, Karl 1910, 'Vorrede', in Karl Marx, *Theorien über den Mehrwert, Dritter Band*, Stuttgart: Verlag J.H.W. Dietz Nachf., pp. v–xi.
Kautsky, Karl 1914, 'Vorwort des Herausgebers', in Karl Marx, *Das Kapital: Kritik der politischen Ökonomie*, Stuttgart: Verlag von J.H.W. Dietz Nachf., pp. viii–xxxv.
Kawakami, Hajime 1928, 'Yuibutsu shikan ni kansuru jiko seisan: Sono kyū' (Settlement of Accounts with Historical Materialism: Part 9), Tokyo: Kōbundō Shobō, pp. 1–35.
Kawakami, Hajime 1946 [1929], *Shihon-ron nyūmon* (*An Introduction to Das Kapital*), Tokyo: Sekaihyōronsha.
Kuczynski, Jürgen 1957, *Studien zur Geschichte des Kapitalismus* (Studies on the History of Capitalism), Berlin: Akademie Verlag.
Kuruma, Samezō 1929, 'Kyōkō ron kenkyū joron' (An Introduction to the Study of Crisis), in *Ōhara shakai mondai kenkyū-jo zasshi* (Journal of the Ōhara Institute for Social Research), Vol. 6, No. 1 (September 1929), pp. 31–81.
Kuruma, Samezō 1930, 'Marukusu no kyōkō ron no kakunin no tame ni' (In Confirmation of Marx's Theory of Crisis), in *Ōhara shakai mondai kenkyū-jo zasshi* (Journal of the Ōhara Institute for Social Research), Vol. 7, No. 2 (September 1929), pp. 1–31.
Kuruma, Samezō 1931, 'Shihon no chikuseki to kotei shihon no shōkyaku: Inomata-shicho *Teikokushugi kenkyū* naka no ichi ron ten' (Capital Accumulation and the Depreciation Fund for Fixed Capital: One Theoretical Point within Inomata's *Imperialism Research*), in *Ōhara shakai mondai kenkyū-jo zasshi* (Journal of the Ōhara Institute for Social Research), Vol. 8, No. 2 (September 1931), pp. 25–62.
Kuruma, Samezō 1932, 'Takada hakase no chikuseki riron no ichi kōsatsu' (A Consideration of Professor Takada's Theory of Accumulation), in *Ōhara shakai mondai kenkyū-jo zasshi* (Journal of the Ōhara Institute for Social Research), Vol. 9, No. 2 (October 1932), pp. 1–21.
Kuruma, Samezō 1933, 'Takada hakase ni yoru chikuseki riron no shūsei' (Professor Takada's Revision of His Theory of Accumulation), in *Chūō kōron* April 1933, pp. 38–50.
Kuruma, Samezō 1935a, 'Kokusai renmei no *Sekai keizai gaikan* o yomu' (A Review of the League of Nation's *World Economic Survey*), in *Gekkan ōhara shakai mondai kenkyū-jo zasshi* (Monthly Journal of the Ōhara Institute for Social Research), Vol. 2, No. 5 (May 1935), pp. 1–20.
Kuruma, Samezō 1935b, 'Gendaiteki tomi no mujun' (Contradictions of Modern

Wealth), in *Gekkan ōhara shakai mondai kenkyū-jo zasshi* (Monthly Journal of the Ōhara Institute for Social Research), Vol. 2, No. 11 (November 1935), pp. 1–16.

Kuruma, Samezō 1936, 'Bassui chō yori' (From My Excerpt Notebooks), in *Gekkan ōhara shakai mondai kenkyū-jo zasshi* (Monthly Journal of the Ōhara Institute for Social Research), Vol. 3, No. 8 (August 1936), pp. 43–66.

Kuruma, Samezō 1946, 'Chingin neage to infurēshon tomi no mujun' (Wage Increases and Inflation), *Kaizō*, May 1946, pp. 16–23.

Kuruma, Samezō 1948a, 'Ōuchi Hyōe, Arisawa Hiromi, Wakimura Yoshitarō, Takahashi Masao kyōcho *Nihon infurēūshon no kenkyū* o yomu" (A Review of *Studies on Inflation* Co-written by Hyōe Ōuchi, Hiromi Arisawa, Yoshitarō Wakimura, and Masao Takahashi) in *Infurēūshon to tōkei hattatsu shi: Takano Iwasaburō sensei no kijyū kinen ronbun shū* (History of Inflation and the Development of Statistics: Collection of Articles to Commemorate Professor Takano Iwasaburō's 77th Birthday), Tokyo: Daiichi Shuppan, pp. 33–51.

Kuruma, Samezō 1948b, *Keizaigaku shi* (History of Political Economy), Tokyo: Kawade Shobō.

Kuruma, Samezō 1949, *Marukusu kyōkō ron kenkyū* (An Investigation of Marx's Theory of Crisis), Tokyo: Kitakōkan.

Kuruma, Samezō 1953a, '*Shihon-ron* to kyōkō-ron to no kankei ni tsuite Uno kyōju ni kotau' (A Reply to Professor Uno Concerning the Relation Between *Capital* and Crisis Theory), in *Keizai shirin* (Hosei Economic Review) Vol. 23, No. 3, pp. 19–39.

Kuruma, Samezō 1953b, *Kyōkō ron kenkyū* (An Investigation of Crisis Theory), Tokyo: Shinhyōronsha.

Kuruma, Samezō 1953c, 'Gakkyū seikatsu no omoide' (Memories of a Scholarly Life: Part 1), in *Shisō*, July 1953, pp. 872–81.

Kuruma, Samezō 1953d, 'Gakkyū seikatsu no omoide' (Memories of a Scholarly Life: Part 2), in *Shisō*, August 1953, pp. 981–89.

Kuruma, Samezō 1957, *Kachikeitai-ron to kōkankatei-ron* (Theory of the Value Form and Theory of the Exchange Process), Tokyo: Iwanami Shoten.

Kuruma, Samezō 1962, 'Sengo no kyōkō ron ni okeru ikutsukano mondaiten' (A Few Problems Concerning Postwar Theories of Crisis), in *Hōsei daigaku ōhara shakai mondai kenkyū-jo shiryō-shitsu hō zasshi* (Report of Reference Room of Journal of the Ōhara Institute for Social Research, Hosei University), No. 82 (October 1962), pp. 1–17.

Kuruma, Samezō 1965, *Kyōkō ron kenkyū* (An Investigation of Crisis Theory), Tokyo: Ōtsuki Shoten.

Kuruma, Samezō (ed.) 1968, *Marx-Lexikon zur politischen Ökonomie*, Vol. 1 (*Competition*), Tokyo: Ōtsuki Shoten.

Kuruma, Samezō (ed.) 1969a, *Marx-Lexikon zur politischen Ökonomie*, Vol. 2 (*Method I*), Tokyo: Ōtsuki Shoten.

Kuruma, Samezō (ed.) 1969b, *Marx-Lexikon zur politischen Ökonomie*, Vol. 3 (*Method II*), Tokyo: Ōtsuki Shoten.

Kuruma, Samezō (ed.) 1971a, *Marx-Lexikon zur politischen Ökonomie*, Vol. 4 (*Materialist Conception of History I*), Tokyo: Ōtsuki Shoten.

Kuruma, Samezō (ed.) 1971b, *Marx-Lexikon zur politischen Ökonomie*, Vol. 5 (*Materialist Conception of History II*), Tokyo: Ōtsuki Shoten.

Kuruma, Samezō (ed.) 1972a, *Marx-Lexikon zur politischen Ökonomie*, Vol. 6 (*Crisis I*), Tokyo: Ōtsuki Shoten.

Kuruma, Samezō (ed.) 1972b, 'Shiori' No. 6 (Insert No. 6), in *Marx-Lexikon zur politischen Ökonomie*, Vol. 6 (*Crisis I*), Tokyo: Ōtsuki Shoten.

Kuruma, Samezō (ed.) 1973a, *Marx-Lexikon zur politischen Ökonomie*, Vol. 7 (*Crisis II*), Tokyo: Ōtsuki Shoten.

Kuruma, Samezō (ed.) 1973b, 'Shiori' No. 7 (Insert No. 7), in *Marx-Lexikon zur politischen Ökonomie*, Vol. 7 (*Crisis II*), Tokyo: Ōtsuki Shoten.

Kuruma, Samezō 1973c, 'Shakai kagaku 50 nen no shōgen' (Testimonies on Fifty Years of Social Science: Interview with Samezō Kuruma), in *Shūkan ekonomisuto* (Weekly Economist), 21 Aug. to 2 Oct. issue, Tokyo: Mainichi Shimbun Shuppan.

Kuruma, Samezō (ed.) 1975a, *Marx-Lexikon zur politischen Ökonomie*, Vol. 8 (*Crisis III*), Tokyo: Ōtsuki Shoten.

Kuruma, Samezō (ed.) 1975b, 'Shiori' No. 8 (Insert No. 8), in *Marx-Lexikon zur politischen Ökonomie*, Vol. 8 (*Crisis III*), Tokyo: Ōtsuki Shoten.

Kuruma, Samezō 1975c, 'Kyōkō ron taikei no tenkai hōhō ni suite (1)' (Method of Unfolding the System of Crisis Theory: Part 1), in *Keizai shirin* (Hosei Economic Review) Vol. 43, No. 3, pp. 1–38.

Kuruma, Samezō (ed.) 1976a, *Marx-Lexikon zur politischen Ökonomie*, Vol. 9 (*Crisis IV*), Tokyo: Ōtsuki Shoten.

Kuruma, Samezō (ed.) 1976b, 'Shiori' No. 9 (Insert No. 9), in *Marx-Lexikon zur politischen Ökonomie*, Vol. 9 (*Crisis IV*), Tokyo: Ōtsuki Shoten.

Kuruma, Samezō 1976c, 'Kyōkō ron taikei no tenkai hōhō ni suite (2)' (Method of Unfolding the System of Crisis Theory: Part 2), in *Keizai shirin* (Hosei Economic Review) Vol. 44, No. 3, pp. 1–32.

Kuruma, Samezō (ed.) 1978, *Marx-Lexikon zur politischen Ökonomie*, Vol. 10, Tokyo: Ōtsuki Shoten.

Kuruma, Samezō 1979, *Kahei-ron* (Theory of Money), Tokyo: Ōtsuki Shoten.

Kuruma, Samezō (ed.) 1985, 'Shiori' No. 14 (Insert No. 14), in *Marx-Lexikon zur politischen Ökonomie*, Vol. 15 (*Money V*), Tokyo: Ōtsuki Shoten.

Kuruma, Samezō 2007 [1954], 'A Critique of Classical Political Economy', translated by E. Michael Schauerte, in *Transitions in Latin America and in Poland and Syria, Research in Political Economy 24*, edited by Paul Zarembka, New York: Elsevier, pp. 295–340.

Kuruma, Samezō 2015 [1977], *Kuruma Samezō to no kaidan* (A Discussion with Kuruma Samezō) in *Hōsei daigaku shi shiryō-shū*, (Materials on the History of Hosei University), No. 36, Tokyoi: Hosei University, pp. 315–41.

Kuruma, Samezō 2018, *Marx's Theory of the Gensis of Money*, translated and edited by Michael Schauerte, Koninklijke Brill NV.

Kuruma, Samezō and Hyōe Ōuchi (eds.) 1948, *Infurēushon to tōkei hattatsu shi: Takano Iwasaburō sensei no kijyū kinen ronbun shū* (History of Inflation and the Development of Statistics: Collection of Articles to Commemorate Professor Takano Iwasaburō's 77th Birthday), Tokyo: Daichi Shuppan.

Kuruma, Samezō and Sutehiro Uesugi 1960, Interview, in *Keizai seminā* (Economic Seminar), No. 39, Tokyo: Nihonhyōron-sha, pp. 34–41.

Lenin, Vladimir Illyich 1964 [1917], *Imperialism, the Highest Stage of Capitalism: A Popular Outline*, in Vladimir Ilych Lenin, *Collected Works, Volume 22*, Moscow: Progress, pp. 184–304.

Lenin, Vladimir Illyich 1972 [1897], *A Chararterisation of Economic Romanticism*, in Vladimir Ilych Lenin, *Collected Works, Volume 2*, Moscow: Progress, pp. 129–265.

Luxemburg, Rosa 2016a [1913], *The Accumulation of Capital: A Contribution to the Economic Theory of Imperialism*, in *The Complete Works of Rosa Luxemburg Volume II: Economic Writings 2*, translated by George Shriver, edited by Nicholas Gray, London/New York: Verso, pp. 1–342.

Luxemburg, Rosa 2016b [1921, written 1915], *The Accumulation of Capital, Or What the Epigones Have Made Out of Marx's Theory – An Anti-Critique*, in *The Complete Works of Rosa Luxemburg Volume II: Economic Writings 2*, translated by George Shriver, edited by Nicholas Gray and George Shriver, London/New York: Verso, pp. 343–449.

Marx, Karl 1967, *Theorien über den Mehrwert. Zweiter Teil* (Theories of Surplus Value Vol. 2), in *Karl Marx Friederich Engels Werke. Band 26, Zweiter Teil*, Berlin: Dietz Verlag Berlin.

Marx, Karl 1973a [written 1857–58], *Grundrisse*, London: Penguin Books, translated by Martin Nicolaus, Harmondsworth, Penguin.

Marx, Karl 1973b [written 1857], 'Introduction' in *Grundrisse*, London: Penguin Books, translated by Martin Nicolaus, Harmondsworth, Penguin, pp. 83–111.

Marx, Karl 1976 [1867], *Capital: A Critique of Political Economy. Volume 1*, translated by Ben Fowkes, Harmondsworth, Penguin.

Marx, Karl 1977 [1847], 'Wage Labour and Capital' in Karl Marx and Frederick Engels, *Collected Works, Volume 9*, New York: International Publishers, pp. 197–228.

Marx, Karl 1978 [written 1885], *Capital: A Critique of Political Economy. Volume 2*, translated by David Fernbach, Harmondsworth, Penguin.

Marx, Karl 1979 [1852], 'Pauperism and Free Trade: The Approaching Commercial Crisis', in Karl Marx and Frederick Engels, *Collected Works, Volume 11*, New York: International Publishers, pp. 357–63.

Marx, Karl 1981a [written 1864–65], *Capital: A Critique of Political Economy. Volume 3*, translated by David Fernbach, Harmondsworth, Penguin.

Marx, Karl 1981b [1858], 'British Commerce and Finance', in Karl Marx and Frederick Engels, *Collected Works, Volume 16*, New York: International Publishers, pp. 33–6.

Marx, Karl 1983, Correspondence 1856–1859, Karl Marx and Frederick Engels, *Collected Works, Volume 40*, New York: International Publishers.

Marx, Karl 1985, Correspondence, Karl Marx and Frederick Engels 1860–1864, *Collected Works, Volume 41*, New York: International Publishers.

Marx, Karl 1986a [1857], 'The Trade Crisis in England', in Karl Marx and Frederick Engels, *Collected Works, Volume 15*, New York: International Publishers, pp. 400–03.

Marx, Karl 1986b [1858], 'British Commerce', in Karl Marx and Frederick Engels, *Collected Works, Volume 15*, New York: International Publishers, pp. 425–34.

Marx, Karl 1987a [1859], *A Contribution to the Critique of Political Economy. Part One*, in Karl Marx and Frederick Engels, *Collected Works, Volume 29*, New York: International Publishers, pp. 7–255.

Marx, Karl 1987b, Correspondence 1864–1868, Karl Marx and Frederick Engels, *Collected Works, Volume 42*, New York: International Publishers.

Marx, Karl 1987c [written 1857–58], *Grundrisse*, in Karl Marx and Frederick Engels, *Collected Works, Volume 29*, New York: International Publishers, pp. 257–417.

Marx, Karl 1988a, Correspondence 1869–1870, Karl Marx and Frederick Engels, *Collected Works, Volume 43*, New York: International Publishers.

Marx, Karl 1988b, *Ökonomische Manuskripte 1864–65*, in *Marx-Engels-Gesamtausgabe Abteilung 2, Band 4.1*, Berlin: Dietz Verlag.

Marx, Karl 1989a, *Economic Manuscript of 1861–63* [Notebooks VII to XII], in Karl Marx and Frederick Engels, *Collected Works, Volume 31*, New York: International Publishers.

Marx, Karl 1989b, *Economic Manuscript of 1861–63* [Notebooks XII to XV], in Karl Marx and Frederick Engels, *Collected Works, Volume 32*, New York: International Publishers.

Marx, Karl 1991a, *Economic Manuscript of 1861–63* [Notebooks XV to XXIII], in Karl Marx and Frederick Engels, *Collected Works, Volume 33*, New York: International Publishers.

Marx, Karl 1991b, Correspondence 1874–1879, Karl Marx and Frederick Engels, *Collected Works, Volume 45*, New York: International Publishers.

Marx, Karl 1993 [1872], *Le Capital*, Livre Premier, Paris: Presse Universitaires de France.

Marx, Karl 1996 [1867], *Capital Volume 2*, in Karl Marx and Frederick Engels, *Collected Works, Volume 35*, New York: International Publishers.

Marx, Karl 1997 [written 1885], *Capital Volume 2*, in Karl Marx and Frederick Engels, *Collected Works, Volume 36*, New York: International Publishers.

Marx, Karl 1998 [written 1864–65], *Capital Volume 3*, in Karl Marx and Frederick Engels, *Collected Works, Volume 37*, New York: International Publishers.

Marx, Karl 2008, *Manuskripte zum zweiten Buch des "Kapitals" 1868 bis 1881*, in *Marx-Engels-Gesamtausgabe Abteilung 2, Band 11*, Amsterdam: Akademie Verlag.

Marx, Karl 2017, *Marx's Economic Manuscript of 1864–65*, edited by Fred Mosley, translated by Ben Fowkes, Leiden: Konninklijke Brill NV.

McCulloch, John 1825, *The Principles of Political Economy*, Edinburg: William and Charles Tait.

Mendelson L.A. 1959, *Теория и история экономических кризисов и циклов Т. 1–2* (Theory and History of Economic Crises and Cycles Vols. 1–2), Moscow: Social and Economic Literature Publishing House.

Mitchell, Wesley 1927, *Business Cycles: The Problem and its Setting*, New York: National Bureau of Economic Research.

Miyake, Yoshio 1974a, *Marukusu Engerusu: Igirisu kyōkō shi ron* (Marx and Engels's History of Crisis in England) Volume 1, Tokyo: Ōtsuki Shoten.

Miyake, Yoshio 1974b, *Marukusu Engerusu: Igirisu kyōkō shi ron* (Marx and Engels's History of Crisis in England) Volume 2, Tokyo: Ōtsuki Shoten.

Nimura, Kazuo 1989, 'Ōhara shakai mondai kenkyū-jo no 70 nen' (70 Years of the Ōhara Institute for Social Research), in *Ōhara shakai mondai kenkyū-jo zasshi* (Journal of the Ōhara Institute for Social Research), Vols. 363/364, (February/March 1989), pp. 2–17.

Nimura, Kazuo et. al 1989, 'Zadankai "Seikei biru jidai no omoide"' (Recollections of the Seikei Bldg. Era), in *Ōhara shakai mondai kenkyū-jo zasshi* (Journal of the Ōhara Institute for Social Research), Vols. 363/364, (February/March 1989), pp. 22–48.

Oelssner, Fred 1949, *Die Wirtschaftskrisen* (Economic Crises), Berlin: Dietz.

Ōhara Institute for Social Research, Hosei University 2020, *Ōhara shakai mondai kenkyū-jo hyaku nen shi* (100-year History of the Ōhara Institute for Social Research), Tokyo: Hosei University Press.

Ōshima, Kiyoshi 1957, 'Shihonshugi-teki seisan no seigen to kyōkō' (The Barrier of Capitalist Production and Crisis), in *Keizaigaku no shomondai* (Problems of Political Economy), Tokyo: Hosei University Press, pp. 255–91.

Ōtani, Teinosuke 1973, '"Naizaiteki mujun" no mondai o "saiseisan-ron" ni zokuseshimeru kenkai ichi ronkyo ni Tsuite – *Shihon-ron* daini-bu chū 32 no "oboegaki" no kōshōteki kentō' (Regarding the Basis of the View that the Issue of the 'Immanent Contradiction' Pertains to the 'Theory of Reproduction': Textual Analysis of the 'Memo' Published as Note 32 in Book II of *Capital*), in *Keizai keiei kenkyū hōkoku* (Bulletin of Research on Economics and Management), No. 6, Tokyo: Tōyō University.

Ōtani, Teinosuke 2003 *Marukusu ni yotte, Marukusu o amu* (Based on Marx, Editing Marx), Tokyo: Otsuki Shoten.

Ōtani, Teinosuke 2016, *Marukusu no rishiumi shihon ron: 3 kan* (Theory of Marx's Interest-bearing Capital: Volume 3), Tokyo: Sakurai Shoten.

Ōtani, Teinosuke 2018, *A Guide to Marxian Political Economy: What Kind of a Social System is Capitalism?* Cham, Switzerland: Springer.

Ōtani, Teinosuke and Noriko Maehata (eds.) 2019, *Marukusu no kyōkō ron: Kuruma Samezō hen 'Marukusu keizaigaku rekishikon' o jiku ni* (Marx's Theory of Crisis: Centered on Samezō Kuruma's *Marx-Lexikon zur Politischen Ökonomie*), Tokyo: Sakurai Shoten.

Ōuchi, Hyōe et. al 1946, *Nihon infurēūshon no kenkyū* (Studies on Inflation), Tokyo: Ōdosha.

Ōuchi, Hyōe 1957, 'Rōyū Kuruma-kun no ashiato' (The Footprints of My Old Friend Kuruma), in *Keizaigaku no shomondai* (Problems of Political Economy), Tokyo: Hosei University Press, pp. 391–402.

Ōuchi, Hyōe and Tatsuo Morito (eds.) 1957, *Keizaigaku no shomondai* (Problems of Political Economy), Tokyo: Hosei University Press.

Ricardo, David 1996 [1817], *On the Principles of Political Economy and Taxation*, Amherst: Prometheus Books.

Say, Jean-Baptiste 1827, 'Messrs. Say and Sismondi', *Asiatic Journal and Monthly Register for British India and its Dependencies*, Vol. XXXIII (Jan. to June), London: Parbury, Allen, & Co., pp. 35–8.

Schauerte, E. Michael 2007, 'Samezō Kuruma's Life as a Marxist Economist', in *Transitions in Latin America and in Poland and Syria, Research in Political Economy 24*, edited by Paul Zarembka, New York: Elsevier, pp. 281–94.

Schauerte, Michael 2018, 'Introduction to This Edition', in Samezō Kuruma, *Marx Theory of the Genesis of Money*, Kuruma, Samezō 2018, *Marx's Theory of the Gensis of Money*, translated and edited by Michael Schauerte, Konninklijke Brill NV, pp. 1–21.

Schmidt, Johann Lorenz 1956, *Neue Probleme der Krisentheorie* (New Problems of Crisis Theory), Berlin: Akademie Verlag.

Sekine, Thomas 1977, 'Translator's Introduction', in Uno Kōzō, *Principles of Political Economy: Theory of a Purely Capitalist Society*, translated by Thomas Sekine, Essex: The Harvester Press Limited, pp. vii–xvii.

Sismondi, Jean Charles Léonard Sismonde de, 1991 [1827], *New Principles of Political Economy*, translated by Richard Hyse, New Brunswick: Transaction.

Smith, Adam 1937 [1776], *The Wealth of Nations*, New York: Random House.

Smith, Henry DeWitt 1972, *Japan's First Student Radicals*, Cambridge, Massachusetts: Harvard University Press.

Takada, Yasuma, 1935a [1932], 'Chikuseki riron no ikkōsatsu' (A Consideration of the Theory of Accumulation), in *Marukusu keizaigaku ronhyō* (A Critique of Marxian Political Economy), Tokyo: Kaizōsha, pp. 285–304.

Takada, Yasuma, 1935b [1933], 'Chikuseki riron no shūsei' (A Revision of the Theory of Accumulation), in *Marukusu keizaigaku ronhyō* (A Critique of Marxian Political Economy), Tokyo: Kaizōsha, pp. 323–45.

Tomizuka, Ryōzō, 1965, *Kyōkō ron kenkū* (An Investigation into Crisis Theory), Tokyo: Miraisha.

Tomizuka, Ryōzō, 1974, 'Kyōkō ron taikei no tenkai hōhō nit suite: Kuruma kyōju e no kōkai shitsumonjō' (Method of Unfolding the System of Crisis Theory: An Open Letter to Professor Kuruma), in *Shōgaku ronshū*, Vol. 41, No. 7, July, Fukushima: Fukushima University Faculty of Economics.

Tugan-Baranowsky, Michael 2000 [1901], 'Chapter 1. The Fundamental Causes of Crises in the Capitalist Economy' of *Studien zur Theorie und Geschichte der Handelskrisen in England*, translated by Alejandro Ramos-Martínez, in *Value, Capitalist Dynamics and Money, Research in Political Economy 18*, edited by Paul Zarembka, New York: Elsevier, pp. 53–80.

Uno, Kōzō 1953 [1952], 'Shihon-ron' ni okeru kyōkō ron no nanten (Problematic Points in the Theory of Crisis in *Capital*), in *Kyōkō ron* (Crisis Theory), Tokyo: Iwanami Shoten.

Uno, Kōzō 1973 [1949], *Shihon-ron no kenkyū* (Investigations of *Capital*), in *Uno Kōzō chosaku shū dai-san kan* (Selected Works of *Kōzō Uno Vol. 3*), Tokyo: Iwanami Shoten, pp. 3–191.

Uno, Kōzō 1973, *Shihon-ron gojū nen* (Fifty Years of *Capital*, Vol. 2), Tokyo: Hosei University Press.

Wilbrandt, Robert 1919 [1918], *Karl Marx: Versuch einer Würdigung*, third edition, Leipzig: Teubner.

Yamada, Moritarō 1948 [1931], *Saiseisan katei hyōshiki bunseki joron* (An Introduction to the Analysis of Reproduction Schema), Tokyo: Kaizōsha.

Yoshikawa, Tetsu 1973, '[Shohyō: Kuruma Samezō hen *Marukusu keizaigaku rekishikon kyōkō 1*' (Review: Samezō Kuruma, Ed., *Marx-Lexikon zur Politischen Ökonomie Krise 1*), in *Keizai hyōron*, March, 1973, Tokyo: Keizai Hyōronsha, pp. 215–8.

Index

abstraction   23, 45, 125, 312
Academy of Science (USSR)   362n
accumulation
   accumulation fund   167–8, 196, 321, 326–8, 330, 332–3, 435
   accumulation of capital   48, 61, 63–4, 68, 97, 142, 167, 171, 237, 241, 242, 244, 314, 316–36, 378, 379, 426, 458, 461–2
   equilibrium rate of accumulation   171, 173, 378n, 404, 451, 454–5, 462, 462n
   rate of accumulation   33–4, 169–73, 177, 197, 383–4, 386, 389, 395–6, 401, 448–52, 454–6, 460–1
Akashi, Hideto   27
amortisation fund   167n
Archiv für die Geschichte des Sozialismus und der Arbeiterbewegung   80
Arisawa, Hiromi   351–4

Babbage, Charles   281, 281n
Bailey, Samuel   125, 458–9
balance of payments   247, 294, 296n
Bank Charter Act   253
banking crisis   302, 304
bankruptcy   44, 47, 236, 301
barrier (*Schranke*) of capital   18, 35–9, 120, 146–9, 152–3, 154, 175, 186, 197–9, 201–6, 209, 211–4, 216, 223, 234–5, 236, 239, 245, 266, 268, 270, 277, 303, 364–5, 372
barter   31, 136, 137, 156, 158, 349–52, 353
Bergmann, Eugen von   49n
Bergson, Henri   2
Berkman, Alexander   14
Bernstein, Eduard   61, 61n
black market   337, 353–4
boom   4, 43, 56, 296, 296n, 302, 363–4, 363n
Boudin, Louis   61
bourgeois political economy   12, 53, 57, 231, 293n
Bukharin, Nikolai   379
business cycle   57–60, 59n, 60n, 146–7, 271–3, 363

capital
   absolute overproduction of capital   184, 453

commercial capital   38, 120, 189, 199, 214, 270
commodity capital   161, 165, 176, 377, 414, 427, 438, 442
concentration of capital   37, 169, 183, 199, 371
constant capital   165, 166–7, 262, 286, 319, 321–4, 326–7, 379, 384, 387–8, 392, 425, 448, 457, 459–60
export of capital   68, 224, 237, 243, 245–7
finance capital   68, 304–5
fixed capital   50–1, 192, 195, 254–5, 261–2, 272, 280–3, 285–6, 317–9, 321–2, 324–7, 329, 331, 437, 445–7, 330, 332–3
individual capital   36, 73, 97, 125, 162–4, 167, 169, 171, 177, 196, 423–4
investment of capital   87, 111, 442, 458
productive capital   120, 143, 160–1, 165, 224, 414–5, 419–25, 426, 428–9
variable capital   33, 163, 165, 323, 342, 379, 387, 392, 420, 442, 454
capital in general   12, 18, 23n, 29, 75, 78–9, 84–5, 88–96, 93n, 94n, 99, 104, 106–7, 109, 112–4, 150
capitalist development   13, 38, 66, 67, 192, 209, 232, 254, 286
capitalist mode of production   45, 50–1, 94, 96, 112, 114, 125–7, 129–30, 198, 200n, 203–5, 237–9, 297, 299–300, 311–2
Cazenove, John   332n
Charles H. Kerr & Co.   74n
Christianity   5
circulation
   circulation of capital   32, 82, 111, 127–8, 129, 139, 156–67, 195–6, 317, 321–2, 378–9, 408–9, 405–32, 410n, 417n, 439, 448, 451, 459
   circulation of commodities   31–3, 545–5, 74, 120–4, 136, 154, 157, 162–3, 177, 195, 320n, 322, 327, 357–8, 408, 411, 412
   circulation of money   47, 125, 158, 165–6, 278, 311, 318–20, 322, 325, 350–9, 358n, 359
class consciousness   43, 56
Classical school   293, 311, 340
Comintern   13

INDEX   473

commerce 2, 44, 119–20, 186, 223, 254, 256–7, 274, 302, 303
commodity
   commodity capital 161–2, 165, 176, 377, 413–4, 427, 438, 442
   commodity form 315, 412
   commodity production 54, 126–7, 157, 158, 314
   world of commodities 163
competition 46, 48, 49, 50, 65, 73, 75, 79–80, 85, 90, 93–4, 94n, 96–9, 127, 129, 173, 194, 200–1, 235, 416–7
competitive battle (struggle) 115, 184
composition of capital 37, 171, 182–3, 342–3, 381, 385–6, 393–4, 387–94, 397–401, 453
Condliffe, John 25, 293–305
consumer goods 295, 296n, 381–2, 384, 387, 391–2, 393–4, 400, 402, 403
consumers 38, 50, 55–6, 119, 158, 165
consumption
   individual (personal) consumption 98, 162, 241–2, 319–20, 392
   limits of consumption 38, 179, 180, 199
   restricted consumption of working class 36, 175, 209, 213, 438
content determination (*Inhaltbestimmung*) 33–4, 155, 159, 160, 161, 164, 165, 166, 195–7, 405, 217, 407, 412, 415, 423–5, 449, 451
contradiction 29–31, 34–6, 38, 56, 62–3, 69–70, 91–2, 113–4, 115, 117–9, 122, 151–3, 156–7, 174–8, 176n, 178n, 180, 185–7, 197–200, 200n, 202–6, 208–9, 211–3, 217–8, 239, 266, 299–300, 299n, 303–4, 312–5, 339, 403
convertibility 235–6
cooperation 71, 208
cotton industry 237–8, 331, 415, 419, 422
credit, credit system 72, 73, 75, 79–80, 85, 90, 93–4, 97, 120, 139–40, 169, 173, 187, 189–90, 199, 204, 223–4, 239, 246, 247, 253, 301, 303–4, 416–7
crisis
   abstract possibility of crisis 33, 122, 156–7, 159, 161, 217
   commercial crises 91, 117, 135, 225–6, 231, 249–50, 253
   essence of crisis 29, 39, 43, 91, 113, 148–9, 152–3

   intermediate crisis 251, 289, 363, 372–6
   international repercussions of crisis 225, 237, 243, 247
   moments of crisis 115, 118, 119, 121, 213, 243, 293, 422
   necessity of crisis 57, 113, 115, 173, 206, 214–8, 233–4, 378, 392, 397, 404
   periodic crises 12, 36, 56, 198, 208, 218, 234, 241, 252, 363, 372
   possibility of crisis 31–4, 37, 122, 137–9, 155–61, 164, 181–2, 195–8, 210, 213–5, 217–8, 405–7, 413, 415–6, 419–20, 422, 423–5, 431
   world market crises 91–2, 117, 135, 228
Currency school 252

debt 296, 298, 300, 360
depreciation fund 167, 167n, 316–36, 435
depression 13, 25, 44, 234, 238, 275, 277, 294–302, 305, 363
Diedrich, Franz 21
Die Neue Zeit
disequilibrium 49, 158, 173, 294–7, 295n, 297n, 304, 305, 344–6
distribution 38, 56, 108, 130–1, 135, 175, 184, 191, 222, 241, 297, 299, 303, 310, 433–5, 451, 456
dividends 247, 301–2
division of labour 8, 164, 208, 313, 349, 424
Dobb, Maurice 74n
Doshisha University 10
Drahn, Ernst 21
Dunker, Franz 83

East Asia Studies Institute
East Germany 194, 372
Eckstein, Gustav 64
Economic Intelligence Service 294n
Économie et politique 372n
Edinburgh Encyclopedia 44
elasticity of production process 38, 119–20, 188, 199, 214, 269, 271, 303
Emperor Meiji 2
Engel, Ernst 16
Engels, Friedrich 15, 88–9, 103–6, 175–8, 205–8, 224–5, 227–31, 251–2, 258–63, 265, 273–5, 280–2, 287, 289, 329–31, 333, 335–6, 365, 371–7, 422n, 442, 443–4

equilibrium 49, 167, 172–3, 294, 296–7, 297*n*, 304, 321, 345, 391–2, 394, 397, 399, 400, 402–3
exploitation 125, 128, 184, 223, 240

fateful events (*Schicksalsfälle*) 282
faux frais of capitalist production
Figurnov, P.K. 363
five-year cycle 375–6
flexibility 237, 269–70, 294, 298, 459
fluctuations 135, 139, 146, 161, 169, 226, 235, 345, 352, 415, 419–22, 425
Fukuda, Tokuzō
Fukumoto, Kazuo 79–80
Fullarton, John 254, 293*n*

German Economic Association (*Verein für Socialpolitik*) 58
Glöckner, Hermann 21
glut 54, 138, 175, 185–6
gold 47, 64, 166, 191, 225, 227, 247, 251, 254, 260, 278, 302, 305, 320, 346, 351–5, 357
Goldmann, Emma 144
goods
    consumer goods 295, 295*n*, 296*n*, 379–82, 384, 387, 391–4, 400–3
    luxury goods 3, 237, 241, 446
    producer goods 379–84, 387, 391–4, 396, 402–3
Gonda, Yasunosuke 7
government expenditures 235, 297
Gray, Nicholas 201*n*
Grossman, Henryk 12, 29, 29*n*, 80–90
ground rent 75, 86–90, 98, 101, 105, 106–9, 111, 113, 221, 432
Grünberg, Carl 80

Habeas Corpus Act 44
Hardy, Thomas 2
Harvard University Committee of Economic Research 59
Hasebe, Fumio 365
Hayashi, Keijirō 5
Hegel, Georg 10, 201–2, 204–5
Heidelberg University 9, 9*n*
Henderson, Francis 8
higher schools 2–3
High Treason Case 2

Hilferding, Rudolf 10
Hirase, Minokichi 251
historical mission of capitalism 63, 69, 205, 208, 222, 237, 248, 303
Hosakawa, Karoku 7, 17
Hosei University 18, 21
Hosokawa, Karoku 7, 10, 17
Hoston, Germaine 13*n*
House of Commons 253
Hugo, Victor 2
Hyōron 19, 20

Ikumi, Takuichi 362–71
Imai, Noriyoshi 362
imperialism 14, 62–69, 316
industrial cycle 38–9, 59, 61, 146–52, 251, 256–7, 259, 261–75, 276–81, 283–4, 286–7, 289, 362–71, 371–3, 373–7, 437
industrial reserve army 364
inflation 18–19, 24, 27, 235–6, 288, 337, 339, 346, 348–50
inflexibility 294–6, 298, 300, 303, 305
Inomata, Tsunao 318
Institute of Economics 59
Institute of Marxism-Leninism 21, 84*n*
Institute of Pacific Relations 294*n*
Institut für Sozialforschung (Institute for Social Research) 80*n*
interest rates 115, 171, 173, 246, 264, 268, 278–9, 301
Internationale Marx-Engels Stiftung 443
International Institute of Social History 440
International Labour Organisation 7
International trade 73, 90
Inukai, Tsuyoshi 4
investment 195–7, 235, 247, 267, 272, 285, 286, 301, 303, 334, 436
Isawa, Takio 16
Ishii, Jūjji 5
Itoh, Makoto 14*n*, 22*n*
Iwanami Shoten 20

James, William 2
Japanese Communist Party (JCP) 7, 8, 8*n*, 13–4, 14*n*, 15, 17
Japanese Socialist Party (JSP) 14, 17
Japan Labour Yearbook 10, 16
Jevons, William Stanley 250

INDEX	475

joint-stock capital   79, 90
Juglar, Clement   58

Kaizō   19
Kaizōsha   15
Karl Dietz Verlag   365
Kautsky, Karl   10, 61n, 69, 73, 75, 76, 110, 76–7, 81–2, 84, 84n, 90, 93n, 107, 365
Kawade Shobō   20
Kawakame, Hajime   3, 6–7, 6n, 19n, 78–9, 79n, 326–8
Kawanabe, Tadatoshi   27
Kawata, Jirō   6
Keio University   2, 4
Keizaigaku kenkyū (Economic Research)   6–7
Keizai hyōron   215
Keizai ronsō   378
Keizai seminā   173
Keynes, John M.   252
Kimura, Sukeyoshi   264
Kobayashi, Naoe   20–1
Kōda, Rohan   2
Komatsu, Yoshio   264
Konishi, Kazuo   27
Kōtoku, Shūsui   2
Kōza faction   13
Kropotkin, Peter   7
Kuczynski, Jürgen   251, 372n, 373–7
Kugelmann, Ludwig   82–4, 93, 96, 111
Kunikida, Doppo   2
Kuruma, Ken   10, 20
Kuruma school   26
Kushida, Tamizō   3, 7–10, 14, 27
Kyōchōkai (Harmonisation Society)   5
Kyoto Imperial University   3, 378n

labour
    labour power   32–3, 116, 125, 160–1, 165, 176, 185, 314, 346, 410, 420, 438, 442
    private labour   122, 208
    social labour   28, 122, 127, 204, 207–8, 314
    wage labour   28, 72–5, 79, 85–6, 87, 88, 90, 92, 95, 101–6, 108, 112–3, 124, 129
landed property   51, 72–4, 76, 79, 85–90, 92, 95, 101–7, 109, 112–3, 129
Lasalle, Ferdinand   73, 81, 82n, 84, 111

Laveleye, Émile   250
League of Nations   25, 288, 294
Lederer, Emil   9
left-communism   14
Lenin, Vladimir   14–5, 62, 66–9, 179
Lexis, Wilhelm   16
Liebig, Justus von   108
limit (*Grenze*) of capital   116, 198, 201–3
limited consumption of working class   36, 209, 213, 438
liquidity   301
living contradiction (*lebendiger Widerspruch*)   34–9, 197–9, 205, 208–9, 212–3
loan capital   262, 285
Luxemburg, Rosa   61n, 63–5, 67–9, 201, 317–318, 320–3, 325–8

Maehata, Noriko   264
Maehata, Yukihiko   26
Maikiyama, Kōhei   250
Malthusians   332
Malthus, Thomas   9, 53, 108
Mann, Tom   8
Marco Polo Bridge Incident   15
marginal utility   3, 217n
markets   43, 165, 175, 185, 223, 237–40, 242, 245–6, 350–1, 361, 411–2, 438, 442
Marx-Engels-Lenin Institute   93n, 374–5, 440
Marxian economists   7, 12, 13, 19, 22, 27, 28, 61, 147, 167, 217, 235, 379
Marxist centre faction   63, 65
Marx-Lexikon zur politischen Ökonomie   1, 3, 20–1, 26, 28, 39–40, 135–289, 396, 400–2, 404–6, 404n, 408, 415, 415n, 422, 423, 432, 435, 451
Marx's plan   75, 78–80, 84, 90, 93–4, 99, 150, 248, 434
materialist conception of history   1, 21, 49, 58, 152, 203, 208, 264–5
Mayr, Georg   16
means of subsistence   184, 240–2, 262, 420, 442, 446
Meiji Restoration   13
Mendelson, L.A.   363, 365
mercantilists   124
metamorphosis
    metamorphosis of capital   33, 123, 125, 156, 156n, 161–4, 410–2, 426–8

metamorphosis of commodities   32, 57–8, 122–3, 163–4, 194–5, 354, 355, 355n, 356, 356n, 425
metamorphosis of money   414
method of crisis theory   153, 195, 405–6
military expenditures   235, 300
Mill, James   53n, 359, 458
Mill, John Stuart   131
Mita, Seikisuke   14n
Mitchell, Wesley   59–60
Mitsubishi   306
Mitsui   4, 17
Miyake, Kikuyo   10, 17
Miyake, Yoshio   18, 251, 273, 289
Miyata, Korefumi   27
modern economics (*kindai keizaigaku*)   217, 217n, 272
money
   Marx's law of amount of circulating money   359
   money as means of circulation   158, 166, 278, 311, 322, 350–8, 358n
   money as means of payment   31, 123, 157, 196, 254, 349–50, 352, 358–9, 359n
   money as means of purchase   318, 322, 349–51, 345–55, 358, 358n, 359n, 360–1
   money hoard   141–2, 166–7, 311, 325, 358–9, 425
   quantity theory of money   358–60, 358n
   riddle of money   19, 23
monopoly   62, 63, 68, 192, 289, 296–7
Morita, Sōhei   2
Morito Incident   6
Morito, Tatsuo   7, 10, 17

nächsten Abschnitt   176–9, 178n, 200, 439–41, 443, 444
Nakabayashi, Shizuko   14
Napoleonic Wars   44, 52
National Bureau of Economic Research   59
national income   297–9
Natsume, Sōseki   2
New Deal   235
New York Daily Tribune   246, 248, 274
Nimura, Kazuo   6n, 14n, 17
North, Dudley   53n
Nosaka, Sanzō   8, 8n

Oberbaum Verlag   194
Oessler, Fred   363n
Ōhara Institute for Social Research   5–6, 14–8, 21, 306, 348, 362, 440
Ōhara, Magosaburō   5
Okayama   2–5, 10
Okayama Orphanage   5
Okayama University   2
Okuda, Hirono   26
Opium Wars   238
Ōshima, Kiyoshi   18, 24, 212
Ōshima, Sadamasu   250
Ōuchi, Hyōe   7, 9, 10, 11, 16, 17, 19, 348, 350–4, 359
Ōtani, Teinosuke   20–1, 22, 25, 26, 27, 27n, 28, 40, 143–81, 173n, 176n, 178n, 200n, 205n, 265n, 268n, 274n, 441n, 442n, 443n, 444n, 447n
Ōtsuki Shoten   20–1, 39, 417
overaccumulation   184, 240, 244, 380, 449, 452–5, 461
overproduction   37, 53, 55, 56, 137, 139, 147, 150, 157–8, 184–5, 199–200, 206, 210, 240, 241–2, 254, 366, 438, 421, 441–2, 453
Overstone, Samuel   274n

Papiermark   350–2
Parvus, Alexander   6n
Peel's Bank Acts   231
Perkeo Restaurant   9
Peterloo Massacre   44
Petty, William   16
Phillippovich, Eugen   3
physiocrats   53, 110
Popular Front Incident   15
potassium mark   353
precious metals   91, 141, 246
price
   cost price   110, 110n
   market price   96, 97, 116, 128, 129, 150, 344–5, 353, 360–1
   production price   80, 89, 93–6, 99, 107–8, 110n, 116, 128, 150, 301, 338–45
private property   112, 208, 304, 349
production departments   34, 143, 169–72, 173n, 237, 241, 379–80, 379, 382, 385–6, 392, 396, 426, 448, 456

production process   32, 34, 125, 127–31, 155, 186–7, 269–70, 406, 408, 412–4, 416–7, 424, 426–7, 445–6
productive power   36–8, 51–2, 198–9, 204–7, 209–13, 239, 242, 299–300, 307, 311, 371–2, 385–6, 398–9
productivity of labour   35, 37, 128, 130, 182, 188, 191, 204, 205, 211, 222, 236, 282, 299, 398–9, 453
profit
 average profit   94–6, 107, 110, 128–9, 338–9, 342, 343, 345
 commercial profit   128
 conversion of profit   94–5
 division of profit   108, 128, 433
 general rate of profit   37, 94–6, 99, 107, 300, 339, 453
 mass of profit   38, 234
 quantity of profit   184, 199, 453
 rate of profit   37–8, 93–5, 97, 107–8, 115–6, 171, 173, 182–4, 211, 234–5, 341–2, 449, 452–3
 surplus profit   110
proletariat   13, 43, 51, 57, 65–7
prosperity   129, 147, 189, 226, 238, 259, 266, 274–5, 277–9, 285, 364, 368, 377
purchasing power   44, 53, 236, 296, 311, 317, 345

railways   142, 246, 271, 426, 446
raw materials   268, 295, 297, 302, 327, 415, 419–22, 445, 459
Red International   8
reification   129
renewal of constant capital   167, 286, 318–9, 321, 324
rent   56, 88–9, 94, 103–6, 108–13, 115, 130
replacement fund   167n
reproduction
 expanded reproduction   33–4, 63, 169–70, 197, 319–21, 323, 325, 327–8, 378, 380, 391–2, 448, 456–61
 reproduction process   13, 33–4, 61, 63, 130, 155, 163–4, 169–70, 170–1, 174, 177, 179–80, 197, 260, 262–3, 319–21, 323, 325, 327–8, 329–30, 378, 380, 391–2, 404–11, 414–5, 417–8, 420–4, 426–33, 439–40, 447–8, 456–61
 reproduction schema   13, 61, 173, 176, 179, 323–4, 422, 432, 461–2
 simple reproduction   33, 170, 318–9, 450, 457–60
 social reproduction   170–1, 196, 435
reserve funds of coin (*Münzreserve*)   357
revenue   33, 50, 98, 108, 140, 162–6, 318–9, 423–5, 433, 439, 446
revolution   13, 48, 61–2, 125, 225, 258
Riazanov, David   10, 15
Ricardian socialism   56
Ricardo, David   50–2, 54–6, 108, 110, 183, 185, 188, 228, 231, 306–8, 310–4, 338–40
rice riots   5
Rikkyo University   20
Rōnō faction   13, 14, 15
Rousseau, Jean-Jacques   44
Rozenberg, David   19n
Ryazanskaya, Salo   74n

Sadler, Arthur   2
Saitō, Kōhei   27
Sakisaka, Itsurō   19, 365
Sasaki, Ryūji   27
Say, Jean-Baptiste   31, 53, 55
Say's Law (*théorie des débouches*)   53, 55
Schmidt, Johann   230, 362n, 365n
Second International   62, 66, 69
Shakai mondai kenkyū (Research in Social Problems)   79
Shao, Yong   313n
shareholders   15
Shūkan ekonomisuto (Weekly Economist)   17n, 24n, 193
sinking fund   167n
Sismondi, Simonde de   44–5, 48–53, 55, 57, 65–6, 80, 108, 179, 188, 206, 470
Sixth Higher School   2
Skambraks, Hannes   194
Slack (*Abspannung*)   277, 277n
Smith, Adam   10, 48, 50, 87, 184, 228, 308, 448
Social Democratic Party   63, 64, 68
socialism   2, 14, 8, 28, 56, 61, 65, 69, 73, 171, 205–7, 208
Solvay Institute   6
Spartacist uprising   9
speculation   275
Spiethoff, Arthur   58

stagnation 147, 231, 257, 268, 274, 277–9, 285, 364–5, 367
state 50, 90
state capitalism 14, 28
Stone, Nahum 74n
student movement 3
Sumitomo Bank 4
Sun, Tat-sen 4
superprofits 66
surplus population 278, 364
surplus value 30–3, 35–7, 95–8, 107–8, 127–30, 135, 137–41, 142, 161–2, 164–6, 182, 183–6, 188, 191–2, 195, 223–4, 228, 241, 319–23, 325–8, 338–9, 341–2, 407–9, 415–8, 425, 457
suspended coin (*suspendierte Münze*) 357
Suzuki, Kōichirō 19
Suzuki, Masaya 4
swindles 275
system of convertibility 235–6

Takada, Yasuma 172, 326–8, 378–403
Takahashi, Masao 348, 349–50, 352–3, 354, 358–61
Takano, Futasarō 7
Takano, Iwazaburō 6, 7, 17
taxes 72, 98, 235
Tennessee Valley Authority 235
ten-year cycle 375–76
Third International 69
Tokyo Imperial University 3–4, 6–7
Tomizuka, Ryōzō 22, 22n, 200n, 216–9, 387n, 404–62
Tooke, Thomas 141, 293n, 411
Trafalgar Square 8
trinity formula 57, 434
Tucker, Josiah 53n
Tugan-Baranowsky, Mikhail 61, 176, 450–1, 456, 461
Turgenev, Ivan 2
turnover 120, 142, 189, 281–2, 286, 327, 432, 446

Uesugi, Sutehiko 18, 173, 173n
underconsumption 36, 38, 179, 185, 186, 200, 210, 213, 252

unemployment 48, 230, 288, 298, 300
University of Michigan 294n
Uno Kōzō 12, 14, 14n, 19, 26, 100–16
Uno school
Usami Seijirō 22, 362

valorisation 35, 124, 173, 175, 204, 208, 213, 269, 303, 426
value form 19–20, 23, 144, 350, 355
variable capital 33, 163, 165, 323, 342, 379, 384, 387, 392, 394, 420, 442, 454
vulgar economics 108

wage labour 28, 72–5, 79, 85–6, 87, 88, 90, 92, 95, 101–6, 108, 112–3, 124, 129
wages 19, 47–8, 73–5, 86–8, 103, 104, 111–3, 115–6, 130, 184, 210, 242, 268, 297–300, 299n, 317, 327, 337–47, 442–3, 453–4
wageworkers 43, 48, 56, 317
Wall Street crash 12
war 16–7, 19–20, 44, 62–3, 67, 68–9, 197, 235–6, 287–8, 298, 362, 366
Waterloo 44
wealth 45–8, 51, 126, 129, 203, 206, 239, 255, 306–8, 310–3, 315, 332
Wilbrandt, Robert 78, 80, 85–6
Wilhelm, Lexis 16
Wilson, John 293n
Wirtschaftswissenschaft 372n
Woodcutter Dialogue 313
workers 33, 36–8, 48–9, 51, 128–9, 184–5, 240, 242, 298–300, 316–7, 341, 343–5, 420
World Economic Survey 25, 293–305
world market 29, 72–3, 75, 90–2, 114, 117, 120, 204, 222–3, 225, 235, 237–40, 242–3, 245, 248
World War I 3–4, 58, 235, 287–8, 350
World War II 2, 251, 288, 366, 371

Yahagi, Eizō 4
Yamada, Moritarō 13, 176, 177, 179–80, 422–3
Yamakawa, Hitoshi 8
Yamauchi, Tamon 15
Yoshikawa, Tetsu 215–6
Yūaikai labour union 7, 8

www.ingramcontent.com/pod-product-compliance
Lightning Source LLC
Chambersburg PA
CBHW070605030426
42337CB00020B/3698